The Stirling Story

Other books by Michael JF Bowyer include:

*Action Stations Revisited – The Complete History of Britain's Military
Airfields: No.1 Eastern England*
Mosquito (with C. Martin Sharp)
2 Group – A Complete History 1936-1945
Air Raid!
Interceptor Fighters
*Action Stations No. 6 – Military Airfields of the Cotswolds and Central
Midlands*
Force for Freedom – The USAF in the UK Since 1948
The Battle of Britain – Fifty Years On
Aircraft for the Few – The RAF Fighters and Bombers in 1940
The Spitfire Fifty Years On
*Aircraft for the Many – A Detailed Survey of the RAF's Aircraft in June
1944*
Aircraft for the Royal Air Force

The Stirling Story

Michael JF Bowyer

Crécy Publishing Limited

Published in 2002 by Crécy Publishing Limited
All rights reserved

A CIP record for this book is available from the British Library

ISBN 0 947554 91 2

Printed by
Bookcraft

Crécy Publishing Limited
1a Ringway Trading Estate, Shadowmoss Road, Manchester M22 5LH
www.crecy.co.uk

CONTENTS

Appendices

Glossary and Abbreviations

A&AEE	Aeroplane and Armament Experimental Establishment (at Martlesham Heath pre-war, Boscombe Down in wartime)
ACAS(T)	Assistant Chief of the Air Staff (Training) responsible for aircraft development
AFDU	Air Fighting Development Unit
AFEE	Airborne Forces Experimental Establishment
AGLT	*Automatic gun-laying turret*
ampg	Air miles per gallon
AOC	Air Officer Commanding
AP	Armour Piercing (bomb)
ASR	Air-Sea Rescue
ASU	Aircraft Storage Unit
bboc	Brought back on charge
BDU	Bomber/bombing Development Unit
cg	Centre of gravity
Circus	Fighter escorted daylight raid designed to encourage enemy fighter response
CRD	Controller Research and Development
CU	Conversion Unit
DDOR	Deputy Director Operational Requirements
DGRD	Director General Research and Development
dr	Dead reckoning (navigation)
DZ	Dropping Zone
ETA	Estimated Time of Arrival
FA	Flying Accident (EFA = category E, write off)
FBE	Flying Battle casualty/accident, categorised E or write-off. Also EFB
F.N.7, etc	Frazer Nash gun turret 7, etc
FS	Full Supercharger (engine gearing in operation)
FTC	Flying Training Command
FTR	Failed to Return
GP	General purpose (bomb)
Grand National	Bombing operation involving OTUs and squadrons
HC	High Capacity (bomb)
HCU	Heavy Conversion Unit
H2S	Navigational radar based upon scanning
IAS	Indicated Air Speed
IE	Initial/Immediate Equipment (of a squadron)
IR	Immediate Reserve (of a squadron)
KG3, etc	*Kampfgeschwader* (German bomber group)
LC	Low capacity/Light case weapon
LFS	Lancaster Finishing School
LZ	Landing Zone
MAP	Ministry of Aircraft Production
MC	Medium Capacity (bomb)
MS	Medium Supercharger (engine gear in operation)
MU	Maintenance Unit
Oboe	Radio blind bombing aid
OTU	Operational Training Unit
PFF	Pathfinder Force

RAE	Royal Aircraft Establishment Farnborough
Ramrod	Fighter escorted daylight raid designed to destroy a specific target
RASC	Royal Army Service Corps
Rebecca	Radio navigational aid
R/T	Radio Telephony
RTO	Resident Technical Officer
SAP	Semi Armour-Piercing (bomb)
SAS	Special Air Service
SBC	Small Bomb Container
SCI	Smoke Curtain Installation (also for gas and smoke laying)
Shaker	Main Force attack led by flare- and incendiary-dropping aircraft fitted with TR 1335 (*Gee*) equipment
SOC	Struck Off Charge
TAS	True Air Speed
Tinsel	Radar jamming device
TRE	Telecommunications Research Establishment (Defford/Malvern)
TTC	Technical Training Command
u/c	Undercarriage
'x'	Suffix to 4lb incendiary bomb signifying high-explosive component included, eg. 2,160 x 4lb etc = 2,160 four-pound bombs dropped, etc

Table Glossary

0+1, 0 1	Figures indicate number of aircraft serviceable plus aircraft unserviceable
28/48 aircraft	Twenty-eight aircraft/crews of the forty-eight despatched were thought to have attacked the primary target. Others may have attacked secondaries, last resort targets, jettisoned loads, aborted or failed to return
XV Squadron	A few RAF squadrons traditionally identify themselves using Roman numerals and XV (15) is one. Nos II (2), IX (9) and LXX (70) are others

Bombing Analysis Tabulations Special Notes

The **Bombing Analysis Tabulations** list each Pathfinder (PFF) and/or Main Force (MF) raid in which Stirling bombers participated.

Following date, target and role, the four figure numbers show first the number of Stirling crews claiming to attack the target and secondly the total number of Stirlings dispatched. For example, '48/54' means 48 crews attacked out of the 54 which set out and crossed the UK coast. These four figure groups will also be found within the text where the dates of operations appear in bold type. Single figures indicate alternative attack(s) or lone sorties.

The following columns show figures for high explosive (HE) loads aimed at what was thought to be the primary target and quantities of incendiary loads/flares dropped. The (FTR) column lists the number of aircraft or the identity of those failing to return.

The right-hand column indicates the total number of bomber crews operating within either the PFF or Main Force (MF) and claiming to have bombed the primary target out of the total number dispatched. Thus, 600/705 indicates that 600 crews claimed to bomb the Primary Target (P/T) out of 705 that crossed the UK coast.

The number of crews shot down and indication of whether they bombed the primary target were always very difficult to establish. Details of aircraft which returned/aborted before crossing the UK coast, failed to start out, abandoned the sortie soon after take-off, suffered technical malfunction and made an early return, or bombed alternative targets for a variety of reasons do not figure in the analysis.

Preface and Acknowledgements

FOR East Anglians like myself, the Short Stirling was an impressive part of wartime daily life, and my recordings and recollections from those years form the basis of this book. Having earlier produced a title on the Stirling I was, in 1997, asked to generate a more extensive edition which emerges here as *The Stirling Story*.

Affection for the aircraft remained strong among the many who wrestled with them, built them, maintained them or just eyed them in awe and this affection brought the Stirling Aircraft Association into being. Many of its members have, over the decades, contributed much to this volume. To the Stirling the words of the well-known song might be truly applied: 'Unforgettable – that's what you are'.

I was able to set personal records against industrial and official material before much of it was disposed of, and at a time when many documents relating directly to Bomber Command policy and operations remained heavily restricted. Times have changed dramatically with Form 540s (Operations Books and Appendices) relating to Commands, Groups and Squadrons being open for inspection in the Public Record Office (PRO), Kew. They may be found placed within CLASS AIR 24, 25 and 27. The all-important returns of daily strength occur in AIR 22. Please treat them all with very great care for many are unique documents, easily damaged. Operational training and station diaries are spread through CLASSES 28 and 29. Sundry Bomber Command files relating to the Stirling are gathered in CLASS AIR 14.

From the vast number of Registered Files, once shrouded in considerable secrecy, and some which have escaped destruction as Secret Waste, those relating to the Stirling can be found within AIR 2, 8 and 20. Performance and evaluation records arising from A&AEE trials appear within AVIA 18. Handbooks relating to the Stirling, its power plants, weapons and equipment form part of the AIR 10 collection. To those of us who had access to such material as indexes in times long gone it seems amazing that one can search for references to such documents (thereby learning much that was hitherto restricted) by reading the listing on the PRO website. A few years ago that would simply have been rated 'incredible, impossible!' Of course, one still has to visit PRO to read a document of interest. Damage received by squadron records as a result of much handling and a despicable case of theft has led to CLASS AIR 27 records and others being available only on microfilm. This makes photocopies easy to obtain.

Outline Service Histories of individual aircraft (the Form 78s) are held on microfilm – but not each aircraft's service file – at the RAF Museum, Hendon. Unlike the PRO's Historical Documents, which have a legal classification, those at Hendon including aircraft handbooks etc can be viewed after making an appointment. To use PRO documents a Reader's Ticket needs to be obtained.

The illustrations in *The Stirling Story* come from many sources. It is to Laurence Haylock that I am deeply indebted for the superb airbrush artwork which has converted some of my wartime notes and memories into sights fine to behold. To Alf Alderson, whose line drawings are always so superbly executed, I extend my gratitude for being able to use them.

Apart from Crown Copyright and Imperial War Museum items, the input to this book is derived from many sources, much of it in private collections. Contributions by the Rochester Branch of the Royal Aeronautical Society, the *Rochester Evening Post* and *Radio Medway* awoke many memories of 'the night bomber'. Shorts of Belfast have contributed photographs reproduced within these pages. Special items include the recollections of Mr J H Lower, one-time manager at Belfast, and John Bull's first hand memories of the prototype's tragic first flight. Geoffrey Tyson, Shorts' test pilot who flew so many Stirlings, recalls the handling qualities of the bomber. Group Captain Paul Harris who commanded No 7, the first Stirling squadron, has contributed his memories as has

John Prentice who flew on the first Stirling operation. George Blacklock, too, recalled for me some of the 1941 Stirling operations, while Frank Griggs and crew of 214 Squadron recalled the night when they destroyed three German night fighters. Mr I J Edwards related the story of a horrendous Stirling crash in Essex, a sortie which, like so many involving Stirlings, demanded great courage. Members of the Royal Air Force Association and the Bomber Command Association have recalled their Stirling days. A most worthy item is Bryce Gomersall's monograph, *The Stirling File*, published by Air Britain, which gives concise listings of many facets relating to the Stirling which he shared with me many years ago. His monograph is well worth acquiring. To John Strangward I extend my thanks for skilled proof reading.

Unique Stirling memories have come from Gerrit Zwanenburg MBE, Royal Netherlands Air Force Salvage Officer who, in attending wrecked aircraft, has thrown light upon harrowing moments and given many airmen a known final resting place. Lt Col Arie de Jong, Royal Netherlands Air Force, recounted being on the receiving end of the very first Stirling raid.

From the many photographs of Stirlings which have flown my way, those selected are from over 400 shortlisted for use. To all who at any time contributed photographs, all of which have brought much interest, a very big "thank you". The Stirling Association has over the years gathered and garnered a large collection of Stirling photographs and would be very pleased to hear from anyone who can contribute to the collection.

Since 1941 so many Stirling 'fans' have provided material and pictures from which I have drawn for this book that it seems invidious to list some contributors. The following have, however, made a clear input of stories or pictures:

Barry H Abraham, Frances J L'Anson, Jim Baldwin, C D Barnes, C R Barrass, E Basford, T Bate, P Bates, P D Beldersen AFC, the late Plt Off Earl Belford RCAF, L v de Bergh, George Blacklock, G Bladon, Sqn Ldr P J S Boggis DFC (who helped so much with the story of MacRobert's Reply which he piloted), E N Bolton, the late J T Breeze, P C Burbridge, P Burke, A A Busby, R Cassingham, Noel Chaffey, E F Chandler, the late 'Cherry' Cherrington, G H Chesterton, J Chinchen, J Chinery, J B Church, D R Clarke, the late Peter Corbell, R W Cox, B Craven, J Vaupell Christensen, Tommy Cushing, Bob Dalton, H A Davenhall, C H Dorrington, I A Downie, D K Dyell, S Edwards, Miss W Few, Dennis Field, A Fuller, P A Gilchrist, Gp Capt D Giles, C Gilks, R Glass, Bryce Gomersall, John Graf, D Green, J E Greenfield, Gp Capt Frank Griggs, Sidney E Groves, Jim Halley, R A Hammersley DFM, Michael Hardwick, Brian Harris (for many fascinating and rare photographs), the late Gp Capt Paul Harris, D H Hardwick, J Helme, C J Hobson, F N Hodson, J P Holden, A A Holland, the late A Hotchkiss, A B R Hudson C Eng MRAeS, G Jeffrey, W Jepson, D Kitchingham, Richard Livermore, J H Llewelly, D A Locket, George Mackie, D C M Marks, the late Bob May, J Miller-Stell, R C Monteith, Arthur Moore, K W Morgan, Gp Capt O A Morris, R W Mortimer, D Murray-Peden QC, A P O'Hara, I Pacey, Phil Pannichelli, G Parry, J Payne, S Phillips, the late B Philpott, David Oddy, the late John D R Rawlings, Bruce Robertson, P J Rowland, M Schoeman, L H D Scott, Roy Scott, Gp Capt B D Sellick, J Shields, Bill Slater, R A A Sloan AFC, J L Smith, W N Sonnfinsrein, the late Sqn Ldr R B Spear DFC, RNZAF, S A Spray, Gp Capt C S G Standbury, R Staton, D B Stephen, M D Stimson, R A Strachan, E S Summers, J Swale, J Thuring, H Todd, E Turrell, the late Mrs Phyllis Walliker, A E Watson, W P Warson, G Webb, T White, Jock Whitehouse and the Stradishall Memorial Association, Florence Willsher, N E Winch, E A Woodger and S Woodward. Contemporary ranks and decorations (where known) are included in respect of listed RAF personnel. In an instance where someone has passed away which is unrecorded above, I express my deepest sympathy to those who knew them well.

Michael J F Bowyer
Cambridge, March 2001

Introduction

Remember the Stirling?

A mere sixpence, a 'tanner' – that is all it cost to prise open the nation's secrets from a little book. *Silhouettes of British Aircraft* it was called; very official and restricted, not just to those with a sixpence, but also to important people with a 'need to know' and the affluent like me who unlawfully managed to acquire a copy. Between the green utility paper covers nestled 1940s state secrets in profusion, among which were silhouettes of a new bomber – the Stirling. Using the book you should have been able to identify it – if you were lucky enough to catch a glimpse of this, Britain's first wartime four-engined bomber. For good measure, and in case the enemy did not know, its wing span was given as 99ft 2in, its length an amazing 87ft 3in.

Not until the Battle of Britain reached its climax did one of these strange, dangly-looking contraptions find a squadron home. Not until six months had passed did it enter the bombing campaign. Even by then only seven Stirlings of the hundred ordered were in squadron hands. Each was handmade, like a flying-boat, by skilled men and women.

First sighting of a Stirling was unforgettable. Its similarity to the Short Sunderland was obvious but slicing away the lower half of the hull had spoilt its predecessor's old elegance. As soon as it banked, its engines whispering, the Stirling's unusual wingspan-to-fuselage length ratio was apparent. The broad chord wing of exceptionally deep section looked too short, correctly suggesting that it had, at some time, been 'clipped' perhaps to improve the rate of roll and maybe reduce weight.

Truth was different, for the Stirling was a victim of what would now be called 'political correctness' – the outcome of a desire to restrict the size of aerodromes to keep the agricultural lobby from complaining too much at the loss of their land and others at the expenditure on 'defence'. Some attitudes never change!

Cutting the take-off run by reducing the bomber's size and weight and shortening its wing span generated a major problem. To obtain sufficient lift during the take-off run the wing incidence needed increasing and was achieved by lengthening the undercarriage which included an amazing array of folding struts, girders and a crate which retracted both backwards and forwards. It looked certain to cause trouble especially on a wet airfield surface and in a strong crosswind. Aided by gigantic tyres to permit flying from grass surfaces, the undercarriage helped to position the pilot over twenty feet above the ground when the aircraft was at rest.

But the Stirling joined Bomber Command at the very time when all seemed lost, when the Battle of Britain had just started, and it came to be a symbol of hope that we might be able to hit back. In the event, two years passed before it effectively established itself. Then, as much as any aircraft, it heaped terrible retribution upon Germany and its people. What follows is the tortuous story of the Stirling and those who took it to war.

Chapter 1
Origins

THERE has never been any other aeroplane quite like the Stirling. Its nose in Heyford style reared towards the sky while its frame rested upon giant and inelegant legs. Once airborne it metamorphosed into a fast flier, a whispering, nimble giant whose broad chord wings supported an incredibly slender and lengthy body. How did such a combination come about?

In the early 1930s the British decided that the heavy bomber was the best weapon for both defensive and offensive operations. Fighters defending bomber bases as well as industrial enterprises, ports and population centres could never win a war which would be the task of the attackers.

Even before the 1914–18 war, British advanced thinkers envisaged aircraft penetrating enemy territory to attack industrial targets and communications and to assault enemy morale. Eleven British heavy bomber designs (six to official specifications) were prepared between 1914 and 1919 and five entered service.

Independent strategic bombing was first contemplated by the Admiralty and, by the end of 1914, Handley Page were working on a 114ft span design able to carry six 100lb bombs when flying at 65mph and at 8,000ft. It entered service in 1916 as the 0/100, its wing span prophetically limited to 100ft due to hangar size. Able to accommodate sixteen 112lb bombs, its top speed was 76mph, ceiling 8,700ft and range 490 miles.

A new variant with additional engine power, the 0/400, was available in 1918. By then 1,650lb bombs were in use and one of 3,360lb was under development. At the end of the war the Handley Page V/1500, designed to drop that large bomb on Berlin, was available. The RAF's first four-engined bomber, and the last until the Stirling arrived, the V/1500 was also its longest spanned aircraft until the 1950s when the B-29 and Blackburn Beverley arrived. Four engines were needed to cope with the large structure and tail defence was now featured. Able to attain 99mph and reach over 11,000ft, the V/1500 which entered service too late for action was withdrawn in January 1920.

By then the Vickers Vimy, carrying a 1,510lb bomb load for around 400 miles at a top speed of 103mph, was the RAF's main heavy bomber from which the similar Virginia was born and which served until 1935. With twice the Vimy's bomb load, more engine power and twice the range, it was only marginally faster. Meanwhile, Handley Page produced their Hyderabad and Hinaidi based upon the 0/400, but not until their Heyford did the speed increase to over 150mph as a result of streamlining and power raised to 960hp.

These biplane bombers had metal or wooden frames over which plywood or cotton/linen fabric was stretched, fastened and doped to seal the airframe. Water cooled, in-line cylinder engines were favoured driving fixed pitch wooden propellers. Flying instruments were basic, electrical needs being met from wind driven generators. From 1920 onwards heavy bombers answered only official requirements, development costs being too high for private ventures. A general outline of heavy bomber basic design parameters – and especially structural strength – was prescribed in AP 970.

Significant change came with the Fairey Hendon, a very heavy, large twin-engined monoplane whose extremely deep-section fabric-covered metal wing carried the bomb load and huge trousers encompassed the undercarriage. Glazing covered the cockpit canopy and forward turret, the aircraft's considerable weight nevertheless being linked with a modernistic looking aeroplane. The crash of the prototype unfortunately delayed development.

Between 1919 and 1932 the Government believed, in successive years, that no war in

Europe was likely in the following decade, and British military aircraft advancement was slow with no major threat evident. The main change came in the mid-1920s when Air Ministry favour switched from wood to metal construction.

Major advancement began when the B.9/32 specification led to streamlined monoplanes, the elegant Vickers bomber and an unusual looking Handley Page design with minimum surface area intended to reduce drag. Both (respectively becoming the Wellington and Hampden) were powered by air-cooled radial engines, flew at 100mph faster than the Heyford, had retractable undercarriages and featured defensive armament in superior traversing gun turrets, the Wellington had heavier multi-gun turrets. Whereas the Wellington was of Barnes Wallis's open 'geodetic' construction, the Hampden had a sheet metal monocoque structure. The former, with lower structural weight, was nevertheless very strong but, being fabric covered, was vulnerable to fire in flight. To reduce landing speed, flaps were introduced and replaced wing leading edge slats.

Advanced innovations led to the Wellington weighing over 28,000lb loaded, making it twice as heavy as a Virginia while the bomb load rose only from 3,000lb to 4,500lb. On the other hand streamlining and reduced skin surface area added almost 150mph in speed, the increased range making attacks on Berlin possible, should they ever be needed. More instrumentation demanded extra electrical power provided by engine-driven generators, while hydraulic pumps supplied other systems. Superior instrumentation included blind flying assistance and autopilot installation.

By 1934, with a threat from Nazi Germany emerging, 'the ten year rule' was cast aside and RAF rearmament began. Emphasis was shared between building a shield of advanced defensive fighters and a powerful independent bombing force. The Air Ministry now outlined a new bomber requirement to four firms – Armstrong Whitworth, Fairey, Handley-Page and Vickers Armstrong – placing emphasis firstly upon a range of 1,260 miles (ie. Berlin and back) and secondly a speed of at least 200mph at 5,000ft. An unfortunate rider called for it to perform as a troop carrier. The Whitley, carrying twice the Wellington's bomb load while flying higher over the same range but more slowly, was the outcome. Since it was intended for use as a night bomber it had reduced defensive armament.

The Hampden, Wellington, Whitley and also the smaller Blenheim and Battle – preferred by the newly established Bomber Command in that order – were all relatively short-range or small load carriers. Aircraft with greater range and much higher load carrying ability were considered necessary. In fact, what should have been developed was 'The Ideal Bomber' towards which thought was directed too late. By the mid-1930s advances in engineering, structures and particularly aero engines were making possible fulfilment of very demanding requirements and permitting development of aircraft able to carry heavy loads at higher speeds and for much greater distances.

As a result, April 1936 saw the emergence of formulations for the next bomber generation, the B.12/36 specialised long-range heavy bomber and the P.13/36 medium-range/load bomber. The former would replace the Whitley, the latter the Hampden and probably the Wellington. A Draft Specification describing the former was drawn up on the 28th of the month outlining the Air Staff's ideas for a heavy bomber. It must carry an 8,000lb bomb load for 3,000 miles, with provision for a 14,000lb load linked with a 2,000 mile range. Such a machine was initially intended to equip only a small portion of the strike force and back a large force of P.13/36s. Carrying the load over the prescribed range, the heavy bomber would inevitably be large, also certainly have four engines, but to contain its size a wing span of 100ft was arbitrarily set. Where, in the case of earlier bombers, hangar containment was a consideration, others factors now came into play.

Much thought was given to preventing over-long take-off runs demanding large, costly aerodromes likely to provoke public resentment in peacetime. To assist, a powerful yet heavy new twin-row, air-cooled radial engine, the Bristol Hercules, was favoured. To ensure the limited take-off run, novel forms of assisted take-off initially found considerable favour. Such a heavy bomber would, for survival, need the highest possible performance. A minimum top speed of 230 mph at 15,000ft was set, at the optimum altitude for combat aircraft of the 1930s. Two nose machine guns, two more amidships and four in the tail, and all in turrets, were thought sufficient to defend the bomber from fighter attack from any direction.

Constraints placed on the bomber force by politicians related to its numerical strength and not the size and type of aircraft. As a result the Air Staff fundamentally altered its plans and opted for the largest number of heavy bombers that it was possible to acquire.

Compared with the medium P.13/36, the B.12/36 had a 50 percent higher all-up weight and twenty-five percent greater wing span to permit it to carry a 100 percent increased load. Plans also took into account the use of the largest bomb in vogue – the 2,000 pounder. Such heavy weapons in their armour-piercing form were envisaged for supporting the Navy, to be suitable for attacking enemy surface warships preying upon merchant shipping at trade focal points. The specification stated that the heavy bomber should be able to carry seven 2,000lb AP bombs.

On 28 April 1936, as he reviewed the Draft Specification, Gp Capt R D Oxland, Operational Requirements Staff, reckoned the proposed aircraft to be unduly large, and argued that the required performance could be achieved by an aircraft spanning less than 100ft. He also expressed the view that suggested catapult launching might hinder performance, even if it did permit a heavy take-off weight.

Air Cdre A Cunningham wondered if a 3,000 mile ferry range was sufficient and he pointed to a need for food, sleeping and sanitary arrangements during a thirteen hour flight. He asked whether more economical diesel engines had been considered, and said that rate of climb was important to ensure the bomber reached operational height well before entering enemy airspace, and with as little fuel consumption as possible. He also suggested heavier-calibre tail guns but the Air Staff considered four .303in guns sufficient. A maximum cruise speed of not less than 230mph seemed a slow setting, he observed, and silencing would be needed to reduce fatigue. Others were uneasy about vertical bomb stowage for it led to inaccuracy. Incendiary bombs, with which the Stirling later operated so successfully, were not considered.

Further comments during a meeting held on of 22 May 1936 pointed out that the normal loaded range of 1,500 miles was low for, with diversions etc, action radius would be only 600 miles. A strong undercarriage was absolutely essential in case the aeroplane had to land in a heavily loaded state, and fuel jettisoning equipment was strongly advised. The Fairey Battle's single Merlin engine was as noisy as nine Bristol Bulldogs, it was claimed, so four engines would produce a cacophony, but silencing them would entail extra weight.

On 18 May 1936, the specification draft circulated at the Air Ministry then an Operational Requirements conference was held on 27 May. Chaired by AVM C L Courtenay CBE DSO, Deputy Chief of the Air Staff, the Committee comprised AVM W R Freeman CV DSO MC, Air Cdre A Cunningham, Air Cdre S J Goble, Air Cdre R H Vernay, Air Cdre A T Harris (later Sir Arthur), Gp Capt R D Oxland, Wg Cdr A W Milne, Wg Cdr B Mcentegart, Sqn Ldr N H Bilney and Capt R N Liptrot with Mr W F Jacks as Secretary.

AVM Courtenay opened the proceedings asking whether there was a need for an aircraft of the size visualised, for the Vickers B. 1/35 (Warwick) had a wing span of 97ft and the new Handley-Page bomber's span was 96ft, their all-up weights being 25,000lb and 29,000lb respectively. One large bomber, though, was said to be worth two smaller ones. Gp Capt Oxland, Deputy Director Operational Requirements, said the aircraft they had in mind would not be much larger than the 1/35. Normal all-up weight would be

31,200lb, 36,000lb overloaded for a 700 yard take-off, 46,000lb when catapult launched. Engines would be Rolls-Royce Goshawks. Deputy Director Plans wondered whether a smaller aircraft would suffice, for two small ones would be cheaper than one large one. The medium bomber envisaged had a 3,000 mile range but carried half the bomb load.

One factor influencing the opinion of the Chairman was the B.12/36's ability to carry 2,000lb bombs. The large number of P.13/36s would be supplemented by a number of heavy bombers. Cunningham felt that the operation of a 50,000lb bomber would be difficult in bad weather. Gayford considered that there should be metalled runways in addition to catapults, for it would take three minutes for one catapult launch and a long time to launch a dozen bombers. The 3,000 mile range was questioned, but it was pointed out that it was needed in case Russia became aggressive,

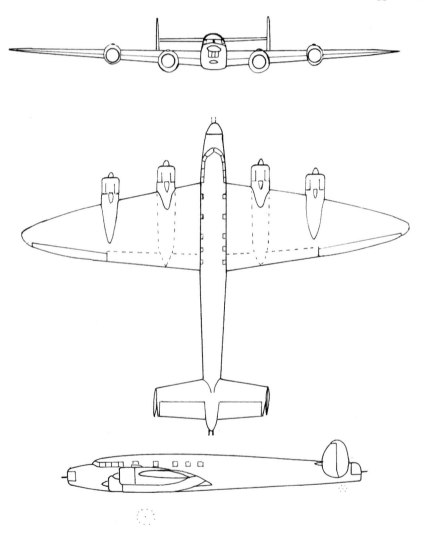

The Supermarine B.12/36 underwent a number of basic changes including a wing plan with leading edge sweep back as an alternative to an elliptical shape. The fuselage shows Wellington ancestry and the narrow fuselage section is apparent. Twin wheels were fitted beneath the inner engine nacelles.

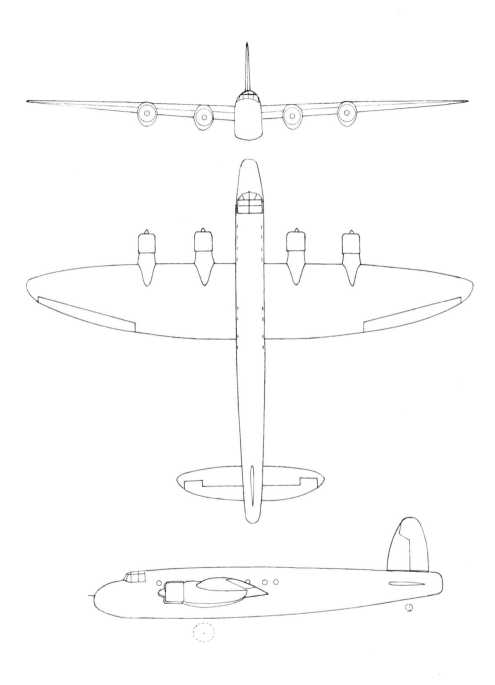

Vickers submitted a geodetic framed B.12/36 scheme based upon the Wellington and Warwick and whose features were repeated mid-war on their advanced Windsor four-engined bomber. Those included the elliptical wing planform and an undercarriage leg beneath each of the four engine nacelles. Among the other contenders was a Bristol four-engined enlarged version of the Blenheim.

as well as for overseas reinforcement.

Maintenance was also discussed. One large aircraft seemed more economical than two medium ones, yet it was possible to maintain a heavier scale of attack with the latter. Heavies would spend longer over enemy territory with more risk of interception. Cunningham suggested speed was a better safeguard than defensive armament, thereby unknowingly promoting the philosophy which produced the de Havilland Mosquito. It was quickly pointed out that politicians gauged the strength of the Air Force by numbers – better to have a large number of heavies! The morning's deliberations had little effect upon the aircraft. When Milne suggested a higher speed, Capt Liptrot said that what was being asked for was the best they were likely to get. Bombs of heavier weight than 500lb would be used against ships, fortifications and magazines.

Liptrot estimated the overload service ceiling would be about 25,000ft, and the landing run, using flaps, about 250 yards at 60mph. Remotely controlled armament was appealing and it was asked whether this could be fitted in the rear of any nacelles. It meant that both turrets could not be brought to bear on any one target, and none under the tail. A ventral station was instead approved.

The Chairman felt there was no need for a dinghy, but the pilots' seats would need armour plating. Soundproofing seemed essential, likewise a toilet.

After a few amendments the specification details were, on 9 July 1936, circulated to the aircraft industry although, initially, only Armstrong Whitworth, Bristol, Vickers and Handley-Page were invited to tender. Boulton Paul were told that they would be invited later to submit their ideas. Shorts were not included on the tender list until a recommendation was received that this flying-boat builder should be invited to participate because the company already had on the drawing board an aircraft answering some of the B.12/36 requirements. When approached, Short Bros stated that they had ample design, drawing office and production staff to cope with the project, along with production facilities, since they were amalgamating with the Belfast firm of Harland & Wolff.

Although the specification was circulated to Messrs Fairey, Westland, Hawker, Rolls-Royce, Napier, Saro, de Havilland, Blackburn, Avro and Gloster, those firms were really only being informed of the latest operational thinking. Acceptable responses were expected only from five regular bomber builders.

Slight amendments to the specification followed. It could have radial or in-line engines, the track must be sufficiently wide to prevent overturning when manoeuvring and tyre pressure must not exceed 35psi since the machine must be able to operate from grass surfaces. The tail wheel could be retractable.

During October 1936 a combined Air Ministry and RAF conference reviewed tenders submitted by Vickers, Bristol, Armstrong Whitworth, Supermarine and Short which, after analysis, were placed in that order of preference. Vickers had based their ideas on the Wellington, Bristol on the Blenheim and Armstrong Whitworth upon the Whitley. Only Supermarine and Shorts had entirely new designs on offer, entirely untried notions.

Supermarine's design was graceful, but the fuselage cross-section was too small to allow a man to stand upright and would thus make movement between stations difficult. It also seemed unlikely ever to have been able to carry the stipulated bomb load. Yet, with its elliptical wing, it was related to an already outstanding product from the firm.

Although last in the line of preferred contenders, the Short design was considered likely to be a highly robust affair closely akin in construction to a flying-boat; a landplane version of the Sunderland.

Three months of intense consideration of the tenders followed, including reviews of the work loads of the firms whose designs had first found favour. Then in January 1937 the decision was made. Two prototypes of the Supermarine design, particularly attractive from an experimental point of view, would be ordered. Originally the Rolls-Royce KV-

26 was to power both, but Bristol Hercules radials were later substituted for one aircraft.

Worried over possible delay, even failure of the chosen contender, the Chief of the Air Staff reckoned that a second '12/36' design must go forward. He suggested the Short bomber because the firm had ample experience of four-engined monoplanes.

It was not such a straightforward decision as it might seem for the Short submission had been subjected to much official criticism. Therefore, the firm was asked to redesign it then resubmit before any order could be considered. When initially submitted, in September 1936, the mid-wing monoplane was to be powered by four Napier Dagger in-line engines already in vogue for the Handley-Page Hereford, a version of the Hampden to be built exclusively by Short & Harland. Great things were expected of the sleeve-valve liquid-cooled Dagger, but as well as delivering insufficient power it encountered many technical problems akin to those of its big brother, the later Sabre. The original Short design incorporated a 112ft and later a 102ft span wing with a net area of 1,300sqft and a fuselage 86ft 6in in overall length. A normal loaded weight of 38,100lb was forecast, overload of 42,900lb and a maximum feasible load of 53,100lb. Bombs were to be carried in four long compartments, two either side of the fuselage centre frames. Provision was for twenty bombs in four tiers of five to be carried in main compartments sited below the pilot's and radio operator's positions. Special arrangements for the carriage of eight 2,000lb HEs were envisaged.

April 1937 saw the submission of a much revised Short design and another from Bristol. The new Short aircraft could now have either Daggers or Hercules HE 1SM engines. Its wing span was set at 102ft, overall length at 86ft 8in. Normal loaded weight had risen to 41,600lb, overload to 46,600lb and maximum possible to 56,900lb. The carriage of twenty-eight 500lb or seven 2,000lb bombs was now provided for and tiered stowage abandoned. Shorts also made provision for their aircraft to serve as a troop carrier. The conference unanimously chose it as the back-up to the Supermarine bomber.

Chapter 2
Appraisal and Refinement

IN June 1937 the decision was made to ask for two prototypes of the Short bomber, both to be delivered within eighteen months. In approaching the Treasury for the funding, the Air Ministry pointed out that the death of R J Mitchell, Supermarine's designer, had introduced a risk that their bomber might run into hitherto unforeseen difficulties. Since other countries were building large four-motor bombers, and the Air Staff was now planning to make the B.12/36 the backbone of its heavy bomber force, successful development and large-scale manufacture were of vital importance. During August and September 1937 the mock-up of the aircraft was examined at Rochester. As work went ahead there was still some doubt as to whether the aircraft would be funded, and not until 6 October 1937 did the Treasury sanction expenditure for two prototypes. The final mock-up conference followed in December.

Fortunate indeed was the decision to go ahead with the second B.12/36 design for, chiefly due to Supermarine's preoccupation with the Spitfire, neither prototype of the company's B.12/36s was ever completed. Both examples were destroyed when the Supermarine Woolston factory was bombed in September 1940. They were by then far behind the planned building programme partly due to the difficulty of producing the large elliptical wing.

So just what had Short Bros of Rochester now let themselves in for? An outline was described as follows, in the B.12/36 Specification:

> The Air Staff require a heavy bomber for world-wide use, an aircraft exploiting alternatives between long range and very heavy bomb load made possible by employing catapult launching in overloaded condition. The aircraft must possess high performance but at the same time have strong defence in all planes.
>
> An aircraft fulfilling these requirements will probably be large, but it should not exceed a span of 100ft. In order to maintain maximum reliability during, and immediately after catapulting, and also to be able to retain height with one engine out of action, the aircraft should be four engined. Since it will be required to operate from bases anywhere in the world, the aircraft must possess facilities for maintenance in the open.

Thus ran the preamble to Specification B.12/36 from which the Stirling stemmed. The requirements continued in detail:

> The speed at 15,000ft at maximum cruise revs must not be less than 230mph, range 1,500 miles at 15,000ft after a take-off run of 500 yards carrying normal loading including 2,000lb of bombs. In overload condition range, after a 700 yard take-off, must not be less than 2,000 miles at 15,000ft at maximum cruise revs, with not less than 4,000lb of bombs. It is hoped that a range of at least 2,000 miles will be obtained when carrying the maximum possible bomb load – ie. 14,000lb. Overload range, after accelerated take-off and at 15,000ft, must not be less than 3,000 miles with not less than 8,000lb of bombs.

Such performance in the mid-1930s would be outstanding, and Shorts must have wondered if it could be achieved. Nevertheless they accepted the challenge.

> Rate of climb is secondary. [This was later amended to read 20,000ft in 25 minutes.] Service ceiling should not be less than 28,000ft carrying normal load and 2,000lb of bombs. The aircraft must be able to fly level at 10,000ft on any three engines with any loading.

Such a ceiling would be difficult to achieve using existing engines, so power plants would be new, untried. Power loading and wing loading would be important, for the aircraft must use a standard-sized field and clear 50ft in 500 yards when fully loaded. Landing run with full normal load must not exceed 500 yards. Difficult figures to meet, some said impossible.

Crew would number six: two pilots (one acting as navigator), observer/front gunner/bomb aimer, relief radio operator, two air gunners (one amidships to monitor engine instruments, one a radio operator.) A twin-gun front turret would allow a field of fire from wing tip to wing tip. A retractable belly turret might be remotely controlled. In the tail must be a four-gun turret, and access between all crew stations was needed.

A wide variety of bomb loads was specified including eight 250lb GP/SAP/AS/LCB, smoke curtain installation; or four 500lbGP/SAP/AS; or twelve 2,000lb AP. In overload condition with a 700 yard take-off run the load could be sixteen 250lb; or eight 500lb or two 2,000lb. Heaviest loads on take-off seemed possible only with the aid of catapult launching and totalled 14,000lb: twenty-eight 500lb or seven 2,000lb. Internal horizontal stowage or positioning in vertical tiers was acceptable. No high degree of manoeuvrability was specified but a good view was needed for formation flying. Among items of equipment would be sun-proof head covering at crew stations to obviate the need for sun helmets in the tropics - a quixotic idea easily met.

By late 1937 performance outlines for the Short B.12/36 had been prepared:

Weight loaded (lb)	Max speed 15,000ft (mph)	Cruise speed (mph)	Wing area (sqft)	Take-off run(yards)	Landing, half fuel, no bombs (yards)
41,600	323	275	1,300	473	494
43,120	327	285	1,300	440	600
44,745	327	285	1,300	450	640
45,300	327	285	1,420	430	600
45,600	323	282	1,480	350	500
48 500	311	273	1,850	350	500

The length of likely take-off and landing runs worried the Air Staff so much that in March 1938 they decided that the wing area of B.12/36 should not exceed 1,320sqft offering a landing run of 600 yards, and prescribed a maximum take-off weight of 45,700lb.

By May 1938 Supermarine's design, with an all-up weight of 44,500lb was forecast to have a landing run of 740 yards. This increase arose partly because the intended Rolls-Royce KV 26 engines were to be replaced by more powerful, heavier ones. Reassessment of wing area led to an increase to 2,145sqft in the Short design, further increasing the structure weight. Long landing and take-off runs seemed unavoidable.

On 13 May 1938, Mr Lipscombe, Short's Chief Designer, asked for a further increase in take-off weight to 60,000lb. Without assisted take-off the undercarriage would need strengthening and tyre pressures increased. Because of the higher weight, new figures were prepared for both B.12/36 designs (See Table A).

The problem of landing run was far from solved, with that of the Supermarine aircraft ever lengthening, and further comparison of the designs was made in August 1938 (See Table B). The Supermarine design now had the edge over the Short bomber but both designs continued.

Shorts considered the take-off run to be longer than was necessary. Sliding Gouge flaps could be increased in area by fitting a second flap aft to take care of the trouble. Nevertheless they decided to investigate by building a half-scale plywood aerodynamic replica of the bomber.

Table A: *Comparison of Shorts and Supermarine B.12/36 designs (1)*

Weight loaded (lb)	Max speed, 15,000ft, 2,000lb load	Cruise speed, 1,500 miles (mph)	Take-off run (yards)	Landing speed (mph)
Short (Bristol Hercules Mk 1 SM)				
43,120	327	285	440	78
48,570	327	284	605	78
59,090	327	282	–	–
Supermarine (Merlin)				
42,640	329	284	475	85
47,910	329	282	605	84
58,380	329	279	–	84

Table B: *Comparison of Shorts and Supermarine B.12/36 designs (2)*

	Load (lb)	Weight loaded (lb)	Range (miles)	Cruise speed (mph)
Short				
	2,000	50,336	1,500	263
	4,000	56,120	2,020	259
	8,000	60,600	2,830	254
	14,000	66,400	3,000	254
Optimum take-off run 1,000 yards:				
	9,000	61,300	2,000	256
Supermarine				
	2,000	44,790	1,500	273
	4,000	50,200	2,000	270
	8,000	60,300	3,000	265
	13,500	58,000	2,000	266
Optimum take-off run 1,000 yards:				
	11,500	58,000	2,000	266

Table C: *Comparison of Shorts and Supermarine B.12/36 designs (3)*

	Short	Supermarine
Take-off over 50ft screen (yards)	790	680
Landing over 50ft screen (yards)	650	690
Max speed 15,000ft (mph)	305	317
Tare (lb)	34,920	29,500

Plans for accelerated take-off were discarded in August 1938 due to tactical inflexibility and the risk of enemy attack destroying the means of launching bombers. Four types had been under consideration, of which rocket assistance was the most straightforward. That was later tried at Boscombe Down, with rockets under a Stirling's wing. One which fired spontaneously ignited the aircraft's rudder discouraging much effort in exploiting the system.

A huge catapult with underground power house was built for the RAE at Harwell. To launch a laden bomber required enormous thrust to generate which a dozen Rolls-Royce Kestrel engines were linked. Although the main installation was completed, and remained intact for many years, the surface catapult equipment was apparently never fitted; the device was certainly not used for any launching. The greatest difficulty in catapulting a large aircraft was reckoned to be obtaining sufficient aircraft strengthening to permit a 2g acceleration. Rapid loading of aircraft onto the catapult would certainly have posed a problem.

An alternative was the 'portable inertia catapult' intended for use where a 1,500 yard concrete runway was available. Two catapults to operate in unison and capable of handling Stirlings would have been needed, one on each side of the main runway. Bomber Command opposed the idea from the start on the grounds that it could easily cause runway obstructions. A plan was then put forward whereby the forward pulley carrying the cable to return the catapult would be housed beneath the surface. That would have entailed some minutes' delay between the launch of each bomber, even if the system was duplicated, and included collapsible arresting cable gear. Since aerodromes would have several runways, duplication of the equipment was necessary and the wells in which the gear would be sited were obviously susceptible to flooding and the gullies dangerous. Such catapults were portable in little more than name.

The fourth system was the rail track along which an aircraft on a sledge would be propelled to lift-off speed then released. Hope was that aircraft could be launched with undercarriages already retracted thereby making greatest use of the equipment. That might have been possible with rocket assistance. Each launch was reckoned to take at least three minutes - assuming loading of the aircraft on the track could readily take place in darkness and that aircraft could be marshalled safely and correctly at the end of the track.

What brought about the end of these exotic ideas was the eventual decision that bomber airfields would have one 1,800 yard runway, and up to three of 1,100 yards for use in strong cross winds. Concrete runways offered smooth, firm surfaces for take-off and were safer when landing heavy bombers. They also avoided airfield grass surfaces being transformed into quagmires. A major problem concerned how a pilot, in wartime, could find a runway at night. In 1938, reliance had to be placed upon Lorenz beam equipment. Once off the runway the possibility of an aircraft becoming bogged down in winter seemed likely. A 1,500yd runway was reckoned to give enough length for any foreseeable heavy aircraft, but if that was overloaded, or operations took place in bad weather, then rocket assistance still seemed the best answer when operating from hard surface runways. Set against this was the risk of both runways and queuing aircraft being bombed. Even so it was clearly easier to mend battered runways than to repair elaborate catapults.

There was a further possibility: the use of composite aircraft with a large machine like the Stirling taking off then launching from its back a small, fast bomber. The Short-built Mayo Composite aircraft promoted such ideas and Shorts proceeded with the design of just such a bomber combination. Again, it was the problem of the time likely to be taken in launching such a force, and its vulnerability in the launch period, that halted the idea before it was seriously considered. Instead, all of these schemes fell by the wayside. Conventional flying was the only realistic method coupled with making sure that take-off weights were kept as low as possible. But revision of the Short bomber's mainplanes had drastically altered calculations, increased power loading and resulted in an aeroplane with increased rate of roll but longer take-off run which was the very thing that the Ministry wanted reduced. A fuselage that was so long in comparison with the wings would bring trouble when taking off and landing in crosswinds.

The Short B.12/36 construction was strong, on semi-monocoque lines. The constant-section fuselage consisted of stringers passing through three main component joints, and was flush riveted. Four fuselage main sections were joined by bolts passing through, and frames reinforced internally by extrusion riveted across joints.

Wing construction was similar to that of the Sunderland and had lattice braced ribs, adopted instead of tie rod torsion box bracing in the upper truss. This continued through the fuselage, with close-tolerance bolted joints at root ends. Wing tips were detachable. For repair purposes, spar booms outboard of outer nacelles were later jointed. Outboard of this, a watertight wing would afford buoyancy on ditching.

Lower section spar booms fitted level with the fuselage decking which was supported by two deep longitudinal girders to form three 42ft long bomb cells. Six long doors in three sections hung from the girders. Fuselage narrowness resulted in cells only 19in wide which could thus never accommodate weapons of greater girth due to the fitting of the strengthening girders.

Pilots sat side by side above the forward end of the bomb cells. The navigator's, radio operator's and engineer's stations were close by. Suspended above the bomb aimer's position was the nose gunner. Autopilot steering controls were fitted below him, and oxygen bottles above the spar in the fuselage. Flares and launch tubes were aft of the bomb cells and a ventral Frazer-Nash FN 24 turret was chosen.

Four large fuel tanks in each wing were marked by external oval shaped access panels. Two more tanks fitted between spars and flap shrouds. Another in the wing leading edge was intended for ferry purposes. The others were later to be covered by rubber and soft latex, preventing fuel leakages caused by enemy fire.

An extremely strong airframe added to the structure weight, but meant that the bomber could absorb great punishment and survive. Shorts stressed the design in keeping with the aircraft's overall specification.

The company was very concerned about a potentially long take-off run. Gouge flaps which slid from the wing trailing edge could indeed be increased in area by fitting a second flap aft but, until flight trials had been undertaken, the necessity for such a drastic cure remained uncertain. To obtain firm evidence Shorts decided early in 1938 to build the half-scale plywood aerodynamic replica of the bomber. With an order for one hundred B.12/36s placed in April 1938, the company was even more eager that the aircraft should be an unqualified success. Included would be a scaled-down version of the then straightforward undercarriage. Originally the 'model' was expected to fly in May or June 1938, six months ahead of the date laid down for the first flight of the full-size aircraft. Instead, it was September before taxiing of 'M4' commenced. The Director of Technical Development was much in favour of building the half-scale model to assess flying qualities of the bomber, and reckoned it much better than relying upon wind tunnel tests.

Powered by four 90hp Pobjoy Niagara engines boosted to give 114hp each, and driving two-bladed propellers, the aircraft designated S.31 was commonly referred to as the 'M4', the Class B identity registration it carried. Shorts listed its loaded weight as 5,370lb, wing area 330sqft, wing loading 16.3lb/sqft and top speed 180mph. Painted silver, what proved to be a very agile aeroplane was first flown by John Lancaster Parker and Hugh Gordon from Rochester on 19 September 1938. On 21 and 22 October 1938 three of Martlesham Heath's test pilots managed ten half-hour flights in the aircraft. Their brief was to examine mainly its stability, trim and stalling when cg was at one position.

Their general opinion was that take-off and landing characteristics were good, although the aircraft swung very readily to the right during the take-off run in which it would lift itself off without need for any trim change. Rudder control faded somewhat in a glide but was otherwise sound. Slow response to aileron movement was experienced,

M4, the half-scale Stirling, had a simplified form of the original undercarriage.

but effective enough in a glide. Ailerons were very light, well harmonised, and little trim was needed when flaps were lowered. No directional change of trim was needed at speed, and longitudinal stability was neutral during climb and cruise. An experimental hinged tab on the elevators was controlled by aerodynamic load exerted on a hemispherical cup.

With the two port engines throttled back only a slight swing developed on landing and, with flaps up, the stall was gentle and there was no clear stall warning. When flaps and undercarriage were lowered, the wing abruptly dropped but, once the flaps were down, control was easy although the tailplane masked the elevators. More positive directional trim was needed.

All of that was very encouraging, until the A&AEE confirmed lengthy take-off and landing runs. This serious situation was coupled with a radical suggestion - wing incidence should be increased by 3 degrees making a total of 6½ degrees which would much increase drag which the initial low setting had been chosen to reduce. It would have improved lift and considerably cut the take-off run.

Tooling and prototype planning was advanced, making such a major change impossible. Instead, Shorts produced the only possible solution: they added 3 degrees to the ground angle by lengthening the undercarriage and introduced the notorious gear which later became so troublesome. The undercarriage legs were already lengthy to allow for loading and to cope with any extension of the belly turret during landing. The imposed shortened wing span combined with this complex undercarriage crippled the design.

The half-scale S.31 was modified and flew with a small version of the new undercarriage on 22 November. Then it was re-engined with Niagara IVs of 115hp with which it first flew on 10 January 1939. Horn balanced elevators were later fitted.

The finalised specification prepared for the production Short S.29 Stirling 1/PI showed it to be similar to L7605, the second prototype. Detailed modifications listed for production aircraft included more rapidly detachable outer mainplanes, no catapult provisioning, dual controls, Bristol Hercules III engines and armour fitted to the pilots'

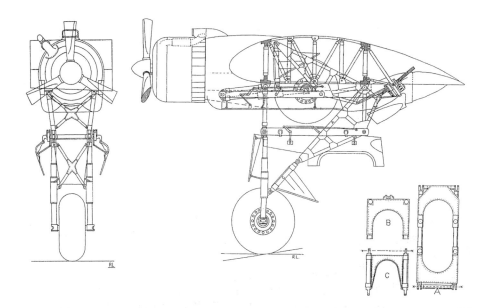

General arrangement of the Stirling's production undercarriage. (Richard Livermore)

and radio operator's seats, oil tanks and both inboard fuel tanks. The crew would number six, one manning the midships retractable turret. The off-duty radio operator would man the rear turret. Cutters would be fitted to wing leading edges to cut barrage balloon cables. Self sealing was to be fitted to the tankage for 1,912 gallons and also to the 308 gallon leading edge tanks. The alternatives for bomb provisioning would be:

(a) 14,000lb SA/B/LC/GP load
(b) twenty-four 500lb GP/SAP/AP
(c) seven 2,000lb
(d) three SCI smoke containers.

There was to be provision for converting bomb racks from 250lb or 500lb carriers to 2,000lb-type in a short time.

The contract now called for a take-off run of 600 yards at normal all-up weight and ranges were specified as:

1,500 miles at 15,000ft two-thirds max cruise revs, 4,000lb bomb load
2,000 miles at 15,000ft, two-thirds max cruise revs, 2,000lb load
3,000 miles at 15,000ft two-thirds max cruise revs after 30 minutes at max power
Maximum range 3,000 miles

Short's original tender quoted a normal operational load of 4,600lb and maximum loaded weight of 56,900lb. Radical modifications now proposed for the bomber meant increases in load/range capability and the following modified figures were agreed on 5 January 1939:

Normal loaded weight: 50,844lb for 1,496 miles
Maximum loaded weights:
56,240lb for 3,000 miles
66,240lb for 2,912 miles
67,000lb for 2,000 miles
At 67,240lb a 10,000lb bomb load was forecast as being carried for 2,000 miles.

All of these figures inevitably suggested a possibly much longer take-off run, something that everyone agreed should be avoided, but the temptation to extract the maximum possible from the aircraft was irresistible.

'M4' aerodynamic test flying continued while construction of the full-sized prototype, L7600, started late in 1938. On 14 March 1939, King George VI and Queen Elizabeth toured the Rochester factory viewing the construction of the Stirling prototype and seeing the mock-up of a possible 'Ideal Bomber' successor, the S.34 to specification B.1/39 and already called the Stirling Mk II. Although it resembled the S.29 Stirling, the potential successor had the desirable greater wing span, twin fins and rudders and two huge midships turrets each carrying two 20mm cannon chosen in place of a tail turret. The turret was also intended for the ventral position on P.13/36 designs - until that idea was abandoned in favour of having two of them, one for the upper hemisphere the other for the lower. Increased strength rear fuselage structure was being included to carry the hefty items, and it was estimated to add about 920lb while offering a better cg outcome. After seeing this advanced project Their Majesties proceeded to Rochester Airport where 'M4' was displayed by Harold Piper. The Queen was so impressed by the little aeroplane's display that she asked for, and was given, a repeat performance.

Mid-November 1938 brought an RAE recommendation that a modified tailplane to improve elevator control be designed. Tested on 'M4' early in 1939 it was partly this which had enabled such a spirited 'Command Performance'. The little aeroplane served for a variety of detail refinement tests prior to their application to the full-sized bomber.

The undercarriage geometry of L7600 involved breaks in the front leg and rear arch. Slight fuselage curvature reduced undercarriage height. (Shorts)

All except L7600 had wheels retracting into a forward swinging 'crate' attached to which were fairing doors. (Shorts)

The half-scale Stirling, M4. Initially painted silver, it became a camouflaged wartime light transport for Shorts.

Early in 1940 it was fitted with a mock-up of the midships cannon turret proposed for the Stirling and other bombers and RAE Farnborough placed it in their 24ft wind tunnel for airflow and drag measurement. About a year later it was again flying and used by Short's pilots travelling between Stirling bases. Worn out by the close of 1942 it came to grief in the hands of Sqn Ldr E J Moreton when, taking off from Stradishall in bad weather, it overturned and was damaged beyond repair. For many months it languished in a Stradishall hangar awaiting demise.

Chapter 3
On Trial

B Y October 1938 prototype building underway was being delayed by failure of the builders to deliver turrets for the aircraft. Arrangements were at this time well advanced for the transportation of the second prototype to Belfast where, after being erected, it was intended to give Short & Harland experience of an aircraft they were to produce. Only the tail turret for the first machine having arrived by late November, plans to fly the second aircraft from Belfast were abandoned. By mid-December 16,332 of the planned 17,000 diagrams needed to guide the workforce had been issued, all fuselage sections were assembled, the mainplanes were well advanced, outer engine nacelles being wedded to the wings, but the nose turret had still not arrived at Rochester. On the day of the Royal visit the mainplanes were complete, the undercarriage was being fitted and engines installed. The first flight had been set for 22 April, but the aircraft was not ready in time. When it was, a fracture in the assembly came about during test retraction of the undercarriage, delaying the first flight until May.

There were other problems too. Throughout 1939 concern within the company had largely switched from a likely over-long take-off run to repeated weight increases which, by January 1939, had added about 9,200lb. Of this, 5,700lb arose from additional structure. Balloon cable cutters and de-icers would add 1,800lb and any additional flaps about 300lb. Normal loaded weight had risen to about 53,000lb bringing the aircraft near to its forecast maximum permissible take-off weight. Air Ministry estimates showed a limiting weight of 63,000lb, which would mean a take-off run of 1,000 yards to clear 50ft which was way beyond the specified limit. The implication might be a reduced bomb load, 7,000lb for a 2,000 mile sortie, a mere 1,000lb load for 3,000 miles and tyre pressures of about 43.5psi. All of this provoked little short of general alarm.

"In view of the disappointing load-carrying capacity to be anticipated from this type," commented N E Rowe, "it may be necessary to review commitments on the Stirling." Detailed investigation followed, and new figures suggested a range of 1,490 miles at 52,954lb take-off weight, 1,980 miles at 58,350lb. At the maximum loaded weight of 69,100lb range would be 1,980 miles. With a 10,000lb bomb load at 64,580lb range would also be 1,980 miles.

Such deliberations were unknown to Short's workers who viewed the aircraft as prestigious. Proud, they were, especially of their flying-boats. However, at the factory Gregg Webb recalls, "concern was felt about the configuration of the main undercarriage with its new-type oleo legs". One of Short's craftsmen was D C Marks. He started work as a boy of fourteen in 1938 at the seaplane works. "There was a road through the centre with the works being divided into 'Shops', running to No 18 during the war, fronting the River Medway for a mile or so. The first Stirling was started in No 1 Shop."

On his first day at Short's he reported to red-haired Mr Shepard.

> "In the Shop the fuselage was being assembled. It was the biggest I had ever seen being put together with a series of large rings of Z-section following the fuselage lines. Each ring had been made by hand in smaller dural sections. All was riveted together to make one ring, which included in its shape the bomb floor and doors. Work on the 'Night Bomber' was to the extent of building the fuselage.
>
> "In early 1939 No 1 Shop moved to Rochester Airport where the prototype was completed. Rumour had it that wingspan had been reduced to allow it out of the hangar! Excitement built. Early summer was boiling hot. The completed Stirling was outside on the grass most days. They seemed to be engine running all day."

There had been a disappointment. Bristol were unable to deliver the Hercules Mk III, and inferior Mk Is were fitted. "Being on piecework," recalls Gregg Webb, "we could not be absent from work long. I used any excuse to walk by the windows near the drawing office to watch what was happening outside. One day excitement mounted as the bomber moved down the field to the other side of the aerodrome. Throttles were opened for what looked like a fast taxi, but it never took off; the first flight occurred at the

Second prototype, L7605, shortly after completion. (Shorts)

weekend when we were not at work."

Aboard L7600 for the maiden flight were John Lankester Parker (pilot), Sqn Ldr E J Moreton (second pilot), George Cotton (foreman of engine installation and flight engineer) and John Bull (flight engineer) who recalls that first flight:

"It took place on Sunday 14 May 1939. The first Form 1909 was issued the previous day. The aircraft taxied on that date to check brakes, and a number of fast runs across the airfield were carried out. For some reason a flight was abandoned. It could have been that the wind was unfavourable as the aerodrome at Rochester was an odd shape and was grass surfaced.

"I don't think any of us had any misgivings about the undercarriage, although it was a strange shape. This, of course, was mainly for convenience of bomb loading. Considerable trouble was experienced with the undercarriage door functioning, and a lash-up with Bungee cord to close the doors when retracted was introduced. I was instructed, prior to the first flight, to see whether the doors closed after retraction, and if not to give a hefty pull on the yards of Bungee running through the fuselage.

"Take-off appeared to be normal and the aircraft flew quite well. But it appeared that, as the weight of the machine came on to the undercarriage on landing, the back arch gave up the ghost, fractured, and L7600 finished up in a belly flop approximately in the middle of the airfield. I would mention that the back arch was of light alloy extrusion. On the second prototype this was changed to steel tubing."

The "concern ... felt about the configuration of the main undercarriage" by Gregg Webb and the others had been fully justified. It meant delay, going back to the drawing board at a crucial time. Morale at the works had been high following the success of the Empire Boats and Sunderland, though some wise folk were concerned at the narrowness of the Stirling's bomb cells. Few realised how serious would be the reduction in span.

"The unfortunate landing produced a wave of depression, expressed forcibly by the old stagers whose opinions I had come deeply to respect," recalls Gregg Webb. "Shorts never could make a landplane," they said. Thereafter, main pride rested in design and manufacturing craftsmanship. It took weeks for the firm to recover from this major blow. The first prototype was so badly damaged it was fit only for scrap, and the whole project was seriously delayed. Some considered that the undercarriage should have been left alone, the long run chanced. There could be no going back now, though: the task was to make the best of the Stirling. The country needed it – and so did Shorts.

The undercarriage had to be put right. It was strengthened, and the door mechanism finalised. Every care was taken with the second prototype, L7605, which made its first flight on 3 December1939 as John Bull records:

> "On this occasion the undercarriage was not retracted, deliberately, although it could have been. Apart from that the flight was normal, like the landing. Then the aircraft was grounded, enabling it to be prepared for Boscombe Down. The task had been just to prove the aerodynamics of the machine. I believe horn-balanced elevators were on for the first flight, and then replaced by the normal type.
>
> "The next flight took place on 24 December 1939 and was successful. The undercarriage retracted, doors closed satisfactorily. Flight trials continued without any incident."

A feature of the Stirling was the use of Exactor throttle controls. Short's pilots had plenty of experience of them in the flying-boats. Exactors were the source of persistent complaint among RAF pilots, and John Bull recalls this feature:

> "In view of the complaints about Exactor throttles when the aircraft was in service, comment seems opportune. I had considerable experience of them. They were fitted in the Empire Boats. It was my job as fitter on those to install, prime, and set up throttle mixture controls. Exactors were also my province on the first Stirlings.
>
> "When the second prototype was about ready for A&AEE, John Parker was of the opinion that the four throttles had become too heavy for one-handed operation, so something had to be done about it. All the units, both transmitters and receivers, were removed and the glands eased off to bring the operating load down to an acceptable poundage. When reinstalled in the aircraft it was found, when the engines were running, that the Exactors would not stay in place, but moved to 'closed throttle' when the hand was removed. The modification to overcome this consisted of four serrated arcs of metal mounted on the throttle box with spring-loaded detents mounted on the throttle levers, so that the throttles would stay in the desired position.
>
> "In service, a further modification was introduced: a hinged top position to the throttle levers which, when pushed or pulled, lifted a spring-loaded detent which registered with an adjustable stop for cruising power. This appeared to be the ultimate answer to Exactor controls."

On 22 April 1940, L7605 was delivered to Boscombe Down for four months' trials, spending a brief time at Ringway for safety in August–September before returning to Shorts on 2 September 1940.

Work on the first production aircraft was hastened in early 1940 in an attempt to recapture lost time. Sufficient Mk I or similar Mk III Hercules engines intended for the first fifteen Stirlings still being unavailable, Mk IIs, which peaked at low altitude, had to be fitted. On 7 May 1940, Parker flew the first production aircraft, N3635, for twenty-five minutes. During take-off an engine cut occurred, investigation of the cause attributing it to rapid throttle movement being met with a lag in the un-pressurised liquid column of the Exactor hydraulic transmission system. The seriousness, and the likelihood that it would become a common problem when the aircraft was in Service hands, was not appreciated. Exactor throttle systems were common on flying boats where power alterations were nowhere as critical as with landplanes operating from much restricted space. Had it been realised that Exactors were unsuitable there is little doubt that they would never have been fitted to any Stirling.

N3636 remained at Rochester for makers' flying tests. On 29 May N3637 was flown to CFS Upavon for the preparation of pilots' notes. On that occasion Hugh Gordon was second pilot to John Lankester Parker. They landed the machine 'uphill' for there was a pronounced slope at Upavon. It was only then decided that Upavon was too small for an aircraft of this size, and in consequence it was flown to Boscombe Down the following morning.

Through the summer of 1940, as the Battle of Britain raged, Stirlings were tested at Boscombe Down and their actual performance was revealed. The initial findings were disquieting for they revealed as follows:

Take-off weight during tests: 57,400lb
Take-off to unstick: 640 yards
To clear 50ft: 1200 yards
Service ceiling: 15,000ft

All of these basic figures exceeded estimates except one, for the Hercules II engines had drastically lowered the service ceiling (the highest altitude at which the aircraft could still climb at 100 feet per minute) to its intended normal operating altitude. That made the bomber, in its present condition, virtually useless for operations.

What of its speed? A&AEE trials revealed these figures:

Height (ft)	Max speed (mph, TAS)	Time to height (min)	Rate of climb (ft per min)
5,000	253	5.6	950
10,000	249.5	12.5	560
15,000	218	27.5	160

Stalling speed: 107mph TAS
Landing speed: 110mph TAS
Glide-in speed: 120mph TAS

Whilst these figures were not exceptionally high, they were better than those attained by the medium bombers in service. The Stirling was, perhaps surprisingly, almost as fast as a Blenheim IV and even in its early condition greatly superior to them all.

For bombing operations, range and cruise performance were generally of more importance than speed – and Boscombe Down's tests revealed more disturbing statistics:

L7605 at Boscombe Down in December 1939.

Aircraft	Height (ft)	Weight (lb)	Cruise speed (2,400 revs, weak mix, mph)
N3635	10,000	57,400	184
N3636	10,000	48,000	194
N3637	10,000	45,000	195
N3644	10,500	53,000	200

Above 10,000ft performance deteriorated. The original specification, it will be recalled, asked for a cruising speed of 230mph at 15,000ft for a range of 1,500 miles carrying a 2,000lb bomb load. Overload take-off run was to be 700 yards for a 2,000 mile range at 15,000ft with a 4,000lb load, with 14,000lb as the maximum load. Maximum range was to be 3,000 miles. How far short of these figures the Stirling fell is all too clear.

Some improvement in cruise performance was obtained after compensation for position error had been incorporated in the figures, suggesting a cruising speed of 232mph at 10,000ft at 54,000lb, the average flying weight after take-off at 57,400lb. Full throttle maximum engine condition for economical cruise was achieved at a mere 10,000ft with the Hercules Mk II, rated at 1,100/1,150hp at 5,000ft with +1 1/2 lb boost, 1,375hp at 2,750 revs at 4,000ft. These figures were close to those of the Hercules HE 1M fitted to the prototype. Mk III engines would have a better output at greater height so high hopes rested on engine development.

N3635 was examined in detail, and tested at 3,000ft and 10,000ft at typical service loading of 57,400lb (41,160lb tare, 48,003lb on landing). The gradual weight rise during design had reduced performance. Take-off weight was restricted to 64,000lb. This included a tankage of 1,935gal from a possible total of 2,293gal and a bomb load of only 3,500lb.

To increase the bomb load, fuel had to be drastically reduced so that with 1,096gal, bomb load was 10,000lb; and with 584gal, 14,000lb. Some 200gal of fuel were needed for run-up and climb to 10,000ft. It was difficult to maintain 15,000ft, the absolute ceiling being considered as barely 14,000ft. At 10,000ft the range obtainable was barely 5 percent more, trials with L7605 showing little difference.

Range and speed trials undertaken at Boscombe Down with the aircraft weighing 64,000lb at take-off and 62,500lb after climb to 10,000ft revealed further disturbing figures:

mph/IAS	mph/TAS	Revs	ampg
184	195	2,400	0.86
161	171	2,200	1.07 (− 3% lb boost, 160gal/hr)
192	207	2,400	0.99 (209gal/hr)

The most economical cruise at 10,000ft appeared to be 158mph IAS/184mph TAS at 2,400 revs using 162gal/hr – ie. 1.34 ampg. Climb to 10,000ft took twenty-seven minutes (145mph IAS to 5,000ft then 138mph IAS to 10,000ft), taking about 150gal to cover about 70 miles. Range in maximum cruise condition (2,400 revs – 1 1/4 lb boost) was 1,740 miles at 187mph IAS. At 170mph IAS range was about 2,020 miles. Absolute range at 60,500lb with hot intakes was 2,140 miles, with cold intakes 2,200 miles.

These depressing figures were being obtained as production came slowly under way. N3638 left Rochester on 8 June 1940, for allocation to Short & Harland, Belfast, who were already starting Stirling production. N3639 went to A&AEE in June, N3640 to 10 MU, Hullavington on 8 July, N3641 to 48 MU on 20 July, N3642 to 19 MU on 25 July, N3643 to 22 MU on 31 July and N3644 to 10 MU on 9 August.

By then the first Stirling squadron had formed, and drew upon the first ten production aircraft with Hercules Mk IIIs, unsuitable for operational use, and Stirling Trainers. One, N3644, was later re-engined with Hercules Mk IIIs for use by XV Squadron. The Trainers had engines in monocoque nacelles making engine change difficult whereas later nacelles were truncated at firewalls just ahead of the wing leading edges. Tubular steel engine mountings on the Stirling Mk III were fitted to the firewalls, allowing the entire engine plant to be detachable.

L7605 in summer 1940 acquired prominent fin stripes. Pitot head is fitted to the radio mast.

The inboard nacelles were slung low to enable the 6ft diameter tyres and the complex undercarriage to retract into the nacelle and wing. On the first prototype the undercarriage hinged on the front spar. In subsequent aircraft a crate hung below the spar and swung forward as the wheels retracted backwards into the crate. The advantage of this arrangement was that the edge of the wheel barely protruded. Undercarriage retraction, flap operation and retraction of the twin tail wheels (chosen to permit more internal space after retraction) was electrical. The undercarriage motors were later sited in the fuselage to permit manual override if motors failed. Just how much the Stirling's performance was below that specified is shown by this simple comparison:

	Specified	Actual
Maximum range/bomb load	3,000 miles/8,000lb	1,930 miles /5,000lb
Maximum bomb load/range	2,000 miles /14,000lb	740 miles /14,000lb
Most economic cruise	230mph/15,000ft	200mph/15,000ft

All along the Short B.12/36 had been viewed as an insurance against the two Supermarine bomber prototypes (L6889 and L6890) but they, too, were in trouble.

Supermarine had interpreted the specification quite differently from Shorts. Their original submission comprised variants powered either by the Bristol Pegasus XVIIII, Hercules, Kestrel KV 26, Merlin F or Napier W108 Dagger. Only two of that listing would have provided enough power. Most of the bombs to be carried in wing cells aft of the single spar, and by not carrying them tiered, the fuselage cross section had, as previously mentioned, been kept small. By spreading the load over half the wing span the bending moments of the mainplane were reduced, promoting a less weighty structure, which gave the Supermarine bomber an advantage over its competitor. Fuel tanks were an integral part of the wing structure and within the metal leading edge ahead of the spar, which feature saved about 1,000lb in weight. According to the company, the aircraft could carry twenty-nine 250lb 'B' anti-shipping bombs, twenty-nine 500lb GP

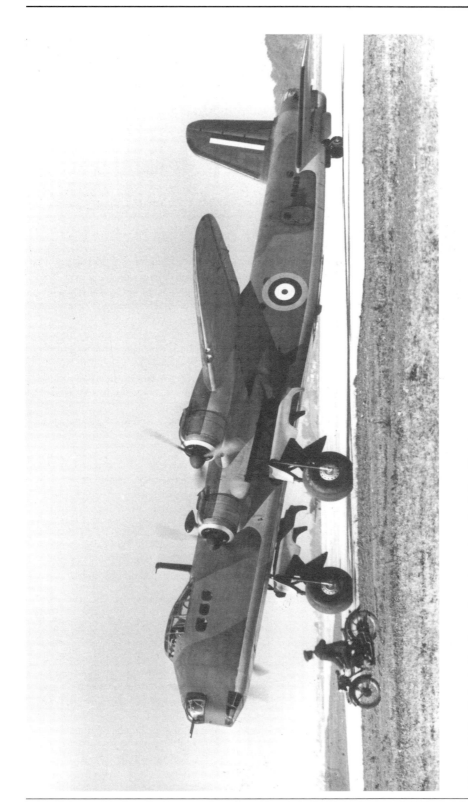

N3638, a 'Stirling Trainer' with yellow under surfaces, pictured at Belfast. (Shorts)

bombs and the required seven 2,000lb weapons. Double main wheels were chosen, since the smaller tyres to be used would take up less space when retracted. In January 1937 it had been decided to increase the wing span substantially from 93ft to 97ft, increasing its wing area from 1,240sqft to 1,358sqft, and also to enlarge the flaps, for it was clear that the original design would have a long field performance. Fitting Hercules instead of Merlin engines meant providing more fuel because of the former's high consumption rate. That was forecast to reduce the top speed from an unlikely 370mph to an equally unlikely 360mph in an aircraft with an all-up weight of over 55,000lb. By autumn 1938, Supermarine were claiming a top speed of 330mph at 17,000ft and a cruising speed of 290mph and a range of 1,980 miles linked with a 2,000lb load being carried at 179mph at 15,000ft. Normal loaded weight would, the company claimed, be 44,000lb and the aircraft's service ceiling would be 32,000ft. Overloaded it would cruise at just over 200mph carrying 8,000lb for 3,680 miles, or 14,000lb for 2,360 miles. Whether it would have lived up to these expectations it is not possible to relate, for the two prototypes whose construction was so delayed as to make them of little value were destroyed during the bombing of the Supermarine Itchen factory on 26 September 1940. In late November 1940 the Air Ministry cancelled its contract for the aircraft. Long delay was not only the prerogative of the Supermarine bombers. Shorts had estimated that the first production Stirling would fly in May 1939. The crash of L7600, a variety of teething troubles and an over optimistic outlook by the firm were all blamed for the first production machine appearing a year late.

Production came under way as the Beaverbrook Plan for concentration only upon aircraft in service was announced. The Stirling had been delayed because of the tooling need, and time taken to build components. It was 18 October before the first Belfast-built machine, N6000, flew by which time the Stirling was in squadron hands. Operations, though, were four months away.

Chapter 4
Into the Grand Ring

GROUP Capt George Blacklock – then a Sergeant Pilot – was among those who arrived at Boscombe Down on 3 July 1940 to form the Stirling Development Flight. "The time we spent there was less inspiring than the title of the unit," George Blacklock recalls, "for due to the poor serviceability, we did very little flying. One of the highlights was the visit of 'Boom' Trenchard and his announcement that we were to become 7 Squadron." On 14 July the Air Ministry had ordered 7 Squadron's resuscitation at Leeming in Yorkshire's Whitley-equipped 4 Group.

Arrival at the station of what was then a huge new bomber was, for those who knew nothing of its problems, grand for morale. Among them was the late Bob May, later Mayor of Cambridge. He recalled:

> We were expecting the aircraft. Engines were heard, and they weren't a Whitley's Merlins. We hurried on to the tarmac, and in the distance glimpsed this lovely aircraft – a beautiful sight.
> I remember so well the high cockpit, long fuselage and tall tail fin, and how absolutely thrilled we were. It circled, made a married man's landing, then taxied slowly to the hangar where we viewed it eyes goggling with amazement. It had looked impressive when flying, but as it taxied in we were amazed to see that undercarriage – gaunt, like a lot of scaffolding. It was huge, much bigger than anyone would have imagined the aircraft needed. It was all tubular spars intertwined and linked. We soon found it to be a dangerous contraption, but to the delight and thrill of 7 Squadron the Stirling had arrived.

It was 3 August 1940 and aboard N3640 on its flight was Sgt Plt Blacklock and crew. As to Bob May's reference to the aircraft's excellent landing, George Blacklock comments:

> I am amused by his description of its arrival and the impression made on the waiting ground crew. To say that I made a married man's landing is perhaps slightly ironic. I had assumed that having the honour of making the first entrance was at least partly due to my having quite the opposite marital status!
> The two other qualified pilots – Fg Off G H Smith and Plt Off R W Cox – were married, and had the privilege of transporting their wives and cars to Yorkshire. As a Sergeant Pilot I was, in every way, the junior bod! Having found a bed and stowed my kit I was having a quiet cup of tea in the Sergeants' Mess when Reg Cox arrived in no mean state of sweat; I was wanted at the hangar immediately. On arrival I found not only the Station Commander, but several Army officers including General Sir John Dill, Chief of the Imperial General Staff, who asked to be shown over the aircraft. He looked a rather aged gentleman and I was doubtful of his ability to climb through the main spar, clad as he was in smart riding breeches and knee boots. However, he managed very well and was quite impressed by his brief tour.
> The following morning the CO made good after parting me from my car, by awarding me the captaincy of N3640. Fg Off Smith was naturally the Flight Commander and poor Reg Cox was to be Squadron Adjutant. Thus, I had become captain of the first four-engined bomber in the Command. But not for long. I did not fly that aircraft again until 28 August, and the next day it crashed in the Pennines.

Placing the Stirling in 4 Group had come about on the basis that, having a long-range capability, it was the obvious Whitley replacement. The latter too had always been viewed as an interim bomber although its service record was as good as, and in some respects better than, other bombers. On other grounds it was an unsuitable idea, for the Group flew Merlin-engined aircraft and held spares for such power plants. Introduction of a Bristol-engined bomber upset that arrangement. Ultimately Merlin-engined Halifaxes more logically replaced the Whitleys.

In *The Stirling Bomber* (Faber & Faber 1980) reference to pilots being drawn from

Cockpit layout of Hercules II Stirling. Exactor controls and fuel mix levers are central, engine rev and boost gauges are on the instrument panel and the Lorenz indicator and repeater compass are to the left of these. Bomb door switches are right of the throttles, propeller feathering buttons to right of the main compass. (Shorts)

Cockpit port side in an early aircraft with the engine maker's plate beyond the 'wheel'. Navigation items are on the left side. (Shorts)

Bomb aimer's compartment in a Mk I. (Shorts)

Retractable FN 25 ventral turret visible in the aft fuselage. (Shorts)

Coastal Command claimed by some sources is incorrect. The Development Flight comprised Sqn Ldr Paul Harris with a skeleton crew who had finished a tour on Wellingtons of 149 Squadron, Sgt Plt George Blacklock with a skeleton crew tour-expired from 99 Squadron and the recently commissioned Plt Off R W Cox who had been instructing on Whitleys at Abingdon. They were joined after a week or so by Fg Off Smith, who had also completed a tour on 149 Squadron. At Leeming, Fg Off Bradley joined them during August, along with Fg Off Henry and Flt Sgt Witt all tour-expired and from 4 Group Whitley squadrons. Fg Offs Larney and Best were both New Zealanders from 3 Group's No 75 Squadron. Larney was something of an 'electrical guru' and, instead of converting to Stirlings, became the Squadron Electrical Officer. Eric Best went to No XV when that Squadron started to re-equip.

Wg Cdr Paul Harris had arrived at Leeming on 3 August, there to command 7 Squadron which, he had been told, would receive eight Stirlings when production permitted; but production was very slow. Despite the Beaverbrook decision to concentrate production upon six well-tried combat aircraft types, other aeroplanes were still being built, including Stirlings. Shorts continued to produce them singly in the same way as they had their magnificent flying boats, applying their craftsmen's skill to produce strong, superbly constructed machines. Such policy might well have suited Imperial Airways; it was most unsuitable for bomber building. Certainly the strength inherent in the Stirling was applaudable; its costs in structure weight and production rate were not.

What of the ground crew faced with maintaining what was, in August 1940, looked upon as a huge, complex machine? Bob May recalled:

> There weren't many of us on the Squadron at that time. We hadn't much equipment, but we were tremendously intent upon our tasks. The Stirling meant a break from the monotony of cleaning hangar floors! Now we had something to work upon, a sort of great status symbol. Fighter Command held the headlines and we felt our turn would come. We had the first four-engined bomber in the RAF, and we were very proud of it. We worked on our one aeroplane whenever we could, for as long as we could. We were supposed to do a daily inspection – we sometimes did twelve. Just to get the trestles around the engines was quite a performance. People somehow liked to do this. We used to put covers on the engines, although we kept the aeroplane in the hangar whilst learning all we could about it. It was all very exciting. We knew little about its past.

The few aircrew shared the machine with the groundcrew, each claiming their priorities. Simple handling came first, then it was time to arm the turrets.

At Short & Harland in Belfast, Stirling production commenced in June 1940. Mr J H Lower had, in October 1936, been appointed by Shorts (who held 51 percent capital, the remainder being put up by Harland & Wolff) as Works Manager. The company locally recruited workers skilled in all branches of engineering, relying upon them for tooling, and for building Bristol Bombays, Blenheim components, and then Handley Page Herefords. Nearly thirty Stirlings were in various stages of construction when, late on 14 August 1940, German bombers visited the works.

About fifteen Heinkel He IIIs of KGr. 100 based at Vannes, Brittany, delivered a sharp night attack which damaged the final assembly shop reducing N6025-28 to scrap and splintering others. But this was only a foretaste of what was to occur next day.

Sydney Groves joined Shorts at Rochester Airport in May 1939 as a time recorder. Transferred to the night shift, he had been at work on 12 July when distant crumps were heard. The enemy was getting nearer. "In daylight," he recalls, "we found a string of small bomb craters, coming from the direction of the Davis Estate and finishing just short of the hangars. One bomb landed in the road close to the duck pond of the farm across the way; a bomb fell in the later big raid in exactly the same place."

Thursday 15 August 1940 brought a massive onslaught against Britain, the Germans mounting a maximum effort. Soon after dawn a Junkers Ju 88 reconnoitred the

Rochester area. Around 2.00pm over eighty Dornier Do 17Zs of KG 3 began taking off from Antwerp, led by Chamier-Glisczinski. Over one hundred Messerschmitt Bf 109s of JG 51, JG 52 and JG 54 took up defensive positions around the bombers which crossed in over Deal at 1530 hrs. Meanwhile, a formation of about sixty Bf 109s sped in at Dover, splitting into two groups to protect the flanks of the bombers. Hurricanes of Nos 111 and 151 Squadrons, and a dozen Spitfires of 64 Squadron patrolling between Manston and Hawkinge, were vectored to intercept. Although they were joined by Hurricanes of 17 and 32 Squadrons, their total strength was insufficient to breach the fighter screen whose top cover, in particular, engaged them driving them off.

Over Faversham at 1535 hrs the Dornier force split into two formations, and Stab KG 3 with I and II/KG 3 ran in to attack Rochester Airport. The bombers had come in from the south-east out of range of Chatham's anti-aircraft guns. As the formation comprising twelve Dorniers in vic formation followed by six slightly lower swung about to attack, a dozen gun sites engaged them firing 235 mixed rounds, many of which burst around the raiders. Ample fighter cover was protecting the Dorniers, but it could not prevent the four 3.7in guns of the 159th Bty, 53 Regt at site S11 from scoring a direct hit on a Do 17 which crashed into the sea north of Garrison Point, Sheerness to the satisfaction of watching fishermen. The bombers released ninety-four high-explosive bombs, others which failed to explode and probably some incendiaries all of which fell in a line across Chatham, Rochester and Rochester Airport, where eight were known to have exploded at Shorts, starting a fire which took two hours to bring under control. One very large bomb exploded in the wing shop at Pobjoy Motors putting a third of the factory out of use. As a result of the crushing attacks, six Stirlings – N3645 and N3647 to N3651 – were destroyed and production at Rochester was halted. The Luftwaffe had dealt a devastating blow to the build-up of the Stirling force, and not until March 1942 did Stirling components begin leaving the rebuilt Rochester airport factory.

In Shorts' factory at the receiving end of the bombing was D C Marks who will never forget the punishing raid:

> It was about 3.30 in the afternoon when we received an alert and cleared the factory. Within minutes the whole air shook in rapid concussion and deafened us in our shelter, for all the bombs came down together. Our charge hand went to the door of the shelter, looked out, and told us solemnly that our factory was burning – but it was actually only a small fire. We apprentices were sent home for the rest of the week.

Sydney Groves had been resting ready for his night shift. He recalls being awakened by his wife about 4.00pm.

> I went out to see, from my home in Strood, a huge pall of smoke over the hills in the direction of the airport. I cycled over Rochester Bridge and along City Way, only to be stopped by another alert as I entered Arethusa Road. I reached the airport gate at about 4.15pm and was able to enter in my capacity as air raid warden. I joined Ron Davies (later landlord of the Prince of Wales in Railway Street) for a tour of inspection. Smoke and water were everywhere. The production Stirlings were a sorry sight with their backs broken. Everywhere were signs of shrapnel-riddled sections and buildings. A fire watcher's post – a large, bell-like device – was peppered with holes made by parts of oxygen bottles exploding, and a very likeable Mr Oakley died at this post. He was the only casualty.
>
> We worked all through the night, and into the next day, and later held a pay parade on the tarmac outside the hangars while soldiers with fixed bayonets hovered around. Invasion seeming imminent, large stakes were now driven in over the airfield to stop Ju 52s landing.

There were many stories of the strange twist of events. Mr Bates, just released from the Army to work at Shorts, placed his shoes by his sandwich case. Returning to the factory he found a piece of shrapnel had removed an eyelet from a shoe, passed through his case and bisected his sandwiches. More ominously several unexploded bombs poked from walls: it was not a healthy place in which to tarry.

Marks returned to work the following Monday to find the detail shop in confusion. Air raid warnings punctuated the day sending everyone hastening to the shelters. There was an enormous hole in the shop roof:

> We were very nervous, and put to work repairing splinter holes in finished parts. I remember a charge hand saying to me, "This makes us all the more determined to go on building the bomber". Craters were everywhere outside the factory.

Sydney Groves recalls:

> Within a week dispersal orders were effected. I was one of the first into Strood Extension. I set up office with a table, chairs and a cabinet surrounded by a screen of sacking over a framework of battens. The unfinished building needed ramps, walls and roofing. The Mainplane Section was eventually established at Strood, which meant that long articulated lorries had to negotiate the narrow streets.

Mr J H Lower appointed to establish dispersed production units for Stirlings recalled that:

> Part of the Gloster Aircraft Co works, Hucclecote, served until Rochester reopened, twenty-seven Mk 1s and a Mk II being completed at Gloucester between July 1941 and November 1941. The Drawing Office dispersed to Kidderminster.

Part of the GWR works at Swindon was acquired, material salvaged from bombing being sent there allowing Stirling manufacture to commence. From other sites – at Blunsdon and Sevenhampton – major components were taken to South Marston airfield where the aircraft were erected and flight tested. Production Control was established in a large house at Stratton St Margarets. Ultimately 351 Stirlings were completed by the Swindon Division, management of which was transferred to Armstrong-Whitworth Aircraft Ltd on 1 September 1943. The new firm supervised the completion of the final 106 Stirlings generated in the Swindon area. Ten Stirlings (Hercules Mk II) had been Rochester built before the bombing. It was obvious that the aircraft's ceiling with these engines was insufficient for operations, yet interruptions to production seemed certain to force their operational employment. On 20 August it was decided essential for succeeding aircraft to have Hercules Mk IIIs. There could be no retrospective fitment, because of the early type special nacelles.

On 12 August N3641 reached 7 Squadron, followed by N3642 on 29 August. Two more joined in September. Bomber Command wanted a Stirling for AFDU assessment of ventral and dorsal defence. None was available, such was the need to equip 7 Squadron. When fuel consumption tests were being conducted using N3641 on 1 September, it was fired upon over the Isle of Man, but no damage was suffered.

Attempted loading of N3641 with 12 x 250lb GP bombs showed that the cables were too short for holding beams to be lowered to accept the weapons. Therefore the bomber took off with a small load, most worrying to the squadron. The full load take-off run was seen to be so long for Leeming that the squadron was told to be prepared to fell trees on the runway line should an invasion come.

Stirling high-explosive bomb loads could be arranged in twelve ways, the main loading being 7 x 2,000lb AP; or 24 x 500lb GP/SAP, 8 x 500lb GP/SAP; 8 x 500lb AS; 24 x 250lb released in two or four salvos; and 5 x 1,000lb or 6 x 500lb GP, SAP. Modification 266 enabled the Stirling to carry 7 x 1,900lb bombs.

Fuel consumption rates needed careful investigation prior to commencement of operational flying so, on 29 September 1940, Fg Off T P A Bradley DFC took N3640 on test. At about 1230 hrs engine trouble developed. With a halted engine the Stirling quickly lost height, and eventually crashed into a Westmoreland stone wall.

Three aircraft now remained with 7 Squadron, and snags were plentiful. Undercarriage motors were burning out, the rear turret was exceptionally cold, rain seeped into the cockpit. Engine plugs brought ignition problems and N3641 encountered tail wheel retracting mechanism troubles, traced to the operating motors. Brackets for gill motors came adrift; and oil leaks during plug changes were serious. Oil temperatures ran high on port motors and oil coolers soon needed replacing.

On 21 August a major policy meeting had taken place at Rochester to review the development of Stirling defensive armament. Although Short's B.1/39 design had fallen by the wayside, development of its huge 20mm cannon turret had continued because it was required for the twin-Vulture-engined Boulton Paul cannon fighter, later bomber schemes and for Saunders-Roe flying boats still under consideration. Early in September 1940 the fighter was cancelled, releasing turrets for other aircraft. A trial installation of 20mm cannon turrets in Stirlings and Halifaxes had been requested at a progress meeting on 17 April 1940 and the Air Staff was still anxious for that work to go ahead.

N3641 at Rochester, summer 1940. (Shorts)

The August meeting with Shorts established that the Stirling and Halifax should, in their Mk II forms, have not two- but four-cannon dorsal and ventral turrets, and that they should then no longer have nose and tail turrets. Estimates suggested that 3,000lb would be added to the aircraft's weight.

Shorts found it exceedingly difficult to find any way of accommodating such huge turrets without drastically altering the Stirling's design and cg loading. Nevertheless they were ordered to forge ahead, but with a twin-cannon turreted aircraft for which, they were told, turrets should be available in five months time. Short's told the Air Ministry that there was no way in which 20mm turrets could be fitted in addition to existing nose and tail guns, but the ACAS(T) replied that he had "no confidence in the elimination of all nose and tail armament". Developed cannon turrets were far from ready even late in the war; even alternative use of .50in guns would have been impossible before 1942.

That defensive armament must be increased there was general agreement at the August meeting. It would be improved but less radical than hitherto suggested – and it would be implemented over a longer time scale than hoped for. Alterations to the ambitious plans formulated on 17 April 1941 were thus:

1st Stage: two nose and four tail .303in guns, two ventral .303in guns and two sets of hand-held beam guns.
2nd Stage: nose and tail guns unchanged; one set of two hand-guided ventral guns and a dorsal turret containing two .303in guns.
3rd Stage: as for Stage 2, but with two .50in tail turret guns.
4th Stage: as for Stage 3, but with a two-cannon dorsal turret.

Introduction of beam guns was causing confusion throughout Bomber Command and particularly among Wellington squadrons. The cause? Failure to issue definite instructions to contractors, as a result of which Stirlings, over many months, left production lines lacking suitable beam gun mountings. As for fitting a dorsal turret, that meant ventral turret deletion. Such a change was many months away although, as early as 24 July 1940, affirmation was reached and high priority awarded to making a trial installation of a dorsal turret in a Stirling.

On 30 September 1940, a report summarised four weeks' 'intensive flying' during which N3638 replaced N3640. Its forthright conclusion? The Stirling was judged unfit for operations in the foreseeable future – a most bitter blow.

As a result N6002 would, when ready, fly to Hucclecote for maker's very intensive trials, and among its modifications would be a revised cabin heating system. Particular criticism had been levelled (as forecast) at the high level of cockpit noise –intolerable during lengthy sorties. Windows were being sucked out by air pressure, and even when in place they produced high noise levels and admitted strong draughts. Sliding windows were therefore stiffened, and covers were placed over the high cockpit canopies at dispersals. Undercarriage selection levers overstrained action cables. Gravest concern, though, surrounded the Exactor throttle.

Throughout test flying at Boscombe Down the throttle controls raised most serious concern, and the Air Ministry questioned their suitability for a four-engined landplane. The matter was raised between the Air Staff and Shorts on 24 August 1940, and discussed again on 4 September. As a result, Shorts agreed to fit rod and chain controls on the forthcoming new Stirling Mk II. That was no longer the radical redesign but the 1939 planned Wright Cyclone-engined version of the Mk 1 envisaged for production by Canadian Associated Aircraft in Canada as an insurance against production loss of Bristol engines. It was impossible to fit different throttles in Mk Is without disrupting the whole production plan.

Just how easily and suddenly a serious throttle problem could arise was shown on 15 October. N3636 force landed at Scampton and the engines failed to respond after being throttled back because the Exactors were unable to translate instructions fast enough. For a flying boat it mattered less than for a landplane with a limited landing run for which the outcome could easily be disastrous.

However, a test pilot with much experience of Stirlings was Geoffrey Tyson, and his opinion remains that:

Slamming open the throttles on airfields with not much more than a 1,200 yard run and some on grass was certainly a cause of many flying accidents. Additionally, the Stirling had a built-in tendency to swing to starboard due to slipstream effect, and if the wind was from a starboard vector as well the opening of the starboard outer throttle (and sometimes the starboard inner too) had to be staggered behind the port ones to prevent swinging. Pilots were reluctant to do this – at least, inexperienced ones – for it increased the take-off run. I think, too, that the Stirling with its stalky undercarriage and high cg was more prone to weathercocking than other bombers. I flew Lancasters and Halifaxes and they were certainly less prone to swinging on take-off in my view. The Stirling had a tall rudder which presented a bigger 'keel surface' to a cross wind. This was an advantage, of course, with a wind from port. I somehow doubt whether Exactors were a contributory cause. Throttles were primed in the forward position, and the first job on sitting in the seat was to prime them; it was almost a religion. And of course they were automatically reprimed on opening-up.

October arrived and still no Stirling had a dorsal turret, the fitment date for trials now postponed to December 1940. Until it was fitted, stated an instruction of 2 October, no under-turrets were to be removed from Stirlings. Expectation was that a more streamlined Frazer-Nash under-mounting would become available in mid-1941. The fitment of retractable under-turrets in all new bomber types was discussed at the Air Ministry on 13 November 1940, the intention still being to have them removed because of their considerable weight and the drag they produced when extended. Their value was questionable, and their field of fire could almost be covered by the 2-gun beam mounting under development. Mounting a mid-upper turret was also reckoned likely to result in a deterioration of longitudinal stability which seemed to make the entire idea impracticable. A single 'hand-held' beam gun for use during day bombing operations was suggested, while a 2-gun semi-power-operated unit was reckoned the best and simplest solution.

Beam defence, all at the conference agreed, was essential and this latter suggestion would avoid cg problems. Orders to proceed were therefore given for a 2-gun mounting weighing 200lb placed to give the best field of fire, achieved from a short way aft of the mainplane. Irrespective of whether a new under turret was fitted, the existing version was ordered to be removed as soon as a mid-upper turret was installed in an aircraft. Beam guns would be an interim measure.

A further conference held on 20 October 1940 at Bomber Command discussed the Stirling, and particularly whether to operate it by day or night. Boscombe Down's report on trials with N3635 and N3637 was available. The truth about the take-off run on 64,000lb was at last known: it was 1,500 yards. Other tests concentrated on flying at 57,400lb, when the service ceiling was reached after thirty-four minutes. Climb started at 132mph, IAS, to 3,000ft, falling by 1mph per 1,000ft. Maximum level speed was 246mph TAS at 4,000ft; most economical cruise speed was 165mph, IAS, at 10,000ft, where fuel consumption was 175 gal per hr. Maximum range was obtained at 160mph, IAS, at 3,000ft.

At these speeds the Stirling would be unable to penetrate far during short summer nights. Some operations would have to be in daylight, and fighters might give some cover. The Commander-in-Chief agreed: he wanted an aircraft to bomb Germany now. "In the immediate future we are confined to night operations," he said, "and must arm a bomber with this in mind." But was the Stirling armed for night operations, particularly as it had been decided to fit pairs of beam guns which were reckoned unnecessary at night? Should they be removed or held in abeyance? The Assistant Chief of the Air Staff (T) pointed out that it had recently been agreed to fit a dorsal turret, but the ventral FN periscopic sight would not be ready for six months. Beam guns seemed of little extra value to a Stirling with two turrets producing a field of fire that converged just beyond the wingtips. Bomber Command since early 1940 had pressed for beam guns on all bombers. It would be bad for industrial morale if they were cancelled. Therefore it was decided that beam mountings, but not guns, would be fitted to Stirlings. No 4 Group were told to withhold judgement on the Stirling until Hercules Mk III-engined aircraft were available. If enough armour was removed, the bomber could carry another 500lb bomb. Representatives of 4 Group retorted that armour gave crews confidence, important if Stirlings operated in daylight. In one respect the new bomber did score well for, from N3640, Stirlings could carry six mines against the Halifax's two. The Manchester carried none, but later could carry four.

To a large extent most of the arguments were academic for, throughout October and November, 7 Squadron held only three Stirlings with little hope of more, although N6000 (Hercules Mk III), the first Belfast machine, had reached Boscombe Down for trials showing the Irish production line was in play. To speed operations No 7 Squadron was to move to Benson to be nearer the Shorts production centre, but when N3641 visited the station on 24 October, a tail wheel collapsed on the rough landing ground.

Problems with the tail wheel unit were never fully overcome, a second failure occurring in November. By then the squadron had been ordered instead to Oakington in 3 Group because their Wellingtons had Bristol engines.

Early Stirlings had leading edge wing tanks interchangeable with leading edge mounted cable cutters. The first thirty Stirlings had tankage without cutters; likewise the first ten from Belfast, all of which had de-icers. Subsequent aircraft had cutters as well as tanks, but no de-icers.

On 11 November 1940 the AACAS Liaison Committee met. ACAS(T) reported serious Exactor trouble, and considered that another system must be fitted. "Unreliability was intolerable." Difficulty came with synchronisation, improvements aimed at remedying hydraulic leaks being insufficient. Servicing was a major problem. Nevertheless, it was again agreed that, since a change to rod and chain could not be brought about easily, all Stirling Mk Is would have Exactors, bad as they were said to be.

The Under Secretary of State at the Air Ministry raised the question of the Stirling's poor performance with Hercules Mk IIs. This engine was limited to a take-off boost of 1 3/4 lb, preventing take-off from an ordinary airfield with full tanks and a reasonable load. Hercules Mk IIs were being replaced by Hercules Mk II (Mod), improving take-off and allowing a bomb load of 3,000–4,000lb for a range of 1,300 miles. Operational height still remained poor, for Hercules Mk IIs had single-speed superchargers rated at 5,000ft allowing an absolute ceiling of 14,000ft – and an operational height of only 10,000ft. Robert Saundby did not consider that use of a valuable aircraft on operations over enemy territory was justified until operational height could be increased by the Hercules Mk III to a minimum of 15,000ft. Future hopes were now pinned on the Hercules Mks X and XI. The weights of aircraft variously powered were compared and forecast:

N6000 – the first Belfast-built Stirling. (Shorts)

	Hercules II (lb)	Hercules III & X (lb)
Tare	39,194	41,938.5
Service load	5,761	16,388
Fuel 1,354 gal	10,155	10,155
Oil 70 gal	630	630
Gross weight	55,740	69,111.5
Max service load	18,135	22,061.5
Gross weight, operational	64,009	?
Max loading weight	57,000	?
Max for take-off	64,000	?

Supermarine's B.12/36 went ahead, it will be recalled, with provisioning for Hercules or Merlin engines. The Stirling entered production suitable only for Hercules power plants. There was, however, a secondary engine distantly considered for the aircraft. That was the 40-litre Armstrong-Siddeley Deerhound in the 1,500hp class and most unusual in that it featured three rows each of seven cylinders. Official favour veered towards four rows each of six cylinders. Having an amazingly small frontal area, and in consequence low drag, the Deerhound appeared ideal for fighters and even shallow enough in cross section to have been buried within the centre fuselage. It would drive a propeller via a long shaft after the manner of the Kestrel in the Westland F.7/30 of long ago. (The Merlin, incidentally, was a 27-litre engine). Setting the Deerhound deeply within the wing of a Stirling was an attractive proposition heightened in autumn 1940 as the engine approached its 100 hour type test. Twice surviving the prospect of cancellation, at the start of the war and again in May 1940, its Mk II form was about to be tested, its future seeming dependent upon the outcome.

All through its existence, development and indeed survival had been prejudiced by the need to concentrate upon, and accelerate, Cheetah production for Ansons. Only by establishing another production source for Cheetahs had the revolutionary engine been so far saved. The Director of Engine Production, and indeed the Air Staff, were strongly in favour of forging ahead with Deerhound development in preference to the high drag 2,000hp Bristol Centaurus in the belief that the Deerhound would eventually deliver well over 2,000hp. That was possible, and the less exotic Centaurus was making slow but fair progress. Facing the Deerhound was the other major hurdle of finding capacity to develop it and, perhaps even more difficult, to establish a suitable production source for such a complex low-drag engine. That, as much as anything else, brought about the demise of a potentially fine and very advanced power plant. The Stirling, then, would have no divorce and continue to be married to the Hercules.

N6001 has the third camouflage style including a straight top line to its matt black. (Shorts)

Experience showed a need for many more less radical modifications discussed at Gloucester on 25 November. They included propeller de-icers, alcohol de-icing for carburettors, rudder pedals nearer the pilot, improved emergency exit, blind flying visor, better weatherproofing, increased chord for rudder trimmer, Marston oil coolers, stronger tail wheel chassis, Hercules Mk II (Mod), stronger wing leading edge between nacelles, Lorenz radio gear for operational aircraft, W/T master aerial and D/F loop, heated windscreen, improved flare chute, and more minor changes.

Boscombe Down had tried bombing up the Stirling. Stations 10, 11 and 12 could each carry a 1,900lb bomb, Stations 1 to 6 and 22 to 27 could also each take a 500lb or 250lb bomb. Nos 1 to 6 and 22 to 27 could also each take various containers as an alternative. A&AEE had done a trial loading of 7 x 2,000lb HC bombs. There was only a 2 1/2 in clearance between the tails of the bombs on stations 4, 5, 6 and 11, and at 10, 11, 12 and 17, only 1/4 in clearance each side of the bomb at door hinge level, owing to the position of the door brackets.

The armament at this time comprised an FN 5A twin-gun nose turret, FN 25A belly turret, FN 4A four-gun tail turret and beam guns on FN 55A mountings. This armament applied to Mk I series i aircraft, the first eighty built, still allowing for twenty-six troops to be carried: three in the bomb aimer's compartment, eight in the centre section, ten on the starboard side aft and two on the port side, with another sitting on the port side ammunition shelf. Fortunately none were paratroopers!

Troubles precluded much flying by 7 Squadron evidenced in November when N3644, with front turret hydraulic problems and troublesome Exactors, needed repositioned bomb door cables. N3642 was grounded due to a weak tail wheel chassis.

Moving to Oakington took several weeks, ahead of which rumours raced around that secret bombers were coming to the station. As the first Stirling circled the aerodrome, I stood on Midsummer Common, Cambridge. The Stirling looked huge at that time and to me seemed a strangely proportioned machine. Through binoculars I saw that amazing, complex undercarriage, and thought how difficult it would be to model! The arrival of the Stirlings came as a great tonic when things were bad. Almost every night German bombers overflew Oakington heading for their Midland targets or for Merseyside. Not many days previously we had watched their contrail processions to and from Coventry. And now, some revenge as the Stirling's size suggested that might could be on our side.

By 30 November, squadron personnel included many who were to be well known in the early operational phase. Wg Cdr Paul Harris was in command, Fg Off L G Bristowe Adjutant. Other officers were Sqn Ldr J M Griffith-Jones, Flt Lt G H Smith, Flt Lt G W Bennett, Flt Lt A Chambers, Flt Lt H S Browne, Flt Lt A C Ward, Fg Off G B Blacklock, Fg Off V F B Pike, Fg Off E W Best, Fg Off S G Stock, Fg Off G K Larney, Plt Off R W Cox, Plt Off F H P Austin, Fg Off B A R H Mathe, Plt Off D T Witt and Plt Off C R Barrett. In December Sqn Ldr P W Lynch-Blosse arrived to command 'B' Flight. The squadron held five aircraft – N3636, N3638, N3641, N3642 and N3644.

Among others who joined the squadron in November was Keith Deyell, and now a retired RCAF Wing Commander, one of the many Canadians who had enlisted in the RAF pre-war and trained as an air observer (navigator/bomb aimer). On completion of his first tour with Marham-based 38 Wellington Squadron, the crew of which he was a member was posted to Leeming's 7 Squadron only to find that all but the Rear Party had moved to Oakington in Cambridgeshire.

He recalls that his:

> ...first look at a Stirling was, indeed, an inspiring sight. There just wasn't a land-based aircraft of that size around anywhere – it was a giant when compared with the Hampden or Wimpey. The pilots sat side by side, and the navigator had the luxury of a large plotting table and easy access to the bomb-aimer's position in the nose. No more crawling under the second pilot's legs as he sat on a dickey seat a la Wimpey. Moreover, the Stirling had on board a technical

marvel of those days, the distant reading compass with its master unit in the rear and repeaters for the pilots and navigators. It was 'light years' ahead of the P4 compass.

Our skipper, Flt Lt Gordon Bennett, had been a civil airline pilot before the war and had many hours under his belt. Consequently, he checked out on the Stirling in short time and was flying as a captain by the end of November. Commissioned in December, I became Squadron Navigation officer. Since 7 Squadron was doing Service Trials of the Stirling this gave an opportunity to offer suggestions to help make navigators' lives more pleasant. These included development of a canopy over the top of the navigator's table permitting use of the astrograph, and also a light which did not illuminate the great 'greenhouse' of a cockpit changing it into a beacon for night fighters. I also suggested that a folding step replace the cumbersome pile of wooden boxes on which the navigator had to stand to make use of the astrodome – a suggestion which was turned down!

Commissioned air-gunners on the squadron included Fg Off Mills, Plt Off Pier, Plt Off Stock and Plt Off Spiller. Experienced navigators included Flt Sgt Halcrow and Sgts Watson and Bolton, all of whom were commissioned early in 1941. Most of the navigators were, however, early graduates of the Commonwealth Air Training Plan who began arriving in 1941 directly from Canada and often taking advantage of trans-Atlantic ferry flights. Among them were Plt Offs Baker, Cotton, Durban, Gillespie, Kennedy, McCauley and Roach, also Sgts Alverson and Webb, along with an Australian, Chris Masters. Flt Lt Walker and Plt Off Bailey, both RAF and British, arrived in spring 1941.

N3637 'K-King' of 7 Squadron dispersed on mud and coke near Oakington railway station in early 1941.

On 21 December N3637 arrived; like all the others so far received it was a Trainer and it was clear that these might have to be used operationally. To cope with them the number of corporals and airmen at Oakington soared. One arrival was Mr R C Monteith, previously at Sullom Voe in the Shetlands, who was a Sunderland electrician. When he arrived at Oakington Station he saw some aeroplanes dispersed close by. He went over to a porter and asked: "What kind of kites are they, then?" The reply was: "They'm be Starlins, they'm be." He'd never heard of them before! He recalls:

> I phoned the guardroom and a truck took me there. When I was asked what section I was for, I said, "Electrical!" "What, another one?" the Corporal replied. When I reached the Section there were between fifty and sixty electricians there. The Stirling was an 'electrical wonder', and we were soon like bees round a honeypot for there were so few aircraft. The station didn't need so many electricians, though: the plan was to familiarise us with the aircraft. We were to become preachers to other stations when they changed over to 'Starlins'.

By January the squadron held N3641: D, N3642: E, N3636: A, N3637: B, N3638: C, N3644: H (the first with Hercules Mk IIIs, and which had arrived on 25 September 1940); N3643: G arrived on 3 January 1941. Icing trouble with carburettor controls manifested itself, and the squadron was told not to fly in icing conditions until modifications had been made. The weather at this time was atrocious, cold and snow greatly reducing flying. Serviceability was low, too. In the first week of January only 21hr 20min flying was completed. Between 7 and 13 January, five aircraft were unserviceable. On five days, when two were serviceable, only 7hr 35min flying was possible.

On 16 January King George VI and Queen Elizabeth visited Oakington and inspected N3652. N3644 was flown. Next day Plt Off Cox left for St Athan to collect N6003 (Hercules Mk X), 7 Squadron's first operational Stirling. It reached Oakington on 22 January to replace N3637 in the intensive flying programme.

Among the Stirling crew was an entirely new member: the flight engineer. He monitored engine performance and generally assisted the captain. The Air Ministry asked that sergeants be posted for special training but it was impossible to find qualified men so the Squadron began training aircraftsmen as flight engineers.

HM King George VI and HM Queen Elizabeth at Oakington on 16 January 1941. (Wg Cdr B D Sellick)

Wing Commander B D Sellick conversing with HM Queen Elizabeth. The AOC 3 Group and Group Captain Adams, Oakington's Station Commander, look on. (Wg Cdr B D Sellick)

Rochester's 160ft production bay looking towards the 120ft bay on 31 January 1941. Aircraft 9 to 20 are under construction. (Shorts)

Experience after six months' flying was depressing. A summary of each week's activity was ordered, that of 27 January showing just how low serviceability was. N3641, awaiting an undercarriage motor, had not flown. N3642 had done only 1hr 45min before the starboard undercarriage motor went unserviceable. Undercarriage motors were being changed on N3638, which had logged 2hr 35min. N3636 (A) was grounded awaiting spares. N3644 had managed 2hr 35min and was awaiting repair of a contact breaker. N6003, upon which high hopes had been pinned, had in all flown only 3hr 10min (1hr 10min on the squadron) and now was grounded awaiting the fitting of a Graviner fire extinguisher and modifications to the rudder balance.

A&AEE Boscombe Down was called upon to investigate repeated tail wheel lowering problems. It was discovered that keys and worm drive shafts had sheared under loads for their design was insufficiently sturdy. The emergency gear incorporated only dealt with mechanical malfunction.

Sunday, 27 January was sunny, 7 Squadron managing some flying so I visited Oakington. Around the aerodrome were hosts of sightseers who were rewarded with views of a Stirling with yellow undersurfaces. Dispersed near Oakington station were two of the huge machines. Someone said they looked like dragonflies, which was an apt description. Among the crowd enjoying a close look some were discussing the Stirling's misfortunes – so much for security.

Times remained hard at Oakington, but soon the unready bombers were ordered into action, which boosted morale. One can surely imagine the feelings of the crews when the order to operate was received.

Extract from A&AEE report on handling trials of N3635 – February 1941:

Before engines are started, each throttle lever should be moved to the priming position slightly beyond full throttle position, should be held in this position for a few seconds against the exactor spring then brought back to the closed throttle position very slowly. When the engine fires on the starter magneto each engine should be switched on. Throttle levers should not be moved during the process of starting up. Then start the engine with the propeller in fully fine position. During run out with engine speed about 2,500 revs., replan airscrew pitch levers by moving them to the fully coarse position and holding them to the stop against the springs, then slowly return levers to fully fine position. For take-off set flaps to point 4 of the total travel, trim elevators as follows: Forward cg 0, no 1 cg 1 1/2 position forward, aft cg 9–10 divisions forward. Apply full brakes, reprime airscrew controls. This may be done by the second pilot. Close gills, release brakes, open throttles as quickly as possible, leaving one outer lever in half-way position. If the aircraft should tend to swing follow up slowly with the remaining throttle so as to counteract tendency to swing to the right. Alternatively, all throttles may be fully opened and the outer engine on the side opposite to the swing may be throttled back slightly. Raise the tail as early as possible and at 100mph ASI ease the aircraft off the ground, raise the undercarriage, which takes 53 to 55 seconds, open cooling gills when undercarriage is up, raise flaps, trim the aircraft while the flaps are closing. Select ASI 135mph on initial climb. At 57,000lb aircraft can be climbed away on any three engines provided undercarriage is retracted. Aircraft has sufficient rudder bar for climbing feet off and sufficient rudder trim to climb hands off.

The aircraft is easy to land if, when approaching, reduced ASI to 160–170mph can be obtained in level flight 2,400 revs and 3lb sq in boost. Set propellers to fully fine pitch, reduce ASI to 140mph by throttling back and, when this speed is obtained, extend flap and re-trim aircraft. Open throttle slightly to give ASI 130–135mph, and retain this until ready to land. When in position lower undercarriage, turn on to path of approach and re-trim. Extend flaps fully, re-trim, keep ASI and glide angle constant by use of throttles. Best glide-in speed 120mph. When ready to touch down close throttles. Easy 3-point landing can be made using elevator alone. Settle brakes quite hard without fear of tail lifting. In event of baulked approach opening throttles with flaps down makes the aircraft rail heavy. It can easily be re-trimmed, and will keep height at 57,000lb.

Chapter 5
Let Battle Begin

MR Churchill was obsessed with the idea, and Lord Beaverbrook had little choice but to go along with sending the Stirlings to bomb Berlin. It was, of course, a very Churchillian idea even if it was impossible to carry out.

Wg Cdr Paul Harris visited Beaverbrook to explain to him why his Stirlings were unable to grant them their desire, then he called on ACM Sir Charles Portal. Explaining that the squadron would be lucky if it managed to despatch three or four Stirlings, he added that it would be fortunate if any returned. Losses due to technical malfunction would be certain, a Berlin raid would be a disastrous failure. Portal replied: "It is not a good thing to be associated with failure." The simple truth was that the Stirling was not ready for operations. On 31 January 1941 Bomber Command held 535 serviceable operational aircraft and another 139 unserviceable of which seven were Stirlings, fifteen Manchesters and three Halifaxes. The new bombers were simply not ready for use.

Weather was bad, Stirling serviceability poor, the heavy aircraft often bogged in Oakington's mud and still the senior authorities failed to curb their impatience and obsessions. On 2 February a Stirling was ordered for mining, but snow prevented that. Postponement only increased pressure for operations and cross-country flights to assess fuel consumption were made as far as Cape Wrath and Portreath. On the 6th another crew stood by for mining. Again, mercifully, it snowed. Next day three crews stood by for a Boulogne raid only to be foiled, and once more when a venture to Antwerp was mooted on the 8th. Then came the first really alarming undercarriage malfunction at Oakington.

Mr Churchill encouraging N6090 to visit Berlin! (Imperial War Museum)

Sunday 9 February 1941 was a dull, raw day, but Fg Off R W Cox managed local flying. Approaching Oakington he selected 'U/C down' and found he was unable to lower an undercarriage leg. For 4 hours 50 minutes N6003 droned around, the crew trying to find a cure and jettisoning all they could. With fuel low, Cox lined up 'V-Victor' for a wheels-up landing, something not previously attempted with a Stirling. He achieved an immaculate belly touch down

Almost certainly V-Victor of 7 Squadron in which Pilot Officer Cox belly-landed in February 1941.

on mud, the aircraft skidding 165 yards before coming to rest little damaged. Fumes from an exploding accumulator filled the aircraft forcing the crew to make a hasty exit to encouraging cheers from onlookers.

Railway sleepers were brought forth and, with the aid of inflatable bags and a large crane, the aircraft was lifted. Then the undercarriage was manually wound down, temperamental retraction motors having caused the failure.

When daylight faded No 7 Squadron was holding nine Stirlings, eight of which were unserviceable. Not even that - nor the day's serious problem - failed to counteract the pressure for operations to begin and next day Bomber Command ordered operations for the night of **10/11 February 1941**.

A brief improvement in the weather was being seized upon, a cold, clear moonlit night being forecast. In total 263 aircraft were to be despatched, 189 of them to bomb Hannover. Another four, 1 Group Wellingtons carrying ' freshmen' crews learning the art of bombing under operational conditions, set forth for Boulogne. A further force ordered to attack oil storage tanks near Rotterdam, comprised six Blenheims, fourteen Wellingtons, nine Whitleys and, going into action for the first time, three Stirlings – thirty-two bombers in all. It was a busy, historic night for Bomber Command.

Eventual analysis of the Hannover raid showed:

Group	Aircraft despatched	Load dropped
1	8 Wellingtons	13 x 500lb, 3 x 250lb, 1,780 x 4lb incendiaries
2	29 Blenheims	55 x 250lb, 122 x 40lb, 2,480 x 4lb incendiaries
3	80 Wellingtons	24 x 1,000lb, 242 x 500lb, 37 x 250lb, 12,760 x 4lb incendiaries
4	28 Whitleys	50 x 500lb, 54 x 250lb, 6,960 x 4lb incendiaries
5	44 Hampdens	15 x 1,900lb, 96 x 500lb, 40 x 250lb, 1,380 x 4lb incendiaries

Of the above, a Wellington of 1 Group, three Blenheims, fifteen Wellingtons of 3 Group, one Whitley and one Hampden were recorded as attacking last resort targets.

A Blenheim crew claimed to have been chased over Hannover by a vic of three biplanes. Another was challenged off Great Yarmouth by an intruding night fighter which followed it to Stradishall then opened fire. A third, a Blenheim, was followed to Bodney where, seeing an unidentified aircraft ahead, its pilot opened fire as a second German intruder fired at the Blenheim overtaking it even when the pilot applied +9lb boost. Night homing could be hazardous.

Getting three Stirlings serviceable was no mean feat. Indeed, only one was ready at 1800 hrs but with a great effort the most portentous event of the night began as ordered when, at Oakington at 1900 hrs, the engines of Stirling N3641 'D-Dog' burst into life. From its dispersal near Oakington Station, it taxied across the rough surface, Flt Lt Howard-Smith in the captain's seat and Flt Lt G B Blacklock as second pilot. At 1905 hrs take-off began and the Stirling at last started its operational career. The crew must have had very mixed feelings and some concern as they climbed out over the Fens.

N3641 as 'D-Dog' of 7 Squadron at Oakington in late 1940 wears early style of camouflage. Note the absence of under-nose pitot heads. (Shorts)

Half an hour later N3644 'H-Harry', flown by Sqn Ldr W Lynch-Blosse left base and at 2000 hrs Acting Sqn Ldr J M Griffith-Jones in N3642 'E-Easy' followed. Each Stirling had 16 x 500lb GP bombs with which to blast oil storage tanks near Rotterdam.

Wellingtons opened the attack, near the receiving end of which was Arie de Jong (lately a colonel in the Royal Netherlands Air Force), who recorded in his diary that "defending searchlights were switched on at 2007 hrs, around the Hook of Holland". What the Germans would have made of a teenager keeping such a diary one scarcely dare imagine! Ten minutes later, Arie recorded that "air raid sirens wailed in Rotterdam, and at 2032 hrs the first bombs fell on a Shell refinery south of Vlaardingen". Tanks were hit, causing fires to rage, then thirteen minutes later another bomber arrived, its flares illuminating the scene. Soon, there were two oil fires at the Pakhuismeesteren Depot, one mile south-west of Vlaardingen. At 2057 hrs a very heavy salvo fell, perhaps from N3641?

In the moonlight ground observers claimed to see five aircraft, three of which turned in for another attack. Heavy flak opened up on them, further flares illuminated the area at 2135 hrs and anti-aircraft guns blazed away while searchlights swept the sky. Two minutes later another heavy salvo of bombs crashed down, possibly from the second Stirling. Bombing continued from 2140 hrs and until 2240 hrs when a final hefty stick of bombs was released.

All three Stirlings made a safe return to Oakington, although N3641 and N3644 each had a bomb hang-up. The most disappointed person at Oakington must have been Gp Capt Harris, for sickness had prevented him from leading his squadron. He returned to duty the next morning, as bad weather returned to halt operations.

Bomber Command's analysis of the Rotterdam/Vlaardingen raid showed the following:

Group	Despatched	Load
2	6 Blenheims	?
3	13 Wellingtons	53 x 500lb, 7 x 250lb, 2,200 x 4lb incendiaries
	3 Stirlings	44 x 500lb
4	9 Whitleys	18 x 500lb, 36 x 250lb, 2,400 x 4 lb incendiaries

Three Wellingtons of the 3 Group Hannover force aimed another 12 x 500lb HEs at Rotterdam. Of 263 aircraft dispatched, 240 dropped bombs and 16 aborted.

Although Stirling operations were underway they were barely sustainable for unserviceability remained so high. Following the first operation N3641 was grounded awaiting electric motors, N3642 managed only fifty-five minutes flying in the ensuing week in which N3638 flew 3hrs 50mins before brake trouble halted its flying. N3636 was then awaiting spares, N3644 had magneto trouble and N6003 was grounded with intercom problems.

During the next week flying hours achieved by 7 Squadron totalled only twenty-eight. N3641 encountered tail wheel retraction problems and, after 10hrs 10min flying, N3642 had a burnt-out under-carriage motor. N3638 suffered a jammed undercarriage. N3636 flew for only thirty minutes and N6003 was still under repair. N3641 had by 17 February logged only another 2hrs 5mins, then needed a replacement gill motor and a new tyre. N3636 was awaiting under-turret removal, N3644 needed an electric motor and Shorts were busy on N6003.

The situation with the RAF's other new bombers was scarcely better. No 35 Squadron had only four Halifaxes, one being unserviceable. No 207 Squadron with Manchesters, still had fifteen, nine of which were unserviceable.

Glimpses of Stirlings aroused much local interest, not to mention rumour, and a splendid view of Britain's secret bombers could be had from the Oakington village to Longstanton road. The sight of a Stirling rearing up from a rise in the runway and resembling a giant monster emerging from the deep remains vivid.

Saturday 15 February was a dull winter day but that did not deter me from wanting more such thrills. Close to the village, N3641 'D-Dog' was on dispersal near to a gate through which personnel passed to Oakington. It was unguarded so I crept in and cautiously headed (watching out for other spies) across the grass and clinker acquired from the Cambridge Gas Company to form a hard dispersal resting area for 'D-Dog'. The Stirling was so gigantic, and I stood in awe dwarfed by one of its colossal 6ft diameter mainwheel tyres. I was amazed at how incredibly shabby the aeroplane looked with its very matt black suede-like coat now extending erratically only half way up the mud-splattered fuselage sides. A repositioned serial number I duly noted was in the brown shade officially named Dull Red.

Summoning more courage, I was closing in on 'K-King' when a young Pilot Officer appeared and enquired of me just what I was doing. I answered honestly: "Having a close look". He must have recognised a keen Stirling supporter for he walked me around N3641 telling me that the pilot sat 22ft above the ground, and gave me my first leisurely look at the amazing undercarriage. "This part folds up into the crate halfway up, then the whole thing is hauled into the nacelle," I was told. Thanking my host, I cycled home to fit a more accurate undercarriage on to my model, as well as streamlined spinners to the propellers. Amazing, surely, that any outsider could have so easily inspected Britain's latest bomber.

A Stirling's nose towered higher than many a modern house.

Maybe others less friendly had been that way. The enemy could have done so with great ease merely by travelling on a train between Oakington and Longstanton. A story losing nothing in the telling circulated around Rampton in 1941 that a German agent had entered a village shop asking, in a foreign accent, about the possibility of being able to buy a wrist watch. The local 'Bobby'

took away the unwanted visitor who had, naturally, been parachuted in to the area to spy on the Stirlings. Like all Germans who ventured to Cambridgeshire in wartime he had, of course, "been at the University before the war". Judging by its Soviet spy production line that tale may well have been founded in truth.

On **15 February** Sterkrade's oil refinery was 3 Group's main target. Another fourteen Wellingtons settled for Boulogne and this time Flt Lt C E Bennett and crew accompanied them in N3641 along with Wg Cdr Harris and crew aboard N3642. Both found the target, Bennett dropping 16 x 500lb bombs across the docks. Twenty minutes later, Harris made an east-to-west run and claimed six hits on Docks 4 and 5.

Differing loadings and individual idiosyncrasies meant that each Stirling had an individualistic performance, but overall they performed similarly to L7605, N3635 and N3643 (all Hercules II powered). That was evident from a further report issued by A&AEE on 20 February 1941 indicating that a fully laden Stirling took an average of 2.4 minutes to reach 2,000ft where its top speed was 249.5mph. By the time 15,000ft was reached that had fallen to 218mph. Brief tests using N6008 (Hercules Mk X) at 50,000lb showed a speed of 200mph and thus no improvement.

The third operation, undertaken on **24/25 February**, was the first in which any flew within the (fifty-three strong) Main Force targeted mainly on a Hipper Class cruiser in Brest hiding in darkness interrupted by plentiful flak and searchlights. From Gordon Bennett's N3636 bombs fell during an east-west run across No 8 dock. Three crews had set off at around 1800 hrs for the five hour flight, with Flt Lt G B Blacklock flying N3642 and Sqn Ldr P W Lynch-Blosse (a Wellington veteran of 149 Squadron) using N3652.

With the Stirling trio were twenty-eight Wellingtons, sixteen Hampdens and six Manchesters. The latter, between them carrying 60 x 500lb GP and 12 x 500lb SAP bombs, were in even deeper trouble than the Stirling, but the Manchester had great development potential. Only two of 7 Squadron's aircraft were able to release their 32 x 500lb SAP bombs, one salvo of which hit the north side of the cruiser's dock. Great alarm seized Oakington when Lynch-Blosse in N3652 was reported missing. Bad weather during return included a snow storm over Wiltshire and Group HQ had misunderstood a signal, for Lynch-Blosse had landed safely at Boscombe Down.

Pilot Officer Keith Dyell (left) and Flying Officer Denis Witt outside Newmarket's Officers' Mess in spring 1941. (D. K. Dyell)

February 25 was cloudy, and a Dornier 17 of KG 2 making use of that made a low-level pass over Oakington and dropped two bombs in front of a hangar. Strafing as it passed, a few of its machine-gun bullets entered N3652 just back from Boscombe Down. A more worthy visitor to the station was Captain Harold Balfour, Secretary of State, who called on 1 March.

Arrival by air was impossible on the airfield's slippery, muddy surface. On the previous day a PR Spitfire pilot of No 3 PRU, based there, died when his aircraft overturned in the mud, so Balfour came via Wyton where he saw lightly loaded Stirlings arriving after struggling off from Oakington to be refuelled and bombed up for operations. He heard from three crews about the intensive flying programme in which N6004 had now replaced N6003, but the Minister had come primarily to see the aerodrome which, because of its awful state, Stirlings had been unable to use for some days. The Station Commander told how he had been pressing for runways since learning, in the previous summer, that heavies weighing up to 70,000lb were eventually to use the grass landing ground.

Oakington was in the grip of 'English permafrost'. It was extremely cold, exceptionally so at night, until March when the thaw at last set in converting Oakington and other airfields into quagmires as bombers churned up extensive areas including the grass runways. So serious was the situation that, on 16 March, 'A' Flight 7 Squadron was ordered to Newmarket Heath, whose very long grass runway had a dry chalk base. The suitability of the Heath for Stirlings was shown on **2/3 March** when Wg Cdr Harris (N3653) and Flt Lt Best (N3652) returning from abortive sorties directed at Brest, landed there on return. Control of operations from the Heath was vested in Stradishall, Newmarket's parent station. Ground crews, also forced to move, were most discontented when their very cold accommodation was established under the grandstand. Arthur Moore, one of them, "never would forget the rats in the one-time stables, and which seemed very interested in the newcomers".

On 29 November 1940, Beaverbrook had written to Sir Archibald Sinclair, the Air Minister, raising the question of concrete runways at bomber bases which, he claimed, were being laid down 1,000 yards in length and at a time when new aircraft entering service needed 1,500 yard runways. Beaverbrook also asked what was being done to improve airfields susceptible to flooding. Could tarmac runways be laid to generally improve the situation?

In his reply, the Minister explained that runways were being provided on a scale of one of 1,400 yards long and two each of 1,100 yards at airfields where such were considered necessary. That included new bomber aerodromes and satellites. Beaverbrook quickly responded, raising an obvious question. Why, he enquired, were heavy Stirlings using an aerodrome with only a grass surface? The answer was that the Commander-in-Chief, Bomber Command, was responsible for their siting, and had decided upon the location after considering the weather, approaches, surface and geographic position. On the best technical advice, the conditions of soil and drainage at Oakington were considered likely to produce a satisfactory grass airfield. Of Gp Capt Adams', Oakington's Station Commander, claim for runways in summer 1940, it was said that no such request had reached Air Ministry. Although the station opened in July 1940, it was 4 January 1941 before Bomber Command asked for runway provision at Oakington.

Although the value of runways was appreciated before the war, it was usually difficult enough to get Treasury funding for a grass landing ground let alone hard runways. Only five British aerodromes had them pre-war, all approved only on the grounds that they were necessary to prevent undue wear and tear or because of unstable surfaces. During the first winter of the war increased flying (which damaged many aerodrome surfaces) showed that metalled runways were essential.

Considerable opposition to runways remained, and particularly in Bomber Command where it was felt that they would be impossible to camouflage. Aircraft queuing for take-off would be vulnerable to intruder attacks, and take-off delayed by the need to suitably position aircraft. In February 1940, the Command listed aerodromes where runways were thought unnecessary because firm surfaces were available – and Oakington was one such site. The C-in-C Bomber Command wrote:

> In the interests of camouflage I do not want to extend (the provision of) runways unless essential. I base my recommendation on normal winter weather and discount abnormal conditions of the past three months. There is only one station where I recommend concrete runways, Stradishall. For the rest, provision of concrete runways can be deferred.

All new Bomber Command airfields were completed with runways because it took eighteen months to two years for a satisfactory grass flying field to become established –

unless there was a ready-made surface. Runway building made heavy demands upon labour and materials, so special priorities had to be arranged. By February 1941 runways were being laid at one hundred aerodromes under construction, they were being added to twenty existing aerodromes and plans existed for another fifty new aerodromes to have runways, the building of twenty coming under way. Insufficient labour was available to provide any more runways, and in any case their construction would have put too many airfields out of use at a vital time. Bomber Command listed, for future attention, thirteen airfields needing runways, and gave Oakington seventh place of priority. The Air Ministry did not accept that the Stirlings could not be moved to a more suitable station, especially as the intention was to introduce sixteen new airfields with perimeter tracks during March 1941, and extensions beyond 1,400 yards being already under way at four stations despite the recent difficult weather.

Undaunted, Beaverbrook gave his weight to the pressure for more runways to suit the increasingly heavy aircraft the industry was producing. The Deputy Chief of the Air Staff weighed in, saying that for five years he, too, had been pressing for runways and larger flying grounds. Not to be completely outdone, Balfour added that he had been supporting the idea for nearly three years. Oakington, it transpired, had been intended to stay as a grass field and was satisfactory – until the huge tyres of the big bombers cut up its surface. Runway building at Oakington was approved in spring, 1941, but it took some six months to complete the task.

Although provision of concrete or tarmac runways superseded ideas for assisted take-off, in November 1940 another possible way of getting Stirlings away carrying full bomb loads on to operational flights had been under consideration. This was to make use of in-flight refuelling (IFR), but it was dismissed in the belief that 1,500 yard runways were suitable for conventional operating. "Bomber Command regard IFR as impractical for night operations," stated a report. "Tied together take-off and operations in bad visibility and cloud would be too difficult to depend upon. There would be difficulty in training crews, which already have as much as they can do in their training and on operational duties. Separate crews could not be maintained for the tankers needed for refuelling work, and it would not appear practical to make use of operational aircraft as tankers, even if they can be converted and restored to standard in comparatively short time. Its use would only be for very exceptional flights requiring heavier loads than can be taken off from a 1,500 yard runway," continued the study. Nevertheless, the cost and the time needed to develop a satisfactory method of in-flight refuelling was ordered to be ascertained. Stirlings always operated conventionally – and, for many months, from grass surfaces.

What 7 Squadron viewed as inevitable came about on **3/4 March**. Three Stirlings, each carrying 4 x 2,000lb bombs, headed within the Main Force for Brest. Flt Lt V F B Pike was forced to jettison his load at sea, Sgt L McCarthy bombed the target area, but N3653 flown by Sqn Ldr Griffith-Jones failed to return. The first Stirling missing from operations had come down in the sea, all but one of the crew perishing.

Much concern centred on the number and variety of undercarriage malfunctions. The AOC No 3 Group, was so worried about problems with N6003 that he gave instructions that no more Belfast (N6) aircraft were to be accepted before their undercarriage gear boxes were modified. A ferry pilot delivering N6001 to Short's modification depot established late 1940 at Wyton joined the circuit then found that the complex undercarriage would not lower. Another wheels-up landing resulted. Then on 13 March Fg Off Blacklock collected N6006 from the depot and, this time over Oakington, another undercarriage failing to mechanically lower was laboriously cranked down by hand.

In the defence field there was some improvement. A Shorts working party was cutting beam gun hatches in the fuselage for incorporation of Modification 215 which, first applied to N3644, allowed the fitting of a pair of guns on each side. This was featured by a number of aircraft pending fitment of a dorsal turret. During the modification work a beam gun was accidentally fired spraying plentiful bullets in the area where the work's team was resting. They were not the only ones who succumbed to panic on such occasions. Motorists on the road across Oakington, which passed close to the perimeter track, were uncomfortably near when guns were tested shortly before operations by the firing of shots into the ground. On another occasion a rear gunner forgot to depress his guns before firing at night and released an arch of tracer bullets over the road causing a motorist to take to a ditch in terror.

Every additional equipment item affected not only the weight but also the trim. The variety of installations in early Stirlings produced at least three basic different tare weight and cg positions. Individual calculations were needed to decide which of the fourteen fuel tanks should be filled, and which bomb positions used for each operation by each aircraft. George Blacklock had the task of working out loadings until a model Stirling balance was produced upon which token weights were hung at their appropriate stations. Plt Off Austin soon took over the taxing task.

It was on **17 March** when the next Stirling milestone was passed. Flown by Lynch-Blosse, N3652 became the first example to penetrate into Germany where it delivered 5 x 1,000lb GPs and 7 x 500lb GPs to Bremen/Doschimag. The load fell on the southern corner of the target to generate five white explosions and a large fire. One wing cell 500-pounder had hung up. Seven months of service life had passed before a Stirling entered the main bombing arena, the lone aircraft being outnumbered by eighty-one Blenheims, Hampdens, Wellingtons and Whitleys in which seventy-four crews claimed to bomb their targets.

Having by now amassed ample flying hours on Stirlings, A&AEE pilots – who had repeatedly produced such damning reports – were at least praising the aircraft's amazing manoeuvrability, and admiring its strong structure. Shortening the wing span had brought about a high rate of roll further enhanced by very effective ailerons. Rudder action, sluggish during the early part of a take-off run, meant that a correcting technique was needed to counteract problems in throttle control handling. Standard procedure before engine start was for each throttle lever to be moved to a priming position slightly beyond full throttle setting, held for a few seconds against the Exactor spring then brought back to 'closed' very slowly. Each engine was started with the throttle set 1 1/2in forward of 'closed'. When the engine fired off the starter magneto, each engine was switched on without moving throttle levers. As the aircraft moved forward, propellers were set to coarse pitch, then slowly returned to fine.

For take-off, flaps were first set to forty percent of total travel and elevators trimmed. Brakes were fully applied and airscrew controls reprimed, usually by the second pilot. Gills were closed, brakes released, and the throttles were opened as quickly as possible. leaving one lever in the halfway position so that if the machine swung to the right, as it tended to, this could slowly be opened, to counteract the swing. The tail was raised as soon as possible and at 100mph IAS the Stirling would be lifted off and gills opened when the aircraft was airborne. Climb-away was at 135mph IAS, and climb at 57,000lb was still possible on three engines.

Because of the assorted problems, short range operations remained the norm. On **23 March 1941**, Sqn Ldr A F Robertson set off for Rotterdam in N3643 loaded with 22 x 500lb HEs. On return, and for reasons never established, the aircraft hit high tension cables at Halewood Common, Leiston. All the crew, except Sgt White, died instantly. Certainly they had been unaware that they were flying so low. The deepest penetration into enemy territory so far came on **27 March** when Flt Lt E V Best in N3652 joined 3 Group's Wellingtons for a 3hr 45min flight to Cologne. His load of 5 x 1,000lb and 6 x 500lb GPs was dropped from 14,000ft after which temperamental bomb doors were wound shut by hand. Later, the undercarriage proved troublesome.

Another of the bomber's annoyances was what Mr Sharman, Short's electrical representative at Oakington, called a 'negative earth'. It manifested itself by lighting the 'bomb door open' indicator whilst the bomb doors were still closed. An aircraft particularly blighted was N6005 which George Blacklock flight-tested eleven times before the trouble was cured. In other respects this was 'a good Stirling' which, during the final test at light loading, surprisingly reached 20,000ft.

Astro-navigation was pushed by Bomber Command in 1940 and 1941 with the introduction of the Mk IXA averaging sextant and the astrograph. Its usefulness as an aid to navigation depended upon the dedication and skill of the navigator and pilot, weather conditions and enemy activity. Pilots did not mind flying straight and level when over water, but were understandably 'quite twitchy and bitchy' about astro sights over enemy territory. The sudden appearance of flak or searchlights would result in evasive action, usually without warning, leaving the navigator with buckling knees trying to find support around the slippery astro-dome.

Politicians and aeroplanes have nothing in common. They cannot be spin-doctored into success; that can only be achieved by leaving it to the professionals. In the case of the Stirling there was an inevitability – sooner or later Bomber Command would have to give way to Churchill and send the Stirlings to Berlin. Whether they were ready for such a hazardous mission mattered not. On **9 April** the dreaded order was given and in the evening three left Newmarket for the 'Big City'. Apart from the long flight, the sorties involved relatively low altitude penetration of flak and searchlight belts, reliance on meagre radio aids and the possibility of weather deterioration. It was an exceptionally risky venture with little chance of success.

Fg Off J F Sach (N6009) encountered propeller trouble which forced him to turn back at the Dutch coast then jettison his load. George Blacklock was making his last flight in N6005, one of whose engines persisted in overheating on the climb forcing spells of level flying to allow it to cool off. What followed is told in his own words.

It was at 16,000ft near Lingen that the aircraft was coned by searchlights. First one caught us, then several more illuminated their target, making me feel certain that they were radar guided. Almost immediately Flying Officer Stock in the rear turret called 'Fighter!' and the guns soon rattled. At that time I had never heard of a specific corkscrew manoeuvre but did just what came naturally, and it probably amounted to much the same thing. I remember quite distinctly seeing a number of white orbs through the windscreen and the canopy above, and realised I was looking directly into the searchlight bowls! An instinctive glance at the instruments showed the artificial horizon hard over on the stops. A strong smell of cordite, a loud bang and it was over. The fighter had broken away with Stock claiming to have hit it, and all the searchlights were out. We resumed course for Berlin, but every attempt to regain height caused the engine to overheat, so I diverted to Emden. It was a beautiful moonlit night with everything in the Germans' favour. Our W/T set had been shot up and the loud bang had been caused by an incendiary bullet entering the No1 starboard tank which had exploded.

From Flt Lt V F B 'Farmer' Pike and crew in the third aircraft nothing was heard – apart from a faint call for instructions. N6011 had, in fact, been shot down near Lingen by Fw Scherling in a Bf 110 of 7./NJG 1,claiming to make the *Luftwaffe*'s 98th night kill. Berlin had escaped a Stirling visit, but for how long?

With production totalling thirty-three aircraft, sufficient were available for the equipping of a second squadron and No XV Squadron was re-established with Stirlings on 10 April. Next day Flt Lt Best took N3644 to them at Wyton while 'B' Flight of 7 Squadron was returning to a drier Oakington. So, things were slightly improving, although the build-up in numerical strength of all squadrons re-arming with new type bombers was slow, as these figures illustrate:

Sqn	Type	1 Jan	14 Jan	2 Feb	9 Feb	13 Mar	27 Mar
7	Stirling	3 + 3	2 + 5	4 + 3	1 + 8	1 + 9	2 + 8
35	Halifax	–	–	2 + 2	3 + 1	6 + 8	9 + 7
61	Manchester	–	–	–	–	–	1 + 1
97	Manchester	–	–	–	–	4 + 4	5 + 4
207	Manchester	–	–	6 + 7	6 + 9	10 + 6	8 + 9

On 15 January establishment of Bomber Command medium and heavy squadrons was raised from sixteen IE + nil IR to sixteen IE + two IR. On 14 March 1941 the Command operational squadrons (all types) held 546 serviceable and 195 unserviceable aircraft.

Wg Cdr Harris's difficult and demanding task of introducing the Stirling being complete, he now handed command to Wg Cdr H Robert Graham DSO, affectionately known as 'der Führer' – or just plain 'Bob'. A truly legendary leader, he left the Service as an Air Commodore and later hit national newspaper headlines after using a rolled newspaper to clout a lion to discourage it from attacking a child.

On **16/17 April** another attempt was made to bomb Berlin and from N6010 flown by Flt Lt Williams 5 x 1,000lb and 7 x 500lb HEs dropped across the centre of the city were the first to fall there from a four-engined bomber.

Lord Trenchard visited Oakington on 18 April to congratulate the squadron before, on the 20th, seventy-five 'other ranks' left for Wyton to join XV Squadron. No 7 Squadron's personnel strength then reverted to normal establishment. The same day Wg Cdr Graham demonstrated N3655 during a display for VIPs at Hatfield.

The next memorable event developed on **20/21 April** when Flt Lt Cruickshank set off for Cologne, failed to locate it and jettisoned his bombs. He homed in N6009 to Marham where, too late, a Ju 88C night intruder was discovered in the area. Cruickshank, a Cranwell graduate and a special 'N' pilot who had flown on the first Stirling raid as a navigator, now faced a very difficult situation for to attract the raider lights were switched on at the Stanbourne 'Q' Site. Cruickshank undoubtedly mistook it for nearby Marham and as the Stirling approached the rough field the bomber struck an obstacle, became inverted, crashed on its back and all aboard were killed. The Ju 88 crew then struck at the burning wreck, their bombs narrowly missing the crashed Stirling.

By this time thoughts were being directed towards the 1941 summer bombing offensive. At Command HQ on 9 April daylight use of the Stirling was considered. Short hours of darkness made speed and defensive armament essential because aircraft

MG-G N6004 dwarfs Wellingtons of 101 Squadron at Oakington in early 1941. (RCAF)

would often operate in twilight which is why bomber losses were proportionately higher in mid-summer than in winter despite more inclement operating conditions. As a follow up Sir Archibald Sinclair visited Oakington on 26 April to acquire first-hand knowledge of operations so far. He enquired about range, speed and general capability relative to summer daylight operations. The decision to attempt cloud cover daylight operations was now taken.

Aircrew of 7 Squadron at Oakington in spring 1941. Identified are: Front row (left–right): 4th Fg Off Sach, 5th Plt Off Dyell, 6th Fg Off Witt, 8th Sqn Ldr Lynch Blosse, 9th Wg Cdr H R Graham, 10th Sqn Ldr Speare, 11th Flt Lt Bristowe, 12th Fg Off Blacklock, 14th Flt Lt Stock, 15th Plt Off Austin, 16th Fg Off Saunders. 2nd row: 2nd Sgt Martin, 3rd Plt Off Bailie, 6th Plt Off Brander, 7th Plt Off Blunden, 9th Plt Off Levine, 10th Fg Off Morley, 12th Plt Off Bolton, 14th Sgt Prentice. Back row: 11th Sgt Austin, 12th Sgt Savage. (D K Dyell)

Next day Sqn Ldr Lynch-Blosse set out from Newmarket at 1130 hrs but lack of cloud cover forced him to abandon the sortie. On 28 April it was the turn of Fg Off Witt and crew aboard N6010, the bomb aimer being Keith Deyell who recalls that these operations for him were the 'most nailbiting'. He recalls that two he flew in were:

> Cloud cover raids on Germany and three fighter-protected raids on northern France. The first was a cloud-cover daylight operation against Emden on **28 April**. We took off at 1115 hrs, remaining in cloud cover with its base 1,000ft all the way to Emden. A heavy barrage of light flak greeted us well before the target and followed us there. I released, on the dock area from about 900ft, 18 x 500lb bombs, while our gunners strafed everything in sight. Delayed action fuses enabled us to avoid our own bomb blast, and we pulled up into the clouds without seeing them burst. Cloud cover gave us safe passage home.

Although operations had not been all that successful, Stirling production dramatically increased when a third source came on line. Austin Motors had built Fairey Battles at Birmingham and switched to the Stirling in late 1940. Bombing of Birmingham impeded progress and it was March 1941 when the first Austin Stirling was completed.

Austin Motors was a separate Stirling production unit set up by MAP. Shorts initially passed on 'know-how' to Austins, but new, very different jigging methods were introduced at Longbridge. Austins were geared to mass production methods, their tooling allowing for faster building than at Shorts. It was a widely held opinion that the workmanship on Short machines was superior to that of Austins, but that the parent builder's airframe was heavier. Shorts were also building Sunderlands, and officialdom exhorted them to build both at faster rates despite their capacity being already fully utilised.

To assess the quality of Austin workmanship, Boscombe Down analysed W7426, the first flown, and tested it at 53,390lb. The controls seemed heavier, ailerons in particular feeling uncomfortably heavy at high speed. Elevator and aileron controls seemed slacker but stability was normal. With flaps and undercarriage down the aircraft dropped the starboard wing, rectification only coming after a dive. Generally the performance was as good as that of parent firm aircraft. About thirty of the first Austin machines were powered by Hercules Mk Xs, also fitted in a Belfast-built batch beginning with N6005.

April's major event was the conversion at Wyton of No XV Squadron which in remarkably short time switched from Wellingtons to Stirlings under the leadership of Wg Cdr H R Dale, ably assisted by Sqn Ldrs Menaul and Morris. Build up was very slow as is shown here (aircraft seviceable + aircraft unserviceable):

11 Apr	12 Apr	17 Apr	20 Apr	25 Apr	27 Apr
0+1	1+1	4+1	3+2	4+2	4+2

Nevertheless, XV Squadron first operated on **30 April** and ambitiously, for its target was none other than Berlin. Each of the four aircraft set off with 15 x 500lb HEs and Flt Lt Raymond (N6018-C) actually penetrated to the city only to discover 10/10 cloud obscuring it. He came home via Kiel where he deposited his load on a searchlight site. Dale in N3654-B was less successful, engine oil temperature rising dramatically in a port engine. Its revs fell so he turned back and bombed searchlights near Hamburg. Sqn Ldr Morris (N6004-F) had such a high rate of fuel consumption that he turned off track and bombed Kiel (the night's main target for 3 Group) from 16,000ft. Sqn Ldr Menaul (N6015-A) was forced back by engine trouble off Borkum. It had been an inauspicious start.

N6004, predecessor LS-F to 'MacRobert's Reply', had very matt black under surfaces crudely extended up the fuselage sides and bombed Kiel during XV Squadron's first operation on 30 April 1941. (Gp Capt W M Morris)

A spate of engine troubles was linked with fuel pump failures. Sqn Ldr W T C Seale (N6019), taking off from Oakington on 8 May, had two engines cut out for that reason and the aircraft slithered to a halt without damage. But 7 Squadron was more sobered on **2/3 May 1941**. Three Stirlings (N3652, N3655 from which bombs were jettisoned at sea and N6012) set out for Hamburg, along with forty-four Wellingtons, sixteen Hampdens, sixteen Whitleys and two Manchesters carrying between them seventy-five tons of HE as well as incendiaries. Twenty other crews were to attack Emden and three Wellingtons some oil tanks near Rotterdam. Another eleven Hampdens mined, and six leaflet droppers of 6 Group trained over France. Eventually 132 aircraft set out, 124 attacked and 8 aborted. Over Hamburg cloud varied up to 6,000ft, fires were started and there was one large explosion. Two Stirlings bombed, dropping 10 x 1,000lb and 14 x 500lb HEs, and as they neared Oakington on returning fearsome trouble overcame them.

A low-flying Ju 88C intruder of NJG2 which bombed dispersal areas at Waterbeach may well have been the same machine that slipped unnoticed into Oakington's circuit. As soon as the presence of the Ju 88C was discovered, runway lights were extinguished and airborne Stirlings were ordered to douse their navigation lights. Unfortunately one crew had left their R/T on 'transmit' and did not hear the warning. Within moments, fire from the intruder raked N6012 as its undercarriage was being lowered. Plt Off Alverson DFM, bailed out, his parachute opening just before he hit the ground. During a desperate attempt to land, N6012 hit trees near Dry Drayton and the remaining crew were killed.

Daylight operations were resumed on **6 May** when Lynch-Blosse attacked a convoy with uncertain results. At Wyton, XV Squadron were also getting into their stride and on **2 May** had been the first to drop incendiary bombs from the Stirling during a Rotterdam raid.

Two crews of No XV set off for Berlin on **8 May**, and once more engine trouble manifested itself. Campbell and crew attacked an alternative target, a canal near Berkenthin ten miles south of Lübeck; Leggate and companions settled for Hamburg. Next night the squadron was more successful for Plt Off Campbell and Sqn Ldr Morris both bombed Berlin. It was far from easy for Campbell and crew for, as N3656-H approached the city at 17,000ft, the starboard inner engine failed and boost fell to -4lb on the port inner. Height was rapidly lost, and the bomb doors had to be opened by hand. After 'bombs away' many searchlights swept the sky and Campbell lost altitude from 11,000ft to 7,000ft. Heavy flak was intense and put both the gyro compass and artificial horizon out of action which meant flying home on three engines while relying on turn and bank indicators.

On **10 May**, XV Squadron yet again despatched two crews to Berlin. Flt Lt Raymond pinpointed Steinhunder Lake and, from above cloud topping 12,000ft, dropped 5 x 1,000lb and 9 x 500lb bombs from 18,000ft. Flak was intense, N6018 being hit in many places as a result of which the port inner motor burst into flames. About twenty miles north of Dummer Lake, searchlights coned the Stirling and a single-engined fighter attacked, firing from 200 yards on the starboard quarter. The rear gunner fired, possibly damaging the fighter. Raymond dived, released a flare which attracted searchlights and also a fighter which possibly believed it to be a burning bomber. Then they headed home.

Wg Cdr Dale and crew aboard N3654 were less fortunate. At 0004 hrs on 11 May, Freya F 42 radar at Medenbilk, Holland, on the west side of the IJsselmeer, picked up an incoming bomber, N3654 of XV Squadron. It had already been detected by *Oblt* Prinz zur Lippe-Weissenfeld of 4.NJG/1, and F42 now guided his Bf 110 as the bomber flew along a reciprocal track about 5km north. The fighter was then directed on to a collision course. As soon as the Stirling came into view, zur Lippe placed himself slightly below the bomber out of range of the tailgunner who did not see the fighter until it delivered its second attack and made a series of fast 'S' turns. After a fifth assault the Stirling turned for the west, by which time it was over the IJsselmeer. Three thick fuel trails streamed from wing tanks as, in the face of return fire, two more assaults were carried out. As zur Lippe came in for the eighth attack the bomber's port inner engine was ablaze; so he took up position alongside the bomber, from which the bombs were being jettisoned near the F 42 installation. N3654 was now quite low, the crew baling out as the port outer engine burst into flames. Left to its fate, the Stirling slipped into a vertical dive, broke up in the air and disintegrated so completely upon impact that the Germans were unable to identify the wreckage. The Bf 110D-0 had used 561 rounds of MG 17 and 53 of MG FF to bring down the first Stirling to fall in Holland. Zur Lippe was credited with fifty-one victories by the time of his death on 12 March 1944.

German fliers believed their quarry cruised at 200mph and had well-protected fuel tanks from which fire had spread slowly. They reckoned the aircraft – which they finally decided to be a Stirling – was able to fly on two engines, and that the attacking position that had been used, from below the rear turret, was outside its field of fire. Wg Cdr Dale's place at Wyton was taken by Wg Cdr B Ogilvie, and about this time Sqn Ldr R D Speare took over 'A' Flight, 7 Squadron from Sqn Ldr Lynch-Blosse. Both squadrons headed for Berlin on **2 June**. Taking off before dusk, they relied upon cloud cover on their outward flight. Fg Off Mitchell and crew of 7 Squadron failed to return whereas Sgt Needham of XV Squadron, making slow progress, instead attacked Kiel. A fighter was vectored on to him but was shaken off.

On 6 June N3663 arrived at Oakington. The first Mk 1 Series iii to enter squadron service with the superior, eagerly awaited Hercules Mk XI engines, it was also the first to enter service featuring Modification 312, the FN7A dorsal turret, and could still accommodate twenty-six troops. The eighty-first and subsequent bomber Stirlings

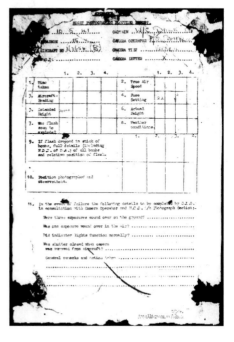

One that got away? A report salvaged from the crash site of N3654 LS-B by a Netherlands Air Force team nearly thirty years after Wg Cdr Dale's crash on 10/11 May 1941. (G J Zwanenburg)

– from N3662 and N6066 onwards – all featured dorsal turrets, although slow delivery rates meant that few entered service for some weeks. By 6 June only forty-seven Stirlings had been accepted by the RAF. Introduction of the other heavy, the Halifax, was also slow as these representative figures highlight:

	1 Apr	9 Apr	11 Apr	12 Apr	17 Apr	20 Apr	27 Apr	2 May
Stirling								
7 Sqn	4+9	4+11	7+5	4+8	4+8	5+7	2+10	8+3
XV Sqn	–	–	–+1	1+1	1+3	3+2	4+2	–+7
Halifax								
35 Sqn	10+7	–	15+6	–	15+3	–	4+2	–
76 Sqn	–	–	–	–	17+4	–	–	–

	10 May	15 May	27 May	2 Jun	6 Jun	12 Jun	15 Jun	28 Jun	30 Jun
Stirling									
7 Sqn	4+6	7+3	6+6	7+5	5+9	9+5	9+4	11+5	–
XV Sqn	3+5	4+3	4+4	6+4	7+4	–	4+4	6+4	7+4
Halifax									
35 Sqn	–+24	1+20	–	–	–	–	–	–	–
76 Sqn	–+4	–+7	–	–	–	–	–	–	–

XV Sqn establishment changed to 16+2 Stirlings on 10 Apr, 76 Sqn to Halifaxes wef 6 Apr

The Hercules XI powering N3663 developed 1,315 max hp at sea level and 1,460hp at 9,500ft. Normally, climb on 2,500revs gave an output of 1,315hp at 2,000ft and 1,185hp at 12,750ft. During cruising, power was 1,020hp at 7,500ft and 920hp at 17,750ft both when running at 2,500revs. For take-off at 2,900revs the output was 1,590hp.

The Mk 1 Series iii, which remained in short supply for some time, was introduced to operations on **12 June** when 7 Squadron dispatched its 100th Stirling sortie with N3663 being among seven (the others were N3652, N3655, N6003, N6005, N6007 and N6013) that headed for Huls. Only three Stirlings of 7 Squadron had so far been lost on operations, and four in accidents. By the end of June 1941 No 7 Squadron had dispatched 135 night sorties and No XV Squadron, for the loss of three aircraft, had sent out 70.

Extract from A&AEE report on Stirling N3662 fitted with FN 7A dorsal turret

Rotation of FN 7A fitted to Manchester caused severe vibration of tail fin and in more than one instance disintegration of the fin took place. Urgent tests were undertaken with the FN 7A on Stirling. In the first flight the turret was taken through 360° both ways, guns depressed and elevating at 150mph to 300mph ASI. Rotation caused slight structural vibration with the maximum at 60 from astern, which increased with speed. No noticeable effect on controls. A further flight to test rotation to 310mph IAS showed vibration greatest between 280mph and 310mph IAS, but it still did not affect controls. The FN 50 was rotated at all speeds up to a dive speed from 250mph to 300mph IAS and the pilot noticed the badly vibrating turret. While it was not excessive it was more pronounced than with the FN 7A.

The conclusion was that the FN 7A was suitable aerodynamically, but that the FN 50 was not suitable for gunnery and needed modifications. More tests were ordered using the FN 50 and a Mk II cupola. During early trials nothing had been placed around the fuselage junction with the turret.

Dorsal Turret – Effects upon Performance

Fitting a dorsal turret on the Stirling 1 was expected to cause a speed loss of only about 4mph with rotation to either side costing another 3.5mph. Comparative speed trials at a take-off weight of 57,680lb, with no turret, an FN 7A and an FN 50 were flown using N3678 (Hercules XI). Results were:

State	Revs	Height	TAS	IAS (mph)
No turret	2,800	12,000	262.5	214.5
FN 7A guns aft	2,800	12,000	258.5	211.5
FN 7A guns to beam	2,800	12,000	255	208.5
No turret	2,800	14,000	258	205
FN 50 guns aft	2,800	14,000	254	202
FN 50 guns to beam	2,800	14,000	250	199.5

Stirling Operations

10/11 February – 30 June 1941

Following each day's operations an analysis of sorties flown, bombs dropped and losses sustained was prepared at HQ Bomber Command. A summary of these items was sent to the Air Ministry War Room for high level perusal. The details included may be judged as a fairly accurate indication of bombing operations, bearing in mind precise accuracy would be impossible to record. Night photographs indicated where some bombs fell and coupled with results achieved by photographic reconnaissance often resulted in the ORS producing bomb plots at the target. The effectiveness of incendiary raids could only be assessed from reconnaissance photographs although areas of conflagration were obvious during attacks. The contribution to attacks made by missing crews was inevitably left open to question. Revised summaries included various adjustments to bomb load dropped in target areas and usually did not alter listing of released loads. The listings here and later give as brief and accurate a listing of attacks as possible.

Stirling Operations 10/11 February – 30 June 1941

Date	Target	Aircraft attacking/ despatched	2,000	1,900	1,000	500	250	FTR	No. attacking/ Total force despatched
February									
10/11	Rotterdam, oil store	3/3	–	–	–	48	–	–	32/33
15/16	Boulogne	2/2	–	–	–	32	–	–	2/2
24/25	Hipper at Brest SAP	2/3	–	–	–	45	–	–	52/58
March									
3	Hipper at Brest	2/3	12	–	–	–	–	N3653	43/50
12/13	Boulogne	1/1	–	–	–	22	–	–	6/6
17/18	Bremen	1/1	–	–	5	7	–	–	50/82
	Doschilrag Rotterdam	0/1	–	–	–	–	–	–	0/1
18/19	Rotterdam oil store	1/1	–	–	–	21	–	–	2/17
19/20	Rotterdam oil store	1/1	–	–	–	22	–	–	1/1
21/22	Lorient	1/1	–	–	–	16 SAP	–	–	?/?
	Ostend	0/2	–	–	–	–	–	–	?/?
23/24	Rotterdam	1/2	–	–	–	16	–	N3643 crashed	1/17
27/28	Cologne	1/1	–	–	5	6	–	–	33/?
April									
3/4	Rotterdam	2/2	–	–	10	24	–	–	?/?
7/8	Kiel	1/2	–	–	10	12	–	–	208/263
8/9	Kiel	1/1	–	–	5	6	–	–	139/159
9/10	Berlin, Emden: one bombed	0/3	–	–	5	3	–	N6011	?/59
14/15	Brest	3/3	–	–	14	25	–	–	89/94
15/16	Brest	3/3	–	–	5	7	–	–	?/68
16/17	Kiel	1/2	–	–	5	12	–	–	?/?
	Emden (alt)	1	–	–	5	12	–	–	?/?
17/18	Berlin	1/2	–	–	5	7	–	–	?/81
20/21	Cologne (alt)	1	–	–	5	12	–	–	?/?
22/23	Brest	2/2	11	–	–	2	–	–	13/13
23/24	Brest	0/1	–	–	–	–	–	–	58/67
25/26	Cologne	1/1	–	–	5	6	–	–	?/?
	Berlin	1/1	–	–	5	7	–	–	2/48
27	Wilhelmshaven (D)	0/1	–	–	–	–	–	–	0/1
28	Emden(D)	1/1	–	–	–	18	–	–	1/1
28/29	Brest	1/3	–	–	–	12	–	–	12/12
29	Wilhelmshaven attacked 29 barges at 52.55N/04.10E	1/1	–	–	–	18	–	–	1/1
30/1	Berlin, alts	3/8	–	–	10	24	–	–	?/?
	Kiel 2, Hamburg 1, Emden 1	4	–	–	–	30	–	–	4/4
May									
2/3	Hamburg	2/3	–	–	10	14	–	N6012	80/?
3/4	Brest	2/3	10	–	–	–	–	–	?/33
4/5	Brest	1/1	5	–	–	–	–	–	91/106
5	Bremen(D) attacked ship off Terschelling	1/1	–	–	–	–	–	–	1/1
5/6	Mannheim	4/4	–	–	20	37	–	–	120/?
6/7	Hamburg (one bombed Vegesack)	2/2	–	–	10	18	–	–	76/81
7/8	Bremen	3/3	–	–	15	32	–	–	3/3
8/9	Berlin (one bombed nr Lübeck)	2/4	–	–	10	13	–	–	2/4
9/10	Berlin	2/2	–	–	10	18	–	–	4/5
10/11	Berlin	0/4	–	–	5	7	–	–	?/98
11/12	Emden	1/1	–	–	–	–	–	–	?/131
15/16	Berlin	2/7	–	–	13	23	–	–	5/15
	Berlin (alts: Hannover, Cologne, Waalhaven)	5	–	–	–	–	–	–	5/5
16/17	Cologne	1/1	–	–	5	13	–	–	?/88

Date	Target	Aircraft attacking/ despatched	Bombs Dropped HE (lb)					FTR	No. attacking/ Total force despatched
			2,000	1,900	1,000	500	250		
23/24	Cologne alts:	3/3	–	–	15	42	–	–	?/40
	Rotterdam 2, Hamstede 1								
27(D)	Search for Hipper – not seen	0/17	–	–	–	–	–	–	?/69
30	Munster(D) (ab, NCC)	0/1	–	–	–	–	–	–	0/1
June									
2/3	Berlin	4/8	–	–	20	18	–	W7430	128/186
	alts: Kiel 1, Wilhelmshaven 1	2	–	–	–	–	–	–	2/3
7/8	Brest	7/7	24	–	71	–	–	–	33/37
9	off Belgium(D)	2/2	–	–	–	28	–	–	6
10	Emden (D) (NCC)	2/2	–	–	–	–	–	–	2
11/12	Düsseldorf	5/6	–	–	15	36	–	–	66/80
	(alts Cologne, Ruhrort, Duisburg)	3	–	–	–	–	–	–	3/3
12/13	Huls (alts:	4/7	–	–	25	52	–	–	224/339
	Emden 1, Rotterdam 2)								
13	'Lutzow' off Norway, recalled	4	–	–	–	–	–	–	4
13/14	Brest	0/4	–	–	–	–	–	–	?/?
15	Hannover	5/5	–	–	25	45	–	–	152/177
16/17	Düsseldorf	7/7	–	–	34	90	–	–	203/223
17/18	Hannover (3 bombed P/T,	5/6	–	–	25	45	–	–	5/9
	alts: Lemgo 1, Bramsch 1)								
18/19	Brest	5/8	12	–	–	12	–	–	48/65
20/21	Kiel	8/13	–	–	38	70	–	–	104/124
21	North sea	1/1	–	–	–	–	–	–	1/1
23/24	Kiel, also one bombed	11/13	–	–	55	18	–	–	54/62
	Wilhelmshaven								
26/27	Kiel	12/15	–	–	?	?	–	–	31/41
28	Bremerhaven (NCC)	0/6	–	–	–	–	–	N6007	0/6
29/30	Hamburg	7/13	–	–	35	55	–	N3664 N6016	15/28
	alts bombed by others							N6001 N6015	

Incendiaries dropped during the period:

2/3 June	720 x 4lb
12/13 June	1,200 x 4lb
16/17 June	1,008 x 4lb
26/27 June	1,380 x 4lb
29/30 June	1,480 x 4lb

Notes:

2/3: 2 claimed to attack primary target (P/T), other aircraft attacked alternative or aborted

ab: abandoned

alt: alternative targets

(D): daylight operation

Final column: Figures refer to total number attacking/number of all types despatched to given target. Such figures can only give a realistic reckoning and can never be precise.

FTR: failed to return

ncc: no cloud cover

P/T: primary target

Some precise weapon loads carried/dropped remain uncertain

Chapter 6
Temptation

NOT only was there a shortage of Stirlings, the targets which had brought the bomber into being were equally sparse. Arsenals, capital ships, distant arms factories and suitable specialised targets which the aircraft could not reach were few. Their absence, the small number of Stirlings and their good manoeuvrability found them, amazingly, participating in operation *Channel Stop* alongside the Blenheims of No 2 Group trying to halt German ships supplying occupation forces in France.

On **9 June**, Wg Cdr Graham and Flt Lt Cox were despatched individually to add considerable weight to the campaign by attacking shipping off the Belgian coast. Each highly vulnerable Stirling carried 14 x 250lb 'B' special anti-shipping bombs. Cox, after a 4,000ton MV and three smaller ships sailing line abreast north-east out of the English Channel, saw his bombs fall a little ahead of them.

German fighters rapidly responded, three Bf 109s tackling N6006 soon after it had bombed. Fighters – none of which was destroyed – scored six hits on the bomber's stern, put cannon shells into the fuselage and punctured its starboard tyre. Graham (N6020) was attacked off Dunkirk by two Bf 109s of 3./JG 52 one of which gave up after a 25 mile chase out to sea after peppering the bomber which had attacked ships of a *Hafenschutzflotille* and Boat 822.

Next day Flt Lt Blacklock (N6022) and Sqn Ldr Searle (N6003) set out individually to make cloud cover attacks upon Emden. Blacklock considers it probably was unwise to have proceeded after cloud ran out, but as there was more ahead decided to press on.

> We were proud of our Stirling, anxious to prove our CO's boast that one Stirling could carry as many bombs as a squadron of Blenheims, but more than anything else remembered that Denis Witt had already done it! My log book entry for the 10th states that we were attacked by two 109s, not the three oft quoted, which persisted in quarter attacks until 'Jock' Graham shot down the leader, *Uffz* K Marz who was killed flying Bf 109F WNr 9540 Black 1 of 2/JG 52. The No 2 then made a wide sweep to starboard before turning in for a beam attack. As the fighter turned, I turned towards him so that Ashton was able to get in a shot with almost no deflection, and possibly just in time, as I think our front turret hydraulics were hit.

The crew had survived an eighteen minute fight, which took place between 7,000ft and sea level, and must surely have been grateful for the excellent manoeuvrability of the Stirling.

Records are conflicting and Blacklock believes the following episode, which he recounts, may have taken place as they returned.

> As we approached the Suffolk coast, 'Jock' Graham asked for, and was given, permission to start cleaning his guns. Ahead of, and below – probably 1,500ft to 2,000ft – two Hurricanes were weaving around. We wondered what they were up to as we could not see any ships for them to be protecting. After we passed over them one tagged on and shortly after starting firing from below us. 'Jock' meantime had been sitting on the platform behind the turret with two of his guns out for cleaning. He had an eye on the Hurricane and when it lined up for attack slid back into his turret, swung it round and replied with a short burst to the fighter's fire. Naturally, he had not wasted time closing turret doors and as soon as the first door cleared the fuselage it swung open and was blown off in the slipstream. On enquiring at debriefing where the Hurricanes came from we learned that they belonged to a Polish Squadron of Debden Sector, and "thought they had hit us because part of our aircraft was seen to fall away". Our next air test included a few circuits of Debden. No one replied to our R/T calls explaining who and what we were!

The next cloud cover foray came on 28 June and involved three crews from each of the two squadrons all operating independently despatched to bomb Bremerhaven. Plt

W7429 LS-J sets forth on a 1941 Circus operation.

Off Campbell's aircraft, N3656-H of XV Squadron, was damaged during a fighter attack while the squadron's other two aircraft, N6021-D and W7429-J, turned back when the cloud began to run out. Sqn Ldr Speare (N6020) also turned back leaving the other two from 7 Squadron proceeding. They became involved in a memorable encounter.

Although cloud cover ran out, Flt Lt Collins (N6007) and Flt Lt Blacklock (N3663) decided that by staying low and keeping well north of the Friesians they could reach the cover visible in the distance.

> We had flown for quite a spell in clear conditions [recalls George Blacklock] when 'Jock' Graham, our rear gunner, reported another Stirling, about a mile behind and south of our track, being attacked by fighters. I turned back to give him support, but before we could reach him we were set upon about 50km north of Schiermonikoog by nine yellow-nosed 109s. Perhaps fortunately our own N6022 was unserviceable that day, and we were using the COs N3663, the first Stirling with a mid-upper turret. 'Taff' Price, flight engineer, needed no urging to man the extra guns, and took great delight in his new role. Again, Graham's directions showed that an agile bomber properly guided had a good chance against fighters so long as their attacks were from the rear. Before we had joined the other Stirling, which proved to be Collins', the fighters had retired, 'Jock' claiming one down and with 'Taff's' help, damaged two others. Into the sea had crashed a brand new Bf 109F-1 Wk Nr 8942 'PB+SU' of I/JG 52 and probably flown by *Lt* Hans Betke.
>
> I was unable to raise Collins on R/T but managed to edge him round until we were on a westerly heading. Then I formated on him to be better placed should more fighters turn up. It appeared that he had probably suffered some damage and maybe casualties, and we had the impression that his starboard outer engine was windmilling. I don't remember any of his props being feathered, but he was flying lower and lower and slower and slower so that I had to put out partial flap to maintain formation.
>
> R/T having failed, we tried the Aldis lamp, but to no avail. We all felt so helpless and frustrated. It seemed obvious that 'Queenie' was not going to get home and indeed it was not long before Collins ditched about 25km north of Texel, but not nose first as reported – at least, not as I recall it. At the speed he was flying, N6007 was obviously in a tail-down attitude and it just flew on to the sea, which was relatively calm. When the spray cleared we could see that the fuselage had broken in two behind the mainplane. The rear half had disappeared and the front half was vertical, nose down, in the water. In a very short time, probably less than a minute, that too had sunk.

> I had the navigator ('Paddy' Kenny) drop a smoke float to mark the approximate position, and we orbited for ten minutes or so in the hope that maybe some of the crew and perhaps the dinghy might come to the surface. I wondered what would happen if we tried to release our dinghy in the air, but perhaps it was as well that we did not put that notion to the test.

Blacklock sorrowfully set course for home.

Another cloud-cover operation flown on **1 July** involved a maximum effort. Two loose formations each of three aircraft set forth to raid Aurich and Cuxhaven. The trio of XV Squadron aircraft turned back when the cloud ran out, but the three from 7 Squadron, headed by Fg Off Witt with Sgt Bolton as second pilot, pressed on in broken cloud whose base was under 1,000ft. When that ceased to give cover they headed for Borkum, their secondary target. Flak ships and six Bf 109s fiercely responded as Witt's aircraft approached, Deyell releasing the bombs from 900ft while a fighter closed upon them. Deyell reached the navigator's seat just as two explosions rocked the Stirling.

Flight engineer aboard was Sgt John T Prentice, another of the original members of 7 Squadron in its Leeming days as well as one of the RAF's first flight engineers known, until early 1941, as Fitters II/Air Gunners. John Prentice recalls:

> When the six Bf 109s first attacked I was acting as Fire Controller. During the course of the engagement I was tapped on the shoulder by Fg Off J L A Mills, the rear gunner, who had been shot in the arm and was not able to continue. I took over his position in the turret and indeed remained there until we reached base.

Denis Witt had meanwhile thrown the aircraft about, taking evasive action to shake off the Messerschmitts as Deyell and Sgt Savage, the radio operator, looked after Mills. Sgt Prentice had raced back to the rear turret which he reached just as a Bf 109 was coming in and during the course of the continuing engagement he shot down a fighter, a highly meritorious effort. As soon as they had entered protective cloud a shot of morphine and a good supply of bandages helped Mills until badly-shot-about N6005 safely landed. The raid had cost the squadron Fg Off J Kinnane and crew aboard N6013, last seen circling a dinghy containing the crew of a 139 Squadron Blenheim shot down by Bf 109s of I/JG 52. German records claim that a Bf 109 of 4./JG 52 destroyed a Stirling at 1452 hrs and that two more were shot down by Bf 110s of 6./ZG 76, Leeuwarden. The Luftwaffe timed their claims as at 1520 hrs and 1521 hrs and admitted losing a Bf 110. The third Stirling (N3655) in fact returned safely.

N6029 LS-K over France and under fire.

Saturday **5 July** brought a watershed, for heavily escorted Stirlings began participating in operation *Circus*, a daylight activity in which they provided tasty bait for enemy fighters. It was an attempt to induce the Germans to bring home fighters from the Russian front. Mercifully, this crazy activity lasted only a fortnight.

Proceedings were opened by XV Squadron fielding Sqn Ldr Menaul, Flt Lt Gilmour and Fg Off Thompson flying, respectively, N6018-C, N3658-E and N6029-K. They set forth from Wyton in formation to bomb the Fives steel works at Lille while Fg Off Marsh, alone and heavily protected by fighters, tackled Abbeville's marshalling yards.

Circus operations were complicated affairs. Two miles above Southend for this, the first *Circus*, the three Stirlings began collecting around themselves fighters drawn from the Kenley and Northolt Wings. Overall cover and close escort was provided by the Hornchurch Wing, and target support (ie. fighters to operate over the target) by Biggin Hill and Tangmere Wings. On some later Stirling *Circuses*, rear support (also called 'withdrawal cover') was provided by fresh squadrons patrolling over the Channel. With No 312 (Czech) Squadron close, the Stirlings made landfall near Dunkirk then faced flak near Gravelines, over Roubaix and in the target area where, due to light cloud, they made a dummy run before turning to drop 15 x 1,000lb and 30 x 500lb HEs from 12,000ft. Anti-aircraft gunners fired, trying in vain to break the bomber formation before it unloaded, the attempt being followed by Bf 109s which from 25,000ft dived upon the Stirlings. Some Bf 109s raced between them, 312 Squadron claiming a Bf 109 trying to latch on to the rear of a Stirling. Target Support Spitfires closed in before Dunkirk was reached on return to keep enemy fighters busy and No 616 squadron eventually drew them off, leaving 610 Squadron to help cover the bombers' withdrawal. The Stirling attacking Abbeville faced far less opposition but unloaded south-west of the target. From this first day it was clear that the Stirlings would be very vulnerable to flak which could not be avoided.

No 7 Squadron's introduction to *Circus* came next day when three aircraft (W7433, N6017 and N6022) left Oakington at 0740 hrs to bomb shipyards at Le Trait. Heavy flak greeted them this clear morning, the bombs from two aircraft overshooting onto the wrong bank of the Seine. The other crew attacked Yainville power station, the alternative target.

Later, six Stirlings of XV Squadron (N6018-C, N6021-D, N6004-F, W7429-J, N6029-K, N6030-P) took part in another *Circus* with Fives/Lille steel works as target. Protecting the six bombers flying in two vics was the Hornchurch Wing which they met over Manston at 1428 hrs. Nearest explosions to the target from the 24 x 1,000lb and 56 x 500lb HEs released were within two sticks which exploded in adjacent marshalling yards. Bf 109s accepting the challenge broke through the fighter protection to damage a Stirling in the second vic. Busy in the fight was 611 Squadron led by Wg Cdr Stapleton (W3246). Flying Spitfire W3247 was Flt Lt Lock who claimed a Bf 109, while Sgt N J Smith (W3311) shot down another and Sgt Gilmore (W3243), after being set upon by no fewer than four 109s, shot down one and seriously damaged another.

Flak was heavy, and Messerschmitts again penetrated to attack the Stirlings. Sgt Ward, Flt Lt Gilmour's front gunner in the second vic, damaged a Bf 109 but the Stirling was hit before the fighter broke away pursued by Hurricanes of Nos 71 (Eagle) and 306 (Polish) Squadrons. Being half a mile behind the leading vic exposed the rear of the forward formation. Three Bf 109s entered that space and one was shot down. No 71 Squadron was continuously in action during withdrawal to the French coast, and No 242 Squadron also attacked Bf 109s pestering the bombers.

Both Stirling squadrons again operated on **7 July**, Plt Off Stokes raiding Hazebrouck where his bombs fell wide. A Bf 109 was claimed without British loss. Meanwhile Menaul, Gilmour and Thompson made for the Kuhlman chemical works at Chocques where 15 x 1,000lb and 42 x 500lb HEs burst around a cooling tower and on the ammonia plant. Four crews of 7 Squadron were despatched to attack the aircraft factory at Meaulte/Albert where HEs and 360 x 4lb incendiaries burst around the works. Although no German fighters reached these Stirlings, their escort claimed two Bf 109s but two Spitfires failed to return.

There was no let up in *Circus* operations, the next early on **8 July** involving three Oakington crews ordered to bomb a chemical works north-east of Lens and also Mazingarbe power station. Their fighter escort took up station over Rye then faced heavy flak near Boulogne which forced the entire formation off track. Two crews assaulted Lens as a line of flak bursts crept up on Plt Off Morley's aircraft. Witt and crew watched in horror as a direct hit overtook the bomber and only two parachutes opened before it inverted itself then entered a steep dive. Two fighters attacking Witt's aircraft were driven off by the top cover. A fierce fighter battle at 20,000ft over St Omer involved fifteen Bf 109s. No 603 Squadron was in thick of the fight, Sgt P Tabor (W3138) destroying a Bf 109 which he chased to south-west of Lille. He then tackled a second one which he watched smash itself into a tree. Another Bf 109 fell to Sgt Plt Jackman in Spitfire R7227. After regrouping, the battle was resumed, the RAF claiming in all five Bf 109Es shot down for the loss of three Hornchurch fighters.

XV Squadron also flew three daylight sorties on the **8th**, to the Kuhlman works at Lille and the town's power station. Heavy flak which prevented accurate bombing damaged all three Stirlings, N6030-P, N3656-H and N6021-D. Three red-nosed Bf 109s were engaged, the tough fighter response costing the RAF seven fighter pilots.

Three Stirlings of XV Squadron operated the next *Circus*, flown on **9 July**, thick haze diverting the attack (by W7428-F, N3656-H and N6030-P) to switch from Mazingarbe to La Buissere. Tenacious *Luftwaffe* fighter pilots again to the fore penetrated to the bombers whose gunners claimed a Bf 109. No 312 Squadron tackled them, one falling to Hurricane Z3742 and another to Flt Sgt Kucera in Z3314. Sqn Ldr (Z3660) claimed another.

On **10 July**, 7 Squadron provided the bait, Fg Off Witt (N6022) leading two other Stirlings (N6017, W7433) to attack the chemical factory at Chocques near Bethune. Dangerous coastal heavy flak battered Fg Off C V Fraser's aircraft (N6017) in the number two position and scored a direct hit on its port inner engine. Almost immediately the bomber was fiercely blazing and only one parachute cast off. Witt and crew pressed on to bomb a marshalling yard, and Plt Off Roach's bombs hit the chemical works. German fighters scored hits on his tail unit, and eight British fighters were shot down or severely damaged.

Despite the losses and obvious risks both squadrons despatched three more day sorties on **11 July**, Wg Cdr Graham leading his squadron's last *Circus* contribution, a relatively uneventful one directed against Le Trait. XV Squadron mounted a three-

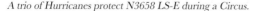

A trio of Hurricanes protect N3658 LS-E during a Circus.

Stirling afternoon raid but thundery conditions caused a diversion to Hazebrouck marshalling yards. Observing from HQ 11 Group was HM King George VI.

Circus 46 flown on **12 July** had as its target an impressive ship lift at Arques near St Omer. It remained, bombs from all three Stirlings (N3658-E, N3656-H, W7429-J) having overshot while the bombers suffered flak damage. For the next three days XV Squadron awaited orders, several times loaded aircraft becoming airborne only to find weather conditions causing abandonment and fuel jettisoning prior to landing.

Circus operations were resumed on **19 July** and another tragedy came about over the French coast. Sqn Ldr T W Piper was leading three aircraft to bomb a factory near Lille where 10/10 cloud over the primary target brought a turn about for the last resort, Dunkirk docks. There the AA gunners awaiting the Stirlings placed accurate fire around them. Piper's aircraft received direct hits which set his port inner engine ablaze. Flames pierced the port wing and pieces began falling away. Piper ordered all aircraft to release their bombs before his aircraft curled away to port. Two of the crew baled out; before, having straightened out, N6018 then zoomed into a vertical dive from 1,500ft and spiralled into the ground.

Early on **21 July** three Stirlings of XV Squadron left for the accumulator factory at Lille but visibility was so poor that their bombs were jettisoned in Barrow Deep. Flak around Dunkirk succeeded in forcing Sgt H Taunton to put down at Manston after his starboard inner was put out of action. He had lost height to 7,000ft over Merville when two Bf 109s sneaked up, fired on him and stopped his starboard outer engine. Shepherded by Hornchurch's Spitfires he lined up on Manston but with only two engines running he was unable to make the customary left-handed circuit. He turned right and on his second attempt safely executed an extremely difficult landing.

The final *Circus*, flown on **21 July**, was a failure. Clouds towered to 23,000ft bringing the fourth consecutive abortive effort – 'a colossal waste of effort, fuel and bombs' in XV Squadron's opinion, not to mention lives. Stirling Circuses had ended; they should never have begun.

Over France, three XV Squadron Stirlings including W7431 LS-A and N3656 LS-H.

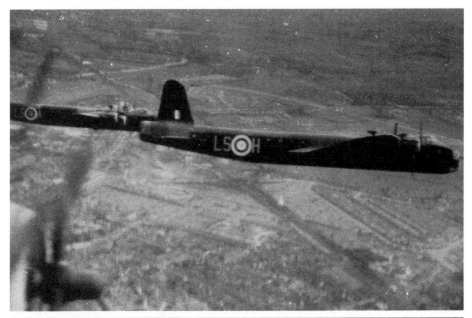

Using Stirlings provoked no more fighter reaction than against Blenheims, and had been very expensive in every way. Chosen targets did not warrant the effort, and the bombers' vulnerability to flak was their Achilles heel, its hazardous nature leading to the withdrawal. This was not, however, the end of Stirling day raids, for something special suddenly developed – a reconnaissance flight over Brest on **23 July** revealed that *Scharnhorst* had sailed. At last the Stirlings would, and for the first time, operate in their prime role, by attacking a capital ship with 2,000lb AP bombs. Her move caused surprise and considerable alarm, for a large scale day raid on Brest had been planned for the very next day. Had there been a security breach, or was it pure (unlikely) coincidence?

Scharnhorst had sailed south, initial belief being that she had gone to La Rochelle, but later information showed the battle cruiser to be in La Pallice. Plans to include fifteen Stirlings in a large-scale daylight raid on 24 July were abandoned; instead, and responding very fast, the Stirlings would attack on 23 July. That meant loading and refuelling the aircraft very quickly and at around 1745 hrs Sqn Ldr R W Cox (N6037), Flt Lt Blacklock (N6035) and Fg Off D Witt (W7434) became airborne from Oakington. Almost simultaneously three other Stirlings left Wyton but misfortune quickly intervened for Plt Off Needham, unable to raise the undercarriage of N6029-K, had to jettison the fuel then land with the large bombs aboard. The other two pressed on, Sgt Jones in W7428-F coming across a large ship by a jetty on an island. He attacked, but his wrong target was by Fromentine and the ship was not the *Scharnhorst*. Fg Off Campbell was believed to have attacked the target but with what success was unknown for he ditched N6038-R about 50 miles from Milford Haven and all aboard died.

By 7 Squadron the event was rated the summer's high spot, as George Blacklock recalls:

> Cox, Witt and I were the only captains to have been with the squadron since its Leeming days. We had passed through the traditional route of aircraft apprenticeship and sergeant pilot and now, for the first time, were to share a daylight operation with each Stirling carrying three 2,000lb armour piercing bombs. I don't remember the amount of fuel required, but it was going to produce a considerable all-up weight, and I do recall expressing doubts about our ability to get off the ground as it was a very hot afternoon and Oakington was, of course, still a grass airfield. However, the problem was solved by arranging to return to St Eval instead of Oakington thereby reducing the fuel and take-off weight. Reg Cox's request for take-off clearance is still quoted by surviving members of the crews: 'Freeman, Hardy and Willis ready for take-off!'
>
> He and his navigator did a first-class job in leading us below radar cover all the way round the Brest peninsula and along the French coast to the right spot from which to make a rated climb to arrive just short of the target at bombing height, where we broke formation and attacked individually. We were not troubled by fighters until after we had bombed, but there was same flak about, one piece of shrapnel coming up through the floor and wrecking Rossiter's W/T set for the second time. I guess he must have thought the next time might be unlucky because he didn't fly with us again, but instead got a posting to Lossiemouth. A 109 latched on to us as we dived for the sea, 'Taff' again enjoying a go in the turret and 'Jock's' shooting persuading the fighter to break off, probably damaged. I remember being struck by the change in light – we had been flying in bright sunlight but by the time we had descended to sea level, which did not take long, twilight was well advanced.

Just after Witt's bombs exploded away from the ship three Bf 109s engaged his aircraft so he dived to a very low level to escape. Cox reckoned one of his own bombs burst on the ship's stern whereas his other two hung up. Two Bf 109s which dived on his aircraft from out of the sun were claimed by the rear gunner who saw them crash in the sea. It was clearly an auspicious end to the Stirling's daylight bombing campaign – for the present.

Summary of Stirling *Circus* Operations – July 1941

Op No	No/Sqn	Bomber's Target	Close Escort	Escort cover	Target support	Rear support	Withdrawal cover
5 July							
C-33	3/XV	Fives Lille (Z183)	258	54	74	19	
	–	–	308	603	92	257	
	–	–	312	611	145	401	
	–	–	485	–	610	–	
	–	–	–	–	616	–	
	1/XV	Abbeville(Z440)	71	–	–	–	
	–	(Diversion)	242	–	–	–	
	–	–	222	–	–	–	
	–	–	–	Fighter pilots lost 2, claims 2-1-5			
6 July							
C-34	3/7	Le Trait (Z363)	?	?	?	?	
	6/XV	Fives-Lille (Z183)	71	74	54	56	258
	–	–	222	92	145	65	312
	–	–	242	609	303	601	
	–	–	306	–	308	–	
	–	–	–	–	603	–	
	–	–	–	–	610	–	
	–	–	–	–	611	–	
	–	–	–	–	616	–	
	–	–	–	(485 at Readiness, Kenley)			
	–	–	–	Fighter pilots lost 6, claims 11-6-5			
7 July							
C-36	1/1	Hazebrouck (Z437)	71	303	54	19	
	–	–	222	308	603	257	
	–	–	242	–	611	401	
	–	–	–	Fighters lost nil, claims 1-3-0			
	–	–	–	–	–	–	
C-37	4/7	Albert/Meault (Z189)	258	74	145	–	
	–	–	312	92	610	–	
	–	–	485	609	616	–	
	–	–	–	Fighters lost 2, claims 2-0-2			
C-38	3/XV	Chocques (Z220)	258	145	303	–	54
	–	–	312	610	308	–	603
	–	–	485	616	74	–	611
	–	–	–	–	92	–	
	–	–	–	–	609	–	
	–	–	–	Fighter pilots lost 1, claims nil			
8 July							
C-39	2/7	Lens (Z526)	258	92	1	222	
	1/7	Mazingarbe (Z301)	312	609	54	306	
	–	–	485	–	603	–	
	–	–	–	–	611	–	
	–	–	–	–	145	–	
	–	–	–	–	610	–	
	–	–	–	–	611	–	
	–	–	–	Fighter pilots lost 3, claims 7-4-7			
C-40	3/XV	Lille/Kuhlman	56	–	258	–	
	–	Lille (Z246)	65	–	312	–	
	–	–	601	–	485	–	92
	–	–	–	–	–	–	609
	–	–	–	Fighter pilots lost 7, claims nil			
9 July	–	–	–	–	–	–	
C-41	3/XV	Mazingarbe	258	145	54	71	
	–	La Buissere	312	610	603	242	
	–	bombed – power	485	616	611	306	
	–	station	–	–	92	–	
	–	–	–	–	609	–	
	–	–	–	–	303	–	
	–	–	–	–	308	–	
	–	–	–	Fighter pilots lost 7, claims 12-0-0			

Op No	No/Sqn	Bomber's Target	Close Escort	Escort cover	Target support	Rear support	Withdrawal cover
				Fighter Squadrons involved			
10 July							
C-42	3/7	Chocques	71	302	54	306	72*
–	–	–	222	308	603	312	92*
–	–	–	242	–	611	485	609*
–	–	–	–	–	145	–	
–	–	–	–	–	610	–	
–	–	–	–	–	611	–	
–			–	Fighter pilots lost 7, claims 11-3-4			
11 July							
C-43	3/7	Le Trait	303	–	–	610	–
–	–	Yainville (Z453)	312	–	–	616	–
–	–	–	602	–	–	–	
–	–	–	485	–	–	–	
–			–	Fighter pilots lost 3, claims 6-2-7			
C-45	3/XV	Fives/Lille (Z183)	72	303	54	222	–
–	–	but bombed	242	308	145	310	–
–	–	Mazingarbe	306	603	–	–	
–	–	–	–	610	–	–	
–	–	–	–	611	–	–	
–	–	–	–	616	–	–	
–			–	Fighter pilots lost 2, claims 3-0-0			
12 July							
C-46	3/XV	Arques ship lift	312	54	303	306	19**
–	–	–	485	603	308	242	56**
–	–	–	602	611	145	–	257**
–	–	–	–	–	610	–	
–	–	–	–	–	616	–	
–			–	Fighter pilots lost 2, claims nil			
19 July							
C-51	0/3 of XV	Lille/Sequedin	3	54	72	485**	312
–	–	bombed Dunkirk	71	603	92	602**	
–	–	docks	222	611	609	–	
–	–	–	–	145	–	–	
–	–	–	–	610	–	–	
–	–	–	–	616	–	–	
–	–	–	–	306	–	–	
–	–	–	–	308	–	–	
–			–	Fighter pilots lost 2, claims nil			
20 July							
C-52	0/3 of XV	Hazebrouck	485	72	54	306**	3
–	–	cloudy	602	92	603	308**	
–	–	–	71	609	611	–	
–	–	–	–	–	145	–	
–	–	–	–	–	610	–	
–	–	–	–	–	616	–	
–			–	Fighter pilots lost 3, claims nil			
21 July							
C-54	3/3 of XV	Lille	485	72	54	306**	3
–	–	–	602	92	603	308**	
–	–	–	71	609	611	–	
–	–	–	–	–	145	–	
–	–	–	–	–	610	–	
–	–	–	–	–	616	–	
–			–	Fighter pilots lost 3, claims nil			
C-55	0/3 of XV	Mazingarbe	71	54	72	19**	485
–	–	–	111	603	92	65**	602
–	–	–	306	611	609	266**	
–	–	–	–	–	145	–	
–	–	–	–	–	610	–	
–	–	–	–	–	616	–	
–			–	Fighter pilots lost nil, claims nil			

* = high cover Wing ** = forward support

Fighter Squadrons – Equipment and Bases

Sqn	Aircraft Type	Base
1	Hurricane IIb	Tangmere
3	Hurricane IIb	North Weald
19	Spitfire IIa	Fowlmere
54	Spitfire Va	Hornchurch
56	Hurricane IIb	Duxford
65	Spitfire II	Kirton-in-Lindsey
71	Hurricane IIb	North Weald
72	Spitfire V	Gravesend
74	Spitfire Vb	Gravesend
92	Spitfire Vb	Biggin Hill
145	Spitfire IIb/Va	Merston
222	Spitfire IIb	Manston
242	Hurricane IIb	North Weald
257	Hurricane IIb	Coltishall
258	Hurricane IIa	Martlesham
303	Spitfire IIa	Northolt
306	Hurricane IIb	Northolt
308	Spitfire Vb	Northolt
310	Hurricane IIb	Martlesham
312	Hurricane IIb	Kenley
401	Hurricane IIb	Digby
485	Spitfire IIa	Redhill
601	Hurricane IIb	Matlask
602	Spitfire V	Kenley
603	Spitfire Va	Hornchurch
609	Spitfire Vb	Biggin Hill
610	Spitfire Vb	Westhampnett
611	Spitfire Vb	Hornchurch
616	Spitfire IIb	Westhampnett

Rocket-assisted take-off tests using Stirling N3635

Loaded to 64,000lb a Hercules II-powered Stirling was reckoned to need a take-off run of about 1,400 yards in order to rise to 50ft and some form of assisted take-off seemed desirable. The most easily applicable seemed to be the use of cordite rockets since they needed no fixed equipment on the airfield and could be easily fitted.

Tests were carried out using the tail portion of the 3-inch UP rocket whose electrically fired propellant delivered a thrust of 11,800lb lasting for about 1.3 seconds. Twenty-four rockets were fitted, twelve in one of two carriers fitted between the engine nacelles. Firing all rockets simultaneously would have put too much strain on the structure and so the rockets were instead fired one under each wing at 0.6 second intervals. Timing was obtained by using two standard Automatic Bomb Distributors in series. When about 60mph IAS was reached, the pilot depressed the firing button and the carriers were jettisoned about two seconds after the last rocket had fired.

Trials started with the aircraft weight at 46,000lb and with increasing numbers of rockets until twenty-four were tried. Take-off weight was steadily increased and eventually two tests were undertaken at 58,000lb at which loading N3635 took off as the last pair of rockets were firing. Testing was limited to 58,000lb by the age and state of the particular aircraft and showed these results:

	Weight (lb)	Ground Run (yards)	Airborne (yards)	To 50ft (yards)
Standard operation (no rockets)	56,600	960	440	11,480
(1) with 24 rockets	57,900	495	540	11,035
(2) No rockets	57,900	625	520	11,145

A demonstration of the system was being given on 16 August 1941 when a firing failure occurred. The first pair of rockets was ignited and then the remainder fired simultaneously, probably as a result of an electrical malfunction. The carriers moved forward damaging the propellers before breaking up.

Although the tests showed the scheme to be quite practicable, the fitting of Hercules XI engines in a 70,000lb Stirling reduced the take-off run to 1,200 yards, making rocket assistance unnecessary. Undercarriage drag was considerable, making desirable the firing of some rockets during the climb when the undercarriage was being retracted. Suggestions were made following the trials that bi-fuel, using a mixture of petrol and liquid oxygen, was likely to be preferable to cordite.

A Rogue Aircraft?

N6040 was tested at Boscombe Down in August 1941 after repeatedly showing very poor climb and cruise performance, and was suspected of being a 'rogue' aircraft. Tests showed its performance to be not unreasonable and produced these results:

Height (ft)	All-up weight (lb)	Supercharger	IAS (mph)	TAS (mph)
14,000	67,000	FS	159	194
11,000	66,750	FS (2,500 revs)	160	194
10,000	66,550	MS (2,510 revs)	177	207
10,000	64,200	MS (2,450 revs)	178	210
Comparative results with N3662 showed:				
10,000	64,200	FS (2,400 revs)	186	223
—	—	MS (2,300 revs)	165	189

Outward Cruise Performance

Tests using N3662 showed a maximum speed for continuous climb at high weights of around 155mph IAS. It was uncomfortable to fly at minimum power, only gentle manoeuvres being possible without height loss. Lowest recommended speed for outward flight was 165mph IAS. If engine speed fell from 2,500 revs to 2,300 revs the aircraft could no longer maintain 15,000ft. At 10,000ft in MS gear there was ample power in hand for weak mix cruising. N3662 (Hercules XI) undertook speed trials in December 1941–January 1942. It was fitted with an FN 50 and an FN 64 ventral turret, exhaust ring shrouds, CS 1941 inter-cylinder baffles, plain open-end exhaust pipes, ice guards and carburettor intakes. Tests at 70,000lb showed speed losses as 7–9mph in MS and 11–18mph in FS gear. Below full throttle height, respective losses were 6–15mph and 7–15mph.

Chapter 7
A Steady Increase

AFTER arrival at Brest, the *Scharnhorst* and *Gneisenau* had attracted much attention. By July 1941 Allied shipping losses had declined sufficiently to free Bomber Command from anti-naval activity for redeployment against German industry. Overcoming Ruhr haze seemed an insurmountable problem, with only moonlit night operations likely to bring worthwhile results. The Telecommunications Research Establishment had by August 1941 evolved the *Gee* navigation aid thought to be usable as a blind bombing aid. Instead, it was insufficiently accurate and attacks would still have to be delivered with the aid of a conventional bomb sight.

When 3 Group's Wellingtons began dropping 4,000lb 'cookies' in March 1941, the Stirling was at once out-performed for its bomb bay longitudinal stiffeners prevented it from carrying bombs of such size. Nevertheless, it could haul a 10,000lb load to the Ruhr and in 1942 it became clear that the most effective raids involved dropping high proportions of incendiary bombs which Stirlings could readily carry and in plenty.

There were still only two Stirling squadrons, and by the close of July 1941 a mere forty-eight Stirlings had reached the RAF. Eight were lost in action in July alone and sixteen so far, with another three written off due to battle damage and five in accidents – half the total number so far delivered. Hope was for improvements in serviceability and performance from Hercules XI-engined aircraft now entering service. N6029, the first from Belfast, joined XV squadron on 15 June and W7432, the first Austin-built, on 4 July.

On **14 July** six crews of 7 Squadron set off carrying 30 x 1,000lb and 33 x 500lb HE bombs along with 42 x 250lb incendiaries destined for Hannover. In all, a force of sixty-seven bombers (a 3 Group Wellington, thirty Halifaxes of 4 Group and thirty-three Hampdens in addition to the Stirlings) were despatched, of which fifty-one claimed to attack the city. Their return journey became alarming when the weather deteriorated, and only one Stirling homed to Oakington. From N6033, unable to land before fuel ran out, the crew baled out at the last moment believing that their aircraft would crash in open country. Instead, it flew on for some distance. Living in Northampton at the time was David L Sharman (later to become an RAF pilot) who remembers the event well.

> I was awakened around 5.00am as a huge aircraft thundered low above our roof top, heading north-north-west. The pilot must have just about been struggling free for he landed on Kingsthorpe Recreation Ground about a mile from my home in Kingsley. He must have baled out at no more than 200ft, with the normal consequences, while the plane completed the circle and finally came to earth after travelling eastwards dead centre along Gold Street. Damage in the street was amazingly minimal, the wrecked aircraft finishing by All Saints Church much to the disgust of the Chief Constable, who remarked "I can't have this".

Meanwhile Flt Lt D A J Sanders in N6036, also short of fuel, had landed at Bircham Newton and overshot. Sqn Ldr Speare put down safely at Waterbeach and Fg Off K O Blunden at Honington, although the tailwheel doors of his aircraft were damaged. The other aircraft was Witt's, and that also crashed. Aboard, Keith Deyell was making his twenty-second operational trip in a 7 Squadron Stirling which turned out to be both his last and very unforgettable.

> We'd flown in good weather all the way to Hannover, where fires were burning by the time we arrived. There was heavy flak and searchlight activity, but we bombed without difficulty. Several aircraft were being coned, which took attention away from us. We encountered heavy flak over Holland en route home, with the usual crumps and puffs nearby. Soon after a burst of flak underneath the aircraft we lost two engines and a third was playing up. For a while it looked as though we might have to ditch, but we managed to

stagger over the English coast at 10,000ft before having to bale out.

I went through the bomb aimer's hatch and stopped with a terrific jerk when I pulled the rip cord. I watched the Stirling going down in a shallow dive, with its last live engine popping and showering the night with sparks. I couldn't see any other parachutes, and was high above a cloud layer and in bright moonlight. The swaying of the parachute was making me feel sick so I pulled on one cord to spill air and speed my descent, whereupon the parachute started to collapse and that really threw me into a fright! I let go and watched the clouds gradually come nearer and was in them for a few minutes and surprised at how wet it was in the foggy fluff. It was as dark as Hades below the clouds, then suddenly I discovered that I was moving backwards. A tree whizzed by just before I hit the ground, landing very hard. I felt my left ankle snap.

It was raining, so I covered myself with the parachute and waited there, since I could not walk. A few cows arrived and sniffed me once, then the rain stopped. I had landed around 0330 hrs and when daylight came I discovered a railway line close by. At last a train rattled past as I waved part of the parachute. Soldiers soon arrived, for the engine driver had reported a German parachutist. I was taken to a Norwich hospital for a week's stay before transfer to the RAF hospital at Ely. The rest of the crew had landed safely and the aircraft had crashed at Newton Slotman, Norfolk.

After talking to many in the hospital, Keith Deyell concluded he was its only battle casualty – until he visited a 7 Squadron friend who had been badly burned in a crash and was in Ely's special section for those who had cruelly suffered. The experience was unforgettable.

> The ward was filled with people bandaged and looking like mummies. The friend I visited had his head and arms completely wrapped apart from openings for his mouth, nose and eyes. I held a cigarette for him and was enormously impressed by his great courage, for he made not a whimper. He was but one of many hundreds who, with terribly serious injuries, were brought to RAF Ely.

So many stories about Bomber Command relate to late war, more sophisticated periods than 1941. Operations, losses and battle and training accidents at this earlier period all seemed, somehow, even more poignant, possibly because numbers involved were fewer. There were still personnel who, as close friends, had served in the RAF for years while many others – civilian and military – suddenly experienced horrific sights, sounds, smells that would stay with them forever. Although the Battle of Britain had been won and pressure reduced when the Germans invaded the USSR, the outcome of the war at this time was very uncertain and there were no signs of victory. That made the impressive sight of the Stirlings a tonic for any watching them roaring off from Oakington and Wyton. They were grand morale boosters, made one feel proud, satisfied that 'we' were fighting back, that 'we' might just win but those views were not shared by some more closely involved.

Flying control in its infancy meant facing difficult decisions – especially at night, and even more so if the weather turned bad as aircraft were homing. Bomber Command was

What happens when the undercarriage won't come down? The crew of LS-L are about to discover on Wyton's grass.

doing its best to damage the German war effort, eagerly encouraged by a nation brutally bombed. The questioning, the doubts, the recriminations, they have come all too often from critics unborn when the events related herein took place, and who lack the experience of those alive at the time and better placed to pronounce fair judgement.

July 1941 ended spectacularly for 7 Squadron when five crews set out for Cologne. Four attacked the city and on his return Wg Cdr Graham, flying at 10,000ft, entered an electrical storm 30 miles ESE of Bexhill. Severe glazed ice formed, for the temperature was minus 4 degrees centigrade. There was a blinding lightning flash, the Stirling fell out of control, most instruments went haywire, the autopilot was switched off, and not until they had fallen 6,000ft did Graham regain control. Both DR and P4 compasses remaining out of use, base had to be reached by dead reckoning, map reading and QDMs. The compass had a 70 degree error and the aircraft retained a lot of induced magnetism. Fg Off C I Rolfe encountered similar trouble and when N6029 was struck the radio burnt out. He landed at Martlesham.

On **2 August** three Wellingtons of 1 Group, eight Halifaxes and fourteen Wellingtons of 4 Group, four Wellington IIs of 3 Group each carrying a 4,000 pounder, and three Stirlings opened a series of Berlin raids. One of the 'Cookie Wimpeys' dived from 16,500ft to 6,000ft to release its large bomb, but of far greater importance was the reckoning that ten bombers attacked simultaneously, showing that swamping the defences was becoming feasible. At the same time Hamburg was attacked by thirty-six Wellingtons, twenty-one Whitleys and a Stirling. Kiel's shipyards were the target for eighteen Hampdens with another twenty-one ordered to bomb the town, while fourteen 'freshmen' flying Wellingtons were practising by bombing Cherbourg docks. Dispersion of effort was meant to cause the defenders to operate over a very wide area, but it meant that the effect of each attack was reduced, especially if accuracy was poor.

Losses were inevitable, one involving Fg Off C I Rolfe and crew aboard N3663, 7 Squadron's first Hercules XI Stirling. Its first operation had been on **12 June** against Huls carrying 5 x 1,000lb GPs, 12 x 500lb GPs and 240 x 4lb incendiaries, and the sortie was abortive. It bombed Ostend on **16 June**, Kiel on three nights, carried out a Bremen day raid on **28 June** and, in the hands of Wg Cdr Graham during the Bremerhaven raid of 29 June, was engaged by a Bf 110 off Texel. Extensively damaged, N3663 did not operate again until **30 July**, with Cologne its target. During the Berlin raid of 2/3 August 1941 it was brought down near Werder in Germany.

Following the famous 2 Group Blenheim 12 August daylight raid on Cologne's power stations, seventy bombers made a further attack during the following night, the participants including nine Stirlings. Three other crews were briefed to bomb Krupps at Essen. None of the Stirling crews claimed to hit that factory, and a single crew sent to Bielefeld made no attack. Four bombed the capital while other Stirling crews claimed attacks on Gusten, Brunswick and a railway siding south of Iserlöhn. Eight Halifax crews claimed to release 24 x1,000lb and 48 x 500lb HE bombs on to Berlin, while the three Stirlings dropped 15 x1000lb and 28 x 500lb HEs as well as 740 incendiaries showing that load-wise the Stirlings were the more productive which was often the case.

No XV Squadron's participants – one for Hannover and two for Magdeburg – were to operate from Alconbury because at Wyton runway building had begun. Sqn Ldr J F Foulsham, having had difficulty raising the undercarriage, set course for the Wash to jettison his load and almost immediately the port inner engine lost power. Unable to maintain height, he crashed near Ramsey. Plt Off Gould swung badly as he took off from Alconbury, and the undercarriage collapsed. Heading home from Magdeburg in W7437, Sgt Stewart signalled at 05.25 hrs that he was ditching off Belgium. It certainly had been a sombre night for No XV.

No 7 Squadron also fared badly, only two crews reaching distant Magdeburg. Plt Off

W N Crebbin (N6042), short of fuel, crashed on Graveley's runway while at Oakington both Wg Cdr Graham and Witt overshot on landing. Soon after, an intruder placed a 250kg bomb on Barrack Block 'E', fortunately without causing casualties.

Weather conditions could be just as treacherous as in winter and, of thirty-seven Wellingtons and twelve Stirlings detailed for Karlsruhe on **25/26 August 1941**, only twenty and four crews respectively reached their primary target. Cumulus clouds gave them a bumpy ride, and icing was so bad that fourteen crews were forced back and eleven selected last resort targets. Those who pressed on found clear weather over Karlsruhe which eight Stirling crews bombed.

Austin-built W7434 was delivered from Longbridge in July 1941. After it crash-landed on 15 August 1941 Sebro reduced it to spares.

Duisburg, the next main Command target for both Stirling squadrons, was attacked on **28/29 August**. No 7 Squadron despatched seven crews of which five claimed to bomb the target area. Fire from a Bf 110 blew Perspex out of Flt Lt D J H Lay's tail turret severely wounding the gunner, Sgt Macree, who baled out when the Stirling began to fall out of control. By united effort Flt Lt Lay and Sgt Tourville regained control but N3666 was now tail heavy and with trim tabs out of action. They located an alternative target, dropped 5 x 1,000lb and 8 x 500lb GPs, then came home at 135mph IAS – the fastest speed they could achieve – and made for Newmarket's long grass runway. After being laboriously wound down by hand, the undercarriage's port gear collapsed on touch-down. Luckily there were no further casualties. Robinson, although wounded, had kept at his station throughout the splendid effort by the entire crew.

On **2/3 September** last-minute weather deterioration caused a scheduled Berlin raid to be switched mainly to Frankfurt. Only forty-nine bombers eventually left for the capital, leaving 125 heading for Frankfurt. Over Germany cloud was 2/10 to 8/10, but more troublesome was widespread fog which forced many aircraft to land on return away from home bases.

Attempts were being made to rationalise the Stirling modification programme. An extra 450gal tankage was considered, the current 1,945gals giving a still air range of 1,800 miles whereas the aircraft was designed for 2,000 miles and an 8,000lb load. Current operational range – 1,300 miles with a 6,000lb bomb load – was less than that of the Halifax, but the Stirling could carry a heavier load for a short range, so tankage remained unaltered.

Operationally the event of the month came on **10/11 September** when Stirlings first raided Italy. All such ventures were highly demanding on crews and aircraft. Oakington sent seven, XV Squadron six, all to bomb the Royal Arsenal, Turin. A long, hazardous mission, it was undertaken in the face of exacting weather conditions. Threading a way through the mountains or skimming over the peaks was impossible – the aircraft's performance prohibited that – so they followed a more westerly route across Lake Geneva. That meant passing close to the Mont Blanc Massif, not a jolly thought in darkness. Yet, the first journey to Italy on 10 September proved surprisingly successful.

Early arrivals found excellent conditions before haze and smoke were generated from fires and a thin layer of stratus at 3,000ft drifted over the target. Bombing was carried out by 8/10 Wellingtons of 1 Group, 24/38 Wellingtons of 3 Group and 10/13 Stirlings of 3 Group, 6/7 Halifaxes (18 x1000lb and 36 x 500lb HE) and 8/8 Wellingtons of 4 Group. Some 25 miles west of the city several single-engined fighters tackled a Stirling at 2308 hrs and at 19,000ft. They were driven off by the rear gunner's fire.

Stirling N3658 'E-Easy' of XV Squadron crashed near Hengelo, Netherlands at 0405 hrs on 8 September 1941 and was the first Stirling to fall reasonably intact into German hands. Richard Pape aboard the aircraft recounted the night in his book Boldness Be My Friend *(G J Zwanenburg)*

All the 7 Squadron crews reached Turin – no mean achievement. Wg Cdr Graham's bombs burst across the town centre, Sqn Ldr Speare's too. Bayley's incendiaries caused three fires, and more were started by Flt Lt Lay and Flt Lt D A J Sanders, and bombs from Ellis-Brown's aircraft burst in a northern area. Oakington's aircraft all safely returned but XV Squadron's contingent was less successful. Only three reached Turin, and on the night that the Station's new satellite, Warboys, was first used as a departure point.

In mid-September one of XV's Stirlings was detached to AFDU Duxford for tactical fighting trials, and found to be more manoeuvrable than expected. "When all the turrets are manned," read the final report, "there is extremely good all-round view." The arc of fire from the three turrets covered the hemisphere above the aircraft. Beam attack could easily be countered now. Attack from below would be dangerous for that was an undefended area except in the few Stirlings that had a gun poking through the emergency rear exit.

Stettin, the most important Baltic port for reinforcing the Russian campaign, was on **19/20 September** the primary target. Docks, railways and industrial plants were aiming points and the motley force of seventy-two aircraft despatched included 5/10 Wellingtons

W7440 MG-W carries markings denoting four operations and the destruction of an enemy fighter – applied more easily by the back door than upon the nose!

of 1 Group, 25/28 Wellingtons of 3 Group (18 x 1,000lb and 46 x 500lb HEs dropped), 4/10 Stirlings, 4/4 Halifaxes (12 x 1,000lb, 20 x 500lb HEs and 480 x 4lb incendiaries), 6 Whitleys and 2 Wellingtons of 4 Group and 2/3 Manchesters of 5 Group, two aircraft failed to return and two were destroyed in crashes.

A second Italian venture, this time to Genoa, came on **28 September**, the only Stirlings being of XV Squadron. No 3 Group called for forty-nine Wellingtons and six Stirlings, but eventually only two Stirlings and forty-five Wellingtons participated. Cloud was 8/10 over the target which both Stirlings reached, and strong winds brought anxiety over fuel states. When Plt Off Jones landed at Thorney Island his fuel tanks were almost dry.

On **3 October** 7 Squadron sent nine crews to Brest while 78/80 3 Group Wellingtons mounted sharp raids on Rotterdam, Antwerp and Dunkirk, with a Stirling joining in the latter attack along with ten Whitleys and a 4 Group Wellington. Two of the 7 Squadron Stirlings bombed Brest using 2,000lb AP. They were now operating from both Bourn and Oakington and, as Sqn Ldr D I McCleod and crew were returning to the former, they were set upon by a Ju 88C. Six times its ace pilot *Fw* Koster opened fire as McCleod tried to evade. Being near the end of the sortie, the rear gunner had left his turret for landing and N6085 was shot down in flames. Two of the crew escaped by parachute even though the bomber was at only 700ft when they baled out.

Bombing-up at Oakington while a Zwicky tanker refuels MG-M. A lorry serving as the runway 'caravan' is attached to the Chance light.

Sgt S G Matkin, on seeing the action, had placed his Stirling in a position for his gunners to engage, and they claimed to damage the Ju 88. It was probably that aircraft which attacked Oakington's flarepath. Night flying was in progress when bombs began to fall too close to the intrepid Wg Cdr H R Graham for comfort. Four night fighters were vectored on to the enemy aircraft which escaped. Just over a week later Hitler ordered the intruder campaign to cease, and the Ju 88 fighters moved to Sicily. He had made one of the most foolish decisions of the entire war.

Graham, by contrast, always showed top quality leadership and courage of the type often associated with a fighter pilot. High-level reconnaissance sorties over Oakington made by a Ju 88 so much irritated him that he announced his intention to "have a Stirling lightened then put paid to the blighter!" Even in the lightest possible condition no Stirling could have flown high enough.

With about sixty Stirlings available it was time to contemplate equipping a third squadron. That required the establishing of a unit to train crews and as a result a third or 'C' Flight was added to 7 Squadron. Formed under Flt Lt P R Crompton, it

Wg Cdr H R Graham of 7 Squadron poses by MG-W.

was removed on 5 October to form the cadre of a special unit, No. 26 Conversion Flight. That soon moved to Waterbeach where it acted as the catalyst of No 1651 Conversion Unit.

Meanwhile a new bombing operations directive had made U-boat building yards priority targets, and it led to 153 aircraft setting out for Bremen on **20 October**, 47 heading for Wilhelmshaven and another 35 (including two Stirlings) making for Antwerp.

Aircrew of XV Squadron at Wyton in late 1941. Front row (left–right): 1st Flt Lt Swales, 3rd Fg Off Ordish, 4th Flt Lt Dyell, 5th Fg Off Ryan, 7th Fg Off Boggis, 8th Sqn Ldr Sellick, 19th Sqn Ldr Wilson, 11th Flt Lt Rogers, 14th Plt Off Laird, 15th Flt Lt Cocheran, 16th Fg Off Fink. Row two: 12th Plt Off Kennedy, 13th Fg Off Hughes, 16th Fg Off Reeves, 19th Plt Off Strachan, 23rd Sgt Henry. Others unknown. (D W Dyell)

Others were despatched to Emden. Bremen was the main target which 11/15 Stirlings attacked with 42.1 tons of HEs. With them were 23/48 Wellingtons of 3 Group, 42/82 Hampdens of 5 Group and 5/8 Manchesters. No. XV Squadron had nine aircraft operating and, as Sgt De Ville crossed East Anglia on his return, the starboard outer of W7431 failed. With fuel short the crew baled out, and the aircraft crashed on Catshole Farm, Methwold, just north of Feltwell.

On **22 October** six crews of XV Squadron, Sqn Ldr Sellick leading in N6042-O along with N3665-B, N3671-H, N6088-Q, N3675-S and N3667, returned to the capital ships at Brest. Proceeding in open formation they approached from the seaward side to achieve maximum surprise but flak hotly greeted them. Although five aimed 24 x 2,000lb AP bombs none of the ships was damaged. Another Stirling bombed Honfleur.

Some of the longest operational sorties yet attempted were made on **28/29 October** when five crews of each squadron made for Pilsen's Skoda works. Weathermen forecast cloud breaks over southern Germany but they were wrong. Instead, violent wind changes

Defensive tactics were explored at AFDU Duxford in late September 1941 using N3667 LS-T. It had flown six operations and crashed during its seventh.

were encountered north of Pilsen and the effort expended resulted in only leaflets being dropped in the target area. Bombs were released around Frankfurt and Nuremberg

Since the first day of the war, 149 Squadron had been flying bombing raids with Wellingtons, and achieved notoriety first in the film *The Lion has Wings* and more so with *Target for Tonight*. No. 149 was a good choice to become 3 Group's third Stirling squadron and, on 12 October, N6093 and W7448 joined them at Mildenhall, premier base of Bomber Command. By the end of the month '149' held eight Stirlings and conversion was well under way. Re-equipment proceeded through November and, on the 26th, N6099 OJ-C carried out the first operational sortie to Ostend. Next day two air–sea rescue sorties were flown. On 30 November, N6099 ventured to Bremerhaven with five of the squadron's Wellingtons. Bomber Command was, at this time, smarting from a terrible misfortune.

Bomber operations on **7/8 November** 1941 were among the most calamitous of the war. They sent shock waves not only through the Command and War Cabinet, but also throughout the nation when high losses were announced on the radio next day. The night's activity is worth special consideration, especially as resulting deductions had a considerable influence upon the continuation of the bomber offensive.

The night produced two records, one for the number of Stirlings despatched, the other an appalling and initially inexplicable loss of thirty-six bombers. Making use of a long period of darkness, Bomber Command had hoped to operate 400 aircraft. Eventually only 332 crews out of 367 despatched were reckoned to have bombed a wide

assortment of targets, including Berlin, target for an intended force of 170 aircraft. As is
so often the case, precise figures for the night's activity vary according to the source
consulted. HQ Bomber Command in their report of the night's operations submitted to
the Under Secretary of State, Air Ministry, claimed that 400 were despatched. Records
compiled by Bomber Command Operations Research Section suggest that on this very
cloudy, windy night only 367 set forth, with the Berlin force comprising 9/20 Wellingtons
of 1 Group, 30/69 Wellingtons of 3 Group (which dropped 2 x 4,000lb, 12 x 1,000lb, 78
x 500lb and 6 x 250lb HE along with 18 x 50lb and 4,400 x 4lb incendiaries), 6/17
Stirlings, 17/42 Whitleys and 6/10 Wellingtons of 4 Group. From those, nine 3 Group
Wellingtons, nine Whitleys, two Stirlings and a 4 Group Wellington failed to return.
Mannheim was bombed by 2/2 Stirlings, some of the twenty-six 1 Group Wellingtons, of
which seven were lost, and three Wellingtons of 3 Group. Cologne was also attacked,
without loss, by thirty-six Hampdens and twelve Manchesters, and Ostend was the target
for 3/4 Stirlings, 14/19 Wellingtons and two Hampdens.

Late 1941 and W7442 MG-M, bomb doors open and dispersed on grass, towers over a train of GP bombs.

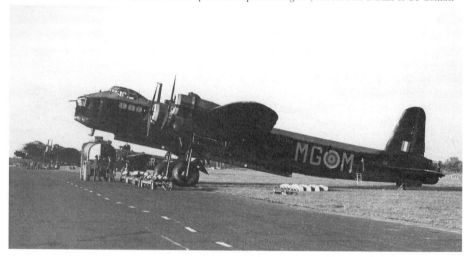

Additionally, nine Wellingtons of 3 Group (two missing), twelve Whitleys and three
Halifaxes of 4 Group (one of each missing) had a *Roving Commission* to attack Ruhr
targets of opportunity. Mining was carried out by thirteen Hampdens, three of which
were missing, and another six Hampdens were given an intruder role involving the
attacking of searchlights on the route taken by the Main Force.

In all 19/23 Stirlings operating bombed, releasing 61 tons of HE, but they could not
individually match the 8 x 4,000lb 'cookies' aimed at Munster by 8/9 Type-423
Wellingtons of 3 Group, and a further three which donated their loads nearby.

It was a grim night for Bomber Command. No 7 Squadron had despatched thirteen
crews, the most yet; and XV Squadron sent ten, seven to Berlin. For them the weather
was poor, and only five of XV Squadron reached the city. The final outcome was that 3
Group lost twenty Wellingtons and two Stirlings, other heavy losses including ten
Whitleys, five Hampdens and a Halifax.

Flak damage was sustained by thirteen aircraft and night-fighter fire peppered
another following five combats and eight interceptions – slightly lower figures than
expected on a moonlit night favouring above-cloud interception. Very accurate AA fire

was reported by the Berlin force, adding weight to the belief that the gunners had radar assistance. Nevertheless, normal opposition did not explain the high loss rate.

A substantially accurate weather forecast had been given to crews, predicting convection clouds rising to 15,000ft over the sea with icing in clouds and possible thunderstorms. Wind speed forecast as 65–70mph at 15,000ft over the sea proved to be 70-75mph, which may have brought disaster to some aircraft for clouds with severe icing billowed to 18,000ft and there were also thunderstorms.

Using previous operations against the same targets as a guide, and coupling them with known weather conditions, Bomber Command did not rate the losses unduly high, although they were 50 percent above those usually expected. The Wellington loss on Berlin was about 10 percent, but the nine Whitleys lost out of forty-two and four abortive sorties (21 percent) was indeed exceptional. On their return, twenty-one aircraft had to land at coastal aerodromes due to fuel shortage even though tanks had been filled to total capacity. Icing, high wind speeds and frequent use of engine superchargers had all taken a toll, eating away at the 1½hr fuel margin.

Losses among those attacking Mannheim were similarly attributed. A strong tailwind was thought to have caused many to over-run the target, two missing aircraft sending SOS messages reporting fuel shortage. None of the Cologne attackers was lost, probably because the target was nearer. Heavy AA defences around Oslo had brought down two Hampden minelayers.

With a low loss rate of 8.65 percent overall, the Stirlings had survived satisfactorily, but 11.6 percent lost raiding Berlin was seriously high. Air Marshal Sir Richard Peirse, C-in-C Bomber Command, in his report, stated that "In my view the operations ordered were practicable on the weather forecast given to me, and were accepted as such, with one exception, by my Group Commanders, who are authorised to cancel or reduce the scale of any operation at their discretion". AOC 5 Group had considered Mannheim too far for his limited-range Hampdens and substituted Cologne for the force.

The wide differences in fuel remaining aboard aircraft which safely returned brought much comment. Some crews had been unable to reach their targets due to 'insufficient fuel' whereas others landed with enough for several more hours of flying. The final conclusions were that the standard of long-range flying and engine manipulation was extremely variable, and that conditions on the night in question, although safe for the majority, would have been taxing for the less skilled. The whole episode highlighted the need for vigorous, first-class training and led quickly to major alterations in the operational training scheme.

Bombing-up W7451 in rough conditions at Oakington in late 1941.

A sobering day for 7 Squadron was **18 November**. Eight crews were briefed for a cloud cover daylight raid on Brest. On take-off O'Brien had an engine fire so he turned back to make a forced landing at base and in doing so hit a telegraph pole then smashed into a wall at Willingham killing his second pilot. The other crews proceeded only to discover 10/10 cloud at 5,000ft protecting the 'Hipper Class' cruiser *Prinz Eugen* in Brest's No 8 Dock. Only one crew saw the ship through a cloud gap and aimed their 16 x 500lb SAP bombs at it. Two other crews released similar loads on estimated position, but the remainder brought their bombs back. W7446 overshot on landing and was written off.

A four-Stirling cloud cover daylight operation was ordered for **24 November**. W7443-J and N3676-U of XV Squadron both turned back at the Dutch coast, whereas the two 7 Squadron crews pressed on and discovered south-west of Borkum a convoy of two large ships and two smaller ones escorted by flak ships despite which they decided to launch an attack. Wg Cdr Graham (N6095-K) ran in first to place his 500-pounders among the vessels but, before Sgt Taylor (W7449-J) could do likewise, eight Bf 109s arrived on the scene and up to three at a time attacked 'J-Johnnie'. To a frontal attack the nose gunner replied. The mid-upper gunner scored some hits and the rear gunner watched the fighter curl away smoking. Taylor's mid-upper and rear gunners in action for over twenty-five minutes claimed two fighters destroyed and one damaged. W7449 came home liberally peppered in the fuselage, wings and tailplane and, if testimony to a Stirling's ability to survive enormous punishment was sought, it could certainly have been found on this occasion.

Nos 7 and XV Squadrons were each ordered to despatch two crews on another daylight cloud cover raid directed against Essen on **9 December**. Absence of cloud forced XV Squadron's pair to turn about, whereas 7 Squadron's duo which, at the last minute, had their target changed to a maritime one. Flt Lt Crebbin (W7451-D) and Flt Lt R Ellis-Brown (W7440) left at noon and came across a tanker, accompanied by two flak ships in line astern 5 miles off the Hook. Flak began as they turned for the bomb run, hits being scored on Crebbin's aircraft as he raced in at 500ft. Sgt H C Cotton, his navigator, was wounded just as he was about to release the weapons. Ellis-Brown made two attempts to hit the ships, during which his aircraft was also hit causing its port undercarriage to collapse on landing. Crebbin's tailwheels failed to lower further damaging his aircraft.

Highly secret work had, for some time, been underway in developing navigation beam radio equipment designated TR3098 (code named *Trinity*) to improve bombing accuracy. Six Stirlings in each of the two squadrons began to have the special equipment installed on 8 November, the intention being to field nine bombers on a chosen night to attack the ships in Brest. Fitment allowed 7 Squadron to test the equipment on 9 November and, although the selected Stirlings could still operate conventionally, the secret nature of the equipment made unnecessary use undesirable.

The plan called for diversionary attacks by 'cookie carrying' Type-423 Wellingtons while the nine Stirlings each carrying 5 or 6 x 2,000lb AP, tried out *Trinity*. No 109 Squadron, skilled in 'beam riding', would provide assistant pilots to ensure that the radio beam was accurately followed. An additional W/T operator working the special radio apparatus would also be aboard.

Instructions outlining tactics to follow during the first raid called for an approach to Brest at 18,000ft, then a loss of 600ft on the run-in at 165mph IAS (210mph TAS) bomb doors being opened five minutes prior to bomb release to help steady the aircraft. Later attacks were to be tried at between 16,000ft and 20,000ft.

A trial installation was undertaken at Boscombe Down in N6090 of 7 Squadron, the equipment eventually leading to the highly effective *Oboe* radio aid. *Trinity* was soon joined by TR1154/1155 *Gee*, a navigation system to be widely used in Bomber Command into the mid-1950s. At Rochester on 21 November the fitting in Stirlings of *Gee* was fully discussed, and N3639 became the first to carry it as Modification 436, with N3681 just off the production line being set aside for Shorts trials.

During much of 1941, Bomber Command persistently and, at times, almost nightly attempted with scant success to damage the German capital ships at Brest, officially referred to as the 'Toads'. One week of intensive effort culminated in a spectacular day raid undertaken by Britain's latest bombers. More portentous was an operation mounted on **7 December** 1941 for it saw the first operational use of *Trinity*.

Aachen was Command's main target and, while Ostend and other French harbours were also raided, the radio beams were secretly focused onto Brest. Along them flew two Trinity-equipped Stirlings of XV Squadron (N6092-O and N3676-U) and four of 7 Squadron (N6094-G, N6095-K, N6032-T and N3672-U). Bombers despatched to Brest invariably followed a south-westerly track for most of the way over England, the sight of them trailing towards Cornwall having become a familiar evening event in 1941. Late that year intelligence information indicated that the *Scharnhorst, Gneisenau* and *Prinz Eugen* were soon to break out to attack British shipping in the Atlantic. It was to prevent such activity that the build-up in raids on Brest occurred.

Eventually only four Stirlings delivered a *Trinity* guided attack, dropping between them 15 x 2,000lb AP bombs. Results were disappointing for the new equipment functioned none too well. Sqn Ldr B D Sellick of XV Squadron bombed as instructed without seeing the results. Bombs from Sqn Ldr Swales' aircraft were released using TR 3098. With the Stirlings flew twenty-three Wellingtons, nineteen of which attacked releasing 6 x 4,000lb, 4 x 2,000lb AP, 45 x 500lb SAP and 24 x 500 pounders. PRU photographs taken shortly after the raid showed the 'Toads' unscathed.

On **11/12 December**, 17/21 Wellingtons and 3/5 Stirlings again called on Brest, and next day six Hampdens carrying 2,000 pounders aborted due to lack of cloud cover. At night the *Trinity* boys followed, 5/6 dropping 25 x 2,000lb AP reinforced by loads from 16/18 Wellingtons before Hampdens unsuccessfully tried again on the **12th** in daylight. Six Stirlings despatched on the 14/15th were unable to bomb due to atrocious weather.

Yet again the *Trinity* force tried, 6/7 Stirlings with 7 Wellingtons aiming fruitlessly at the vessels. On the **16/17th**, 12/17 Wellingtons and 3/5 Stirlings using 2,000lb AP and standard 2,000lb HEs faced the ever increasing flak and searchlights to damage the warships, and made their final attempt before the major day raid. Overnight on the **17/18th** it was the turn of Hampdens, other Wellingtons and Whitleys, to deliver a heavy onslaught, this time intended to wear down the defenders, reduce their effectiveness and empty their smoke-generating cylinders to limit the effectiveness of a daylight smokescreen.

On **13 December** each station involved in the big raid was sent a copy of Bomber Command Operations Order No 138 giving details of *Veracity*, a bold fighter-supported day raid on Brest. Nos 3, 4 and 5 Groups would each despatch eighteen bombers, over which four long-range fighter squadrons (later amended to six of Spitfires and two of Hurricanes flying at between 17,000ft and 20,000ft) would provide thirty minutes of target support. Three squadrons of Spitfire short-range fighters would cover the bombers' withdrawal, while two Spitfire Wings carried out a sweep over the Straits of Dover. It was essential that bomber crews held close formation, and remembered that RAF fighters would be supporting them.

Accurate timing was vital in order to deliver the attack before the smoke screen became fully effective and enemy fighters could be called in from further afield. Each bomber formation would have an eight minute follow-on slot, Stirlings leading followed by Manchesters then the Halifaxes. Fifteen minutes before bombing began a dozen Blenheims would fly with a large-scale *Circus* over the Pas de Calais. To have height in hand the heavy bombers would be permitted to climb to 20,000ft – if possible – on their journeys to their exit points between the Lizard and Scillies, then proceed from either to the target to attack in sections of three.

Halifaxes and Stirlings would carry maximum 2,000lb AP loads and as many 500lb SAP as possible, while half the Manchesters would be similarly armed leaving the remainder each carrying a 4,000lb HC bomb. After bombing, the force would withdraw to Start Point not losing less than 3,000ft within the first 30–40 miles to enable long-range high-flying fighters to protect them. The intention had been to mount the raid on or after 21 December, but in the belief that the warships were about to sail it was advanced to **18 December**, Wg Cdr H R Graham leading in N3669-E.

Both 7 and XV Squadrons each despatched nine crews, take-off being around 0945 hrs and the flights in vics of three formed up with Wg Cdr Ogilvie leading XV Squadron. Stirling rendezvous was over Wyton from where they set course for Lundy Island over which planning called for the Halifaxes to turn in behind them at 1120 hrs. The Stirlings arrived a little early so they tracked out west then turned south. The eighteen Halifaxes swung in behind, after which came eleven Manchesters showing a change in planning.

Just after 1230 hrs the Stirlings commenced the bomb run from the south-east, each vic having planned to cross the target at one minute intervals then break for shallow dive bombing from 14,000ft. Radar, however, alerted the enemy fighter force before the bombing began and as Wg Cdr H R Graham in N3669-E saw his 4 x 2,000lb bombs burst across the twin docks, Bf 109s were already in action. His aircraft was being hit both by their fire and by flak and Plt Off G E Mitchell, the rear gunner, claimed a Bf 109. Sqn Ldr W V Jennens (W7436-D) was soon shot down, some of the crew baling out. Plt Off G C Baylie (N3668-B) saw two of his bombs burst north-east of the docks as fighters hotly engaged him. His rear gunner, Sgt J M Smith, was credited with a Bf 109.

As Plt Off T G T Heard (N6095-K) bombed, shrapnel struck the astrodome, badly wounding Sgt Hayward, the flight engineer. The rear gunner, Sgt Inman, hit in the shoulder, kept to his post and did not report his injury until later.

WO N L Taylor's aircraft, N6089-L, suffered extensive flak damage and crash landed at Bourn. Its port inner fuel tanks had been pierced, turrets put out of action and intercom damaged. A mainwheel tyre and tailwheel tyre both burst on landing.

Flt Lt B Parnell in N3680 was shot down, but Plt Off S G Matkin (N6121) saw his bombs burst across the ships. His aircraft, too, was extensively damaged. Hydraulics and undercarriage were hit, and a large portion of the rudder shot away. The port undercarriage would not lower and he crash landed at Oakington. His gunners claimed a Bf 109 and

W7436 MG-D at Oakington, autumn 1941.

damaged another. Plt Off H G Pilling saw his bombs burst on a road at the north-west end of the docks, before his aircraft W7454 was hit by flak in the mainplane, fuselage and rear turret in which a gunsight was put out of use.

Piloting N6086, the famous 'MacRobert's Reply', was Sqn Ldr P J S Boggis.

> It was a clear, crisp sunny day [he recalls] without a cloud in the sky. We flew into the target at about 17,000ft in vic formation, a long line of Stirlings, Halifaxes and Manchesters. I was leading my vic of three when we left England, but my No 2 aborted and over the target my No 3 was shot down, whether by flak or fighters we never knew. There was a heavy box barrage from about 12,000ft to 18,000ft and enemy fighters attacked us through this barrage. My aircraft was attacked several times, and my gunners shot down one Me 109 and claimed another. In the course of this battle we became separated from the rest of the formation. As soon as we completed the bombing run, we put our nose down and headed for the Channel.
>
> Once back over the sea and down almost to sea level in case there were still fighters about and not long after crossing the French coast our rear gunner suddenly reported a formation of six aircraft approaching from behind and about 2,000ft up. Before we had time to think the worst, someone came through with the news that these aircraft were Halifaxes obviously returning from Brest and, like us, having lost height to gain speed. In our solitude they were a welcome sight, and when they came nearer they opened up their formation in invitation and gratefully we climbed and soon were enfolded in their midst. Thus we returned in grand style.

This was Boggis's last operation with XV Squadron.

By the time XV Squadron attacked, the opposition had become intense. Fg Off Vemnieux in N3676-U and Plt Off D A Parkins both claimed hits on the ships, in addition to which two fighters were claimed and others damaged. Fg Off G Bunce's

Early Mk I, N3665, was modified to have an FN 7A dorsal turret.

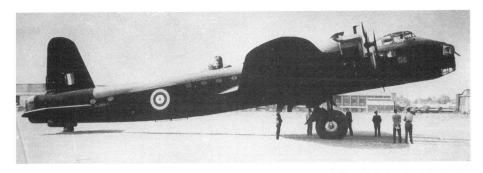

W7428-Z was last seen with a wingtip on fire and diving towards the sea, harried by fighters. Flt Lt G G Heathcote's aircraft, N3665, was also shot down. N6092 had earlier aborted, with oil covering the rear turret. N3700 of 7 Squadron had also turned back.

Crews in the Halifaxes had watched as the Stirlings disappeared behind a wall of flak, themselves flying in among stragglers. Being first, the Stirlings had attracted much of the enemy response, and though they were the best armed of any bombers, four

Reconnaissance photograph of Brest after the 18 December 1941 raid shows smoke rising from buildings in the dock area.

were shot down, along with a Halifax and a Manchester. Back from the raid, the squadrons received a signal from C-in-C Bomber Command: "My warmest congratulations on a very successful and gallant action this afternoon".

Bomber Command ORS analysis showed the following:

16/18 Stirlings dropped 64 x 2,000lb AP, 7 x 250lb GP
15/18 Halifaxes dropped 60 x 2,000lb AP, 18 x 500lb SAP
8/11 Manchesters dropped 5 x 4,000lb HC, 1 x 2,000lb AP and 24 x 500lb SAP

In total 39/47 aircraft had released 88 tons of HE and still the ships were little affected.

Stirling gunners claimed three Bf 109s destroyed, three probables, nine damaged, and the fighter support claimed another four. Six bombers (two of 7 Squadron, two of XV Squadron and a Manchester of 97 Squadron) were shot down; a Halifax of 35 Squadron crashed in the sea and a Manchester of 97 Squadron crashed at Coningsby, all the crew being killed. Top cover was given by ten fighter squadrons, the 10 Group Polish Wing, Exeter based, claiming four Bf 109s without loss. The only fighter missing was a Hurricane of 79 Squadron.

Stirlings participants were:

No. 7 Squadron: N3669-E (Wg Cdr Graham), N3668-B, N3680-Y(FTR), N3700-A (aborted near Oxford with engine problems, bombs jettisoned at Berner's Heath), N6089-L, N6095-K, N6121-W (crash landed at Oakington), W7436-D(FTR) and W7449-J.
No XV Squadron: N6093-C (Wg Cdr Ogilvie), N3665-B (FTR), N3673-D, N3676-U, N6088-Q, N6089-F, N6092-O (aborted, bombs jettisoned), N6098-G and W7428-Z.

Still no success having been achieved, the pressure on Brest was maintained, six crews of 7 Squadron making another night attack on **23 December**. Searchlight beams drenched the sky, dazzling the crews, and Matkin's beam gunners tried unsuccessfully to shoot them out. Again, no hits were confirmed on the ships.

Next day XV Squadron put up a nine-aircraft formation – a very impressive sight – and for bombing practice preceding another special day effort. Suddenly *Gneisenau* sailed from her one-time dry dock and in mid-afternoon the squadron was ordered to be at three hours' readiness. They stood by throughout Christmas Day, navigators working out square search areas in case the ships slipped out during the festive season. For three days they stood by then, at 0800 hrs on 30 December, were called to readiness. At 0915 hrs they were briefed for operation *Veracity II* but at 0945 hrs the show was called off just as the crews were about to leave for Alconbury from where operations were currently being mounted because runway building had begun at Wyton on 12 December. At the satellite, weather was too poor for take-off, visibility being below 1,000 yards and expected to deteriorate. Cancellation was the only option.

On 31 December 1941 the positioning of the new bombers in squadrons (serviceable + unserviceable) was: Stirling 29 + 22, Halifax (including Mk II) 32 + 28 and Manchester 35 + 22, Stirling numbers remaining well below the 100 originally required. They had only rarely been employed as intended. Good defence and excellent manoeuvrability had prompted more daylight operations than other large bombers rarely attempted. There was, however, a newcomer on the scene because shortly before Christmas 1941 the first production Lancasters had joined No 44 Squadron at Waddington. This second generation four-engined bomber based upon the unfortunate Manchester would prove to be superior to the Stirling in almost every way.

Come January 1942 there were still only two full Stirling squadrons, both of which were undertaking experimental *Trinity* raids on Brest. Another three modified aircraft reached XV Squadron on the 5th giving it a total of seven all awaiting the call to mount a day raid in which a new bombsight could also be tested. Instead, the standby tailed off because the weather was poor and 7 Squadron on 5 January was taken off operations while the aircraft were fitted with *Gee*.

Bomber Command's basic problem had long been finding even large targets at night. Reliance had been placed on moonlight but *Gee*, the new radio aid, was expected to deliver greater accuracy, and to this highly secret equipment Flt Lt 'Ted' Jones of XV Squadron was introduced early in 1942.

> No XV Squadron was one of the first to have *Gee*. We were shown it by WO Lambert at Alconbury and in strict secrecy. "This is IT", he said. "This is THE GEN". To us it at once became the 'Gen Box', or 'Gee' for short. Detonators were installed in the aircraft to destroy secret parts of the equipment to prevent enemy capture, and included was an electric furnace in which one was supposed to destroy the special lattice charts! The detonators had a nasty habit of sometimes going off accidentally and completely upsetting the poor navigator trying to get a fix.

Steadily increasing Stirling production rates, while allowing for more squadrons to equip, also called for an appropriate supply of trained crews. For financial reasons Operational Training Units were not equipped with expensive four-engined bombers. Instead, a new training scheme came into being towards the end of 1941 by which, after leaving OTUs or on being seconded from twin-engined bombers, crews would assemble at Conversion Units equipped with four-engined bombers which were allotted a quasi-

1651 Conversion Unit's first aircraft were 'war weary' examples with previous unit letters sometimes visible through the paintwork.

operational role. As an interim measure bomber squadrons included Conversion Flights using the squadron number as prefix. Prior to the introduction of that policy No 26 Conversion Flight, formed at Waterbeach in November 1941 was, on 2 January 1942, renamed No 1651 Conversion Unit,

Two early Stirlings of 1651 Conversion Unit. 'B', nearest, has no dorsal turret.

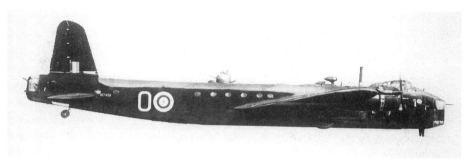

The troublesome tail chassis led to many 1651 Conversion Unit aircraft flying with theirs permanently fixed in the 'down' position.

the first of its type in Bomber Command. Soon it was to Waterbeach that personnel were posted to form Stirling crews and receive operational training in the use of the aircraft. Little wonder that it was at Waterbeach where the Stirling accident rate was highest. Pilots needed to know about the lag of the Exactor throttle's instruction transmission, and the necessity of adjusting swing on take-off. Over 220 Stirlings met with serious undercarriage problems at Waterbeach.

To convert crews to Stirlings on operational squadrons Conversion Flights formed at Oakington, Alconbury, and also Lakenheath and Marham where Stirlings would soon fully re-equip Nos 149 and 218 Squadrons. Each functioning squadron was ordered to surrender four aircraft reducing its strength to 14 IE + 0 IR, and set them aside for the Conversion Flight whose aircraft usually carried individual letters taken from the end of the alphabet.

A distinctive Stirling modification introduced to squadrons in January 1942 was the Frazer Nash FN 50 dorsal turret. Although not so cramped as the FN7 'Botha' type, the newcomer (more difficult to enter and exit from) became the standard type retrospectively fitted to some aircraft.

Poor weather in January 1942 meant sometimes flying between cloud layers during operations. The French coast was being crossed at the wrong point during line up to attack the ships in Brest, and at a time they were forecast to sail. Thick cloud protected them from prying photo reconnaissance flights.

Seemingly invulnerable in Brest, could they be somehow enticed out for a showdown at sea?

A cunning plan was devised: a Commando attack on the Lofoten islands off Norway carried out at the end of December 1941. As intended, it convinced Hitler that the British were planning an invasion of Norway, so he ordered the *Tirpitz* and the capital ships in Brest to be made ready to thwart it. RAF reconnaissance aircraft found *Tirpitz* in Aasfjord, 18 miles ENE of Trondheim, and in a narrow part of the fjord close to land. Attempts had been made to camouflage her, and the only possibility of successful bombing would be on a moonlit night. The British considered the ship as a threat to Atlantic shipping, but the Germans had other plans for her.

Bomber Command issued orders for an attack on the *Tirpitz*, operation *Oiled*, on the first suitable night beginning **29/30 January** 1942. A force comprising twelve Stirlings – eight of XV Squadron and four of No 149 – and ten Halifaxes was to operate from Scotland because of the distance involved.

Sgt Stanley Smith recalls:

On 28 January 1942, ten Stirlings left Alconbury for Lossiemouth. Each carried 2,000lb armour-piercing bombs and two ground servicing personnel. I was flying in N6086-F, piloted by Fg Off 'Red' King.

To ensure secrecy, radio silence covered the move. Next day eight of the crews were detailed to attack the *Tirpitz*, take-off time being fixed for 0030 hrs on the **30th**. Although poor over base, the weather over Norway was expected to be good and eventually five crews flying N6086-F, N6092-O (Sqn Ldr Sellick), N3674-T, N3676-U and N3673-D (Sqn Ldr Wilson) set off. Icing rapidly increased, cloud thickened to 19,000ft and in deteriorating weather there was no choice but to turn back about 100 miles from the Norwegian coast.

At Lossiemouth they awaited better weather but it never came. Their sojourn, though, was not without high drama. N6098 was being refuelled and aboard was Stanley Smith.

> With the tanker attached to the port wing the aircraft was having a pre-flight inspection. I was in the nose section, a fitter was monitoring the fuel going into the tanks, and an electrician was somewhere in the fuselage. Suddenly, someone put his head in the rear hatch and yelled "Fire!" As we hurtled out of the back door, the electrician pulled out the cable of the external power supply (trolley accumulator) and ran.
>
> When I got out, an armourer ran to me and said, "Let's jettison the bombs", so as he entered the aircraft, we restored the external supplies then he jettisoned the bombs (safe). I pulled out the power cable and we both ran for our lives as the fire engine arrived. The fire damaged the port wing and undercarriage.
>
> I can still see and hear in my mind the thump of the 2,000 pounders hitting the ground flat, the aircraft rising as its undercarriage extended, and the bent tail fins on the bombs. In hindsight I think the fire was probably caused by static, as the petrol tanker was not properly earthed to the aircraft.

For Stanley Smith the return flight to Wyton was even more dramatic:

> After the abortive operation by those five aircraft, we left for Wyton on the morning of 7 February. When the aircraft became badly iced up, four diverted into Peterhead and stayed overnight. One was N6086, probably the best known of all Stirlings and named 'MacRobert's Reply', which was the second of the four aircraft taking off on the morning of the 8th. Just before getting airborne, we lost power on both port engines, slewed off the runway at about 70-knots, and crashed through a Spitfire dispersal. We finished up with our nose in the mud, the port undercarriage bent, and a Spitfire jammed under our tail for we had dragged it off its dispersal. Luckily, we had only a few bruises.

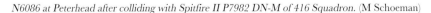

N6086 at Peterhead after colliding with Spitfire II P7982 DN-M of 416 Squadron. (M Schoeman)

The Spitfire rammed against 'MacRobert's Reply' and is pictured on 7 February 1942 the day after the event.
(M Schoeman)

After jettisoning the upper hatch we ran down the wing to the ground, released the dinghy and all had a good swig of rum from the bottle in the survival pack. The aircrew took off in the other two aircraft when the fuss had died down. I was left behind with the bent aircraft and instructions to remove the MacRobert's crest, the clock and the bombsight. An aircraft would call and collect me in a few days, I was told, and I was glad of that for I did not fancy carrying the heavy tool kit and equipment back by train.

Unfortunately, when I removed the metal plate with the MacRobert's arms I overlooked painting out the words 'MacRobert's Reply' on the fuselage. A corporal photographer at Peterhead took four photographs of the wreck, and I took these back and handed them to the CO for the squadron diary.

Fg Off Peter J S Boggis (left) and
crew look at copies of Lady
MacRobert's letter explaining the
significance of N6086 received by
XV Squadron on 10 October 1941.   *Fg Off Boggis in the cockpit of 'MacRobert's Reply'.*

Lady MacRobert, the widow of Baronet Sir Alexander MacRobert who had died in 1922, had three sons. The eldest was killed flying his own aircraft before the war (not in the RAF as many accounts wrongly indicate) and the other two were killed during wartime operations. Each inherited the title in turn. In memory of her gallant sons, Lady MacRobert had given money for the purchase of four Hurricane fighters and a Stirling which created a wave of admiration and interest at the time. N6086 was chosen as the Stirling to carry the emblem of the MacRobert family and the name 'MacRobert's Reply'.

'MacRobert's Reply' banks low over Wyton, N3705 and other Stirlings.

There was nothing particularly special about N6086 assigned to XV Squadron on 15 September 1941. After acceptance checks and updating to current service standard, N6086 received the identity letters LS-F. In a ceremony at Wyton on 10 October 1941, Wg Cdr Ogilvie, commanding XV Squadron, formally turned N6086 over to Fg Off Peter Boggis. Why he was chosen for this particular honour, Peter Boggis remains unsure, but he had survived fifteen operational sorties to that time and thinks that this might well have been a factor.

Mighty impressive on approach as N6086 confirms.

N6086 flew its first operational sortie on **12 October** 1941, with Nuremberg as target. Two nights later, heading for the same city, icing at 12,000ft became so severe that Mannheim was bombed instead. On **20 October** bombs and leaflets were dropped over Bremen and, on **22 October**, Flt Lt Gilmour took the place of Fg Off Boggis for an attack on *Prinz Eugen* at Brest. The night of **28/29 October** found Fg Off Boggis and N6086 making the long haul to Pilsen. The weather was bad and the temperature fell to -26ºC, the poor heating system bringing terrible punishment to the crew who bombed Frankfurt after finding Pilsen cloud clad. Crossing Nieuwpoort on return, flak opened up, and the tail unit was damaged. This put the aircraft out of use for some weeks.

Patched up, 'MacRobert's Reply' bombed Cologne on **13 December** with Fg Off Boggis once more at the helm. Poor weather prevented Brest from being bombed when they arrived there on **16 December**. Then came delivery of 4 x 2,000lb bombs during the big daylight raid, after which Fg Off Boggis ended his tour of operations. Three Bf 109s had tried unsuccessfully to bring down the bomber. Finally came the detachment to Lossiemouth, when the take-off accident occurred.

N6086 was dismantled and loaded on to 60ft 'Queen Mary' transporters which set off on the very long trek to the Sebro (the Short Bros Repair Organisation) works at Cambridge. As the convoy passed through Aberdeen, a lot of people saw the huge aircraft bearing a familiar name and on its low loaders, a rare sight in those parts. Many phoned Lady MacRobert at her home at Dounside 30 miles away tell her what they had seen.

About ten days after getting back to the Squadron, Sgt Smith was sent for by a none too happy CO and, to quote him, "was given a flea in the ear. I was told that Lady MacRobert had raised a query with the Air Ministry and it has come down the line to me. 'Well Sir,' I answered, 'everyone makes mistakes'."

When the fuselage reached the Sebro Madingley Works, word spread fast from the guardroom. Within minutes much of the work force had streamed from the shops. "It mustn't be our 'MacRobert's Reply'" was the general sentiment. As the sad wreckage passed slowly, many wept. Mrs Phyllis Walliker remembers: "Yes, I cried, and I thought of the young men who might have been in her at the time. We were all very distressed, for the very special Stirling was in a terrible state."

In fact N6086 was repairable, and gave useful service at 1651 Conversion Unit Waterbeach. Meanwhile, a replacement aircraft, W7531 also LS-F now carried the name and spirit of 'MacRobert's Reply'. However, the legend, like that brave family, seemed ill-fated. Sqn Ldr J C Hall took off in W7531 on 17 May 1942 to drop mines in the Baltic and at 0210 hrs as he passed over the Little Belt Bridge, flak opened up and the bomber

W7531 LS-F, the replacement 'MacRobert's Reply', at Wyton in 1942.

was brought down at Gaisklint, near Middelfart. Three mines were found in the wreckage, a fourth having exploded. One member of the crew, Sgt D J Jeffs, was taken prisoner, but the others, including two of the crew of the original 'MacRobert's Reply' were killed. Seven were buried in Odense cemetery. One crew member, Sgt Ronald Maycock, had no known grave and is commemorated on the Royal Air Force Memorial at Runnymede. There was, unusually, a crew of nine on this occasion.

Stirlings were not noted for long operational careers although many accumulated commendable flying hours during training duties. In assessing the number of sorties flown by individual aircraft one has little choice but to base judgement mainly upon the serial numbers listed in Operations Record Books (Form 541), although there is no doubt that these are not absolutely complete and do contain errors. Both those features are, however, not as extensive as is sometimes claimed. On available evidence, W7429 to this time had been the most successful Stirling with twenty-two sorties to its credit followed by W7436 with twenty, W7428 with nineteen and N3669 with eighteen. The latter, destined to fly many more, was later exhibited outside St Paul's Cathedral in London. W7429 flew its first sortie, to Kiel, on **23 June** 1941, and in the hands of Sqn Ldr Boggis who retained it for several more sorties. It took part in raids on Berlin, Karlsruhe, Cuxhaven and, flown by Plt Off Jones, reached Turin on **10 September**. On **28/29 October** it set out for Nuremberg but, because of bad weather, bombs were dropped on Frankfurt. Returning over Rotterdam the Stirling ran into heavy flak which damaged both port engines so badly that it had to land on the starboard engines only. Not surprisingly, on touching down at Warboys the undercarriage collapsed, and although W7429 was taken to Sebro for repair, this proved impossible and it was written off on 15 February 1942. W7428 and W7436 were both lost during the Brest day raid on 18 December.

N3669's bomb tally of sixty-seven sorties. (B Harris)

Famous N3669 'H-Harry' of XV Squadron on display outside St Paul's Cathedral, London late in 1943 having completed sixty-seven sorties.

W7461 QJ-N of 149 Squadron crashed in Yorkshire on 16 January 1942 when returning from operations.

On **28 January** four of 149 Squadron were ordered to Lossiemouth for operation *Oiled* and next day two were detailed for the raid. They failed to locate the *Tirpitz*, W7462 'T-Tommy' crashing on landing and being written off.

Fears that the 'S & G' would slip out of Brest had reached fever pitch by early February. Daily alerts for operation *Fuller* under which raids at sea would take place, plagued the three Stirling squadrons. Without the slightest warning they suddenly received the executive order for Fuller. It was given at 1100 hrs on bleak, rainy **12 February** 1942. By that time the three large warships screened by the atrocious weather had completed most of their passage from Brest through the Channel and when the Stirlings reached

At the start of 1942 W7455 QJ-B was in service with 149 Squadron.

N6090 awaits collection from Belfast watched by Blenheim I, K7062, of 13 OTU. (Shorts)

them it was also dusk. No 7 Squadron sent two crews, Plt Off S G Matkin in R9300 and WO W Nicholls in R9297 who brought home their loads. Matkin's crew saw nothing, and Nicholls caught only a glimpse of the flotilla through a cloud break at 800ft and lost it soon after. Four crews of XV Squadron and two of No.149 fared no better. Of the latter, N6102-G searched low for the ships and the other, N6124-R, crashed on return with bombs still aboard. Not surprisingly there was tumultuous fury that these ships managed to sail through the English Channel undetected and in impunity. Equally, there was anger at the wastage of lives and material during the abysmal episode.

There was also mounting concern over the activity of the Stirlings. In February 1942 they managed only thirty-nine operational night sorties, yet two aircraft were written off and thirteen damaged. Write off thus accounted for 5 percent of the operational effort, while 33 percent of the aircraft suffered damage. Many Stirlings were awaiting repair, and damage at this rate would prevent further squadrons from equipping with Stirlings. Sebro would need to expand if more squadrons were to equip.

Little increase could be made to the Sebro civilian labour force in an area where engineering skill was difficult to recruit. Instead, service personnel were posted into the works, while Sebro working parties did their best on RAF stations. Estimates suggested it would take eight weeks to repair the thirteen damaged aircraft.

One of the problems besetting the aircraft was a steady flow of new modifications. On 27 February the ACAS discussed with VCAS an often mentioned Stirling 'quirk': the hydraulic pipelines to the mid-upper and tail turrets were very easily shot through by aiming at the centre of the fuselage roundel during beam attacks. This vulnerability weighed considerably on the minds of crews, and led to an urgent review of the positioning of these pipes. It was pointed out, however, that most night attacks were delivered from astern.

At the start of 1942, and with Bomber Command poised to open a new sustainable offensive, there were still only three Stirling squadrons and three with Halifaxes. Total Stirling production amounted to 210 examples of which 20 had been written off due to battle damage and 40 in flying accidents. Another 35 had been lost in action, giving a loss rate of about 4 percent per operation, lower than the figure normally judged as acceptable. It was slow production that caused shortages, so the RAF and other official bodies issued numerous exhortations for it to be speeded up. The problem was that the quality of the finished product was such that it took time to build. Too much time, some said. Meanwhile, Short's drawing office team were working on an alternative more modern bomber much larger than the Stirling.

Growth in Bomber Command Squadrons and Aircraft
September 1940 – 1 January 1942

	Stirling		Wellington		Halifax	
	Sqns	aircraft	Sqns	aircraft	Sqns	aircraft
1 Sep 40	1	3	9	151	Nil	–
1 Jan 41	1	6	19	254	1	2
1 Apr 41	1	10	20	309	1	16
1 Jul 41	2	25	21	402	2	36
1 Oct 41	2	38	22	370	2	20
1 Jan 42	3	50	23	407	3	56

Operation *Trinity* – by Group Captain K J Somerville DSO DFC AFC

The request we were about to receive from Chiefs of Staff was most welcome since it allowed us to test our special equipment under operational conditions. The request was, "Can 109 Squadron and its beam flying pilots and highly trained wireless operators take part in the bombing of Brest by Stirlings from Oakington, in an attempt to hit the two battle cruisers 'blind'?" The answer from our young commanding officer, Squadron Leader Hal Bufton, was, "Yes, of course we can". He, incidentally, had already passed into history as the pilot who, with his wireless operator, found and plotted the positioning of the German pathfinder beams code-named 'Knickebein'.

Flight Lieutenant George Grant, myself and one or two others were called in to be told what the 'flap' was all about. We were to fly at maximum Stirling height, with full bomb load and along our British beams. Acting on a special bomb release signal the hope was that we would be able to drop our load on the ships. We knew, even if others did not, that such operations meant flying straight and level at a predetermined air speed and height on the beam. That really meant 'straight and level' with no weaving, no avoiding action, while the controlling ground radar station plotted the exact release point from which we would drop the armour piercing bombs.

We also knew, and so did the Chiefs of Staff, that it was very likely that German radar operators would have ample time to locate us, and that we would be boxed in by concentrated Ack-Ack fire well before we reached the target. So important was the task that a calculated risk was necessary. Although the normal Stirling crews did not like other pilots taking over their aircraft on the bombing run they joined the special operations with commendable keenness.

Tests included opportunities for the '109' pilots to get used to handling the heavy Stirlings on the beam – no easy task, for we were used to operational beam flying using Wellingtons. George Grant and I left our base at Boscombe Down on 4 December 1941, and headed for Oakington and the first operation which took place on 7 December 1941. I was in Stirling N6032 with Flight Lieutenant Crebbin as senior Stirling captain, Pilot Officer Cotton as navigator and five crew including my special operator whose task was to listen for the bomb release signal.

Take-off was in daylight at 2.30pm just two hours before darkness, with the total flight estimated to last about five hours which meant landing at Oakington at about 7.30pm.

As you can imagine, tension was high, for the Stirling boys already used to heavy punishment did not like the idea of dead straight and level flying for ten minutes at a set air speed and height. Bomber Command Special Operations had ensured that the special Stirlings would have maximum cover and interference with German radar by using some fifty Wellingtons flying just below the Stirlings' flight path. This after-thought was much appreciated. I received no flak hits on my aircraft, but I believe Grant's received a peppering and returned safely. As for damage to the ships, it was estimated as amounting to one or two very near misses and slight damage.

We left for Boscombe Down on 8 December then next day returned to Oakington to carry out our second bombing operation, on 12 December. This time I was in N3669 with Flight Lieutenant Parnell as Stirling captain. My third *Trinity* operation was on 15 December, the fourth on the 23rd, with Plt Off Collins and Plt Off Matkin respectively.

Some flak damage was received but nothing to really hurt. As for our bombing, we certainly did some damage to the ships. One further operation planned for 28 December was cancelled.

Both George Grant and 'Slim' Somerville finished the war as Group Captains (as did Hal Bufton) having completed further full operations tours as Commanding Officers of one or other of the two *Oboe* Mosquito squadrons. All three became proud recipients of the DSO and DFC.

Daily State of Stirling Squadrons 1800 hrs on given dates July – December 1941
(Establishment: 16 IE + 2 IR)

Sqn	1 Jul	5 Jul	7 Jul	11 Jul	19 Jul	22 Jul	23 Jul	24 Jul
7	3 6	2 7	5 6	4 6	5 4	6 4	6 5	3 8
XV	4 5	8 4	6 6	5 6	8 6	5 6	7 4	6 4

	10 Aug	11 Aug	12 Aug	14 Aug	15 Aug	25 Aug	28 Aug	2 Sep
7	8 5	9 4	7 6	7 5	2 7	5 5	7 4	3 8
XV	6 7	6 8	7 7	4 8	1 8	7 5	8 5	9 4

	10 Sep	19 Sep	30 Sep	1 Oct	3 Oct	4 Oct	12 Oct	20 Oct
7	10 3	9 5	6 9	9 10	13 6	12 7	16 0	13 6
XV	8 6	6 6	10 7	11 6	11 8	12 7	13 4	14 4
149*	–	–	–	–	–	nil	nil	nil

* 149 Sqn established 4 Oct 41 at 8 + 1 Stirlings; first on charge 22 Oct 41

	22 Oct	28 Oct	1 Nov	8 Nov	18 Nov	26 Nov	29 Nov	30 Nov
7	12 6	13 5	19* 7	12 8	9 7	12 6	13 10	9 –
XV	10 8	11 8	18* 11	8 11	7 7	9 7	8 9	6 –
149	0 1	0 1	3* –	7 –	7 1	13 8	6 6	8 –
26 Flt	–	–	3 2	n/a	n/a	n/a	3 4	n/a

* total holding
n/a: not available
26 Flt established at 8 aircraft

	6 Dec	13 Dec	17 Dec	18 Dec	31 Dec
7	13 6	7 5	15 2	8 5	8 7
XV	11 7	7 8	13 4	4 11	12 4
149*	6 7	11 6	5 12	8 9	6 9
218*	nil –	2 –	2 –	– 2	3 2
26 Flt	3 5	2 5	n/a n/a	n/a n/a	n/a n/a

* both established at 16+2

Sample on-strength comparisons with other bombers (1941)

	1 Jul	19 Jul	28 Aug	19 Sep	31 Dec
Halifax					
10 Sqn	– –	– –	4 11	– –	– –
35 Sqn	8 12	9 7	7 3	5 2	17 2
76 Sqn	6 10	8 6	5 5	8 0	11 8
102 Sqn	– –	– –	– 7	– –	– –
Manchester					
61 Sqn	– 8	– 5	1 2	0 0	12 6
83 Sqn	– –	– –	0 8	– –	– –
97 Sqn	– 11	– 9	3 3	6 3	10 5
207 Sqn	– 15	– 17	11 4	13 5	13 3

NB No 10 Sqn, established as a Halifax squadron on 25 August 1941, was the first to receive the Halifax Mk II. By 13 December No 10 Sqn had eleven Mk II, 35 Sqn held nine Mk 1 and eight Mk II, 76 Sqn held thirteen Mk 1 and six Mk II and No 138 (SD) Sqn had two Mk II. The period also saw the introduction of the Wellington III (Hercules), the first squadron example joining No 9 Sqn (established at 16+2) on 7 September 1941.

Summary of Stirling Operations 1 July – 29 December 1941

Date	Target	No of Stirlings used	HEs (lb) 2,000	1,900	1,000	500	250	Incendiaries (lb) 30	4	4X	Missing	Crews claiming to attack primary target/ Total force sent
1-Jul	Borkum (D)	2/3	–	–	–	–	–	–	–	–	N6013	2/3
	Cuxhaven (D)	0/3	–	–	–	–	–	–	–	–	–	0/3
1/2 Jul	Bremen	4/6	–	–	15	33	3	–	–	–	–	142/153
	Deutsche s/yd, 1 alt Rotterdam	1/1	–	–	–	–	–	–	–	–	–	1/1
5/6 Jul	Magdeburg	1/3	–	–	5	4	1	–	–	–	–	9/16
7/8 Jul	Frankfurt	3/3	–	–	5	1	–	–	720	–	–	3/3
8/9 Jul	Merseburg/ Leuna, I-G Farben	0/1	–	–	15	21	–	–	–	–	–	10/14
14/15 Jul	Hannover and one alt	4/6	20	25	6	–	1260	–	–	–	–	51/65
18 Jul	Cloud cover attacks detailed: Aachen, Rheyt, Krefeld, Munster abandoned no cloud	0/5	–	–	–	–	–	–	–	–	N6030	0/5
20/21 Jul	Cologne	0/3	–	–	–	–	–	–	–	–	N6038	77/113
23 Jul	La Pallice (D) and Fromentine	4/6	–	–	10 AP	–	–	–	–	–	–	4/6
25/26 Jul	Berlin	?/7	?	?	?	?	?	?	?	?	N6029	?
		?/?									N6035	?
30/31 Jul	Cologne	?/5	–	–	–	–	–	–	–	–	–	–
2/3 Aug	Berlin	3/5	5	7	15	18	–	–	–	–	N3663	32/39
	Missing aircraft load	–	5	7	–	–	–	–	–	–	–	–
5/6 Aug	Hamburg	1/1	35	–	–	–	–	–	–	–	–	1/1
	Karlsruhe	7/8	–	–	42	–	–	–	1920	97	–	59/97
7/8 Aug	Essen	5/8	25	37	–	36	1500	–	–	–	N3658	65/106
	Hamm	0/1	–	–	14	–	–	–	–	–	–	–
	Alts: Homberg Duisberg Dorsten	3	–	–	–	–	–	–	–	–	–	–

Date	Target	No of Stirlings used	HEs (lb) 2,000	1,900	1,000	500	250	Incendiaries (lb) 30	4	4X	Missing	Crews claiming to attack primary target/ Total force sent
12/13 Aug	Berlin	4/9	–	–	15	28	–	–	740	–	N3659	32/70
	Bielefeld	0/1	–	–	–	–	–	–	–	–	–	1
	Essen & alts: Gusten, Brunswick, Iselohn	3/3	–	–	15	18	–	–	–	–	–	?/28
14/15 Aug	Iselohn	3	–	–	–	–	–	–	–	–	–	
	Magdeburg two others bombed, alts	3/9	–	–	12	25	–	–	420	–	W7437	17/?
		2/	–	–	15	17	–	–	960	–	–	
19/20 Aug	Kiel	4/7	–	–	10	23	–	–	–	–	–	65/108
22/23 Aug	Le Havre	2/2	–	–	20	40	–	–	480	–	–	19/23
25/26 Aug	Karlsruhe	4/12	–	–	20	20	–	–	1320	–	N6020	23/49
	7 more bombed alts		–	–	20	15	21	–	–	480	–	
26/27 Aug	Boulogne	1/2	–	–	–	17	–	–	240	–	–	?/11
	Other Crotoy	1	–	–	–	19	–	–	240	–	–	
28/29 Aug	Duisburg	12/13	–	–	45	124	–	–	1500	–	W7438	84/118
	Other jettisoned over Germany		–	–	–	–	–	–	–	–		
30/31 Aug/ 31 Aug/	Cherbourg	1/1	–	–	5	8	–	–	–	–	–	
1 Sep		1	–	–	5	6	–	–	480	–		1
2/3 Sep	Cologne 1 abortive	5/6	–	–	15	24	–	–	360	–	–	69/120
	Berlin, 1 attacked alt, 1 aborted	4/6	–	–	–	–	–	–	–	–	–	24/24
3/4 Sep	Brest 1 aborted	3/4	13AP	–	10	22	–	–	960	–	–	52/65
7/8 Sep	Berlin	7/0	–	–	30	31	–	90	420	–	N6045 N6046	113/176
10/11 Sep	Kiel	1/3	–	–	5	3	–	–	–	–	–	43/?
	Turin 3 aborted	10/13	–	–	16	62	8	24	78	–	–	56/76
12/13 Sep	Frankfurt and 1 alt, Trier	8/9	–	–	35	54	–	72	620	–	–	86/130
13/14 Sep	Brest	3/3	10AP	–	–	–	11SAP	–	–	–	–	133/155
15/16 Sep	Hamburg	6/8	–	–	28	38	–	–	–	–	N6021	99/159
	Le Havre	1/1	–	–	5	8	–	–	–	–	–	1/1
	West of Hamburg	1	–	–	–	–	–	–	–	–		
18/19 Sep	Le Havre	2/2	–	–	4	21	–	–	240	–	–	10/10

Date	Target	No of Stirlings used	Bombs dropped from Stirlings (number of each type)								Missing	Crews claiming to attack primary target/Total force sent
			HEs (lb)					Incendiaries (lb)				
			2,000	1,900	1,000	500	250	30	4	4X		
19/20 Sep	Stettin, 1 attacked	4/10	–	–	16	14	–	–	–	–	–	50/72
	Wismar, 1 alts, 1	–	–	–	–	3	–	9	–	–	–	
	aborted		–	–	8	6	–	–	–	–	–	
26/27 Sep	Cologne 1 attacked	5/10	–	–	10	18	–	–	–	–	–	11/104
	Hagen	1	–	–	5	6	–	–	–	–	–	
	4 aborted											
28/29 Sep	Genoa	2/2	–	–	4	6	–	–	240	–	–	30/68
		0/1										
29/30 Sep	Emden	8/10	–	–	25	21	–	–	2160	–	W7433	84/139
	Stettin, 1 attacked		–	–	–	16	–	–	360	–	W7441	
3/4 Oct	Le Havre	1/1	10	–	–	–	–	–	–	–	–	
	Brest	2/9	–	–	–	–	–	–	–	–	N6085	2/9
	Dunkirk 1/7 aborted	5/6										
10/11 Oct	Cologne 1 aborted	5/6	–	–	23	35	–	–	480	–	–	53/88
12/13 Oct	Nuremberg (also dropped 12 x 40lb APB)	6/7	–	–	30	41	–	–	–	–	N6047	69/85
13/14 Oct	Dusseldorf	5/7	–	–	14	44	–	–	720	–	–	35/60
	Boulogne	1/1	–	–	–	9	–	–	630	–	–	
	1 alt, Siegburg	–	–	–	–	13	–	–	–	–	–	
14/15 Oct	Nuremberg	0/4	–	–	–	–	–	–	–	–	–	14/80
	3 bombed nearby	–	–	–	11	18	–	–	–	–	–	
15/16 Oct	Cologne	5/7	–	–	25	37	–	–	–	–	–	29/34
20/21 Oct	Bremen (also dropped 6 x 40lb HE)	11/15	–	–	50	88	–	–	–	–	–	75/153
	Antwerp	1/2	–	–	5	6	–	–	–	–	–	
	3 alts (also dropped 6 x 40lb HE)	–	–	–	14	35	–	–	–	–	–	
22/23 Oct	Brest	5/6	24AP	–	–	–	–	–	–	–	–	5/6
	1 bombed alt Honfleur	1/1	–	–	5	6	–	–	360	–	–	
23/24 Oct	Brest	7/9	35AP	–	–	–	–	–	–	–	–	7/9
	2 aborted											
24/25 Oct	Brest	6/6	–	–	–	119	–	–	–	–	–	6/6

Bombs dropped from Stirlings (number of each type): HEs (lb) = 2,000 / 1,900 / 1,000 / 500 / 250; Incendiaries (lb) = 30 / 4 / 4X

Date	Target	No of Stirlings used	2,000	1,900	1,000	500	250	30	4	4X	Missing	Crews claiming to attack primary target/ Total force sent
28/29 Oct	Pilsen; 8 bombed alts	0/10	–	–	27	27	–	24	720	–	–	0/10
31 Oct/ 1 Nov	Bremen	4/8	–	–	18	49	–	–	720	–	–	12/20
	Boulogne	2/3	20AP	–	9	13	–	–	240	–	–	
	one alt: le Touquet	–										
1/2 Nov	Brest	4/8	–	–	4	5	–	–	–	–	–	4/17
3/4 Nov	Boulogne	0/1	–	–	–	–	–	–	–	–	–	0/1
	Dortmund	0/11										0/11
5 Nov	Essen	0/1										
	Day raids; no cloud cover											
7/8 Nov	Berlin	2/2	–	–	30	24	4	–	–	–	N3677	68/158
	Mannheim	2/2	–	–	10	12	–	–	–	–	N6091	
9/10 Nov	Ostend	3/4	–	–	5	30	–	–	–	–	–	
	Hamburg B&V shipyards	3/5	–	–	15	24	–	–	2160	–	–	68/106
15/16 Nov	Kiel	1/6	–	–	5	5	–	–	–	–	–	8/18
18/19 Nov	Brest; 3 abortive	3/6	–	–	–	48SAP	–	–	–	–	–	3/6
23/24 Nov	Brest	9/12	31AP	–	–	16	–	–	–	–	–	9/12
24-Nov	Ruhr (2); Osnabruck; 2 abortive; 1 attacked shipping	1/4	–	–	–	–	–	–	–	–	–	4/4
25-Nov	NW Germany; Day attempt, no cloud cover	0/3	–	–	–	–	–	–	–	–	–	3/3
25/26 Nov	Brest	6/7	?	?	?	?	?	?	?	–	?	?/35
26/27 Nov	Ostend	0/2	–	–	–	?	–	–	–	–	–	?/5
27/28 Nov	Dusseldorf; 4 alts Ostend; Bombed Dunkirk	0/5; 0/1	–	–	20	43	–	–	–	–	–	51/?
30 Nov/ 1 Dec	Hamburg	2/2	–	–	10	12	–	–	900	–	–	131/181
	Emden; and 1 alt	2/3	–	–	–	19	–	–	–	–	–	
7/8 Dec	Brest	4/7	15AP	–	–	–	–	–	–	–	–	23/30

Bombs dropped from Stirlings (number of each type)

Date	Target	No of Stirlings used	2,000	1,900	1,000	500	250	30	4	4X	Missing	Crews claiming to attack primary target/Total force sent
			HEs (lb)					Incendiaries (lb)				
09-Dec	Roving commission / 2 attacked shipping	2/4	—	—	—	16	—	—	—	—	—	4/4
11/12 Dec	Cologne	6/9	—	—	30	60	—	—	—	—	—	34/60
	Brest	3/5	11	—	—	—	—	—	—	—	—	
	Le Havre	/2?	—	—	—	—	—	—	1440	—	—	
12/13 Dec	Brest	5/6	25AP	—	—	27	—	—	—	—	—	34/36
	Dunkirk 3/3	—	—	—	—	—	—	—	—	—	—	
14/15 Dec	Brest abandoned	0/6	—	—	—	—	—	—	—	—	—	1/31
15/16 Dec	Brest	6/7	26AP	—	—	—	—	—	—	—	—	13/?
	Ostend	1/1	—	—	—	—	13	—	—	—	—	
16/17 Dec	Brest	3/5	9+5AP	—	—	—	10	—	—	—	—	15/22
	Ostend	1/2	—	—	—	—	7	—	—	—	—	
18 Dec (D)	Brest	16/18	64AP	—	—	—	—	—	—	—	N3665 N3680 W7428 W74236	39/47
		—	—	—	—	—	—	—	—	—		
23/24 Dec	Brest	8/9	24AP	—	10	16	—	—	—	—	—	43/47
27/28 Dec	Brest	4/6	15AP	—	5	7	—	—	—	—	—	18/29
28/29 Dec	Emden	1/1	—	—	5	8	—	—	—	—	—	31/40

Explanatory notes:
4/6 etc = Number known to have attacked/number despatched
alt = alternative target(s) attacked
AP = armour piercing HE
(D) = daylight operation
SAP = semi-armour piercing HE
Final column lists total number of aircraft despatched for operations on given date. In many cases it was not possible to ascertain with certainty the number attacking against Stirling's primary target.

Chapter 8
Super Stirling

Arthur Gouge and several of Shorts representatives, the Director of Technical Development, Director and Deputy Director of Operational Requirements, Director of Armament, Stedman Willot the Resident Technical Officer, and Wg Cdr Hutton the Overseer, met on 9 July 1941 to consider a 'Stirling Mk III'. Shorts had in mind a 'Super Stirling' utilising 2,000hp Bristol Centaurus engines, a landplane version of the giant Shetland flying-boat carrying 'a modern bomb load'. Maybe an incredible official suggestion to employ the hefty, slow Shetland as a main stream heavy bomber had given impetus to the idea.

A far better scheme would have been an unarmed high-flying bomber relying upon speed and not heavy turrets for defence, a complete break from the Stirling concept. Before the war Shorts projected such a machine as a top component in a composite. Instead, they were making a big mistake by going for an even larger conventional, relatively slow bomber whose heavy defensive equipment compromised its offensive load.

Increased span and mainplanes with 6.25°incidence were proposed to improve take-off performance, further aided by having a fuselage curiously cranked upwards by 3.5°aft of the wings. A redesigned undercarriage would be more compact and much stronger that the Stirling's.

Shorts also were working on an improved version of the existing Stirling powered by much superior Mk VI Hercules engines. A circular of 29 July 1941 gave instructions that this – and not the aforementioned design – was to be known as the 'Mk III'. The new 'super bomber' then became the Short S.36, and outline details were reviewed by the Air Staff who produced a draft Specification B.8/41 for such a bomber.

The S.36 (four Centaurus CE38Ms) would need to be suitable for world-wide use. A realistic, quite low, weak mixture cruising speed of not less than 210mph (substituted for the original 240mph) was linked with a range of 2,100 miles on maximum tankage when carrying 12,000lb of bombs, a 23,000ft ceiling with normal load or 3,000 miles using auxiliary tankage. The take-off run from grass would be 1,400 yards, the landing run (light) 1,100 yards.

A major switch would be to .50in gun nose and tail turrets. To avoid cg problems the dorsal turret would carry .303in guns. Bomb loads would be:

(a) 1 x 8,000lb HC + 4 x 2,000lb AP/HC or 6 x 1,000lb GP in the fuselage
(b) 6 x 4,000lb HC + 6 x 1,000lb GP in wing cells
(c) 9 x 2,000lb AP/HC + 6 x 1,000lb GP in wing cells
(d) 9 x 1,900lb GP + 6 x 1,000lb GP
(e) 9 x 1,500lb Type A mines
(f) 18 x 1,000lb GP
(g) 18 x 1,000lb SBC or equivalent

Conscious of criticism of the Stirling's vulnerability to fighter attack, armour plate would be built on the bulkhead behind the wireless operator to protect from belly attack. Pilots' seats would have 9mm plating, as would vital engine areas. The eight-man crew – two pilots with dual controls, navigator/observer, four air gunners and a flight engineer – would include two gunners to act as radio operators. Troop carrying and glider towing were featured.

Ralph Sorley considered the overall specification "attractive and well worth adopting", but that the cruising speed was too low for night operations. He considered a four .50in gun dorsal turret might well be needed during moonlight sorties, and rated weight of fire more important than its duration. He also suggested sacrificing 2,000lb bomb load for additional armour. One tailwheel was preferable to two, and bigger flaps to cut the landing run.

Although this was far from the 'ideal bomber' the Air Staff wanted, the ACAS considered it advanced enough for adoption. With possible 2,000 yard runways the take-off run was acceptable, and arrester gear could deal with landing problems. The span must not be increased, and the armour would be essential. Production could not possibly begin in under eighteen months, and service entry in under thirty months by which time night fighters would have improved, making protection against 20mm cannon fire necessary.

Ralph Sorley wrote to the CRD on 24 September 1941, stating that "the B.8/41 looks very attractive", then the VCAS agreed that it should be an Air Staff Requirement. The S.36 looked to have a future.

Shorts had submitted a detailed design study on 15 July 1941, a week after the first conference. They outlined a bomber of 80,000lb all-up weight, span 136ft, wing area 2,145 sqft and aspect ratio 8.62. The calculated performance was as follows:

Weight (lb)

Structure 36,630
Fuel: 22,810
Crew: 1,400
Equipment: 22,940
Power plants: 17,100
Total all-up weight: 103,100

Loads, range and speed:

Bombs (lb)	Fuel (gal)	Range (miles)	Mean Speed (mph)
12,000	3,000	2,000	221
11,000	4,350	3,000	221

Performance at these two weights:

All-up weight (lb):		80,000	103,000
Max. speed, 3,200 revs, mph			
MS gear		282	275
FS gear		311	300
Economical cruise speed			
MS gear, mph,	6,000ft	243	234
	24,000ft	262	237
Max. ceiling, max. power for climb,			
'S' gear, ft:		29,300	23,800
Service ceiling, ft:		28,300	23,000
Max. economical cruise power ceiling,		21,000	14,700
Take-off run, yards:			
to unstick		390	810
to clear 50ft		710	1,275

Maximum possible bomb stowage was 30,000lb, comprising the ultra 'modern load' of 6 x 4,000lb, with a further 6 x 1,000lb bombs in wing cells. The MAP, reckoning that Shorts weight assessments optimistic, suggested that at normal operating weight with 3,000 gal fuel and a 5,000lb bomb load, the all-up weight would be nearer 105,000lb. Drag estimates also seemed optimistic, but range might be greater. Although the S.36 was a logical step in heavy bomber development, its landing run seemed disturbing.

Extrapolated figures based on a flying weight of 105,000lb and 3,000 gals fuel were:

	MAP forecast	Short's forecast
Max. speed mph	295	300
Max. cruise 15,000ft weak mixture mph	214	222
Max. economic cruise at 15,000ft	190	not listed
Range miles	2,000	not listed
Cruise range, weak mix miles	2,000	2,120
Service ceiling, normal weight (ft)	22,500	23,000
Service ceiling, mean weight (ft)	27,000	not listed
Take-off run, normal weight, (yds)	1,400	1,500
Landing run, half fuel, no bombs (yds)	1,100	1,200

The B.8/41 Draft Specification reached Shorts on 24 January 1942 and, at the end of January, a fuselage mock-up was officially inspected. Lack of layout originality was criticised for it differed little from the Stirling. The blunt nose was anachronistic, the .50in dorsal turret huge. A 4 x .303in type or even a power mounting for 2 x .50in guns was suggested instead of Short's heavy, fully rotatable 4 x .50in dorsal turret with 35°downward fire and just aft of the cg. The flight engineer needed to be positioned ahead of the armoured bulkhead, and only two engines were armour protected, not the stipulated four. The belly FN 64 turret would have to be periscopically sighted. Oil coolers needed to be moved to the wing leading edges to reduce vulnerability, and dinghies stored in the wing to avoid a blow-out in the fuselage

A usual bomb load only 2,000lb more than the Stirling's would have been acceptable had performance been much superior. Instead, a high price was being paid merely for .50in guns. All agreed that the aircraft's all-up weight must certainly not be allowed to rise.

Production possibilities were considered on 22 February 1942, in the knowledge that prototypes could not fly before late 1942. Increased range and bomb load would be useful in the Far East, provided airfields and maintenance facilities were available, for the Stirling was fast becoming outdated, making a successor necessary. About two years were needed for a production switch to the S.36, meaning that 172 Stirlings would be lost for a gain of 46 B.8/41s. Monthly output of eight would replace the twelve Stirling rate. Production was unlikely to start before January 1944, thus Stirling production losses would begin about January 1943 and progressively increase. The VCAS suggested the start of production be retarded allowing highest Stirling production cuts to come in winter.

All agreed that the B.8/41 must not be launched unless production was certain. CRD favoured introducing the S.36 when MAP production staff and Sir Henry Tizard had reservations feeling that a better heavy replacement would be a Lancaster derivative. Their views marked a turning point.

On 2 May 1942 B.8/41 was discussed with the C-in-C Bomber Command who did not want to lose twelve real Stirlings for one possible B.8/41. He favoured 4 x .50in tail guns, 4 x .303in dorsal guns and a retractable ventral turret as preferable to .50in guns throughout, and reckoned it better to go for a 170,000lb ultra-heavy bomber.

On 4 May 1942, Ralph Sorley received new B.8/41 estimates from the DGRD. Original bomb load expectations had not taken into account weight of the aircraft fully operationally equipped, and the adjusted load showed a reduction to 12,000lb for 1,600 miles. Increased armour and .50in guns would further reduce that to under 11,500lb for 1,600 miles. Even more alarming was a new predicted ceiling of only 16,000ft for 1,600 miles range showing no improvement on the Stirling's performance. Flexibility between 16,000ft and 20,000ft needed rich mixture setting, which would increase fuel consumption and reduce the range. Further Centaurus development would probably increase fuel consumption, might demand more tankage and cut the offensive load. Additional equipment could even further cut the B.8/41's average bomb load. While 24,000lb could be carried, that was linked with only a 400 mile range. It seemed best to forget B.8/41, and concentrate on the Hercules Mk VI Stirling, with a forecast 19,000ft ceiling.

On 22 May 1942, the CAS said that they should cancel B.8/41 for "it was not as promising as at first hoped". Shorts were instead pressed to build Avro Lancasters, but reluctant to do so. They wished to build the successor which evolved as the Avro Lincoln for which they eventually received an order only to have it cancelled – like the S.36. Although they tried to produce Stirling successors in post-war years – some sound in concept too – no more of the company's bombers would see RAF service. Meanwhile, making the Stirling as effective as possible was the path to tread.

The Stirlings of '218' – Some Personal Memories

Some of the problems met when No 218 Squadron at Marham began converting from Wellingtons at the end of 1941 are described here by Eric Basford.

A Stirling with 'HA' markings first took off for air testing on Christmas Eve 1941, and its undercarriage could not be fully retracted after take-off. Fortunately there was no difficulty in lowering it for a safe landing. That proved to be just one in a series of undercarriage difficulties during the conversion period.

The first Stirlings were allocated to 'B' Flight, and it was understood that the squadron would be taken off operations for a period of two months, January–February 1942, during which time each crew was expected to acquire twenty-five hours flying the new type. To achieve that, an intensive flying programme was laid on, but ice and snow on the airfield made all flying impossible for many days in January. Furthermore, attempts to do the necessary practice flying from other airfields was thus frustrated, and keeping the Stirlings serviceable soon became a major headache.

Vicious weather in Norfolk that January, combined with serviceability problems and the unsuitability of a grass airfield for the heavy Stirlings, soon demonstrated how ambitious that conversion programme really was.

All trades were affected during the conversion period. Airframe fitters, riggers and electricians were continually beset by undercarriage retraction problems. Engine fitters and mechanics had their problems too. When the first aircraft needed a routine change of sparking plugs, most of the brass terminals on the ends of the HT ignition leads fell off – along with the porcelain insulators – as soon as the retaining nuts were unscrewed and the leads pulled clear of the hollow upper portion of the sparking plugs. Thus, a standard replacement job became an extensive repair operation. The eccentric vane fuel pumps on the engines presented other difficulties, and so on.

Engine operating temperatures seemed generally higher than we had known on the Wellingtons' Pegasus. Maximum permissible engine temperature on the Hercules XI was 280°C, but there were reports that this was being reached and even exceeded during take-off. However, that tendency seemed to become less of a problem on the Mk B. III with Hercules XVIs. Nevertheless, for many months on the Mk 1s an endless variety of cooling air baffles were fitted around the plugs, not to mention the fitting of plugs of different designs.

The saga regarding the Exactor controls seemed endless, and there were sighs of relief from all quarters when the Mk IIIs arrived with more conventional engine and propeller controls. Matters were so serious in 1942 that the squadron set up a small section to specialise in the rectification of Exactor defects. Pipelines connecting the transmitters in the cockpit to the receivers on the engines were very long, particularly with the outer engines, and every joint had to be regarded as having the potential to produce an air leak. Then there was the possibility of vibration causing cracks in the pipes. The section of small-bore copper pipe that weaved its way through the banks of engine cylinders to the receiver at the top of the propeller constant speed unit, which was mounted on the engine front cover, had to be removed periodically and examined for cracks then either renewed or sealed. Air in the throttle Exactor system resulted in the throttle in the carburettor being pushed open, ultimately to take-off boost, even though the throttle lever in the cockpit was being held hard against the running stop. In such circumstances, the engine cut-off lever became ineffective and the only way to stop the runaway engine was to switch off both magnetos and then turn off the fuel supply to that engine. I found the experience very disconcerting when ground testing, but it was surely more alarming when it happened in flight.

It was standard procedure on the Mk 1 Stirling for ground crews to ensure that the throttles were in the take-off position when the aircraft was left overnight and then to check their positions next morning. If a throttle lever had 'crept' back along its quadrant, that was taken as an indication of air in the system and some investigation was necessary. The propeller controls, which were always left in fine pitch, were similarly checked for 'creep'. Air in a propeller Exactor control would set the propeller at its fine pitch stops, irrespective of the control lever in the cockpit. The result in flight was a screaming engine. Again, the only action possible was to shut down the engine completely and investigate as soon as possible.

Some servicing difficulties in the early days could perhaps be put down to maintenance personnel dealing with unfamiliar aircraft. For instance, it was very quickly discovered that the very low temperatures experienced at Marham in 1941–42 froze the universal joints in the double-cranked drive between the electric motor and the chain drive in the engine cooling gills. This resulted in one or other of the universal joints shearing when the gills were opened. A Flight Order to that effect stated that when low temperatures prevailed, cooling gills on engines should not be opened until the engine temperature reached a minimum of 130°C. It went a long way to ending that difficulty.

Yet in spite of all the problems, both air and ground crews still held a lot of goodwill towards the Stirling and wanted it to be a success story because it did have many good points. It was a big, modern all-metal aeroplane (apart from the fabric covered control surfaces). Its size alone was impressive, the tallest person could walk freely beneath the propellers whether they were rotating or not, and the roomy interior made the Wellington seem poky by comparison. Many of the Stirling's facilities were an improvement on those provided on the Wellington, eg. priming the Stirling's engines with fuel for starting was done from within the fuselage, whereas on the Wellington you did that job from underneath the engine itself with your back pressed against the mainwheel and the propeller turning a few feet in front of your eyes. The draught air intakes of the Hercules engines eliminated the possibility of air intake fires which we had long accepted as a regular hazard with the updraught intakes on the Wellington's Pegasus engines, particularly when starting in very cold weather or sometimes simply as a result of 'finger trouble' in the cockpit. Then the introduction of the power plant concept simplified maintenance and so on.

Of course, with the arrival of the Stirling the deployment of ground crews changed. The squadron establishment for Wellingtons was for a Corporal Fitter E/A to be in charge of each aircraft and its ground crew of mechanics and riggers; one Sergeant Fitter Engines and one Sergeant Fitter. Airframe workers were then employed in a supervisory role for the entire Flight of aircraft. But squadron establishment for the Stirling was much increased and allowed for a Sergeant Fitter E/A and a Corporal Fitter E/A to each aircraft then its ground crew consisted of four mechanics and two riggers. Also, because of the additional work load, one electrician was allocated to each aircraft as well, although they were still responsible to their NCO i/c trade for that particular Flight. Consequently, expansion in all trades and ranks up to Sergeant began immediately. Many more electricians soon arrived on the squadron, since the use of electrical power on the Stirling was much greater than on the Wellington. Flaps, bomb doors, undercarriage, cooling gills, all were driven by electric motors as well as the usual electrical services. In fact only the landing lights were hydraulically positioned on the Stirling, as I recall. Also, the virtual doubling of the numbers of engine and airframe tradesmen on the squadron soon created difficulties on 115 Squadron, who had re-equipped earlier with Wellington IIIs, and were still resident on the Station. All newly arrived personnel were therefore billeted in huts in the grounds of nearby Narborough Hall, and had to be transported to and from the Station daily.

Chapter 9
All Change

So far the Stirlings had operated in a somewhat ad hoc manner, and sometimes in daylight because they were manoeuvrable and rated fairly fast. All was about to change, for Bomber Command was to have a new manager carrying out new Directives.

Forceful, single-minded, highly accomplished tactician and impressive during every encounter, Air Chief Marshal Sir Arthur Harris became C-in-C Bomber Command on 22 February 1942. A superb leader, he was regarded by tens of thousands with the greatest possible respect and admiration. Scant recognition later awarded him by feckless politicians evading their decisions, and harsh criticism often from folk not even alive during the war and incapable of understanding Bomber Command's wartime sacrifices and achievements remain a national disgrace.

From his underground headquarters, the only example of their type in Britain purpose-built to withstand air attack and nestling in woodland five miles from High Wycombe, Sir Arthur waged an increasingly tough battle campaign. He took command as equipment was improving, and a week after orders were issued for a major policy change. Wholesale destruction of German cities, industrial areas and the workers' homes around them at night by means of short, intensive onslaughts had been decided upon, the aim being total destruction of the enemy war machine. Harris, the professional, neither devised nor initiated the idea of area bombing and destruction of German cities, he merely carried out the instructions given to him. It was Winston Churchill, his War Cabinet, the Air Ministry and the Air Staff who, on 14 February 1942, demanded what amounted to a brutal bombing campaign and later credited Harris with the scheme. Before Harris took command the order to ravage by fire four large German industrial cities in the Ruhr, then fourteen elsewhere, was masterminded by the Air Ministry and given to Bomber Command which was then instructed to complete within three months Part 1 of the Government's orders – as soon and effectively as possible.

Such destruction had long been proposed by some senior Air Force officers and politicians, but the 4,000 heavy bombers needed to destroy German industry and break the morale of its people were impossible to produce. Sir Arthur inherited what he correctly called a force 'too small and poorly equipped' for, upon taking command, he had 529 aircraft of which an average of 378 were serviceable aircraft and crews. Of an average of forty-seven serviceable heavy bombers, thirteen were Stirlings. Another seventy aircraft were 2 Group's Blenheim light bombers. Harris could thus realistically expect to field about 250 medium and 50 heavy bombers. Such was his organising ability that within a few weeks he managed to launch a 'thousand bomber' raid.

In any assessment of the effectiveness of Bomber Command's war effort, and indeed that of the Stirling, basic aspects of the overall campaign need to be borne in mind.

As the bomber force was strengthened so were German defences, preventing unescorted day raids by very heavy bombers on the large industrial areas now selected for attack. That meant night bombing, when target location was difficult. If necessary a listed alternative and, if all else failed, any 'military objective' was to be attacked. Although skilled bombing had damaged some worthwhile targets, raids had so far not constituted an effective campaign. Estimates suggested that only one load in ten fell within five miles of a Ruhr A/P and strong evidence indicated that British bombs often failed to explode or disintegrated upon impact.

The overriding need to find the primary target was, in February 1942, thought soon to be answered by *Gee*, a new navigation system whose long development period was the result of the need to first introduce airborne interception radar in Fighter Command.

Tail high, N6124 OJ-R gets airborne in typical style from Lakenheath.

A master station and a slave station each transmitted a pulse signal received by equipment able to measure the time difference in reception and indicate the distance from source. A chart showing grid lines allowed position of the aircraft and distances to be deduced. Another master and second slave station transmitted synchronised signals which the navigator plotted on another line, the aircraft being at the intersection of the lines.

Gee tests had been undertaken by the Command during June 1941 then halted, to maintain secrecy while equipment was produced for widespread use. Jamming was expected after about five months. 'False' radio beams were being transmitted to confuse the Germans as to the reason for improved bombing accuracy expected from 'TR 13357 *Gee*'.

On 26 August 1941, approval was giving for fitting the equipment in Halifaxes, Wellington IIIs, Stirlings and soon Lancasters while on production lines. Dynatron received an order for 200 sets all to be ready by 30 November 1941 and 300 were expected to be built by Cossor by 31 December. Operational launch – set for 1 January 1942 – was postponed to 1 February, and the target number of squadrons using *Gee* cut from twenty to ten because production was slower than anticipated. On 14 December 1941 the TR 1335 Development Unit formed, and re-established itself as 1418 Flight on 5 January 1942. At Tempsford and Gransden Lodge they investigated *Gee* operational techniques. Training navigators of Nos 7, 9, 44, 57, 75, 76, 101, 115 and 218 Squadrons to use *Gee* had commenced on 17 December 1941.

Gee was introduced in February 1942 although it was to be many months before all operational bombers carried it. Two tests *(Crackers I and II)* assessed its likely effectiveness, the first using the Isle of Man on 13/14 February 1942, as 'target' showing ground station operation to be far from satisfactory. The second, on 19/20th February using Brynkir railway station in North Wales as target, was more successful and two days later a general directive authorised operational use of *Gee*. On 25 February nine squadrons were told to stand by for operations.

Very extensive operational changes were initiated during the trials. Every aircraft in a small raid-leading element would carry six flares, each to burn for four minutes. Relying upon *Gee* they would drop marker flares for the following Main Force. Each in the lead element would then make five back-up passes over the A/P releasing a flare every time to maintain marking. It was already clear that *Gee* was incapable of leading aircraft to a very precise target, and that many bombs would still fall two or three miles away. Brilliant dazzle from the flares in use resulted in the introduction of 'hooded flares.'

To be effective, attacks needed to be concentrated in time and space, with 100 aircraft over a target within an hour being something to try for. An idea also being pursued was having a large concentrated group of bombers delivering a high proportion of incendiaries – which the Stirling was well able to do – within a brief period. A belt of fighter control stations stretched through Denmark then along the coast to the Netherlands before following the frontier of Germany. Each station controlled a fighter in a small 'box' and only one bomber could be intercepted at one time. Breaking through the belts would obviously be done easier en masse.

The habit of seeking the target would be replaced by one *Gee*-assisted bombing run over the flare-lit area and possibly directed mainly against Ruhr targets because *Gee* range was limited to 350–400 miles. Stirlings carried a good load during short-range operations, although vulnerability due to the low ceiling remained.

Renault's Billancourt factory near Paris was chosen for a *Gee* trial on 3 March 1942, twenty-eight Stirlings being in the force. The moon was full, the night clear, defences weak. Bombing of the factory on an island in the river Seine was carried out from a low level, Stirling contribution being introduced by 218 Squadron which had received its first example on 16 December 1941. For one crew with Fg Off Allen as captain the Billancourt raid ended horrendously for, as N3720 touched down, two 1,000lb bombs still aboard exploded and the aircraft burst into flames. Two of the crew died, the flight engineer was seriously injured and the others clearly had a miraculous escape.

No XV Squadron attacked at between 2,000ft and 2,500ft and claimed that every bomb hit the factory. No 7 Squadron dropped 100 x 1,000lb bombs scoring hits on a power station and gasometer. High explosive bombs were used because machinery was particularly susceptible to blast damage.

A high average load of 10,611lb was dropped by each of the twenty-seven Stirlings attacking and damaging the power house, assembly shops and press shops. Of 235 aircraft which set forth, 222 attacked, among them 18 Halifaxes (which dropped 4 x 4,000lb HCs and 120 x 1,000lb HEs), 25 Manchesters and 105 Wellingtons. Among the latter's' loads were 28 x 4,000lb bombs, which had to be released between 1,200ft and 4,000ft to prevent them from breaking up as they fell.

The attack lasted for a little over an hour for *Gee* was not yet ready. Wellingtons comprising the marker force of 3 Group were divided into a flares-only contingent of about twenty aircraft, a dozen carrying bombs as well as flares and an incendiary force of about fifty operating in rudimentary 'pathfinder' style. Later, incendiaries mixed among HEs stoked the fires, creating more. About half of the factory buildings and over 2,000 lorries were destroyed, but there were heavy casualties among French civilians living nearby.

Bomber Command's diverse equipment complicated its effort, the assortment used being:

1 Group: 18/19 Wellington 1c, 9/10 Wellington III, 5/5 Wellington IV, one Type 423 Wellington
3 Group: 24/25 Wellington 1c, 8/8 Wellington III, 5/5 Wellington Type 423, 27/29 Stirlings
4 Group: 21/23 Wellington 1c, 14/16 Wellington II, 18/20 Halifaxes (average load 7,555lb)
5 Group: 47/48 Hampden, 25/26 Manchester (average load 5,280lb)
Average Wellington load was about 3,600lb.

Stirling participants were:

7 Sqn: W7466-B, N3708-E, N3709-K, W7471-J, N3710-M, R9297-P, N3706-S, W7468-W and W7501-Z
XV Sqn: N3699-C, N3673-D, N6065-G, R9303-P, N6094-R and N3674-T
149 Sqn: W7452-A, R9296-D, N62103-E, N3682-F, R9295-G, N6127-N, W7460-O, N6122-Q and N6068-T
218 Sqn: N3720-B, W7473-F, W7469-M and N3710-Y

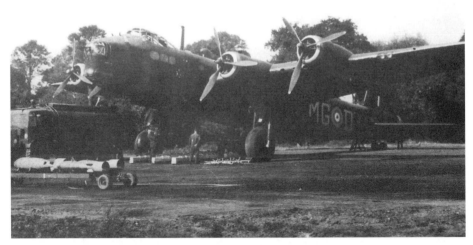

Loading incendiary bomb containers aboard 'D' of 7 Squadron, summer 1941.

Much satisfied, Essen – a major target area – was similarly attacked on **8/9 March 1942** by 211/230 aircraft, including sixty-three flare dropping and fire raising Wellingtons of 3 Group. Participating in the first larger scale Stirling raid were 22/27 of them which dropped mixed loads including 13,500 x 4lb and 48 x 250lb incendiaries, the latter being used for the first time. Six Manchesters added another 21 x 250lb fire bombs, and 10/10 Halifaxes brought along high explosives. Photographs showed that, although aircraft passed close to the primary target, damage was mainly 600 yards south of the Krupps factory.

A repeat raid took place next night when Stirling loads averaged 7,865lb. Nos 7 and 218 Squadrons carried mainly incendiaries leaving 149 Squadron to deliver HEs. Haze, considerable cloud and a lot of smoke led to the bombing drifting onto Hamborn and other nearby town. That proved fortuitous because part of the Thyssen Steel Works was damaged and some sections gutted while less important adjacent factories and dwellings suffered worse. Stirlings delivered 15.7 tons of HE, 45 x 250lb incendiaries and 8,100 x 4lb incendiaries.

'East India III' R9295 QJ-G which joined 149 Squadron in February 1942 and crashed at Holywell Row on 11 March. All aboard died.

The next night, Bomber Command tried a third time for Krupps only to find, as so often, that cloud and mist were protecting it. For 149 Squadron it was a bad night, N6126-U 'Uncle' failing to return and R9295, unable to lower its undercarriage, crashing at Holywell Row, just short of Mildenhall. Although a smaller force was deployed, it was a highly portentous and historic night, for included were two Lancasters, the first to participate in a Main Force operation against Germany, during which they unloaded 2,520 x 4lb incendiaries.

A sixth and accurate attack in the trial period came on **13/14th**. Cologne was the target, the TR 1335 guided force running in from the East with the leaders releasing flares on *Gee* fixes. Fire raisers bombed visually on the eastern side of the city, or on a blind fix if the river could not be seen. Of the thirteen Stirlings operating (average load 6,630lb), ten attacked Cologne while 9/11 Halifaxes (6,424lb) unloaded 10 x 250lb and 13,590 x 4lb incendiaries. A lone Lancaster added a 1,260 x 4lb load. PRU photographs confirmed serious damage in Cologne/Nippes, at Kalk Chemische Fabrik, in the large Cologne/Kalk marshalling yard and some 1,000 yards west of the cathedral. *Gee* had improved navigation accuracy and been effectively exploited.

Heavy bomber effectiveness over the next two years was currently being reviewed. Good reserve performance at 16,000ft to 17,000ft was needed, along with engines suitable for operations around 22,000ft. Only the Lancaster – yet to prove itself – was to achieve that. The Air Staff felt that while little could be done to improve the too-specialised Stirling, and that a replacement was desirable, careful operating techniques might improve its performance and make it more suitable for general employment. Current practice was for Stirlings to climb out on weak mixture only and be unable to get above 16,000ft. Would it be better to climb to operating altitude at full power, then switch to cruising at 16,000ft, it was asked? Only by fitting Hercules Mk VIs, rated at 17,000ft, did improvement seem likely. Four-bladed propellers which might have improved climb produced too high a weight penalty.

Further investigations revealed the 16,000ft ceiling was not simply due to weak mixture climb, so HQ Bomber Command recommended that climb remain in weak mixture and an MS gear change to FS in rich mix when boost had fallen to -1lb. This avoided a painfully slow weak mix climb. Service ceiling of the Hercules Mk XI-engined aircraft at starting weight 70,000lb was confirmed by A&AEE as 16,500ft, the weight by then having fallen to 67,500lb. More use of rich mixture still resulted in slow climb and high fuel consumption. Recommended altitude on the outward runs was ordered not to exceed 16,000ft, gradually reached. A slower outward cruising speed than Command wished for was recommended.

On **25/26 March** came the next major raid, 7 Squadron despatching eight Stirlings to Essen out of the twenty-six operating (average load 5,626lb). Sqn Ldr Legh-Smith and crew, unsure of their position during return, ran out of fuel and prepared to bale out over North Wales. One pulled his 'chute too soon and, as it billowed in the fuselage, Legh-Smith ditched N6074 off Barmouth after four others of the crew had satisfactorily jumped. From the incident useful information about Stirling ditching became available.

A most effective March raid came when incendiaries were sown over the highly combustible old Hanseatic port of Lübeck. Of 257 bombers operating on **28/29 March**, 234 had it as their primary target, 186 claiming to attack on a narrow front in a tight pack. Much of Lübeck's timber was left burning after Bomber Command's most effective raid yet for the marker force performed well yet ironically the target lay beyond the range of *Gee*.

In bright moonlight XV Squadron dropped 250lb incendiaries for the first time, and enemy fighter response – very limited – located Plt Off N L Taylor's Stirling over Heligoland. The intercepting Ju 88 was claimed as shot down. Huge fires were burning by the time 218 Squadron arrived, Flt Lt Humphries pressing home his attack even though W7507 had been shot about by a fighter over the Kiel Canal. First shots hit his starboard wing, then the fuselage was peppered and a shell which passed through the cabin Perspex exploded on the armour plate just behind the pilot's head. Rear and mid-upper turrets were put out of action, the rear gunner was wounded and finally the Stirling was forced down to 200ft. Only after a running fight was the fighter shaken off, the target bombed, and a miraculous flapless landing made.

Bomber Command's Tactics Report/ORS summarised the Lübeck raid thus:

	Fighters attacking	Enemy aircraft seen	Other aircraft seen	Failed to return
1 Group				
15/16 Wellington II	–	2	3	1
14/15 Wellington IV	2	–	–	2
17/ Wellington Ic	2	1	1	1
3 Group				
49/57 Wellington III	5	–	12	3
17/20 Wellington Ic	4	1	2	–
24/26 Stirling	2	–	3	3
4 Group				
14/17 Wellington II	1	1	2	–
5 Group				
36/41 Hampden	–	1	–	1
20/21 Manchester	2	1	–	1

Average loads carried (attack levels in brackets) were:

Wellington 1c: 2,160lb (15,000ft)
Wellington III flare force: 3,043lb (12,500ft)
Hampden: 1,961lb (6,500ft)
Manchester: 5,500lb (9,000ft)
Stirling: 5,828lb (14,000ft)

Stirlings despatched for the raid were:

7 Sqn: N3679, N3706, N3710, R9300, R9305 (FTR), W7466 (FTR), W7468, W7470, W7471, W7501 (FTR)
XV Sqn: N3669, N6065, N6076, R9304, W7504, W7505
149 Sqn: N6068
218 Sqn: N3721, N3725, N6070, W7473, W7475, W7502, W7503, W7506, W7507

April's operations began on the **2nd** with 8/10 Stirlings participating in a raid on Ford Motors Matford/Poissy works. Then on the **5th**, 22/29 – the largest number yet despatched to one target – attacked the centre of Cologne releasing 35 x 2,000lb HE and 305 x 250lb incendiaries while thirty-nine Wellingtons of 1 Group attempted to destroy the Humboldt Deutz Motoren Werke at Köln/Kalk. Two days later Gp Capt C D Adams, Station Commander at Oakington, with Gp Capt H R Graham, attended a luncheon in London given by Short's Directors. Graham reported that 7 Squadron had flown 525 sorties, dropped 1,600 tons of bombs, lost 29 aircraft and suffered 199 aircrew casualties. They had claimed thirty-four enemy aircraft, and had been awarded a DSO, twelve DFCs and twelve DFMs. The operational loss rate of 5.6 percent was about normal for the period.

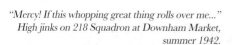
"Mercy! If this whopping great thing rolls over me..."
High jinks on 218 Squadron at Downham Market, summer 1942.

March 1942 and hardstandings remain in short supply at Oakington, with the main weight of the aircraft placed upon the perimeter track. Visible are N6075 MG-A, N3710 MG-M and W7517 MG-Z. The public railway passes close by! (Imperial War Museum)

High-explosive MC bombs heading for MG-Y N6073 in early 1942. (Imperial War Museum)

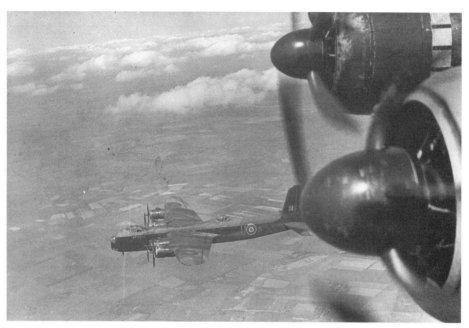

R9304-U joined 1651 Conversion Unit in April 1942 and was written off following a landing accident at Oakington on 28 February 1943.

On **8/9 April** another major Stirling participation was included. The 12/22 operating dropped 17,700 x 4lb and 185 x 250lb incendiaries as well as 22.3 tons of HE, and 18,000 incendiaries on Hamburg. They returned to Essen on **12/13** and three nights later Dortmund was raided and again the following night. The most important raids of the month came on **23/24, 24/25** and **25/26 April** when punishing onslaughts in Lübeck style overtook Rostock, home of Ernst Heinkel GmbH, and deeply disturbed the Nazi hierarchy.

The first of those saw a record number of Stirlings despatched, 28/31 being within the 143 aircraft operating. Only three bombers failed to return. The weather was fine, some attackers unloading from as low as 3,000ft. By the end of the raid huge fires were raging.

Sgt Runciman, his aircraft engaged by a night fighter near the target, jettisoned his 4 x 2,000lb bombs and, doubtful of the state of his aircraft's undercarriage, ordered the crew to bale out. Four did so before Runciman landed safely at Newmarket. One who baled out

W7505 LS-V following its crash at Alconbury when landing back from Rostock on 26 April 1942.

called at a farmhouse requesting use of a telephone to contact Oakington. Somewhat reluctantly the occupant agreed, then demanded 2d for the call. Such generosity was richly rewarded when the airman generously donated a florin to the helpful farmer. XV Squadron's Wg Cdr Macdonald in 'V-Victor' was also set upon by a fighter which so damaged his aircraft, already hit by flak, that a wheels-up landing at Alconbury resulted.

On **25/26** April, Bomber Command again called on Rostock. This time within the 128 raiders were nineteen Stirlings. Another six (N3721-C, N3722-E, W7506-K, W7469-N, R9313-Q and W7521-U of 218 Squadron), carried out the type of long-range operation for which the Stirling had originally been intended by heading for Pilsen's Skoda arms works.

Aboard one was Sgt A H Hotchkiss who recalls that:

> The raid was to be carried out with the help of the Czech Underground movement which was to light a beacon fire near the Skoda works. I was flying in N3722, and as we reached Pilsen we could see the fire burning, so dropped our bombs. We were the only crew to reach Pilsen. The Underground fighters began their planned sabotage, but the Germans soon caught and executed some, if not all, of them.
>
> Skoda of Pilsen was the target for a repeat operation on **4 May**. Opposition was fierce, but we bombed a power house. Two crews attacked 'last resort' targets at Mannheim and Mainz. Only two crews attacked Pilsen, and one other was lost. This time I was flying in W7469, captain Sqn Ldr Oldroyd. Our aircraft was shot up over the target after having been held by searchlights. Over Belgium on the way home as dawn broke, a Ju 88 located us near Brussels. Oldroyd began to weave, flying lower for protection, with the Ju 88 on our tail. The engagement came to a peak with the Stirling tightly circling a village church until the German fighter broke off combat. The Stirling's fine manoeuvrability saved us. The fighter's fire damaged our oil tanks and port undercarriage, and as fuel was running low – for the tanks had been punctured – we forced landed at Manston.

The previous Pilsen raid cost '218' W7506-K, captained by Plt Off Millichamp, which came down at Hugelsheim, Germany.

A late 1941 trainee crew at 1651 CU dwarfed by a Stirling. Sgt A Hotchkiss is third from the right.

April had been a busy month, Stirling squadrons operating on twenty nights and despatching 383 sorties. No 214 Sqn had joined them, but increased Stirling operational activity inevitably needed backing from the special repair organisation with unserviceability on Stirling squadrons remaining high. Marham had eight aircraft damaged in four months, Mildenhall fifteen in five, Wyton thirty-five in one year and Oakington thirty-eight in the same period. Most of the trouble concerned main and tail undercarriages – along with flak damage beyond unit capacity to repair.

Sebro, the Short Brothers Repair Organisation, was now fully established. Early in 1941 Short's had fortunately taken space in cold, draughty rooms at Trinity College Great Court, Cambridge. A factory site was obtained by Madingley Road just outside Cambridge and near the present Veterinary School. There metal T2 hangars were erected, some being joined which resulted in long halls where wings and fuselages could be repaired. Under Hugh Gordon as General Manager, a skilled work force numbering almost 5,000 men and women was assembled but with difficulty. Workers came from Rochester and other parts of the country for Sebro had to compete with Marshall and Pye Radio in the small local labour pool. Expansion meant employing people with neither factory experience nor knowledge of aircraft construction and who needed training at a critical time. One was the late Mr S Phillips. Preferring to serve in the Forces, he was instead drafted to Sebro of which he had never heard. Involved in the transport service of a local store, he soon found factory work alien to his way of life.

A big problem was assembling and maintaining sufficient stores items without which aircraft waited long for repair. Phillips remembers how he once travelled to London just for a small, vital pump. Sebro did not have the capability to manufacture major components, but was able to construct new items such as wing ribs. A lot of activity involved replacing flak damaged panels, and parts damaged in accidents. Large components came from the main factories.

Mid-war Stirling mass production at Austin's Longbridge works with EH883 nearest and EH884 ahead.

It would be unfair to declare Sebro inefficient. Once underway it proved very competent, but that took time, and in 1942 streamlining the organisation had a long way to go. What impressed local workers was the skill and devotion of Shorts personnel.

> They were magnificent, with very high standards. We relied upon their skill and guidance [recalled Mr Phillips]. If the aircraft were brought in categorised 'E' – write-off – all usable parts were removed and stored for future use. Fuselages retained their identity, whereas mainplanes, tail units and other parts were interchangeable. Aircraft often left with repaired wings taken from another machine. If a fuselage was struck off charge, the aircraft's identity was lost too. After repair the Stirlings were moved on 'Queen Marys' for re-erection at Bourn airfield and test flown from there.

Repair needs and too much unserviceability worked against the Stirling bomber going overseas. Engine cylinder temperatures were high when taxiing and taking off, meaning that heavy extra tropical cooling gear would have been essential, increasing the take-off run to about 1,680 yards. That, too, precluded tropical service.

By May criticism of Sebro was extensive. One RAF officer noted: "On my recent tour of squadrons I collected nothing but complaints". The truth was not as bad as imagined, as these 1941/42 figures indicate:

Date	Cumulative input to date	Output 9 weeks later
25.1.41	2	1
22.2.41	3	2
29.3.41	5	5
26.4.41	7	10
31.5.41	11	17
28.6.41	19	20
26.7.41	31	24
30.8.41	34	30
27.9.41	41	31
26.10.41	48	37
29.11.41	55	41
27.12.41	64	48
31.1.42	71	61

Additional repair work was undertaken by working parties at Stirling bases.

It was now that the expense of the Stirling force was raised, as a result of which a Parliamentary Select Committee studied specific items. One was the cost and value of the ventral turret. The PSC report of 23 April 1942 recalled that the ventral turret was seldom extended because of its adverse effect upon performance. Although in early 1941 ordered to be removed from all except a few aircraft held for daylight operations, instructions to finally remove all ventral turrets were not promulgated until Modification 492 approved in November 1942. Additional armour and self-sealing tank covers imposed considerable extra weight, as did beam and dorsal defence, altering the cg. Serious maintenance problems arose because spares were not interchangeable among early Stirlings, and minor undercarriage defects were forever being followed by others. Cures – complicated to effect – could only be effectively achieved by redesign, further delaying already slow production.

To assess the overall picture in the light of the PSC Report Bomber Command representatives visited each squadron in late April 1942 collecting information on aircraft states. No 218 reported an average serviceability among its eighteen aircraft of 75 percent after flying Stirlings for about two months, and achieved with only 75 percent of the servicing personnel establishment. This high level was due mainly to the use of new aircraft. Ice guards were breaking on air intakes, and turret hydraulics were troublesome as were undercarriage 'up' locks. Fuel contents gauges were inaccurate, there were Exactor throttle problems, flak damage repair was not readily available, ignition leads were burning out and there were primary pipe fractures.

Similar complaints were reported by other squadrons, No 149 with 95 percent servicing personnel on strength, reported only 50 percent serviceability and frequent posting of personnel. No XV Squadron with an average of fourteen aircraft against its IE/IR of eighteen and an average of 10 percent above the normal full strength of groundcrew establishment, was also managing only 50 percent serviceability. Many mechanical failures had involved the undercarriage and tailwheel chassis. No 7 Squadron, with 25 percent above prescribed groundcrew strength, managed 60 percent serviceability. Overall low rates were attributed to having so few aircraft in service. Wellington serviceability was around 75 to 80 percent. Persistent complaints surrounded the FN 20 tail turret especially after an untrue rumour attributed losses during the April 1942 Lancaster daylight raid on Augsburg to it.

N3752 OJ-O which crashed possibly due to altimeter trouble on 17/18 May 1942 at Risegaards Mark, Denmark. (J Vaupell Christensen)

Despite serviceability levels, the squadrons operated on twelve nights in May 1942, five times they laid mines and No 218 Squadron again tried to bomb Pilsen's Skoda works. The month's highlight came at the end when Bomber Command mounted one of its most famous raids. Details were signalled to stations in Bomber Command Operations Order No 148 of 26 May 1942, stating that:

It has been decided an attack of exceptional weight is to be made on an important German industrial city, to be known as 'Thousand Plan', and is to take place on **27/28** or **31 May/1 June** or a suitable night until **1–16 June**.

Coded names indicated that either Hamburg or Cologne would be targeted.

ACM Sir Arthur Harris, C-in-C Bomber Command – preparing to use the entire strength of Bomber Command including training units – had decided to unleash one thousand aircraft against one target. The greatest number so far employed in one attack had been 228, while the average available front line strength was only 350. Thus, Bomber Command achieved in the closing days of May 1942 a state of readiness hitherto seemingly impossible and masterminded by the dynamic new commander.

The first fifteen minutes of the attack on the city centre would be carried out by *Gee*-equipped aircraft of 1 and 3 Groups, and the final fifteen minutes onslaught by the heavies of 4 and 5 Groups. OTU aircraft and others would form the interim bulk. Mixed bomb loads would include explosive headed 4lb incendiaries designed to improve penetration and discourage fire fighters. Fire bombs were to form two-thirds of the Stirlings' loads. Throughout Bomber Command feverish activity ensued amidst strict security difficult to maintain because OTU aircraft needed to set out from operational stations.

Thundery conditions and cloud over the Continent persisted and it was not until midday on **30 May** that the C-in-C give the go ahead for Operation Millennium. Weather at bomber bases seemed likely to remain good throughout the night but thundery conditions over Germany had not entirely cleared, although the Rhineland was forecast as likely to be clear.

At 1800 hrs the Operational State of the squadrons showed:

Stirling	Serviceable	Unserviceable
7	16	2
XV	14	2
101	–	–
149	10	6
214	14	1
218	15	1
Others types:		
Halifax		
6 squadrons at 16 + 2	105	7
Hampden		
408 Sqn (24 + 3)	20	0
420 Sqn (16 + 2)	15	1
Lancaster		
6 Squadrons at 16 + 2	71	8
Manchester		
2 Squadrons at 16 + 2	27	5
Wellington 1c		
None established	46	5
Wellington II		
12 Sqn (24 + 3)	30	1
305 Sqn (16 + 2)	16	6
Wellington III		
7 Squadrons at 16 + 2	115	4
Wellington IV		
3 Squadrons at 16 + 2	59	6

Notes:
Manchester: Nos 61, 83, 106, 408 and 420 Squadrons not established but held 17 serviceable and 9 unserviceable
Wellington II: No 158 Squadron non-established held 9 serviceable and 2 unserviceable
Wellington III: No 101 Squadron non-established held 12 serviceable and 1 unserviceable

Stirling stock in hand on 28 May 1942 was seventy on squadrons, thirty-eight in Conversion Units, twenty-eight variously under repair by contractors and nine under repair in works giving 153 in total.

Returns show 1,091 bombers as operating against Cologne on 30/31 May, 338 of them new heavies and Manchesters. The five Stirling squadrons despatched eighty aircraft and 1651 CU a further eight.

There was icing on route with cloud thinning over the Netherlands. Heading the Stirling contingent was Wg Cdr Macdonald (W7516) of XV Squadron who took off at 2234 hrs and was first over the city, closely followed by Sqn Ldr Gilmour in N3707. Arriving at about 0045 hrs, they found moonlight bathing the city's streets, the railways and the centre where Macdonald's crew placed 12 x 90 x 4lb incendiaries and 12 x 8 x 30lb incendiaries (the cluster loads prescribed for XV Squadron) which lit a beacon for those following.

Two of XV's contingent, Fg Off Phillips in W7536 and Flt Sgt McMilland, had Exactor trouble and turned back. Fighters attacked several XV Squadron aircraft, Sgt Melville's crew driving away a Bf 110. So numerous were the bombers that clearly the defences were, as forecast, overwhelmed.

No 7 Squadron, flying at between 12,000ft and 15,000ft, had alongside Stirlings of 101 Conversion Flight. Plans were for 101 Squadron to re-arm with Stirlings, but aircraft shortage was preventing it. Seven Oakington Stirlings carried loads of 4 x 2,000lb bombs and one 1,000lb GP, leaving the remainder to each take 2,160 x 4lb incendiaries with the overall load totalling 122,760lb. 'S-Sugar's' bombs had to be jettisoned in the Wash, and Sgt Templeman's R9324-X was attacked by a fighter during the second pass of which the crew jettisoned live their load 20 miles north-east of Antwerp. The rest of 7 Squadron attacked without loss.

No 149 Squadron's seventeen aircraft were plagued by engine troubles. Bombs from N6083 were jettisoned near Tilburg; N6079 and N6080 both returned early with engine trouble, and the crew of R9296 were forced to jettison their bombs when the aircraft entered a spiral dive as a result of slow climb. The dozen left attacked with 103,680lb of bombs.

No 214 Squadron's first Stirling sorties had been flown on 18 May when the Rosemary area was mined. Since then No 214 had bombed St. Nazaire, Mannheim and Gennevilliers. During the Cologne raid thirteen aircraft delivered 84,560lb of bombs.

A special honour befell 218 Squadron which carried AVM J E A Baldwin, AOC 3 Group, in R9313 'Q-Queenie' flown by Wg Cdr Hodder DFC. The AOC was able to observe an attack unfold, a rare experience for a senior officer. The squadron despatched nineteen aircraft which attacked from between 13,000ft and 17,000ft dropping 145,280lb of bombs. Sgt Davis and crew failed to return.

Participating in a raid for the first time was 1651 Conversion Unit, which despatched eight Stirlings one of which turned back a few minutes after take-off leaving the others to attack. W7465 shot up over the target landed at Coltishall with fuel remaining for only five minutes' flying.

The total weight of bombs dropped during the raid was 1,455 tons. According to German records 486 people were killed in Cologne and 55,027 injured. Some 59,100 were left homeless, 18,432 buildings were destroyed and 9,156 heavily damaged. Another 31,000 buildings received some damage. Of 12,000 fires, 2,500 were major. Missing were forty-three bombers – 3.8 percent of the force – and 116 were damaged of which 12 had to be written off. Two Stirlings failed to return and some were damaged by flak which accounted for the bulk of all losses. The Stirling loss rate of 2.5 percent was very low. Bomber Command's analysis of the loads dropped showed:

'SR-X' with ground personnel of 101 Conversion Flight, Oakington, bears traces of having been MG-W.
(J Shields)

Analysis of loads dropped during the Cologne raid

Group	Aircraft	HE (tons)	Incendiaries 30lb	4lb
1	154/181 Wellington	54	128	87,990
2	38/49 Blenheim	16.3	nil	nil
3	138/171 Wellington (includes 15 of			
	91 Group and 20 of 92 Group)	80.3	312	70,095
	71/88 Stirling	76.1	3,016	61,280
4	108/131 Halifax	138.7	25,236	82,370
	3/9 Wellington	1.8	48	1,080
	2/7 Wellington	nil	32	960
	16 Whitley			
5	31/34 Hampden	nil	–	11,160
	35/46 Manchester	nil	1,364	25,470
	60/73 Lancaster	119.5	112	42,270
91	171/194 Wellington (includes 27 in 91 Group)	31.5		–
	42,536			
	21/21 Whitley	9.4	–	6,980
92	29/40 Wellington (includes 20 in 3 Group)	2.2	–	14,760
	40/45 Hampden	5.6	–	14,310

The Bomber Command Tactics Report showed:

	Aircraft intercepted	Enemy aircraft seen	Other aircraft seen	Failed to return
1 Group				
23/24 Wellington 1c	1	–	–	1
32/36 Wellington II	3	1	1	–
16/17 Wellington III	–	–	1	–
62//69 Wellington IV	1	1	2	2
5/5 Wellington '423'	–	–	2	–
2/3 Whitley V	–	2	–	–
3 Group				
33/36 Wellington 1c	4	–	8	1
86/91 Wellington III	5	15	5	6
6/6 Wellington '423'	–	–	–	1
75/88 Stirling	3	2	14	2
4/4 Wellington 1a (FTCmd)	–	–	–	1
4 Group				
5/9 Wellington II	–	–	–	2
3/7 Whitley V	–	–	–	1
110/131 Halifax	4	1	12	3
5 Group				
31/34 Hampden	1	1	2	–
39/46 Manchester	–	2	1	4
68/73 Lancaster	2	2	2	1
91 Group				
21/21 Whitley V	–	–	–	–
172/194 Wellington 1c	3	5	4	7
with 1 Group:				
22/26 Wellington 1c	–	–	–	1
1/1 Wellington IV	–	–	–	–
with 3 Group:				
15/17 Wellington 1c	–	–	–	–
92 Group				
42/43 Wellington 1c	1	1	4	1
43/45 Hampden	–	–	3	1
with 3 Group:				
15/21 Wellington 1c	–	–	–	3
Intruder force:				
35/49 Blenheim IV	–	–	6	2

Periods of attacks by the heavies: Stirling (first) 0037 – 0204 hrs, Halifax 0100 – 0240 hrs, Lancaster 0134 – 0310 hrs

Average load/height of attack: Stirling 7,716lb (15,500ft), Halifax 6,724lb (13,500ft), Lancaster 6,504lb (14,000ft), Hampden 1,140lb, Manchester 4,373lb.

Extract from Bomber Command Form 'G' –
Aircraft and Crew Availability 1800 hrs 30 May 1942:

	Aircraft fit	Crews fit	Total aircraft establishment	Total crews	Aircraft with crews
1 Group					
Wellington	156	126	170	168	147
3 Group					
Wellington	119	93	140	133	109
Stirling	70	60	100	80	64
4 Group					
Halifax	97	92	140	143	93
5 Group					
Hampden	35	27	50	51	30
Manchester	21	16	60	54	21
Lancaster	50	47	100	80	42
Blenheim	38	34	60	68	38
Boston	47	–	60	82	47
Mosquito	–	8	20	8	–

Stirlings available in Bomber Command – 1800 hrs 30 May 1942:

Squadron	Serviceable	Unserviceable
7	16	2
XV	14	2
101+	–	–
149	10	6
214	14	1
218*	15	1

+ squadron in process of forming
* relates to 29 May, none for 30th held

The final analysis of the operation indicated that 919 crews had claimed to attack out of
1,092 despatched, later altered to 1,091. Total loads dropped amounted to 555.4 tons of
HE, 7,548 x 30lb and 461,961 x 4lb incendiaries, with forty-three missing aircraft
carrying a further 17.7 tons HE, 948 x 30lb and 19,430 x 4lb incendiaries for which no

MG-S N3706 formating upon another 7 Squadron aircraft, a manoeuvre easier in a Stirling than in many
aircraft. (Imperial War Museum)

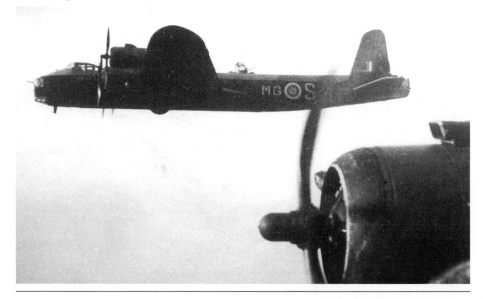

bombing analysis could be prepared. Abortive sorties included thirteen by Stirlings. Only two Stirlings failed to return, W7502 of 218 Squadron which crashed at Huppenbroich in Germany, and W7534 of 214 Squadron which crashed near Aachen, possibly after colliding with Wellington X3670 of 101 Squadron. The operation cost two other Stirlings, one being 218 Squadron's R9311 whose port mainwheel tyre was ruptured on take-off. The aircraft belly landed at Marham on return. The other was R9325 of 214 Squadron which, following an engine failure, swung off Stradishall's runway when landing. Stirlings had performed well for in addition to incendiaries they dropped 32 x 2,000lb, 35 x 1,000lb and 143 x 500lb HEs. Loads varied between squadrons, many of 7 Squadron aircraft each carrying 2,160 x 4lb incendiaries. 'C', 'L', 'P', 'S' and 'SR:W' of 7 Squadron all carried 4 x 2,000lb and 1 x 1,000lb HE loads. Of 149 Squadron's seventeen aircraft, all of which carried full incendiary loads, four turned back with engine trouble.

Stirlings officially listed as setting forth were:

7 Squadron: R9238-A, W7500-B, W7472-C, N3750-D, N3708-E, W7533-G, W7471-J, W7539-K, R9300-L, W7563-M, N3754-0, R9297-P, R9301-Q, N3706-S, W7470-U, W7529-W, R9324-X, W7517-Z and N6075-SR:W

XV Squadron: W7504-A, R9318-B, N3756-C, W7524-D, W7525-E, W7561-F, W7536-G, N3707-N, W7513-R, W7516-S, N3728-T and N3758-V

101 Conversion Flight: see N6075 above

149 Squadron: W7510-B, N6084-C, W7508-D N3723-E (engine trouble, bombs jettisoned near Tilburg), N6079-F (engine trouble, bombs jettisoned), N6080-G (engine trouble, bombs jettisoned near Nijmegen), N6081-H, N6083-N, R9300-0, N6082-Q, R9321-R, N3755-S, R9314-T, R9296-W (engine trouble, bombs jettisoned), W7455-X and R9299-Y

149 Conversion Flight: N3682, W7455, R9296 and R9299. One returned early

214 Squadron: DJ973-A, N3769-B aborted, R9322-C, R9323-D, R9325-F, R9326-G, W7537-H, W7526-M aborted, W7527-0, N3751-P, R9319-S and W7538-T

218 Squadron: DJ976-A, N3720-B, N3725-D, N3722-E, W7575-H, W7474-K, R9311-L, W7469-M, W7502-N (FTR), N3700-0, N6078-P, W7530-Q, W7503-R, DJ974-T, N3753-U, N6077-V and N6129-X

1651 Conversion Unit: 8 aircraft (7 attacked) including W7465 which crashed on landing at Coltishall.

N6101 of 1651 Conversion Unit participated from Waterbeach in the 1942 'Thousand Plan' raids. (Imperial War Museum)

For years Bomber Command provided the only means Britain had of hitting the Germans hard, of disturbing them in their lair and proving ever more convincingly that they were not as secure as their leaders had promised they would be. A 4,000lb blast bomb dropped anywhere, detonating very loudly, provided at the very least a noisy, highly unwelcome jolt. In post-war analyses of the bomber offensive one aspect repeatedly overlooked is Bomber Command's tremendous morale boost for the battered British public, many of whom derived much satisfaction from knowing that the enemy was suffering a dose of his own medicine. In the case of the Cologne raid, hundreds unusually stood in the streets of Cambridge expressing unbounded delight while watching an unusually large number of bombers setting forth, and stayed until the engine notes faded, which took almost an hour. Memorable dusk indeed, and coupled with a very surprising aspect for some were openly naming Cologne as the target for an 'impossible' thousand bombers! So much for the strict security.

With the bomber force not much scarred but precariously marshalled, Harris decided to strike again although the weather by **1/2 June** had deteriorated. Essen was chosen for there was the least likelihood of low cloud in that area. This time the 956 aircraft participating (347 from OTUs) carrying mixed HE and incendiary loads took off and found thin cloud covering the target. Tactics applied to the Cologne raid were repeated, seventy-seven Stirlings opening the show and including seven from 1651 Conversion Unit. Although *Gee* was in use, the cloudy conditions caused bombing to spread away from Essen lessening the raid's effectiveness. Defences were again saturated, thirty-one bombers (3.8 percent) failing to return including a Stirling.

No 7 Squadron's eighteen aircraft each carried either 2,160 x 4lb incendiaries or 4 x 2,000lb HC and 1 x 1,000lb GP bombs. For several of XV Squadron's twelve crews the night was very eventful. WO Cowlrick was unable to start his engines, Wg Cdr Macdonald had trouble with his bomb release gear and Sqn Ldr Gilmour unable to identify his target returned with his load. The other nine found widely scattered fires and bombed by the aid of Rhine pinpoints and *Gee*. On their return in R9318, Flt Sgt MacMillan's crew claimed a fighter, and over Antwerp Flt Lt Parkin's rear gunner was wounded by shrapnel, W7513 having to crash land at base. N3728 took 4 x 1,900lb and 1 x 500lb GP bombs; the rest of XV's contingent carrying incendiaries. Of 149 Squadron's fifteen aircraft, one had engine trouble leaving the remainder to deliver incendiaries.

Stirlings which participated were:

7 Squadron: W7500-B (FTR), W7472-C, N3750-D (FTR), W7533-G, W7471-J, R9300-L of 7 Con Flt, W7563-M, N3754-O, R9301-Q, N3706-S?, W7470-U, R9306-V, W7529-W, R9324-X, W7517-Z, N6075-SR:W and two uncertain, possibly MG-A and MG-K
XV Squadron: W7504-A, R9318-B, N3756-C, W7524-D, W7525-E, N3757-G, N3707-N, N3759-Q, W7513-R, N3728-T (FTR), W7518-U, N3758-V
149 Squadron: W7510-B, N6084-C, W7508-D, N3723-E, N6079-F, N6081-H, N6083-N, R9300-O, N6082-Q, R9321-R, N3755-S, R9314-T, R9299-Y and two of **149 Conversion Flight**: N3682, R9299
214 Squadron: N3769-B, R9322-C, R9323-D, R9325-F, R9326-G, W7537-H, W7526-M, W7527-O, N3751-P, R9319-S
218 Squadron: N3720-B, N3725-D, R9332-G, DJ976-H, W7474-K, W7469-M, N3700-O, N6078-P, W7530-Q, W7503-R, N3755-U, N6077-V, N6129-X, N6089-Y, W7464-Z.
1651 Conversion Unit: E, L, O, Q, V, X, Y. Total unit load 53,000lb.

Showing by Stirlings on the *Millennium* raids was encouraging, their crews drawing satisfaction from attacking above the height of the Wellingtons. 'My memory of the Cologne raid was peering through the aft escape hatch upon thousands of twinkling lights, the burning incendiaries,' recalls Sgt A H Hotchkiss. 'I felt safer in the Stirling than I had in 99 Squadron's Wellingtons because it had four engines. There were many of us who felt the same way.'

W7513 LS-R tipped onto its nose after touch down at Wyton early on 2 June 1942. Flak damage had been sustained over Antwerp. (J Helme)

Bombing analysis for the Essen raid showed that sixty-two of the seventy-seven Stirlings operating attacked the primary target dropping mixed loads and the second largest consignment of fire bombs, some 2,884 x 30lb and over 60,000 x 4lb incendiaries. Three Stirlings bombed secondaries, eleven aborted and N3750-D of 7 Squadron, flown by Fg Off N E Winch with Gp Capt Massey as second pilot, came down off the Dutch coast. The squadron claimed a Ju 88 over Ghent at 0310 hrs at 7,000ft and a Bf 110. W7513-R of XV Squadron captained by Flt Lt Parkins and damaged over Antwerp by AA fire crash landed at base.

After the two big raids, the Stirling stock on 2 June 1942 was: On squadrons – 69, In training formations – 33, In Class 2 ASUs – 4, In Class 3 ASUs – 4, In CRO hands – 48, For repair on site – 31, Under repair in works – 17, In CRD hands – 10.

On 6 June 1942 the Airframe and Modification Committee urgently met to discuss Modification 549, the improved undercarriage retraction gear with a redesigned gearbox in the fuselage. It affected component inter-changeability, for the old wing unit would not mate with the new. Shorts had stopped producing the earlier type, so the modification had to go ahead.

Main Force operations took place on thirteen nights of fair weather in June. Apart from the last 'Thousand Plan' Bremen operation of **25 June** when seventy-two Stirlings operated, the busiest nights were **5/6th**, when Essen was again raided and on **6/7th** Emden was the target and again bombed on **22/23rd**. Four Stirlings out of forty-four despatched failed to return from the Bremen raid on **29/30th**. On that night R9330-OJ:R crashed on take-off, S/7 Squadron ditched 50 miles off Cromer. The night of **5/6th** was chastening for 149 Squadron. Eight of their aircraft bombed Essen, two others did not return, and Flt Sgt Whitney was forced into the sea off Belgium after colliding with a Wellington which severed the Stirling's fuselage and killed the rear gunner. Next afternoon the remaining crew were rescued by an ASR launch.

Although '1,000-bomber' raids were impossible to sustain for long, the third involved 1,077 aircraft of which eventually 1,006 took off including 272 from various training units, 102 aircraft of Coastal Command and 71 intruders of 2 Group to suppress night-fighter activity. A cloud layer topping 5,000ft made target identity difficult and only 742 aircraft were credited with attacking the P/T. This included 40/69 Stirlings which dropped high explosive bombs including 2,000lb HCs and some 60,000 incendiaries. Alternatives attacked were Bremerhaven, Vegesack and Wilhelmshaven. Stirling abortive sorties totalled sixteen and three aircraft failed to return.

Lead Stirlings bombed aided by *Gee*, and the Focke-Wulf works were damaged. A Bf 110 poured shots into N6079 of 149 Squadron over the sea, and its 1,800 x 4lb incendiaries were jettisoned. Throughout the engagement great coolness was shown by Sgt J Barrett, the rear gunner, who had to cope with faulty guns. Enemy fire stopped the port outer engine, and despite damaged flaps and ailerons the Stirling still brought the crew home. Stirlings were outnumbered by the 348 Wellingtons attacking, and by 124 Halifaxes and 96 Lancasters.

The Stirlings operating were:

N7 Squadron: N3701, N3708, N3754, N3764, N3765, R9297, R9301, R9321, R9328, W7470, W7529, W7533, W7539?, W7563, and two from **101 Conversion Flight** N6039-SR:Z and N6075-SR:W

XV Squadron: N3756, N3757, N3758, N3759, R93 8, R9351, R9353, W7504, W7516, W7518, W7524, W7525, W7561

149 Squadron: N3723, N3755, N6079, N6082, R9161, R9329, R9330, R9334, BF310, BF311

214 Squadron: N3751, N3766, N3769, R9323, R9335, R9356, W7526, W7532, W7538, W7567, DJ975

218 Squadron: N3718, N3720, N3721, N3763, N6077, N6089, R9332, R9333, R9354, R9357, W7503 (FTR), W7575, DJ974

On **27/28 June 1942** there came to 214 Squadron one of the most memorable Stirling sorties of the war. Nine aircraft set out from Stradishall to bomb Bremen, one of them N3751 P-Peter. Over the target flak hit the starboard outer engine causing rough running then about halfway across Holland during the homeward run a twin-engined night fighter attacked from the cloud below the Stirling killing the rear gunner, Sgt Sewell, set fire to the to the starboard outer engine and wrecked the radio compartment. The wireless operator, Sgt Wiley, was wounded in the arm. Now the crew had no radio intercommunication system.

Sgt Frank Griggs recalls:

> I had been taking normal weaving action above the cloud layer and now put the Stirling into a steep spiral corkscrew. Initially this brought the attacking night fighter very close, enabling the mid-upper gunner, Flt Sgt Waddicar, to bring effective fire to bear. I continued the spiral corkscrew through the shallow cloud layers, occasionally glimpsing a twin-engined aircraft, either a Ju 88 or Bf 110, also spiralling down. During this time I operated the fire extinguisher on the starboard engine and feathered its propeller. At about 7,000ft another twin-engined night fighter attacked and scored hits on the Stirling with its cannon, causing the propeller on the starboard inner engine to fly off, luckily ahead of the aircraft. A gun mount in the mid-upper turret was damaged but the gunner managed to cope with this. As the Stirling levelled out at about 500ft, the mid-upper gunner sighted an explosion on the ground, which he attributed to the first night fighter to attack.

N3751 continued on its way home with the navigator, Sgt O'Hara, standing beside the pilot and acting as the lynchpin to co-ordinate crew action. On occasions he was heard to yell to the pilot "Bloody close!" when enemy fire was accurate, and guided Frank Griggs between flak positions and on to the Dutch coast.

Sgt T Prosser, the flight engineer, carried out orders to feed the good engines on the port side from the tanks in the starboard wing, and acted as runner to check the other crew members. He was unable to operate the rear turret emergency entry controls from inside the fuselage and could not get to the rear gunner. Subsequently it was found that the tail gunner had been killed instantly, most likely from the initial burst of fire from below.

Although the navigator had led them to evade the main flak positions the mid-upper gunner replied to some AA fire. With two engines out on the starboard side the aircraft was not very manoeuvrable and the pilot kept it at about 500ft. After crossing the Dutch coast the engineer gave the wireless operator morphine and did his best to bandage his smashed arm. He also bandaged the thumb of Sgt Watson, the front gunner.

The first signs of daybreak were visible when about 20 miles out to sea two Bf 109s in loose formation appeared on the starboard beam. They flew ahead of the Stirling, then turned for a frontal attack, flying loose line astern.

Griggs intended to try to ram the leading Bf 109 as it commenced firing so Sgt O'Hara grabbed the front gunner and pushed him into the front turret yelling at him to "fire the guns!" Half in and half out of his turret the gunner fired his guns now fixed and forward firing. The leading Bf 109 flew into the hail of fire, disappeared under the Stirling and hit the sea. His No 2 pulled up above the Stirling providing an easy target for the mid-upper gunner. It, too, was also soon in the sea.

As the Stirling continued homewards there came yet another Bf 109 flying above and behind and which opened fire well out of range. The mid-upper gunner fired a long burst at this aircraft which broke off the attack and was not seen again. In evading this assault Sgt Griggs flew so low that "the tail end of the Stirling's fuselage kissed the sea".

The rest of the trip was relatively uneventful until near Stradishall where Sgt Griggs tried a straight-in approach with the wheels down and

Sgt Frank Griggs points to damage inflicted upon kangaroo-decorated N3751 'P-Peter'. With him are (left) Sgts Waddicar, Watson and P O'Hara. (P O'Hara)

The port side of N3751 relatively unscathed after its crash. (P. O'Hara)

In the crash most of N3751's starboard wing was wrenched off. (P. O'Hara)

quickly discovered that he could not control the aircraft. To gain height and to avoid crashing he re-started the starboard outer engine, then had another go at landing wheels down. All looked good until the starboard outer engine caught fire again on the approach so Griggs cut its fuel supply and feathered the propeller. Back to two engines on one side, and with wheels down, control problems arose again which led to the aircraft touching down off the runway, running off the airfield and tearing off its wheels in a ditch and coming to rest in a wheat field. All the crew were evacuated including the dead rear gunner. Thus ended the life of P-Peter, acknowledged as the squadron's best aircraft.

Throughout July, activity remained high with operations on fifteen nights. A *Shaker* on Wilhelmshaven on **8 July** included 113 aircraft of 3 Group but only 33/34 were Stirlings. During the month 3 Group received some FN 64 belly turrets for aircraft delivered with provision for it, but fitment problems were many and the plan was abandoned. Modifications were applied to prevent FN 20 jamming during rapid rotation.

Unusual operations were about to commence: dusk raids by heavy bombers on U-boat building yards along the coast of north-west German and by the Baltic. An attempt

Troublesome tailwheel doors on HA-U. (Gp Capt O A Morris)

by Lancasters to bomb Danzig was spoilt by thunderstorms. On **16 July** Stirlings were used in operation *Pandemonium* their target the Lubecker Flenderwerke AG at Herrenwyk, 4.5 miles north-east of Lübeck and sited by the river Trave, where 500-ton U-boats and associated floating docks were built. Initial plans called for thirty Stirlings, but twenty-one eventually set forth each loaded with 2,100gal of fuel and 6 x 1,000lb GPs. Experienced crews chosen from all six squadrons to fly in lose vics of three until 7°E then, if cloud cover was 8/10, they would proceed individually.

Take-off came just before 1900 hrs allowing a daylight crossing of the North Sea and Denmark, 10/10 cloud at 6,000ft giving good cover. Visibility was fair at the target, but the attack was far from successful. Sgt D R Barrett in W7524 of XV Squadron succumbed to heavy flak five miles south-east of Esbjerg. Fg Off King of XV Squadron ran out of cloud cover and aborted at Haddersley. 'H-Harry' of 214 Squadron broke cloud over Denmark and Sgt Flemming met intense flak which killed his front gunner.

Only seven Stirlings each carrying 6 x 1,000lb bombs finally attacked the ship yard, at between 600ft and 5,000ft. Three were of XV Squadron whose Flt Lt Barr and Plt Off Shoemaker bombed from 900ft and 500ft respectively. Flt Lt Hockley (OJ-O) and crew were the only ones from 149 Squadron to claim hits on submarine slips and reported fires in some of the sheds. An aircraft of 149 Squadron came home peppered by flak and

Stirlings of 218 Squadron thunder low across Downham Market whilst training for operation Pandemonium. (Gp Capt O A Morris)

the crew of W7425 of 218 Squadron which survived attacks by no less than five fighters bombed a 'last resort' target on Fynn Island.

Bomber Command's ORS analysis of the operation eventually concluded that between 2222 hrs and 2248 hrs the Stirling crews had aimed 48 x 1,000 pounders at the submarine slipways. During the attack heavy rain and searchlight dazzle created problems, not to mention the night fighters. Five crews scored hits in the target area, but only three bombs exploded on slipways and another thirty burst on wharves or in the dock area. Bombs from two Stirlings fell on Flensburg, but nine crews aborted and two Stirlings failed to return from the force which comprised:

> **7 Squadron**: N3764-J (bombs jettisoned), W7533-G and W7529-? (latter two bombed Flensburg)
> **XV Squadron**: W7504-A, W7525-E, R9351-R, W7518-U, N3758-V and W7524-D (FTR)
> **149 Squadron**: BF320- H, R9143-O and BF512-A (FTR)
> **214 Squadron**: BF318, R9141, R9358
> **218 Squadron**: BF319-C (bombs jettisoned), W7425-H (engaged by fighters), W7562-P (bombed a train at Graatsten), N3763-Q (Wg Cdr Hodder – bombs undershot), ?-F (bombed the edge of Luberdock) and W7562-R (Plt Off Sanderson – one bomb on slipway)

On **19 July** thirty-one Stirlings were prepared for another dusk attack, operation *Bedlam* aimed at the Stettiner Vulkan and Oderwerke U-boat yards. During preparations the operation was abruptly altered into a Main Force attack on shipyards at Vegesack by 33 Halifaxes, 26 Lancasters and 22/32 Stirlings which bombed through 10/10 cloud on ETA. Loads also fell at Norden, Bremerhaven, Pappenburg and Bremen. Subsequent operations were more conventional.

Duisburg, Germany's largest inland port, was attacked on **21/22** and on **25/26** July, when 252/313 aircraft attacked, including 37/48 Stirlings of which only one did not return . This time they released over 130 HE bombs and 18,000 incendiaries. Next night heavy damage and casualties were caused at Hamburg raided by 304/403 bombers of which 24/39 were Stirlings. That night 359.2 tons of HE fell on the city along with 1,504 x 30lb and 156,420 x 4lb incendiaries. Stirlings contributed 19,350 of the latter. Then on **28 July** the Stirling squadrons struck again during what turned into a disastrous night.

To maintain the offensive, OTUs in No 91 Group provided fifteen Whitleys and thirty-two Wellingtons and 92 Group nine Whitleys and thirty-five Wellingtons to participate

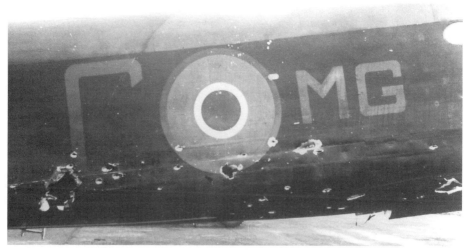

Flak damage like that of well-peppered 'MG-C' could put aircraft out of action for lengthy periods.

with front-line squadrons in operation *Derby*. Fielded were 302 bombers and a strong intruder force to maraud over night-fighter airfields. Eventually only 259 bombers set forth, 71 of them Stirlings. Over the sea dense cloud and severe weather led to a desperate recall signal being sent. Only 113 crews received and heeded it; the remainder proceeded among them twenty-seven Stirlings and fifty-eight 3 Group Wellingtons.

Included was Flt Lt E E Jones of XV Squadron flying in an aircraft captained by Sqn Ldr Walsh. He recalls it as:

> My most hazardous trip. We took off at 2230 hrs to attack the docks at Hamburg and battled through appalling weather for most of the way across the North Sea. We ran out of cloud and into a clear sky under bright moonlight. Visibility was excellent; we could see the target but no other aircraft. All was quiet and being ahead of time we circled a small wood north of the city, to await our briefed time on target, and to see if any other bombers were around to share the flak when we went in.
>
> Nothing happened so we headed in and, promptly coned by searchlights, ran the gauntlet of heavy and accurate flak. Twisting, turning and losing height to 3,000ft we roared over the city, dropped our bombs and turned out to sea. There were plenty of holes in the aircraft and both turrets were put out of action due to severed hydraulic lines. Fortunately, no fighters appeared and we made our way home still wondering where all the other aircraft had gone.

Others had reached Hamburg including eighteen Stirling crews and forty-two 3 Group Wellingtons all of which claimed to have attacked the target. Of the 91 Group contingent only one Wellington crew made such a claim. Possibly 61 of the 256 aircraft which had proceeded from the English coast dropped their bombs anywhere near Hamburg. From the largest number of Stirlings despatched since the Cologne '1,000 bomber' raid eleven failed to return. The night's total was twenty-five aircraft. For 3 Group the raid was catastrophic.

Trouble had struck from the very start when just after take-off Wellington X3668:SR-G of 101 Squadron collided with Stirling N6075:SR-W of 101 Conversion Flight, operating under 7 Squadron control and with 4 x 2,000lb HCs and a 1,000lb GP bomb aboard. After N6075's tailplane was ripped away only Flt Lt Butterfield's outstanding airmanship controlled the situation long enough to allow the crew to bale out. The Wellington crew was killed.

Stirlings of 1651 Conversion Unit had so far flown thirty-four sorties mainly dropping leaflets. On **28 July** nine bombers took off from Waterbeach but heavy icing a forced three to turn back and two others with mechanical troubles also aborted. Profound shock overtook the station when the other four did not return, this being one of the highest loss rates ever sustained by any Stirling unit.

Another *Derby* was mounted, on **31 July/1 August** and in better weather. This time Düsseldorf was the target for 470 bombers including for the first time over 100 Lancasters along with 40/61 Stirlings. Not for many months would Stirlings again operate in such strength. Absence of cloud and the good visibility were marred by slight haze and later by smoke rising from nearly 1,000 fires. Some 574.8 tons of HE, 8,780 x 30lb and 119,840 x 4lb incendiaries had been aimed at the city in the complex operation. Of the front-line aircraft 78 percent attacked and a high proportion, 71 percent, from the OTUs.

Throughout 1941 intensive development of a new bomb sight eventually led to the stabilised Mk XIV introduced to service in summer 1942. Slow production resulted in only sixty-five sights being built in July 1942 and fifty in August. Forecast output was for 60 in September, 90 in October, 120 thereafter building to 900 per month by June 1943 and 1,400 by December 1943. First to have the new sights were 35 and 405 Pathfinders squadrons using Halifaxes and which were joined in August by XV Squadron. September 1942 saw 149 Squadron getting them. No 7 followed suit in October and 218 in November 1942 with thirteen squadrons having the Mk XIV by the end of the year.

On 7 August 1942, another piece of equipment – the FN 50 turret – was approved for general use in Stirlings and as a replacement for the FN 7. Some elderly Stirlings repaired at Sebro emerged with FN 50s.

July and August thus saw tactical and technical change and, since the *Trinity* trials, considerable advances had also been made with *Oboe*, a superior derivative, intended for use in very-high-flying Wellington VIs which would offer maximum radio range. On 9 July 1942, the decision was changed, *Oboe* would be carried by Mosquito pathfinders of 109 Squadron and as soon as possible. Heavy bombers dropping special coloured markers, flares and incendiaries would backup their initial marking and drop high explosive and incendiary bombs to confuse the enemy as an attack opened.

As important as these new developments were, it was the introduction of a special marker force during August 1942 which brought to a close the phase of disappointment during which *Gee* failed to deliver the hoped for improvement in bombing accuracy. Well over half the bombs dropped at night still fell way off target. Additionally, the German practice of lighting decoy fires too readily lured bombers from their targets, something greater accuracy in target marking and the use of special coloured flares was to help defeat. After the fire raids on Lübeck and Rostock German night defences were strengthened, both in respect of night fighters and AA guns and in consequence of which the loss rate reached 5 percent on too many occasions.

Harris did not much like the idea of an élite band leading the main bomber force for it implied that many crews were inferior to such hand picked leaders. He maintained that every squadron needed skilled crews setting a good example to others. ACM Sir Charles Portal, CAS, came along with a compromise whereby one squadron in each bomber Group was posted to a station near Huntingdon. These crews would work in unison to carry out marking. To help with grouping the chosen squadrons XV Squadron moved to Bourn making way at Wyton for Lancasters of No 83 Squadron on loan from No 5 Group.

No 3 Group designated No 7, the senior Stirling squadron, for the marker force in which, because of the specialised nature of the task, crews would undertake longer tours. For the Stirling Group there was another change when in the autumn AVM Baldwin, their long serving highly respected and popular commander, retired. His place was taken by AVM The Hon Ralph A Cochrane. Facing him and the others managing the bomber offensive was the question of whether to rely upon *Gee* and the new pathfinder force and carry out attacks on precise targets, or concentrate upon area bombing at night.

Summary of Stirling Operations 1 January – 24 August 1942

Date	Target	No of Stirlings Used	HEs (lb) 2,000	1,900	1,000	500	250	Incendiaries (lb) 250	30	4	4X	FTR	Crews claiming attacked primary/ force despatched
JANUARY													
2/3	Brest	7/9	18AP			48 SAP						—	/36
3/4	Brest	1/4	4AP									—	1/18
5/6	Brest	2/2			5	15						—	/138
	Cherbourg	1/1			5	7						—	/16
10	Brest	3/4			18	16 SAP						—	/82
10/11	Wilhelmshaven	2/5			14	3						—	86/124
	Emden	1/1			5	5						—	23/29
	Leeuwarden afd	1			7	4						—	alt
11/12	Brest	3/3				54 SAP						—	24/26
14/15	Hamburg	1/7			5	9						—	49/95
	Emden	2/4			10	6						—	14/18
	NW Germany	4			28	12						—	alt
15/16	Hamburg	3/4			15	22						—	/48
17/18	Bremen	0/1										—	44/83
	Emden	0/2										—	14/24
	Soesterberg	0/1										—	/2
21/22	Bremen	0/1										—	24/55
	Emden	2/2										—	/16
22/23	Munster	2/5				14				960		—	35/47
	Dunkirk	2/2			14	40						—	/5
26/27	Brest	3/3	9AP			21 SAP						—	21/23
28	von *Tirpitz*	0/2										—	0/2
29/30	,,	0/5										—	0/16
31.1/1.2	Brest	0/2										—	54/72
FEBRUARY													
6/7	Brest area	3/3	5AP			45 SAP						—	23/60
10/11	Brest	5/8	5AP			21 SAP						—	14/20
12	Channel Dash	1/8				11 SAP						—	38/242
13/14	Cologne	2/4			14	18						—	25/85
14/15	Mannheim	0/2										—	64/98
	Le Havre	2/2				29						—	/4
17/18	Ruhr	3/3			21	16						—	4/13

Date	Target	No of Stirlings Used	Bombs dropped from Stirlings (no of each type)									FTR	Crews claiming attacked primary/force despatched
			HEs (lb)						Incendiaries (lb)				
			2,000	1,900	1,000	500	250	250	30	4	4X		
25/26	Kiel	1/6			7	6						—	/42
	Nickel												
27/28	Paris-Lsille	1/1											
	Wilhelmshaven guns	1/2				20						—	/33
MARCH													
3/4	Billancourt	27/29			157	252						—	/243
8/9	Essen	22/27		27	28	32	42	48		13,500	—	1	211/230
	alt-2												
9/10	Le Havre	1/1										—	/13
	Essen	10/21		5	18	19		45		8,100		1	145/187
10/11	Essen	8/12		15	12	15				5,130		1	/150
	Boulogne	0/1											/3
13/14	Cologne	10/13				12	32	112		9,270			/110
	Dunkirk	2/3											7
25/26	Essen	18/27			32			263		6,030		1	191
	St Nazaire	2/3											37
26/27	Essen	10/11		15				232				1	85/115
	Le Havre	1/1					15					1	8/8
28/29	Lübeck	24/26						547		2,160		3	186/234
APRIL													
2/3	Poissy	8/10		28	24	19						—	44/50
5/6	Cologne	22/29	35					305				—	188/223
	Le Havre	0/1											14/18
6/7	Essen	8/19	10	9			78					1	72/157
8/9	Hamburg	12/22	4	18	6			185		17,700			163/272
	Terschelling		4										alt
10/11	Essen	11/18	11			2	180			810			173/254
	Le Havre	2/3				32							32/34
12/13	Essen	21/27	36				216			1,890			67/251
	Le Havre	3/4				47							22/22
14/15	Dortmund	13/20	6				168			9,450		1	110/208
	Nickels Lille	1/1										—	
15/16	Dortmund	9/15	6	8	1	14	72		192	3,780		1	102/208
17/18	Hamburg	18/23	9		24	3		285				—	105/175
	Baltram alt	1/1											alt
	Le Havre	0/1			6							—	13/14

Date	Target	No of Stirlings Used	Bombs dropped from Stirlings (no of each type)									FTR	Crews claiming attacked primary/force despatched
			HEs (lb)						Incendiaries (lb)				
			2,000	1,900	1,000	500	250	250	30	4	4X		
22/23	Cologne	3/5	8	—	—	—	24	—	—	—	—	—	47/69
	Le Havre	2/2	—	—	—	35	—	—	—	—	—	—	19/23
23/24	Rostock	28/31	33	—	—	—	—	—	—	—	—	—	?/145
24/25	Rostock	10/11	8	—	—	—	192	450	—	—	—	—	111/125
	Dunkirk	2/2	—	—	—	32	—	—	—	—	—	—	24/47
25/26	Rostock	15/19	24	—	—	—	72	72	—	—	—	1	110/128
	Pilsen	5/6	—	—	30	—	—	—	—	—	—	1	5/6
	Dunkirk	3/4	—	—	—	52	—	—	—	—	—	—	21/32
26/27	Rostock	8/8	—	32	—	—	—	—	—	—	—	1	96/107
	Dunkirk	1/1	—	—	—	16	—	—	—	—	—	—	22/24
27/28	Cologne	15/19	*	—	—	—	—	—	—	16,200	—	—	63/92
28/29	Kiel	6/15	11	—	—	—	—	—	192	3,150	—	—	62/88
29/30	Geneevilliers	6/6	—	5	31	40	—	—	—	—	—	—	85/88

* bombing analysis not available; tonnage dropped 26.8

MAY

Date	Target	No of Stirlings Used	2,000	1,900	1,000	500	250	250	30	4	4X	FTR	Crews claiming attacked primary/force despatched
3/4	Hamburg	8/13	—	—	—	—	—	—	768	8,370	—	—	37/53
	St Nazaire	1/1	—	—	—	—	—	—	—	—	—	—	?/7
4/5	Stuttgart	7/14	—	—	—	—	—	—	—	12,330	—	1	49/?
	Pilsen	2/5	—	—	12	12	—	—	—	—	—	1	2/5
	Nantes	1/1	—	—	—	—	—	—	—	—	—	—	/4
	Nickels	1/1	—	—	—	—	—	—	—	—	—	—	/2
5/6	Stuttgart	12/17?	—	—	—	—	—	—	758	7,660	—	—	51/77?
	Nickels	1/1	—	—	—	—	—	—	—	—	—	—	10
6/7	Stuttgart	7/15	—	—	—	—	—	—	696	6,210	—	—	56/97
	Nantes	1/2	—	—	—	14	—	—	—	—	—	—	11/19
	Nickels	2/2	7/9	—	—	—	—	—	—	—	—	—	
7/8	St Nazaire	0/1	—	—	—	—	—	—	—	—	—	—	2/6
8/9	Warnemunde	26/27	—	—	164	94	—	—	—	—	—	1	127/184
17/18	Boulogne	1/1	—	—	—	18	—	—	—	—	—	—	1/1
	Nickels (Vicky)	1/1	—	—	—	—	—	—	—	—	—	—	1/1
19/20	Mannheim	23/31	—	—	—	87	—	—	192	41,400	—	4	154/197
	St Nazaire	6/8	—	—	—	24	—	—	—	—	—	—	28/65
29/30	Gennevilliers	7/9	—	13	25	—	—	—	—	—	—	1	65/125
	Cherbourg	2/12	—	—	—	32	—	—	—	—	—	—	/26
30/31	Cologne	71/88	32	—	35	14	—	—	3,016	61,280	—	2	919/1092

Date	Target	No of Stirlings Used	Bombs dropped from Stirlings (no of each type)									FTR	Crews claiming attacked primary/force despatched
			HEs (lb)						Incendiaries (lb)				
			2,000	1,900	1,000	500	250	250	30	4	4X		
JUNE													
1/2	Essen	62/77	28	4	28	135	–	–	2,884	60,440	–	1	729/957
2/3	Essen	14/21	–	–	–	–	–	–	480	27,540	–	2	195/215
3/4	Bremen	6/15	–	–	–	30	–	–	250	6,300	–	2	130/170
4/5	Dieppe	0/3	–	–	–	–	–	–	–	–	–	–	0/3
5/6	Essen	15/25	–	–	–	–	–	–	482	27,780	–	3	118/181
6/7	Emden	34/40	–	–	–	–	–	–	1,895	38,160	–	2	104/134
8/9	Essen	7/14	–	–	–	–	–	–	214	10,720	–	1	?/170
	Dieppe	6?	–	–	–	?	–	–	–	–	–	–	6?
10/11	Nickels	1/1	–	–	–	–	–	–	–	–	–	–	1
16/17	Nickels	1/1	–	–	–	–	–	–	–	–	–	–	?
	Essen		–	–	–	–	–	–	–	–	–	–	
17/18	(alt. Bonn, 2)	3/12	4	–	–	–	–	–	–	–	–	1	?/106
	Nickels	4/4	–	–	–	–	–	–	–	3,600	–	–	4
	St Nazaire	5/10	–	–	–	66	–	–	–	–	–	–	/16
	Nickels	2/2	–	–	–	–	–	–	–	–	–	–	
19/20	Emden	16/26	–	–	–	–	–	–	524	23,040	–	2	119/196
	Nickels	2/2	–	–	–	–	–	–	–	–	–	–	
20/21	Emden	13/21	–	–	–	–	–	–	384	22,140	–	2	93/116
21/22	Nickels	1/1	–	–	–	–	–	–	–	–	–	–	
22/23	Emden	31/36	8	–	–	18	–	–	1,288	41,490	–	1	185/225
	Nickels	2/2	–	–	–	–	–	–	–	–	–	–	
23/24	St Nazaire	0/4	–	–	–	71	–	–	–	–	–	–	7/14
24/25	St Nazaire	3/8	–	–	–	46	–	–	–	–	–	–	16/21
25/26	Bremen	40/69	12HC	–	5	–	–	–	968	58,950	–	2	742/1,006
	Nickels	2/2	–	–	–	–	–	–	–	–	–	–	
27/28	Bremen	21/26	–	–	–	16	–	–	–	–	–	1	118/144
28/29	St Nazaire	1/4	–	–	–	–	–	–	–	–	–	1	7/19
	Nickels	1/1	–	–	–	–	–	–	–	–	–	–	
29/30	Bremen	37/47	–	–	–	–	–	–	5,016	20,700	–	3	206/251
JULY													
2/3	Bremen	20/34	–	–	3	–	–	–	3,200	21,240	–	2	269/325
8/9	Wilhelmshaven	33/34	64	–	4	–	–	6**	384	25,170	–	–	241/290
13/14	Duisburg	9/9	20HC	–	12	13	–	–	–	3,960	–	–	161/194
16	Lübeck	8/21	–	–	48	–	–	–	–	–	–	2	8/21
19/20	Vegesack	22/31	–	–	81	16	–	–	45	19.710	–	–	81/99
	Nickels	1/1	–	–	–	–	–	–	–	–	–	–	

Date	Target	No of Stirlings Used	Bombs dropped from Stirlings (no of each type)									FTR	Crews claiming attacked primary/force despatched
			HEs (lb)						Incendiaries (lb)				
			2,000	1,900	1,000	500	250	250	30	4	4X		
21/22	Duisburg	35/36	56	12	25	39	—	—	1,568	13,860	—	—	250/291
23/24	Duisburg	32/39	64	4	32	27	—	—	992	11,610	—	2	186/215
25/26	Duisburg	37/48	42	16	45	30	—	—	1,568	16,200	—	1	253/313
26/27	Hamburg	24/39	6	—	2	2	—	—	1,024	19,350	—	2	304/403
28/29	Hamburg	18/71	8	—	12	3	—	—	64	17,830	—	9	67/256
29/30	Saarbrucken	23/24	17	4	10	10	—	—	1,536	15,120	—	2	238/287
31/1.8	Düsseldorf	40/61	34	12	35	87	—	—	1,276	18,000	—	—	470/636
** 50lb incendiaries													
AUGUST													
5/6	Essen	0/5	—	—	—	—	—	—	—	—	—	—	77/97
6/7	Duisburg	34/44	18	4	8	8	—	—	3,272	23,760	—	2	177/216
	Le Havre	0/1	—	—	—	—	—	—	—	—	—	—	/5
9/10	Osnabrück	30/40	78	25	47	22	—	—	480	38,280	—	—	166/192
	Le Havre	1/2	—	—	18	18	—	—	—	—	—	—	14/15
11/12	Mainz	25/28	12	19	18	18	—	—	1,184	16,800	—	1	?/154
12/13	Mainz	17/27	7	8	19	16	—	—	1,344	5,310	—	—	?/138
15/16	Düsseldorf	11/18	10	4	—	2	—	—	64	1,026	—	—	98/131
17/18	Osnabrück	25/29	18	8	18	6	—	—	1,392	23,590	—	1	112/128
18/19	Flensburg	14/16	—	12	—	15	—	—	192	12,870	—	1	100/127
24/25	Frankfurt	33/42	—	—	18	—	—	—	2,880	31,680	—	4	187/226

NB. The right hand column shows where known the number of aircraft attacking/number which took off to raid the listed target. In the case of missing aircraft point of unloading was often not known. In some cases the figures were later updated in the light of intelligence material. The numbers of weapons quoted are those known to have been released within the target zone. **These criteria apply to similar listings elsewhere within this volume.**

Chapter 10
Lighting the Way Ahead

Spring 1942 had seen the Stirlings committed to the more intensive night bombing campaign in which they played a leading role within the new marker force. Gone their role for specialised bombing ventures, they were now well and truly playing a major part in the main force night strategic bombing campaign.

While the pathfinder force assembled, operations continued, Stirlings being out on fifteen August nights although with some tempo reduction. Fine weather and short nights aided defenders as much as attackers, high flying bombers silhouetted against the lighter sky prompting some crews to opt for a low-level passage home. Thereby they became easier targets for AA fire.

On **6/7 August 1942**, 34/44 Stirlings were among 193/216 bombers which hurled 261.3 tons of HE, 556 x 30lb and 63,000 x 4lb fire bombs at Duisburg, aided by 576 flares. On **9/10th** 192 bombers, including 101 heavies, headed for Osnabrück, 30/40 Stirlings among them, and dropped 106.7 tons out of the total of 308.4 tons HE delivered. Two particularly damaging raids were made upon central Mainz, the first on **11/12th** and the second including 17/27 Stirlings on the following night, by the end of which 61.4 tons of HE had fallen on the city.

It was **17/18 August** when No 7 Squadron flew its final Main Force sorties, during the raid on Osnabrück. The change did not mean that the squadron's loads would be only flares and incendiaries, for mixed high-explosive loads were often carried. No immediate improvement in bombing accuracy came when the PFF formed, but it lit the way to future punishing accuracy. Expected jamming of *Gee* was first suspected on the night of **6/7 August 1942**,and confirmed during the Osnabrück raid of **9/10 August**. Existing techniques would still have to be exploited until more accurate marking came from *Oboe* and marker weapons.

W7612 HA-T of 218 Squadron after updating to have an FN 50A turret on dispersal at Downham Market.

PFF administered by HQ Bomber Command through HQ 3 Group at Exning, went into action on **18/19 August**, when thirty-one Pathfinders (ten Halifaxes, eight Wellingtons, seven Stirlings and six Lancasters) led in an attempt to halt U-boat production at Flensburg. Dark and hazy the night, and only sixteen markers managed between 2315 hrs and 2350 hrs to illuminate the target area assisting the 100/127 Main Force to attack, including 14/16 Stirlings. Accuracy was less than hoped.

On **24/25 August**, 226 bombers were dispatched to Frankfurt including forty-two Stirlings in Main Force and eleven among the thirty-seven Pathfinders. Three nights later 306 aircraft headed for Kassel, when the 33-strong Pathfinder force included 4/8 Stirlings to back up initial marking with 192 x 30lb incendiaries as well as 6 x 1,000lb and 44 x 250lb HEs. Bright moonlight much improved the PFF effectiveness while 27/40 Stirlings took part in more effective bombing, along with fifty-six Lancasters. Night fighters were active too, including those of III/NJG2 Twenthe, III/NJG4 Juvincourt and I/NJG2 from Bergen/Alkmaar, and six of the sixteen missing bombers are thought to have fallen to them. Five were Pathfinders, two were Main Force Stirlings.

Nuremberg and Saarbrucken were attacked on **28/29 August**, 159 bombers heading for the former. Included were thirty Pathfinders – 2/7 were Stirlings – and 16/27 Stirling bombers, only one of which took part in the 111-aircraft Saarbrucken diversion. Night fighters responded including those of I and III/NJG1 operating from Twenthe and Venlo, II and III/NJG2 from Gilze–Rijen and Leeuwarden and Juvincourt's II and III/NJG 4. Three Stirlings failed to return from Nuremberg.

Analysis showed that in the six months ending 30 September 1942, 3 Group had despatched 7,096 sorties – 2,637 by Stirlings – making it the most active Group in Bomber Command. The next highest total was 4,674, achieved by 5 Group increasingly operating the efficient Lancaster. The pathfinder Stirling squadron flew 65 sorties in September, compared with 110 by No 149, the 'top sortie' squadron in the Group that month. As regards strength, 3 Group held thirty-six Stirlings with another ten being in 7 Squadron. On 27 September the totals had fast risen to sixty-four and sixteen respectively.

N3725 HA-D which crashed near Stoke Ferry on 15 September 1942 returning from Wilhelmshaven. It is pictured, engine running, at Marham. Removing the long 'warning' tapes from the pitot tubes proved tedious. (Imperial War Museum)

September had opened with a concentrated attack on Saarbrucken, the thirty-six Stirlings taking part being from all five squadrons. Next night, twenty-five operated against Karlsruhe and on the **4th**, thirty-six against Bremen. The biggest night attacks, each including thirty-eight Stirlings, were directed at Frankfurt on the **6th**, Düsseldorf on the **10th** and by forty-three Stirlings against Bremen on the **13th**. Subsequent smaller scale night raids included one aimed at Munich by eighteen Stirlings on the **19th**.

The Düsseldorf raid of **9/10 September**, carried out by 360/476 aircraft, included Stirlings of 1651 Conversion Unit and aircraft of OTUs. For Fg Off J Trench and crew in W7564 'T-Tommy' of 7 Squadron, the night became unforgettable, the events being related here by Sgt I J Edwards the wireless operator:

> We had done the trip a few times before, and with some scorn it was called the 'Milk Run to Happy Valley', and to the target it had been easy. We were at about 14,000ft when we were coned by searchlights. Strategy was then for AA fire to fill the top of the cone, and it was very effective. The Stirling, though, was highly manoeuvrable, our skipper a very sound pilot. His normal method of escape was a stall turn, at which he was very expert. After quite a few this time, we came out at about 4,000ft, and were happy with our luck. The engineer, Sgt Mallett, soon stopped the joy with bad news of the oil pressure on the port inner.
>
> The next move was to feather the prop, but we found we had too little pressure for this, so it had to be allowed to windmill until the engine seized up and we lost the prop. We, like others, had lost a prop before and were not too worried. The whole operation would not take too long. As it had happened on my side, the engineer awaited my running commentary. The port prop would go up and over when metal melted and fell away. Once the red and white hot bearings started coming out it would go – and did. The snag in this case was that our prop had not conformed to pattern. The whole arc was slightly behind the outboard in the Stirling, and there was a little overlap. In going off it had fouled the outer prop. The next sensation was of someone out at the wing tip shaking it, and the order to 'bale out' was given.
>
> Before this came underway there was a loud crack to port. It was then quiet, and we could see the whole power plant had left the bulkhead; so it was a case of a very low ride home. We threw out all movable objects and were down to 150ft over the Dutch coast. I can remember a rowing boat tied to a jetty in a river mouth. When you looked from the pilot's seat through the bomb aimer's window and saw phosphorescent wave tops, you really were low. We had ditched all ammunition magazines. (The rear turret was served from large magazines forward of the door, and there was quite a lot of ammunition.)
>
> We were aiming for Martlesham Heath, and it was obvious we would have to do a wheels-up landing. We climbed to cross the coast almost touching a haystack with our starboard wingtip.
>
> The rest was very fast. The engineer, one of the best in the squadron, had worked the fuel to the last drop and his power timing was perfect. We almost got the middle of Weeley

BF382 withdrawn from 214 Squadron for equipment trials at A&AEE from October 1942 to November 1943.

village, but saw it before it was too late, and in a cloud of dust we hit the ground.

Then it was that real tragedy struck. Crash drill, which we had done many times, was perfect. The crew were aft of the mainspar, except the navigator, who was on the bed. The aft escape hatch and astrodome were off and everybody got out. Our captain and myself were knocked unconscious, but the navigator, Plt Off C L Selman, dragged the pilot clear. I came to and gave him a push up, and also had to disconnect the oxygen and R/T lines to his helmet. Then the three of us just sat on top of the cockpit glasshouse.

The fire started rather slowly, but was enough to make us jump off and land in some bushes. After that it was run, run! We didn't know that the others also thought it was a piece of cake and had gone back in, the rear gunner telling me afterwards that he went back for his peaked cap, the engineer for his tool kit and the bomb aimer for some coffee. Suddenly, the whole aircraft exploded. The rear gunner was blown out, badly burned, but the others were not so lucky. The front gunner, Sgt F A Thorln went in to try some rescue. The rear gunner, Plt Off W N Gledding, was pulled clear by the mid-upper gunner, Flt Sgt Jenner.

The Home Guard rounded us up and the 'local' opened up rather early that morning. Everyone was wonderful, giving us beds for the night. The rear gunner went off to Colchester Military Hospital, the other survivors to Oakington.

Officially the incident was recorded as "an outstanding example of courage and determination on the part of the captain and crew".

In gathering dusk 218 Squadron awaits operational take-off from Downham Market.

An unusual multi-target operation took place on **23/24 September**, twenty-four Stirling crews being briefed to attack the Bremer Vulkan Shipyard in Vegesack, while eighty-three Lancasters attended to the Dornier works and town of Wismar and sixteen Halifaxes the U-boat building yards at Flensburg. Whether all twenty-four Stirlings set out is uncertain, but twenty-one certainly operated, each taking two containers of incendiaries and maximum 1,000lb GP loads. As during *Pandemonium*, the route out was below 1,000ft to evade radar detection, followed by a climb at the coast, the bomb run and a fast, low return run. Only seven Stirlings reached the target due to thunderstorms and thick 7/10 cloud down to 150ft. Pin-pointing was therefore difficult and mostly alternative targets were bombed, including Wangeroog and Baltram.

During the eighteen months in which Stirlings had been operational plans for a shortened, simpler landing gear had been cast aside, likewise a twin-tail layout allowing dorsal and ventral twin-20mm cannon layouts. Complaints had steadily increased concerning the Stirling's overall performance amid claims that it was the only mainstay bomber to enter service in a form inferior to that which was contracted. Suggestions of deterioration in handling and performance brought a general investigation into overall effectiveness in summer 1942.

Stirlings in flight were whispering giants – except for noisy Wright Double-Cyclones in the Mk II, also identifiable by different shaped cowlings and exhaust stacks. Visible on N3657 (depicted in August 1941) are ventral turret foot wells and an SBA aerial.

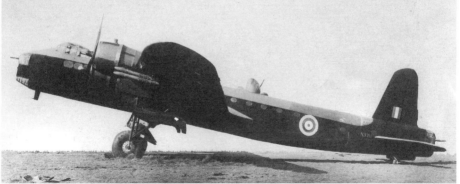

Flame damping exhaust stacks added to another Mk II, N3711, for A&AEE trials. Shorts later returned it to Mk I standard.

Main drawbacks were listed as its inability to fly high enough for operational safety, a tendency to fly at trim laterally, its low power/weight ratio when compared with other large bombers, and a low rate of climb when heavily loaded. Trim difficulties were encountered during contractor's testing when lightly loaded.

All was not bad. While the bomber did not possess the extremely long range/heavy bomb-carrying capacity originally envisaged, it was able to convey heavy loads of incendiaries during short/medium-range operations, and the Air Staff called it "the Ideal Ruhr Bomber", for which reason they stated that they were "content with its performance".

Summer 1941 saw the possibility of a re-engined variant, with the overall designation 'Stirling Mk II', given considerable attention. Radical re-design abandoned, support was given to fitting the American Wright Cyclone 2600 engine in mind since pre-war times for production of Stirlings in Canada. Engines of that type were now installed for trials in three British-built aircraft which became the real, ultimate Mk II flight trials of which showed them highly unsatisfactory. Indeed, in September 1942 CRD pointed out that the Mk II's ceiling was 2,000ft lower than that of a standard Mk I, and that range was less. Engine cooling problems were also experienced, and engine life was thought likely to be much shorter than that of Bristol engines. Flame damping was hard to achieve, and the Cyclones produced excessive cockpit noise.

CRD was not alone in his condemnation, Shorts wanting the Mk II abandoned on technical grounds. Cancellation followed in September 1942, leaving the Stirling I (Hercules XI) to continue in production until a new version, the Mk III, was ready. Later Hercules engines earmarked for lacklustre Armstrong Whitworth Albemarles were now to be diverted to Stirlings and replaced in that type with Cyclones.

The Hercules VI-engined Stirling III was eagerly awaited. Not only were its engines expected to confer the longed-for increased ceiling and generally improved high-attitude performance, it would feature mechanically operated engine and propeller controls in place of hated Exactors. Long in the development stage, CRD had in May 1942 complained about the slow Mk III development rate suggesting that it would be December 1942 before trials were completed. Meanwhile, what was the truth about the current Stirling I, and was it so very inferior to other bombers?

In June 1942 Sir Henry Tizard carried out an investigation. Construction appeared to be wasteful in man hours when compared with the Halifax and Lancaster, but condemnation based purely upon that aspect took no account of operational efficiency, which Tizard next considered. His research produced a very different picture of the Stirling from that so often presented, as this summary of his report illustrates:

Fuselage assembly of Stirling Is, turrets wells and full window arrangements clear.

Period reviewed – Night Raids, June 1941 to May 1942

Bomb tonnage delivered per missing aircraft:

	Stirling	Halifax	Manchester
Germany	71.3	51.2	33.8
Other targets	92.5	42.6	35.8

Bomb tonnage per aircraft missing or written off due to enemy action:

	Stirling	Halifax	Manchester
Germany	65.0	49.7	32.0
Other targets	82.9	41.0	34.2

Bomb tonnage per aircraft operationally written off to all causes:

	Stirling	Halifax	Manchester
Germany	49.1	38.1	28.8
Other targets	59.4	32.7	29.9

Time-expired LS-H in use for ground training at Halton.

Compared with its peers the Stirling can clearly be seen to have been, perhaps surprisingly, more effective! Write-offs due to enemy action were less with the Stirling than the Halifax, although the number of aircraft damaged was greater. That suggested the Stirling to be far more robust, as was always claimed. Stirling gunners shot down more enemy aircraft than those of Halifaxes, suggesting it was easier to intercept and attack than the Halifax. Stirling crews reported three times as many interceptions as Halifax crews, so it seemed possible that the shape of the Stirling rather than operating height made it easier to locate at night.

Tizard's contention was that there was no justification for fading out Stirling production, but that a case *could* be made for fading out the Halifax as soon as Lancaster production allowed. He considered that while the current Halifax had a markedly inferior operational performance when compared with the Stirling, there was absolutely no reason to think the same would be true of the Lancaster, a much later design.

Digestion of Tizard's somewhat unpopular conclusions took time. Indeed, it was not until 29 December 1942, that the Chief Executive of the Aircraft Supply Council provided MAP's response and fielded some preposterous ideas.

"The Stirling," he stated, "is uneconomical to produce, its elimination is desirable. It has some aerodynamic faults, but to stop production would mean a loss in bombing effort." Therefore, it was to be retained in production at Belfast and its development would continue. Swindon production source, linked with Rochester and also Austin Motors, should switch to building Lancasters. He accepted that the Halifax had been unsatisfactory, that it would never achieve a really acceptable performance, but that production could not be entirely switched to Lancasters because loss of so much bomber output would be damaging for Bomber Command. The Stirling, though, must partly go.

Accepting the value of a really heavy bomber, MAP then made an incredible proposal, the introduction of the American B-29 of which they had very little knowledge. If the Boeing B-29 proved satisfactory during trials, MAP officials proposed that licence production should start, initially at the English Electric Preston works, then at Rootes of Speke and eventually at Short & Harland and Vickers. The Lancaster would definitely be replaced by a new British 75-ton bomber. A MAP team had already left for the USA there to 'anglicise' the B-29 for UK production, while English Electric would form the parent company in Britain and have to establish a design team recruited from pre-war aircraft industry staff. Design of a 150,000lb bomber was rated as an "undertaking of great importance since it must eventually replace all heavies and may form the basis of our post-war civil aircraft".

Had further comments in the MAP report been leaked in modern manner their effect would surely have caused uproar. It stated:

> Re the Anglicisation of the B-29, a number of our designers have proved themselves ineffective, or have personal peculiarities which make them unsuitable to undertake a visit to the USA. It is thought that Lloyd of AWA would be a suitable leader. We cannot afford two designers and must make available the best brains for our own 75-tonner. It is proposed, therefore, to ask certain firms experienced in design and manufacture of bombers for their rough views on a layout of such an aircraft which will be referred to a committee.

The eventual outcome was a bomber project from which the huge Brabazon 1 airliner emerged post-war.

Meanwhile the Stirlings, doubtless encouraged by Sir Henry Tizard's favourable calculations, had been actually fighting the enemy but not in such increasing numbers as other types, as the following comparison shows:

Bomber stock (Home) 3 September 1942 – included features:

	Total	In service	With MAP
Stirling	178	116	62
Halifax	302	225	51
Lancaster	243	187	56
Wellington	1,914	1,378	280

(Another 420 Wellingtons were in transit and 236 were in service overseas.)

Enlargement of the Stirling force meant formation of another conversion unit, so a new airfield at Chedburgh in Suffolk was opened to accommodate 214 Squadron, which moved in from Stradishall on 1 October 1942. No 101 Squadron scheduled to be established with Stirlings on 30 September 1942 instead left Stradishall for No 1 Group to rearm with Lancasters. No 1657 Conversion Unit formed and replaced it under Wg Cdr B R Kerr, its strength being sixteen IE (later thirty-two IE) aircraft achieved by absorbing sundry Conversion Flights. On 28 September, Marham passed to 2 Group

R9358 BU-A, 'The Saint' of 214 Squadron. (R Glass)

and No 218 Squadron was moved to the station's satellite at Downham Market which, on 1 December, was raised to fully self accounting station status.

On **1/2 October** another triple target attack was mounted. While twenty-seven Halifaxes headed for Flensburg and seventy-eight Lancasters for Wismar, 16/25 Stirlings attacked submarine yards north of Lübeck. Cloud layers at 4,000ft and 8,500ft, also plentiful searchlight glare, made accurate bombing difficult and three aircraft failed to return.

Next night, 8/10 Stirlings of 7 Squadron formed half the Pathfinder force leading 188 bombers to Krefeld. Darkness and haze made marking difficult, some crews taking too long for safety in locating the target. Eventually, the Main Force bombed on several fires, prescribed aiming points being impossible to locate. Marking techniques required perfecting and the flares burst too high preventing accuracy. Stirlings of 7 Squadron, which dropped a dozen 250lb incendiaries, also released 216 flares along with 2,000lb HC and 1,000lb HEs, while 9/13 of 3 Group dropped incendiary loads. Four Stirlings had gone in first laying lead-in lines of reconnaissance flares. Then came the illuminators, the fire raisers, a 10-minute bombing attack by 3 Group and finally the rest of Bomber Command. High approach was followed by rapid descent on the run-in, and a return at around 7,000ft.

The most successful other Stirling attacks of the month were against Osnabrück on the **6th** when thirty-one Stirlings took part and illuminating was good and on **13/14th** when, in good weather, 233/288 aircraft raiding Kiel included 23/28 Stirlings carrying over 17,000 incendiary bombs. Against Cologne on **15/16th**, when a dozen 7 Squadron aircraft again formed part of the marker force, 26/32 all with fire bombs were part of the 289-aircraft force. Thick cloud accumulated during the attack and, although it was clear towards the close, strong winds dispersed the parachute flares.

It was now that the Stirling squadrons faced a most frightening ordeal – bombing Italy in support of operation *Torch*, the invasion of north-west Africa. Mounted to force the enemy to hold back fighters, bruise morale, inflict material damage to Italian ports and cities, they included operation *Haphazard*, the delivery in total of over 15,000,000 leaflets to the French explaining operation *Torch*.

A high-flying jet nowadays crosses the Alps with impunity and in a few moments. In wartime, in a Stirling, in darkness and cloud and aware of the need to avoid neutral territory, it meant flying close to, and even between the fearsome, vicious alpine pinnacles making the journey fraught with great danger.

After entering France somewhere near Boulogne the bombers crossed many miles of night-fighter infested hostile territory over which return would have to be made. Their tracks then led them to the Annecy area then along the edge of Lake Geneva and close to Mont Blanc whose summit was higher than the Stirling's ceiling. Then came the run to the chosen northern Italian target. Wandering off course in darkness would have been fatal.

Chosen first for attack, on **23/24 October**, was Genoa. Only 4/13 of the 7 Squadron Stirlings operating located and marked the target for the Main Force comprising thirty-eight Stirlings, eighteen Wellingtons of 3 Group also fifty-three Halifaxes of 4 Group. The length and exacting nature of the journey took a heavy toll, for the alpine region was covered by 10/10 cloud although northern Italy was clear. Over Genoa the target area was hard to locate because of 9/10 cloud at 9,000ft and apart from the pathfinders only twenty other Stirlings, six Wellingtons and forty-four Halifaxes unloaded somewhere around Genoa. Later evidence suggested most crews had bombed Savona. Three of 7 Squadron and a lone Wellington attacked Turin. Both 214 and 218 Squadron each lost an aircraft, and W7628 of 149 Squadron ended its sortie in the Thames Estuary killing the crew.

Of 214 Squadron's nine participants, five made early returns. Of those, Sgt L T Richards was shot up over the French coast and forced back, BF343 abandoned due to engine trouble, W7614 was attacked by a fighter north-east of Paris, and W7612 had to return from the Alps with engine trouble. R9184, flown by Plt Off Studd, failed to return.

EF427 posed for a special presentation picture given to some of the Sebro work force. Later operated by XV Squadron, it succumbed to AA fire near Mannheim.

First to operate Mk IIIs was XV Squadron, Bourn, where LS-V was photographed.

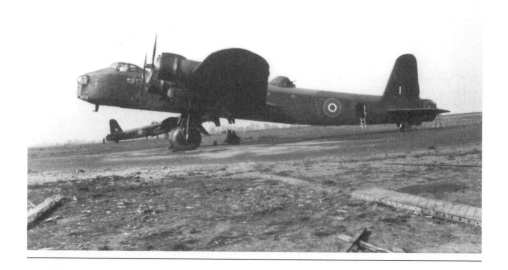

Out of XV Squadron's ten, only five bombed; and the Commanding Officer, Wg Cdr D H Laye, crash landed at Bradwell when an engine cut in the circuit. Flt Lt Baignot's aircraft was attacked by two fighters and the mid-upper gunner claimed a Ju 88. Six out of the nine crews from 149 Squadron reached Italy, but not all of their loads fell on Genoa. Engine failures and fuel shortages also plagued the operation. Lancasters were absent from the night's effort because a gaggle of 73/88 were needed for a dusk attack on Milan next day.

Half an hour after nightfall, seventy-one bombers flew a follow-up raid. Led by 3/10 7 Squadron pathfinders and 7/13 3 Group Stirlings and ten Halifaxes of 35 Squadron, a dozen Wellingtons of 1 Group, with five Halifaxes of 4 Group and eleven Wellingtons of 3 Group raided Milan. Only thirty-three crews claimed to attack, several below cloud level. Reliance upon *Gee* fixes had little value because they were obtainable only to within 200 miles of Milan so that the most difficult part – around the western edge of the high Alps – had to be flown on dead reckoning. Forecast was of a front likely to be encountered about halfway to the target with cloud base down to 1,000ft and heavy icing up to 7,000ft. Very strong winds from the west were expected, and the front was thought likely to break before the high mountains. Half the outward track was flown at 3,000ft for safety before the climb across part of the Alps. Then the bombers were to descend below icing level to avoid upper winds and night fighters. Instead, it was very cloudy for almost the entire journey causing mainly wasted effort. No 7 Squadron attacked built-up areas, although the flares were widely scattered. Some aircraft could not climb as intended owing to icing, and only two crews of 218 Squadron reached Milan. Another failed to return. The harrowing nature of the flights to Italy is recalled here by Flt Lt E E Jones:

> This was my last operation with XV Squadron and I flew with Sqn Ldr Claydon. The weather was bad with fronts across France and 100mph winds forecast for the alpine area. We never saw the Alps, just a huge wall of cumulus towering up to 25–30,000ft which we flew along looking for a break while conscious that the Stirling's ceiling was less than the height of Mont Blanc. We made one attempt at penetration but soon started icing up. On our second try the build-up of ice was very rapid on wings and propellers and we lost height fast. Lake Geneva suddenly appeared below so into it we jettisoned the bomb load, un-fused and hopefully in the French half, This gave us breathing space. We managed to hold altitude and get back to clear air then returned to base.

On 29 October 1942, the total holding of Stirlings by the RAF was 154 of which ninety-eight were in squadron hands, fifty-one in conversion units, one in transit, three at State Class III in MUs and one being used for miscellaneous trials. For comparison, total holding of Lancasters was 265 (209 in squadrons), of Halifaxes 297 (168 in squadrons) and Wellingtons 1,314 (208 held in UK squadrons and 734 in OTUs).

November's wintry weather limited operations. Apart from small scale attacks on Hamburg on **9/10th**, and Stuttgart on **27/28th**, the effort was mainly devoted to mining and seven more raids on Italy. The small-scale Hamburg raid was a failure, high winds forcing many aircraft off track.

Genoa was 3 Group's primary target three times in **November** and Turin twice. On the **7/8th**, **13/14th** and **15/16th** No 7 Squadron helped lead the way. Flares from 10/11 of the leaders were well placed for the first attack carried out by 175 aircraft including 16/28 Stirlings. Two major fires were started, but a high proportion of the force turned back on meeting severe icing and snow on reaching the Alps. On the **13th** only 7 Squadron's Stirlings were involved, 8/9 claiming to successfully mark for 5 Group. For the third raid seventy-eight bombers set forth and sixty-seven crews claimed to attack. This time only 8/11 7 Squadron Stirlings were involved.

Turin was four times the target during the month, in operations that cost a dozen Stirlings. A small-scale raid on **18/19th** was followed on **20/21st** by a large raid mounted by 239 bombers including 179 heavies. Among them were 27/33 Stirling which were reckoned to have bombed the target, marking of which was attempted by twenty-eight Pathfinders including 10/12 Stirlings. XV and 214 Squadrons each lost an aircraft.

On **20 November** the weather was kinder, the moon bright, visibility good, Nine crews of XV Squadron attacked, and seven of 218 Squadron. When W7584 was nearly back at Chedburgh, two Exactor controls failed. Flt Sgt Corlett ordered his crew to bale out before the Stirling crashed and killed him.

A new Stirling formation was soon to join the fray, No 75 (New Zealand) Squadron which had a distinguished record flying Wellingtons. With Stirling production increasing faster and two conversion units functioning, 75 Squadron began conversion and with the help of No 7 Squadron at Oakington, the 'Kiwis' received their first Stirlings at their Newmarket Heath base on 16 October.

At 1820 hrs on 20 November, four crews of 75 Squadron, captained by Plt Off L G Trott, Flt Sgt J M Bailey, Sgt B A F Franklin and Flt Lt C W Parish started the new campaign bravely participating in a long haul to Genoa. Trouble soon overtook Franklin whose crew jettisoned their load in the Wash. Flt Lt Parish had to abandon his sortie over the south of France leaving only two crews to complete 75's first Stirling raid.

Also out that night and against Turin were ten Stirlings of 7 Squadron. In one was Plt Off Boylson from whose machine the starboard outer transmission pipe sheared off carrying away the constant speed unit. Sqn Ldr Cribbin's aircraft had its port and centre bomb bays damaged by flak which ignited the flare load. Fg Off Duro's machine was also hit, his escape hatch being blown in and the starboard elevator almost shot away.

Flight Sergeant Rawdon Hume Middleton of 149 Squadron posthumously awarded the Victoria Cross. (Australian War Museum)

The next Stirling foray to Turin came on **28 November**, and was the biggest for 12/13 of 7 Squadron and 11/34 other Stirling bombers participated. Abortive sorties on the dark night were many. Five crews of XV Squadron set out, their orders being to attack from a lower level than usual. Only two reached Turin, W7585 turning back at the mountains with engine trouble. The bombs from 'T-Tommy' were jettisoned near Dijon because of engine trouble. Three out of 214 Squadron's seven crews attacked, and one was missing. No 218 fared little better, only three crews out of six reaching Turin. Of the night's episodes, one would long be remembered with pride.

At 1814 hrs Flt Sgt R H Middleton, an Australian pilot, opened the throttles of BF372: OJ-H. Within moments the heavily laden Stirling had cleared Lakenheath, and around 2130 hrs was running up on the Alps with fuel consumption rate causing concern. Middleton turned in the darkness on to his Turin run which had to be repeated. During a third pass he descended to a mere 2,000ft and entered a hail of flak. A shell burst in the cockpit and a splinter smashed into his face tearing part away and ripping out his right eye along with the flesh about it. A second splinter pierced his chest, a third a leg. By his side was Flt Sgt L A Hyder who received severe leg and head wounds. Most of the windscreen had been shot away allowing bitterly cold air to pour in.

As Flt Sgt Middleton fell unconscious from his appalling wounds the Stirling plunged down. Hyder, summoning great strength and courage, seized the controls and managed to level out the aircraft at 800ft. The bombs were released then, despite the alarming fuel state, a climb to 1,500ft was made and course set for home. Again the aircraft was hit by flak. Despite his horrific injuries Middleton by supreme effort recovered consciousness. and insisted on taking over allowing Hyder's serious wounds to receive attention. There seemed little possibility of reaching England, but Middleton stayed at the controls to afford the others a chance of survival.

So sorely wounded, Middleton almost impossibly nursed the crippled Stirling around the alpine region and across France only to encounter more flak over Boulogne where BF372 was hit yet again. By the time it reached the coast, near Dymchurch, 'H for Harry' had fuel for about five minutes' flying. Middleton flew along the coast allowing the crew – apart from the front gunner and flight engineer – to bale out. Those remaining had elected to stay with their courageous captain. Within a few minutes the aircraft plunged into the Channel, and not many hours later bodies of both who had stayed behind were recovered. Middleton, it was thought, had gone down with the aircraft.

On 1 February 1943, Middleton's body was washed ashore. He was taken to St. John's Church, Beck Row, where he was lain in state. On 5 February he was buried in the churchyard as the Band of Bomber Command played in tribute to his bravery. A special salute from Fighter Command was given by Wg Cdr Strange. Representing C-in-C Bomber Command was Gp Capt H R Graham. Surely there could have been no more suitable person to represent all those who flew in Stirlings, or indeed served in Bomber Command. The inscription on the headstone soon read 'Flight Sergeant R H Middleton VC'. He was the first Stirling crew member to receive the highest award for bravery, and his body remains in the small War Cemetery, Beck Row. Flt Sgt Hyder was awarded the DFM and four others of the crew were also decorated.

The terrible nature of the flights to Italy was insufficient to halt them, and a further attempt to destroy Turin's Fiat works took place on **29/30 November**. Nine Stirlings of 7 Squadron and seven Lancasters of 83 Squadron led the Main Force which included twenty Stirlings. Treacherous weather enveloped the mountains, producing the usual story of fast dwindling fuel and aircraft so heavily ice encrusted that thirteen Main Force crews had to turn back.

Of the four Stirling bombers which reached the Turin area none claimed to bomb Fiat. None of 149 or 214 Squadrons reached the city, but one crew who had braved the terrifying conditions briefly glimpsed the Fiat works from 10,000ft, banked, lost it, found it again then ran in very low in an attempt to bomb it. Superior performance which permitted all the Lancasters to reach the target area could not defeat the dense haze and smoke from the previous night's fires now hiding the factory. Six pathfinder Stirlings which reached Turin dropped 378 flares and 18 x 1,000lb HEs. The final tally showed three Stirlings to be missing. When the sums were worked out it was found that about 223 tons of bombs had been dropped by Stirlings that month, but of the courage and misery brought by those alpine ventures there could be no measure.

November saw one unusual attack, carried out on the **3rd** and relying on cloud cover. Three crews of 218 Squadron set off from Downham Market to make a daylight attack on the railway installation at Lingen. Reaching the town they found an 800ft cloud base which meant that each crew could safely make only one pass. One load undershot and the next careered beyond the rail yards into a built-up area. The third crew, seeing accuracy impossible to achieve, called off their attack.

December's wintry weather reduced that month's sorties to 199. Despite the forecast of likely haze and cloud, Turin was nevertheless twice bombed by Stirlings and with moderate success. No 7 Squadron marked for a third attack. Nine markers and thirteen Stirling bombers were sent to Frankfurt on **2 December** when a trial radio commentary was given by the marker leader in an attempt to improve accuracy. It led later to the 'Master Bomber' concept. Thick haze had caused the raid to go astray.

Bad winter weather which reduced the number of aircraft operating made them easier for fighters to find. On the **16th**, Diepholtz airfield was selected for attack by eight Stirlings including three of XV Squadron. Flt Sgt McMonagle in BF355 was three times intercepted by Bf 110s the first of which was shot down, the second shaken off before the third gave up the fight. The Stirling landed, with a wounded crew member, at Coltishall. R9168 was shot down near Aalsmeer, all but one of the crew evading capture. All aboard R9186 were more fortunate for, although flak set fire to incendiaries in the wing cells, they managed to reach home.

On **17/18 December** 104 bombers operated, some engaged in a mining operation while others, including sixteen Stirlings, set out for the Opel factory in Fallersleben. In moderate visibility, with rain and ample cloud at around 5,000ft, four Stirling crews eventually claimed success, leaving others to call upon alternative targets. Cloud and moonlight produced fairly good operating conditions and not only for the bombers – night fighters destroyed five Stirlings. Only by flying very low might the fighters have been evaded. One of the missing was BF396, captained by Wg Cdr V Mitchell, Commanding Officer of 75 Squadron, from which four of its five Stirlings operating failed to return. It was also a bad night for XV Squadron when returning from mining, one of its aircraft crashed near Bourn and another burst into flames during landing. Two aircraft of 149 Squadron were also involved in crashes.

On **20/21 December** Duisburg was very successfully hit, partly because the Stirling element within the 192/232 aircraft force kept fairly closely together. Of twenty-six Stirlings which set forth, twenty-one bombed the primary target and all returned safely. On this night 3/6 Mosquitoes of 109 Squadron first tried out *Oboe*, successor to *Trinity*, in a strike on Lutterade power station, near Sittard, in a highly portentous operation.

Munich, not attacked since 19 September 1942, was the last German city to be visited by Stirlings that year. Only six of the nine 7 Squadron aircraft operating were thought to have attacked, the other three being shot down. The raid, much of which strayed from the target, was the first in which Stirlings dropped specially devised target indicators instead of modified flares.

Personnel of 218 Squadron by the tail of N3721 HA-J. Symbols denote fifty bombing sorties flown. (E Basford)

Stirling losses had of late been high, but the future looked a little safer. On 2 November, Bomber Command gave instructions that *Moonshine* should be brought into use on 1 December and, in the case of Stirlings, first fitted in aircraft allocated to 75 Squadron. It would soon be fitted to aircraft of Nos 149, XV, 214 and 218 Squadrons and in that order, and was already installed in Defiant fighters, which had been flying ahead of bomber missions and working with ground stations in Kent. *Moonshine* equipment was intended to jam German long-range *Freya* early warning radar able to detect incoming bombers when they were about 120 miles from the coast. That was a great advance over the 30-mile or so range of *Wurzburg* radar. Use of *Moonshine* was credited with the likely reason for the absence of losses during the recent Duisburg operation.

As the year closed expansion of the Stirling force was at last well under way. On 1 November 1942, Newmarket Heath returned to Mildenhall's control from Stradishall to make way for its use by 75 (New Zealand) Squadron. At Mildenhall, on 24 October 1942, a special unit had formed to undertake major inspections of Stirlings, but no personnel establishment was ever listed. Instead, it was staffed for the time being by reducing Stirling squadron personnel strength to support fifteen IE aircraft thereby releasing one maintenance crew.

Another new squadron, No 90, began forming on 1 November under Sqn Ldr J C Claydon and commenced receiving its *Moonshine*-equipped aircraft at Bottesford on 1 December. A borrowed 5 Group station well out of the 3 Group area, it was used because of airfield shortage caused by the arrival of American forces in East Anglia's 3 Group area. No 90 Squadron's first Stirling was BK644 which, and as it taxied along the perimeter track, collided with a roller whose driver jumped to safety before the vehicle crashed into the Stirling's tailplane. On the 29th the Squadron set out for Ridgewell, second satellite of Stradishall and its operational base, where the first to touch down was Flt Sgt Freeman in BK625. The all too familiar swing on landing overtook the aircraft which ended its arrival in a ditch. Remaining orbiting Stirling crews were evidently of the opinion that Bottesford was a safer known haven for they turned back. They moved south next day.

Earmarked for a Stirling conversion unit formed elsewhere, Great Ashfield opened on 26 October 1942, as the satellite of Mendlesham but regarded as a fully accountable station until its parent was ready. Instead, both were switched to USAAF use. Another intention was that 115 Squadron should rearm with Stirlings at Mildenhall, but that station closed on 7 November 1942, for runway building and 115 Squadron's Wellington IIIs moved that day to East Wretham which was transferred from Honington to become Mildenhall's third satellite station. On 8 December a Flight from 115 Squadron arrived at Oakington to commence conversion flying where a second Flight was scheduled to arrive on 28 December. Intention was for the squadron to start operating from Oakington on 10 January 1943. Several Stirlings were delivered for '115' and had the squadron's 'KO' identity letters applied. By late December it was clear that there were insufficient aircraft to permit full conversion, and 115 Squadron continued operating fourteen Wellington IIIs. In spring 1943 the squadron re-armed, on a trials basis, with Bristol Hercules-engined Lancaster IIs. There was a proposal to re-equip all Stirling squadrons with them on the basis that those already had experience of the engines. Another squadron deprived of using Stirlings was No 166, the intention being that it would transfer to 3 Group and receive them at Oakington in January 1943. On 1 December, RAF Waterbeach ceased to exist as such and became 'No1651 Conversion Unit, Waterbeach', thereby bringing its administration into line with Operational Training Units.

On 3 December 1942 the total stock of Stirlings amounted to 222 including 99 in squadrons, 55 at CUs and 48 in MAP hands. Total holding of other bombers showed Halifax 457, Lancaster 373 and Wellington 2,087 emphasising how much easier or faster it was to build them. On 31 December 1942 Stirling stock amounted to 223 aircraft of which the MAP held 60.

Depending upon the records consulted, the precise number of Stirling sorties flown in 1942 varies. This may in part be due to the manner of gathering and sorting data. Bomber Command ORS statistics submitted to the Cabinet Office show the following:

Total sorties despatched: 3,984
Missing: 159
Lost, all causes: 220
Despatched at Night: 3,157
Attacking at night: 2,154(?)
Tonnage dropped: 71,706
Missing: 128

Squadron Operations Record Books suggest a loss of 162 aircraft. Files and ORB listing by 3 Group provide similar totals and it seems likely that accuracy may never be achieved. Aircraft withdrawn from operations at the last moment, abortive sorties, omissions, recording of sorties landing away from base, all may well contribute to conflicting totals. Logically, it might seem that the Squadron ORBs would be the most accurate since they were compiled closest to the scene of action, but there are numerous instances when this is certainly not so.

What cannot be disputed is the bravery displayed on a great scale during operations, that all participating in the bombing campaign were mixing skill with courage. Perhaps best of all, the Alamein rout showed the possibility of ultimate victory to be brighter. To that the Stirling crews, at considerable cost, had contributed to the best of their ability.

Summary of Stirling Bomber and Pathfinder Operations 27 August – 31 December 1942

Date	Target	PFF/MF	No of Stirlings Used	Bombs dropped from Stirlings (no of each type)									FTR	Crews claiming attacked primary/force despatched
				HEs (lb)						Incendiaries (lb)				
				2,000	1,900	1,000	500	250	250	30	4	4X		
AUGUST														
27/28	Kassel	PFF	4/8	—	—	6	—	—	44	192	—	—	—	22/33
		MF	27/40	3	—	—	—	—	—	—	16,024	—	1	87/273
28/29	Nuremberg	PFF	2/7	2	—	1	—	—	24	—	—	—	—	17/30
		MF	16/27	—	3	5	4	—	—	1,100	19,600?	—	2	60/159?
	Saarbrucken	—	1/1-	—	6	5	—	—	—	—	—	—	—	70/111
SEPTEMBER														
1/2	Saarbrucken	MF	27/29	3	—	12	—	—	—	1,816	16,024	—	1	208/231
2/3	Karlsruhe	PFF	4/4	3HC	—	—	6	—	—	—	—	—	—	18/20
		MF	20/23	6	—	12	2	69	—	1,288	13,320	—	1	?/?
3/4	Emden		2/3	—	—	16	—	—	—	—	—	—	—	?/11
4/5	Bremen	PFF	6/6	—	4	1	—	—	180*	—	—	—	—	22/25
		MF	28/30	15	—	19	6	55	—	1,160	14,220	—	1	187/226
6/7	Duisburg	PFF	4/5	—	—	—	—	—	126*	—	—	—	—	19/24
		MF	23/25	14	—	12	10	—	—	1,296	10,800	—	1	155/183?
8/9	Frankfurt	PFF	7/8	—	—	—	—	—	?*	—	—	—	—	24/29
		MF	25/30	—	—	7	84	—	—	2,056	20,500	—	—	166/225
	(190/249)													
10/11	Düsseldorf	PFF	6/10	—	12	21	—	—	126*	—	—	—	1	?/29
		MF	28/35	—	—	6	69	—	—	1,136	34,020	—	3	?/447
	(360/476)													
13/14	Bremen	PFF	7/8	—	8	24	—	—	126**	—	—	—	—	?/31
		MF	34/45	—	4	—	74	—	—	2,880	23,940	—	1	?/417
	(338/448)													
14/15	Wilhelmshaven	PFF	4/4	—	4	18	—	—	84*	—	—	—	—	15/23
		MF	17/23	—	—	—	—	—	—	112	17,540	—	—	121/179
	(157/202)													
16/17	Essen	PFF	2/6	—	—	—	—	—	144*	—	—	—	1	?/19
		MF	22/27	—	—	—	—	—	—	2,064	19,890	—	5	?/350
	(233/370)													
19/20	Munich	PFF	2/2	—	—	—	—	—	216*	—	—	—	—	9/9
		MF	15/19	8	—	—	4	24	—	1,088	2,970	—	3	68/80
	Saarbrucken	PFF	1/1	—	—	—	—	—	—	192	3,420	—	—	7/15
		MF	3/4	—	—	—	—	—	—	192	3,420	—	—	56/65
23/24	Vegesack	MF	7/24	—	—	46	3	—	—	64	540	—	1-	7/24

* = flares

Date	Target	PFF/MF	No of Stirlings Used	Bombs dropped from Stirlings (no of each type)									FTR	Crews claiming attacked primary/ force despatched
				HEs (lb)						Incendiaries (lb)				
				2,000	1,900	1,000	500	250	250	30	4	4X		
OCTOBER														
1/2	Lübeck	MF	16/25	–	–	86	–	–	–	224	12,960	–	2	16/25
2/3	Krefeld	PFF	8/10	15HC	–	10	–	12	216*	–	24,860	–	–	16/20
5/6	Aachen	MF	9/13	–	–	–	–	–	–	768	18,750	–	1	144/171
6/7	Osnabrück	MF	17/23	9HC	–	6	–	–	118*	768	14,850	–	–	192/257
		PFF	8/12	–	–	–	–	–	–	–	–	–	–	?/20
13/14	Kiel	MF	22/26	–	–	–	–	–	–	2,584	–	–	1	?/185
15/16	Cologne	MF	23/28	–	–	–	6	–	504*	2,544	–	–	–	233/255
		PFF	10/12	12HC	–	–	–	–	–	–	–	–	–	?/33
		MF	26/32	–	–	–	–	–	–	3,246	18,720	–	2	?/256
23/24	Genoa	PFF	4/13	–	–	–	8	12	84*	–	2,160	–	–	4/13
		MF	26/38	7HC	–	16	5	12	–	1,910	7,290	–	1	70/109
24/25	Milan	PFF	3/10	–	–	–	15	–	93*	–	540	–	–	6/20
		MF	7/13	–	–	6	–	–	–	768	–	–	–	27/51
NOVEMBER														
3	Lingen	PFF	2/3	–	–	12	–	–	–	18	–	–	–	2/3
7/8	Genoa	MF	10/11	–	–	48	35	78	252*	296	2,630	–	–	?/33
		PFF	16/28	2	2	3	3	–	–	–	–	–	3	?/160
9/10	Hamburg	MF	2/10	–	–	–	–	–	69*	624	4,140	–	1	?/36
13/14	Genoa	PFF	6/9	–	–	14	–	–	378*	304	–	–	–	?/177
15/16	Genoa	PFF	8/9	–	–	14	7	–	432*	120	–	–	–	13/15
		MF	8/11	–	–	–	–	–	–	–	–	–	–	14/17
			67/78	4HC	–	–	4	–	420*	–	–	–	–	22/40
18/19	Turin	MF	2/2	–	–	36	–	–	–	–	–	–	–	?/28
20/21	Turin	PFF	10/12	17	–	3	–	–	–	–	19,000	–	2	?/211
		MF	27/33	5	–	10	–	8	561*	–	15,840	–	–	?/196
22/23	Stuttgart	MF	18/27	–	–	36	44	–	–	–	–	–	–	?/20
28/29	Turin	PFF	12/13	–	–	34	16	–	378*	–	–	–	2	?/208
29/30	Turin	MF	11/34	–	–	18	–	–	–	–	–	–	1	13/16
		PFF	6/9	–	–	4	–	–	–	–	–	–	1	4/20
		MF	4/20	–	–	–	–	–	–	–	–	–	–	

Date	Target	PFF/MF	No of Stirlings Used	Bombs dropped from Stirlings (no of each type)									FTR	Crews claiming attacked primary/force despatched
				HEs (lb)						Incendiaries (lb)				
				2,000	1,900	1,000	500	250	250	30	4	4X		
DECEMBER														
2/3	Frankfurt	PFF	6/9	–	–	7	12	69	102*	–	–	–	–	21/34
		MF	10/13	6	–	–	6	–	–	–	13,300	–	1	/78
6/7	Mannheim	PFF	6/11	2	–	21	–	–	240*	–	–	–	1	22/31
		MF	30/38	6	–	46	3	–	–	–	34,650	–	–	186/241
8/9	Turin	PFF	6/7	–	–	24	–	–	252*	–	–	–	–	/38
9/10	Turin	PFF	5/5	–	–	15	–	–	315*	–	–	–	–	23/26
		MF	18/20	2	–	14	2	–	–	–	14,040	–	1	140/175
11/12	Turin	PFF	1/8	–	–	3	–	–	63*	–	–	–	–	/26
		MF	20/54	–	–	–	–	–	–	–	–	–	–	
16/17	Diepholtz	MF	3/8	–	–	28	–	–	–	–	5,606	1,354	1	3/8
17/18	Fallersleben	MF	4/16	–	–	43	–	–	–	–	–	–	6	5/22
20/21	Duisburg	MF	21/26	–	–	10	3	–	–	–	29,300	1,410	–	178/198
21/22	Munich	PFF	6/9	–	–	10	–	–	2*+4TI	448	–	–	3	20/28

* = flares   TI = target indicators/markers

Notes: In many instances the number of crews attacking their primary targets remains uncertain. Some typical returns, applying to PFF and Main Force numbers combined and extrapolated by Bomber Command ORS shortly after the listed 1942 raids are these:

total attacking force

8/9	September	190/249
9/10	September	360/476
13/14	September	338/448
16/17	September	233/370
24/25	October	33/71
28/29	November	161/228
8/9	December	117/136

Chapter 11
Behold – the Long Awaited

DISAPPOINTMENT surrounded the Hercules XI Stirling. Boscombe Down's tests with N6000 so fitted showed that at 70,000lb and with gills open, climb fell away to 430fpm at 15,000ft at 175mph TAS. The greatest height reached was 17,000ft in just under 70 minutes, the change from MS to FS gear coming at 13,150ft. The take-off run had been 1,380 yards and the climb to 15,000ft made over a run of 100 miles consumed 275gal of fuel out of the 1,940gal carried. About 60 percent of the fuel would be consumed en route to the target, with the weight then being 61,000lb. After bomb release it would fall to around 53,000lb, and to 47,500lb on arrival over base. Return could thus conceivably be made at 20,000ft.

The fastest speed, weak mixture at 15,000ft, was about 226mph TAS outward, fuel consumption about 1.22gal per mile, allowing a journey of about 1,740 miles and flight time of about 7hr 45min. The homeward speed would be 217mph TAS. If outward indicated airspeed were reduced at 15,000ft to 155mph IAS (192mph TAS), fuel consumption would fall to 1.03gal per mile, allowing a 9hr 30min flight. Maximum possible still air range at 70,000lb at 10,000ft was computed as 2,110 miles at 200mph TAS, using 1.07gal per mile outward, and 1.27gal on return which permitted a duration of 11hr 15min.

Additional new equipment – flame dampers and extra turrets – was not accounted for in these figures. Drag from the dorsal turret would cut speed by about 5mph, and range by 6 to 8 percent, at 15,000ft.

N3662, the first with FN 7 and FN 64 turrets and new equipment, began trials at Boscombe in May 1941. Weighing in at 70,000lb for take-off, it could barely maintain 15,000ft making it no better than the rogue aircraft N6040 loaned for comparison by XV Squadron. Compared with N3662 that one did not now look so bad. Comparative results were as follows:

	Height (ft)	Weight (lb)	Supercharger gear	Revs	Speed (mph) TAS	IAS
N6040	10,000	64,200	MS	2,450	178	210
	10,000	66,500	MS	2,510	177	207
	11,000	66,750	FS	2,500	160	194
	14,000	67,000	FS	2,500	159	194
N3662	10,000	66,000	FS	2,500	186	223

An altitude of 15,000ft could only be maintained in summer, when 12,500ft would be comfortable for cruise. Unmodified Mk 1s could hold 15,000ft at 66,000lb. To cruise at heavy weights at 15,000ft an increase in boost of 1psi was needed.

Unmodified N6000 was also compared with N3662, next fitted with FN 50 dorsal and FN 64 turrets. Full throttle speed loss on N3662 varied from 7mph to 9mph in MS, 11mph to 18mph in FS gear. Both aircraft were then raised to similar modification states, with mock-up turrets being fitted to N6000 whose maximum speed then fell by about 11mph, and by 8mph to 14mph in weak mixture.

Overall speed reduction with the additional features was accepted by Shorts early in 1941 who concluded that no improvement was possible without better engines. With Hercules Mks II/III, operation altitude had been a mere 10,000ft, with Hercules XI the usual cruise altitude was between 12,000ft and 15,000ft on outward journeys. With ever improving enemy defences much better performance was essential. How could that be achieved?

Bristol were bench running the more powerful higher-rated Hercules Mk VI, so hopes were now pinned upon this long awaited power plant, and especially so when performance of the Cyclone-powered Mk II proved inferior to the Mk I. A decision to re-engine with the Hercules Mk VI was taken in May 1941 as soon as N3662 proved disappointing, but it was not until the spring of 1942 that Mk VIs reached Rochester. R9309 was re-engined and a number of other modifications were incorporated.

The Hercules Mk VI had a revised cooling layout, and 12in diameter oil coolers were placed below each nacelle replacing leading edge intakes. Thermostatically controlled shutters could close the duct exits. Extended air intakes were sited above cowlings, containing ice guards and cleaners – useful during overseas employment. Barrage cutters remained on early machines, but there was no de-icing equipment. A small blister was placed on each side of the forward fuselage for better view fore and aft. Turrets installed were FN 5 nose, FN 50 dorsal, FN 64 ventral and FN 20 in the tail.

R9309 serving as the prototype Mk III flew in June 1942, and proceeded to A&AEE on 14 July, its performance of particular importance now that the B.8/41 had been dropped. At the maximum all-up weight of 70,000lb, Boscombe's tests showed the rate of climb to be only 500fpm at 5,000ft reached after 9.3min at 161mph TAS. This was alarming, and worse was to follow, for R9309 took 44.5min to reach 15,000ft (176mph TAS) where climb rate was a mere 90fpm.

Stirling I, R9309, modified to Mk III was being flown on 6 September 1942 by Polish Flt Lt Reise when its starboard outer engine caught fire. The aircraft crashed on Porton Down. (Shorts)

During August 1942 tests were directed to improving the oil cooling. Then, with dramatic suddenness disaster struck during a flight test on 6 September. Following a cylinder fracture the starboard outer engine burst into flames which quickly spread forcing the crew of six to abandon the burning bomber which soon crashed on Porton Down.

Shorts rapidly re-engined R9188, a Cyclone prototype, and had it flying by late September, and Austin Motors converted BK648 and BK649 (intended to be the first production Mk IIIs with Hercules VIs) into development aircraft. BK648 passed to 19 MU on 1 December 1942, and to XV Squadron on 31 December for intensive trials. BK649 went to Boscombe Down for further Mk III tests early in December. As well as the engine change these aircraft differed from the Mk I in another very important respect. They had cable throttle controls in place of Exactors. Hopes that this change

Central throttle arrangement in a Stirling III. (B Harris)

might reduce accident rates were quickly dashed. Strong take-off and landing swings arose in particular from the design configuration when the wing span was reduced while the fuselage remained proportionately very long and the stabiliser did not sufficiently compensate. However, a time-consuming maintenance problem had been removed by fitting the new throttle system

BK649 wearing prototype colours had none of the yellow ochre Kilfrost de-icing paste common on operational Stirlings in 1941 and 1942, and its armament was as fitted to R9309. Climb and level flight assessment revealed the maximum rate of climb (gills open and in MS gear) as 740fpm to 5,850ft. A change to Full Supercharger came at 9,000ft, the climb-rate of 400fpm being maintained to 12,800ft. Service ceiling was 16,750ft, estimated absolute ceiling 18,000ft and thus only slightly above that of a fully equipped Mk I. Above FS full throttle height (cooling gills closed) the rate of climb rose

BK649, third Stirling III and fitted with an FN 64A belly turret, wore yellow under surfaces which bore an incongruous Type A roundel.

by 155fpm when the service ceiling became 18,500ft, absolute ceiling 20,000ft, again during an outward journey. In FS gear at maximum all-up weight the top speed was 262mph TAS at 13,000ft, with the maximum reached in MS being 254mph TAS at 5,800ft, and 215mph TAS in weak mixture cruise in FS gear at 18,500ft. A more comfortable cruise was achieved at 16,000ft. The maximum MS cruise speed reached was 228mph IAS at 12,000ft.

Dry reading though such figures may make they were important for they showed that the performance of the Stirling Mk III was little better than that of the Mk I. True, it took about twelve minutes less to attain 12,800ft, and its operational cruise ceiling of 16,700ft showed a 2,300ft improvement. Although the Hercules Mk VI gave more power at high altitude that was largely nullified by its weight being in excess of the Mk XIs.

Comparative figures for the engines were:

Engine (Hercules)	Dryweight (lb)	Take-off power	Max power level, 5mins	Normal climb	Max level econ cruise
Mk XI	1870 lb all-up	1,590hp 2,900 revs	1,315hp 2,800 revs sea level	1,315hp 2,000ft 2,500 revs	1,020hp 2,500 revs 7,500ft
			1,460hp 2,800 revs 9,500ft	1,815hp 2,500 revs 12,750ft	920hp 2,500 revs 17,500ft
Mk VI	1,930lb	1,615hp 2,900 revs	1,675hp 2,900 revs 4,500ft	1,355hp 2,400 revs 4,750ft	1,050hp 2,400 revs 10,250ft
			1,445hp 2,900 revs 12,000ft	1,240hp 2,400 revs 12,000ft	955hp 2,400 revs 17,750ft

Both engines had a capacity of 2,360 cu in and diameter of 52in

BK650, the first of the production Mk IIIs left Austin on 9 December. Some others were powered by Hercules Mk XVIs similar to the VIs but having fully automatic Hobson 132 ME carburettors with differential carburation characteristics. Performance differed little, tests showing this version's maximum MS speed, reached at 11,600ft, as 219mph TAS. In FS it was 244mph TAS at 15,000ft making it a little faster than Mk VI engined Stirlings.

90 Squadron preparing for night operations from Ridgewell. (D Giles)

Sixteen Mk IIIs reached the RAF in January 1943, initial deliveries being to XV Squadron, Bourn, where climb performance at operational loads was explored. On 7 February the squadron despatched fifteen Stirlings to Lorient and among which were three Mk IIIs operating for the first time. They were BK654:W flown by Sqn Ldr R English; BK657:C (Flt Sgt J Shiells) and BK658:K (Sgt Irwin). The load aboard the first aircraft was 1,500 x 4lb and 30 x 4lb 'X' incendiaries, the others each carried 2 x 500lb GP, 423 x 4lb and 27 x 4lb 'X' incendiaries. All three attacked Lorient, Shiells from around 16,000ft, the others from about 13,000ft.

90 Squadron later operated from Tuddenham where LK516 WP-J was photographed. (Denis Field, via G Jeffrey and 90 Squadron Association)

Thereafter small numbers operated and Mk IIIs and attacked Germany (Wilhelmshaven) for the first time on **18 February 1943**, when BK654, BK657 and BK667:H set forth. The first one returned. Four more took part in the Essen raid of 5 March, mining with IIIs commenced on **17 March** and on **29 March** six operated against Berlin.

Deliveries of Mk IIIs (Hercules Mk VI) to squadrons in the first quarter of 1943 were:

	7	XV	75	90	149	214	218
January	–	7	–	–	–	–	–
February	–	10	–	2	3	3	5
March	4	6	2	6	13	10	8

Deliveries from the second production source began with BF457 on 24 January 1943 and this, like all Mk IIIs, had an FN 50 dorsal turret.

Introduction to operations, total sorties flown by Mk IIIs, losses and accidents to 3 April 1943 were:

Squadron	First op	Target	Aircraft	Sortie total	First loss	Write-offs after flying accidents
7	2.4.43	St Nazaire	BK724:I	–	–	–
XV	7.2.43	Lorient	BF547:B	129	18.2.43 BF547:B	22.3.43 BK667:H
			BK657:C			
			BK685:K			
			BK654:W			
75	3.3.43	Hamburg	BF456:J	17	–	8.3.43 BK770
90	13.2.43	Lorient	BK693:B	22	–	–
149	28.2.43	St Nazaire	BK696:K	32	1.3.43 BK692:W	–
			BK692:W			
			BK701:G			
214	16.2.43	Lorient	BK690:V	40	5.4.43 BK662:V	–
218	13.2.43	Lorient	BK650:L	52	29.3.43 BK716:J BK702:O	1.3.43 BK666

The Mk IIIs entered battle at a turning point in Bomber Command's capability. Improved enemy defences necessitated operations on dark nights to evade fighters, and at greater heights to avoid flak. Those precious feet that the Mk III attained were valuable.

The first two months of 1943 saw reduced action while 3 Group integrated Stirling IIIs into its ranks and the Pathfinder Force exploited the Mosquito's target marking potential. There was a general improvement in overall efficiency in Bomber Command and the strength of the Stirling force increased faster as these figures indicate:

	Establishment	In squadrons	Operationally fit
31 December 1942			
3 Group	80	45	26
PFF	16	9	8
27 January 1943			
3 Group	96	81	59
PFF	16	23	15
13 February 1943			
3 Group	112	99	78
PFF	16	23	18

Force expansion was now increasing quite fast and by 1 March 1943, squadrons held 122 Stirlings – ten above establishment. No 7 Squadron had a third Flight, increasing its strength to twenty-four aircraft.

Sir Arthur Harris was little heeded when in 1942 he stressed the importance of preventing the enemy from building massive concrete shelters for U-boats. By the start of 1943 bomb-proof structures had been constructed and, too late, attempts were in January and February 1943 made to destroy them. On **14/15 January** 99/123 aircraft, led by Pathfinders including 7 Squadron and 16/19 Stirlings of 3 Group, the latter attacked Lorient in two groups bombing from 10,000ft and 11,000ft during a twenty minute attack. After passing through rain and ice they reached a moonlit target which made visual bombing possible. Fires were started by the estuary and in the south-east target area, but 72.7 tons of HE and 85,860 x 4lb incendiaries failed even to dent the U-boat shelters. Next night a similar sized force – 130/147 aircraft including 92 heavy bombers of which 29/36 were Stirlings and 10/10 Wellingtons of 3 Group led by eighteen

Mk III BF509 served with 149 Squadron from March 1943 to February 1944. It ended life resting among Woburn Abbey's trees tended by 6 MU – and presumably the estate gardeners. (Shorts)

Pathfinders including 4/4 Stirlings of 7 Squadron – returned and bombed through cloud gaps and light of flares, incendiaries, moonlight and some of the previous night's fires. Some 140.4 tons of HE, over 90,000 incendiaries and 276 flares were used during the raid costing one Stirling also a Wellington of 427 Squadron.

Lorient was again raided on **23/24 January 1943**, this time by 109/160 bombers led by 22 Pathfinders. With the Main Force were twenty-nine Stirlings, fifty Halifaxes of 4 Group and another fifty from 6 Group. Clear conditions again enabled good visual marking and only one Stirling, from 75 Squadron, failed to return. Comparison of the loads dropped by the twenty-five Stirlings and forty-seven Halifaxes on this occasion supporting Sir Henry Tizard's analysis, viz:

Stirlings: 2 x 2,000lb HC, 15 x 1,000lb, 7 x 500lb, 36,960 x 4lb incendiaries
Halifaxes: 103 x 1,000lb, 30 x 500lb, 29,970 x 4lb incendiaries

February 1943 proved to be a far busier month for the Stirling squadrons which operated on twenty nights and were engaged in bombing during fifteen of them. Six times the total despatched exceeded sixty, including twice during Lorient raids.

Stirling I BF350 LS-O viewed at Bourn from the cockpit of LS-D. (B Harris)

Viewed from the cockpit a Stirling's engines and propellers seemed mighty close. (B Harris)

Biggest Stirling involvement of the month came on **14th/15th** when Bomber Command despatched 204/243 aircraft to Cologne, among them 9/10 of 7 Squadron and 49/58 Stirlings. Thick cloud extended to 8,000ft over the city imposing blind bombing on sky markers, while moonlight exposed the force to fighters nine of which were lost, among them three Stirlings.

The second largest scale Stirling operation had taken place on **3/4 February**, but only 126/263 participants were thought to have attacked Hamburg, where they dropped, blind, 121.2 tons of HE also fire bombs. Conditions en route were extremely bad, 7–10/10 cloud up to 20,000ft producing severe icing conditions which forced many crews to turn back. Pathfinders, including 4/9 of 7 Squadron, which released 4 x 250lb TIs and fifteen flares to back-up marking the target area between 2102 hrs and 2114 hrs for the bulk of the attackers, which released their loads between 2100 hrs and 2120 hrs. Among those were 26/57 Stirlings of 3 Group which dropped only incendiaries, over 45,000 x 4lb type. Cruel indeed was the weather, mainly responsible for a very heavy loss of eight Stirlings.

Another costly raid came on **19/20 February** when 41/56 Stirling crews claimed to attack and five did not return. Wilhelmshaven, the target, was obscured by a smokescreen but Pathfinders managed to pick out the Bauhafen over which they positioned eighty-four sky markers and thirty-two flares visible through the clouds and smoke. Between them the force of 302/338 bombers dropped 349.6 tons of HE, 6,868 x 30lb and some 170,000 x 4lb incendiaries.

Two deep penetration operations were flown in **February**. On **4th/5th** 151/188 aircraft (41/50 Stirlings) set out for Turin and claimed to hit targets in the city. After meeting cloud on the run up to the Alps, the weather luckily improved and became excellent over the target. A concentrated attack was at last possible despite considerable AA fire and two searchlight concentrations.

From the Nuremberg raid of **25/26th** three Stirlings out of 42/53 operating failed to return, a third of the total loss. All told 277/337 bombers were involved in what could have become yet another a disastrous operation. The Pathfinders,

When we were young – Sgt Naylor, flight engineer, aboard LS-D. (B Harris)

Sgt Ware relating events to his wife in a letter? (B Harris)

LS-D's crew enjoy viewing a photograph of the wife of their skipper Sgt Ware. (B Harris)

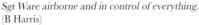

Sgt Ware airborne and in control of everything.
(B Harris)

Sgt Brian Harris, XV Squadron. Seen here at his navigator's table, he not only braved flak and fighters but was also courageous enough to take some splendid personal photographs!

including 4/9 Stirlings, arrived late and many Main Force bombers were compelled to orbit awaiting them. So hazardous was such a practice that some crews unloaded before marking took place.

Concentration upon maritime targets was marked at the end of the month by 52/60 Stirlings trying to cripple U-boat facilities at St Nazaire. Among the raid leaders were 2/2 Stirlings of 7 Squadron and 2/4 pathfinder Mosquitoes, one of which was operating at 28,000ft. At such altitude it was almost immune from enemy interference and being guided by *Oboe* which was about to transform Bomber Command's Ruhr campaign.

Sergeant Geoff Ware inspects BF439's tailplane which gives a bomb tally of twenty-three sorties flown so far. (B Harris)

Features of the Stirling Mk III
Construction

Mainplanes: Mid set two-spar all-metal cantilever structure similar to that of the C-Class flying boat, each mainplane designed to be assembled in one piece. Spar flanges of extruded T-section, and top and bottom flanges connected by a tubular girder arrangement similar to that of the flying boats. Inter-spar bracing was, however, of the same tubular form as that of the spars. Top wing skinning continued across fuselage. Gouge-type trailing edge flaps with chord equal to 48 percent of total wing chord. Armoured wing leading edges which could be fitted with cable cutters.

Fuselage: All-metal structure built of transverse frames covered with aluminium alloy sheet with intercostal stiffeners and all joints joggled flush and flush-riveted. Frames of Z-section, and longitudinal stringers a cross between V- and U-sections. Continuous stringers attaching to notched frames. Bomb bay 42ft 7in long fitted with six hinged doors. Two dinghies carried – one in fuselage the other in wing.

Tail unit: Cantilever monoplane type, similar to that of C-Class flying boat but reduced in area.

Accommodation: Crew of seven normally carried – two pilots, navigator/bomb aimer, front-gunner/wireless operator, two air-gunners and a flight-engineer/air-gunner. Pilot's coupe designed for both good forward view and to permit fighting controller to operate with minimum of interference during enemy fighter attack. Navigator seated within coupe boundary. Retractable astrodome superimposed with escape hatch just aft of back end of coupe. Armoured bulkhead with hinged door separated flight compartment from engineer and wireless operator. First pilot had additional armour to his back and head and fighting controller had armour protection to his chest when superintending air gunner's action. Crew rest quarter amidships, bunk on starboard side of compartment. Multi-flare chutes aft of bomb bay, walkway to tailplane spar frames and through them to tail turret.

Dimensions

Wing span	99ft 1.12in
Wing area gross	1,322sq ft aerofoil section Gottingen 436(mod)
Wing root chord	21.888ft, incidence at fuselage chord centre line 3º
Dihedral	top surface front spar 2º25', long spar datum 4º15'
Wing sweep	5º
Aileron area	117.6sq ft
Flap area	405sq ft
Fuselage length overall (datum horizontal)	87ft 3.5in
Fuselage maximum width	6ft 7.5in
Fuselage depth, central	8ft 8in
Fuselage bomb cell length	42ft 7in
Height (maximum possible)	28ft 10in
Height tail down	22ft 9in
Height to wing tip	15ft 6in
Height to outer prop boss	16ft 6in.
Propellers	DH Hydromatic 55/9, 13ft 6in diameter.
Mainwheel track	25ft 7.85in
Mainwheel tyres	Dunlop AH 2233 Type IBB.14, diameter 70.8in
Tailwheel track	23.5in
Tailplane span	40ft 8.5in
Tailplane root chord	9ft 2.5in
Tailplane aerofoil	RAF 30 (mod)
Tailplane incidence	1.45º
Tailplane/elevators area	239sq ft
Fin/rudder aerofoil	RAF 30 (mod)
Fin/rudder area	77.68sq ft
Height over fin	9ft 10.75in
Rudder area	33.35sq ft

Power plants
Fuel loads   4 x Bristol Hercules VI/XVI two-row sleeve-valve radial engines.

Fuel tankage (100 octane)

No 1 tank (two) – inner rear	2 x 80 gals
No 2 tank (two) – inboard	2 x 331 gals
No 3 tank (two) – outer rear	2 x 63 gals
No 4 tank (two) – inboard middle	2 x 254 gals
No 5 tank (two) – outboard	2 x 164 gals
No 6 tank (two) – outboard	2 x 81 gals
No 7 tank (two) – leading edge	2 x 154 gals
Total	2,254 gals normal
Auxiliary tanks:	
Inboard wing cells	269 gals
Fuselage (ferrying)	3,292 gals.

Tare weight   44,856lb

(undercarriage down, flaps one-third extended)

Maximum permissible flying weight   70,000lb

Maximum landing weight   60,000lb

A Multitude of Modifications

Stirlings differed in detail as many modification states were applied. BK761, whose performance was assessed by A&AEE pilots at Oakington, typified a 1943 Stirling III. FN 5A, FN 50A and FN 20A turrets were carried, also an astrodome amidships, Perspex blisters on either side of the pilot's cabin, no barrage cutters, extended/tropical air intakes with ice guards but no filters, oil coolers normal 12in diameter Martson type fitted with segmental blanking plates 4in deep on inboard engines and 5in deep on outers. All engines had standard exhaust rings, shrouded blackout panels with heat isolation cuffs, 13ft 5in diameter Type 55/1 DH propellers without de-icing and DTD 308C finish on good surfaces panels.

A comparative Mk III tested was EH949, similar but fitted with double rimmed anti-shimmy Marstrand tailwheels instead of normal round section type. BF501, a third Mk III also tested at Oakington, had no front cylinder baffles on its engine cylinders, flames dampers on outer engines of a modified pattern terminating in a conical point. Inboard propellers were Type 55/9 DH hydromatic of 13ft 6in diameter, outer propellers were Type 55/1 of 13ft 5in diameter.

Performance of Typical Stirling BIIIs

A later Mk III, LJ483 from Armstrong Whitworth, Swindon, was tested at Stradishall. Its Hercules XVIs featured a fully automatic Hobson 132/ME carburettor giving much different carburation characteristics. Bristol Mod E.139 made the port carburation air cock inoperative in each engine. Stepped power valves were not used. Marstrand anti-shimmy tailwheels were fitted, DH Type 55/10 propellers in lieu of Type 55/1 and an FN 120 rear turret (externally unchanged from the 20A). There was a small deflector modification to ramp modification 1072 4in deep below the fuselage ahead of the forward escape hatch. All exhaust rings had anti-glow paint.

Handling was undertaken at between 64,000lb and 70,000lb and level weak mix cruising speeds recorded were:

Height (ft)	TAS (mph)	IAS (mph)
MS gear		
4,000	210	203
8,000	218	198
11,600	224	192
13,000	220	183
15,000	210	168
FS gear		
10,000	210	184
13,000	216	189
15,000	219	177
16,800	213	174

Rates of climb

MS gills open	750 fpm at 2,000ft
FS 2,500 revs	430 fpm at 8,000ft
Time to 12,000ft	21 minutes
Service ceiling	16,900ft

These results were considered typical.

EF229 (Hercules XVI) showed a cruising speed of 216mph at 11,300ft in MS gear and 203mph in FS between 13,000 and 14,000ft.

LK450 (Hercules VI) had a service ceiling of 16,400ft and took 22.3 minutes to reach 12,000ft, had a maximum weak mix cruise speed of 217mph TAS at 11,000ft and 215mph in FS at between 14,000 and 16,000ft.

Chapter 12
Fire Raiser

THREE years' bombardment of the Ruhr and Rhineland had brought limited success. Finding specific targets at night in an area frequently disguised by industrial haze had been difficult and enemy defences steadily improved, but all was about to change. Devastating, concentrated night raids delivered in the shortest possible time by large forces flying at differing heights and saturating defences were planned, calling for very accurate time keeping especially by pathfinders. Late arrival would dangerously degrade any attack which, if executed to plan, was intended to incinerate Germany's cities, destroy the workforce, obliterate her industry.

Oboe was now available for Mosquito markers of 109 Squadron and three Stirling squadrons had Mk XIV stabilised bombsights by March 1943. No 90 Squadron had equipped first with the sights which, it was said, would make it possible to 'hit a beer barrel from 15,000ft'.

Bomber production was sufficient for large forces to be deployed and varying performance capabilities were exploited. Overall excellence of the Lancaster – its load carrying, range, good altitude performance and high reliability made it by far the Allies' best heavy bomber – was obvious, but for Ruhr raids the Stirling, able to drop huge incendiary loads, was very useful. Somewhere between the two came the Halifax which, like the Stirling, could not carry large girth bombs. Around 230 Wellingtons able to operate at 17,000ft remained in front-line Bomber Command squadrons, and many had Type 423 provisioning allowing carriage of a 4,000lb bomb. Flying very high, leading them all, fast and almost invulnerable were the superb little wooden *Oboe* Mosquitoes, the very antithesis of the Stirlings.

Stirling IIIs were slowly entering squadrons. Apart from 7, XV and 218 established at 24 + 3 aircraft, holding was of 16 + 2 giving a total establishment of 136 IE + 17 IR. Strength at 1800 hrs on 5 March 1943 was:

Squadron	Serviceable	Unserviceable
7	20	3
XV	14	13
75	14	2
90	8	12
149	9	8
214	12	3
218	15	8
Totals	92	49
		(37.4% of holding)

Other types in Bomber Command at this time were:

	Established (IE + IR)	Strength (IE + IR)	Percentage unserviceable
Halifax	200 + 25	147 + 77	34.4
Lancaster	288 + 36	232 + 84	26.6
Wellington	224 + 28	181 + 80	30.0

Just how effective the new bomber force could be was first demonstrated at Essen on **5 March 1943**. Some 442 bombers set forth – fifty-one of them Stirlings – to lay waste the vast Krupp armaments emporium. *Oboe* would, for the first time, be used to mark for a Main Force onslaught.

Zero hour at Essen was 2100 hrs BST at which time, despite the haze, 5/8 Mosquitoes began accurately marking the target area. During the three-phase attack twenty-two backers-up of the PFF – including two Stirlings of 7 Squadron – placed green target indicators (flare bundles had now been replaced) on the positions where red ones were initially placed.

The attack was carried out as follows:

Group	Aircraft	Time (hrs)	Average bombing (ft)	Average bomb load per aircraft (lb)
8	Mosquito	2058 – 2131	28,000	1,000 (4 x TIs)
	Lancaster	2103 – 2138	20,000	3acft:6,880
				16acft:6,910
	Halifax	2109 – 2121	19,500	6,750
	Stirling	2118	14,300	7,200
1	Lancaster	2119 – 2131	17,000	7,840
	Wellington III	2116 – 2126	13,000	3,428
	Wellington (423)	2116 – 2123	15,000	1 x 4,000
	Wellington IV	2115 – 2133	16,000	2,880
	Wellington X	2120 – 2133	13,000	2,880
3	Wellington III	2115 – 2126	12,000	3,493
	Stirling	2105 – 2128	13,000	7,828
4	Halifax	2100 – 2119	17,000	6,200
	Wellington III	2113 – 2117	15,000	3,460
	Wellington X	2104 – 2124	16,000	3,420
5	Lancaster	2111 – 2138	19,000	7,600
6	Halifax	2102 – 2136	17,000	6,840
	Wellington III	2110 – 2129	17,000	3,612
	Wellington X	2111 – 2117	17,000	3,420

Additionally, 3/3 Halifaxes and 2/4 Wellington Xs laid mines at sea from 4,000ft.

For many crews the night's spectacularly effective operation was straightforward, but Plt Off R F Bennett, heading 75 Squadron's nine participants, had an early engine seizure. Aboard was a 2,000lb bomb and 2 x 1,000lb bombs, supplemented with 1,740 x 4lb and 32 x 30lb incendiaries, he and his crew being very lucky in safely landing, load aboard, at Newmarket.

One of 214 Squadron's ten aircraft, coned by searchlights, was hit by flak so the crew jettisoned their load leaving seven others of the squadron to bomb at between 12,500ft and 15,000ft. One aircraft carried 6 x 2,000lb bombs and three had 3 x 2,000lb, 2 x 1,000lb and 1 x 500lb bombs. Others each took 1,890 x 4lb incendiaries. Only three Stirlings failed to return making the 3.9 percent loss rate lower than expected. Stirlings operating were:

7 Sqn: W7529-R, W7617-A
XV Sqn: R9193-S, BF439-B, BK652-V, BK656-A, BK657-C, BK694-O, EF339-Y, EF470-G*
75 Sqn: R9243-C, W7513-G, BF437-L (Sgt Davey FTR), BF451-Z, BF455-Y*, BK602-R, BK619-O, BK646-N, BK664-M* (Plt Off Bennett forced landed)
90 Sqn: R9271-Q, W7627-E, BF407-S, BF414-F, BF462-F*, BK665-Z*, EF334-U
149 Sqn: R9327-U, BK696-V*, BK698-S*, EF327-M, EF340-D (early return), EF342-A
214 Sqn: R9186-F, R9285-J, R9358-A, W7465-W, W7621-G, BF466-B*, BF469-M*, BK662-K* (FTR), BK690-V*, EF331-H
218 Sqn: R9203-D, R9333-Y (FTR), BF440-U, BF446-H, BF447-F, BF452-V (early return), BF468-K* (early return), BK596-B, BK650-L*, BK687-R* (early return), BK700-W*

* Mk III

Bomber Command's summary stated that 'the PFF technique was unanimously considered to have been perfectly carried out' and that a solid circle of fire 2 miles in diameter in one place 'looked like an immense pot boiling over'. The glow visible from 150 miles looked like a red sunset.

The ORS Bombing analysis showed:

Group	Aircraft despatched	Attacked primary	Enemy aircraft attacked	Enemy aircraft encountered	Missing
8	8 Mosquito	5	–	1	–
	19 Lancaster	19	–	–	2
	6 Halifax	5	–	–	–
	2 Stirling	1	–	–	–
1	41 Lancaster	37	–	1	–
	22 Wellington III	14	2	–	1
	3 Wellington (423)	3	–	–	–
	9 Wellington IV	6	2	–	–
	4 Wellington X	3	–	–	–
3	4 Wellington III	3	–	–	–
	50 Stirling	39	–	1	3
4	68 Halifax	60	3	–	2
	7 Wellington III	5	–	–	–
	25 Wellington X	23	–	–	1
5	97 Lancaster	90	–	2	2
6	20 Halifax	17	–	1	1
	52 Wellington III	46	–	1	2
	5 Wellington X	5	–	–	–

Bombs dropped:

Aircraft	4,000lb HC	2,000lb HC	HE 1,900lb HC	1,000lb	500lb	30lb	Incendiary 4lb	4lbX
1 Group								
Lancaster	36	–	–	–	–	1,180	24,220	1,440
Wellington	38	–	–	–	18	456	9,690	570
3 Group								
Stirling	–	30	4	44	7	1,384	32,242	1,958
Wellington	1	–	–	–	–	–	1,620	–
4 Group								
Halifax	–	–	–	1,118	–	1,856	44,430	2,520
Wellington	1	–	–	4	72	384	8,010	540
5 Group								
Lancaster*	85	–	–	–	–	2,784	54,585	810
6 Group								
Halifax	–	–	–	46	–	512	9,600	–
Wellington	10	–	–	–	111	576	12,460	860

*5 Group Lancasters also dropped 3 x 8,000lb HC
In addition a PFF Lancaster dropped one 4,000lb 'Pink Pansy' incendiary
Total HE tonnage: 467.7
Total 250lb target indicators used: 45
(NB. The three missing Stirlings carried 2 x 2,000lb HC, 4 x 1,000lb, 1 x 500lb, 192 x 30lb, 1,980 x 4lb X)

Stirling squadron records reveal the following picture:

Squadron	Despatched	Attacked primary	Early return	Crashed	Failed to return
XV	8	?	?	–	–
75	9	8	–	1	–
90	7	5	2	–	1
149	6	4	2	–	–
214	10	7	–	–	1
218	11	9	2	–	1
7PFF	2	2	–	–	–
Totals	53	35?	6?	1	3

Nuremberg, so steeped in Nazi folklore was, on **8/9 March**, the target for the next large-scale raid. In a cloudless sky, route markers showed the way with fine visibility apart from ground haze suggesting another gruesomely effective strike. But Nuremberg lay beyond *Oboe* range, and with few *H2S* aircraft available, scattered marking (which began at 2312 hrs and included 8/12 Stirlings of 7 Squadron) led to dispersed bombing. Several Stirlings encountered fighters, one Bf 110 being claimed by a Stirling crew. Of only seven bombers missing, two were from 7 Squadron, one being BK610-V.

Over northern France its captain, after calculating a low fuel state, told his crew to abandon aircraft. The mid-upper gunner failing to hear the order stayed aboard with the pilot as the Stirling followed a wayward path. Sgt Spanton clambered from V-Victor after it alighted on a sandbank 11 miles off Dungeness and later reached shore. The other missing aircraft was R9270 carrying Flt Lt J P Trench and crew of 7 Squadron.

The next main target was Munich. Despatching greater numbers inevitably led to more losses, one of which this night was R9149-B of 7 Squadron fitted with *Tinsel* and one of ten markers that set forth on **9 March**. Reaching 9,000ft operating height while crossing the Thames Estuary, blackout within R9149 became a problem, but all was well by the time the German fighter belt was reached and through which the Stirling gently weaved at about 155mph TAS. Suddenly at around 2212 hrs near Charleville, and in moonlight, a twin-engined fighter pounced pouring a three-second burst into the bomber's starboard wing. R9149 entered a steep dive in an attempt to extinguish the resultant fire, for the starboard outer engine was still working. Instead, the blaze took greater hold. Sgt Goddard, the bomb aimer, left via the front hatch, parachuting to safety while watching the bomber go steeply down trailing fire then exploding after hitting small trees. Others of the crew safely baled out, but the pilot was killed in the aircraft and buried at Elan, 9 miles ESE of Sedan.

Stuttgart had been bombed by **mid-March**, but Stirling loads were considerably lower when compared with other bombers when the target distance was greater, viz:

Target	Average load/attack height		
	Stirling	**Halifax**	**Lancaster**
Stuttgart (ll/12th)	6,200lb/16,500ft	7,680lb/13,500ft	5,550lb/13,000ft
Essen (12/13th)	6,000lb/17,500ft	7,733lb/17,500ft	8,591lb/12,000ft
Berlin (27/28th)	5,000lb/18,000ft	6,400lb/19,000ft	5,900lb/14,000ft
St Nazaire (28/29th)	6,200lb/14,000ft	7,760lb/13,000ft	7,260lb/13,000ft
Berlin (29/30th)	5,000lb/18,000ft	7,800lb/18,000ft	4,980lb/15,000ft

After a period of bad weather Berlin twice became the target. During the raid of **27/28th** Stirling pathfinders dropped 40lb anti-personnel bombs mixed in with 2,000lb HCs and target indicators while the Stirling Main Force unloaded incendiaries. That was the first of three occasions when small AP bombs were dropped by 7 Squadron, the others being on **4/5 April** and **20/21 April 1943**.

A trio of XV Squadron Stirlings over Bourn. (B Harris)

Over Chedburgh early on **30 March** two returning Stirlings of 214 Squadron collided, their occupants baling out except for one member in each of the crew who died. March losses were eighteen Stirlings, giving a rate of 4 percent.

March was a month for new features for it saw the introduction of the Base Organisation scheme. Under an Air Commodore, Mildenhall, Lakenheath and Newmarket were closely linked as 31 Base (ie. 3 Group No 1 Base) enabling squadrons to borrow aircraft from one another.

Personnel at Bourn gather logs for the Nissen hut stove. Life was quite hard on temporary wartime airfields. (B Harris)

Bombs for Berlin being loaded aboard BF439 of XV Squadron at Bourn on 27 March 1943. One is covered with National Savings stamps. (B Harris)

The Bomber Development Unit (BDU) which had acquired its first Stirling in October 1942 for H2S Mk IIG trials, moved from Gransden to Feltwell in April 1943 by which time BK594 (which became a most meritorious aircraft) was testing Monica radar for the future 100 Bomber Support Group. That Stirling also tested Oboe, Boozer, Mousetrap and Fishpond. BDU moved to Newmarket on 13 September 1943, then BK594 began high-level mine delivery techniques before becoming the vehicle for testing ventral gun installations for night bombers.

Increased production permitted formation of third, or 'C' Flights, from which new squadrons would form, making 100 Stirling sorties per night feasible. That benchmark was first attained on 23 May. Third Flights doubled operational effort within two months.

75 (NZ) Squadron re-equipped with Stirlings at Newmarket Heath before transfer to Mepal.

On 1 April No 75 Squadron became the first to expand having eight Stirlings added to strength. 'C' Flights on Nos 149 and 214 were declared operational on 10 April. To support a faster rate of crew output on 1 May 1943 a 32-aircraft 'Stirling half Conversion Unit', No 1665, was formed. Mepal being unready, it opened at Waterbeach and placed lodger Flights at Stradishall and Great Ashfield (loaned by the USAAF) before consolidating after moving on 7 June to Woolfox Lodge, a newly opened satellite of North Luffenham.

Stirlings at dawn after safe return to Bourn.
(B Harris)

On nine **April** nights Stirlings bombed. They mined on eleven and in total operated on seventeen nights. Small-scale attacks on St Nazaire and Lorient on **2/3rd** preceded the first major raid on **4/5th** when Kiel was the target for Stirlings carrying only incendiaries and 7 Squadron pathfinders delivering mixed loads. Nearly 70,000 fire bombs were released between 2306 hrs and 2337 hrs from between 13,000ft and 16,000ft. Soon after midnight a Bf 110 slipped out of cloud, lights on, to intercept a Stirling which neatly escaped by corkscrewing downwards.

LS-J which failed to return on 4 April 1943.
(B Harris)

The month's second large-scale raid flown by 289/392 aircraft on **8/9th** was on Duisburg. Cloud billowed to 22,000ft, flak was intense and loads had to be released on ETA. The Stirling PFF contingent included R9199 lost without trace. That misfortune may have been due to the weather which caused seventy-one crews (fourteen flying Stirlings) to abandon the operation. Main Force Stirlings were carrying the highest average load of any types operating, ie. 8,547lb.

Frankfurt – next listed for assault – escaped due to dense cloud, 479.9 tons of HE and many fire bombs bursting wide of the city. Bomber Command ORS recorded that 69/82 (or 72/82 according to Tactics Report No 74/73), were 3 Group Stirlings delivering 44 x 2,000lb HCs, other HEs and over 43,000 incendiaries. Other records suggest that 84 No 3 Group aircraft participated, along with 10/16 of 7 Squadron which, if true, means that for the first time 100 Stirlings were despatched for bombing while another four (possibly seven) were mining. Average Stirling loads were only 6,899lb against the Lancaster's 7,600lb. Six Stirlings failed to return.

Included was BK760-X of 7 Squadron, flown by Sqn Ldr Chesterman. Arriving fifteen minutes early at the target, his aircraft was hit three times by AA fire before it attacked from 17,000ft. The aircraft was hit again heading homewards, then the rear gunner reported searchlights following it. When very low over the village of Bree in the Maescyck area a searchlight illuminated the bomber and light machine-gun fire riddled the central and forward parts of the fuselage. Then a fighter raced in to finish it off and set fire to at least four of the wing tanks. A second strike probably killed two gunners. BK760 then briefly climbed before plunging into a canal. Sgt Ferguson, the flight engineer, and Sgt Moore, the navigator, escaped and evaded capture.

Flt Sgt Rothschild of 75 Squadron in BF455 was also among Frankfurt's attackers. Flak hit his aircraft, fighters chased it, then a prolonged track led to a low fuel state resulting in ditching 3 miles off Shoreham. Sgt E R Todd's radio messages had raised a flight of Spitfires to provide a dawn escort before the crash after which BF455 floated for twenty-five minutes. That gave the crew ample time to board their dinghy, but a Walrus which alighted collided with it hurling the crew into the water. All were soon safely ashore.

Weather conditions always play a major part in success or failure of air operations and the night of **14/15 April** was cloudless when Stuttgart was the target. Effectiveness also depended upon the accuracy of PFF marking which was good at the start. Ground markers were dropped but the backers-up released their TIs too soon and the bombing crept back along the run in track. Nevertheless, fires in Stuttgart and nearby towns caused by over 154,000 incendiaries were visible 80 miles away. Three Stirling Pathfinders failed to return, and five of the 56/67 (possibly 69) drawn from 3 Group, giving an overall loss of some 9.5 percent. Track distance reduced the average Stirling load to 4,800lb compared with 9,000lb carried by Lancasters.

On 13 April 1943 XV Squadron moved to
Mildenhall making way for 8 Group at
Bourn. Here BK654 LS-W is seen leaving.

Reduced effort ensued due to
organisational changes. Oakington
and its satellite stations transferred
to No 8 (PFF) Group on 15 April
1943, a day which unusually saw
two Horsa gliders help move XV
Squadron   from   Bourn   to
Mildenhall to make way for 97
Squadron's Lancasters loaned by 5

XV Squadron's memorable moving day involved two
Horsas with Albemarle and Whitley tugs.

Group to the PFF. But future prospects for the Stirling force improved when some
squadron establishments increased to 24 IE + 6 IR and thirty-three crews.

A two-pronged attack was launched on **16/17 April,** when 239/327 Lancasters and
Halifaxes, thirty-seven of which failed to return, attempted to bomb Skoda's Pilsen works.
Another force, 197/271 strong and including 8/10 Stirlings Pathfinders and 63/85
bombers, unleashed a highly damaging attack upon Mannheim. With them were 159
Wellingtons and 17 Halifaxes. Losses that night totalled fifty-five including seven Stirlings,
the heaviest yet in one night.

Among those was BK725 'M-Mother' of 90 Squadron flown by Fg Off P D White.
Returning home very low, they climbed on reaching Laon for searchlights beaming almost
horizontally illuminated and held the aircraft as it banked steeply at a mere 200ft. German
machine-gun fire injured the pilot before the rear gunner could shoot out the searchlights.
A damaged starboard engine meant the propeller needed feathering and White ordered the
crew to prepare for forced landing. Five minutes later both starboard engines were useless
and soon after the aircraft crashed near a wood and erupted in flames. Fg Off White,
seriously injured, became a POW. His companions had lucky escapes from the bomber.

BK653-A of 214 Squadron captained by Flt Sgt D E James left Chedburgh at 2150
hrs with a load including 2 x 2,000lb HEs and a 500lb long delay bomb. During the
9,000ft outward run two Ju 88s were evaded before another fighter made three
damaging attacks. Bombs were jettisoned, dives at up to 300mph followed, but still the
fighter tenaciously held on then closed from starboard pouring shots through the
Stirling's cockpit windows and between the pilot and navigator. The mid-upper turret
was damaged and bullets even whistled through the gunner's seat. He used all his
ammunition in a 2–3 minute burst whereas the front guns couldn't be brought to bear.
Instead he tried to scare off the fighter which had used all its ammunition. Heading for

home the crew discovered Nos 5 and 6 petrol tanks were leaking. Nine minutes later the crew began to abandon the aircraft while two helped the pilot to keep the Stirling aloft. Leaking fuel soon set the starboard wing alight and although the engines kept running they were surrounded by fire which no extinguisher could cope with. All the crew abandoned the aircraft which exploded on hitting the ground near Bonneuil, France.

A five-pronged assault on **20/21 April** resulted in a battering for central Stettin while 9/11 Mosquitoes bombed Berlin in moonlight, small numbers mined or dropped leaflets and 53/84 Stirlings attempted unsuccessfully to disable Heinkel's Rostock plant marked by two crews of 7 Squadron. A smokescreen fast cloaked the factory causing caused Stirlings to bomb alternatives. Eight others did not return.

Duisburg wrapped in ground haze was the main target on **26/27th.** PFF ground marked but still many bombs fell short of the APs although fires were started and considerable damage was caused. In the month's final Stirling venture, on **30 April/1 May,** eight PFF Stirlings practising marking further disturbed Bocholt's residents by dropping 9 x 2,000lb HC bombs.

Analysis of the **April** effort showed that No 218 had despatched the most Stirling sorties, 127, and No XV Squadron's 117 was outstanding considering it had changed bases. The highest sortie success rate, 92 percent, was claimed by 214 Squadron, which dropped 375,000lb of bombs. Shorter nights reduced operational radius, with 549 bombing and 120 mining sorties by Stirlings judged as successful, but at a cost of forty-three aircraft missing.

R9254 – one of the few with H2S radome – was at A&AEE for radio and radar development between November 1942 and June 1943.

No 7 Squadron should by now have had all its Stirlings equipped with *H2S*, with other squadrons following as sets became available. Installation meant removing the few ventral turrets in situ, but *H2S* equipment and radomes also prevented the bombers from fulfilling their secondary paratrooping role. *H2S* in belly radomes was eventually fitted to only a handful of Stirlings. Arrester gear, proposed for heavily laden aircraft and installed at Waterbeach in an attempt to reduce excessive tyre wear, was also abandoned.

Defensive armament was repeatedly revised. Stirlings now had FN 20 tail turrets with improved gunners' view but slower rotation. For each gun, including those in the FN 50s, 2,500 rounds were available. Arthur Edgley, a XV Squadron gunner, recalls that:

> The FN 20s had a reflector sight with spare bulbs, a bright and dimming switch and a circle with a central dot focused at infinity. The views from the mid-upper and front turrets were really exhilarating! Before take-off the rear gunner had to harmonise his four guns, for

which purpose a large board with four different-coloured roundels was placed same 400 yards from the rear turret. Then the gunner took the firing pins out of each gun before adjusting and lining up each barrel on its coloured dot. After all four guns were harmonised they were locked into position. We had two different kinds of toggle to cock the guns for firing, one being a length of wire with a loop in one end whereas the other was a piece of metal with a hook which engaged the cocking stud.

We also had to check the links joining the ammunition rounds. There were Type B1 and B2 links, and if any were wrong then changing them could take a considerable time. On one occasion making such a change on BF533-LS:H took me a whole afternoon! Another task was the checking of the recuperator. This ensured that there was enough oil in the system to drive the turrets and, when all was well, that the plunger would be at its highest level. If there was a leakage, or pressure was low, the plunger would be down or partly so.

Another job for the tail gunner was to take a drift reading for the navigator. The gunner locked his turret central then pointed his gun sight, or watched his sight, as it passed through something on the ground such as a tree, farmhouse, etc. He then unlocked his turret and pointed the sight at the chosen object. Then he read off the drift from a red or green scale in a hole in the bottom of the turret. The turret gunner waited a few seconds before training his sight on the picked object.

All gunners needed to know where the escape hatches were, the release point for the large dinghy, the storage points of tools, axe, oxygen points, etc. The rear gunner had his own one-man dinghy.

BF476 of XV Squadron brought down by flak during a Rostock raid and set ablaze by the crew. Prior to the operation it had flown only 18 hours 10 minutes. (J Helme)

A solitary WAAF smiles upon the safe return of many youngsters of 199 Squadron.

During March 1943 the fitting of an FN 82 carrying 2 x .50in guns had been discussed, and the effect of this and AGLT radar on trim was being explored. Proposals were made for it to be accommodated in Stirling Mk IIIs, along with arrester gear, a B.12 dorsal turret, radio modifications, a Tricell flarechute and another five flarechutes moved forward. Such changes would have shifted the cg position 1.5in aft of the extreme already accepted.

To make the change the ventral FN 64 – unpopular because it altered the cg – would need removal, rounds per gun reduced to 1,000 in the FN 82, the rear gunner would need to move to the rest bunk during landing and arrester gear taken out. Arguments about fitting the FN 82 droned on until early July 1943, by which time it was decided that its introduction when Stirling production was at its peak was unwarranted. Installing the B.12 would have little effect on cg, but its weight with 5,200 rounds was 550lb more than that of the FN 50 meant sacrificing bomb load or fuel. Arthur Edgley tried the B.12 and recalls that "as the gunner's seat went up, the guns came down and vice versa. I didn't care much for that!"

May 1943 saw seven major bombing operations. Squadron aircraft now mostly having Mk XIV bombsights were at their peak strength. On 30 April 1943, 3 Group's Stirling establishment stood at 136, whereas strength was159 aircraft. Peak strength was attained on 12 May, a fall to an establishment of 104 being ordered next day when strength stood at 103 aircraft. Throughout May, No 7 Squadron's establishment was held at 24 IE + 3 IR Mk IIIs, strength equated on most days. Ironically, the establishment reduction came as the Stirling force was at its most efficient. Strength and distribution of the Stirlings at 1800 hrs on 23 May was:

Sqn	Establishment	Serviceable	Unserviceable	
			Non-operational	Operational
7	16+4	29	–	4
XV	24+6	19	–	5
75	24+6	17	6	4
90	24+6	12	7	4
149	24+6	15	3	5
214	24+6	17	–	9
218	24+6	13	7	6
Totals		122	23	37

The first of the months' punishing assaults came on the **4/5th**, when in excellent weather Dortmund was terribly tortured. Placing of initial red TIs a little to the north of the aiming points were soon corrected, and very soon enormous fires were visible 150 miles away. The raid cost thirty-one aircraft, among them six 3 Group Stirlings and one of 7 Squadron's six. A training operation was carried out by six Stirling Pathfinders three of which aimed a dozen 2,000lb HCs at workshops in Rheine.

On **12/13 May** Bomber Command made its fourth major raid on Duisburg. Weather again was good, PFF marking accurate and on time. Very heavy concentrated bombing followed and at 0217 hrs there was a spectacular explosion flames from which rocketed high enough to illuminate aircraft flying at 18,000ft. Extensive heavy damage was caused throughout Duisburg, to the Thyssen steel plant and in Germany's major inland port. The 63/70 Stirlings, fewer than of late, attacked from around 13,000ft dropping mixed loads averaging 7,500lb, whereas the 227/238 Lancasters averaged 9,133lb and attacked from over 18,000ft. The 121/142 Halifaxes each delivered an average 6,097lb load. Five Stirlings failed to return, and one of 75 Squadron crashed soon after take off from Newmarket. Six of the crew died, and two were seriously injured.

Just how effective a German intruder campaign could have been was shown when Plt Off F Shippard and crew (BF473-B/75 Squadron) were intercepted home-coming 15 miles off the East coast. Rear and upper turrets were damaged and only by firmly holding the column between his knees could Shippard prevent the aircraft from climbing. The crew were lucky to have made their safe return to Stradishall.

Next night, again fine, the action switched to Bochum. Reports of twenty-seven night fighter interceptions were filed, one Stirling being twice fired upon at 0157 hrs over Harderwijk and another four times over Egmond. A second engagement, by a Fw 190, took place at 13,000ft over Harderwijk at 0203 hrs, and near Solingen at 0212 hrs the mid and rear gunners of 0/75 Squadron shared a Bf 110. Meanwhile the rear gunner of Y/149 Squadron shot down a single-engined fighter at 0207 hrs near Munster after a Ju 88 had fired upon the Stirling. A third success was attributed to the rear and mid-upper gunners of R/218 Squadron who, at 0251 hrs and 3 miles north of Terschelling, saw their attacker explode on the ground. Near Apeldoorn at 0240 hrs a Fw 190 engaged H/75 Squadron in an inconclusive fight and at 0259 hrs a Bf 110 was shaken off over Hertogenbosch with the corkscrew manoeuvre. It was certainly a night packed with night-fighter activity.

Landing back after any sortie was always a testing time demanding much concentration as shown when Sgt T J Nichols of 218 Squadron was about to line up with Chedburgh and EF367-G developed a major problem. Aboard as navigator was Flight Sergeant Price, who only too well remembers that night:

> We were on our first operation to Germany. As we crossed from Belgium into Germany we were attacked by a night fighter. Our rear gunner, Sgt Hovards, was killed, and although the aircraft was badly damaged none of the rest of us was injured.

We dropped our bombs on the nearest German village then turned back towards England, crossing the Scheldt Estuary at low level. The maximum height we reached over the North Sea was 8,000ft and over England Chedburgh responded to our 'Mayday'. As we were in the funnel approaching the runway, without flaps or undercarriage down, an engine cut. The aircraft hit a tree, broke in half and caught fire, two of our crew being thrown out and instantly killed. Another died in Bury hospital six hours later. Jameson, the trapped wireless operator, lost his life in the burning fuselage, while Sgt Nichols was flung under the burning wing from where one of the crash tender crew, at considerable risk to himself, pulled him clear. He spent many months in hospital suffering from burns and other injuries. Fate was very kind to me for I only had a sprained ankle and was soon back at Downham Market, where I joined the crew of Sgt G Jenkins (later Pilot Officer, DFC) who was killed during the Nuremberg raid of **27/28 August** when our crew was shot down by a fighter. The rest of the crew that night became POWs.

At 1800 hrs on **23 May**, the following night of which brought another highpoint in the Stirling's career, the strength of the force was:

| | | Unserviceable | |
Sqn	Serviceable	Non-operational	Operational
7	31	3	–
XV	16	5	8
75	16	3	10
90	14	3	5
149	16	5	6
214	23	4	–
218	15	8	8
620	–	–	–
Totals	131	31	37

Of the Stirlings, 34 percent were unserviceable compared with about 23 percent Halifaxes and Lancasters and 36 percent Wellington Xs.

Comparative totals on 18 May 1943 for other operational bombers were: Lancaster 353, 7, 96 (of which 19 were Lancaster Mk IIs of 115 Sqn); Halifax 133, 1, 22; Wellington X 101, 16, 20.

Mk IIIs featured a useful 'bubble' window on both sides of the forward fuselage. Nose turret is an FN 5A. Prominent engine cooling gills 'Open' or 'Closed' had considerable performance effects.

On the night of **23/24 May** not only was the largest number of bombers despatched since 1942's '1,000 bomber' raids, but for the first time 100 Stirling bombers operated with 17/20 more in the marker force. Accurate marking in excellent weather allowed 584/632 aircraft to deliver a devastating onslaught upon Dortmund with returns suggesting that eighty-two Stirlings bombed the primary target. So extensive were the fires that they rapidly consumed the ground markers, brightly lit the sky to a height of 3 1/2 miles and were visible from over 100 miles away. Average Stirling load was 7,590lb compared with the 9,120lb of the sixteen Lancaster IIs of 115 Squadron and the 11,420lb carried by the 48/51 Lancasters of 5 Group which emphasises the increasing efficiency of the second generation four-motor bomber. Fighter defences not surprisingly responded over a wide area bringing 3 Group twenty assorted brushes with the enemy.

On this special Stirling occasion those operating were:

7 Sqn: R9249-H, R9257-R2, R9258-K, R9260-O, R9266-J, R9267-S, R9283-Q, R9289-F, BK723-E, EF361-B, EF363-G, EF364-X, EF368-A, EF369-Z, EF384-U, EF387-D, EF388-M, EF390-T, EF392-N, EF402-Y

XV Sqn: BF439-D, BF460-C, BF470-G, BF482-R, BK648-J, BK654-W, BK656-A, BK533-H, BK719-B, BK774-K, BK815-V, BK818-O, EF339-Y, EF348-N, EH875-S

75 Sqn: BF443-V, BF459-JN:E, BF461-B, BF561-O, BK434, BK646, BK776-B, BK777-?, BK778-U, BK783, BK817, EF398-A, BK810 and two unknown

90 Sqn: BF404-V, BF407-Q, BF435-X, BF464-C, BF504-F, BF527-N ?, BF566-T, BK665-D, BK693-A, BK718-M, BK779-L, BK781-E, BK784-P, BK811-B, EF334-U, EF397-K, EH876-J

149 Sqn: BF477-D, BF503-U, BF507-S, BF509-N, BF573-W, BF530-B, BF531-M, BF576-Y, BK703-K, BK710-A, BK713-X, BK799-O, EF336-F, EF389-Q, EF395-L

214 Sqn: W7465-W, W7610-A, BF478-G FTR, BF481-M, BF511-V, BF516-U, BF528-L FTR, BF574-B, BK659-N, BK689-E, BK690-V, BK717-U, BK720-Y, BK763-F, BK771-L, BK800-Z, BK801-?, EF394-H, EH882-O, EH886-S, MZ261-? (FTR)

218 Sqn: N3721-J, BF472-V, BF501-N, BF522-F, BF565-H, BF567-P, BF568-B, BF572-K, BK687-R, BK688-A, BK706-Y FTR, BK712-D, BK722-G, BK761-O, EF352-Q, EH878-I, EH884-X

Most were Mk IIIs. A worthy Mk I, N3721 of No 218 Squadron by far the oldest Stirling operating, was on squadron strength from February 1942 to November 1943.

On **25/26 May** it was Düsseldorf's turn but two thick cloud layers protected it, and illuminators and bombs fell well dispersed and over a wide area. May's most destructive raid came instead on **29/30** when 608/719 bombers using 856.6 tons of HE and 345,500 incendiaries virtually wiped out Wuppertal's Barmen district. Conflagrations with astounding rapidity engulfed thousands of buildings and over 3,000 people died. Bomber Command ORS assessment reckoned the raid caused twice as much damage and five times as many casualties as any previously. Stirlings (eight of which did not return) carried average loads of 7,320lb, compared with a 6,362lb average aboard the 172 Halifaxes. Two combats were reported, one by the crew of G/7 Squadron who at 0052 hrs and 7 miles east of Rotterdam, claimed a Bf 110 shot down on fire after it twice attacked them. The other was an unidentified fighter which tackled U/214 Squadron over Diest at 0223 hrs and which was driven off in flames. A total of thirty-three aircraft were missing, and a 90 Squadron Stirling crashed 8 miles south-east of Newmarket killing all except the rear gunner.

Stirlings flew 627 successful bombing sorties in May, 214 Squadron being top of the league with 129, and 149 Squadron second with 121. In addition, over 700 mines were laid during a further 143 successful sorties.

A second Base, No 32, had formed comprising Stradishall, Ridgewell and Chedburgh, During the month Ridgewell passed to the 4th Bomb Wing Substitution Unit, USAAF and 90 Squadron moved on the 31st to newly opened West Wickham, renamed Wratting Common on 21 August 1943.

*R9147 operated from Waterbeach and
Wratting Common by 1651 Conversion Unit.*

*In 1943, 1651 Conversion Unit aircraft began
displaying unit identity letters like BS-O shown
here at Wratting Common.* (G Mackie)

Not only had squadrons expanded to three-Flight level, their establishment was unexpectedly raised in May by the addition of three extra aircraft and crews, making Stirling squadron establishment 24 IE + 6 IR along with thirty-three crews. Faster and increased output from conversion units was essential, No 1657 turning out thirty-seven crews in April, who achieved 1,309 flying hours, while 1651 Conversion Unit generated thirty-five crews who flew 1,223 hours. A lot of training involved 'circuits and bumps'. In April 1943, 1657 CU recorded 2,017 landings and 1651 CU a further 2,070.

Accident rates at conversion units were high, many attributed to pilot error on landing or taking off. A necessary deep ancient drainage ditch skirted the Cambridge–Ely road bordering Waterbeach. It is said to have caught and collapsed over 200 Stirling undercarriages.

The increase in effective aircraft strength at Conversion Units is shown by these 1943 figures:

CU	7 Jan	18 Feb	1 Apr	21 Apr	29 Apr	27 May	30 Jun
1651	27	33	35	13 op 27 non-op	12 op 24 non-op 1 x MkIII	9 op 24 non-op 1 x MkIII	9 op 26 non-op 1 x MkIII
1657	26	27	20	22 op 16 non-op	17 op 14 non-op	17 op 16 non-op	12 op 25 non-op
1665	–	–	–	–	Estab 16 Has nil	Estab 32 Has nil	17

May 1943 had brought a welter of courageous action. Early on the **13th** Plt Off G W Young of 90 Squadron, four times attacked by a fighter, had aboard his aircraft Sgt W Davine who, although seriously wounded, continued to play an active part while Young nursed home the damaged aircraft. Plt Off Shippard also of 90 Squadron and flying BF473 loaded with 1,080 x 4lb and 90 x 30lb incendiaries (standard for 90 Squadron that night) was flying at 190mph IAS at 11,000ft, 15 miles off the enemy coast, when a fighter scored hits on the rear and mid-upper turrets. The badly shot about Stirling kept adopting a nose-up attitude, and only by clasping the control column between his knees could he keep it level. Over Stradishall a main wheel began vibrating badly, nevertheless a safe landing was achieved.

Night fighters did not have it all their own way. On **13 May**, Sgt J R Mitchell of 75 Squadron flying BK619 was attacked by a Bf 110 from 400 yards below and astern. The mid-upper gunner replied as the fighter curved away below the Stirling then the rear gunner finished off the fighter.

On 1 June 1943 Stirling squadron total establishment stood at 104 aircraft in 3 Group and 24 in 7 Squadron with 96 and 21 aircraft respectively fit for operations. Although up to strength, the reduced operational effort at this time was partly due to squadron movement and introduction of new airfields. Although Mepal did not officially open until 30 July, No 75 (New Zealand) Squadron, had arrived from Newmarket Heath on 26 June. Close-by Witchford was also occupied well before formal opening on 31 August.

Stirlings carried a large inflatable dinghy in the wing. If it came adrift in flight it could wrap itself around the tail bringing disaster.

Only on the **11/12th** within the first half of June did 3 Group Stirlings set forth in strength, their target being Düsseldorf. Many factories were hit and the half-hour raid left a gigantic fire engulfing the city centre. Over 1,400 large fires had been started, and more than 140,000 people became homeless. Dropped from 15,000ft, the average Stirling load was 7,334lb compared with 9,220lb of the 5 Group Lancasters. Although thirty-eight aircraft were missing, only two were Stirlings.

LK380 XY-Y of 'C' Flight 90 Squadron crashed at Sedge Fen, Shippea Hill, after colliding with AFDU Hurricane KW800 during fighter affiliation training.

German aircraft had recently launched half-hearted intruder activity against British bomber bases particularly East Anglia's. At 0320 hrs on 15 June 1943, Stradishall came under attack from a lone single-seat Fw 190 fighter-bomber of SKG 10 operating at extreme range. Its single bomb exploded in a field 300 yards east of the aerodrome, and the pilot poured cannon shells into two Stirlings of 1657 Conversion Unit.

Failure to mount a sustained intruder campaign allowed Bomber Command to continue dealing out punishment on a grand scale, Le Creusot's Schneider arms factory coming under attack on **19/20 June**. The 266/290 raiders included 18/18 PFF Stirlings and 83/87 3 Group Stirlings all of which safely returned. Command Operations Order No 175 called for twenty Stirlings carrying 100 percent incendiary loads to drop them from 4,000ft 15 minutes after the raid began to start a fire in the north-east corner of the Schneider factory, leaving other Stirlings to drop 100 percent HE loads. Many bombs fell wide of specified APs because drifting parachute flares and not TIs were used for attacks on France. Another 3/3 7 Squadron Stirlings marked the Henri Paul transformer station at Montchanin but instead a nearby factory was bombed. The power station escaped damage due to its small size.

Krefeld was next to experience incineration, and on a dark night with good visibility. Correctly placed ground markers were well backed-up, but PFF losses were high due to night fighter activity. Although 15/19 8 Group Stirlings are thought to have attacked, four did not return and No 3 Group lost three Stirlings. Krefeld joined the set of fire ravaged towns with its centre incinerated, over 5,500 houses destroyed, more than 1,000 inhabitants killed and 4,500 injured. Some 72,000 people lost their homes in one of the most horrific raids so far.

Fine and clear was the night of **22/23 June** which allowed very accurate ground marking of Mulheim upon which a ferocious onslaught was unleashed cutting its links with rescue services beyond and destroying over 60 percent of the town. Of 557 aircraft setting out, 35 never returned. No 75 Squadron lost four aircraft, other Stirling losses totalling seven. Among the missing was BK712 which, straying from the prescribed course, fell prey to a Bf 110 of II/NJG 1 whose pilot, *Major* Heinz-Wolfgang Schnaufer, brought down the bomber near the Belgian village of Langdorp.

Elberfeld/Wuppertal attracted attention on **24/25 June.** Bombing wiped out 94 percent of the target, casualties reaching around 1,800 killed and 2,400 injured. No 3 Group lost seven Stirlings. Ground marking commenced at 0101 hrs and within fifteen minutes a gigantic explosion was seen by many crews. A bomber had crashed in Gelsenkirchen which, on **25/26 June,** became a Main Force target. Stirlings of 3 Group released all-incendiary loads, but the result was less than in some raids due to considerable cloud, *Oboe* failures and drifting sky markers. Five Stirlings were missing out of a total loss of thirty aircraft.

Accurate ground marking generally led to the most successful raids but the other major raid of the time, directed at Cologne on **28/29 June,** involved sky marking and turned out to be the city's most devastating experience of the war. The 510/608 attackers released 604.4 tons of HE and a huge load of incendiaries which led to the destruction of forty-three industrial premises, the deaths of 4,377 people and around 10,000 injured and left an horrific 230,000 homeless. Ju 88 fighters were probably responsible for three losses sustained by 149 Squadron and two by XV Squadron.

One missing aircraft on the **28/29th** was EE880-O of 149 Squadron. En route it only reached 14,500ft and was very late for the 3 Group assault timed to run from 0155 hrs to 0159 hrs. With EE880's tailplane and port wing flak damaged, the pilot guided by his rear gunner began weaving among more flak bursts directed blind at the aircraft flying above cloud. Clear of Cologne, 'O-Orange' headed homewards at 13,000–14,000ft and at around 160mph IAS. Just after crossing the Belgian frontier the flight engineer heard the rattling sound of bullets striking the aircraft. The intercom system had failed so no warning of attack could come from the gunners. Within moments bursts of flame streamed from both mainplanes and fire rapidly spread into the fuselage. From the doomed aircraft the bomb aimer and navigator baled out of the front hatch and the flight engineer left as the Stirling began rolling. EE880 crashed near Thielt, Brabant. By heading home 25 miles south of the prescribed route the Stirling had become easy picking for a fighter.

Expansion of the Stirling force was still underway. No 199 Squadron brought their Wellington Xs from Ingham to join 3 Group at Lakenheath on 20 June, the squadron having flown their last two Wellington sorties on 13 June and then began work up on Stirling IIIs. Another new Stirling squadron was No 620 based at Stradishall's Sub-Station Chedburgh. Commanded by Wg Cdr D H Lee, they first operated on **19 June** during the Schneider factory raid when eight crews participated and against Krefeld on

21 June. Sgt P O'Connell flying BK724 faced a Bf 109 over the target, his gunner, Sgt C Doig, firing a 30-second burst to drive away the fighter. O'Connell's adventures for the month were not over, for on the 24th his aircraft was hit by flak, forcing it so low that a gunner, Flt Lt Weston, was able to pour fire into searchlights from 700ft. Two of the crew sustained superficial wounds, and O'Connell was forced to crash at Chedburgh.

Stirlings sometimes flew daylight ASR sorties. An eventful one took place on 13 June when Sgt J M Steel was flying BK781 of 90 Squadron. A dinghy holding six men was spotted and Steel circled until a relief Stirling arrived. A Walrus alighted close to the dinghy, and the occupants scrambled aboard. As the second Stirling prepared to leave the heavily laden Walrus made frantic unsuccessful attempts to get aloft. Smoke flares were dropped to give the Walrus pilot clear wind direction, and then a second Walrus circled. An ASR launch soon reached the scene and took aboard the rescued men, allowing the alighted Walrus to depart.

An amazing event had occurred during a Ruhr attack by 75 Squadron on **19 June**. Flt Lt J Joll was flying EH880 when an anti-aircraft shell burst inside the port mainplane severing a petrol cock, oil pipe and control cables. Oil poured into the fuselage so Sgt G Fallon, the flight engineer, unable to ascertain the fracture point, decided to enter the wing to locate it. With the aircraft still under fire in the target area he cut a 2ft square hole out of the fuselage metal, then crawled into the wing, turned off the fuel pumps and investigated the leak. While in the wing, he inspected the mainwheel tyre. All was well, so he crawled back to report. He had shown complete disregard for his own safety, and the aircraft made a safe landing at Newmarket.

July 1943 brought no let up as the vicious campaign headed towards an horrendous climax. Stirlings participated in seven major attacks including the most destructive and harrowing of all conventional bombing raids – those directed at Hamburg. Four other operations were against Ruhr targets, and Stirlings also flew 103 mining sorties over nine nights. Sorties for July totalled 1,026, with 90.7 percent of the crews claiming to bomb their primary targets during 5,040 flying hours. Bomb tonnage amounted to 1,466.21 tons, and 199 Squadron flew its first Stirling operation when six crews mined on **30 July**.

During those four Ruhr raids, Cologne, Aachen, Essen and Remscheid came under attack, the Cologne operation being mounted on the **3/4th** when 59/76 Stirlings dropped only incendiaries. On this one night Bomber Command ORS reckoned that a minimum of 331,647 such bombs showered onto the city in addition to 915.2 tons of HE weapons. Over 500 people were killed, 1,000 injured, some 2,200 houses were destroyed, 72,000 were made homeless and twenty factories wrecked for the loss of thirty bombers including five Stirlings. Nine in the Stirling force aborted and five attacked last-resort targets including Euskirchen, Bruges and Antwerp. Such 'small-scale' raids should never be underrated, for an assault by one Stirling could produce enormous damage with just one incendiary bomb load being able to destroy a quite large area, whereas during very heavy onslaughts many bombs fell on to areas already suffering savagely during the same raid.

BF530-B of 149 Squadron, captained Flt Sgt G A Cozens heading a crew of eight, left Lakenheath at 2330 hrs, headed for Cologne in the dark sky, crossed the enemy coast at 14,000ft and took moderate evasive action. As Flt Sgt R Hodge, the wireless operator, stepped from the astrodome stand he heard bullets striking the aircraft and, looking upwards, saw the reflected glow of flames. The pilot called out "Quick, abandon aircraft!" as both mid-upper and rear gunners spotted the German fighter.

Fire in the port wing root spread into the fuselage close to Hodge's seat, burning him when he grabbed his parachute. Aboard the aircraft was a full incendiary load which, like the aircraft, was probably alight by the time he was wearing his 'chute pack. When Hodge reached the forward hatch he found the bomb aimer had jumped and that the navigator was about to do so. Suddenly the pilot lost control and the Stirling entered an almost vertical dive. Fg Off E G Redman baled out, but Hodge was hurled around in the aircraft, which was soon spinning. He was then flung from the bomber, pulled his 'chute ripcord at about 2,000ft and lost his flying boots before landing in a wheatfield at Geet Betz. Only Redman and Hodge survived the appallingly event, and the bomb aimer died in hospital.

Against Aachen on **13/14 July**, Bomber Command fielded 327/374 aircraft including Stirlings of 7 Squadron. Strong tail winds brought too many aircraft simultaneously on to the scene as PFF markers opened the assault. A gigantic fire engulfed much of the city causing very high casualties. Flt Lt C E Coombs flying EE873-D of 90 Squadron was carrying out his twenty-first operation. After take-off from West Wickham at 2230 hrs, and carrying 80 x 30lb and 1,080 x 4lb incendiaries, he climbed to 15,000ft in bright moonlight while weaving continuously. About 40 miles from Aachen the mid-upper gunner noticed a twin-engined fighter shadowing them so the pilot corkscrewed after diving to port. From starboard below a second fighter closed firing a one-second burst scoring hits on the starboard mainplane and outer engine which soon was burning.

Sgt W G Dawson, the bomb aimer, called "Dive!" and the captain responded. Sgt R Clarke, the mid-upper gunner, hearing no more, assumed that the intercom was dead and seeing fire fast spreading, decided it prudent to prepare to bale out. On reaching the rear hatch he was uncertain whether to leave then the bomber suddenly lurched hurling him out. Believing he had landed near Maastricht, he began walking and covered over 200 miles before making contact with anyone! He had seen nothing of the crash, but concluded that a fuel tank had been hit. Although EE873 was fitted with *Boozer* only one indication of enemy activity had been detected, over the enemy coast.

H2S was the prime navigational aid but, it will be recalled, fitment precluded installation of ventral guns. With the rapidly improving night fighter defences, such guns were a worthwhile asset, but only Lancaster Mk IIs carried the ventral FN 64 turret so unpopular that BDU devised a simple ventral defence in the aft escape hatch of a Stirling. It consisted of a .50in gun on a simple mounting behind a triangular protecting windscreen. Command examined it on 20 July, approving it for non-*H2S* aircraft and future production heavies. Downward search provision was required, so trials continued into autumn of 1943.

It was surprising how few Stirlings were struck by bombs falling from higher operators, but 149 Squadron's aircraft seemed prone to the misfortune. Plt Off G W Macdonald over Aachen on **13 July** in EH894 had several incendiaries strike his aircraft severing fuel leads. The aircraft also suffered flak damage and, short of fuel and flying on three engines, he forced landed at Tangmere.

No raids so far became as horrific as those directed in late July upon Hamburg, second city of the Reich and which accommodated over 3,000 industrial units and undertook 45 percent of U-boat production giving it much legitimacy as a target. Bomber Command's Stirling force still at high strength could inflict awesome fire raids upon relatively close targets like Hamburg despite improving German defences. In response Bomber Command introduced *Window*, the metal foil – now commonly called 'Chaff' – and designed to prevent radar tracking.

Bomber Command Operations Instruction No 70 of **17 July 1943** described this new 'weapon'. Bundles weighing 2lb each and comprising 2,200 wafer thin metal strips each measuring 25cm by 2cm would be released at a rate of one bundle per minute per aircraft and by 600 aircraft per hour. Each bundle would take 20–30 seconds to disperse, fall at between 300 and 400 feet per minute and be effective in jamming enemy radar for between 15 and 20 minutes during which time individual aircraft would be effectively protected by a huge metallic cloud. Fear of German use of the idea had hitherto caused it not to be used, but mounting bomber losses led to its introduction now.

Details of *Window* were announced to crews during briefing for the first Hamburg raid and by each Station Commander using these authorised words:

> Tonight you are going to use a new and simple countermeasure, *Window*, to protect yourselves against the German defence system. *Window* consists of dropping packets of metal strips which produce almost the same reactions on RDF equipment as do your aircraft. The German defences will, therefore, become confused and you should stand a good chance of getting through unscathed while their attention is being wasted on the packets of *Window*.
>
> There are two points which I wish to emphasise. Firstly, the benefit of *Window* is a communal one; the *Window* which protects you is not so much that which you drop yourselves as that which is already in the air dropped by the aircraft ahead. To obtain full advantage it is therefore necessary to fly in a concentrated stream along the ordered route.
>
> Secondly, the task of discharging the packets of *Window* will not be an easy one. You are hampered by your oxygen tube, intercom connections, the darkness and the general difficulties of physical effort at high altitudes.
>
> Despite these hardships it is essential that the correct quantities of *Window* are discharged. So important is this new Hun-baffling device considered, that special semi-automatic machines are being produced to ensure a steady flow from each aircraft. Two-thirds of our present losses occur on the way home, *Window* can only reduce these homeward losses if each one of you makes a special effort to adhere strictly to the ordered return route.

During the ensuing night Stirling brushes with enemy aircraft amounted to only six.

The Hamburg raids, planned in **May 1943** and covered by Ops Order 173, were intended to completely destroy the city. Stirlings and Halifaxes would carry two-thirds incendiary loads including 50 percent 30lb weapons and 15 percent 4lb Type 4X explosive bombs and Lancaster IIs of 3 Group would deliver 8,000lb HC bombs. Other Lancasters would drop mixed loads.

Crews were ordered to approach from well out to sea, after over-flying the Cromer exit point and following the course 54° 45N/07° 00E – 53° 55N/09° 05E – Hamburg – 53° 15N/10° 00E – 54° 30N/06° 00E – Cromer – bases. The plan was for the first wave to comprise 117 aircraft, the second 18 Lancasters of 115 Squadron with 72 Halifaxes of 4 Group and 27 Lancasters of 5 Group. Then would come 114 Stirlings of 3 Group. With adjustment the operation followed these lines.

At 1800 hrs on 24 July, the chosen day, Stirlings available at 1800 hrs for operations were:

Sqn	Establishment	Serviceable		Unserviceable
		Operational	Non-operational	
7	Nil	15	–	3
XV	24 + 6	16	12	4
75	24 + 6	18	21	1
90	24 + 6	20	10	1
149	16 + 4	22	–	1
196	16 + 4	2	–	1
199	16 + 4	–	12	7
214	16 + 4	20	–	3
218	24 + 6	32	–	2
620	16 + 4	20	–	1
Totals	176 + 44	165	55	24

Totals of other types available:

Halifax II/V	304 + 70	323	14	36
Lancaster				
Mk 1/III	400 + 63	429	4	39
Mk II	32 + 8	18	6	22
Mosquito	58 + 11	43	9	16
Wellington	152 + 21			
Mk III	–	4	2	–
Mk X	104	4	7	–

The Stirlings operating that night were:

7 Sqn: R9283-Q, R9288-P, R9293-F, EF363-G, EF364-X, EF368-A, EF369-Z, EF388-M, EF393-B, EF406-U along with eight Lancasters
XV Sqn: BF470-G, BF521-P, BF569-Y, BK652-Q, BK654-W, BK719-B, BK764-R, BK766-T, BK774-K, BK805-U, BK816-X, BK818-O, EE908-V, EF427-A, EF428-N, EH875-S, EH893-J, MZ264-DJ:A
75 Sqn: BF443-V, BF465-JN:K, BF518-E, BF564-W, BK777-U, BK778-U, BK809-T, EE878-P, EE881-JN:G, EE890-L (FTR), EE891-Q, EE892-F, EE893-N, EE897-G, EE898-D, EE915-X, EF435-JN:J, EH901-JN:O, EH905-R, EH928-A, EH935-K, EH936-W
90 Sqn: BF464-C, BF524-N, BF532-W, BK693-A, BK723-D, BK779-L, BK784-P, EE896-J, EE900-Y, EE904-S, EE916-F, EE951-B, EF431-Q, EF441-G, EF443-M, EF446-O
149 Sqn: BF509-B, BF512-E, BF570-H, BK711-O, BK765-P, BK798-Q, EE872-N, EE879-G, EF360-R, EF411-M, EF412-F, EH883-A, EH903-L, EH904-K, MZ260-C
214 Sqn: BF562-Q, BF574-B, BK686-C, BK689-E, EE874-G, EE876-N, EE899-O, EE901-L, EE902-P (FTR), EH899-X, EH921-J
218 Sqn: N3721-J, BF472-V, BF522-N, BF567-P (WO D T Saville, FTR), BF568-B, BF578-A, BK687-R, BK700-L, BK761-O, BK803-D, EE895-S, EE888-K, EE909-H, EF352-Q, EF410-Z, EH878-I, EH884-X, EH892-U, EH923-W, MZ263-Y
620 Sqn: BF525-Q, BF576-F, BK690-P, BK713-E, BK801-?, BK802-Z, EF433-W, EF442-O, EF457-A, EH945-P, and one unknown

Late on **24 July,** a total of 791 bombers set out for Hamburg and, to further confuse the enemy, thirteen Mosquitoes dog-legged towards other cities while thirty-three Lancasters made for Leghorn in Italy. Mining took place, and crews under training dropped leaflets. With little or no cloud, good visibility, light winds and a half moon rising at about 0100 hrs, Hamburg's fate was sealed. Marking the centre of the large city by approaching along the line of the river Elbe was aided by *H2S* and so devised that the bombing would inevitably creep back along the approach route. Although the huge port along with shipbuilding and U-boat yards were important targets, the series of raids on Hamburg now beginning were intended to obliterate the entire city.

Within the force were twenty-one Stirlings drawn from 75 Squadron which included EH935 flown by Fg Off G Turner. He was avoiding searchlights when a Ju 88 approached head-on and careered into his starboard wing tip knocking off a four foot piece and rendering the aileron useless. The Ju 88 rolled and fell to earth. Controlling the Stirling proved very difficult, the unbalanced bomber only being kept on an even keel by the combined strength of the pilot and the bomb aimer. Nevertheless the three-hour flight ended in a perfect landing at Mepal.

Command ORS summarised this Hamburg raid thus:

Group	Aircraft	Attacked /no sent	Missing	Average height (ft)	Average bombing load (lb)
8	Stirling	9/10	–	14,000	4,050
	Halifax	32/37	–	17,500	4,500 + 16 flares or 5,254
	Lancaster	64/65	–	19,500	8,000 + 12 flares or 7,500 + 16 flares or 8,570
1	Lancaster	117/123	4	20,000	10,720
	Wellington X	32/35	1	17,500	2,700
3	Stirling	106/115	3	15,000	5,650
	Lancaster II	15/16	–	20,000	8,400
4	Halifax	144/158	4	18,000	6,480
	Wellington X	17/17	–	19,000	3,330
5	Lancaster	137/143	–	19,000	10,096
6	Halifax	47/51	–	19,500	6,900

In all 794 out of the 850 aircraft operating that night did so effectively, and thanks to *Window* the loss rate was only 1.4 percent. Flak damaged fifteen Hamburg attackers but only one was damaged by German fighter fire. All thirty-three Lancasters of 5 Group bombed Leghorn through haze while 6/6 Wellington Xs each laid two mines in the Elbe and 5/7 Wellington IIIs of 92 Group dropped leaflets. The bombing analysis showed the weapons drop on Hamburg from 724/791 aircraft as 1,349.6 tons HE, 263 x 250lb TIs, 184 flares. Incendiaries used were 26,402 x 30lb, 281,895 x 4lb and 42,115 x 4lb X. A final summary of the participating force showed:

1 Group	113/123 Lancasters, 31/35 Wellingtons
3 Group	100/115 Stirlings, 15/16 Lancasters
4 Group	139/158 Halifaxes, 17/17 Wellingtons
5 Group	138/143 Lancasters
6 Group	47/51 Halifaxes, 19/21 Wellingtons
8 Group	64/65 Lancasters,32/37 Halifaxes, 9/10 Stirlings

Losses totalled 12: 51 Sqn – 1; 75 Sqn –1; 76 Sqn – 1; 102 Sqn – 1; 103 Sqn – 3; 158 Sqn – 1; 166 Sqn – 1; 214 Sqn – ; 218 Sqn – 1; 460 Sqn – 1. Nine bombers were destroyed by fighters, three by AA fire.

A staggering 92 million strips of *Window* had been dropped confusing *Wurzburg*, *Wurzburg-Reise* and *Lichtenstein* radar wavelengths making firing control and air reporting radar useless. Failures caused the Germans no mean panic, for they could not have new radars available for many weeks. Therefore fighter response was to fly within the bomber stream or operate 'Wild boar' freelance style over the target.

Smoke from Hamburg's fires billowed to no less than 22,000ft – hardly surprising since over a third of a million incendiaries had rained down, representing in effect a mighty retribution for the *Luftwaffe*'s cruel past blitz on Britain. Viewed from half a century on, such attacks killing over 1,500 people seem incredibly hideous but at the time they generated plentiful satisfaction throughout Britain. Passing judgement fifty years later without personal experience of those times leads to misconceptions. Terrible deeds had been and were still being perpetrated by the foe, and many 'civilians' living in Hamburg were employed within the German war machine. All warfare is criminal folly, but a stand against evil regimes has to be made.

Next night, **25/26 July**, the offensive switched to Essen which received its heaviest onslaught so far, 7 Stirling pathfinders and 103 Stirling bombers being within the force according to squadron F.541s – 104 according to Bomber Command ORS survey. A high proportion, 628/705 of the bombers despatched, were reckoned to have bombed the primary target including 84/96 or 75/96 Stirling bombers and 8/8 of 7 Squadron. Certainty was that Krupps factories suffered a very heavy pasting, probably the worst of the war. Essen suffered widely too, and casualties were heavy. Of the twenty-three bombers missing, six were Stirlings, making their loss rate about 6.25 percent, much higher than the total Halifax bomber rate of 3.53 percent. Additionally, a Stirling crashed in the sea 6 miles off Lowestoft, the crew of six drowning. Of the 294 Lancasters operating only five were lost, a rate of 1.7 percent attributed particularly to *Window*. Although twenty-five bombers had flak damage, only one was hit by fighter fire.

On **27/28 July**, following American day raids on **25** and **26 July**, Hamburg received another massive Bomber Command onslaught. After heading in from between Denmark and Lübeck the bombers delivered a forty-three minute onslaught and left smoke and heat haze rising to over 5 miles, a mile higher than during the previous night raid. South-east Hamburg was burnt out on this, the night of the infamous gruesome firestorm. Low humidity and high natural temperature made much of the city very dry making it easy for the concentrated incendiary loads to induce huge fires which combined consuming oxygen at a staggering rate which engulfed a vast residential area including some 16,000 dwellings. In Hamburg's streets the conditions were horrific, raging fires raising the temperature to 1,000°C and

producing an uprush of hot air including a suction effect which generated a ferocious
gale. Not only did that drive flames through the city, trees were torn up and people
swept off their feet were hurled into the torturous blaze. In their shelters carbon
monoxide poisoned and killed on a vast scale. Six districts of Hamburg were
destroyed and few residents survived in the firestorm area. About 40,000 died, many
from oxygen starvation. Within a few hours the vast firestorm uncontrollably itself
faded for it had consumed all it could encompass.

Returns suggest that 722 crews, maybe 736, attacked. Among them were 119 Stirling
bombers and 4 pathfinders. Unable to be radar guided towards the raiders because of
Window's effectiveness, night-fighter pilots had to rely upon skill, chance and good
eyesight. They did well to destroy seventeen bombers, one of them Stirling EH893
brought down near the target area.

Comparison of losses by types involves many factors and on this occasion they were
highest were among Lancasters of 5 Group, 6 of the 155 operating being brought down.
As regards operational efficiency there remained little to chose between the Halifax and
Stirling, although the latter had a poorer serviceability record. Halifaxes had a height
advantage, bombing on this occasion from around from 19,500ft while Stirlings were
flying at about 14,500ft. Both carried similar loads.

To lighten them, many Halifaxes had nose turrets removed or were completed
featuring a clear, streamlined nose. Some even operated shorn of a dorsal turret. Such
radical armament reduction was considered to be unwise in the case of Stirling, and
may explain why so many to the end of the type's operational career had running
battles with night fighters.

From Mepal twenty Stirlings were despatched on the second large Hamburg raid.
One flown by Flt Sgt E J Roberts was approached by a Ju 88 which came in from port
facing a barrage from all the bomber's guns. It quickly broke away to port, but not before
its shots had blown off a bomb door and pierced some of the Stirling's fuel lines.
Nevertheless, Roberts managed to nurse his charge home.

While the city continued to burn Bomber Command returned and between 0023 hrs
and 0152 hrs on **30 July** at least 699 and possibly 724 out of 777 bombers operating in
very favourable weather unleashed yet more destruction upon the stricken city.

Losses this time were higher, twenty-seven aircraft being posted missing, some 3.5
percent, and four were Stirlings. Average loads and heights on this occasion were:

Type	No used	Average attack height (ft)	Average bomb load (lb)
Halifax	244	19,000	5,870
Lancaster	340	19,750	9,587
Stirling	119	11,250	4,684
Wellington X	70	18,500	2,824

Deterioration in efficiency of the older bombers was partly due to their additional
equipment, reducing load-carrying.

German night fighters stung to desperation just had to do their best. A Ju 88 attacked
Sgt Hartstein's aircraft with cannon. Fg Off G Duncan's mid-upper gunner drove off
another and Flt Sgt Wilkinson's crew accounted for one. All were members of 75
Squadron, and other crews had similar tales to recount of what was reckoned to be 'the
best raid so far'.

Stirlings used were:

7 Squadron: EF363, EF393, EF388, EF368, R9283, R9660-O, R9257-R EF406-U,
EF364-X operating with the squadron's Lancasters
XV Squadron: MZ264-DJ:A, EE907-C, BF460-F, BF470-G, BF533-H, BK774-K,
EF351-L, EF391-M, EF428-N, BK818-O, BF521-P, BK652-Q, BK764-R, EF875-S,
BK766-T, EE912-U, EE908-V, BK654-W, EE339-Y

75 Squadron: BF461-B, EF435-J, BF465-K, EE893-N, EE878-P, EE891-Q, EH905-R, BK809-T, BK778-U, EH936-W, BF564-W, EE915-X, EH880, EE881, BK777, EE893, BF458

90 Squadron: EF439-B, BK7621-E, MZ262-K, BK779-L, BF524-N, EF426-O, BK784-P, EF431-Q, EH908-R, EH937-S, EE889-V, BF532-W, EE900-Y

149 Squadron: EH883-A, BF509-B, MZ260-O, EF438-D, BF512-E, EF412-F, EE879-G, BF570-H, EH904-K, EH903-L, EF411-M, EE872-N, BK711-O, BK763-P, BK798-Q, EF360-R

214 Squadron: EF407-A (FTR), EH921, EE899, EF404, BF574, EF409, EE914, EE876, EF401

218 Squadron: BF578-A (FTR), BF568-B, BK803-D, BF519-E, EH898-G, EE909-H, EH8778-I, EF449-J, EE888-K, BK700-L, BF522-N, BK781-O, EF448-P, EF352-Q, EF825-S, BK650-T, EE892-U, BF472-V, EH923-W, MZ263-Y, EF410-Z

620 Squadron: EF437, EF440, EH945, EE905, EF433, BK802, EF442, EF429, BK801, EF896

Hamburg's torture was not completed until **2 August**, when bombers then paid a higher price. Sour weather, icing and storms were so severe that only about half the force of 740 aircraft, maybe 422, bombed the target. Among them were only 44/99 Stirlings and at least 3/6 pathfinders – possibly six of the thirty bombers missing – were PFF Stirlings. Average Stirling load was about 5,400lb, attacking height between 8,000ft and 15,000ft. Within fifty-one minutes another 636 tons of HE and about 40,000 incendiaries – small by recent standards – had fallen upon what little remained of Germany's second city, seaport and industrial centre.

Bombing had destroyed about 61 percent of all accommodation in the city, post-war Allied surveys concluding that 275,000 houses, 2,632 shops, 24 hospitals, 277 schools, 58 churches and 83 banks were wiped out. Casualties amounted to about 41,800 killed, and 37,439 injured many of whom later died as a result of the raids. Goebbels wrote in his diary that it was "a catastrophe the like of which staggers the imagination". Yet, within days – and despite the loss of one third of its population – life somehow resurged from ruination at an astonishing rate. That should have raised little British surprise for it was merely a repeat of what happened following heavy air attacks on Britain. The devastation also brought another mirroring response, a rapid increase in the strength and efficiency of German night defences.

The Hamburg raids were a watershed for the Stirling for they were almost the climax of the bomber's most intensive operational phase. It had raised fearsome fires in German cities and would continue to do so for several months ahead. Numerically its strength was fast increasing, as the following figures show. Squadron establishments had changed on 17 June 1943, Nos 7, 149, 214 620 being set at 16 + 4 and Nos XV, 75, 90 and 218 set at 24 + 6. Squadron strength during July 1943 was:

Sqn	7 Jul			14 Jul			25 Jul			27 Jul			30 Jul		
7	18	–	1	16	–	3	13	–	4	11	–	6	9	–	6
XV	16	6	8	16	8	6	15	11	5	16	8	6	20	–	8
75	17	8	4	17	12	5	18	19	22	24	11	1	19	10	5
90	18	8	3	20	8	4	20	10	1	19	10	1	15	8	6
149	19	–	2	20	–	2	19	–	4	19	–	3	2-0	–	2
196		Nil			Nil		1	–	3	–	1	3	–	1	3
199	–	–	14	–	7	12	–	11	8	–	13	6	14	4	3
214	17	–	3	19	–	1	17	–	8	20	–	4	16	–	6
218	14	8	10	13	10	10	30	–	3	23	5	3	22	–	7
620	16	–	–	17	–	1	20	–	1	14	–	5	15	–	5

Notes:

7, 199, 620 Squadrons established at 16 + 4

199 Squadron, established on Stirlings wef 20.6.43, held no aircraft in June

196 Squadron, established on Stirlings wef 25.7.43 at 16 + 4, held no aircraft yet

7 Squadron came off Stirling establishment 23 June when still holding 17 - 1 examples

New Stirling squadrons were being formed to absorb the much faster output. This followed MAP take-over in March 1943 of the management of all Shorts factories under the Defence of the Realm (General) Regulation No 78. In effect the company had been nationalised to improve its organisation. This was now complex due, in part, to the 1940 bombing and to the extent of sub-contraction to factories which were geographically spread. Loss rates were fairly high yet not prohibitively so. Its performance was increasingly seen to be inferior to the Lancaster's, and there was no possibility of Stirling bomber development. Only a lengthy, complete redesign and an unacceptably long development phase could have achieved a variant superior to the Lancaster by which time upgraded versions of that aircraft would be available. Placing Stirlings in training units where accident rates were high was clearly pointless especially as most crews proceeded to Lancaster and Halifax squadrons. Was there, then, any other use for the Stirling? A conference held in late July 1943 decided that the Stirling would completely change its career.

Summary of Stirling Bomber and Pathfinder Operations 14 January – 22 November 1943

Date	Target	PFF/MF	A/c	HE 2,000	1,900	1,000	500	250	250	Incendiaries 30	4	4X	FTR	Attacked primary/force despatched
JANUARY														
14/15	Lorient	PFF	0/1											16/19
14/15	Lorient	MF	16/19			37					18,648	882		62/104
15/16	Lorient	PFF	4/4					72*			5,076	324		18/18
15/16	Lorient	MF	29/36			61	21				31,948	2,277	1	111/129
23/24	Lorient	PFF	4/4											17/17
23/24	Lorient	MF	25/29	2		15	7				34,890	2,070	1	109/116
26/27	Lorient	PFF	1/3					18*						12/15
30/31	Hamburg	PFF	3/7					12*+18TI			3,580	240		82/130
FEBRUARY														
2/3	Cologne	PFF	5/8					42*+20TI						2/28
3/4	Hamburg	PFF	4/9					15*+4TI						20/33
3/4	Hamburg	MF	26/57								42,479	2,620	8	126/230
4/5	Turin	PFF	7/9			12	3	80*+12TI						24/29
4/5	Turin	MF	33/41			40	14				16,378	812		132/159
7/8	Lorient	PFF	6/6								10,080	723		30/30
7/8	Lorient	MF	51/56			81	8				63,380	2,262		267/293
11/12	Wilhelmshaven	PFF	7/8			4		12*+16TI		64	590	40		33/39
13/14	Lorient	PFF	2/2								3,780	180		23/25
13/14	Lorient	MF	59/64			251	8			992	42,017	2,453	1	410/441
14/15	Cologne	PFF	9/10			14		42*		64	3,060	180		17/18
14/15	Cologne	MF	49/58	12		148	7			776	54,089	3,211	2	183/225
16/17	Lorient	PFF	1/1				4			14	1,350	90		23/23
16/17	Lorient	MF	39/43	22		75	10			880	36,253	177		331/354
18/19	Wilhelmshaven	PFF	6/9					21*+10TI		16	660	60		27/30
19/20	Wilhelmshaven	MF	41/56			120	3			1,592	34,703	1,927	5	302/338
21/22	Bremen	PFF	4/8					12*+16TI						23/27
24/25	Wilhelmshaven	PFF	9/9			18		27*+28TI						17/17
25/26	Nuremberg	PFF	4/9					12TI						36/46
25/26	Nuremberg	MF	42/55	4		69	8			1,104	19,260	1,120	2	243/291
26/27	Cologne	MF	40/46	6		125	15			918	33,673	2,357	1	349/399
28/1-1/3	St Nazaire	PFF	2/3	4HC							1,680	120		30/33
28/1-1/3	St Nazaire	MF	52/60	4HC		132	13		4	1,711	41,656	4,460	1	379/404
MARCH														
1/2	Berlin	PFF	7/10	6HC				18*+32TI			630			31/39
1/2	Berlin	MF	36/50	3HC		27	12			784	21,290	11,624	3	208/263
3/4	Hamburg	PFF	10/13			5		15TI		288				32/37
3/4	Hamburg	MF	38/49		10	23	6			1,680	30,606	1,180	2	312/390
5/6	Essen	PFF	1/2								1,692	108		28/35
5/6	Essen	MF	36/50	30HC			4			1,180	24,220	1,440	3	340/407

Date	Target	PFF/MF	A/c	HE 2,000	1,900	1,000	500	250	250	Inc. 30	4	4X	FTR	Attacked primary/force despatched
8/9	Nuremberg	PFF	8/12						93*+2TI			288	1	32/40
		MF	42/50	29	3	29	17			896	20,970	1,440	3	260/295
9/10	Munich	PFF	5/10						75*+6TI			160	1	24/34
		MF	27/31	13		20	4			400	13,280	940		193/212
11/12	Stuttgart	PFF	8/10						192*+16TI				1	28/32
		MF	37/40							866	30,550	1,950	2	239/282
12/13	Essen	PFF	1/2			38				192	31,254	1,506	1	28/31
		MF	32/40	26	3	28	11			1,096				28/31
22/23	St Nazaire	PFF	4/5						3TI					44/46
		MF	4/58				9				4,950	289	1	244/311
26/27	Duisburg	PFF	2/2	4HC			4	48**		168				10/17
27/28	Berlin	PFF	8/15	4HC					24TI				1	40/54
		MF	54/66	21/15HC		49	9			2,024	14,349	2,571	1	289/341
28/29	St Nazaire	PFF	4/4				2		12TI					24/25
		MF	29/31							1,360	36,828	2,222		255/298
29/30	Berlin	PFF	7/11	2HC					28TI					39/48
		MF	32/53	13HC		22	5			1,296	8,702	1,748	3	174/281
APRIL														
2/3	St Nazaire	PFF	3/3			24								16/22
		MF	4/5			27	4							26/33
4/5	Lorient	MF	4/5			30	2							30/47
	Kiel	PFF	12/14					24*+44TI					2	37/44
		MF	65/76	3HC		1		224**		5,672	57,854	5,396	1	470/533
8/9	Duisburg	PFF	3/4	10HC			1							27/39
		MF	31/52	19HC		46	10			1,928	23,612	1,942	2	362/383
10/11	Frankfurt	PFF	10/16	3HC		14			32TI				2	39/50
		MF	69/82	44HC		58	11			4,548	35,356	3,344	2	397/452
14/15	Stuttgart	PFF	10/16	3HC			8		144*+40TI				3	39/52
		MF	51/67					28		3,248	27,407	3,463	5	325/410
16/17	Mannheim	PFF	8/10	8HC			4		177*+51TI					13/16
		MF	63/85	59HC	6	93	32			1,336	12,880	2,240	7	188/255
20/21	Rostock	PFF	2/2	4HC			7							2/2
		MF	53/84	11HC		36	2	64**		2,344	17,880	601	8	51/84
26/27	Stettin	PFF	9/11				6		144*+47TI					?/46
	Duisburg	PFF	5/6	20HC			72		12TI				2	65/72
		MF	63/72	20HC		116				4,130	53,281	1,539	2	434/489
30-1/5	Bocholt		3/8	9HC									1	?/23
MAY														
4/5	Dortmund	PFF	5/6	20HC			45						1	62/74
		MF	58/74	33HC		81				3,936	39,024	2,276	6	433/522
	Rhein workshops		3/6	12HC										5/9

Date	Target	PFF/MF	A/c	HE					Incendiaries				FTR	Attacked primary/force despatched
				2,000	1,900	1,000	500	250	250	30	4	4X		
12/13	Duisburg	MF	58/70	11HC	–	46	6	–	–	4,738	61,942	4,428	5	400/494
13/14	Bochum	PFF	16/17	3HC	–	–	15	–	60TI	840	–	–	–	32/41
23/24	Dortmund	MF	54/78	–	–	66	–	–	–	3,152	42,898	3,822	4	318/360
		PFF	17/20	21HC	–	–	60	–	35TI	1,440	–	–	–	115/119
29/30	Wuppertal	MF	82/100	9HC	–	136	16	–	–	6,152	51,666	5,914	6	603/708
		PFF	18/19	20HC	–	–	40	–	26TI	1,976	–	–	–	101/116
		MF	80/99	25HC	–	97	14	–	–	5,878	57,151	4,939	8	507/603
JUNE														
11/12	Düsseldorf	MF	86/99	60	–	98	28	–	–	4,949	48,880	6,469	2	?/692
	Munster	PFF	6/6?	6HC	–	–	12	–	72*+30TI	–	–	–	1	60/72
19/20	Le Creusot	PFF	1/1	–	–	–	–	–	–	72	540	180	–	42/45
		MF	57MC	–	–	222	35	–	–	1,560	10,855	4,005	–	224/245?
	Montchanin	PFF	3/3	–	–	–	24	–	–	–	–	–	–	320/32
21/22	Krefeld	PFF	15/19	40HC	–	–	10	–	20TI	760	87,580	7,860	4	?/113
		MF	90/98	–	–	29	–	–	–	8,144	–	–	5	?/592
22/23	Mulheim	MF	4/4	–	–	8	–	–	–	608	–	–	–	?/64
		MF	71/89	–	–	–	–	–	–	6,580	72,590	5,990	11	?/493
24/25	Wuppertal	MF	68/69	–	–	–	–	–	–	6,640	70,002	46,084	7	517/630
	Elberfeld	MF	6/10	–	–	–	–	–	10TI	960	–	–	2	51/75
		MF	69/88	–	–	–	–	–	–	6,640	70,002	46,084	9	497/552
25/26	Gelsenkirchen	MF	64/73	–	–	–	–	–	–	6,168	64,794	5,356	6	388/461
28/29	Cologne	PFF	7/8	–	–	–	–	–	–	400	–	–	–	62/72
		MF	53/67	12HC	–	–	–	–	–	4,888	51,716	4,624	5	448/536
JULY														
3/4	Cologne	MF	59/76	–	–	–	–	–	–	4,980	46,269	2,951	5	?/578
13/14	Aachen	PFF	6/6	–	–	–	–	–	–	1,232	–	–	–	?/47
		MF	41/49	–	–	–	–	–	–	1,792	40,340	3,350	1	?/327
24/25	Hamburg	PFF	9/10	92	–	–	35	–	34TI	256	–	–	–	102/112
		MF	100/115	–	–	5	21	–	–	4,680	41,850	9,180	3	621/676
25/26	Essen	PFF	8/8	–	–	5	30	–	24TI	384	–	–	–	?/87
		MF	75/96	67	–	4	66	–	–	4,144	33,190	5,180	6	?/718
27/28	Hamburg	MF	?/9	–	–	–	–	–	–	–	–	–	–	?/107
		MF	98/107	–	–	–	–	–	–	6,608	72,156	6,324	1	?/680
29/30	Hamburg	PFF	8/9	–	–	–	30	–	–	256	–	–	1	?/114
		MF	96/110	–	–	–	–	–	–	6,832	74,340	1,530	3	?/663
30/31	Remscheid	MF	67/87	–	–	–	–	–	–	4,632	45,657	2,825	8	?/246
AUGUST														
2/3	Hamburg	PFF	3/6	–	–	–	12	–	8TI	128	–	–	3	?/109
		MF	39/99	–	–	–	–	–	–	2,520	28,080	810	3	?/626
10/11	Nuremberg	PFF	4/4	–	–	–	–	–	–	320	–	–	3	?/103
		MF	104/115	–	–	–	–	–	–	4,912	48,485	5,445	2	?/550

Date	Target	PFF/MF	A/c	2,000	1,900	HE 1,000	500	250	250	Incendiaries 30	4	4X	FTR	Attacked primary/force despatched
12/13	Turin	MF	105/112	6HC	–	72	84	–	–	3,656	31,700	1,200	3	143/152
16/17	Turin/Fiat	MF	8/24	–	–	4	2	–	–	880	–	–	1	?/24
	Turin/City	MF	?/79	–	–	47	99	–	–	5,878	–	–	1	?/154
17/18	Peenemunde	MF	48/54	10	–	49	58	–	–	1,800	12,980	450	2	436/510
23/24	Berlin	MF	81/124	6HC	–	63	94	–	–	2,304	27,660	60	16	462/593
27/28	Nuremberg	MF	85/104	–	–	–	–	–	–	4,568	43,694	3,580	11	484/564
30/31	Munchen-gladbach	MF	94/107	–	–	–	–	–	–	8,428	100,920	4,626	6	?/598
31/1.9	Berlin	MF	66/106	1HC	–	45	57	–	–	2,176	22,800	2,610	17	?/512
SEPTEMBER														
5/6	Mannheim	MF	88/111	–	–	718	520	–	–	4,849	48,855	2,915	9	?/502
9/9	Boulogne area	MF	103/118	–	–	193	53	–	–	–	–	–	–	?/233
15/16	Montluçon	MF	117/127	4	–	342	36	–	–	6,408	69,830	6,830	1	?/304
16/17	Modane	MF	119/127	–	–	183	36	–	–	1,336	12,240	1,980	1	?/277
22/23	Hannover	MF	112/137	26	–	–	–	–	–	563	68,310	2,160	5	?/533
23/24	Mannheim	MF	94/115	–	–	–	–	–	–	9,032	48,410	4,650	7	?/539
27/28	Hannover	MF	90/111	–	–	–	–	–	–	7,840	81,890	4,770	10	?/594
OCTOBER														
3/4	Kassel	MF	96/113	–	–	–	–	–	–	6,149	71,330	3,210	5	397/464
4/5	Frankfurt	MF	55/70	–	–	–	–	–	–	3,952	41,915	2,815	1	?/342
8/9	Bremen	MF	84/95	5HC	–	96	77	–	–	2,384	42,090	2,640	3	104/119
NOVEMBER														
18/19	Mannheim	MF	88/114	79HC	–	–	–	–	–	2,368	57,420	5,310	8	?/351
19/20	Leverkusen	MF	74/86	63HC	–	62	–	–	–	2,884	53,330	4,620	1	?/252
22/23	Berlin	MF	28/50	5HC	–	20	1	–	–	644	91,714	1,806	5	?/642

* = flares. ** = 40lb anti-personnel anti-firefighting bombs. TI = 250lb target indicators

Notes: In many instances the number of crews attacking their primary target remains uncertain. Some typical returns, applying to PFF and Main Force numbers combined and extrapolated by Bomber Command ORS shortly after the listed 1943 raids are these:

total attacking force

25/26	July	600/705
29/30	July	697/777
2/3	August	399/735
10/11	August	589/653
5/6	September	512/605

Stirlings on strength in bomber squadrons January to December 1943

January – February

Sqn	5 Jan			15 Jan			21 Jan			1 Feb			18 Feb		
7	7	11	4	6	11	7	8	6	8	21	–	2	18	1	5
XV	7	–	7	12	–	4	5	–	7	11	7	5	12	1	9
75	5	–	3	10	–	2	5	–	4	12	–	4	11	–	6
90	7	–	4	9	1	3	6	4	3	9	–	6	13	–	2
115	–	1	1	–	–	–	–	–	–	–	–	–	Nil		
149	3	–	8	7	–	6	5	–	5	14	–	4	9	–	10
214	8	–	5	10	–	3	6	–	4	12	–	3	11	–	4
218	10	–	4	12	–	4	7	–	7	14	–	3	17	–	3
Total	47	12	36	66	12	29	42	10	38	93	7	27	91	2	39

No 115 Squadron establishment ceased 8 Feb 43

All established at 16 + 2 except for 7 Sqn at 24 + 3

March – April

Sqn	1 Mar			12 Mar			31 Mar			10 Apr			24 Apr		
7	23	–	1	13	–	6	16	–	8	22	–	9	16	–	13
XV	16	–	12	19	–	7	25	–	1	23	–	5	16	–	9
75	12	–	5	7	–	9	13	4	2	15	4	7	12	3	9
90	11	–	3	15	–	4	20	–	5	15	6	5	16	–	12
149	13	–	5	7	–	10	17	–	8	16	7	4	18	–	10
214	12	–	6	9	–	8	16	–	6	12	4	9	14	–	11
218	15	–	3	20	–	5	21	–	6	20	–	8	19	–	4
Total	102	–	35	90	–	49	128	4	36	121	21	47	111	3	68

Establishment on all Stirling squadrons was raised to 24 + 3 wef 8 Mar 43

Establishment further changed on 15 Apr 43. 7 Sqn remained at 24 + 3, others raised to 24 + 6. No 7 Sqn raised to 24 + 6 wef 24 Apr 43. The second main Halifax variant, the Mk V, was entering service in April, 76 Sqn holding 7 - 12 and 408 Sqn one along with 16 Mk IIs. Thus, the Stirling III was just ahead of this rival. The Hercules-engined Lancaster II had also entered service first with 61 Sqn. No 115 Sqn, the second, held thirteen in mid-April.

Columns one and two indicate number of aircraft serviceable – operational, non-operational. Third column indicates number unserviceable.

Stirlings on strength in bomber squadrons January to December 1943

May – September

Sqn	15 May			23 Jun			1 Jul			24 Jul			14 Aug			8 Sep			15 Sep		
7	29	–	4	13	–	6	17	–	1	15	–	3	Nil			Nil			Nil		
XV	19	–	5	16	4	12	16	6	7	16	12	4	15	–	6	10	–	9	23	1	5
75	17	6	4	16	7	2	17	8	2	18	21	1	17	1	10	19	–	1	23	–	6
90	12	7	4	25	1	5	18	10	3	20	10	1	29	–	–	25	–	3	17	–	3
149	15	3	5	16	–	8	16	–	7	22	–	1	16	–	4	14	–	4	14	–	6
196	Nil			Nil			Nil			2	–	2	–	2	15	11	–	8	16	–	3
199	Nil			Nil			Nil			–	12	7	17	–	3	14	–	8	20	–	6
214	17	–	9	16	–	7	19	–	3	20	–	3	26	–	2	20	–	6	18	–	4
218	13	7	6	14	3	9	15	6	13	32	–	2	17	–	6	11	–	11	15	–	5
620	Nil			17	–	1	17	–	2	20	–	1	13	–	6	13	–	3	13	–	7
622	Nil			Nil			Nil			Nil			7	–	2	10	–	3	9	–	3
623	Nil			Nil			Nil			Nil			9	–	–	8	–	1	7	–	2
Total	122	23	37	133	15	50	135	30	38	165	55	15	145	3	54	155	–	57	176	1	49

Establishments changed a number of times. On 17 Jun 43 Nos XV, 75, 90 and 218 Sqns were set at 24 + 6 the remainder having been reduced to 16 + 4. On 24 Jul 43 Nos XV, 75, 90 and 218 Squadrons stood at 24 + 6 while Nos 7, 149, 214 and 620 were set at 16 + 4.

No 196 Sqn Stirling established wef 25 Jul 43, No 199 Squadron wef 20 Jun 43

No 620 Sqn wef 17 Jun 43 and Nos 622 and 623 Sqns wef 10 Aug 43

No 513 Squadron Stirling established wef 15 Sep 43 at 16 + 4.

No 7 Squadron ceased to be Stirling established at 2359 hrs 23 Jun 43 but still held 17 - 1 Stirlings. The one remaining on 31 Aug 43 came off holding that day.

Columns one and two indicate number of aircraft serviceable – operational, non-operational. Third column indicates number unserviceable.

Stirlings on strength in bomber squadrons January to December 1943

October – December

Sqn	7 Oct			26 Oct			27 Oct			2 Nov			16 Nov			4 Dec			16 Dec			28 Dec		
XV	13	–	6	15	–	8	16	–	8	19	–	5	19	–	3	6	1	2	–	6	1	–	1	–
75	19	–	12	21	–	13	21	–	13	25	–	7	24	–	8	17	–	12	24	–	7	21	–	9
90	24	–	4	27	–	5	28	–	4	27	–	5	27	–	6	21	–	5	20	–	7	21	–	10
149	15	–	5	19	–	3	19	–	3	21	–	1	17	–	4	16	–	8	17	–	3	15	–	3
196	12	–	5	16	–	4	16	–	4	17	–	3	–	19	1	Nil			Nil			Nil		
199	16	–	4	20	–	–	20	–	–	19	–	1	16	–	6	5	–	3	13	–	4	18	–	4
214	19	–	2	2	–	5	22	–	3	25	–	2	22	–	6	20	–	8	12	–	7	13	–	8
218	16	–	7	18	–	5	19	–	4	19	–	3	20	–	2	13	–	5	17	–	2	16	–	6
513	Nil			–	–	5	–	–	–	–	2	7	–	7	4	Nil			Nil			Nil		
620	15	–	4	18	–	3	20	–	1	21	–	1	21	–	2	4	–	1	Nil			Nil		
622	17	–	3	14	2	8	14	2	9	11	11	–	11	11	–	7	–	1	–	7	–	–	1	–
623	8	–	7	10	8	5	10	8	4	10	8	5	10	10	2				Nil			Nil		
Total	174	–	59	178	10	64	205	10	53	214	21	40	187	47	44	110	1	45	103	13	31	104	2	34

No 513 Squadron off establishment 26 Nov 43, Nos 196 and 620 Squadrons transferred to No 38 Group 18 Nov 43

Establishment was 16 + 4 for all squadrons except for Nos 75 and 90 established at 24 + 6.

On 31 Dec 43 establishment of the six Stirling bomber squadrons totalled 112 + 28 and strength totalled 102; 1; 41.

Strength, other bombers on 2 November was Lancaster 473; 19; 84, Halifax 284; 6; 27, Mosquito 49; 6; 16 and Wellington X 18; 14; 4 all with 300 Squadron. On 28 Dec 43 the respective totals were Lancaster 543; 7; 129, Halifax 270; 65; 87, Mosquito 51; 7; 21 and Wellington totalled 21 all with 300 Squadron.

No 623 Sqn ceased Stirling operations on 6 Dec 43. No XV Squadron establishment changed to Lancaster 18 Dec 43. No 622 Squadron establishment changed to Lancaster 1 Jan 44

Columns one and two indicate number of aircraft serviceable — operational, non-operational. Third column indicates number unserviceable.

Comparative figures for other bomber types in Bomber Command in 1943

	17 Apr	24 Jul	28 Sep	28 Dec
Lancaster	249 16 117	447 10 57	345 50 125	543 7 129
Halifax	171 23 42	223 14 36	231 16 75	284 6 27
Wellington	188 15 55	104 8 9	30 1 11	20 – 1
Mosquito	35 – 11	43 9 16	39 7 30	51 7 21

On 24 Jul 43 the mixed Wellington III/X force equipped seven established squadrons with some aircraft remaining in seven other non-established squadrons. Halifaxes equipped 15 squadrons, Lancasters 22 squadrons two of which flew Mk IIs (equipment 18; 6; 22)

On 28 Sep 43 five squadrons were still established with Wellington Xs (Nos 300, 420, 424, 428 and 432). No 300 Squadron held 15; 1; 5 and 423 Sqn 15 - 4. No 466 Sqn, although not established, still held two. Halifax Vs (43; 8; 22) were being used by Nos 76, 427, 431 and 434 Sqns and No 428 had a mix of Mk IIs and Vs. Other squadrons held Mk II variants. Lancasters 1/III equipped twenty-two squadrons and another four had Mk IIs none of which were operational. Those were Nos 115, 408, 426 and 514 which between them held – 47; 36.

Total RAF holding of Short Stirlings in 1943

Date	In Squadrons	In CUs	FTC	Misc	UK transit	I	II	III	IV	Total
28 Jan	115	50	–	1	1	2	1	9	–	179
25 Feb	133	62	–	1	–	–	1	15	–	212
1 Apr	173	72	–	1	–	1	1	5	3	256
29 Apr	185	68	–	6	–	–	–	–	–	259
3 Jun	B: 199	83	–	6	–	1	8	–	9	306
	SD: 1	–	–	–	–	–	–	–	–	1
1 Jul	B: 203	88	–	7	–	–	–	8	–	306
	SD: 1	–	–	–	–	–	–	–	–	1
29 Jul	B: 239	90	–	1	–	–	–	–	–	330
	SD: 2	–	–	–	–	–	–	–	–	2
2 Sep	B: 217	104	–	–	–	–	–	10	–	331
	SD: 4	–	–	–	–	–	–	–	–	4
30 Sep	B: 273	102	–	5	–	–	–	–	–	380
2 Dec	B.III: 179	124	–	5	–	68	3	15	2	396
	SD/IV: 39	20	–	–	–	–	–	–	–	59
30 Dec	B.III: 148	178	–	4	–	3	46	55	8	442
	SD/IV: 39	22	–	–	–	–	–	–	–	61

Note: ASU columns cover I, II, III, IV.

Chapter 13
The Way Ahead

ALTHOUGH certainly making a major, valuable contribution to the 1943 offensive, the Controller Aircraft (Research & Development) expressed a widely held view that, while the Stirling was likely to be an unsatisfactory bomber a year hence, its numerical strength would remain high. A conference was convened for 30 July 1943, to discuss four possible future roles for the aircraft: transport, special duties, maritime and meteorological reconnaissance. Transport found most favour and two schemes were decided upon, an initial short-term modification to be followed by production of a dedicated transport with civilian potential. These ideas were discussed with Shorts at Cuxton on 6 August, and it was agreed that present production of Stirling bombers by Shorts and Austin Motors should continue unaltered, and that the bomber would not be phased out of 3 Group until mid-1944. Only if Lancaster production fulfilled all needs would a switch to only Stirling transport production be considered. News of the plan was greeted on the shop floor with mixed feelings for although the bomber of which so many were proud was to be side-lined, a transport might prolong employment. Meanwhile, the Stirling's contribution to the bomber campaign increased – and so did the loss rate.

On 23 July 'C' Flight, 75 Squadron became operational, and was joined on 26 July by 'C' Flight, XV Squadron. Aircraft were available to allow for 'C' Flights of XV and 218 Squadrons to respectively become, on 10 August 1943, the nuclei of 622 Squadron at Mildenhall and 623 at Downham Market, each established at 16 IE + 4 IR. Seven aircraft of XV's 'C' Flight became 'A' Flight of 622 Squadron, and with crews already fully operational both this and 623 Squadron were able to operate the following night against Nuremberg.

No 623 Squadron's origin was more complex, for as well as receiving crews and aircraft from No 218, it acquired personnel from No 3 Lancaster Finishing School and 1653 Conversion Unit when they disbanded. More effort was simultaneously being put into beginning the conversion of 3 Group squadrons to Lancasters. No 214 Squadron would move from Chedburgh to replace 623, some of whose aircraft would be switched to Wigsley under the 3 Group 'Ladder Plan'. These remained on 623's charge and, others allotted, would be passed to 214 Squadron. No 623's operations remained small scale.

Stirlings of 3 Group participated in nine major bombing attacks during **August 1943**, and mined on nine nights, the first big raid coming on **10/11 August** when 589/653 bombers set out for Nuremberg. Of those, 4/4 were 7 Squadron Stirlings and 104/115 3 Group bombers carrying incendiaries. Thick cloud spoilt ground marking and loads were aimed into the glow. Among the three missing Stirlings was BF516 whose Channel ditching resulted in the drowning of two crew members.

For the Stirling the night was very special because No 7 Squadron, the premier Stirling squadron, was operating them for the last time. While eight of the squadron's Lancasters helped mark Milan, EF393-B, R9283-Q, W7259 and EF406-U were among the Nuremberg raiders. The squadron had received its first Lancaster on 11 May 1943, operationally introduced them on 19 June and saw Stirling establishment cease on 23 June although some remaining aircraft saw operational use. The last Stirling to leave the squadron, W7529, did so on 2 September 1943.

On **12/13th** August it was Fiat's factory among others in distant Turin that were the targets for 143/152 bombers while another 473/504 headed for Milan. Raiding Turin were 105/112 Stirlings with loads averaging only 3,360lb. Release was made from between 14,000ft and 18,000ft. Again, losses totalled three, one being EF452 'O-Oboe' of 218 Squadron which featured in a headline event.

At Downham Market thirteen crews of 218 Squadron had begun take-off at around 2130 hrs. At 2135 hrs it was the turn of EF452, piloted by Flt Sgt Arthur Louis Aaron DFM. Even with the Mk III's improved operating height Alpine transit remained dangerous, and the circuitous route around the western side was followed.

Eric Basford, stationed at Downham Market, was the Corporal engine fitter on 218 Squadron's 'O-Oboe' at this time, and recalls that EF452 was a replacement for BK761 received in April 1943. He remembers well that this:

Was the aircraft that Aaron flew back to Downham Market after incendiaries had dropped through the wing during a raid on Remscheid on 30/31 July 1943, an action for which he was awarded the DFM. BK761 had completed seventeen operations and the damage was so extensive that it had to be taken off squadron strength for repair on site by 54 MU before returning to strength as 'O-Oboe'.

EF452, our instant replacement for BK761, flew only two operations before the fateful Turin raid of 12/13 August. The first, skippered by Aaron, was to Hamburg on 2/3 August, the second to Nuremberg on 10/11 August when our new CO, Wing Commander Oldbury, was captain.

On **12/13 August** Flt Sgt Aaron had completed a safe transit of the Alpine region, and was running in towards Turin when his aircraft was suddenly raked from ahead by gunfire. Official sources maintain that the firing came from a night fighter; yet fighters were few in Italy at the time, and there have been suggestions that the fire came from the tail guns of another bomber.

Whatever the origin, the outcome was horrific for Aaron received terrible facial wounds, had a lung punctured and his right arm was broken. As for his aircraft, three engines were hit and the pilot's windscreen shattered. Two turrets were put out of action and elevator cables were damaged.

As Aaron fell over the control column the flight engineer snatched control of the battered machine and set course south-easterly, deciding they might be able to reach North Africa despite the fact that only three engines were functioning. Aaron, carried to the rest bunk and treated with morphia, rallied and as captain insisted on returning to the cockpit where he was lifted into his seat. His feet were placed upon the rudder pedals, and although twice he tried to take over he was too weak. By now the bomb aimer was controlling the aircraft, with Aaron at his side. Together, they coaxed the Stirling along until it was crossing the Mediterranean.

After five hours flying and fuel state low, the lights of Bone mercifully came into view, causing Aaron to summon his remaining strength to assist with landing. Four times they attempted it and on the fifth try managed to put the bomber down wheels-up. Although Aaron was on the point of collapse he fought a tremendous battle to survive, but tragically passed away nine hours later. His outstanding courage won for him a posthumous Victoria Cross, the first to be awarded to an ex-member of the Air Training Corps and the third to a 3 Group member.

Had Louis Aaron lain on the bunk to conserve his strength he might, despite his terrible wounds, have survived. Instead, he gave his life for his comrades, saving them all except one. His award citation spoke so truly of "an example of devotion to duty which has seldom been equalled and never surpassed".

On **16/17th** Stirlings again headed for Fiat's Mirafiore works, 103 attacking out of a total force of 154 aircraft. The occasion was historic, for Bomber Command was reaching out to bomb Italy for the final time prior to that country's surrender on 8 September 1943. All the

Flight Sergeant Arthur Louis Aaron, 218 Squadron, posthumously awarded the Victoria Cross. (Imperial War Museum)

Stirlings, except EH884 of 218 Squadron, came safely home. Meanwhile, planning was almost complete for one of Bomber Command's most important operations.

Intelligence material, backed with results from PR sorties, proved beyond doubt that very important work was going on at Peenemunde, a rocket and jet experimental station on the enemy's Baltic Coast. The grave threat posed by such activity led in July to plans for a moonlight precision attack on the site. Orders for operation *Hydra* were issued on **9 July** and called for 3 and 5 Groups to attack the experimental station, for 1 Group to raid the workshops and for 6 (Canadian) Group to bomb the workforce thereby disposing of specialised staff working there. Mosquito bombers would mount a 'spoof' raid on Berlin which, in the event, very successfully drew off German night-fighters till much of the Main Force had attacked their targets. Participating Stirlings would carry 75 percent 1,000lb/500lb MC/GP bombs and 25 percent incendiaries. The date chosen for the operation was **17/18 August** when the strength of the Stirling force was:

Squadron	Establishment	Serviceable Operational	Non-operational	Unserviceable
7	Nil	1	–	10
XV	16 + 4	15	–	6
75	24 + 6	13	1	5
90	24 + 6	25	–	2
149	16 + 4	12	–	8
196	16 + 4	–	8	10
199	16 + 4	15	–	5
214	16 + 4	20	–	8
218	16 + 4	10	–	12
620	16 + 4	15	–	5
622	16 + 4	6	–	1
623	16 + 4	7	–	2
Totals	192 + 48	139	9	74

Notes:
622 Sqn came onto establishment at 16 + 4 on 10 Aug 43 holding 9 – 1
623 Sqn came onto establishment at 16 + 4 on 10 Aug 43 holding 8 – 2
Although Establishment was much exceeded, the unserviceability figures were high.

Eventually 597 aircraft set off for Peenemunde, and eight 'spoof' Mosquitoes for Berlin. Reaching Peenemunde involved a long flight through well-defended areas making heavy losses likely. Nevertheless, the objective worth maximum effort involved some of the most skilled personnel and most reliable Stirlings in 3 Group.

Among the fifty-four of the latter were fifteen from 90 Squadron, whose 'C' Flight had been declared operational on 8 August, the day before 199 Squadron also became operational with Stirlings. Lancaster production and delivery rates were declared 'critical' on 12 August 1943, therefore Stirlings were to continue as front-line bombers for several months longer than recently intended. For 7 Squadron there would be no going back to

A Stirling silhouetted by fires at Peenemunde on 17/18 August 1943. Photographed from a Mosquito.

De-brief of a
90 Squadron
crew.
(D Giles)

Stirlings. Authority from the Air Ministry on 22 July 1943 called for re-equipment of two Flights of 7 Squadron with Lancaster I/IIIs. By the time of the Peenemunde raid all three Flights had them, squadron strength being set at 24 IE + 6 IR *H2S* Lancaster I/III.

Some official sources quote the number of Stirlings bombing the target as only 48/54 which, between them, delivered 10 x 2,000lb, 49 x 1,000lb, 58 x 500lb, 1,800 x 30lb, 12,980 x 4lb incendiaries and 450 x 4lb 'X' incendiaries. Surprisingly, only two Stirlings failed to return, EE908 of XV Squadron and EF457 of 620 Squadron. German night-fighters were first vectored to engage the Berlin feint, tackling the Peenemunde force only when the bombing was well under way. The Stirlings were protected by *Tinsel*, *Window* and *Boozer*.

Their crews met neither searchlights nor flak at the commencement of their attack, but guns began opening up as the raid developed. Several fighters arrived too, and EE896, on its run-in, encountered a Ju 88 400 yards astern which fired a four-second burst, and to which the rear gunner replied before the Ju 88 corkscrewed away to starboard. EF426 was also fired upon. Both crews of 149 Squadron reported good visibility and attacked on DR runs from Ruden aiming at green target indicators. While bombing they witnessed two large explosions at 0028 hrs.

Stirlings despatched to Peenemunde were:

XV Sqn: EE908-V (Sgt Lundy, FTR), EE912-E, EE940-Y, EE954-J, EH929-F
75 Sqn: BF564-W, BK778-U, BK809-T, EE893-M, EE938-X, EF435-J, EF454-A, EF465-H, EH880-J, EH901-O, EH905-R, EH949-G
90 Sqn: BF566-G, BK781-X, BK723-D, BK781-E, BK811-V, EE896-J, EE932-F, EE951-B, EF426-W, EF443-M, EF446-O, EH908-R, EH937-S, EH944-A, MZ262-K
149 Sqn: BK798-Q, EE872-N
199 Sqn: EE913-F, EH927-E
214 Sqn: EE914/G-C, EE956-J, EF385-N, EF404/G-Z, EF445/G-K, EF405/G-R, EH895/G-Q
218 Sqn: BF522-N, BK650-T, BK700-L, EE888-K, EH923-W
620 Sqn: BF525-Q, BK802-Z, EE945-S (crew claimed a Do 217), EF440-B, EF457-A (FTR)
622 Sqn: EE461-C

Bomber Command Tactical Summary – Peenemunde Raid

Group	Type	Despatched	Attacked	Missing	Average bombing height (ft)	Average load (lb)	Average track (miles)
8	Lancaster	75	70	–	14,000 56 a/c 8,280 8,000 + 16 flares,	14a/c	1,317
	Halifax	21	19	2	12,000	4,416	1,317
1	Lancaster	113	107	3	8,000	10,175	1,284
3	Stirling	54	50	2	8,000	3,956	1,250
	Lancaster II	12	12	1	8,000	5,000	1,250
4	Halifax	145	130	3	8,000	5,448	1,580
5	Lancaster	117	97	17	7,000	10,884	1,248
6	Halifax	53	41	10	9,000	5,498	1,290
	Lancaster	9	8	2	8,000	6,751	1,290

The next major raid involving Stirlings came on **23/24 August** and this time the ten squadrons between them despatched 124 aircraft to Berlin, part of the force of 727 bombers operating. Visibility was excellent, and the moon was rising over the city as the bombs began falling. *H2S* aboard many bombers did not display clear images of the city, and markers were wrongly released over its most southern areas. As a consequence there was less damage than expected, whereas the loss of sixteen Stirlings – close to 13 percent and more than prepared for – was the highest rate yet on a Main Force operation. Lancasters and Halifaxes had on average attacked from around 19,000ft whereas the Stirlings at about 14,500ft were far more vulnerable to flak. Nevertheless their average bomb loads of 3,696lb compared favourably with the 3,820lb aboard the 4 Group Halifaxes.

One Stirling, BK816 of 622 Squadron, was attacked three times by fighters. Its port elevator was shot away, the port inner engine set ablaze and the rear turret hydraulics severed. After Flt Sgt G Marsh, the injured pilot, was removed from his seat, Plt Off A C Richards, the navigator, managed to get the aircraft under control. Accidentally feathered, the port outer engine was restarted, then between them the crew nursed the

The Duke of Gloucester inspects 149 Squadron with OJ-P as backdrop. Pictured, he is about to shake hands with Plt Off L C 'Hank' Woollet RAAF, Fg Off S R Pryor and Flt Sgt D W Oddy under EE963 OJ-N which completed over fifty sorties. (David Oddy)

Stirling III BK309 AA-T of 75 Squadron photographed on Newmarket Heath, summer 1943. Allocated to No 75 on 24 April, it joined the squadron on 2 May 1943 and was the aircraft which, on the night of 8/9 September 1943, swung off Mepal's runway and horrendously crashed into a petrol browser. (Kevin Mitchell)

aircraft home on three engines, flying dangerously low at 4,000ft while the navigator gave the pilot first aid. Plt Off Richards and Sgt S E Meaburn, flight engineer, managed to restart the damaged engine over the sea and eventually a perfect landing was made – a quite incredible achievement. Only 75 gals of fuel remained in the tanks.

Flt Sgt O H White of 75 Squadron and crew, in EF435, also flew a memorable sortie. Approaching Berlin their aircraft, coned with searchlight beams, was repeatedly hit by heavy flak which seriously damaged the port mainplane. Nevertheless, they pressed on even when searchlights guided a Ju 88 to attack them. Its fire hit the rear fuselage killing the rear gunner, Sgt J Poole, and soon the Stirling entered an uncontrollable dive as a result of which the captain warned the crew to prepare to bale out. Then the intercom failed and, unable to contact their captain, the navigator, air bomber and radio operator decided they should abandon the aircraft. Flt Sgt White jettisoned his load in the dive as a result of which he managed to regain control at 6,000ft. Then he and the remaining crew took stock of the damage and decided to attempt the long haul home. That involved a nerve racking four hour journey through German defences and across the sea in a terribly battered bomber. Yet without flaps, and with the undercarriage up because the electrical leads had been shot away, the Stirling brought them home – albeit to a crash landing at Mepal. Sebro repaired EF435, converted in to a Mk IV and then it awaited a further call to battle which never came.

The Berlin raid was extremely costly, Bomber Command losing fifty-seven aircraft and having many others damaged. Initial assessment suggested that only eighty-one Stirlings bombed the city, a figure increased when analysis of raid photographs showed that 3 Group had positioned 52 percent of its bombs within 3 miles of the aiming point. No 1 Group was credited with the most accurate bombing, followed by No 5. As always, it was impossible to assess the accuracy of the incendiaries.

For the whole of Bomber Command, and particularly the 3 Group Stirling squadrons, the fight was now extremely tough with losses too high to sustain for long. Nevertheless they battled on, fielding 98/104 Stirlings within the 620/674 heading for Nuremberg on **27/28th**. This time the total cost amounted to thirty-three aircraft, 4.9 percent of the force, eleven of which were Stirlings – 10.5 percent of their commitment. Of the Stirling average 3,912lb loads, about 54 percent fell within 3 miles of the A/P, putting 3 Group in third place for accuracy. Although Halifaxes were on average carrying only 3,630lb, they were flying at least 4,000ft above the Stirlings. The crippling penalty from which the Stirling suffered is highlighted by comparison with other types operating that night including Whitley Vs leaflet-dropping from 14,000ft with Wellington Xs at 16,000ft.

Scheduled for operations on the **27/28th** was EE944, replacement for 'O-Oboe' flown to Bone, Algeria, by Flt Sgt Aaron and crew. Eric Basford recalls:

> Although this one was to last only twelve days, they were very busy days. During that time it completed two minelaying trips and a raid on Berlin. We also changed two of its engines – the port outer and the starboard inner – because we had found metal in the oil filters.
>
> Its time as 'Oboe' finished most spectacularly on the evening of 27 August when it crashed taking off on operations. I was on 'seeing-off' duty that evening and watched Sgt Bennett taxy EE944 to the long east-west runway. As EE944 gathered speed during its take-off run and the tail began to lift, there was an orange flash followed by a loud bang. The port wing dipped, the aircraft slewed to port and it hurtled across the grass towards the Maintenance Flight Hangar. I dashed past the aircraft waiting behind one on the end of the runway in readiness for take-off, and hurried across the grass to where 944 had come to rest. The port wing was only three or four feet above the ground, and there was a huge pile of soil in front of the port leg which had gouged a track through soft earth.
>
> Just as I arrived, a small pick-up truck was leaving and the crew, uninjured, were standing around looking shaken and recovering their composure. Already, the rest of the squadron had resumed take-off. Apparently, whilst swinging in readiness to turn on to the end of the runway, Bennett had run over one of the FIDO pipes being laid at Downham that summer. He and the Flight Engineer had looked at the port wheel and decided to press

on with the take-off. As soon as the tail lifted and the full load went on the mainwheels, the port tyre had burst with disastrous consequences.

EE944 was eventually destroyed in a crash at Tempsford in March 1944.

On the **30th** 185 Halifaxes, 297 Lancasters and 107 Stirlings were despatched to destroy Mönchengladbach and its Rheydt district. Half the two targets were wiped out including over 2,200 buildings. Six of the Stirlings failed to return including EH938 'F' of 75 Squadron captained by Flt Sgt V T Parkin, and which crashed at Overpelt. On their sixth operation, and manning a new aircraft, they met AA fire at the target and, although the aircraft did not seem to be hit, it left in a very shallow dive. After about five minutes – during which time it had descended to 12,000ft and the bomb aimer had resumed releasing *Window* – there was an explosion in the fuselage near Sgt T Silcock, flight engineer. Flames appeared, and the crew concluded that No 7 petrol tank was on fire. When Sgt R V C Johnson, the bomb aimer, tried his intercom he could make no contact. Silcock was trying to put out the fire while the wireless operator lay slumped over his table. Then the Stirling entered a steeper dive and apparently the engines stopped. Johnson, uncertain of the outcome of the situation, decided to bale out but instead fell from the aircraft as it went out of control. The cause of EH938s misfortune was never established.

If proof were needed that the Stirling was becoming dated, the large scale Berlin raid of **31 August/1 September** provided it. Although 106 Stirlings set out, and at least sixty-six bombed the city, sixteen did not return, an unacceptable loss rate of 15.1 percent. *H2S*, useful against targets with clear geographical features, was of less value over Berlin, and PFF markers were again placed too far south and the bombing gradually spread ever more southerly. Even so, nearly 3,000 people were bombed out of their homes during the costly venture for Bomber Command. Of 331 Lancasters involved, ten never returned, along with twenty of the 176 Halifaxes. Overall, the loss rate was 7.65 percent. No 75 Squadron, which despatched twenty aircraft, the largest number by a Stirling squadron, lost three of them. Enemy defences were certainly improving and making inroads into the effectiveness of *Window*. Losses arising from the two Berlin raids convinced Bomber Command not only that the Stirling's days were numbered, at least against distant heavily defended targets, but that it would not again attack Berlin. The rise and fall of Stirling numbers in August can be seen from the following:

Date	Establishment	Strength	Operationally fit
1 Aug	136	126	90
4 Aug	160	127	120
15 Aug	160	160	111
24 Aug	160	160	108
31 Aug	144	144	115

Stirlings in Bomber Command at 1800 hrs on 31 August were distributed as follows:

Sqn	Establishment	Serviceable Operational	Non-operational	Unserviceable
7	Nil	–	–	1
XV	16 + 4	12	–	6
75	24 + 6	22	–	8
90	24 + 6	22	–	9
149	16 + 4	13	–	5
196	16 + 4	9	–	11
199	16 + 4	7	–	13
214	16 + 4	(21)	–	(7)
218	16 + 4	10	–	7
620	16 + 4	14	–	5
622	16 + 3	9	–	6
623	16 + 4	7	–	4
Totals	192+47	146	0	82

By way of comparison:

> There were twenty-three Lancaster squadrons, establishment 448 + 7, strength 399 + 19 + 78, of which Mk IIs established at 48 + 12 totalled 24 + 18 + 21.
> There were fifteen Halifax squadrons, establishment 304 + 76, strength 252 + 19 + 70, of which Mk Vs totalled 64 + 5 + 22 and were in Squadron Nos 76, 427, 428, 431, 434.
> There were nine operational Wellington X squadrons, establishment 136 + 19, strength 52 + 2 + 11.

Defence against German fighters was of ever-increasing importance and there were no grounds for complacency. Claims arising from combats during the month were as follows:

By type	Destroyed	Probably destroyed	Damaged
Lancaster	18	6	25
Halifax	13	3	13
Stirling	14	2	10

These figures permit various interpretations, although fewer Stirlings were operating, indicating a high interception rate. Claims by Stirling gunners during September included these:

September	Aircraft	Time (hrs)	Place	Notes
5/6	**Mannheim** – 111 Stirlings despatched, 9 failed to return			
	C/75 Sqn	2313	Mannheim	1 destroyed
	Y/75 Sqn	2313	Mannheim	1 damaged
	Z/196 Sqn	2317	Mannheim	Ju 88 destroyed
16/17	**Modane** – 127 Stirlings despatched, 1 failed to return			
	B/75 Sqn	0225	Alencon	Ju 88 destroyed, 1 damaged
22/23	**Hannover** – 137 despatched, 5 failed to return			
	O/XV Sqn	2157	Hannover	1 damaged
	P/218 Sqn	2134	Hannover	Ju 88 claimed
	R/622 Sqn	2139	Hannover	1 destroyed
	A/623 Sqn	2136	Hannover	1 claimed
23/24	**Target Berlin** – 124 Stirlings despatched, 16 failed to return			
	Y/75 Sqn	2154	Mannheim	1 shot down
	L/214 Sqn	0004	off Cherbourg	Ju 88 shot down
	0/622 Sqn	2149	Bad Kreuznach	1 shot down
27/28	**Target Nuremberg** – 104 Stirlings despatched, 11 failed to return			
	H/75 Sqn	2218	Hannover	Ju 88 shot down
	R/75 Sqn	2228	Hannover	Ju 88 shot down
	V/90 Sqn	2213	Hannover	Bf 110 damaged
	F/214 Sqn	2213	Hannover	Fw 190 shot down
	G/620 Sqn	2221	Hannover	Fw 190 claimed at 17,000ft

On 8 September 1943 a proposal was discussed whereby all bombers would have *H2S* radomes fitted, except those like the Lancaster II with a bomb bay modification to carry an 8,000lb bomb. Although the Stirling had an advantage in that the long fuselage would allow both the radome and a .50in ventral gun to be installed, most Stirlings were withdrawn before the plan was implemented.

The 'Stirlingaires', Sebro's popular mid-war strict tempo band. The photo includes Charlie Bull, Charlie Wynn, Allen Talbot, Leon Circuit, Vincent Wright, Sid Todd and Jeff Cooper. (I Pacey)

September saw a third 3 Group Base opened. As No 33 Headquarters Waterbeach it controlled Witchford and also Mepal where 513 Squadron formed on 15 September under Wg Cdr G E Harrison, whose place at 149 Squadron was taken by Acting Wg Cdr C R B Wigfall. The first crews for 513 Squadron were drawn from 75 Squadron but not until 21 October did they receive any aircraft – also from 75 Squadron. Before 513 Squadron was operationally ready, 3 Group was re-arming with Lancasters and the Squadron dissolved, personnel being posted to 1653 Conversion Unit, Chedburgh formed in December 1943.

Early September 1943 found the Stirling squadrons busily mining, then on the **5/6th** 96/111 were among the 546/605 heavies that delivered an hour long onslaught released upon Mannheim and, as planned, slid across to Ludwigshafen. Although cloud layers at 12,000ft and 21,000ft were encountered over France, route markers reliably lit the way to Mannheim where searchlights surrounded the city and, as well as generating intense glare, co-operated with night fighters. Such activity brought about by the effectiveness of *Window* resulted in thirty-four bombers being brought down – 13 out of 299 Lancasters, 13 out of 195 Halifaxes and 8 out of 111 Stirlings including three of 149 Squadron. The 3 Group contingent unloaded over 55,000 incendiaries from around 14,500ft. Over 280,000 fire bombs in all rained down along with 709 tons of HE. Stirling individual loads averaging 4,400lb, some 400lb above those carried by 4 Group's Halifaxes. As the raiders retired, destruction in both cities was vast. Three conflagrations had been created and in all 1,993 had been lit. The centre and southern sections of Ludwigshaven were devastated, its famous I G Farben chemical plant had been seriously damaged.

There was now a pause in the night campaign. To unnerve the Germans and try out plans for the invasion of France, a large scale tactical feint, operation *Starkey*, was mounted against the Pas de Calais at the start of the second week of September. Intensive day raids intended to rouse German fighters into battle were none too successful even when many Allied ships paraded off the Pas de Calais. After dark on **8 September** 234/257 bombers were despatched to attack two military zones including heavy gun batteries close to Boulogne in pretence to be paving the way for troop landings. Among the raiders were 5/8 B-17s of the USAAF's 422nd Bomb Sqn, 305th Bomb Group, operating at night for the first time and which joined Wellingtons drawn mainly from OTUs and 109, 112 or 103/118 Stirlings – the total varying according to data source. Operating close to home, the Stirlings carried heavy loads, 53/56 attacking AP 'A' averaging 9,545lb per aircraft, and the 51/56 tackling AP 'B' averaging 9,500lb. Marking was provided by sixteen Mosquitoes and ten Halifaxes of the PFF during the cloudless, moonlit night. Although the gun batteries escaped destruction, two huge ammunition dumps spectacularly exploded, a dull red fire at 2248 hrs lighting the sky and preceding a giant pillar of smoke. Particularly responsible were 718 x 1,000lb and 520 x 500lb HEs dropped from the Stirlings, all of which returned.

Starkey was not without tragedies. As BK809 'T-Tommy' commenced take-off from Mepal engine trouble struck, the bomber careered off the runway, hit a petrol bowser then hurtled into two houses close to the perimeter track. A fire ball erupted and within seconds there was a tremendous explosion as the bombs detonated. Miraculously only three of the crew died, but the casualties also included a WAAF officer, a sergeant and two civilians dead. Others were injured.

Bad weather prevented operations until **15 September** when 349/369 bombers delivered an hour-long attack on the Dunlop rubber factory at Montluçon in central France. Five USAAF B-17s again participated, along with 121 Halifaxes of 4 Group and 63 from 6 Group. No 3 Group provided the backbone of the force, its 117/120 Stirlings tracking for 1,000 miles and averaging 6,165lb bomb loads, exceeded only by the Lancasters. This was an extremely accurate raid, much of the Dunlop factory disappearing in the flames of a huge fire. Only one Stirling failed to reach home, BF569 of XV Squadron which came down at Vaux in France. Marking for the attack had been undertaken by 37/41 Lancasters and 24/25 Halifaxes of 8 Group.

With the Germans fighting a fierce rearguard action as they slowly retreated in Italy, it was imperative that supplies to their forces be cut. That was to be achieved by attacking the seven rail routes providing links with northern Europe, with the Mont Cenis route being allotted to 3 Group for moonlit attention.

Modane, its most vulnerable point, consisted of a large international railway station and goods yard. Maximum strength was ordered against this difficult target for which the initial run-in was from Lake Bourget, a turning point on many Italian raids. Modane being 3,467ft above mean sea level and within 5 miles of ground rising to 11,257ft meant that the attack needed to be delivered, regardless of wind direction, from between 12,000ft and 14,000ft and on an easterly heading along the valley. The chosen aiming point was halfway between two target areas so that half the bombs could be released to overshoot, half to undershoot. Loads were 80 percent HE (mainly 1,000 pounders) and 20 percent mixed incendiaries.

Bombing became concentrated at the ENE end of the aiming point and negligible damage was done to the yards. Several rail tracks to the Mont Cenis Tunnel were, however, cut. The inaccuracy arose because of a gap after marking before the Stirlings arrived, and when new target indicators fell they did so away from the aiming point just as the bulk of the bombers arrived.

On **22/23 September** 655/711 bombers set out for Hannover on a night that, for the Stirling, witnessed its operational climax. Performing with 226 Halifaxes and 322 Lancasters were 120/137 Stirlings, the largest number ever directed upon one target, and they were carrying average loads of 6,466lb. Results of the 45-minute attack, which incurred an overall loss of twenty-six aircraft (3.5 percent) were disappointing for, although the visibility was good, strong wind blew the markers away to the south-east of the town. Bombing took place along a 3-mile long corridor, spread slightly to the east, and resulted in fires – some very fierce – on the southern perimeter of Hannover. Carrying out the bombing run on a south-easterly track meant facing some 200 searchlights encircling the city over which a flak barrage was set for around 19,000ft to deal with the Lancasters and Halifaxes. Searchlight guided night fighters were reckoned to have brought down five of the eight missing Stirlings, and gunners aboard the Stirlings claimed four night fighters.

Returning from the raid was something Geoff Parry would not readily forget. It was his sixteenth operation and it ended peculiarly, as he relates:

> Waiting to land, we heard the rear gunner say: "Some silly so-and-so is going round the wrong way". Suddenly, control warned us of bandits, and all airfield lights were extinguished. As we milled around in the darkness, we heard control tell the first aircraft to land and switched on the flarepath. As No1 made his approach to land, a Ju 88 clearly silhouetted in the flarepath lights followed him down the runway at low level, and dropped a stick of bombs along Chedburgh's runway.
>
> Control now had a large number of aircraft short of petrol yet unable to land. Diversions therefore had to be made to stations all over East Anglia. We in 'C-Charlie' were sent to Newmarket where they hadn't lit the flarepath when we arrived. On the final approach, wheels and flaps down, the two starboard engines cut dead out of fuel, and the other two faltered. Miraculously the flight engineer found a few gallons of petrol in the two rarely used wingtip tanks. The engines re-started, we landed; but before we were off the flarepath all four engines stopped. All the other aircraft found safe havens too.

Being cloudless and with excellent visibility, the PFF was able accurately to mark Mannheim the next night for 571/622 bombers. Lines of flares again marked the approach, but this time enemy fighters confusingly sowed theirs too. Flak burst as high as 25,000ft at the raid's commencement before German fighters homed in guided by the

PFF route markers. Nevertheless, more heavy damage was caused particularly in the northern parts of Mannheim, and over 2,000 fires raged. As in the previous raid bombing again crept into Ludwigshafen where I G Farben was again hit.

Of the thirty-two British aircraft lost, seven were from the force of 104/115 Stirlings, and three were of 75 Squadron. Attacking from an average height of 14,500ft, the Stirlings carried loads averaging 4,200lb. By way of comparison, the 5 Group 136/139 Lancasters again showed their superiority with bomb loads averaging 10,060lb released from around 19,000ft. Even so that Group lost ten aircraft, showing that height alone did not confer safety. In all Mannheim, hideously tortured previously, this time received a further 905.6 tons of HE and almost 600,000 incendiaries.

On **27/28 September** it was back to Hannover, and with German night defences recovering the loss totalled thirty-eight (5.6 percent) of the 611/678 aircraft despatched. Unexpectedly strong winds shifted the markers and the bombing was scattered. During the 33 minute raid 959.2 tons of HE and 1,219 tons of incendiaries were unloaded onto the highly combustible town. Among the raiders were 101/111 Stirlings from which the loss of ten was again heavy embracing one each from XV, 149, 199, 214, 620, and 622 Squadrons while 75 and 218 Squadron each lost two aircraft. From 4 Group's force of 123/138 Halifaxes eleven failed to return. In all 130 Stirlings were operating that night for 17/19 were mining.

Running in to attack Hannover, EE509 was engaged by a Bf 110. Return fire from the Stirling entered the fighter's wing, but it attacked again – yet the Stirling survived. 'V-Victor' of 90 Squadron was also intercepted, enemy fire raking its fuselage and wounding the rear gunner's foot. Return fire hit the fighter which, after a third burst, dived away trailing smoke. The night's drama for 90 Squadron did not end there for Sqn Ldr M I Freeman's EE952 crashed near Bartlow.

Throughout September the Stirling force had been at peak strength as these counts for 1800 hrs on given dates show:

Date	Establishment	On strength	Operationally fit
7th	160	160	118
14th	168	168	158
21st	176	176	174
28th	176	176	120

During October the Stirling force was at its strongest, as these figures illustrate:

Date	Establishment	On strength	Operationally fit
1st	184	176	155
7th	176	176	168
14th	176	176	166
22nd	176	176	185
29th	184	182	200

Hybrid Mk III LK403 (Hercules VI), posted to 622 Squadron in October 1943 and 196 Squadron in November, had a protective strap unusual on the bomber.

Three heavy attacks were launched in the first eight days of October 1943. On **3/4 October** Kassel, an industrial city not attacked since August 1942, was the target. Of the 540 bombers despatched, 102/113 (possibly 115) were Stirlings. Only 4 Group contributed more, 118/127 Halifaxes. Pathfinder 'spoof' route markers pointed towards Hannover, but 40 miles from there the Main Force line turned towards Kassel. Enemy fighters took fifteen minutes to react to the course alteration, and concentrated their interceptions on the flanks of the Bomber stream where *Window* cover was inadequate. During engagements XV Squadron gunners claimed two night fighters, one near Kassel and the other north-west of Giessen. Within half an hour, and despite marking which went partly astray this time due to ground haze, heavy and widespread damage was caused in Kassel by at least 472 bombers. Among the industrial plants hit were the Fieseler and Henschel aircraft factories. Some 656.1 tons of HE were dropped during one of the largest fire raids of the war. The total recorded numbers of incendiaries loaded on to the whole bomber force prior to take-off was a staggering 340,956 x 4lb, 15,493lb x 4 'X' and 20,787 x 30lb. From the night's activity twenty-four aircraft, 4.4 percent, failed to return including six Stirlings (two each of 90 and 623 Squadrons and one each from XV and 218 Squadrons), a loss rate of about 5.3 percent. Two more were destroyed in battle accidents. Meanwhile another 7/7 Stirlings laid forty-two mines. Only on one more night would the number of Stirling bombers operating exceed 100.

With the weather still fine, Bomber Command struck again with Frankfurt chosen for treatment following a USAAF daylight raid. A smaller force than of late, 351/402 bombers (possibly 406) operated and only 57/70 were Stirlings. Unbroken cloud on route gave way to clear weather over a target slightly protected by haze. PFF markers went down accurately, on time, and again the 599 tons of fire bombs considerably exceeded the 460.9 tons of HE. A huge explosion rocked the city at 2137 hrs and, after the 35-minute raid which caused enormous damage, huge fires were visible 200 miles away. The Stirling force attacked at between 11,000ft and 17,500ft, each aircraft carrying an average load of 5,580lb. Only two Stirlings were missing – one each from XV and 75 Squadrons.

October's other Stirling bombing raid fell on **8/9th** and this time 84/95, led by twenty-four Lancasters and Halifaxes of 8 Group, delivered a punishing diversionary blow on Bremen while the Main Force dealt with Hannover. Because of the raid's nature, this time the Stirlings carried mixed HE and incendiary loads. Night fighters homed in and four combats resulted in four uncertain claims. Two Stirlings were shot down and a third, from 196 Squadron, came down in the sea not far out from Hemsby.

On **7 October** a new activity for Stirlings was introduced when 214 Squadron initiated supply dropping to the French Resistance. No 3 Group's 138 and 161 Squadrons had long carried out that role, the newcomers acting on the advice of Tempsford's experts.

Resulting damage of a night collision on 6 November 1943 between Wellington X3637 of 27 OTU and Stirling R9192 which managed to land at Stradishall.

Just as the Stirling force reached peak strength, poor weather including fog cut the bombing effort for a fortnight. Not until **18 November** did better improvement set in and last for nine days, during which the Battle of Berlin commenced. The new bombing phase began on **18/19 November** when Stirlings again attacked Mannheim and nine failed to return. This was the last time when over 100 participated in a bomber operation.

Although 98/114 operated, the Operations Order called for the Stirling squadrons to generate 138 aircraft as follows: No XV – 12 aircraft, No 75 – 20, No 90 – 17, No 149 – 13, No 199 – 13, No 622 – 12, No 214 – 7, No 218 – 11, No 620 – 13, No 622 – 12, No 623 – 8. It was asking a lot, the layout of the operation being thus:

Target Chubb A – Area I:
8 Group Pathfinders and supporters: 28 markers, 33 Main Force, 7 Mosquito 'spoofers'
1st Wave: 45 Lancaster of 1 Group, 35 Lancaster of 3 Group, 52 Lancaster of 5 Group, 10 Lancaster of 6 Group
2nd Wave: 45 Lancaster of 1 Group, 3 Halifax of 4 Group, 59 of 4 Group, 9 of 6 Group
3rd Wave: 44 Halifax of 1 Group, 4 of 3 Group, 60 of 5 Group, 10 of 6 Group

Target Chubb B – Area II:
8 Group Pathfinders and supporters: 24 markers, 15 backers-up, 5 Main Force, 7 Mosquito spoofers
1st Wave: attack Z to Z+4: 126 Stirling of 3 Group
2nd Wave: attack Z+4 to Z+8: 7 Lancaster of 3 Group, 59 Halifax of 4 Group, 46 of 6 Group
3rd Wave: attack Z+8 to Z+12: 6 Lancaster of 3 Group, 59 Halifax of 4 Group, 46 of 6 Group

Yellow TI route markers were to be dropped at 49°08N/08°25E. Newhaven ground marking through cloud – deliberately chosen – involved yellow TIs and white flares marking the areas for the PFF with supporters dropping red TIs on aiming points and backers-up supplying green TIs. Stirlings carried as many 2,000lb bombs as possible, their main track taking them from bases to Beachy Head – Cayeux – 49°48N/08°25E – target – 49°12N/08°08E – 48°50N/05°00E – 50°00N/00°15E – Beachy Head – bases.

Bombing from around 15,500ft, with some attacking from as low as 10,000ft and the highest claiming to be at 19,000ft, they were aided with sky markers and again dropped mixed HE and incendiary loads. Cloudy conditions and fog reckoned likely to discourage night-fighters from operating led to some scattered bombing, but factories hit included the Daimler-Benz works. With the Stirlings were Halifaxes, while Lancasters headed for Berlin. Night fighters were active, the crew of 'C-Charlie' of 214 Squadron claiming an Fw 190 over Mainz while nearby three of its compatriots tackled 'L' of 214 Squadron, whose crew claimed one of them. A/75 Squadron was also attacked.

The Bomber Command Tactics Report No 437/43 outlined the Mannheim/Ludwigshaven attack (carried out between 2021 hrs and 2108 hrs) as thus:

Group	Type	Force	Bombed between (ft)	Average load (lb)
8	Lancaster	20/23	14,500 – 19,000	7,150 and flares
	Halifax	18/21	10,000 – 18,000	4,431 and flares
3	Lancaster	8/10	18,000 – 19,000	5,348
	Stirling	98/114	10,000 – 19,000	5,393
4	Halifax	116/133	13,000 – 20,000	5,971
6	Halifax	65/94	18,000 – 23,000	6,133

Average tracks flown in each Group were:

8 Group 1,010 miles; 3 Group 1,010 miles; 4 Group 1,314 miles; 6 Group 1,354 miles. These figures naturally had a bearing on overall performance.

A detailed raid survey showed the following:

8 Group PFF force despatched: Halifax II 1, Halifax II series 1a 12/15 (3 bombed alternatives), Lancaster III 19/23 (3 bombed alternatives, one FTR, 1 damaged by flak)
8 Group Main Force: Halifax II 1, FTR; and Halifax II series 1a 4/4
3 Group: 88/114 Stirlings III (3 attacked alternatives, 4 aborted at target, 10 aborted elsewhere, 9 FTR, 19 flak damaged and 2 by fighters, 4 attacked and 5 reported seeing fighters not attacked)
4 Group: Halifax II/V 22/33 (4 attacked alternatives, 6 aborted, 1 FTR, 3 had flak damage), Halifax II 1a 91/100 (2 attacked alternatives, 5 aborted, 2 FTR, 10 flak damage and 2 by fighters, 5 attacked and 8 reported fighters)
6 Group: Halifax II/V 22/37 (10 bombed alternatives, 4 aborted, 1 FTR, 1 flak damaged and 1 by fighter), Halifax II series 1a 37/57 (5 attacked alternatives, 8 aborted, 7 FTR, 7 flak damaged and two fighter damaged, 2 attacked by fighters), 303/395 attacked Ludwigshaven (30 alternatives, 8 aborted over target and 31 elsewhere, 23 FTR, 45 variously damaged one becoming Cat E (Stirling), 13 attacks on bombers by fighters 23 of which were variously encountered)

Stirlings known to have participated were:

XV Sqn: EH930-A, EE907-C, EF183-D, EH929-F, BK707-G (FTR), EH940-H, LJ451-K, EF518-P, BK818-R, EF177-S, EF186-W, EF161-Y
75 Sqn: EF512-A, LJ442-F (FTR), EH880-J, EF163-JN:L, EF507-P, EH949-P, EH943-Q, EF148-R, EF181-JN-S, LK396-JN:U, ?-U, EF152-V, EF462-W, BK695, LJ457 (given twice), EF137, EF152 and three unknown – possibly EF163-JN:L, EF217 and LJ422
90 Sqn: EF159-B, EF511-C, EF431-Q, EJ122-E, EF346-G, EH996-H (FTR), LK379-H (FTR), EF147-J, EF162-K, EF441-N, EH958-O, BK784-P, EF188-R, EH947-S, EH906-T, EF182-V, LK383-XY:W
149 Sqn: EF140-A, EH993-D, EE969-E, BF570-F, EF502-G, EJ107-K, EH903-L, EF411-M, EH922-O, EH904-P, BF509-R
199 Sqn: ?-B, EE953-E, EJ115-H, EF192-J, EE910-K, EF450-N (crashed on return), EE957-Q, EE943-X, LK381-Z
214 Sqn: EE958-C, EH959-F, EF445-J, EE961-L, EF125-X
218 Sqn: LJ448-A, MZ263-B, LJ125-C, LJ447-F, EF410-I, EE888-K, BK761-O, EJ112-Q, EF185-L, LJ446-R
620 Sqn: EF143-C, EF134-G, BF503-H, BF525-Q, EF456-R, EF197-Z, LJ456, LJ459, LK391-X, and two others – possibly EF336 and EF429
622 Sqn: EF123-A (crashed on return), BK816-B, EF461-C, EF128-D, EF150-E, EH921-L, BK766-G, EF127-N, EJ113-U (FTR), EF151-P, EJ114-R, EF144-S
623 Sqn: BF568-B, EE899-C, LJ454-E, EF489-F, LK387-P, EF155-O (FTR), EF194-W

Next night 74/86 Stirlings were among the bombers ordered to attack Leverkusen, and operated with ninety-eight Halifaxes of 4 Group, sixty-seven of 6 Group and a PFF contingent. Cloud increased along the way in, and target marking was none too good because of very difficult weather as expected and also due to problems with *Oboe*, all of which resulted in scattered bombing. Intensive flak was ineffective, few fighters showed up and only one Stirling was missing. What happened to its load of 1 x 2,000lb HC, 1 x 1,000lb HE, 40 x 30lb, 7,200 x 4lb and 90 x 4lb 'X' bombs remains uncertain. When they returned to their bases some of the bombers found them fog bound, and one Stirling crashed as a result, on a morning that saw FIDO used for the first time at Graveley.

Probably unknown to most crews, the operation of **22/23 November** was, for the Stirling, historic. For the last time they were participating in a Main Force raid on Germany, and symbolically, for their target was Berlin for which the original call for a Stirling attack had been strongly demanded in January 1941. What an enormous outpouring of courage, fear, determination and horror had ensued. What changes, too, in Bomber Command's effectiveness – its plight, its might.

At the time of take-off Stirling strength was 152 established, 159 on squadrons of which 133 were operationally fit. Total Bomber Command aircraft strength stood at 1,032 established, 1,025 on squadrons, 962 operationally fit.

The Operations Order for 22/23rd called for 764 bombers to take part that night, instructing the PFF to despatch ninety Lancasters and twenty-one Halifaxes, with eleven Mosquitoes flying a 'spoof'. Main Force was to comprise: 1 Group 169 Lancasters, 3 Group 50 Stirlings and 18 Lancasters, 4 Group 130 Halifaxes, 5 Group 165 Lancasters and 6 (Canadian) Group 83 Halifaxes and 27 Lancasters. Groups were ordered to operate as many aircraft as prescribed wherever possible, and 3 Group called its squadrons to field the following Stirlings:

XV Sqn –1, 75 Sqn – 6, 90 Sqn – 5, 149 Sqn – 2, 199 Sqn – 2, 214 Sqn – 8, 218 Sqn – 10, 622 Sqn – 8 and 623 Sqn – 5, and 3 Group Lancaster IIs 6 of 514 and 14 of 115 Squadrons, all to attack target codenamed 'Whitebait B'.

Take-off began at 1710 hrs for the Stirlings whose ordered track took them out over Cromer then by way of 53°10N/04°00E – 52°40 N/09°00E – 52°36N/12°21E to Berlin where Z hour was 2000 hrs. Their homeward journey was to be via 52°25N/13°50E – 52°23N/12°00E – 52°40N/09°00E – 53°10N/04°00E, in over Cromer, thence to bases.

Eventually the Berlin PFF force was composed of 1/1 Halifax II, 13/14 Halifax II series 1a (six missing, five of them lost to AA fire), 50/60 Lancaster III (six missing) and 9/11 Mosquito IVs. The 8 Group Main Force comprised 27/29 Lancaster IIIs, 5/6 Halifax II series 1a and a Lancaster X of 405 Squadron. Six blind markers opened the raid, their red sky markers falling on time and clustered closely. Backers-up maintained the marking to the end of the planned period. Assorted pyrotechnics soon formed a solid concentration covering about a square mile into which a huge shoal of bombs was hurled bringing vast destruction, heavy casualties and a fire storm, all of which combined to give Berlin its worst air raid so far and delivered by the Main Force ordered to operate as follows:

1st Wave: attack Z to Z+4: 121 Lancasters
2nd Wave: Z+4 to Z+8: 68 Halifaxes of 4 Group and 47 Stirlings
3rd Wave: Z+8 to Z+12: 120 Halifaxes
4th Wave: Z+12 to Z+16: Lancasters of 1 Group, 10 Lancasters of 3 Group, 52 Lancasters of 5 Group, and 15 Lancasters of 6 Group
5th Wave: Z+16 to Z+20: 44 Lancasters of 1 Group, 10 Lancasters of 43 Group, 52 Lancasters of 5 Group and 15 Lancasters of 6 Group

Berlin, 'The Big City', was a distant, difficult target for the Stirling squadrons and only thirty-two crews were credited with attacking it. Two others bombed alternatives, five aborted due to technical problems in the target area, seven aborted earlier and one was intercepted but still attacked. Of twenty-five aircraft lost that night, giving an overall rate of 3.2 percent – lower than might be expected and mainly because bad weather kept many night fighters grounded – four of the losses were Stirlings, two to AA fire and two to fighters, giving a loss rate of 8 percent. It was only a moderately satisfactory finale for the Stirling as a deep-penetration Main Force bomber, those involved being:

XV Sqn: EF177:S making the squadron's final Stirling bombing sortie
75 Sqn: EF148:R (Flt Sgt Turner and crew FTR), EF163-JN:L, EH935, LJ453:K (Flt Sgt A Single and crew FTR)
90 Sqn: BF526-G, BK781-X *, EF147-J, EF196-L, EF443-M, LK382-U
149 Sqn: BF509-R, EE963-N, EF411-M, EJ109-H, EH943-B, EH992-D, LK382-W*, LK388-S
199 Sqn: EE957-Q, EF138-S*, EF505-R, EJ111-P (burnt out at dispersal after landing)
214 Sqn: EE950-C, EE960-Q*, EF125-X, EF444-D, EF445-J (Flt Sgt Atkinson and crew FTR, ditched 60 miles off Cromer 0010 hrs), EH959-F, EH977-R*
218 Sqn: LJ446-R*, EF141-H (bombed from 17,000ft), EF180-D (Sqn Ldr W G Prior and crew FTR), EH923-E*, EH942-M, EJ112-Q, LJ452-S and BK803-U (on loan from 623 Sqn), MZ263-B (early return, icing)
622 Sqn: BK766-G, EH956-F, EF132-Q, EF150-E (FTR), EF461-C, EH921-L, EH992-O, LJ444-A
623 Sqn: EJ123-A, LJ443-G, EF199-I
* made early return for varied reasons - icing, turret problems etc.

Bomber Command's Tactical Analysis, eventually prepared, concluded that 651 bombed the main target, twenty attacked secondaries, nineteen aborted in the target area and forty-nine aborted prior to the target being reached. It also showed the wide assortment of Main Force bomber variants operating that night against Berlin:

1 Group: 24/26 Lancaster I, 131/143 Lancaster III
3 Group: 32/50 Stirling III, 18/24 Lancaster II
4 Group: 25/34 Halifax II series 1/V, 75/96 Halifax II series 1a
5 Group: 34/39 Lancaster I, 118/126 Lancaster III
6 Group: 14/32 Halifax II series 1/V, 35/43 Halifax II series 1a, 26/27 Lancaster II

The bombing analysis showed:

Group	Type	Sorties	FTR	Attack height (ft)	Average load (lb)	Average track (miles)
8	Lancaster	83/90	7	17,000 – 21,000	6,240 + flares	1,260
	Halifax	19/21	–	15,500 – 19,000	4,500 + flares	
	Mosquito	9/11	–	22,000 – 29,000	833 + flares	
1	Lancaster	152/169	–	15,000 – 24,000	10,600	1,240
3	Stirling	32/50	4	13,000 – 19,000	3,640	1,220
	Lancaster	16/18	2	18,000 – 22,000	7,840	
4	Halifax	107/130	6	14,500 – 21,000	6,200	1,295
5	Lancaster	153/165	2	17,000 – 23,500	10,900	1,240
6	Halifax	71/83	4	18,000 – 22,500	6,260	1,330
	Lancaster	26/27	–	17,000 – 22,000	6,640	

Of those that failed to return, two were known to have been shot down by fighters controlled from Deelen, three by fighters near Berlin and five were brought down by flak in the target area, which also damaged ninety aircraft. Fighters damaged another and five were hit by falling incendiary bombs. Two of the six Halifaxes lost by 4 Group collided en route and seven others were variously damaged. On their final raid the Stirlings had performed as well as the others. The crew of damaged J/214 were at 50ft over the IJsselmeer at 2310 hrs and preparing to ditch when a German fighter closed, firing. The rear gunner replied and claimed to bag the attacker. There was nevertheless no denying that although the 'Queen of the Skies' could often still survive enormous punishment she was showing her age.

On 1 November 1943, the establishment for 3 Group Stirlings stood at 184, a peak figure attained in late October. It was not held for long, for on 18 November both 196 and 620 Squadrons were switched to 38 Group, reducing on the 18th front line Stirling bomber strength to an establishment of 168 aircraft. On 22 November it fell as mentioned to 152. Aircraft held by squadrons totalled 180 on 6 November; by the 27th they had only 142 and a month later 112.

Mepal was a sea of mud when '75' arrived in late 1943 as AA-K has discovered.

Another late convert was 90 Squadron whose Mk III WP-B is seen flying near Newmarket.

The decline in Stirling strength can be seen from this November listing:

Day	Established	Actual strength	Operationally fit
17	184	194	179
18	168	186	179
22	152	159	133
25	152	138	115

Total Command strength on 25 November was 1,072 established, 989 actual strength and 857 operationally fit aircraft.

Decisions made in July 1943 were biting; Lancasters were about to start replacing Stirlings in 3 Group. No XV was declared Lancaster-armed with effect from 18 December and 622 Squadron from 1 January 1944. To compensate for the loss of 196 and 620 Squadrons, 514 Lancaster II Squadron was upgraded to a three-Flight squadron Waterbeach-based causing 1651 Conversion Unit to move to 31 Base and Wratting Common.

The superior operational efficiency of the Lancaster IIs, when compared with the Stirling, was apparent when October 1943's assessment showed the following:

Sqn	Sorties	Effective (%)	Op hours	Tons delivered
90	65	93.8	320.44	84.45
75	65	89.2	332.27	89.73
115 (Lancaster)	60	81.7	267.05	191.88

December's returns further emphasised the point:

Sqn	Sorties	Effective (%)	Op hours	Tons delivered
90	56	85.7	320	93.71
75	69	92.7	360.43	101.07
115	62	83.9	312.55	184.25
514	43	90.7	246.03	70.02

An interesting aspect was the steady decline in the Stirling accident rate during 1943. In August, with operations at their peak, the accident rate was 1:455 hours flown whereas in August 1942 it was 1:170 hours. This improvement was attributed to the superiority of the Mk III and the change from the Exactor throttle system, although increased Service experience must have been a factor. In December the accident rate rose to 1:220 flying hours, wintry weather taking a toll and resulting in thirty-six Stirlings being badly damaged, the highest rate for any aircraft type in the Command. Most of the Stirling accidents were attributed to take-off problems or landing swing.

Attention to detail and small modifications at this time brought some slight improvement in overall performance. A smoother paint finish added about 6mph to speed, the D/F loop was removed, sealing was fitted around the front turret and the starboard pitot head was removed – all of which added about 15mph.

No 3 Group's official historian wrote at this time:

> While enthusiastic admirers of the 'Queen of the Air' will probably object to the definition of metamorphosis (ie. a change of form from a chrysalis to a winged insect), Lancaster fans will no doubt endorse the result of this change in character. Those who regard the Stirling as an old and trusted friend will view the new equipment with a mixture of satisfaction and regret.

And the Stirling most certainly was trusted. Those who had previously flown in Wellingtons had regarded it as a massive advance. Massive indeed, for coming face to face with a Stirling for the first time was unforgettable. There seemed much more of it that there was of a Lancaster, and no Lancaster was ever so well built. Nor could the newcomer match the manoeuvrability of the Stirling; but the Lancaster could cruise higher affording additional protection and tactical flexibility. Also, the Lancaster could accommodate large weapons which made it much superior from an operational point of view, and crews found it much easier to master. If the Stirling's wing span had not been altered, if the bomb bay had been designed differently, if engines had been developed to give more power – but history is littered with 'if' and misfortune.

'Winco', the mascot billy goat of the aircrew of LJ513 ('E-Easy') 'En Avant' of 199 Squadron, North Creake. Three horn rings denote his rank, the squadron thus uniquely having two COs. In the back row are Denny Savegar, ?, Stan Roberts, 'Ozzie' Osborne, Jack Turner, ?, Jim Francis, Wally Ascott, Ken Moore; Front row: Bill Smithers, Frank Podd, Ray Varley, Bill Davies, Phil Panichelli, flight engineer and first Secretary of The Stirling Association, and 'Corky' Corcoran. LJ513 managed eighteen operational sorties in the hands of the above aircrew. (Phil Panichelli)

The Lancaster, it must also be remembered, was a second generation four-engined bomber which resulted from a clever design possessing excellent development potential which the Stirling did not. The last envisaged as a bomber transport for use in colonial territories, was born in pre-radar times when adversaries were day fighters and not sophisticated radar-guided night operators. 'Cookies' were undreamed of, although for firebomb Ruhr raids the Stirling had much to commend it. With ever more complicated tactical planning the Stirling was at increased disadvantage particularly when a higher ceiling was essential. Best compared with the Halifax II, it equalled and in some respects bettered it. The Halifax survived longer in bomber squadrons because it had some development potential and could be produced faster. Politics, production facilities, economics; all played a part in the situation leading to the Stirling's withdrawal.

Writing in *Intercomm*, the Aircrew Association Journal, S N Freestone of 199 Squadron drawing upon personal experiences recalled some of the Stirling's main failings:

A considerable drawback to the 12,000ft cruise levels (sometimes less) was the rapid build-up of ice on the airframe as cloud was regularly encountered at these levels. With night upper air temperatures, summertime (Aug/Sep), giving a freezing level of around 8,000ft to 13,000ft, conditions for a rapid build-up of ice were ideal. Sufficient ice build-up in ten minutes' flight was often experienced to cause a marked loss of airspeed during decreased aerodynamic performance, and of course the attendant increase in weight. An increase in engine power was necessary to maintain height and airspeed with the consequent increase in fuel consumed. On longer operations deep into Germany (Berlin and Nuremberg) this caused serious inroads into an already tight fuel contents situation.

The Stirling was a delightful and very manoeuvrable aircraft when unladen and flying below 10,000ft. The short wing span gave a wing loading that was too high for the engine power available. When fully laden there was little reserve airspeed when needing to 'jink' or corkscrew to avoid the attentions of either ack-ack or fighters respectively. The vulnerability of the very long undercarriage is shown by the many incidents when an aircraft was written off with the final comment – 'under carriage collapsed'. In order for this very long leg to be retracted into the wing it actually hinged in two positions; these became the weakest points and many a Stirling sank to its knees after standing in the dispersal for some 20 minutes, when, as a result of turning the aircraft too sharply, the undercarriage leg on the inside of the turn would be left with a very high torsional strain and ultimately gave way, frequently to the great surprise and horror of the groundcrew. As a personal opinion, I consider the high losses on the Stirling, both operational and general handling, were caused by the relative inexperience of wartime pilots. Controlling the swing on take-off and landing gave many pilots – some with only a total of some 250 hours flying – their biggest concern.

The leggy undercarriage also caused serious incidents when taking-off at full weight. It was retracted by electric motors and on one occasion I experienced the real total drag effect of this when still building up airspeed after take-off. The operation was to Turin in August 1943 and planned with a maximum bomb load coupled with a large fuel load because of the distant target. Whilst the normal weight restrictions were observed the conditions at take-off were, I am sure, not as assumed.

A warm summer evening coupled with no wind to assist take-off resulted in a situation where every inch of the runway would be vital. This was at Lakenheath in Suffolk. Every inch of the runway was used and the take-off normal as far as that goes, but upon selecting the u/c up nothing below moved. At this critical stage of flight the Flight Engineer was closely monitoring his instrument panel. After a re-selection of the u/c lever it was decided that the fuse covering the motor circuits had blown. This was the case, but by the time this was realised some two, vital minutes had passed during which time the aircraft had literally gained no height and airspeed barely 5 knots above minimum safety speed. By this time all four engines had exceeded their maximum cylinder head temperatures. There was no reserve of speed to allow a reduction of engine power with the aircraft barely 100ft above the ground. Thus, full power was maintained until the wheels began retracting. Some ten minutes later a height of some 1,000ft had been gained after careful nursing of the engine power within maximum limits. That evening the little town of Brandon, Suffolk had a very close view of a Stirling since the town was overflown at a height not exceeding about 50ft. It was a very unnerving incident precluding a long flight over enemy territory and another 8 1/2 hours to go before we were to see base again. A second incident of this nature took place only days later, when the top of an oak tree suffered damage as one of the dangling legs took a very neat 'V' slot portion out of the top, fortunately missing the inboard propeller, and produced no lodging debris to prevent ultimate retraction.

During November 1943, 3 Group's Stirling strength steadily declined as is evident from these figures:

Date	Establishment	Strength	Operationally fit
17th	184	179	194
18th	168	179	186
21st	152	159	133
25th	152	138	115
Total Command strength			
25th	1,072	989	857

Re-equipment of 3 Group took many months and brought about movement of squadrons and units. No 1651 Conversion Unit moved to 31 Base, Wratting Common making way for Lancaster IIs of 514 Squadron. Some retired Stirlings were earmarked for the new 1653 CU, Chedburgh, which opened under Wg Cdr Crompton on 21 November as the third Conversion Unit in 31 Base now administered only training units. The last Stirling bomber squadron to form, No 513, was ordered to disband on 21 November and pass its aircraft to 1660 CU, Swinderby. No 623 Squadron, which ceased to be operational on 6 December, disbanded to provide aircraft for a conversion unit controlled by 5 Group. With a glimpse into the future, though, North Creake opened on 23 November 1943, in 3 Group, and passed to 100 Group on 3 December 1943. Two squadrons, 196 and 620, had transferred to 38 Group and 1665 Conversion Unit at Woolfox Lodge would now supply crews for transport duties. No 90 Squadron moved to Tuddenham where it awaited its quota of Lancasters. While these changes took place, Stirling bomber squadrons maintained full operational programmes carrying out mainly mining and special duty sorties.

Chapter 14
'…and mines were laid in enemy waters'

THAT laconic phrase ended many a wartime Air Ministry communiqué outlining Bomber Command's previous night's activity. In total 47,307 sea mines – 13,845 by Stirlings – were sown by bombers in routes leading to prominent ports, and was no mere second-class activity. Initially regarded as defensive weapons, mines were introduced for offensive purposes late in World War 1, and by 1918 Britain had developed the magnetic mine. Hitherto the sound of a ship's engines or propellers acoustically caused the mine to explode, but now it could be activated by a magnetic field.

Aerial mining, envisaged as a task for second generation bombers of the 1930s and Coastal Command's new Beaufort and Botha general reconnaissance/torpedo bombers, was no simple activity. As Coastal Command in 1940 possessed so few suitable aircraft with sufficient range to reach worthwhile harvest areas, Bomber Command became involved and had to apply aircraft already in service.

Existing mines needed strengthening to withstand impact upon striking the water, and certainly so if dropped from above 1,000ft. Their ballistics also needed attention and a forward nose fairing was attached to the 17.7in diameter charge section and a drag-inducing parachute for deployment from a detachable 27in diameter section all of which added 50 inches to the mine's overall length. Most suitable bomber for accommodating the 164in long 1,500lb Type A (ie. airborne) Mk I mine was the Handley Page Hampden.

April 1940, therefore, saw mines reach 5 Group as pressure mounted to halt delivery of iron ore to Germany from Narvik. Sensitive political questions concerning mining in neutral international waters were sidelined when on 9 April 1940 the Germans invaded Norway. On 13/14 April, Hampdens laid fourteen mines in the Great and Little Belts off Denmark, and a further twenty-eight the next night while Beauforts placed six in the Elbe Estuary. Throughout the war sowing areas were chosen by the Admiralty, Naval personnel attached to bomber stations assisting with the activity usually undertaken in areas too vulnerable for minelaying by warships.

Most profitable zones at first were Baltic shipping channels, the Kattegat, seas around Denmark and Kiel Bay which remained areas of attention to the end of hostilities. Beauforts and naval aircraft started in 1940 to sow in the estuaries of the Weser, Elbe, Scheldt and Maas. August 1940 saw Beauforts extend their activity to the approaches to Biscay French ports, to which U-boats and blockade runners were homing. By the end of 1940 a total of 1,167 mines had been sown – one per aircraft – by Hampdens, Beauforts, Swordfishes and Albacores. Success, difficult to accredit, was optimistically reckoned as amounting to a mixed bag of 137 vessels sunk.

By 1941, with many more U-boats using ports in western France, emphasis had switched to the Biscay area and increased after the *Scharnhorst* and *Gneisenau* arrived at Brest on 22 March 1941. Some seventy mines were sown monthly in its approaches between March and June 1941. Nevertheless, when the capital ships escaped from Brest on 12 February 1942, they sailed unscathed until, off the Belgian and Dutch coasts, they were damaged by three aerial-laid mines probably delivered by 5 Group and as late vindication of mining's value.

March 1942 saw Bomber Command become solely responsible for the mining campaign, but the Commander's commitment to a strategic bomber offensive led to mining being regarded as "part-training for inexperienced crews and veterans" and acceptable "in so far as it does not prejudice the normal bombing effort". The Air Ministry Directive ordered a great increase in mining by using Wellingtons, each carrying two mines, Manchesters and Halifaxes each with four and by Lancasters and Stirlings each able to carry six. It was now that crews of the latter began 'gardening'.

Introducing Stirlings to operations through minelaying had been proposed in January 1941, but bomb door modifications were necessary allowing five or six mines to be carried. On 8 January 1941 Air Ministry authority called for existing Stirlings to be modified to carry three mines as alternatives to SCIs or 1,000lb bombs with the proviso that the load must later be doubled. N3640 was the first Stirling able to accommodate six mines.

Political pressure demanded that Stirlings drop bombs and although mines were delivered to Oakington in February 1941 they remained in storage. Their use by Stirlings had only been postponed and on 14 May 1941 the Air Ministry decreed that the aircraft could, on 2,000lb bomb carrier Type B2 slings, carry up to seven Type A Mk I-IV mines, one on any of bomb station Nos 4, 5, 6, 7, 10, 11 and 12. So few Stirlings were on strength that diversion from bombing raids were not allowed until the night of **23/24 March 1942** when, in company with nine Hampdens and two Manchesters, they began planting 'vegetables'.

Mines dropped 'live' or 'safe' were fuzed by electro-magnetic means. As the weapon fell away a static cord whipped from a pocket on the parachute housing, snatched a retaining pin and freed flaps of the housing allowing a parachute to be drawn out by a

The Stirling towers above armourers about to load mines on a 199 Squadron aircraft at Lakenheath.

cord attached to its container and which remained on the mine. Forces on the parachute tended to keep it tangential to the weapon's trajectory retarding its fall. Upon striking the water the wooden or metal nose fairing fractured, the impact operating the inertia weight release mechanism, causing the weapon to move away forward.

The forward section of the mine comprised a steel shell made in two parts welded to a forward steel plate bulkhead. Made of 1in thick steel, the nose was also welded, externally, to the mine's shell and at an angle to its longitudinal axis. After the fairing was released in the water an exposed sloping nose tended to bring the mine horizontal during descent through water and prevented it from nosing into the seabed. Alternatively, a hollow tail was fitted creating a long cylindrical body with its centre of gravity well forward.

The nose fairing which broke off when the mine hit the water was contoured to prevent planing. Inertia release mechanism discarded the tail and ensured that the mine entered the water at the correct angle. It was essential that its longitudinal axis during flight was always at a tangent to the curve trajectory. Nose and a tail needed to be fitted parallel to the charge section. Retarded descent made sowing possible from an altitude of about 1,000ft at a speed slow enough to prevent damage on striking the water.

Precise weights of mines varied, a typical example of the Mk I-IV, with a parachute, weighed 1,572lb including about 750lb Amatol filling, and 1,649lb when carrying 775lb of Minol. The later, smaller 1,000lb Mk V magnetic mine with 625–675lb of explosive, was introduced in 1941. By 1943 acoustic or magnetic mines were available that could be timed to become immediately operational or have very long delay fuzing, and they could also be set ultimately to neutralise themselves. Mines Mks I-IV (independent and not contact mines) were seabed resting weapons for use against surface craft and submarines. With an unlimited storage life, they could also be used as delayed or direct-action bombs and, if needed, could be sown by surface ships.

To the end of 1943 mines were generally released from below 1,500ft to ensure accuracy. Mks I and II, constructed of a special tough quality 1/8in thick steel, had a diameter of 17.7in. Then came the Mk III built of a commercial quality 3/16in mild steel, the additional thickness giving the mine extra strength. As a result, its diameter increased to 17.83in and its weight exceeded that of the Mks I and II by about 90lb. The 18.3in diameter Mk IV in use by 1941 differed from the Mk III by being of pressed-steel construction.

Use of the term 'sowing' led to mining being code-named 'Gardening'. Great secrecy surrounded specific reasons for many mining sorties, sometimes flown to very precise positions in an attempt to sink particular vessels within any one of some eighty carefully defined areas identified by horticultural or fishery names.

In March 1942 HQ 3 Group diary recorded that they had 'acquired packets of seed, implements and catalogues,' noting that on **23/24 March** three aircraft of XV Squadron (N3669-C, N3674-T and R9303-P) and two the following night (N6065-G and N6076-D), carried out the first spring sowing. Their 'gardens' were off the French coast near Groix, where, on **23rd/24th,** three crews of 149 Squadron dropped twelve mines from W7460-O, R9296-Q and N6124-R which faced heavy tracer and AA fire from Lorient and more from flak ships in the Channel. Only eight out of ten sorties that month were 'effective' and involved sowing thirty-two mines.

In the course of sixty sorties during seven April nights another seventy-two mines were released but locating a precise dropping position was never easy. The biggest Stirling effort so far came on **22/23 April** when twenty-four set out, along with three Wellingtons of 3 Group and twenty-three bombers of 5 Group. A total of seventy-two mines were sown by eighteen Stirlings - equivalent to the remainder of the month's total effort.

Flak ships in port approaches and anchorages usually fiercely greeted the 'gardeners' who, often operating close to the shore, frequently ran the gauntlet of coastal defences. Guns aboard other ships opened fire, and the small numbers of bombers easy to locate were ready prey for night fighters. Early operations found each Stirling carrying four mines, leaving ample space for several 500lb bombs – useful for intimidating flak ships and coastal military targets. In that respect **3/4 May,** when 11/12 Stirlings planted thirty-nine mines, was typical of the period, for 7/8 Stirlings mined the Langeland Belt where one aimed 2 x 500lb HEs at a flakship. Two others put eight mines in the Little Belt then strafed a minesweeper from 500ft. Such activity was possible because of the Stirling's manoeuvrability.

7/8 May 1942 was a busy night. Some eighty-one minelayers operated, of which forty-three of 3 Group and twenty-three of 5 Group claimed accurate drops. A dozen Stirlings planted forty-seven mines off Denmark, eight put thirty-two into Kiel Bay and another three sowed eleven in the Great Belt. Using their HE loads, two crews announced their presence Sylt and Brondum aerodromes.

On 17/18 May another mining operation embraced fifteen Stirlings, half their thirty-two mines falling around Horn's Reef and the others by Heligoland. Three Stirlings failed to return, one each of XV, 218 and 149 Squadrons with Sgt Jim Jerman piloting the latter. He recalls:

A naval officer came to persuade us that minelaying was a profitable form of warfare, if a very precise kind of exercise. We trained for it during normal air tests, then on 17 May set off for Kiel Bay with four magnetic mines. Shipping channels are very narrow, just a hundred yards wide or so, and mines had to be laid accurately. The technique was to make for some known landmark on a certain course at a steady speed, then fly at 1,000ft altitude straight and level and with bomb doors open. The bomb-aimer calculated the exact moment for release and pressed the button. Down went the mines, guided by their little parachutes, into the hundred-yard-wide lane. Of course, the Germans carefully briefed their night-fighter crews as to the whereabouts of the shipping lanes, making a minelayer a sitting duck. No 149 Squadron carried out the most minelaying operations in the Command, and the overall casualty rate among the squadrons was 37 percent.

When I was flying operationally on bombing raids the casualty rate for all sorties was 3.7 percent. This meant that out of 100 crews only fifteen men could be expected to survive a first tour of thirty ops plus a second tour of twenty. The chances were far less if minelaying was the main occupation. We did not know it at the time.

Vital to survival was an accurate altimeter, an aneroid barometer. Atmospheric pressure over any given target involved inspired guesswork. When bombing a major target from a considerable height an error did not make all that much difference, and a correct QFE would be obtained before a night landing. When laying mines, however, it was essential to have an accurate barometric reading in order to set the altimeter accurately. One millibar difference in pressure means 30ft difference in height reading, thirty means 900ft. Put another way, one inch of mercury represented 1,000ft, making slight errors disastrous when flying low at night - as was the case when mining.

On 17 May 1942 five Stirling crews of 149 Squadron were briefed to mine Kiel Bay, in the Baltic. We were warned that there was a deep 'low' over the area, but just how 'low' the air pressure was could not be ascertained. It was deepening steadily and worse than anything yet experienced. Secondly, we were warned of night-fighter activity supported by radar. To confound them both we were to try to fly under the radar screen. We were to cross the North Sea at 1,000ft then descend to 50ft to cross the Danish coast and Denmark until we reached the island of Langeland. Then we were to climb to 1,000ft again and fly straight and level for 'x' minutes before planting our mines.

Setting out we adjusted the altimeter to Lakenheath's QFE, each crew taking a different set of magnetic mines. Over Southwold we turned as usual, setting course for Denmark at 1,000ft. Just under three hours later 'Fairey' Battle, our observer/navigator, said, "The Danish coast is coming up any minute." I saw it – and could scarcely believe my eyes as I pulled back the stick and just cleared the sand dunes. In the 400-mile sea crossing we had lost 1,000ft.

I climbed to 50ft and set the altimeter at zero. We crossed one or two roads and I saw cars with hooded lights passing beneath. Then, after a few minutes, a church steeple flashed past the starboard wing tip. I thought we were a bit low, so I climbed a little and re-set the altimeter to zero.

Then 'Fairey', down in the belly of the plane staring through the observation hatch trying to get a fix said, "It's no good. I can't make landfall anywhere. Can you turn round and have another go?" "Sure," I replied – and a few minutes later another church steeple (actually the same one again, in Flensburg) told us we were perilously low. Finally the navigator called, "It's no use, we'll have to break orders and climb, so I can get an accurate landmark that will give us a course to Langeland".

I pulled on the stick, lifting the nose. Just as well, because there was a metallic noise as the airscrews touched the top of a little knoll and were bent double. Nobody told us there was a 50ft hill in Denmark! An eerie silence overtook us as the engines stopped and we scraped along the ground for a hundred yards. We had 'landed' near Abenraa, dead on course.

The port inner was on fire and we were sitting on hundreds of gallons of high-octane fuel and four magnetic mines. We were out in a flash through the top hatch, Stan Butcher and I, looking for the others. Then we remembered 'Fairey,' downstairs. I got Stan to take our small fire extinguisher to tackle the engine fire if he could, while I climbed in to pull 'Fairey' out. The hatches were jammed, but Stan climbed back in, grabbed the axe and started chopping. 'Taffy' and Jack Sloan joined us. I noticed the gravity switches on our secret equipment had not worked in the gentle belly landing so I started pressing buttons and setting off explosives which created almighty bangs. By then they were lifting 'Fairey' out. Then we heard Frank Hoyland – he had been flung out as the plane broke its back.

Once together we all made for a hedge thinking we could get the injured behind it while I fired the plane. Lauris, the Flight Engineer, was standing in the astrodome as we hit the ground, and had bumped his nose on the edge. It was bleeding and his eye started to swell. 'Fairey' had been dragged along the ground but inside the aircraft. In fact, he had a fractured skull and broken arm.

A local farmer, hearing the crash and fearing for his horses, had rung the *Kommandatur*, and they had piled into cars to find us. I sent the crew off to try to escape, and except for Laurie and 'Fairey' they all turned back when they came to a river. Meanwhile I tried to find a means of burning the aircraft, but we had no matches. The explosion as the mines went off would probably have killed 'Fairey,' but at the time I did not know the extent of his injuries. I went back to find the crew had returned, and in so doing walked into heavily armed Germans. The two injured men were taken into hospital while the rest of us were eventually sent to Stalag Luft III.

A few days later, at Sagan, more POWs arrived, among them Sgt Wodehouse and crew. They had flown into the Baltic where two of their companions drowned. A year later we heard what had happened to three other mining crews. One disappeared without trace probably in the sea whereas the other two reached home, one with high tension cable around the tailplane, the other with a fir tree stuck in a wing leading edge. All had obeyed orders scrupulously and flown into that deepening low. Nine men had died and eleven were to be POWs for three years. As the Russians advanced westwards we were moved, finally to Fallingbostel, 11km from Belsen from where for a year, when the wind was in the south-west, we faced the stench from the crematoria. We saw Russian troops treated like animals and licking out the rusty empty tins left over from our Red Cross parcels. I remember too the escapers, and the day we were lined up to face heavy machine-guns while we were told about the fifty officers of Stalag Luft III shot while trying to escape.

EF353 HA-C about to take on board its mine quota. Taking off on its fourteenth sortie the aircraft crashed into Downham Market's operations block. (Gp Capt O A Morris)

Much of the Stirling mining activity took place around Denmark. However a new 'gardening' plot, the Gironde Estuary, came into cultivation on **21/22 May 1942.** Of 10/15 Stirlings taking part, one crew instead mined off La Rochelle, indicative of the difficulties minelaying imposed. Two more 15-strong night operations followed before May ended, by which time delivery of 128 mines had cost four Stirlings and crews.

'Thousand Plan' raids and other bombing operations cut June's effort to four nights, 203 mines falling during 52/57 effective sorties. On **11/12 June,** sixty-eight mines were dropped and a Stirling of 214 Squadron failed to return. During July's five mining nights Stirlings made 37/41 effective sorties, laying 184 mines, eighty-six of them on **7/8 July.** One of the busier occasions was the **14/15th,** when 48/52 aircraft operating laid mines, although only 3/3 of them were Stirlings.

After mining off Borkum on 16 August 1942, N3705 MG-F came down near Gorinchem in the Netherlands. Barely damaged it was flown from the crash site to Rechlin for tests after which its under surfaces were sprayed yellow. (G J Zwanenburg)

Increased mining came but slowly, for even in August 1942 available Stirlings totalled only around forty-five. There were operations on six nights in the month, resulting in 53/63 successful drops. Less satisfactory was an increased loss rate and on **10/11 August,** when sixteen Stirlings delivered sixty-eight mines, R9162-Q of 149 Squadron failed to return. Heavier losses came on the **20th/21st** when sixty mining aircraft including fourteen Stirlings again encountered very bad weather. Only eight crews claimed successful sorties, one aborted and Sgt Robertson's R9329-V of 149 Squadron crashed near Cornwood in Cornwall. For 218 Squadron operating off Denmark it was a particularly bad night with four Stirlings failing to return.

September saw a further increase in 'gardening', Stirlings participating on seven nights and completing 39/65 sorties during which 174 mines were sown. A very busy night was **18/19 September** when the total Bomber Command effort was devoted to mining and 99/115 of the aircraft despatched managed successful sorties.

Heavy bombers were now needed for strategic bombing and to support operations in north Africa to the close of October, Italian targets involved the Stirling force. Only small scale mining took place fairly frequently, 77/108 Stirlings delivering 299 mines. The number of weapons released was such because Stirlings had been cleared to each carry five or six mines instead of four. November's busiest night was **10/11th** when 100 percent drops were achieved by twenty-two Stirlings which between them delivered 121 mines.

Despite the onset of the frosty conditions, 'gardening' occupied seven December nights, but again the effort was low with the **8/9th** the busiest when 18/26 Stirlings made drops out of the sixty-one aircraft despatched. On **16/17 December** ten 75 Squadron crews were detailed for mining off Bordeaux. R9245, piloted by Sgt B A Franklin, failed to clear the Devil's Dyke, at Newmarket, marks 4ft from its summit showing where a tyre had hit the ancient earthwork. Parts of the undercarriage were torn off, taking with them the starboard inner engine's oil tank causing engine seizure as a result of which the aircraft spun into the ground a mile away. Two exploding mines produced an enormous eruption of fire and all the crew died. Only three other 75 Squadron aircraft, already airborne, operated that night from Newmarket. During December 1942, 67/78 effective Stirling mining sorties saw 371 mines deposited.

Official statistics surveying the 1942 effort differ in detail. According to Bomber Command ORS, 567 out of 716 sorties flown by mining Stirlings in 1942 were effective, 2,441 mines were laid and twenty-nine Stirlings failed to return.

By March 1943 Stirlings had completed a year's mining, 3 Group having sown over 5,500 mines – some 5,000 successfully – and all Stirling squadrons were participating. The value of such operations was such that in March 1943 Bomber Command Operation Instruction No 69 described in detail areas worth mining, and giving these reasons for the choice:

| Codename | Area boundaries | | Notes |
	N	E	
Silverthorn 10	57°45'		Eastern half too deep except for mining against large ships. Mine in S-SSE Skaw and Western swept channel
Silverthorn 11	57 °10'	11° 50'	Area by Grovis Flak and SW of Fladen Whistle Buoy, east & west along swept channel 7 miles N of Anholt and in SW corner swept channel NE Anholt Knob Light
	56°45'	11 00'	
Silverthorn 12	56° 45'	12° 10'	All except NE deep water. Mine swept channel.
	56° 20'	11° 00'	Drop stocks on other areas.
Silverthorn 13	56° 20'	12° 10'	All suitable, as for No 12
	56° 05'	11° 00'	
Silverthorn 14	56° 18'	10° 40'	All suitable, special channel from Great Belt and Aarhus, anchorage NE of Sejro Puller Whistle Buoy. Much shoal water in area
	55° 44'	10° 40'	
Yewtree	57° 30'	11° 00'	All suitable particularly swept channel flanked by shoal water
	57° 00'	To 5 fathom line	
Kraut	57° 10'	11° 00'	All suitable, especially channel from Aalborg, N/S by Oestre Flak LV
	56° 40'	To 5 fathom line	
Melon	54° 40'	?	
Forget-me-not	?	?	All suitable especially by Kiel LV and channels running NW and E, N from Kabels Flak, SW of Gustav Flak, channel junction 54°35N/10°45E. Flugge Whistle Buoy to coast south and to 55°35N/10°45E
Wallflower	?	?	

Additional to those very carefully selected areas were also the following:

> **Endives** – waters off Brodningen and a swept channel on the eastern side
> **Wallflower** – east of Breda Grund, over Veisnaes Flak and entrance to Flensburger Fjord
> **Pumpkin** – deep water area, mines sown to either side of line joining Linshage, buoy near
> Fals Bolsax, at 55°40N/10°47E, Asnaes Rev and in anchorage 5 miles WNW Asnaes
> **Broccoli** – within area 55°25N – 10°56E – 55°19N – 5 fathom soundings to west
> **Asparagus** – north of Sprogo Island and south of island to 11°00E and N of 55°15N, in
> anchorage within southern area although deep water there required very sensitive mines
> **Melon** – all suitable with channels to Schonhagen Buoy and approaches to Eckernförde
> Bucht needing preference

All were on Denmark's eastern side to where many Stirling mine sorties were despatched.

On the western side of Denmark three areas were designated, codenamed **Hawthorn I,
II, III**. Between Sylt and the mouth of the Elbe coastal shipping lanes lay within the
Rosemary area and, along the Frisians, **Nectarine** mining took place. The other main
region for Stirling mining was off the entrance to Brest (**Jellyfish**), within **Artichoke** off
Lorient, **Beech** off St Nazaire, **Cinnamon** off La Rochelle, **Deodar** being the mouth of
the Gironde, **Elderberry** off Bayonne and **Furze** off San Sebastian. Along the French
side of the English Channel only very limited mining was carried out by Stirlings.

The extent of mining activity between March and June 1943 is shown by these
figures extracted from the relevant 3 Group Operations Summary:

Squadron	March			April			May			June		
	a	b	c	a	b	c	a	b	c	a	b	c
XV	27	–	149	13	–	45	22	–	106	19	–	83
75	6	1	32	20	5	90	28	1	157	13	1	56
90	8	1*	42	13	1	59	14	–	54	12	–	51
149	8	–	30	14	–	53	31	2	126	20	–	78
214	13	1*	42	15	–	54	21	–	107	19	–	90
218	12	–	54	26	3	92	26	1	125	28	–	111
620	–	–	–	–	–	–	–	–	–	14	–	52

Key:
a – mining sorties despatched. **b** – failed to return/crashed during operation
c – number of mines planted. * aircraft crashed

Attributing particular sinkings of enemy shipping to certain squadrons let alone a crew
was rarely possible, but the outcome of one night's activity seems fairly certain.
Unfortunately it was coupled with a very heavy loss rate for on **28/29 April 1943** Nos
75, 90, 214 and 218 Squadrons fielded between them twenty-five aircraft to mine Kiel
Bay. Flak ships were in the area and six Stirlings failed to return, a loss rate of 24 percent.

Air raid warnings were sounded over Denmark between 2240 hrs and 2355 hrs as
sixty-five bombers passed over Jutland between Hallingen and Limfjord, twenty setting
course for the Skaw and Kattegat, another twenty for Langeland and the western Baltic
and twenty-five for the Central Belt. Marine flak units engaged some, encountering
return fire from the raiders, three of which were claimed.

Three Stirlings went to the Great Belt, Nyborg, seven to the Kjalundborg area,
sixteen to Langeland Belt (one of which was lost), forty-two to Cadet Channel where
three were lost, and twenty-two to the Bornholm island area. In all, 227 aircraft were
'gardening' around Denmark that night and twenty-three failed to return.

At 0600 hrs *Kreigsmarine* vessels *Annkrista*, *Diana* and *Sicherungsboot JK 10* took
over the escort of a floating dock towed by two tugs, *Holland* and *Taifun*, on route for
Narvik. At 1032 hrs two mines exploded, one below the *Holland* which sank in four
minutes. Only nine of the crew were rescued. *Taifun* also sprang a leak due to an
exploding mine and sank, and the floating dock remained at Copenhagen. At noon the
Swedish ferry *Malmo*, operating between Malmo and Copenhagen, was damaged by a
mine and beached near Barsebaek, Sweden.

Responding, the Germans extended night-fighter operations against the minelayers and brought along more guns. They also made frequent attempts using Ju 52/3m (MS) aircraft to locate mines and explode them from the air. That did not prevent Bomber Command's 'gardeners' from harvesting the 16,160-ton liner *Gneisenau*, sunk in the Baltic by one mine on 2 May as it headed for the USSR.

Not surprisingly by May 1943 every vessel passing the Frisians carried a wreck buoy to position should it fall prey to a mine. During that month 88 percent of 3 Group's mining sorties were rated successful, 93 percent of the mines reckoned to have been correctly positioned. In all 783 mines were laid that month, 729 successfully, a total of 490 tons. The June effort, extending over fourteen nights, resulted in the successful delivery of 616 mines, with 620 Squadron joining the campaign on **19/20 June.** Busiest nights were the **22nd/23rd** when eighty-eight mines were laid, and the **27/28th** when seventy-seven were dropped.

A long line of mines await loading at Downham Market.

Appreciation of mining's potential led, on 12 June 1943, to the issue of Bomber Command Operations Order No 176 outlining three overall zones for mining, the strength of attack and the number of mines to be sown. Area 1 'Pruning' was to attract 673 mines dropped from 205 aircraft including thirty-six Stirlings and Lancaster IIs of 3 Group. Area 2 'Weeding' would receive 662 mines from 241 aircraft, including forty Stirlings, and Area 3 'Plucking' was to be saturated using 342 aircraft (including seventy-three Stirlings/Lancaster IIs of 3 Group) sowing 1,057 mines. Tactics for minelaying were changing too with Stirling crews making releases, from June onwards, at heights of between 700ft and 5,500ft with 800ft being the norm. All was far removed from the initial intent that mining would be for 'trainees', a sideline to bombing activity.

The risks involved in mining operations are again well illustrated by events which, on **14/15 June 1943,** overtook Fg Off J L Edwards and crew manning BK646-N of 75 Squadron. They left Newmarket at 2253 hrs taking three mines to sow off Bordeaux in clear moonlight. They climbed over the Channel to 4,000ft and dived across the French coast just east of the Cherbourg Peninsula as flak burst on either side. When their *Gee* apparatus became unserviceable, navigation had to be by astro fixes and pin-pointing. At 500ft the lone Stirling roared across France, altering course when the Loire was reached and, heading out to sea, they climbed just south of Les Sables d'Olonne. Slightly off track they ran into plentiful light flak at 4,000ft so dived to gain speed only to be again fired on. Three heavy bumps were felt then Sgt A F Jones, the mid-upper gunner, called up to say that a large chunk of the rudder had been shot away. Having little control left, Edwards ordered the mines to be jettisoned 3–4 miles off shore before they turned for home. Feeling it unsafe to fly fast and low the pilot climbed to 9,000ft where one engine was soon running rough. They were uncertain of the aircraft's position until about 15 miles south-east of Rennes when a fighter three times attacked the Stirling. Edwards called, "We've had it!" so the crew abandoned the aircraft. Searchlight beams illuminated the parachute of Plt Off R G Kirby and he landed near La Haye from where he began a perilous dash to freedom. He heard the aircraft explode, and watched it burn for four hours. Four of the crew became POWs.

During **July 1943** Stirlings managed 103 sorties and dropped 305 mines over seven nights with 199 Squadron 'gardening' for the first time on the **30th.** The level of effort was sustained in August when over another seven nights 306 mines were sown, 75/107 crews claiming to have released them in the prescribed positions but at a cost of two Stirlings.

One was BK690-G of 620 Squadron carrying a crew on their first operation. They set off from Chedburgh at 2157 hrs on **6 August,** mined the Gironde mouth then set course for home. Over Nantes and well west of their intended course they ran into AA fire. Their radio was hurled across the cabin and wing tanks were set on fire causing a blow-torch effect across the fuselage giving them no option but to abandon the aircraft. As the wireless operator left his seat another shell burst above the canopy, probably killing the pilot and bomb aimer. Getting out was far from easy, for the aircraft fell tail first before entering a spin. The injured navigator, Plt Off D D Donkin, became a POW and four others escaped.

Stirling bomber squadron strength was at this time approaching its peak allowing mines to be laid on six nights in **September 1943.** On the **4/5th,** while 111 Stirlings set out for Mannheim, thirteen others successfully dropped sixty-one mines. On the **22nd/23rd,** with 174 Stirlings operationally fit and 112/137 of them sent to bomb Hanover, 12/13 mined from between 1,300ft and 2,500ft.

Although re-equipment with Lancasters was approaching, the Stirling force attained peak strength on 31 October 1943 when establishment stood at 184 aircraft, squadron strength 182 and aircraft fit for operations and available for the Command totalled 204. On **2/3 October,** when 99/117 bombers laid 291 mines, 54/56 were Stirlings responsible for placing 116 weapons. On **7/8 October** 59/79 aircraft laid mines, 34/43 being Stirlings, two of which – from XV and 149 Squadrons – did not return. From a 90 Squadron aircraft, six of the crew were rescued after it ditched 12 miles off Cromer. Next night, while 84/95 Stirlings bombed Bremen, 16/17 dropped 62 mines. Another busy night was **17/18th** when 154 mines were sown by 32/36 Stirlings.

The wind-down in Stirling bomber squadron strength began on 22 November 1943 when front-line establishment was reduced to 152, just two days after the last major Stirling bomber raid. Only five mining operations were undertaken that month, for although release from Main Force bombing meant that a large number of aircraft were available for mining and supply dropping to Resistance forces, many crews were converting to Lancasters. Stirlings would continue to lay mines, and sowing took place during seven December nights. No 623 Squadron ceased the task on 4 December, 622 on the 20th and XV Squadron on the 22nd.

To improve survival rate, release of mines from 12,000ft commenced on **30/31 December 1943** when three Stirlings sowed eleven mines in the Gironde Estuary. January 1944 saw the introduction of *H2S* in an attempt to improve drop accuracy. On **20/21 January** 125 mines were released from twenty-one aircraft, with the **27/28th** proving even busier for 67/74 Stirlings mined approaches to Heligoland and Frisian Area II along with two regions of the Kattegat. Sowing from an average 10,000ft, fifty-two Stirlings each carried five mines leaving the remainder each operating with three. Another busy night was **28/29th** when 58/63 Stirlings dropped 162 mines in an attempt to seal the Kiel Canal two aircraft failed to return. Mining remained no easy option, but the hazardous low-level operations were almost a thing of the past. On this occasion releases took place from between 7,000ft and 17,400ft producing a norm of 13,500ft for the average delivery of three mines.

Mining declined during February in line with the reduced Stirling establishment. There was also a gradual territorial shift, more sowing occurring off the Frisians and Texel, also in the Seine Bay and especially off Le Havre and Cherbourg and in the mouth of the Adour. Nevertheless, the Gironde Estuary, Bayonne and St Jean de Luz, all long frequented by Stirlings, remained good for gardening. Not, however, by 199 Squadron which in February switched to *Window* dropping during Main Force raids before passing to 100 Group for RCM activity.

On **18/19 March** 37/39 Stirling crews successfully dropped 189 mines out of 331 laid that night by Bomber Command. Activity was concentrated around the Cherbourg Peninsula, although the Frisians, Texel, and the French west coast ports still attracting U-boats were not neglected.

The busiest mining night of the month was the **18/19th** when 40/48 Stirlings laid 117 mines off Rostock and off Arcona Light. Bomber Command effort resulted in the sowing of 497 mines that night with the Stirling force forming the largest component. Most of the mining still took place off west or north-west France.

During May it occurred on twenty-two nights in three areas: a) Bordeaux-La Rochelle; b) Cherbourg-Rouen and c) Texel and the Frisians. On three nights there were unusual drops in the IJsselmeer, in Limfjord, off Morlaix and off Dunkirk. After operating on **19 May**, 218 Squadron – withdrawn from bombing operations after the Chambly raid of 1st/2nd – ceased mining and began training for a specialised role during the Normandy landings. Participation in raids on rail centres occupied the remaining Stirlings although in May 1944 they managed 148 'gardening' sorties as well as 140 SOE supply-drops to the French Resistance.

After D-Day, mining was resumed by the remaining Stirling bomber squadrons, Nos 149 and 218. On **17 July** they commenced daylight raids on flying-bomb sites with the cessation of 'gardening' close. No 149's sowing ended on **11/12 July 1944,** eight crews mining off La Rochelle. It was left to Stirlings of 218 Squadron, on **23 July 1944,** and sowing off the entrance to Brest, to complete the Stirling's contribution. Its extent is portrayed by the following statistics taken from Bomber Command ORS records.

Almost to the end, mining operations exacted a toll from those who participated. The closing rounds involving drops by Stirlings came on the nights of the **6/7th, 7/8th** (twenty-two mines), **8/9th** and **11/12th August.** From the first of these, when 12/13 aircraft sowed forty-eight mines off Brest, LK383-A of 149 Squadron and flown by Fg Off D A Adams failed to return. There was often ample flak to face, spectacularly proven when a mine falling from BK816-C received a direct hit soon after it left the aircraft which nevertheless safely landed at Chivenor. On the **8/9th** sixteen mines were planted in the Gironde by eight aircraft and on the last two occasions off La Rochelle, where on **11/12th** eight Stirlings positioned twenty-four mines to round off what had been an arduous campaign. What it precisely achieved none can tell; but the cost in terms of crews losses was only too apparent to all who served on the Stirling squadrons.

Overall Stirling Mining Effort 1942–44

	1942	1943	1944	Total
Despatched	716	1,675	1,410	3,801
Effective	567	1,419	1,210	3,196
No of mines laid	2,441	6,118	5,286	13,845
Failed to return	29	39	16	84

Analysis of Mining Effort (Source: Bomber Command ORS)

	Despatched A	Effective N	Mines laid	FTR	Cat EA	Cat EN
Area A						
1942	193	164	605	5	–	4
1943	722	609	2,100	11	1	3
1944	634	557	2,406	4	1	5
Area B						
1942	319	276	1,362	7	–	2
1943	751	649	3,541	11	–	8
1944	398	375	1,977	2	–	1
Area C						
1942	188	118	447	16	–	1
1943	197	157	465	17	–	1
1944	378	278	903	10	1	1
Area D						
1942	16	9	27	1	–	–
1943	5	4	12	–	–	–
1944	–	–	–	–	–	–
Total	3,801	3,196	13,845	84	3	26

Meaning:
Cat EA – Written off after damage in action
Cat EN – Written off after damage non-attributable to battle

Total mines laid by Bomber Command (for comparison):

	1942	1943	1944
January	62	1,285	1,101
February	306	1,129	1,661
March	356	1,159	1,472
April	569	1,869	2,643
May	1,023	1,148	2,760
June	1,167	1,174	1,178
July	897	927	708
August	968	1,103	1,586
September	1,101	1,188	748
October	982	1,076	1,133
November	1,156	976	750
December	987	800	1,160

A further 4,482 mines were laid in 1945, although minelaying using Stirlings ended in July 1944.

Stirling casualties during mining operations:

Failed to return: 84
Category E: A – 3; N – 23
Category B and AC: A – 21; N – 12

A – Written off after damage in action
N – Written off after damage non-attributable to battle

Chapter 15
Bomber Finale

THE intention had been to re-equip three Stirlings squadrons with Lancasters in February 1944 and another three in March. A counter proposal was to disband all six then reform them as Lancaster squadrons, but neither scheme proceeded. Instead, all six were gradually re-equipped with two being held as long as necessary and practicable for mining operations.

On 1 January 1944, a total of 100 fit Stirlings were available with 100 crews ready to fly them. Squadrons had on total charge 112 aircraft equating their IE, making the three-Flight squadron structure and improved serviceability evident. When, on 16 January, 214 Squadron became non-operational pending transfer to 100 Group and re-equipment with B-17 Fortresses, the Stirling total establishment fell to ninety-six and available crews to eighty. By the end of January, Stirlings ranked third numerically in Bomber Command which, on 21 January, held 585 Lancasters and 285 Halifaxes. Stirlings remained a potent force – even though they had been withdrawn from Main Force operations over Germany – for a part in the Transport Plan attacks on nearby Occupied Countries.

There had, however, been an unscheduled diversion for on **16/17 December 1943** – a small force variously listed as comprising twenty, twenty-six or twenty-seven aircraft, operating with nine Lancasters of 5 Group and guided by twelve Mosquitoes of 8 Group, had been despatched to bomb two V-1 sites under construction near Abbeville. The Stirlings are thought to have dropped 475 x 500lb HEs, a 106-ton load, whereas the Lancasters delivered nine huge 12,000lb HC bombs providing a vivid example of the contrast between the two types.

A further attempt to destroy two V-1 sites under construction by using heavy bombers at night made on **22/23 December 1943,** attracted 24/29 Stirlings led by 6/7 Mosquitoes and three Halifaxes of 8 Group. Stirlings, forming the main bombing force, delivered 507 x 500lb MC and 44 x 500lb GP Long Delay (LD) HEs. Visibility was good but low cloud reduced bombing accuracy. The targets were small and area bombing in Allied territory was obviously unacceptable.

Four times in January Stirling bombers supplied Resistance forces although their main preoccupation now was minelaying, which reached its climax in the final days of the month. Meanwhile, ever increasing concern was aroused by the enemy's preparation of many specialised sites in northern France from which to bombard Britain with novel weapons. Officially designated 'construction works', they varied in size and by January 1944 were under fierce attack in daylight by tactical aircraft and at night by strategic bombers. Four times in **January 1944** 3 Group was involved.

On **4/5 January 1944,** a dozen Mosquitoes marked four flying-bomb sites for attack by 40/57 Stirlings operating with Lancasters of 5 Group. Split into almost equal groups, the Stirlings aimed about 148 tons of HE at each of their two targets. Following a similar raid on the **14/15th,** craters were quickly filled and the simple buildings and concreted areas soon replaced. Attacks therefore needed to be repeated.

Mosquito-led Stirlings went again to France on **21/22 January** and met accurate AA fire to which the Stirling force responded by climbing from 11,000ft to 13,000ft on the bombing run.

The other operation took place on **25/26 January** when 45/56 Stirlings attacked three sites and again relied upon Mosquito marking. By the end of the night they had delivered 951 x 500lb MC HE bombs and 98 long-delay fused aged 500lb GP weapons to delay damage repair, loads almost identical to those carried by Halifaxes also

Stirling IIIs, HA-N, -O and –U in 1944 and featuring the ventral gun position.

operating. Although the vast quantity of bombs being delivered by day and night failed to prevent the V-1 campaign from opening, it prevented commencement prior to D-Day.

February 1944's operations comprised twelve nights of minelaying and nine during which a total of 199 sorties were flown to supply Resistance forces mainly in central and south-eastern France to increase their strength for post D-Day activity. Crews believed these drops were of questionable value because all too often the parachuted containers and large packets fell into German hands. Lone, skilled low flying to very precise co-ordinates made the task perilous and of twelve Stirlings written off during operations in February seven suffered as a result of SOE activity.

Nevertheless, over the first three weeks of **March 1944**, the three remaining operational Stirling bomber squadrons – 75, 90 and 149 – continued supply drops to Resistance groups over thirteen nights, and to the extent that on **10/11 March** a maximum effort was launched by seventy-three crews.

There had been a further reduction in Stirling establishment which by 1 March had fallen to eighty with available crews numerically declining fast. On **1 March**, seventy-three stood by whereas three weeks later the number was around fifty. In mid-March front-line strength had been cut to seventy-six Stirling bombers in Bomber Command whose overall holding of aircraft included 1,050 heavies.

It was now that the Transport Plan came into play involving the Command's use to destroy important rail centres in France and Belgium. The aim was to neutralise them thereby preventing troop reinforcements and supplies from being rushed forward to halt the future Allied invasion. Such short-range operations were ideal for Stirlings, and five times in March they participated in such raids for which Mosquitoes marked the A/Ps.

Rail installations at Amiens were attacked first by 140 bombers which including thirty-eight Stirlings, forty Halifaxes of 4 Group and fifty-four aircraft of 6 Group. There was up to 9/10 cloud, searchlights were very active, some *Oboe* equipment in Mosquitoes became unserviceable and the TIs were released too soon. Night fighters patrolling north of Amiens picked off three bombers, among them a Stirling of 149 Squadron. Eventually 122 crews claimed to attack Amiens, the Stirlings' 800 x 500lb HEs falling on the south-west A/P.

A far more successful raid on the same target was unleashed by 130 bombers on **16/17 March**, when forty-one Stirlings operated with eighty-one Halifaxes of 4 and 6 Groups for which eight Mosquitoes marked. Enemy fighters were absent, marking accurate and on time. Stirlings delivered 178.1 tons, twenty-one Halifaxes of 4 Group dropped 115.9 tons and the 6 Group element released another 249.1 tons. Superior load carrying by Stirlings over the Halifaxes is apparent, the former each dropping about 8.4 tons and the latter around 5.5 tons. Stirlings, however, had the advantage of shorter tracks than the Yorkshire-based Halifaxes.

The third raid in the series, on **23/24 March**, was directed at two A/Ps in Laon's marshalling yards. Of the 143 participants forty-eight were Stirlings. Fine weather allowed the seventy aircraft in the first wave to bomb on two clusters of green markers accurately placed whereas failure of *Oboe* in the second marker force resulted in their attack being called off. Those aborting included 24/48 Stirlings. None of the 3 Group raiders encountered the quartet of active German fighters.

For **25/26 March** Aulnoye marshalling yards were chosen for closure by forty-nine Lancasters with ninety-two Halifaxes joining thirty-seven Stirlings. Again, the force concentrated its assault upon two A/Ps. *Oboe* Mosquitoes marked punctually, and 805 tons of HE were accurately released. Flak and fighter defences were absent, and while 182 crews attacked, seven Mosquitoes of 100 Group flew intruder patrols in support of the raid, a new feature during such operations. Next, it was the turn of Courtrai's undefended marshalling yards upon which 472 tons of fell in clear conditions.

At the start of April 1944, the Stirling IE strength stood at sixty-four with forty-two crews available to man them. An average of fifty-six were operationally fit. By the end of the month establishment had fallen to fifty-six aircraft of which forty-five were fit. The Lancaster establishment in 3 Group had by then risen to ninety-six, of which sixty-seven were operationally ready. On 28 April Bomber Command, established at 1,200 aircraft, had 1,064 operationally ready.

Supply and equipment drops to the French Resistance for their part in the forthcoming invasion continued throughout **April 1944**, and mining was undertaken on thirteen nights. On the 10th No 75 Squadron began operations using Lancasters, and after five further nights of mining their Stirlings were withdrawn, the last leaving the New Zealanders on **26 April**. While 149 Squadron visited many towns to drop leaflets explaining to the French and Belgians the reasons for heavy night bombing raids on railway installations, 218 Squadron participated in three sharp attacks on Chambly and the depot at Volvorde. Four nights of SOE operations by 90 and 149 Squadrons rounded off the month's Stirling bomber activity.

Lille rail installations were attacked on **9/10 April** by a force 226/239 bombers including twenty-three Stirlings which aimed 95.1 tons of HE at the southern A/P. On the **21st/22nd** fourteen Stirlings participated in the Chambly raid, then came the final major Stirling bombing effort when rail installations at Laon were attacked by 160/181 bombers on **22/23 April**. The 40/48 Stirlings involved delivered 173.4 tons of bombs. Red and green TIs were scattered but accurate flare drops transformed the target area into daylight. Flak was slight, but fighter activity resulted in nine bombers failing to return, among them three Stirlings one each of 90, 149 and 218 Squadrons. Another Stirling dropped leaflets over Paris and more southerly regions of France.

A less usual Stirling raid took place on **23/24 April**, their target the German Air Force signals depot at Brussels/Villeborde. For this operation they were relying upon the newly introduced *Gee-H* navigation aid and clear conditions to deliver 88 x 1,000lb MC which started a large fire in the target area. A few fighters responded, gunners aboard EH939-M of 90 Squadron damaging a Bf 110.

Mk III LK615 was shown to the Soviet Acceptance. Commissioned on 1 March 1945, it was rejected as incomplete. It received attention at RAF Habbaniya before handover at Tehran in summer 1945. Flight tested at L11 NKAP (Flight Test Institute of the People's Commissariat of the Aviation Industry) by G M Shiyanov, he considered it far more difficult to handle than the B17/24 tested at L11 Zhukovsky (Kratovo). The Soviet Air Force never tested it.

It was back to Chambly on the **24/25th** with the 3/4 Stirlings again relying on *Gee-H* to hit the depot's shops and stores with 9.4 tons of bombs. A similar operation attempted on the **26/27th** was abandoned when the equipment failed and bombs were jettisoned at sea.

Three Stirling bomber squadrons (Nos 90, 149, 218) remained operational in May 1944, the month that saw 199 Squadron depart for North Creake and 100 Group. On 1 May total squadron strength stood at fifty-six aircraft still equating the establishment. That figure was reduced to thirty-two on 25 May when 199 Squadron became non-operational in order to train in the use of *Mandrel*. Nevertheless, thirty of their Stirlings and crews remained operationally fit on 28 May.

Apart from yet another Chambly raid by sixteen Stirlings of 218 Squadron, the last in the transport attack campaign, the month's effort amounted to 148 mining and 140 SOE sorties. No149 Squadron moved to Methwold between 13 and 15 May to allow the preparation of Lakenheath for Boeing B-29s or alternative RAF very heavy bombers.

Stirling numbers within squadrons increased to forty-eight aircraft to enable them to fulfil special roles on D-Day but soon fell to forty and to thirty-two on 17 June.

On 1 June 1944 the total overall holding of Stirlings (all marks) was as follows:

Total bombers:

Metropolitan Air Force	In MAP hands	Transit UK	Overseas	Total
353	100	6	Nil	459

In squadrons and units:

						Aircraft Servicing Units		
Sqns	CUs	TTC/FTC	Misc	Transit UK	Class I	Class II	Class III	Class IV
62	213	6	5	6	1	22	14	10

Total Stirlings SD in squadron hands: 20

R&D Mk 3/4:

CRO	CRD	On site mods
34	21	45

Obsolescent Mk 1:

MAP holding two on site in the UK, sixty-six in Metropolitan Air Force hands.

While Stirling transports of 38 Group prepared for their major role on D-Day, Bomber Command's Stirlings in 3 and 100 Groups were also waiting to undertake very special tasks. The layout and holding of the force at 1800 hrs on 5 June was as follows:

90 Sqn: Not established 15 – 6
149 Sqn: 20 established 16 – 4
199 Sqn: 20 established 19 – 1
218 Sqn: 20 established 16 – 4

Led by Sqn Ldr J Overton, heading a crew of thirteen aboard EF133-A, No 218 Squadron (also using EF207-F, LJ632-G, LK401-I, LJ472-K, LJ522-N with two reserves LJ449-E and LJ517-U), took up a deceiving position off Boulogne during the night of **5/6 June**. The six special *Window* droppers orbiting precise positions gradually advanced towards the French coast. Strips of metal foil falling from them presented a radar image similar to that generated by an approaching convoy of ships, this feint continuing as the real invasion force crossed to the Seine Bay.

In an arc from 50°42N/00°23E to 51°04N/02°33W eight pairs of Stirlings of 199 Squadron, flying at 18,000ft, established a *Mandrel* screen to cloak the vital incoming attacks by RAF heavy bombers planned to neutralise Normandy's coastal guns. The Stirlings involved were LJ510-A, LJ514-B, LJ544-D, LJ513-E, LJ542-G, LJ560-H, LJ518-K, LJ569-C, LJ543-J, LJ538-T, LJ531-N, LJ536-P, LJ565-Q, LJ525-R, LJ578-S, LJ562-V, LJ580-X, LJ557-Y and LJ520-Z.

Another seven Stirlings, this time of 149 Squadron and led by Wg Cdr M E Pickford, left at around midnight to drop dummy paratroopers and pyrotechnics to simulate an airborne landing near Yvetot in north-west France. Used were EF140-A (Pickford), EJ109-G, LK388-L, EF161-R, EF193-T and two which failed to return – LK385-C and LJ621-M.

Their D-Day feints completed, the squadrons resumed mining and special support operations. On **15/16 June** 29/30 Stirlings joined Lancasters and Mosquitoes in a Master Bomber led night attack on Lens rail centre. Although cloud base was at 7,000ft the raid was well executed, and 135 tons out of the 417.6 tons of HE unloaded fell from the Stirlings. Luck was with them, whereas six Lancasters failed to return.

A night of mining followed, during which thirty-six mines were sown. Then on the **17/18th** a small force, including nineteen Stirling bombers, set forth to block a rail cutting south of Montdidier. On arrival they found the cloud base to be at 800ft. The Master Bomber flying at only 400ft ordered that no more bombs should be dropped after one Stirling crew had unloaded. For 90 Squadron this was its last operation using Stirlings. Since 10 June they had been operating Lancasters alongside the Stirlings.

On **24/25 June** the two remaining bomber squadrons, 149 and 218, each despatched fourteen aircraft to attack V-1 sites, the former to Rousseauville, the latter to Rimeux although mining remained the main occupation, with six aircraft sowing thirty-six mines on **30 June/1 July**.

On **23 July**, 218 Squadron ended their part in the Stirling mining campaign when LJ449-E and EF207-F sowed in Brest Roads. Supply dropping continued and during one of these operations Stirling EF431-B of 149 Squadron was challenged by a night fighter on the same night as LJ477-M was brought down. Such engagements were rare, for much of the German fighter force and radar warning system in France had been overwhelmed.

W7463 of 1657 Conversion Unit was written off after belly-landing at Woodbridge on 5 July 1944.

Stirlings had become involved in a new operational activity. To add more realism to training, crews at the Heavy Conversion Units of 3 and 5 Groups were now flying night diversion feints backing the *Mandrel* screen. On **15/16 July**, for instance, Command fielded 162 aircraft – including thirteen Stirlings – off the east coast. Still used for such activity were a few 91 Group OTU Whitleys, a type of aircraft the Stirling was planned to replace. These operations usually involved eight to ten 3 Group Stirlings, and Conversion Unit aircraft were also often found participating in *Bullseye* exercises which gave practice to night defences. These sometimes provided an operational spoofing.

Over Europe, German defensive power was so greatly stretched that Bomber Command at long last resumed fighter protected daylight raids. Destruction of V-1 sites and depots at night being very difficult escorted Stirlings, on **17 July,** began attacking them in daylight. As part of *Ramrod 1099*, the two remaining Stirling squadrons, at 1900 hrs, despatched between them twenty-eight bombers which joined twenty-two Halifaxes of 4 Group. Led by Lancasters and Mosquitoes of 8 Group, they attacked A213 Mont Candon V-site while other Halifaxes bombed the Bois de le Haye. Protecting them was a huge array of fighters. Detling, so heavily bombed in the Battle of Britain, provided twenty-four Spitfire IXs drawn from 118 and 504 Squadrons, and West Malling a further twenty-four in the hands of 80 and 274 Squadrons, and all providing close support.

Target support was provided by thirty-six Spitfire IXbs of 145, 329, 340 and 341 Squadrons. The Evreux area, from where opposition was forecast as possible, was swept by twenty-four Spitfire Vbs and a dozen Mk IXbs of Merston's 130, 303 and 402 Squadrons. Apart from the bombing of the target, and a Spitfire which crashed and was written off, *Ramrod 1099* proved straightforward.

On the evening of **27 July**, 19/24 Stirlings of the two squadrons flying in close formation, tackled *Noball* targets at Les Landes/Lanvielles-et-Neuss and on the **28th** two more, at Wimereux-Capelle and Fromental, each of which received about 45 tons of 500 pounders dropped in both cases by ten Stirlings during early evening and clear weather. This use of Stirlings or Lancasters was an option signalled to 3 Group by HQ Bomber Command for use against targets Z3318 and Z3319 in Bombing Area 1, over which three squadrons of Spitfires gave target support.

Fielding two dozen Stirlings called for considerable servicing effort from the remaining two squadrons. When next day the IE figure fell to twenty-four Stirlings they represented only 2.5 percent of Bomber Command's 1,256 nominal aircraft strength. Within 100 Group were another sixteen Stirlings.

Two more daylight raids against V-weapons targets were flown, the first taking place during the late evening of **29 July** when 15/16 had the Foret-de-Nieppes as their target. The second, a repeat raid by 20/20 Stirlings on Z3246 Mont Candon, was part of large-scale *Ramrod 1152*, carried out on **2 August**, during the course of which Halifaxes bombed Le Nieppe l'Hey and Foret-de-Nieppes, while 5 Group raided Troissy/St Maximim, and the Bois de Cassin. Bomber Command had asked 3 Group to attack five V-sites using twenty-five aircraft against each. There were, of course, insufficient Stirling bombers to attack in such strength for on 1 August only twenty-four remained in squadron service. To provide area cover for the 3 Group array the Merston Wing of 11 (Fighter) Group fielded twenty-four Spitfire IXs and a dozen Mk Vbs of 130, 302 and 402 Squadrons.

During the first week of August, 218 Squadron moved to Methwold to join 149 Squadron and ease servicing. By now the new navigation aid, *Gee-H (GH)*, had been installed in the Stirling designated to lead each vic. The other two crews depended upon its accuracy in target finding. *GH* equipment continued to be used by Bomber Command to the late 1950s and was employed during the 1956 Suez campaign. Its operational flirtation with the Stirling was brief, for during the Mont Candon raid 218 Squadron had operated its faithful 'aerial battleships' for the last time. In the following week the squadron was rearmed with Lancasters. No 149 Squadron, probably best remembered as star of the film *Target for Tonight*, was left to soldier on alone. Although mining was now finished, Bomber Command's Stirling bombers still had a few more rounds to fight.

On the night of **12/13 August**, while a large force of bombers penetrated to Brunswick and Russelheim, a dozen Stirlings joined Lancasters of 1, 5 and 6 Groups, thirty-six Halifaxes and the markers of 8 Group – a total force of 138/144 aircraft – to open the bombing of a major road junction at Falaise. Through thin cloud the well-placed TIs could be seen and although the force faced flak, all returned. A further fall, to 16 IE, had come on 9 August. That total was halved on the 27th, and the end of the Stirling's main force bombing days was nigh.

In September, Bomber Command made life unbearable for the Germans remaining in Le Havre by unloading huge tonnages of high explosive bombs upon the port during daylight raids. On **5 September**, 5/5 Stirlings joined 183 Lancasters, 130 Halifaxes and 30 Mosquitoes in their six-wave onslaught on troop concentrations and guns at the port. The weather was good like the marking, and opposition only minimal as the Stirlings hurled 136 x 1,000lb bombs, mainly of American origin, on to the target.

On **6 September 1944**, bombers – 344 of them – again headed for six A/Ps in Le Havre including gun positions and strong points. Five were identified from below cloud, but the sixth was not attacked because of the spread of low cloud and bad visibility. Only 2/3 Stirlings released their loads.

At 0505 hrs on the morning of **8 September 1944**, four Stirlings of 149 Squadron – LJ632-P, LJ481-U, LK401-G and LK396-M – took off from Methwold carrying between them 22 x 500lb bombs intended for Le Havre. They joined a stream of 260 Lancasters headed by twenty-eight Mosquitoes, and with a 5 Group Mosquito filming the proceedings. The weather was far worse than forecast, and only 109 aircraft attacked, including three Stirlings. Low cloud made it very difficult for initial markers to be backed up, so the Main Force was ordered to abandon its attack. Flak remained hazardous with low fliers being fired upon by German machine-gunners. Between them the gunners brought down two bombers.

By 0925 hrs the four Stirlings were circling Methwold preparatory for landing. Last in line was LK396 being flown by Fg Off J J McKee RAAF, who brought the Stirling bomber's operational squadron career to a close as he made the final safe home touch down at 0931 hrs.

The end of the Stirling bomber in the Command did not come until it was withdrawn from Heavy Conversion Units. Over its East Anglian homeland the Stirling remained an ever familiar sight well into 1946. But some of those were Stirlings being test flown from Sebro at Bourn, others were from 199 Squadron and the majority were Mk IV transports. The fight, for which the RAF's first wartime four-engined bomber had been designed, reached its victorious conclusion without one of its prime weapons.

Stirling Bombing Operations December 1943 - September 1944

Date	Target	Attacked/ despatched	1,000lb HE	500lb HE	FTR	Total force
December 1943						
16/17	Abbeville V-1 works	21/27	–	475	–	27
22/23	Pas de Calais V-1 works	24/29	–	551	–	29
January 1944						
4/5	V-1 sites a)	20/28	–	659	–	28
	b)	29/29	–	664	–	29
14/15	V-1 sites a)	30/30	–	678	–	30
	b)	28/29	–	668	–	29
21/22	V-1 sites a)	28/30	–	642	–	30
	b)	24/29	–	515	–	29
25/26	V-1 sites a)	16/20	–	410	–	20
	b)	12/19	–	264	–	19
	c)	17/17	–	375	–	17
March						
14/15	Amiens rail centre	33/38	–	735	EJ124	120/132
16/17	Amiens rail centre	36/41	–	798	–	106/128
23/24	Laon rail centre	24/48	–	441	–	66/131
25/26	Aulnoye rail centre	37/37	–	679	–	182/192
26/27	Courtrai rail centre	30/32	–	660	–	102/109
April						
9/10	Lille rail centre	21/22	–	426	–	226/239
20/21	Chambly rail centre	4/14	–	88	LJ448	14
22/23	Laon rail centre	42/48	–	777	EF159	
					EH942	
					EH943	160/181
23/24	Villeborde GAF signals depot	11/12	88	–	–	11/12
24/25	Chambly rail centre	3/4	231	–	–	4
26/27	Chambly rail centre	0/10	–	–	–	10
May						
1/2	Chambly rail centre	16/16	–	348	EF259	
					EF504	/132
June						
15/16	Lens rail centre	29/30	–	605	–	107/116
17/18	Montdidier	1/19	–	22	–	105/117
24/25	Ruisseauville	?/14	–	?	EF140	
					LK394	/14
	Rimeux	10/10	–	227	–	10
July						
17	Mont Candon	28/28	–	670	–	56/57
27	Les Landes	19/24	–	973	–	24
28	Wemers/Capell	10/10	–	204	–	10
	Fromental	10/10	–	207	–	10
29	Foret de Nieppes	15/16	–	?	–	16
August						
2	Mont Candon	20/20	–	414	–	20
12/13	Falaise roads	12/12	–	250	–	138/144
September						
5	Le Havre	5/5	136	–	–	335/348
6	Le Havre	2/3	–	44	–	271/344
8	Le Havre	3/4	–	70	–	109/333

Stirling IIIs on strength in bomber squadrons January - September 1944

January – April

Sqn	14 Jan	30 Jan	21 Feb	17 Mar	7 Apr	30 Apr
75	20 – 10	21 – 10	21 – 11	11 – 12	8 – 3	Nil
90	27 – 5	23 – 9	21 – 9	21 – 7	22 – 8	2 – 7
149	17 – 3	17 – 3	13 – 4	12 – 6	18 – 2	15 – 3
199	18 – 2	19 – 4	12 – 7	17 – 3	15 – 6	12 6 4
214	13 – 7	– – 1	Nil	Nil	Nil	Nil
218	13 4 8	15 5 3	8 8 6	14 – 3	16 – 4	16 – 4

Stirlings were withdrawn from 214 Squadron establishment on 2 Jan 44 and from 75 Squadron on 13 Apr 44

May – 15 September

Sqn	31 May	5 Jun	5 Sep	15 Sep
90	15 – 7	15 – 6		
149	15 – 7	16 – 4	7 – 3	– – 2*
199	17 – 3	19 – 1	19 – 10+	16 – 4
218	17 – 2	16 – 4		

6 June - September

Falling numbers of aircraft and crews were now very apparent. Cover for this period is better portrayed in different tabulation:

Date available	IE establishment	Aircraft in squadrons	Operationally fit	Crews
6 Jun	40	40	42	41
	100 Group 16	16	17	
21 Jun	32	32	36	34
	100 Group 16	16	18	
7 Jul	32	32	31	31
	100 Group 16	16	16	
28 Jul	24	24	20	20
	100 Group 16	16	15	
9 Aug	16	24	13	13
	100 Group 16	16	15	
28 Aug	8	8	8	8
	100 Group 16	16	15	
1 Sep	8	8	8	7
7 Sep	10	5	4	4
13 Sep	10	7	1	1
	100 Group 20	28	14	14

Bomber squadrons were established at 16 + 4. Establishment for bombing operations ended 14 Sep 44. On 16 Nov 44 No 199 Squadron holding was 14 – 5

+ established at 30 Stirlings. * none established.

Both 149 and 218 Squadrons established at 20 Lancasters on 5 Sep 44
Both 138 and 161 Special Duties Squadrons administered by 3 Group were established at 16 Stirling IVs. On 5 Sep 44 No 138 held 15 – Stirling IVs and on 15 Sep 44 No 138 had 11 – 4 and No 161 had 5 – 1

Comparative Bomber Production 1939 – 1945 (MAP figures)

	Stirling	Lancaster	Halifax	Wellington	Whitley
1939	–	–	–	269	157
1940	13	–	6	997	387
1941	153	18	162	1,816	504
1942	461	693	802	2,702	540
1943	881	1,848	1,824	2,536	95
1944	240	2,933	2,333	2,342	–
1945	–	1,447	527	753	–

Stirling Transport output: 1943 – 11, 1944 – 407, 1945 – 201

Stirling I, N3644 (the first with Hercules III engines), wears the initial style of paintwork, very matt Dark Earth–Dark Green upper surfaces with thick ultra matt (Night) under surfaces terminating at the base of the fuselage. Medium Sea Grey identity letters supplemented Dull Red serial numbers. Tall tail identity stripes applied in summer 1940 were removed before, in December 1940, MG-H reached Oakington. There, its under surfaces were soon mud splattered. Note the numerous rear fuselage windows, absence of central guns, mast head pitot tube and foot wells of the retracted ventral turret. Delivered to 10 MU Hullavington on 9 August 1940, N3644 joined 7 Squadron on 25 September for intensive flight trials. Flown by Sqn Ldr Lynch-Blosse it was one of the three Stirlings employed during the first Stirling raid in February 1941. That was its only operation. N3644 on 10 April 1941 became XV Squadron's first Stirling which, on 21 May 1941, suffered an undercarriage collapse when taxying. It was SOC on 17 June 1941.

N3653 (Hercules III), although allotted to 23 MU Aldergrove on 27 November 1940, was not collected from Gloucester/Hucclecote temporary works (where it was completed) until 23 February 1941. Note the irregular extension of ultra matt black (Night) under surfaces to the fuselage sides, soon mud coated. Dull Red serials and Medium Sea Grey identity letters were features, also fuselage windows aft without gun ports. N3653 briefly served with 7 Squadron as 'Q-Queenie' from 24 February. Flown by Sqn Ldr Griffith Jones, it failed to return from Brest on 3/4 March 1941.

N3671 (eighth in its batch to have Hercules XI) was delivered direct to XV Squadron on 25 September 1941 and became 'H-Harry.' Note twin under-nose pitot heads placed there on most Stirlings to reduce 'position error'. It is depicted in 1943's 'green-brown-smoother black' paint scheme with Dull Red codes and serial numbers, typically mid-war. XV squadron moved on 13 December 1941 from Warboys to their new upgraded satellite, Alconbury, to utilise its longer runways. N3671 arrived next day and, on landing, its undercarriage collapsed. Sebro assigned the aircraft on 31 December 1941, repaired it, despatching N3671 to 44 MU Edzell on 14 June 1941. On 18 May 1943, N3671 came on the strength at 1651 Heavy Conversion Unit Waterbeach, and was soon flying as 'BS-F' and thus recorded on 24 July 1943. Moved with the Unit to Wratting Common, it crash landed at Woodbridge one leg 'up' and was declared a write-off on 9 May 1944.

EH949, a standard Mk III, wore smooth mid-war finish, had Dull Red letters and the usual reduced number of fuselage windows aft. Assigned to 75 (NZ) Squadron, Mepal, on 18 July 1943, it was recorded on 20 August carrying the identity letters JN-P of 75 Squadron 'C' Flight. EH949 participated in some of the last Main Force raids, against Turin (16th) and subsequently Peenemunde (18th), Berlin (23rd and 31st), Mönchengladbach (30th), Mannheim (5 September), Montlucon (15th), Modane (16th) and Hannover (22nd). When low flying on 4 December a propeller blade clipped a tree top and the aircraft landed back on three engines. Soon repaired, EH949 laid mines in Biscay on 16 December 1943. After more such activity its final operation, against Aulnoye marshalling yards, was flown on 25 March 1944. EH949 was assigned to 1651 HCU on 29 April upon which day, when taking off from Witchford, its port undercarriage leg collapsed and the aircraft was categorised AC. It returned to training service and then on 6 November 1944 was transferred to 1660 HCU. This active Stirling was struck off charge on 24 April 1945.

EF441/G, a Mk III, flew with 90 Squadron from 23 June 1943 first as WP-G then WP-N.
Prematurely allocated to 1653 HCU on 13 July 1943 it was somewhere (possibly to the BDU) and
instead unusually fitted with an additional tall radio mast and an *H2S* radome (hence the /G 'guard'
identity change) for trials. In late October 1943 I noted it at Witchford marked 'CS-S' and possibly
carrying the markings of 513 Squadron formed there on 15 September 1943 and which began
receiving Stirlings on 21 October. On 30 November all personnel of '513' were posted to 1653
HCU, then forming, and 513 Squadron disbanded on 24 December 1943. EF441/G was officially
recorded as passing to 6 MU on 15 November 1943 where it was struck off charge on 24 April 1945.
Its unusual modifications, whereabouts and markings show that Form 78 aircraft histories, although
usually and basically correct, can reveal contradictions and anomalies.

EF305 completed on the line as a GT Mk IV was delivered to 23 MU Aldergrove on 30 November
1943. It joined 299 Squadron on 24 February 1944 and participated in D-Day operations, hence the
AEAF stripes. On 7 August 1944 it overshot Keevil then the undercarriage collapsed. It was
declared Cat E on 15 September and struck off charge on 21 September 1944.

PJ996, a C Mk V, wore a paint scheme of Dark Slate Grey and Extra Dark Sea Grey with Azure Blue under surfaces which suited it for overseas use. Under wing black serial numbers were later applied, black letters DK-H were worn and on the nose were white radio call sign letters O-H on a black rectangle. These applied to 196 Squadron Stirling Vs, yet the aircraft was flown from 21 June 1945 first by 242 Squadron before joining the newly formed 1588 Heavy Freight Flight, Transport Command, on 24 September 1945. PJ996 arrived at St Mawgan on 6 October 1945 and, after lengthy unserviceability, reached India in March 1946. No 1588, alias 'K' Heavy Freight Flight, operated two flights each of five aircraft. By 31 July 1946, PJ996 had flown 481.55 hours, the most by any Stirling of 1588 Flight. The Mk Vs' main task was to carry spares for aircraft disabled when flying on Far East trunk routes.

Chapter 16
Operational Miscellany

Special Duties Northern Europe

IT was 138 and 161 (Special Duty) Squadrons who were mainly responsible for SOE operations. Their Whitleys and Halifaxes ranged widely in supporting and supplying Resistance forces in occupied countries. By mid-1944 their trusty Merlin-engined Halifaxes were showing their age while all available Mk IIIs were required for bomber squadrons so the Stirling Mk IV was chosen as a replacement. No 138 Squadron received its first Stirling at Tempsford on 11 June 1944 and flew its first operation using the new type on 11 August. Supply drops to France, Belgium, Denmark and Norway followed. On 8 September re-equipment of 161 Squadron commenced, 'B' Flight receiving Stirlings while Hudsons remained in 'A' Flight for pick-up duties.

During October 161 Squadron operated over Denmark and Holland, flying eight sorties and losing Sqn Ldr Abecassis. No 138 Squadron operated over the same areas as required. Sortie rates were lower than for bomber squadrons, 138 successfully completing thirty-nine out of forty-four in November and 161 Squadron seventeen out of thirty-five. Weather conditions and the difficulty always of locating and definitely identifying friends on the ground made high success rates hard to achieve. In December, 161 Squadron flew twenty-two sorties, among them 'spoof drops' in the Ardennes. Stirlings used by the two squadrons were fitted with long-range tanks, and *Rebecca* radio responders to enable them to make contact with Resistance forces on the ground.

January 1945 was a bad weather month, 138 Squadron in consequence managing only eight sorties. With much of Europe in Allied hands, drops were now to forces in Denmark and Norway. February's better weather allowed 138 Squadron to fly eighty-three sorties during 700 hours' flying. Loads usually comprised at least sixteen containers and three packages.

There was a particularly distressing accident near Tempsford on 14 February. Fg Off Timperly was returning from an exercise in LK236 and on the outer circuit when a P-51 pilot of the USAAF's 363rd Squadron made an unauthorised pass during which he smashed into the tail of the Stirling causing the transport to crash near Potton. All involved were killed.

In March 1945 No 161 Squadron flew thirty-five successful sorties out of seventy-one, at a cost of three crews. In April they managed forty-seven successfully out of seventy-nine and flown mainly to Norway. Final sorties were despatched on 15 April.

The late Jim Breeze in the cockpit of 138 Squadron Stirling LK119.

Spy centre Tempsford was home of 138 Squadron's Stirlings. (J T Breeze)

During 307 Stirling sorties by 161 Squadron, 190 successful drops were made and six Stirlings lost. No 138 Squadron was withdrawn from SOE duty on 9 March 1945.

Four nights previously Flt Sgt J T Breeze had been flying with that squadron and it was a night to remember. He recalls:

> Our crew's last operation from Tempsford, on 4 March, was typical. Five days after full moon, we were looking forward to a good trip. We were briefed at 1030 hrs and from the fuel load I knew the DZ to be somewhere in Denmark taking twenty-four containers and seven packages. We would carry 1,946 gals of fuel and operate at 70,000lb.
>
> We were none too happy on two counts. We were detailed for 'Q-Queenie', not our beloved 'R-Roger', LK119. Our navigator reported sick and we were allotted one on his first operation.
>
> After my section briefing I went to do the usual checks on the aircraft's engine runs, etc, then returned to the crew room about lunchtime reporting all was well to the skipper. Our take-off time was 2350 hrs, so we had a long wait. Full briefing was in the late afternoon, our dropping zone about 15 miles south-west of Copenhagen. We assembled in the crew room about 2130 hrs, and were taken to the aircraft about 2300 hrs.
>
> We took off at 2350 hrs and climbed to 2,000ft, the normal height for the crossing to Denmark, and left the English coast at Cromer for an uneventful sea crossing. About 20 miles off the Danish coast our bomb aimer, 'Jock' Kyle, went forward into the nose to prepare for map reading to the DZ. I moved into the second pilot's seat, which I usually occupied until we crossed the coast on our return. We crossed the enemy coast, on track by now, at about 50ft. No problems, apart from a little light flak which curled lazily and fell short of the aircraft. It was a beautiful night as we crossed Jutland to the waiting reception. In such

Stirling IV NF-R of 138 Squadron. (J T Breeze)

> bright moonlight one could see the silhouette of the aircraft scudding across the ground. We climbed to 500ft, the usual height for drops, static lines being used.
>
> The bomb aimer had done an excellent job in guiding us to the DZ. We circled the field until we were satisfied that the reception committee was flashing the correct letter, then dropped our load. A final circle of the field, then down to 50ft and home to eggs and bacon – or so we thought. We had a good flight back across Zealand and Jutland, and were dead on track when the bomb aimer called, 'Coast coming up'. The skipper asked for 2,400 revs which I gave him, and with the speed around 240-knots we crossed the coast at Ringkobing Fiord and, without warning, we suddenly crashed. Mystery still surrounds the crash, but two of the crew said they heard an explosion just before we went in. It was all rather weird: one minute we were flying, the next brought the sensation of diving. I remember pulling back on the second pilot's control column shouting, 'Pull her up, skipper', realising where we were. The skipper replied, 'What a silly place to land.' I replied that we'd better get out. I pushed open the escape hatch in the cockpit, then we climbed out, took our helmets off, inflated our Mae Wests and dropped to the water. It was only about 3ft deep! The rest of the crew evacuated, the rear gunner by revolving his turret. He climbed on to the tail, and then fell into the sea. Then he realised its depth. It was all quite funny. Good job it was shallow, for nobody had given a thought to the dinghy. We were close to an island, and left 'NF-Q' with two of its engines on fire as we walked away to captivity with only a few bruises. Remarkable aeroplane, the Stirling; a 240mph crash and it was still intact! Fortunately for us the war was nearly at its end.

Special duty operations were also and frequently carried out by the Stirling bomber squadrons of 3 Group and Mk IVs of 38 Group.

Special Duties Overseas

Complex maintenance and the need for plentiful logistic support worked against using Stirlings overseas. But when Merlin-engined Halifaxes dwindled in number, Special Duty squadrons overseas had to re-equip. No 148 Squadron was to receive Stirling Mk IVs in August 1944, but shortages and delivery complications delayed conversion until November. From Brindisi, Italy, only one operation was flown by LJ181-F on 5 November before the Stirlings were withdrawn.

No 624, the other Middle East special duties Squadron, was born as 1575 Flight at Tempsford on 28 May 1943 and equipped with four Halifaxes and two Venturas. Within days they moved to Maison Blanche in North Africa and started flying special supply drops to Resistance fighters in Corsica and Sardinia on 13 June. On 22 September 1943 the Flight, now based at Blida, became 624 Squadron.

In June 1944 the squadron were informed they would be converting to Stirlings, and on 28 June Wg Cdr C S G Standbury flew to 144 MU with Flt Lt Fairey to collect the first Stirling. The new aircraft arrived in small numbers during the month, conversion not being completed until the end of July. Wg Cdr Standbury, in LJ938, flew the first operational sortie on 29 July.

During re-arming the squadron had seven accidents. First, an undercarriage unit jammed in the 'up' position. Next came take-off swings, with pilots failing to close throttles to counteract side forces and which resulted in sheared undercarriages. One pilot held his Stirling down on take-off, even though he had reached 105mph, whereas the Stirling would unstick at 95mph even at 70,000lb. The third trouble, which resulted in two fatalities, came about when pilots returned short of fuel. Tanks were filled for nine hours' flying, when operations normally took about seven hours giving a fair safety margin. One eight hour operation by the CO revealed sufficient fuel left for two hours' flying. Most troubles seemed attributable to pilot error but, to be fair, they had not been through conversion units in Britain.

By the end of August, 624 Squadron's Stirlings had flown seventy-two supply-dropping sorties, but with the spate of accidents it seemed unwise to prolong the use of Stirlings. In any case Vichy France, the main dropping area, was being overrun. The last operation was the most impressive for the Stirlings set off in formation in two flights to drop supplies in daylight in the Alpes de Haute, Provence, where 235 containers fell. On 24 September the squadron disbanded.

Screening Bomber Command – the Stirlings of 100 Group

Stirlings of 199 Squadron operating under 100 Group flew what would now be classed as electronic warfare or radio countermeasure sorties. A late recruit to Bomber Command, 100 Group formed at Radlett on 23 November 1943, moved its headquarters from Radlett to West Raynham on 3 December 1943 and to Byleagh Hall near Aylsham on 18 January 1944. No 100 Group comprised special-duty squadrons seconded from 3 Group until Fighter Command night fighter squadrons flying Mosquito II fighters and a few even more weary Beaufighter IIs were transferred to the new Group. Mosquito VI fighter-bombers were later introduced, also a handful of Boeing B-17F/G Fortresses and a few Liberator VIs. Although the B-17 carried a far smaller bomb load than British bombers, and in some respects was outclassed by the Stirling, it could be rapidly built and had a far superior altitude performance, the latter making it useful for ECM/RCM operations.

No 199 Squadron joined 100 Group at North Creake on 1 May 1944 to operate Stirling IIIs fitted with a selection of 'Mandrel' jammers. These produced an electronic barrier preventing enemy early warning radar from detecting an approaching bomber force. Such activity had hitherto been carried out on a small scale using Moonshine equipment carried in Boulton Paul Defiant fighters. Beaufighter IIs had also been used, but both types had insufficient space for enough equipment to make their activity really worthwhile. The new squadron was also required to fly 'spoofs' using a new type of *Window*.

By mid-April 1944 four Stirlings were being fitted with *Mandrel* equipment at the Telecommunications Flying Unit, Defford, where the prototype was complete by the end of the month. Five B-17s flown by 803rd Squadron, USAAF and Sculthorpe based, already had the equipment.

By the time 199 Squadron was transferred to 100 Group a dozen Stirling IIIs were being modified, and to support establishment of 16 + 4 a further eight were modified by 100 Group at Foulsham. Hope was that operational flying would start on 20 May 1944 to acquire experience to apply on the eve of D-Day. Despite a rapid modification programme, only thirteen *Mandrel* Stirlings fitted with the latest IFF equipment had joined 199 Squadron by 25 May 1944. Three were still being modified at Defford and four at Foulsham, while at BDU Newmarket a special chute linked with an American automatic *Window* dispenser had been tested. Stirlings of 199 Squadron were to have this fitted once it had been cleared for use.

It was on **5/6 June 1944** that 199 Squadron with all twenty Stirlings in hand commenced *Mandrel* operations by jamming German early-warning radar stations around the invasion zone. Eight pairs of aircraft orbited carefully chosen positions over the Channel and succeeded in jamming seven of the most important radar stations. Four USAAF B-17s gave similar successful cover for American forces landing in Normandy.

Effectiveness of the screen being beyond doubt, it was to be frequently employed with ever greater sophistication with cunning adjustments ensuring continuing success. On **16/17 June** and **17/18 June 1944,** pairs of Stirlings carrying jammers to cope with the band 7-200MHz, and working with a lone B-17 whose equipment was designed to handle the 120-140MHz range operated paired jamming centres spaced in an arc set 80 miles from the enemy coast. Stirlings were placed, usually in pairs, 28 miles apart to produce a wide screen to nullify German *Freya* radar stations, with single B-17s of 803 Squadron operating between the pairs and against narrow-beam radar looking between the jamming centres. Beginning over Coltishall, the Stirling cover extended in an arc north-eastwards and reaching 80 miles off the enemy coast. Estimates suggesting that the screen would conceal the bomber force until it had passed beyond the jamming centres were proven correct when German night-fighter crews were heard reporting their confusion. In both the operations referred to 199 Squadron fielded a dozen Stirlings and with few problems apart from the loss of LJ531-N on the night of 17/18 June and

Briefing crews of 199 Squadron.

Stirling III EX-B at North Creake features Mandrel *aerials below its fuselage.* (F Smith)

in apparently somewhat unusual circumstances. By 21 June Stirlings had flown thirty sorties and 199 Squadron had received supplies of special *Window* for use against *Freya* stations during special 'spoof' flights. Over 100 *Mandrel* sorties had been flown by the end of June, its success certain. With so few *Mandrel* Stirlings and likely unserviceability, the screen could be sustained only for two nights out of three.

In July *Mandrel* protection was in position on seventeen nights, twelve for major operations and five for minor raids, with the attackers passing through a screen combined with a diversionary 'screen' presented by operational bomber training organisations and using *Window* to mislead the foe. Such was the confusion caused that on 17/18 July *Mandrel* was used in conjunction with a *Bullseye* exercise during which a *Window* force created a spoof attack to force the enemy to fly his night fighters without good cause. While still jamming the radar, the screen slowly advanced from its usual East Coast position to within 15 miles of the enemy coast before slowly moving back to England. *Serrate*-equipped Mosquito night fighters nosing ahead of the Stirlings reported that German fighters were active, but completely confused by the 'strange' activity. Its only limitation applied to its use over the English Channel where it could not be used without upsetting Allied communications in France. Not until 7/8 August was it again used for a short time in that area.

By early August 199 Squadron was producing an incredibly effective activity, reducing the effectiveness of *Freya* stations from 180 miles to about 40 miles, and with low loss rates during attacks on the Ruhr and Kiel being attributed to the squadron's success. To be really effective the jammers needed to directly face the radar beam and clearly there was a need for more *Mandrel* Stirlings particularly in view of the wide frequency range employed by the *Freya* chain. Therefore, late in August, a third Flight was added to 199 Squadron, but its existence was short-lived for it was hived off to form the basis of a second *Mandrel* squadron, 171. They used Stirlings to fly '*Window* spoofs,' but their Stirling days were brief, for on 21 October 1944, they were promulgated as now rearmed with Halifax IIIs. By that time the *Mandrel* screen was often positioned far forward, and frequently over liberated territory.

On nine nights in October 199 Squadron set up the screen for large-scale operations, its positioning protecting minelayers as well as small scale 'spoofs'. There were fifty-seven sorties by 199 Squadron, which also undertook *Window* drops.

In January 1945, No 199 Squadron operated on twelve nights and flew eighty-nine sorties. On the 18th the screen was placed near the southern battlefronts before they formed into a stream for *Window* dropping and proceeded to Stuttgart with a second wave of attackers. The last *Mandrel* Stirling sortie was flown during the evening of **14 March** when, in co-operation with five Halifax IIIs, it fell to Sqn Ldr J J M Button to make this final sortie. Using LJ516-H he touched down at 2350 hrs to bring the end of the Stirling's operational front line career in Bomber Command.

EE948 EX-T after tipping on its nose at Nutt's Corner on 12 April 1945. (F Smith)

After 'Henrietta' had landed, 199 Squadron – one of the most spirited of Stirling squadrons – recorded their sorrow at the passing of a revered friend in these words:

Goodbye, old Stirling, goodbye old friend,
You've never let us down from beginning to end,
Whate'er it was, where'er you went,
On bombing, mining, supporting bent,
You did a grand job, the best on Earth,
You're Stirling by name – you were sterling in worth.

'Jane' painted on the nose of LJ543.

199 Squadron's 'B-Beer' had operations recorded on the nose in beer mugs.

LJ542 EX-G, veteran of over sixty sorties, carried artwork and the name 'The Gremlin Teaser'.

Mandrel Screen Sorties Flown by Stirlings of 199 Squadron

Date	Sorties	Date	Sorties	Date	Sorties
June 1944		**September**		**December**	
5/6	16	1/2	6	1/2	8
14/15	2	5/6	5	2/3	13
16/17	16 (LJ531 FTR)	6/7	11	4/5	11 (LJ567 FTR)
17/18	14	8/9	8	5/6	10
22/23	11	9/10	10	6/7	9
27/28	14	10/11	6 (LJ578 FTR)	9/10	10 (LJ559 FTR)
28/29	14	11/12	7	12/13	10
		12/13	15	15/16	8
		13/14	14	17/18	8
July		15/16	14 (LJ536 FTR)	18/19	12
4/5	14	16/17	5	22/23	13
7/8	16	17/18	16	23/24	13
9/10	14	18/19	17	24/25	7
12/13	20	19/20	9	27/28	7
14/15	19	22/23	6	28	8
15/16	6	23/24	16	29/30	8
17/18	17	25/26	12 (LJ518 FTR)	30/31	10
18/19	15	26/27	12	31/12-1/1	10
20/21	17	28/29	13	**January 1945**	
21/22	14	29/30	10	1/2	11
23/24	15			2/3	9
24/25	14	**October**		5/6	11
25/26	16	5/6	17	6/7	11
28/29	18	6/7	14	7/8	16
29/30	8	7/8	14	8/9	2
		9/10	16	9/10	2
August		12/13	4	14/15	14
6/7	8	14/15	21	16/17	12
7/8	20	15/16	16	17/18	9
8/9	4	19/20	20	22/23	8
9/10	15	23/24	14		
10/11	7	24/25	3	**February**	
11/12	8	25/26	3	1/2	8
12/13	13	26/27	14	2/3	5
16/17	13	28/29	3	3/4	7
17/18	8	30/31	15	4/5	7
18/19	15	31-1/11	14	7/8	8
25/26	14			8/9	6
26/27	13	**November**		13/14	8
27/28	10	1/2	10	14/15	6
29/30	14 (LJ560 FTR)	2/3	12	18/19	5
30/31	4	4/5	14	20/21	6
		6/7	14	21/22	7
		10/11	14	22/23	4
		11/12	10	23/24	7
		15/16	10	24/25	2
		18/19	12	25/26	4
		21/22	11	27/28	4
		25/26	12	28-1/3	3
		26/27	4		
		27/28	12	**March**	
		28/29	12	1/2	3
		29/30	11	2/3	3
		30-1/12	10	3/4	3
				5/6	4 (LJ617 FTR)
				7/8	3

Chapter 17
To Lift and Deliver

THE British Empire went to war in 1939 with hardly any military transport aircraft able to link overseas possessions with the home base. There, the transport force of light transports, including DH89s, Miles Mentors and Vega Gulls, was almost entirely concentrated within 24 Squadron and under the control of HQ Fighter Command. It was intended for the use of senior officers and government officials within Britain's shores – except when they needed to venture to France.

True, the RAF was acquiring Bristol Bombay 'bomber transports' while in Egypt, the Middle East and India, trusty stately Vickers Valentias, which ambled along at a leisurely 100mph, were on hand to transport troops to native trouble spots. For slightly faster movement of persons and materials the British Government relied upon Imperial Airways whose Ensigns, HP 42s and C-Boats conveyed personnel not only to France but also to the outposts of Empire. Employing aircraft in civilian markings for warlike purposes – which allowed them ready passage through neutral territory – can not but be viewed as cynical. The so often sad saga of British commercial aircraft development meant that there was, in 1939, little alternative to using outdated machines.

German airborne forces deployed during the invasion of Norway, then the delivery of troops by glider to capture Belgium's Eben Emael fortress in May 1940 fast propelled many British minds into the realisation that similar tactics would probably be used during any invasion of Britain. Dropping paratroops on to the Netherlands, and landings by Ju 52s on Dutch beaches added a further dimension to the value of airborne forces.

Rapidly responding in July 1940 to such activities, the British Government ordered the formation of a parachute regiment, and was soon discussing the production of gliders to carry paratroops. There was no alternative, for suitable British transport aircraft to airlift them were non-existent. That raised another problem: finding tugs to tow the gliders. An answer for the training phase was to employ ex-army co-operation Hawker Audax and Hector biplanes to tow the eight-man gliders. Antique Avro 504s of First World War parentage would drag sailplanes around as pilots took their first tentative steps towards glider flying.

Paratroop training commenced at Ringway, and soon the volunteers were jumping from aged Whitleys. Tightly packed in the square-sectioned fuselage they made their exit – aided by a static line – through a hole in the floor.

After much argument, plans for paratroops to jump from the small Hotspur or the proposed 40-seater Horsa glider were abandoned. Carrying sufficient airborne troops into battle would have required gliders towed in a stream one behind another, operationally very hazardous and dangerous at any time. Instead, paratroops would jump conventionally from aircraft of which, apart from Whitleys, Britain had none suitable. As for the gliders chosen to carry heavy stores and equipment as well as men, they now would be towed singly to the prescribed landing zone by suitable aircraft which again meant the Whitley. Britain had no other type – unless some four-engined bombers yet to enter service could be snatched from the strong grip of Bomber Command whose leaders fiercely resisted any such notion.

Winston Churchill, the Prime Minister, who from the start had vigorously backed the idea of developing airborne forces, demanded a solution be found to the shortage of aircraft. Accordingly, on 15 April 1941 Air Vice-Marshal Linnell, the Vice-Chief of the Air Staff, enquired about the feasibility of converting scarce Wellingtons into troop transports. Vickers told him that eighteen men and 3,000lb of freight could be airlifted

1,900 miles in a much-stripped Wellington produced one-for-one alongside the bomber version, with the first example becoming available a mere six weeks from the date of any order. In reality it was not that simple because of complex production plans covering the output of various versions of the Wellington for Coastal Command, bombers urgently needed to carry a 4,000lb bomb, examples with tropical gear, etc. Rapid discussion followed before it was decided not to go ahead with production of Wellington transports whose geodetic construction seemed likely to become distorted by aerodynamic loads. A number of Wellingtons were later modified into interim transports.

By mid-1941 there was a desperate need for transport aircraft, particularly in the Middle East and, soon after, in India. As yet there was less need for them in north-west Europe, and such transports would still be mainly based overseas.

Paratroopers prepare for a drop from 299 Squadron Stirling 5G-N. (Imperial War Museum)

On 31 July 1941, the Prime Minister asked the Secretary of State for Air to produce a consultation paper outlining the RAF's likely transport strength over the next two to three months to allow the War Cabinet to discuss what was an increasingly serious situation. The resultant document presented a gloomy picture:

Home based

24 Squadron, Hendon: one DH 84, one DH 86B, nine DH 89As, five Flamingos and two Lockheed Electras
271 Squadron, Doncaster: fifteen Harrows and two DH 91 Albatrosses
Total: thirty-five aircraft, in addition to Whitley paratroop trainers and such impressed ex-civilian aircraft as were from time to time suitable for employment. Those included DH 86s, DH 89s and lumbering HP 42s

North Africa and the Middle East

117 Squadron: four ex-Italian Savoia Marchetti SM 79s, three DC-2s and seven Bombays
216 Squadron: fourteen Bombays
267 Squadron: one Anson, one Caudron Simoun, two Hudsons, one Lockheed 14, two Electras and seventeen Lodestars, two of the latter soon to be passed to the Free French
Total: fifty-two plus sundry light transports

India

31 Squadron: twelve DC-2s, twelve Valentias, six of each type being temporarily based in Iraq
Total:24

Far East

Nil.

On the vital Takoradi–Egypt supply line a motley collection of four Lockheed 14s, two Lockheed 10as, six Lodestars, a South African Ju 52 and nine DH 86s carried ferry crews, and ex-SABENA (Belgian Air Lines) with six Ju 52s, an Italian-built SM 83 and two more Lockheed 14s helped.

The current USA supply programme offered little hope, deliveries for all theatres likely to be:

Type	1941	1942
Lockheed 14	8	–
Lodestar	12	13
Electra	8	–
Hudson	30	170
DC-2	6	–
DC-3	12	38

Total numbers of those listed as IE in all theatres for each month of 1941–42, calculated on a wastage rate of two aircraft per month for each sixty on IE was reckoned as:

1941		1942		1942	
August	101	January	122	July	311
September	112	February	169	August	317
October	110	March	198	September	322
November	115	April	222	October	327
December	119	May	281	November	331
		June	304	December	312

The dramatic change in the 1942 strength was based upon expected delivery that year of 347 Douglas C-47 Dakotas for RAF use.

On 26 August 1941, the decision was taken to form ten heavy or medium transport squadrons to carry 5,000 fighting men and their basic equipment. Finding enough aircraft for such activity remained a major problem, with the obvious solution being conversion of existing heavy bombers, but Bomber Command complained bitterly whenever that was suggested. Nevertheless, during September 1941 the use of the Stirling as a paratroop transport was considered and quickly rejected because of paratroop exit problems.

The need had not been solved when the Japanese attacked Pearl Harbor forcing the USA into the war. The Americans now needed all the transports they could get and notions of Douglas C-47 Dakotas joining RAF squadrons in 1942 vanished.

Then came a flash of inspiration. On 9 January 1942, A V Roe presented to the Air Staff ideas for an Avro Air Express based upon the Lancaster. The company had designed a curvaceous fuselage able to carry passengers or freight and which could be slung below a normal Lancaster wing to produce a very effective medium or long- range troop, passenger, freight transport. The Air Staff at once accepted this sensible idea and ordered a prototype almost immediately. Forecast as able to carry twenty passengers each with 50lb baggage for 2,500 miles at 270mph at 20,000ft, or 10,000lb freight for similar distances, the aircraft which became the Avro York could also operate as a paradropper, conveying thirty troops and gear for 3,000 miles at 200mph. It seemed also likely to make a suitable glider tug, always assuming that there was sufficient productive capacity without cutting back Lancaster output.

Emphasis remained concentrated upon finding a suitable operational paratroop-dropping aircraft because it was easier to train paratroopers than to generate a glider-borne one, although gliders delivering heavy equipment were increasingly favoured for airborne operations.

Neither the Lockheed Lodestar nor Dakota, nor any British type, could satisfactorily tow a loaded Horsa until on 29 January 1942 the Stirling was cleared – on paper – to

Stirling Mk V PJ943 wears two tone 'grey' and Azure Blue paintwork making it suitable for tropical service. Its serial number is in Dull Red.

tow a train of up to three Hotspur training gliders or one Horsa. Hope was that it would also be able to operationally tow a Hamilcar tank-carrying glider. Certain of the Stirling's tug capabilities, orders were given even before much testing for glider-towing equipment to be introduced on production Stirlings from 31 March 1942.

On 19 April 1942, assessing the overall situation as very serious, the Air Staff told the Air Ministry that the only remaining source for possible 'Douglas C-47/C-53' supply was within America's airlines. Too late the British enquired about those; some 300 had already been requisitioned for the US forces, and only small Lockheed types could now be supplied. They were useless, even for paratroop purposes. The Americans had decided to form three Ferry Groups each equipped with seventy-five C-47s, the first to form in India with twenty-five examples. The RAF could only look enviously at twenty-five C-47s in US hands flying in Britain by mid-July 1942.

August 1942 saw an interim choice for the RAF's glider tug fall with unease upon the Armstrong-Whitworth Albemarle, a bomber made from wood and steel but whose performance was not good enough for front-line bomber service. From the 100th example, glider tug equipment would be featured. Far from satisfactory in a towing role, the Albemarle's twin-engines readily overheated when a loaded Horsa was towed. In the Mediterranean theatre that problem would be serious.

Recent proposals were for equipping 38 Wing, the new RAF airborne force, with ninety aircraft: forty Albemarles, forty Whitleys and ten Halifaxes. Such a force was half the size of that recommended by the Directorate of Tactical Operations which meant adding 130 Whitleys. Alternatively, more Albemarles could become available by reducing the proposed allotment of eighty to the USSR and upon which work was proceeding. Another possibility reviewed on 17 September 1942 was linked with the entire future of the Stirling.

From conception its fuselage was planned to carry up to twenty-six troops. N3702 had towed three Hotspurs at AFEE at a time when the importance of finding a suitable tug loomed very large, for on 12 May 1942 orders for 2,345 Horsas and 140 Hamilcars were confirmed. Even more alarming, the Army soon called for 3,500 Horsas and 360 Hamilcars for two airborne operations against the Continent. That meant establishing a pool of about 500 tugs and a similar force of paratroop aircraft even if paratroops descended from Horsa gliders. Further consideration of the Stirling's potential as a tug and paratroop aircraft led to the conclusion that it would be at least five months before a transport version could materialise. Bomber Command did not, however, want to form any more Stirling squadrons, so if the aircraft was satisfactory for transport and glider towing, then it looked a likely candidate for 38 Wing, and was judged a better tug than the C-47 would ever become.

A year after that first major survey of British transport aircraft, the situation was again reviewed. There had been little improvement. On 31 August 1942 a summary listed aircraft needed in place by December 1943 to support Allied plans. Needed were:

In the UK

Thirty long-range transports serving North Africa and the USSR
Thirty long-range transports to carry urgent stores/personnel to Malta and the Middle East
Fifty medium-range transports on ferry routes to West Africa via Gibraltar, for Northern Ireland, Iceland and internally
270 medium-range transports for Army and RAF use during operations against the Continent, and to supply part of an 830-aircraft force needed to lift the Army into operations, some aircraft being released from bomber operations against Germany

In the Middle East

Forty-eight long-range transports to carry stores between Australia, India, North Africa, the Middle East and the UK

In India

Fifty medium-range transports for strategic mobility of fighter and torpedo bomber squadrons in the area West Africa to the Persian Gulf
Twenty-five ambulances, 245 internal ferry aircraft and, for the ferry run Gibraltar–India and for airborne forces, to minimise any requirement from the main bomber force that a large-scale operation would entail
144 for strategic mobility for fighter and torpedo bomber squadrons, and to augment US forces between India and China, and for ambulance work

In South Africa

Thirty for ferry work between Africa and Madagascar and Mauritius, and another thirty for ferry work between South Africa and the Middle East

Total: 144 long-range and 844 short-range transports.

Additional plans for the British Overseas Airways Corporation (BOAC) called for 50 long-range and 100 short-range aircraft.

An updated listing of the transport aircraft situation in India showed one squadron comprising thirteen DC-2s, eight DC-3s, a Lodestar and five Valentias. Civilian aircraft directly backing them were four Stinson Trimotors, nine single-engined Wacos, two single-engined Beech D-17s, a Beech 18 twin and a Percival Gull Six. Hardly an impressive force.

A Stirling with a bifurcated tow rope waits to tow Horsas.

Another conference to consider transport aircraft needs held on 29 December 1942 heard that BOAC was to have forty-five Yorks, ten long-range landplanes and ten long-range seaplanes along with sixty-one medium-range landplanes of which twenty-three might also be Yorks. Consideration had been given to BOAC operating Albemarle freighters on the Sweden–UK run, but five C-47s were allocated instead. A dozen Liberators were used on the transatlantic service, two of which were currently operating the UK–USSR run. Around Australia it was proposed to use Coronado flying-boats and Sunderlands.

For the RAF, the suggestion was that six squadrons should use Yorks and twenty-four squadrons should fly C-47s, each squadron being established at 16 + 4 aircraft. That assumed that the planned delivery of eighty C-47s monthly by 1944 would come about. The airborne forces would have another eight squadrons, a total 240 aircraft. At least three of the airborne squadrons would operate Albemarles. In India there would be eight transport squadrons and another in South Africa. Each airborne and transport squadron would hold 20 + 5 aircraft apart from Albemarle squadrons each of which would have thirty UE. In Britain there would be one squadron of twenty-five Yorks. In the Middle East there would be two of Yorks and five of Dakotas, two of Yorks in India and eight of C-47s. As a make weight, in case Dakota supply failed, a modified transport version of the Vickers-Armstrong Warwick Freighter would be produced after 150 earmarked for ASR squadrons were delivered.

January 1943 saw paratroop dropping trials from a Lancaster, but Bomber Command demanded every Lancaster and indeed every Halifax built. Both types had development potential, whereas the Stirling bomber could not be much improved.

Between February and May 1943 AFEE looked further at N3702. Its bomb bay readily accommodated panniers, twenty-four Mk III or twenty-one Mk I and three Mk IIIs, and no problems arose. Indeed, it seemed ideally suited.

More important were trials assessing the ability of Stirling BK645 to tow a loaded Horsa, in particular its climb and level performance. Conducted in April 1943, they showed no snags with the tug at 54,300lb and the Horsa at 15,250lb, its normal loaded weight. This permitted the tug 1,160gal of fuel and 70gal of oil and a crew of five. During the trial all turrets were left in place making signs good for an unarmed Stirling tug. Unstick was achieved at 950 yards at 90mph IAS and climb-away at 110mph IAS after a run of 2,040 yards to clear 50ft. The combination took 16.32 minutes to reach 6,000ft, 26.2 minutes to reach 8,000ft, after which it fast reduced to 150fpm. The Stirling, with no yet evident overheating problems, was a fair answer to the glider tug need.

A 196 Squadron aircraft tows a Horsa from Harwell. (Imperial War Museum)

Prototype Mk IV LJ512 with a fairing replacing its rear turret. (Shorts)

The results were to hand when a committee examining its future role met on 30 July 1943 during the period of the Stirling's most productive service with Bomber Command. Shorts, who had been asked to prepare schemes for Stirling transports, outlined plans for the Stirling 'A', a conversion of existing Mk IIIs into transports, the Stirling 'B', or Mk IV, which was a fully redesigned Mk III with some or all turrets deleted and intended as a glider tug or paratroop carrier, and the Stirling 'C', or Mk V, whose fully redesigned fuselage for passenger and freight work included a large freight door aft. Some soundproofing would be fitted in the fuselage and an up-swinging nose installed to permit freight loading. The Stirling 'C' could become Shorts post-war civil aircraft.

They were asked how long it would take to get the first two schemes into operation at Rochester and Belfast. Conversion at RAF maintenance units would also take place with unnecessary equipment, including nose and dorsal turrets, being removed. Provision

Stirling IVs of 196 Squadron await embarkation by paratroops.

would be made for external carriage of bulky equipment, for troops, and for paratroops who would clear via a door in the rear floor. Aero engines and perhaps jeeps could be lashed to the belly since there was such good ground clearance. The future for the Mk IV looked bright, and events proved it to be a very useful machine.

Other proposed modifications to Stirling bombers were cancelled, including adding *H2S* radomes, allowing Shorts to proceed with all speed on the stripped transport, the Mk IV, and work upon the Mk V. Then came misgivings. The Air Ministry were uncertain about going ahead with the Mk V, but the Mk IV prototype, first flown in August 1943, strengthened its case. A month later they wondered whether Short & Harland should build the Avro York rather than the Mk V. In October 1943's reckoning there would be ample Stirling Mk IVs for the foreseeable future and, in any case, stripped Lancasters and Halifaxes from Bomber Command could surely be made into troop transports.

A further decision came on 14 October when it was proposed to produce fifteen 'A' transports a month beginning in January 1944. Short & Harland would switch entirely to producing Type 'B' as soon as practicable and Stirling glider-tug squadrons could commence build-up in April 1944.

Such an alteration would allow Stirling squadrons to remain in Bomber Command until December 1944, their numbers steadily declining from thirteen in October 1943 to ten in June 1944, eight in August and six in December 1944. Sufficient Stirlings would be available to allow them to replace Halifaxes in an SOE role from January 1944, while Stirling 'B' production was thought likely to reach 200 by the end of 1944 and 375 by June 1945. In the event Stirling bombers left the squadrons sooner than planned because Lancaster production increased faster than expected.

On 20 October 1943, the decision to drop the Stirling Mk V seemed final in view of Short's incapacity to cope with the design work on this variant as well as the much wanted Lancaster Mk IV (later named Lincoln) which it was intended that Shorts should build.

Yet, to have perhaps 575 Stirling Mk IVs by June 1945 instead of some of the much superior Mk Vs seemed a pity. Shorts were pinning hopes on a civil version of the Mk V so it was reprieved and orders were placed for production at Belfast.

Late 1943 brought the plan for re-equipment with Lancasters of three of the last six Stirling bomber squadrons. Three would receive them in February, the remainder in March 1944. An alternative was to disband all six then reform them using existing crews and within 38 Group but it was abandoned as being too bad for morale. On 23 December 1943, HQ Bomber Command raised the idea of retaining Stirlings for mine laying until June 1944, by which time the intensity of that task was expected to have fallen considerably.

In the Stirling 'A' and 'B' the War Office recognised the only aircraft likely to be available for dropping quite heavy equipment – maybe a jeep, 6-pounder guns and tactical loads. Trials were requested to see if heavy drop loads might be carried externally, but nothing came of that idea.

Before the end of 1943, the recommendation to remove the Stirling from Bomber Command was confirmed, mainly on the grounds that it was difficult and costly to maintain and not simply because of its general performance. In the plan of 31 December 1943 two Stirling squadrons were to re-arm with Lancasters, two would release their crews for No 3 Lancaster Finishing School and two would transfer to 38 Group. That would leave seven operational Stirling squadrons in Bomber Command, one of which would receive Fortress IIIs upon transfer to 100 Group. At the same time high hopes for the Stirling 'C', alias Mk V, were being expressed, although spares and maintenance aspects would remain. The question now was: would Transport Command want further orders placed for what was officially considered to be 'the best transport conversion' of any British bomber?

Chapter 18
Enter the Stirling Transport

THE first two Stirlings converted from Mk III bombers to Mk IV transports emerged, rapidly, in August 1943. EF506 came on charge 26 August, and EF503 on the 28th. The former, after tests at Rochester, was sent to A&AEE on 18 October for four months acceptance trials and operational clearance. EF503 proceeded to A&AEE for handling trials before returning to Rochester in late February 1944.

EF503's nose fairing replacing its turret.

The latter was devoid of all turrets, those in the nose and tail being replaced by Perspex fairings. Lower all-up weight and crew reduction to five conferred an increase of 1,100ft in service ceiling and 3,000ft in cruise ceiling. At weak mixture power an extra 12mph to 15mph was achieved. A take-off weight of 70,000lb was still possible allowing a sizeable load. At that weight, service ceiling was 19,100ft, and with cooling gills closed and the engines running at 2,400 revs, maximum weak mix cruise speed was 235mph TAS, in MS gear at 11,800ft.

Range trials using EF503 were conducted early in 1944 at a take-off weight of 66,000lb in paratrooping mode although take-off weight was usually 58,000lb. Maximum still air range was as follows:

Weight (lb)	Fuel (gal)	Range (miles)
58,000 (paratrooper)	1,640	1,980 at 2,000ft
57,900 (transport/glider tug)	2,245	2,360 at 10,000ft

To cool the engines in hot climates, fans and spinners were tried, some production aircraft featuring both. They brought little significant reduction as tests using BK651 revealed. Flared propeller blades were also tried on BK649, in October and November 1943. These, too, had little effect on cooling which was always a problem with glider tugs.

After plans to equip 3 Group with Lancasters were agreed, much production was switched from the Stirling Mk III to the Mk IV, but because bombers were still required by squadrons and conversion units their production was not halted. By the end of October 1943, six Stirling Mk IIIs had been delivered to 23 MU Aldergrove, for turret removal and conversion to Mk IV standard. Generally only the nose and dorsal turrets

EF506, another Mk III–IV conversion tested at AFEE, typically retained an FN 20A tail turret.

were removed. Another eight aircraft for conversion arrived in November, twenty-one in December and five in January 1944 by which time the first Mk IVs were ready for delivery. A switch to completing Stirlings as Mk IVs at Belfast began in December 1943 with EF317 to EF323 inclusive.

On the line 120 Mk IIIs were converted and completed as Mk IVs and 190 Mk IIIs were converted after completion to Mk IV. A further four were completed as Mk IVs for trials, and were complemented by seven Mk IIIs converted on the production line for various trials.

Probably it was EF318, which left 19 MU St Athan for 299 Squadron at Stoney Cross on 2 January 1944, that was first to join a squadron. 299 Squadron had formed there on 4 November 1943 with Ventura glider tugs and on 29 December 1943 twenty-one crews went for Stirling conversion training at Woolfox Lodge.

Second to equip was 190 Squadron reformed at Leicester East on 5 January 1944 with the usual strength of 16 IE + 4 IR. Crews had to train using operational Stirlings, and received their first six aircraft on 21 January 1944 allowing training to begin in February. To reinforce the transport force, 196 and 620 Squadrons had left Bomber Command in November 1943. 620's first Mk IV was received at Tarrant Rushton on 30 January 1944.

John Payne, flying with 620 Squadron at the time, recalls that:

About October 1943 a large bunch of slightly bewildered aircrew were posted to Leicester East, an awful quagmire on a hill above Oadby, a suburb of Leicester. Primitive was the accommodation we in 38 Group were to endure until the end of the war – that is, those of us who survived the longest unbroken wartime tours of operational flying.

We were intrigued to discover that we were now to be engaged in 'Special Duties' – something we had previously only associated with a mysterious group of ace pilots who did hairy things like landing Lysanders in fields in France under the noses of the Jerries.

But we had no aircraft, so the burning question during the subsequent weeks of inactivity was: "WHAT are we going to fly?" We had star-studded dreams that at least we would get Lancasters, but more likely some extra special type so far unveiled.

Imagine the near mutiny which took place when something like 600 aircrew, representing an almost equal number of Commonwealth countries, were told we would be getting…shudder…Stirlings! The CO gained a slightly better hearing when he said: 'Ah, but wait till you see THIS mark, the IV.'

We waited with growing impatience until the day when a strange and gleaming Stirling appeared fresh from Shorts. We piled into any vehicle, even rode two to a bike, to get to the airfield. It was a Stirling all right, no doubt about that '22ft above the ground' posture, no doubt about that enormous undercart, that tall fin. But where was the front turret, the dorsal, and what on earth was that enormous, horseshoe-shaped lump of steel wrapped round the belly just below and forward of the tail? It all began to look more impressive – particularly with those four Hercules XVI radials.

The first trial flights ended with the skippers outwardly reserved but inwardly jubilant. This 'ugly duckling', built like a battleship, had a TAS which proved it could outpace any other four-engined type we knew of.

Other crew members were also happy, though the general pleasure was tempered, in the case of the veterans, with the knowledge that they were to lose their gunners as 'surplus to establishment'.

Then the questions began. "What is the purpose of the horseshoe?" "It is a strop guard to prevent strops, which serve to pull open paratroopers' chutes, from lashing holes in the fuselage." "So we're to carry paratroops?" "That's right." "In daylight ops?" "That's right" (and remember, all those crews were ex-Bomber Command). This information was supplanted by news that we were also going to tow gliders – and again, all Hell erupted.

With 190 Squadron was Fg Off G H Chesterton. He had trained on Venturas at Pennfield Ridge. The day he and his crew arrived at Bournemouth, a holding station, was that of a disastrous raid by Venturas which were soon withdrawn. A conversion course on to Bostons followed; meanwhile questions were raised as to what should be done with the Venturas, but when one was used for glider-towing trials the aircraft stretched. That happened just as Stirlings were starting to be retired from Bomber Command.

Fg Off Chesterton was posted to 1665 HCU Woolfox Lodge, for Stirling conversion, and on to what he felt to be his most concentrated course ever. He recalls:

> Much of my training was on Stirling Mk Is lettered OG. I felt that the Exactor controls were a fine example of a brilliant idea that went wrong. Certainly the serviceability was poor, and I vividly remember the constant priming of the throttles. One night in three hours' circuits and bumps we used three separate aircraft, although admittedly I had just signed on a new, nervous, meticulous flight engineer. On New Year's Eve 1944 we finished our last landing in someone's chicken run amid a load of feathers. We soon had our introduction to Stirling Mk IIIs – letters NY – which seemed blissfully easy after the Mk Is.
>
> I was one of the founder members of 190 Squadron. We were a cosmopolitan lot, 'A' Flight having seven British captains and seven mixed Australian and New Zealand ones, and hardly a crew without a Canadian. The crews established during March were each six strong. The three of us who had started at Pennfield Ridge were joined by a bomb aimer, engineer and air gunner. In the early months a very happy family atmosphere developed, and unlike Bomber Command we didn't lose anyone – a very popular New Zealander and his crew – until June.
>
> The Squadron was commanded by Wg Cdr Harrison and 'A' Flight by Sqn Ldr Gilliard who did much to engender the splendid atmosphere. This was still in the days when each captain had his own aircraft and groundcrew, another feature that led to a real spirit of unity and loyalty.

During February the squadrons were raised to full strength, and Mk IV operations commenced on the 3rd/4th, when EF469 and EJ110 of 196 Squadron flew night supply drops to the French Resistance. Such 'cloak and dagger' operations were undertaken by Stirling Mk IVs on many succeeding nights. Indeed, on the night after 196 Squadron began operating, 620 Squadron despatched EF203, EF495, EF121 and LK395 from Tarrant Rushton, generally used as the advanced base.

Fg Off Chesterton began his SOE flying in April 1944:

> Each full moon period was the time for SOE and SAS operations. These were highly secret; indeed, each was entered in one's log book as 'operations as ordered'. My first trip was on 14 April 1944 when we dropped twenty-four containers south of Caen. We received the code letters necessary, made our release, and later had an acknowledgement that the containers were received. One wonders whether they fell into the right hands.
>
> We operated alone on these flights crossing the Channel as low as possible. Then we climbed to about 10,000ft to cross the enemy coast, subsequently dropping down to carry on to the DZ at 200ft or 300ft almost always in bright moonlight. We were directed to Boscombe Down on return from our first trip, the static lines trailing from the empty bomb bays. Rather pompously I refused to be debriefed there, and had to wait until we flew on the next morning. Really a rather good place, of all places, to withhold secret information – one of life's good moments!

During these low-level operations AA fire could be a great hazard. On 8/9 February Flt Lt Hannah of 620 Squadron (EF197) was fired upon by light flak when at 500ft over his DZ. His rear gunner had the satisfaction of silencing the enemy gunners. Fg Off Bell, in EF121, also encountered flak which his rear gunner silenced; and Flt Sgt McNamara of 620 Squadron, in EF203, on the same night was attacked by concentrated light flak over Tours when at only 200ft. His starboard inner oil cooler was shot away and the propeller

EF317, a Mk III–IV conversion used for radio and radar trials. (Shorts)

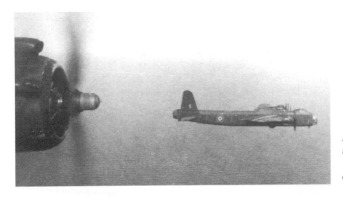

Notable absence of a dorsal turret made the Mk IVs like 7T-F vulnerable during daylight operations.

was hurled against the lower side of the fuselage, making a large hole by the second pilot's seat and engineer's position. Back at Tarrant Rushton he encountered the old problem. He could not lower his undercarriage, and had to make a belly landing.

March was a busy month for the Stirling Mk IV squadrons which took part in a number of large-scale glider exercises. Indeed, 190 Squadron flew 179 glider towing flights before moving forward to Fairford on 25 March 1944, then on 31 March commenced SOE drops out of Tarrant Rushton. 196 Squadron, which flew fourteen SOE sorties in March, took up operational residence at Keevil on 15 March. Three days later 620 Squadron joined 190 Squadron at Fairford.

Both 196 and 620 Squadrons were staffed by experienced Stirling crews, whereas 299 Squadron which had been flying Venturas visualised as possible paratroop aircraft, had to spend February working up on Stirlings. The squadron flew its first glider-towing exercise on 18 February, moved to Keevil at the end of the month and started operations on 4/5 March 1944. Aboard Stirling 'A' flown on that night by Flt Sgt Robotham, was a New Zealander, Lloyd Sparrow, who remembers it only too well:

> Our first operation, even though it was unsuccessful, remains a very vivid experience. Our crew was chosen to fly 299 Squadron's first operation. We were sent to Hurn for loading and briefing and were not allowed to talk to anyone even on our squadron about our trip. Flying out via St Catherine's Point our track took us to Pt de Lerece, Tours and Angoulan, most of it at a rare 500ft – in moonlight, of course. Our dropping zone close to the Pyrenees called for almost seven hours' flying. We carried a cage of pigeons and special notepaper to fasten to their leg capsules, to release if things went wrong. There were often cases of supplies falling directly into enemy hands and on this occasion, although we were certain we reached the prescribed drop zone, all we had for our trouble was to be met with a barrage of machine-gun fire.

Alarming moments in warfare often bring flashes of bright humour, and 299's first long-haul trip was no exception, as Lloyd Sparrow recalls:

> We were each provided with a good meal including canned orange juice, Mars bars, sandwiches, etc, and I had my special issue Thermos flask filled with coffee. Jeff Joyce, the tail gunner, was very much feeling the cold so I sent him the flask, which he much appreciated. Sufficiently warmed he continued flashing V-signs to French locals who were doing likewise.
>
> When we reached home I asked for the flask, but he had 'lost it'. He soon admitted that desperate to 'pay a call', and knowing it imprudent to vacate his guns, he made use of the flask which, complete with contents, he had dropped overboard – hopefully to the Germans.

For Lloyd the matter did not end there. When obtaining clearances prior to his return to New Zealand after the war, he was asked to produce a flask booked out to him about August 1943. That he could not do and despite a full explanation he had to pay 3/4d in lieu of the goods he was unable to produce.

All manner of items were carried by crews on operations. Lloyd kept some of his, including a multi-language phrase book, escape pack with water purifying tablets and high-energy chews, silk escape maps some of which depict much of north Africa and the Spanish Rio de Oro, a .38in Scott Webley (for which he obtained a licence), a Longines wrist watch and, in case the chance ever arose, a simple guide on how to fly a Ju 88!

It is pertinent to include at this juncture a reminder that while squadrons of 38 Group were beginning to supply Resistance forces, Stirling bomber squadrons of 3 Group had been busily undertaking such activity when they were not mining or attacking rail centres. SOE sorties were lonely, quite daring ventures, and thus it is worth recalling the events which overtook another.

Donald Farrington was aboard EH906:XY-T captained by Flt Lt C V French of 90 Squadron based at Tuddenham. Another crew being sick, French and crew took their place, and were for their pains awarded unforgettable experiences, as Donald Farrington recalls:

> We were delivering arms, ammunition and supplies to the French Resistance in the Haute Savoie region. Such operations always involved flying only at full moon and at low-level to the dropping zone. Our trip was uneventful until, somewhere over Central France and with our height approximately 300ft, our aircraft was suddenly enveloped in a blinding light swiftly followed by more from other searchlights. Cannon fire from the ground immediately followed and although our pilot took evasive action we were a sitting target. After receiving direct hits on our port wing, our pilot gained a little height then ordered us to bale out while he struggled to maintain control of the aircraft. Six of us managed to get away, but unfortunately due to the lack of height our pilot was unable to bale out. He tried to land the aircraft but was killed on impact. It was only his skill, coolness and courage that enabled the rest of us to survive. We were so low that when I baled out my parachute had only just opened when my feet hit the ground.
>
> I wasn't captured, and after travelling around the French countryside for four nights, I decided to try my luck during daylight and eventually made contact with the French Resistance. With their help I was able to evade capture for some three months until I was taken prisoner by the Germans on 11 June 1944.
>
> During the three months of my evasion I was passed from one safe house to another. At some I would stay only two nights, at others two or three weeks. During this time I came to know certain families well, people who risked their lives for me. I was clothed, sheltered, fed and treated as one of the family wherever I went. When the invasion started it was decided that it would be too dangerous to stay in the safe houses and I was moved to a *Maquis* retreat organised by a British

Stirling IV EF429 7T-B of 'B' Flight, 196 Squadron, at Shepherd's Grove in 1945.

> agent for the Vierzon region who, to my surprise, was a woman. She had been parachuted into France to organise guerrilla-type warfare. Her name was Pearl Cornioly, code name 'Pauline', and her headquarters were at a farm in a large wooded area.
>
> I was soon joined by two RAF and two American airmen and, separated from the Resistance fighters, we slept in a barn. Our meals we had with Pearl, her husband and the farmer and his family. After a couple of days we were joined by two more evaders, one RAF and the other a Dunkirk veteran. Left behind in 1940, he had got a job, worked for four years as a farmhand and was now trying to link up with our forces.
>
> At about 5am on 11 June we were awakened by the sound of machine-gun fire and immediately ran for cover in the woods. When the firing stopped we thought we had got away with it. Instead, German army patrols searching the area captured us. I had at the time no idea what happened to Pearl, only later discovering that she had avoided capture, then reformed her group to continue the fight.
>
> After the war, and with the help of a French lady translator, I made contact with some of my helpers, all of whom had survived. Our flight engineer managed to locate our pilot's grave and sent me a photograph, and I vowed that someday I would visit it. When I retired

in May 1985, I resolved that I would make that journey my first priority. It would also be marvellous if I could visit some of my old friends! Would they still be alive, forty-one years on, and how could I contact them?

At a social get-together at Blackpool held by the North-West Caterpillar Club, I met someone who had a similar experience, and who had been assisted by the RAF Escaping Society. I contacted that organisation, giving the names of the agent and my helpers.

In a reply they said they did not have any records of them, but forwarded the address of Pearl. She was living in Paris! Can you imagine her surprise when she received a letter from me, for she had no idea whether or not I had survived. From that moment the link was established. She immediately offered to try to locate my helpers and, after countless enquiries, hit the jackpot. She finally located the previous *Maire* of one of the villages where I had stayed, and he knew not only the people who had helped me but their present whereabouts. Pearl then arranged a reunion for us, in a restaurant near to the cemetery where my pilot was buried.

I had meanwhile written to tell the Escaping Society about our visit and they asked me to contact the brother and sister whose parents were wartime Resistance leaders in Nevers, close to the place we were to visit. By coincidence they were holding their annual reunion of Resistance workers and wrote to Pearl asking if they might join our event! Eventually the numbers swelled to thirty, and the luncheon was to be followed by a visit to the pilot's grave.

The brother and sister, Genevieve and Raymond, arranged to met us at Nevers station. The day arrived when my wife and I flew to Paris, me full of apprehension about how it would all turn out. As we stepped off the train at Nevers I could hear a female voice calling a 'Monsieur Farrington' and soon after we made contact with the usual embraces and kisses.

Following a celebratory drink they took us to our hotel and later out for an evening meal. Next morning, 2 July and a beautiful summer's day, my ambitions were about to be realised. Imagine my feelings when I was greeted by Pearl, her husband and my old friends for the first time in forty-one years. I was also greeted by a Col Escriennes, who served with General de Gaulle in London, and a Dr Chanel, who had survived the Malthausen concentration camp.

After lunch we made our way to the village cemetery where the *Maire* was waiting to greet us, along with a charming lady who, although only a child at the time, remembered vividly seeing our aircraft on fire and crashing. The *Maire* placed a wreath on the grave on behalf of all present and I laid a plaque on behalf of our crew. Memories flooded back during a few moments of silence, then the *Maire* took us to the spot where the Stirling had crashed.

During the following days my wife and I were wined and dined by each of the families and friends in turn. Champagne flowed, and we were transported freely everywhere. When we met the helper who had first made contact with me he took us back to the exact location where he found me, and then to the cafe where I had stayed for several nights – and even into the bedroom where I had slept. The night before he contacted me I tried to sleep, unsuccessfully, in the pulpit of the village church, for I was able to get access. It gave an uncanny feeling being there again.

Our visit was reported in French newspapers, one of which commented that we were here to try to relive the wartime period and explain the untarnished friendship which exists between the former members of the RAF and the men who welcomed and aided them. In recalling that hard and painful period of the occupation, the grievous episode, how can we forget the brotherhood, the friendship that united all members of a Resistance, the sole aim of which was to liberate the country? Pearl had, we learned, been decorated by the French Government with the Croix de Guerre with Palms and with the Legion of Honour. This very courageous lady was also awarded the MBE by our own Government.

There were some curious ironies concerning Donald Farrington's adventure. Cyril Vincent French was always Frank French to his crew. As Donald awaited removal to Germany he met another POW – named Frank French. The day he and his wife had arrived in Paris for their return to Nevers they reached the Gare du Nord exactly forty-one years to the day since Donald had stood on the same platform with about 700 other POWs for transportation to Germany and Stalag Luft VII, Bankau. A third coincidence concerned a work colleague who had bought a book entitled *Into the Silk*. It contained a story about a flight engineer of 90 Squadron who had baled out and who was none other than Joe Cashmore, Donald's one-time crew mate.

Cashmore had indeed a remarkable tale to tell. After his POW release he was, in 1946, put in charge of a camp at Melbourne, Yorkshire, housing German POWs where he happened to enter into a conversation with *Unteroffizier* Heinz Ulrich. When Ulrich learnt that Cashmore had flown Stirlings he said, with some pride, that he had been awarded the Iron Cross for shooting one down in 1944, and that he had been NCO in charge of a gun-site in France. Then Ulrich mentioned the date of 4 March 1944. Cashmore, hardly able to contain himself, brought out a map then asked Ulrich to point out Avord, where his unit had been stationed. Unhesitatingly he pointed to a spot between Bourges and Nevers, and then to the village of Hilaire de Gondilly, 6 miles from his gun position, and to Beau Renard where the bomber had crashed. Finally Cashmore asked him what time it happened and his answer confirmed that here indeed was the man who terminated his flight. What irony that Ulrich should have now become his prisoner. Of the six who survived that night three became POWs and three made their escape.

Meanwhile, the huge exercises and the SOE drops had continued in 1944 as squadrons worked up their role in the Normandy landings. On 4 April, 190 Squadron took part in a typical training mission, Exercise *Dream*. Thirteen Stirling/Horsa combinations took off at night in eighteen minutes then, after 3½ hours' flying, the gliders were released.

> By the time D-Day came [recalls Fg Off Chesterton] we had done twenty-four glider lifts. They were a fascinating business. The tug taxied out, and within seconds the ground crew hooked up the Horsa's towrope (nylon by this time) and a batman – as on a carrier – beckoned one to take up slack. Traffic lights to the left gave the signal to take off, and meanwhile the rear gunner told his pilot when the rope was fully taut. Take-off was surprisingly easy, the glider being airborne after about 200 yards. The drag directly astern limited the amount of swing, and the tug lumbered happily into the air well before the end of the runway. Cruising speed with a Horsa was about 140-knots. The gliders then assumed what was called the 'high tow position', but many glider pilots preferred to move down to the low position below the tug's tail as soon as practicable. There was a primitive communication cable between tug and glider, which seldom worked with satisfaction. After exercises, the tow ropes were dropped at the DZ on the edge of the circuit. In May my companion squadron lost two aircraft in collision when rope dropping – a grim day for the whole station.

Massed glider-towing training flights often at dusk were almost complete by the start of May, but SOE flights by the four 38 Group squadrons continued, over fifty more being flown. By the close of the month the squadrons were at peak readiness as the invasion drew near.

Detail planning for the Normandy landings had commenced in 1943 as a result of which Stirling squadrons at Keevil and Fairford would carry paratroops of the 5th Paratroop Brigade in Phase II of operation *Tonga*, with each Stirling carrying twenty troops and their equipment.

At Keevil on 5 June, a day of gloomy weather, cloudy sky and strong winds, the station was very tense for, if the weather did not soon improve, the momentous operation would have to be called off.

At 1400 hrs crews of 196 and 299 Squadrons were called for briefing. Despite the weather, said Air Vice-Marshal Hollinghurst, AOC 38 Group, the operation would take place the following night. The aim was to drop troops on DZ 'H', a space about 21 miles square on the east side of the River Orne near Ouistreham. Their task would be to hold bridges crossing the river Orne and the Caen Canal.

Last-minute preparations as groundcrews swarmed over the forty-six Stirlings would, for all involved, be memorable. The aircraft had to be lined up in correct sequence, close, diagonally facing each other and tightly packed along the edge of the active runway's end. By late evening, troops were busily engaged fitting their parachutes, aided by scores of airmen and WAAFs. They would never forget the enthusiasm of these men of 12 Battalion, 6th Airborne, who seemed relieved that the long wait for battle was ending.

At 2300 hrs the engines of the Stirlings burst into life. Run-up complete, the first

Stirling rolled at 2319 hrs and the whole force was soon away at half-minute intervals, and made straight for the DZ. Light flak streamed up from Ouistreham and Cabourg, but a line of guns by the DZ had already been silenced in a Lancaster attack. All the crews delivered their passengers, except possibly Flt Sgt T Gilbert who was shot down. Several aircraft suffered flak damage and WO Ellis, bomb aimer in Flt Lt Taylor's aircraft, was seriously wounded. After the drop the Stirlings turned eastwards to exit over Fecamp for safe return to base. Considering the importance of the night's delivery, all had gone extremely well.

At Fairford, take-off in the black-and-white-striped Stirlings – thus adorned three days earlier – was set for 2330 hrs on 5 June. Cloud, 5/10 over Britain, thinned over the Continent as the transports flew in low, loose formation, in moonlight and good visibility, for their 3 1/2 hour round trip. The two Fairford squadrons, led by 620, encountered light flak which shot down Sqn Ldr Pettit and two other crews. Four more aircraft had flak damage, but expectation of heavy losses was, fortunately, unfulfilled.

Stirlings involved on that stupendous night included:

190 Squadron: twenty-three aircraft, including EF214, EF242, EF260, EF263, EF270, EF316, LJ818, LJ820, LJ823, LJ824, LJ825, LJ827, LJ829, LJ831, LJ832, LJ833, LJ939, LK431, LK433, LK498, LK513
196 Squadron, used for Operation Tonga IV: EF234, EF276, EF?*, EF309, LJ810, LJ835, LJ836, LJ837, LJ841, LJ843, LJ845, LJ846, LJ848, LJ851, LJ924, LJ925, LJ943, LJ944, LK440, LK502, LK505, LK510, LK564. (* either EF248, EF261, EF311 or EF429)
299 Squadron: aircraft (identities remain uncertain) were drawn from the following: EF243, EF267, EF305, EF318, EF320, EF321, EF323, EH950.
620 Squadron: EF237, EF296, EF256, EF275, EF268, EF293, EF295 (FTR), EJ116 (FTR), LJ847, LJ849, LJ850, LJ865, LJ866, LJ869, LJ872, LJ875, LJ878, LJ892, LJ899, LJ917, LJ921, LK432, LK588

During the daylight hours of 6 June crews snatched their rest while groundcrews patched up the aircraft, refuelled them and made them ready for the next adventure. It came early in the evening.

At Fairford and Keevil seventy-one Horsa gliders were marshalled into position alongside their tugs, and shortly after 1800 hrs troops of 6th Airborne emplaned in the gliders. The aim was to deliver the Horsas to DZ 'W', the object to reinforce paratroops dropped to seize the Orne and Caen Canal bridges. From Fairford thirty-five gliders were towed aloft, and from Keevil another thirty-six Horsas were shared among 196 and 299 Squadrons.

There was a surprising lack of enemy interference. It seemed that both sides had stopped fighting for a moment to marvel at the spectacle as operation *Mallard* unfolded. These reinforcements, the crews learned later, arrived just in time. Many of the gliders, however, ran into 15ft-high poles at the DZ, which caused casualties and equipment damage.

On the afternoon of 6 June [recalls D. H. Hardwick with 299 Squadron] we towed a glider full of supplies and troops to reinforce the paratroops. The sight over the Channel that afternoon was unforgettable, for there were ships and aircraft as far as the eye could see. Each of us seemed to have a squadron of fighters as escort. Two incidents come to mind. The naval barrage balloons were supposed to be lowered to let us through as we approached, but nothing happened. So we had to press on. A fair number of balloons went up towards the moon that afternoon.

Wg Cdr G E Harrison had led 190 Squadron from Fairford. His squadron met intense machine-gun fire which killed the bomb aimer in Sgt Coeshott's aircraft. Six others suffered flak damage, but all eighteen Stirlings released their gliders. Another eighteen of 620 Squadron also took part.

Flt Lt F Thoing's machine, hit by light flak, was forced to land in a French field. The crew escaped, and everyone at Fairford was delighted when they turned up a few days later.

Stirlings involved in operation *Mallard* included:

190 Squadron: EF214, EF263, EF264, EF270, LJ816, LJ818, LJ823, LJ824, LJ825, LJ829, LJ831, LJ881, LJ927, LJ939, LK405, LK431, LK433, LK513
196 Squadron: EF248, EF261, EF276, LJ836, LJ837, LJ843, LJ846, LJ848, LJ923, LJ924, LJ928, LJ937, LJ945, LJ954, LK461, LK505, LK564
299 Squadron: aircraft identities uncertain, but drawn from among EF243, EF267, EF305, EF318, EF320, EF321, EF323 and EH950
620 Squadron: EF237, EF296, EF256, EF268 (FTR), EF293, EF303, LJ847, LJ850, LJ866, LJ872, LJ873, LJ875, LJ892, LJ914, LJ917, LJ970, LK432, LK?

Barely had the squadrons touched down when a number of crews left on SOE and resupply missions, something undertaken on many nights in June and July. Sometimes these entailed container drops in Normandy. Such operations remained hazardous and in three months 38 Group lost eight Stirlings, and 3 Group lost two.

During July, 190 Squadron dropped ninety-three paratroops and operated on eleven nights, participating in small-scale, very secret operations with curious code names such as *Grog*, *Percy* and *Stationer*. As many as eighteen Stirlings would operate on one night. On 10 and 18 July, 196 Squadron was similarly busily engaged.

Although aircraft establishment for each 38 Group squadron totalled 22 + 4 aircraft, on 11 July actual strength of each squadron was:

Fairford: 190 Squadron – 39, 620 Squadron – 35, together with 94 Horsas
Keevil: 196 Squadron – 37, 299 Squadron – 38, together with 93 Horsas

An important feature of the month was the commencement of the replacement at Harwell of the Albemarles of 295 and 570 Squadrons with Stirling IVs. The former had received its first Stirlings on 14 June and, by 11 July, 295 held ten Stirlings and 570 had nine, at a station where another eighty Horsas were available. In all, on 11 July, 128/168 Stirling IVs were serviceable. A total of 850/870 Horsas were ready for use, but their turn to operate was still some way off. Crews for more Stirling IVs were being trained at 1665 HCU Tilstock where the establishment called for thirty-six aircraft. While the two new squadrons converted to Stirlings, Albemarle SOE operations continued. 295 Squadron despatched its first two Stirling operational sorties on 27 July. Next night, LJ951, being flown by the squadron, was shadowed off the French coast by a Ju 88.

570 Squadron began Stirling conversion on 1 July, crews being trained at 1665 HCU Tilstock. By 5 July the unit held nine Stirlings in addition to thirty-two Albemarles. This squadron also commenced Stirling operations on 27 July, when the CO, Wg Cdr R J M. Bangay, delivered twenty-four containers and packages to the Brest Peninsula. Next night, with enemy fighters active, LK133, flown by Plt Off D Robson, was missing, but LJ622 delivered a load in the Massif Central. Then they operated in the Sens area and, on the 30th, around Dijon.

On 1 August the establishment for Stirlings in 38 Group called for 156 aircraft and the Group was at full strength with 149 of the aircraft serviceable. 295 Squadron already had nineteen examples.

Throughout August, SOE support activities continued, and by the end of the month 190 Squadron had dropped 216 parachutists. The squadron participated in an unusual activity on the 5th when ten aircraft set off with containers but dropped only two because of bad weather. Meanwhile Wg Cdr Harrison and Sqn Ldr Gilliard dropped HE bombs and incendiaries on a special target, an unusual activity for 38 Group. Fighters were still around and on 9/10 August Flt Lt Gardiner was chased by a Ju 88. His rear gunner fired, and the Ju 88 gave up the chase.

Night drops continued until 11 September when the squadrons began to prepare for the next momentous event, the Arnhem operation. At noon on 12 September the Stirling IV squadron strength was as follows:

Station	Squadron	Strength Total	Horsas on station Serviceable	Unserviceable
Fairford	190	36	24	} 96
	620	36	26	
Keevil	196	37	34	} 99
	299	37	29	
Harwell	295	33	25	} 130
	570	32	20	

Glider tugs in 38 Group – comparative strength, 12 September 1944

	Establishment	On strength	Serviceable
Albemarle	52	102	95
Halifax	110	67	59
Stirling	156	213	158
Horsa gliders*	1,040	1,117	1,098

* Planned Establishment was for 100 at each station

Chapter 19
Adventure over Arnhem

O N 17 September 1944 the second major Allied airborne assault was mounted, its purpose to capture ahead of the advancing Allies three important bridges. One crossed the Maas at Grave, the second the Waal at Nijmegen and the third bridged the Rhine at Arnhem some 60 miles ahead of the Allied front line. The latter task went to 1st British Airborne Division, the Airborne Corps HQ, a Polish Parachute Brigade and 878th US Aviation Engineering Battalion who would build landing strips.

Initially all was to be achieved through operation *Comet* planned at the end of August 1944 for which purpose, on 6 September, 38 Group Operations Order 524 was despatched to its stations at Fairford (190 and 620 Squadrons), Keevil (196 and 299 Squadrons) and Harwell (295 and 570 Squadrons). They held about 210 Stirling Mk IVs, establishments of 22IE + 4IR (total 156) being well exceeded because D-Day losses had been low and production more than adequate. At each station the Horsa establishment stood at 100 gliders; Keevil had 130 on its dispersals.

Operation *Comet* called for landings before and just after dawn. In a manner akin to the capture of the Caen Canal bridge on 6 June 1944, six gliders would land close to each main bridge which troops would quickly seize and hold until a large number of paratroops, along with others and ample equipment, were brought in 700 gliders. 38 and 46 Groups would mount the lifts aided by the US IXth Troop Carrier Command (TCC). A further lift of 157 IXth TCC tugs and gliders, 26 more transports of 38 Group towing gliders and 100 aircraft of 38 Group making resupply drops would take place the following day. All was to be ready for 8 September.

The assumption was that the Americans could carry out night operations for which the British were trained. Unfortunately the Americans were unready for that, the scheme fell through and a new plan was drawn up on 15 September called operation *Market*. It remained centred on the seizure of three bridges, and two more US Airborne Divisions were added to the force. Delivery of the 'pathfinder gliders' to Arnhem along with the backup force and its resupply would be undertaken by 38 and 46 Groups. American C-47s would undertake paratroop drops, and deliver airstrip builders and defenders. The operation would be in daylight despite greater vulnerability. Insufficient aircraft being available for one assault, the operation would take place over two days, with a third day seeing resupply. Fair weather was essential.

Arnhem's bridge, key to the entire operation, had to be captured and then held at all costs until ground forces fought their way through, as quickly as possible, to join the airborne troops. German reaction would surely be to try containing the latter and in particular to liquidate these troops holding the bridge. A large force would therefore have to be landed to support those holding it.

Four miles north of Arnhem was an area suitable for glider landings, but being in a heavily defended zone it was rejected. South of the river lay soft ground but crossed by ditches and dykes preventing its use by gliders. Only to the north-west of Arnhem was

570 Squadron Stirlings towing Horsas to Arnhem on 17 September 1944. (A Holland)

there a tract of country, shielded by trees, where gliders could readily land in force and be naturally protected. The area was, however, too small for two glider lifts to be landed upon it. In any case, the landing ground would have needed to be held for the second day's arrivals tying up a large proportion of those landed and leaving the bridge-holders on their own for too long. Discussion surrounded use of LZs by the bridges, but finally Maj Gen R E Urquhart DSO opted for the landing of gliders north-west of Arnhem, near the present site of the Oosterbeek War Cemetery.

Meanwhile the enemy was, by chance, concentrating AA defences along routes planned for the transport aircraft, so the Allied Tactical Air Force was ordered to deliver an onslaught on them. Nevertheless, heavy losses were still expected during the first lift. To help course keeping, *Eureka* beacons were set up at sea and some of the first troops to land were to establish more to aid resupply forces.

The first suitable day as far as the weather was concerned appeared to be **Sunday 17 September 1944**, and so operation *Market* was ordered to be launched then. E F Chandler recalls:

> The whole of Keevil was more or less confined to camp for five days prior to 17 September. The only visitors at that time were food suppliers, coalmen and brewers' lorries which usually raised a cheer when seen. Several crews, including ours, were seconded to US 1st Airborne units around Grantham, to get the feel of things. As aircrew NCOs, we were very well treated, whereas in an RAF mess one was one out of hundreds.

September 17 was a beautiful day with a few patches of low cloud. Leading the operation were 190 and 620 Squadrons carrying between them twelve loads of pathfinding troops to be landed close by the bridges at Arnhem and Nijmegen.

Shortly after 1100 hrs departure by 295 and 570 Squadrons began at one-minute intervals, tow ropes being attached after the Stirlings turned on to the runway. With a tremendous surge of power, and a 'green', the heavy gliders lurched as the line went taught and they were hauled away. They circled Harwell gaining height before leaving in a stream in loose pairs at 2,500ft and 175mph. The long procession headed for Hatfield where other squadrons tagged on as course changed for Aldeburgh, the Exit Point. Those from Fairford had commenced take-off shortly after 1000 hrs, Keevil's contribution a few minutes after 1100 hrs.

> At Keevil [recalls Chandler] everything seemed to go smoothly, the only mishap coming when a towrope went taut and hurled a Fleet Air Arm fitter 15 feet into the air. Fleet Air Arm fitters were working in 38 Group to gain radial engine experience prior to Far East service. At least one of them, from HMS Daedalus, took part in the actual operation and, losing his life, was later buried in Oosterbeek cemetery.

There were the inevitable early towing problems. One glider accidentally cast off from a 190 Squadron Stirling over South Cerney, another from 295 Squadron over Melksham. The stream took about an hour to pass over the coast at Aldeburgh where the lines of participating transports converged then flew to West Schouwen almost without incident. Over the Dutch coast 295 Squadron lost another Horsa, but the defences were almost inactive. A host of Allied fighters closed in to protect the transport force as it headed for s'Hertogenbosch and the start of the run-in to the LZs.

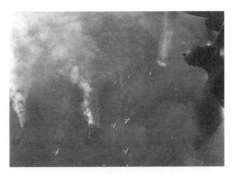

An Arnhem DZ viewed on 17 September 1944 from a 570 Squadron Stirling with a Dutch castle burning in the foreground. (A Holland)

The transports approached in loose formation carrying mixed loads. 190 Squadron, for instance, had six aircraft airlifting ninety-seven pathfinder troops and another nineteen towing gliders in which there were 130 troops, 17 Jeeps, 7 lightweight motorcycles, a heavy motorcycle, 17 trailers, 7 guns and a bicycle. 196 Squadron had two tow ropes break, as a result of which one glider ditched and another cast off, whereas all twelve gliders towed by 570 Squadron were successfully released over the LZ.

Such was the complete surprise achieved that the German *Wehrmacht* commander was comfortably chatting in the course of Sunday pre-lunch drink on the steps of his somewhat palatial Hartseim headquarters when suddenly the operation evolved almost on his doorstep as gliders were released over Oosterbeek.

That task completed, tow ropes were dropped before the Stirlings climbed away for home at 180mph. Despite the long haul over enemy territory, there was little hostile response thanks to the Tactical Air Force. By mid-afternoon the Stirlings were back at their bases bearing a few scratches from desultory flak. During the remainder of the day groundcrews worked feverishly on the tug aircraft and prepared some 300 more gliders for passage next day. The weather had remained clear, and at the LZs the troops had deplaned effectively to ordered positions.

When dawn broke on **18 September** a very different scene presented itself revealing fog-clad airfields which caused no mean alarm. A five-hour delay to re-supply was enforced, and even then there were cloud patches and hazy conditions to face. AA guns had also been rushed to the likely approach lanes and when the Stirlings headed into the Netherlands things were nowhere near as easy as on the preceding day.

This time 190 Squadron successfully towed nineteen Horsas carrying 92 troops, 19 Jeeps, 7 x 5 cwt cars, 4 x 6lb guns, 6 Bren carriers, 21 trailers and a heavy motorcycle. 196 Squadron towed twenty-two Horsas, two of which were released prematurely. Containers were carried by eighteen Stirlings of 295 Squadron and two more towed Horsas. Containers were dropped at LZ 'X'. All 299 Squadron Stirlings towed Horsas, and so did ten of 570 Squadron. Nine gliders were released but at Opheusden LK121, captained by Flt Sgt C W Culling, was hit by flak and crashed. Its Horsa was cast off and landed safely though fired upon at Zetten. Another of the squadron's Stirlings, hit by flak in the same region, eventually crashed near Deelen. 620 Squadron towed twenty-two gliders but the tow rope of one broke over England.

E F Chandler in a Stirling recalls that:

> After take-off we had our glider in high position, but many glider pilots preferred the low state. It fell to the flight engineer to peer from the astrodome and signal to the glider pilot with an Aldis lamp the time for release, following instructions from the bomb aimer who was map reading. We ran in for release at 2,000ft, but supply droppers were going in at around 1,000ft or less, and were drawing most of the anti-aircraft fire. This enabled most of the tug aircraft to return safely to base.

The route taken was as on 17 September, and flak certainly had increased considerably since the preceding day. 570 Squadron's fifteen supply droppers proceeded in vics of three, line astern, at about 15-second intervals, and went in from s'Hertogenbosch at 1,500ft descending to a mere 700ft and 140mph for the drop. Over the dropping zone the cloud base was between 2,000ft and 3,000ft. Flak

Wing Commander Bangay's Stirling LJ977 V8-B of 570 Squadron homeward bound from Arnhem over the North Sea on 17 September 1944 as seen from Flt Lt Hudson's aircraft. ('Cherry' Cherrington)

claimed another Stirling and damaged LK555 which crash landed at base.

190 Squadron had an eventful time. Moments after take-off, Plt Off Sellers had his starboard outer engine fail, so he cast off his glider then landed. Plt Off Beberfeld had his towrope break just after leaving the English coast because the glider placed itself in the wrong position. Both glider and tug touched down safely at Woodbridge and later returned to base. Over Holland, Flt

Initials WES on LK171 'Shooting Star' identify this as Wing Commander W E Surplice's aircraft. (Bob Dalton)

Sgt Herger was drawn into the slipstream of a Dakota. His glider rose as he put his nose down to avoid the Dakota and the towrope snapped, the glider landing near Over Flakkee. Violent slipstream effect of the stream was encountered by many combinations, and in Fg Off T Farren's case the glider he was towing cast off and crash landed 25 miles short of the LZ after the towrope broke. Unlucky, too, was Fg Off Chesterton, one of whose engines was hit by flak.

Ground aids gave a useful lead-in for the crews, who released gliders into increasing flak and small arms fire. German troops fired upon the glider troops as they attempted to unload the Horsas, about fifty of which were burnt out mainly after unloading. Although only three Stirlings were lost, over thirty were damaged by flak. Communication with troops on the ground was impossible, also with the Airborne Corps HQ at Nijmegen. Photographs showed the Arnhem Bridge still intact, and battle in progress.

Back at their bases crews recollected seeing a Stirling spewing smoke. Another, hit by flak, was seen to crash and explode, a third was reported burning on the ground, a fourth had crash landed and from a fifth, hit by flak, only one crewman baled out. A sixth was reported as having fuel streaming from its starboard tank.

By **19 September** American forces had seized the bridge at Grave, whereas the Nijmegen bridge remained in German hands. 1st Airborne Division at Arnhem remained cut off from the planned land advance, no surprise element remained and large enemy forces included unexpectedly Panzers in the Arnhem area formed a formidable foe. Additionally, plentiful AA guns were in position. The idea of dropping Poles south of Arnhem was abandoned, and so was any notion of engineers building landing strips. Only resupply drops and using gliders to bring in heavy equipment were authorised. Once again low cloud and generally poor visibility prevented take-off until around noon. This time twenty Stirlings were involved, some towing gliders. Although enemy fighter interference was prevented by the strong fighter cover, crews encountered along the approach route enemy fire coming from small arms and 40mm guns. From the Waal, waterborne guns opened up.

Approaching the Dutch coast, Plt Off Beberfeld ran into cloud and the Horsa he was towing suddenly closed rapidly on the tug nearly forcing it into the sea. Then the towrope broke, the glider smashed into the water and three men clambered into a dinghy dropped from the Stirling. The sixteen supply droppers of 190 Squadron carrying 384 containers and sixty-four panniers ran into very heavy flak and many were damaged. Shrapnel wounded WO Pelater in Fg Off Pascoe's crew, Flt Sgt Coeshott was shot down, and Sqn Ldr Gilliard's aircraft was hit over the DZ by two shells which severed his controls. He ordered his crew to bale out while they had time, but Gilliard and Fg Off McKewon were still aboard the Stirling when it crashed and were killed.

All seventeen aircraft of 295 Squadron carried containers. Before reaching the DZ two aircraft were badly damaged, one by flak and the other by falling containers. All but three of the Squadron's aircraft returned to base badly damaged. One was shot down in flames near Eede, the crew being casualties. Another made a forced landing at Woodbridge with an engine out of use. 570 Squadron's seventeen aircraft, each carrying twenty-four containers and two packages, followed a new route: Base – Bradwell-on-Sea – Ostend – Ghent Helinthal – Veghel – DZ then descended to 800ft for their drop.

Most of the Allies' Continental fighter airfields were covered by haze and mist, and general opposition had increased. Around the DZ 88mm guns were in operation and three Stirlings were brought down. One, with port engines failing, made a belly landing at Ghent. LJ647, flown by Plt Off E D Hincks and hit over the DZ, successfully crash landed at Haren, the crew scrambling out to make a getaway to Allied lines. Less fortunate were those aboard EH897 who were taken prisoner after crashing behind enemy lines at Arnhem.

By the time 620 Squadron reached the DZ there were many supply droppers in the area, some making second low-level runs to ensure that supplies reached the right hands. 620's crews were crowded out and forced to fly too high for accurate releases. Some of these aircraft were hit by flak, but they all reached home.

By the evening of Tuesday the 19th losses among the Stirling personnel were all too noticeable, aircraft losses for the day being ten. A Stirling had been seen to crash on DZ 'L', and those aboard 'X9-Y' reported seeing 'N-Nan' of their squadron fall in flames. Three men baled out, but no parachutes were seen to open. There were insufficient Allied fighters available to silence flak positions which resulted in some loads being released from as high as 4,000ft as a result of which many containers drifted into enemy hands.

LJ566 'Yorkshire Rose II' of 620 Squadron at Fairford on 19 September 1944. (Noel Chaffey)

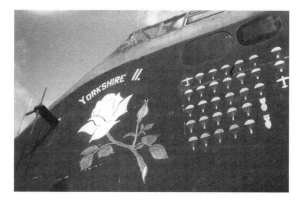

It was not only the loss of thirteen Stirlings that worried 38 Group. Equally disturbing was the alarming number of machines with severe flak damage. Fortunately, many were readily repairable, and Group ample strength at the start of the operation proved a blessing.

On **20 September**, the fourth day, 38 Group fielded 101 Stirlings for supply drops. From Fairford thirty-four drawn from 190 and 620 Squadrons took part; from Harwell thirty-four of 295 and 570 Squadrons and from Keevil thirty-three of 196 and 299 along with a crew from 1665 HCU Tilstock. In all they achieved eighty-seven successful drops unloading 63 containers, 325 panniers, 3 packets, 2 kitbags and a sack load. The cost was high for nine Stirlings and two 46 Group Dakotas were lost. No interception by enemy fighters was reported on the 20th but ground defences had stiffened and again the number of aircraft damaged caused grave concern.

Reports described the use of rocket projectiles from two positions, and returning crews spoke of a number of Stirlings in various difficulties which produced a confused picture. Containers again had to be dropped from high levels and often fell short of the aiming area which was as depressing to the crews as to those enduring Hell on the ground. Bunching as the Stirlings converged on the DZ led to them soon being squeezed out over a wide area.

For E F Chandler the day brought an end to his part in the Arnhem affair:

We had a load of twenty-four parachute containers, three in each wing cell and eighteen in the bomb bay, plus several large wicker baskets carried in the fuselage, along with two RASC Air Despatchers.

Nearing the DZ, we were all alerted. Most pilots and bomb aimers had quite some task trying to concentrate on positioning with so much heavy flak around. At the back of the Stirling Mk IV, near the port side entrance door, was a despatch hatch built within the depth of the bomb bay. The radio operator and flight engineer usually lifted the floor cover off, and then it looked like the inside of a galvanised bath. Through this opening army despatchers would, after seeing the red warning light flash to green, push the supply baskets attached to static lines hitched inside the aircraft. With the hatch open, pieces of shrapnel would race into the aircraft, and the smell of cordite and exploding shells was quite pungent. Luckily, none of us was hit.

With only two more baskets to release, we realised the aircraft had been hit in the port wing and engine, and was on fire. We pushed out remaining supplies before the pilot ordered, "Prepare to bale out!" We grabbed fire extinguishers and I managed to direct mine into a gap where the mainplane was attached to the fuselage. Meanwhile another crew member had extinguished a small fire, flames from which were creeping along the main interbalance fuel line, which was lagged, and which connected the two sets of fuel tanks in each wing. As the smoke had cleared, I told the skipper that I thought the fire was out. He replied, "No it isn't, all the hatches have been opened, that's why the smoke has cleared." The port inner had been feathered earlier. He said, "It's quite serious." We were now heading west and climbing on three engines.

At 5,000ft the pilot ordered everybody to bale out. The army despatchers were first away via the rear exit in the floor, followed by the rear gunner. The pilot, bomb aimer and navigator went from the front exit. The RAAF radio operator told me they had all gone: I rather stupidly decided I could work better with the intercom disconnected – and the skipper had left the autopilot flying the aircraft. I made my way safely to the rear exit followed by the radio operator/air gunner.

Chandler landed on the Allied side of the lines.

Fg Off Chesterton was flying LK431-F 'Fox' (or 'Ferdinand' as 190 Squadron knew it) as he had done on the first two days' operations at Arnhem. On the 17th they had taken paratroops, on the 18th a Horsa. The 20th saw them dropping supplies and on this drop he and his crew had the first indication that all was not going well when the reception was very warm. He recalls:

During all these operations the fighter cover was superb at high, medium and low levels – until Wednesday, the 20th.

The losses of the previous day and general unserviceability, coupled with battle damage, cut 38 Group's effort to a total of sixty-four aircraft making resupply sorties. Of these, only forty-seven crews reported success. Three sorties were abortive, but it was the loss of eleven transport aircraft that made the day so disastrous.

During the previous evening clear reports had been received from Arnhem revealing that only a handful of troops had held the Arnhem bridge but that the main body from the DZs and LZs outside the town had been unable to fight their way through to it. On the third day these stronger groups were forced back to the LZs where supplies had hitherto been dropped. An urgent call for more supplies had been received, and on the fourth day the Stirlings set forth again. Flak was even more intense and a lower dropping height had been ordered for precise accuracy. It called for great courage, the hall mark of the entire Arnhem venture for there was no prospect of land forces being able to fight their way through to the airborne forces in time to save them.

Widespread fog and low stratus again cruelly covered central England early on **21 September**. By mid-morning it had lifted to 1,000ft giving a visibility of one to three miles. Again the southerly route was chosen for resupply aircraft which at noon set off in four waves. A new supply dropping point some 200 yards east of the previous one had been selected which shows the precision demanded of crews. As if that was not enough, far more worrying events distinguished the day.

Mostly carrying containers and assortments of panniers and packages, the Stirlings of 570 Squadron being led by Sqn Ldr Cleaver climbed to 2,500ft and formated behind 299 Squadron heading the formation. As they ran in on the new dropping point flak became even more intense than hitherto, and it was soon apparent that Allied fighters were not interfering with the Germans some of whom had 88mm guns. Transit over the Netherlands had been at 7,000ft, but nearing the dropping point 570 Squadron, in bad visibility, descended to 1,500ft then to 800ft at 140mph for the drop before racing away at deck level. In the face of a tremendous flak barrage almost all of the supplies overshot into enemy hands. Heavy fire seriously damaged two of 299's aircraft and Flt Lt R T Turner crash-landed near Arnhem. Two of the crew became POWs while the others escaped to Allied lines.

This Stirling force-landed on 24 September 1944 during the Arnhem operation. The crew escaped. (Lv dr Bergh)

295 Squadron delivered 237 containers, 34 panniers and 8 packages. Some had been hurled from Plt Off D M Peel's aircraft before it belly landed south of the dropping point. The crews of 620 Squadron, encountering poor visibility en route, noticed an absence of covering fighters at the rendezvous where there should have been seventeen squadrons of Spitfires, three of Mustangs and one of Tempests. Almost immediately Fw190s closed in and Fg Off H M Mcleod, in LJ830, and Fg Off J C L Carey, in LJ946, were soon shot down at Renkum and Bennekom.

It was apparent that although the first and second waves of Stirlings had some fighter support, the other two were without any to silence flak and guard them against enemy fighters. Just after dropping, and as 196 Squadron's Stirlings were leaving at treetop height, in came five Fw190s. LJ810 was raked by enemy fire, and so severely that all the crew except the pilot, WO M Azouz, and the tail gunner, abandoned the aircraft which was savaged by flak and more fighters until it was brought down. Soon, LJ843 and LJ928 had also been shot out of the sky.

Events were unfolding fast as ten crews of 190 Squadron waited their turns to make drops. As they approached the dropping point it was clear that they were heading into a major disaster. The flak was terrifying enough, but some ten Fw190s were intent on making a kill. Fg Off Sigert dropped his load just before two Fw190s attacked. He dived almost to ground level and his aircraft was badly shot about. His rear gunner, Flt Sgt Welton, claimed one enemy fighter before they made their getaway. In a rapidly confusing melee Wg Cdr Harrison was soon shot down, and Fg Off Beberfeld's aircraft was so badly holed by flak over Elst that its load had to be jettisoned. Six Bf109s swarmed around them, set the Stirling on fire and, seeing it doomed, looked elsewhere for trade. The aircraft began to climb, but from it only the radio operator, Flt Lt Munro, and the rear gunner, WO Morris, baled out. They sheltered in a village before making a safe getaway to Allied positions, Morris having the melancholy satisfaction of having driven off a burning Bf109 which partly avenged the deaths of his crewmates.

As Fg Off Pascoe crossed the dropping point, intensive flak enveloped his Stirling, severing the control wires and setting the port wing ablaze. With great effort he retained control but then the fighters again attacked and started another fire. He ditched his

Stirling in the River Maas near Appeltern, all the crew being drowned save Sgt Smith, the flight engineer, and the bomb aimer, Flt Sgt Orange, who managed to get into the dinghy and reach the bank.

Seven of 190 Squadron's ten Stirlings had been shot down. An eighth, Fg Off Farren's machine badly hit by flak, crashed on landing. Farren, hurled through the windscreen in the crash, was seriously injured.

The loss for the day had been fourteen Stirlings, making a total of twenty-nine brought down during operation *Market*. On the **21st** the operation loss rate was 14 percent – almost as high as any which overtook the Stirling. It showed the vulnerability – always expected but hitherto avoided – that a transport force might endure. Had the fighters attacked the Dakotas of 46 Group, the casualty rate would have been even higher: the Stirlings at least had a rear gunner.

On **22 September** the weather was too poor for resupply. Some respite was afforded 38 Group, but not the men on the ground at Arnhem. On the **23rd** the weather cleared again, and a final effort was made using the southern route despite the fact that the enemy was acquainted with the run-in track which it was almost impossible to vary.

This time the force consisted of 123 aircraft of the two Groups, 38 and 46, seventy-three of them being Stirlings. Between them they delivered 1,540 containers, 235 panniers and 50 packages. Effective fighter support was provided by eighteen Spitfire and three Mustang squadrons. Although single-engined enemy fighters were seen, they kept their distance, but the flak could not be avoided. Resupply drop was timed for 1600 hrs, and it took the column – including American C-47s – an hour and a half to cross the dropping point. This time 190 Squadron's seven aircraft – all they could muster – returned safely. The fourteen crews of 295 Squadron unloaded 332 containers and 52 packages and one Stirling, hit over the target area, landed at Ghent with an engine out of action.

Crews of 620 Squadron witnessed all too clearly the enemy's vicious onslaught on the troops below. Some Stirlings were damaged by flak, and Wg Cdr D H Lee, in LJ847, was shot down. 299 Squadron had three aircraft badly damaged and one forced down 6 miles south-west of the dropping point; the crew escaped safely. Among 196 Squadron's thirteen crews operating was that of Fg Off J A Norton which met a hail of flak as a result of which his port propeller flew off. He limped into Manston. LJ949 crash landed at Leende, whereas EF272, seriously shot up, made base; so did LJ502 and another, also severely mauled.

Fighter ground support for 570 Squadron was poor, and 88mm guns poured out their fire. Fg Off B S Murphy crash landed LJ996 at Ghent; EF298 flown by Fg Off W Baker was shot down; so was Plt Off W Kirkham in LJ883, near the dropping point. Stirling V8-A landed at Manston with serious flak damage, and Sqn Ldr R W F Cleaver, in LK191, came down in Holland and he and his crew reached Allied lines. From LJ991, which came down near Heteren, only the radio operator and pilot escaped, the others being killed. In all, 570 Squadron had lost four aircraft and two others were forced to land away from base.

At Arnhem, 1st Airborne Division had been so weakened that further resupply seemed pointless, although the RAF transport force did not desert the troops. Dakotas of 46 Group were moved to Belgium from where resupply continued, and on the **24th** five Stirling crews of 620 Squadron tried to deliver aid despite poor weather.

The cost to 38 Group had been high. By the last day of resupply sixty-three of its aircraft had either been shot down or seriously damaged, a 56 percent loss of effective strength. Details of crew casualties remain confused, for while the records of 38 Group suggest a loss of 159 aircrew members missing, a confirmed twenty-one killed and twelve seriously wounded, later figures suggest higher casualties. By the end of the resupply missions, ten crews had made their way back to Allied lines.

Despite heavy losses the Stirlings available allowed a rapid rise to established strength. By 30 September squadron holding of aircraft stood at: 190 Squadron – 33 aircraft (20 serviceable); 196 – 34 (20); 295 – 7 (6); 299 – 39 (32); 620 – 36 (22); 570 – details not known.

Those who participated in the Arnhem venture tell of their desperation and powerlessness to aid those on the ground, an appalling situation they could not alter. To their everlasting glory 1st Airborne had captured and held the Arnhem bridge whilst displaying great courage. Stirling crew's of 38 Group did all they could to support an almost impossible task.

Arnhem losses were high. Mk IV QS-H burns on the ground near Oss, the Netherlands, on 23 September 1944.

'Just Jane' LJ591 8Z-J takes the strain at Rivenhall. (Roy Scott)

Operation *Market* – A Numerical Survey

Delivery and Re-supply Sorties flown by Stirling Squadrons, 17–23 September 1944

Sqn	17th	18th	19th	20th	21st	22nd	23rd
190	24/25	17/23	16(2)	17(2)	10(7)	–	7
196	24	22	14/15	16/17(7)	6/10(3)	–	13(1)
295	25	20	17(1)	16/17(1)	10/11(1)	–	14
299	23	21	17(2)	16	11(1)	–	14
570	20	25	18(2)	16	11	–	14(4)
620	20	22	17	17(2)	11(2)	–	11(1)

Key:

24/25, etc = 24 sorties effective out of 25 (effectiveness not always recorded in surviving documentation). 10(7), etc = 10 despatched (7 failed to return).

Typical loads, as carried by 190 Squadron

17th: towed 6 PFF gliders with 97 troops, 19 Horsas carrying 130 troops, 17 jeeps, 7 light/heavy motorcycles, 17 trailers, 7 guns, one bicycle

18th: towed 21 Horsas carrying 92 men, 19 jeeps, 7 scout cars, four 6-pounder guns, 6 Bren guns, 21 trailers and a motorcycle

19th: towed 2 Horsa (one crashed in sea), 384 containers and 64 panniers

20th: 408 containers and 68 panniers

21st: 240 containers and 40 panniers

23rd: 168 containers and 28 panniers

Listing of the identities of tugs and the gliders they towed into battle seems not to have survived. During operation *Market I* gliders bearing chalked identity numbers ranging between about 185 and 600 appear to have been towed to Arnhem by Stirlings and during operation *Market II* gliders bore identity numbers between about 900 to 1065.

Planning for operation *Market* called for a first lift (*Market I*) to carry 1st Airborne Division 'pathfinders' in twelve 38 Group combinations, and 228 tugs of 38 Group and 130 of 46 Group between them towing 13 Hamilcars and 345 Horsas, Stirlings towing many of the latter.

Market II was designed to transport HQ Airborne Corps with forty-two 38 Group aircraft towing forty Horsas and two CG-4As with another four CG-4As towed by 46 Group and more of 1st Airborne Division with 164 tugs of 38 Group.

During *Market III* sixteen tug/Horsa combinations were planned, after which 38 Group and others would re-supply the ground forces mainly by day. Glider-tow flying was undertaken at about 145mph, re-supply at about 175mph.

Stirlings Involved in the Operation

Market I: 17 September
Market II: 18 September
Market III: 19 September
Market IV: 20 September
Market V: 21 September
Market VI: 22 September (abandoned)
Market VII: 23 September

190 Squadron

Market I: EF242, EF260, EF263, EF264, EF316, LJ818, LJS31, LJ876, LJ881, LJ934, LJ936, LJ982, LK405 and twelve more unknown

Market II: not known

Market III: EF242, EF263*, EF316, LJ816, LJ818, LJ831, LJ902, LJ934, LJ939*, LK405 and eight unknown

Market IV: included LJ829, EF260, the rest unknown

Market V: EF260*, LJ829, LJ831, LJ982*, LK433, LK498*

Market VII: LJ816, LJ823*, LJ881*, LJ916*, LJ943*

196 Squadron

Market I: EF234, EF272, EF429, LJ440, LJ502, LJ583, LJ836, LJ837, LJ843, LJ848, LJ851, LJ888, LJ440, LJ894, LJ925, LJ926, LJ928, LJ937, LJ945, LJ949, LJ954, LJ988 LK505, LK510
Market II: EF146, EF234, EF248, EF276, EF318, EF429, LJ502, LJ810, LJ837, LJ840, LJ843, LJ846, LJ848, LJ851, LJ894, LJ928, LJ937, LJ945, LJ954, LK440, LK556, LK557
Market III: EF234, EF246, EF248, EF249*, EF318, LJ502, LJ836, LJ848, LJ894, LJ922, LJ945, LJ989, LK510, LK556, LK557
Market IV: EF272, EF318, LJ505, LJ810, LJ851*, LJ853, LJ894, LJ925, LJ926, LJ945, LJ947 cr, LJ988*, LJ840*, LK146, LK510, LK556 cr
Market V: EF272, LJ502, LJ583, LJ810, LJ843*, LJ928*, LJ945, LJ949, LK505 and one unknown
Market VII: EF272, LJ502, LJ583, LJ836, LJ894, LJ923, LJ925, LJ946, LJ949*, LK146, LK147, LK193, LK557

295 Squadron

Market I: EF446, LJ576, LJ590, LJ612, LJ633, LJ638, LJ652, LJ950, LJ951, LJ975, LJ976, LJ986, LJ995, LK115, LK120, LK128, LK129, LK134,,LK141, LK144, LK170, LK543, LK553, LK567, LK575
Market II: EF470, LJ576, LJ633, LJ652, LJ950, LJ951, LJ975, LJ986, LK115, LK128, LK132, LK134, LK137, LK141, LK144, LK543, LK553, LK567, LK575
Market III: EF470, EF446, LJ590, LJ618, LJ633, LJ652, LJ951, LK120, LK132, LK141, LK144, LK170*, LK543, LK567, PW255
Market IV: EF446, EF470, LJ591, LJ612, LJ618*, LJ950, LJ951, LJ986, LJ995, LK115, LK120, LK128, LK129, LK132, LK134, LK575, PW255
Market V: EF446, EF470, LJ612, LJ638, LJ950, LJ951, LJ986, LJ995, LK115*, LK120, LK134
Market VII: EF446, EF470, LJ638, LJ950, LJ951, LJ975, LJ976, LJ986, LJ995, LK128, LK132, LK1345, LK575, PW255

299 Squadron

Market I: EF323, LJ235, LJ629, LJ815, LJ821, LJ874, LJ879, LJ891, LJ893, LJ896, LJ919, LJ948, LJ955, LJ971, LK118, LK130, LK135, LK141, LK148, LK254, LK439, LK544, LK669
Market II: EF323, LJ235, LJ629, LJ815, LJ891, LJ896, LJ948, LJ955, LJ956, LJ971, LK118, LK130, LK135, LK148, LK153, LK241, LK428, LK439, LK544, LK669
Market III: EF267, EF318*, EF321, EF322, LJ239, LJ815, LJ829, LJ868*, LJ879, LJ893, LJ919, LJ948, LJ955, LK118, LK124, LK135, LK148, LK153, LK254, LK287, LK428, LK439, LK544
Market IV: 'NY-A' EF321, EH950, LJ239, LJ669, LJ874, LJ893, LJ956, LJ995, LK118, LK124, LK135, LK241, LK254, LK544, LK645
Market V: EE966, EF321, EH950, LJ874, LJ929, LJ955, LK284, LK428, LK439, LK544, LK645*
Market VII: EF321, EH966, LJ812, LJ815, LJ821, LJ829, LJ874, LJ891, LJ893*, LJ896, LJ919, LJ971, LK135, LK153

570 Squadron

Market I: EF298, EF306, LJ615, LJ616, LJ622, LJ645, LJ883, LJ913, LJ977, LJ985, LJ992, LJ994, LK117, LK136, LK138, LK140, LK199, LK555, LLK559, LK560 cr
Market II: BF464, EF298, EH897, LJ594*, LJ616, LJ620, LJ647, LJ883, LJ890, LJ913*, LJ944, LJ977, LJ985, LJ992, LJ994, LK117, LK121*, LK122, LLK126, LK136, LK138, LK140, LK190, LK555, LK559
Market III: BF464, EF292, EF298, EH897*, LJ616, LJ620, LJ645, LJ647*, LJ890, LJ944 cr, LJ992, LK117, LK122, LK126, LK136, LK140, LK199, LK559
Market IV: EF306 cr, LJ567, LJ576, LJ622, LJ883, LJ890, LJ977, LJ985, LJ991, LJ994, LJ996, LK136, LK138, LK140, LK190, LK199
Market V: EF298, LJ622, LJ677, LJ883, LJ890, LJ985, LJ991, LJ994, LK138, LK140, LK559
Market VII: EF298*, LJ620, LJ622, LJ645, LJ652, LJ883*, LJ977, LJ991*, LJ996 cr, LK117, LK120, LK140, LK191 cr, LK199

620 Squadron

Market I: EF237, EF293, EF303, LJ566, LJ580, LJ588, LJ847, LJ866, LJ872, LJ873, LJ875, LJ887, LJ917, LJ918, LJ930, LJ935, LJ946, LJ980, LK116, LK508
Market II: EF293, EF303, LJ566, LJ588, LJ847, LJ866, LJ871, LJ872, LJ873, LJ875, LJ892, LJ899, LJ917, LJ918, LJ921, LJ930, LJ935, LJ946, LJ970, LJ980, LK116, LK127
Market III: EF237, EF293, EF303, LJ566, LJ580, LJ588, LJ847, LJ865, LJ872, LJ873, LJ875, LJ892, LJ921, LJ930, LJ952, LJ970, LK508
Market IV: EF237, EF293, EF303, LJ548*, LJ588, LJ847, LJ865, LJ866, LJ872, LJ873, LJ875, LJ892, LJ918, LJ930, LJ954*, LJ970, LK127*, LK432, LK508
Market V: EF237, LJ580, LJ588, LJ830, LJ873, LJ892, LJ917, LJ946*, LJ952, LJ980, LK116
Market VII: EF237, LJ847*, LJ865, LJ871, LJ873*, LJ887, LJ930, LJ952, LJ970, LJ973, LK123, LK509

* = Failed to return
cr = crashed during the operation

The Squadron Form 541 for **190 Squadron** does not fully list the aircraft used by the squadron during operation *Market*. The Stirlings on strength during the operation were:

EE900, EE962, EF214, EF242, EF260 (FTR 21st), EF263 (FTR 19th), EF315, LJ563, LJ816 (damaged 22nd returned to strength 30th), LJ818, LJ820 of 1665 CU 'NY-A' (damaged in action 21st), LJ823 (FTR 21st), LJ825, LJ826, LJ829 (FTR 21st), LJ831 (belly landed Ghent 21st), LJ832, LJ833 (FTR 21st), LJ881 (FTR 21st), LJ895, LJ898, LJ899?, LJ916 (FTR 21st), LJ943 (FTR 21st), LJ982 (FTR 21st), LJ997, LK405, LK431, LK433 (damaged 21st), LK498 (FTR 21st), LK513

Stirling Glider Tug Mk IV on Strength (Establishment 26)

Sqn	15th	19th	20th	21st	22nd	24th	25th
190	32+4	17+6	22+13	16+18	12+13	15+11	13+15
196	36+1	11+24	8+25	15+14	27+5	27+7	25+6
295	27+6	9+22	7+18	14+6	17+5	10+8	10+7
299	36+3	11+26	17+17	19+14	25+3	27+6	27+6
570	29+7	9+15	4+22	11+14	12+12	11+9	11+8
620	29+7	17+19	24+12	20+13	17+10	16+10	16+10

Gliders on 38 Group strength

	15th		19th	
Hamilcar	84	4	56	8
Horsa	1,108	14	479	17

Chapter 20
Over the Rhine to Victory

FOLLOWING the Arnhem operation, 38 Group was rapidly rebuilt. To be ready for any future airborne assault the squadrons moved to East Anglia, such was the pace of the Allied ground advance. Therefore they occupied bases vacated by the US IXth AAF, 295 and 570 Squadrons to Rivenhall, 196 and 299 to Wethersfield (and later to Shepherd's Grove) leaving Great Dunmow to 190 and 620 Squadrons. Although low-level night supply drops for SOE were resumed, the squadrons' main tasks were to prepare for future airborne operations. Large-scale training glider towing exercises were flown between November 1944 and March 1945, impressive events to observe and experience, for the long trains of tugs and gliders flew quite low.

Stirling D4-Y in the snow at Great Dunmow circa Christmas 1944. (Noel Chaffey)

'Goofy II' EF446 8E-O at Rivenhall in 1945. (J Swale)

There was never any reason why the Stirling Mk IV should not carry bombs. Crews trained for that role at Wainfleet bombing range and Denghie Flats, bombing accuracy being aided by *Gee-H* and *Rebecca*, and soon learned that they were to fly night bombing operations in support of the Army but under 2 Group control.

The first operation was ordered for **21 January 1945.** 190 Squadron, led by Wg Cdr R H Bunker, sent four crews to Rees, each aircraft taking 11 x 500lb MC bombs plus incendiaries, though the more normal load was to be 24 x 500lb MCs. The Rees raid supported Allied forces in Belgium.

Conditions were clear over Britain when 620 Squadron set off the same night for Arsbeck, but soon after crossing the French coast the six crews progressed through 30 miles of towering cumulus to attack from between 7,000ft and 11,000ft. All agreed on one thing: it was a very cold night out, severe icing causing a lot of coring in the engine oil coolers.

When the Stirlings left their bases on **1 February** for another raid, a strong gale was blowing which, at the operational height, reached 75mph. Next night fog and low cloud at the target forced blind bombing of Arsbeck. As Flt Sgt W R Halford was taking off from Rivenhall on the **4th** for Grevenbroich, the aircraft swung violently and crashed. The crew quickly evacuated, getting clear before the bombs burst. On **7 February,** about 30 miles from the target, Fg Off D P J Torens of 196 Squadron spotted a German jet fighter. Crews of 299 and 570 Squadrons also saw it, but no attack developed. The purpose of their mission had been to bomb German troops, either in billets or as they moved through three towns.

On **21 February,** it was 196 and 299 Squadrons' turn to operate and Sqn Ldr Speir and Wg Cdr Baker failed to return. German night fighter activity had been reported and when Flt Lt Campbell arrived overhead at Shepherd's Grove around 2230 hrs, his aircraft – unbeknown to him – had been located by one of the now rare intruders over Britain, possibly an Me 410. As he lined up on final approach, the German pilot opened fire setting the Stirling ablaze. Campbell managed a satisfactory landing, the crew – apart from the rear gunner WO J McGovern – escaping from the burning wreck. The intruder then four times fired without success upon Flt Sgt Payne's aircraft flying over Shepherd's Grove. Payne was diverted to the safety of Foulsham.

One who flew these bombing operations in 1945 was I A Downie. Detailed for the bridge at Rees in 'I-Ivor' of 196 Squadron, he recalls that:

> The take-off, the first we had done with such a heavy load as 24 x 500lb bombs, was frightening in the extreme. After brakes were released the aircraft hardly seemed to move. I felt that its tyres were so compressed they were behaving like a wheelbarrow wheel being pushed through a muddy field. Everything was slower than usual, and the end of the runway was just under the nose as the needle crept to minimum speed for take-off. The controls also felt much heavier than usual.
>
> Tension built as we crossed into Belgium; and then we spotted flak, a single stream of tracer. The odd thing was that its arc remained unchanged, and we turned away. Had some *Oberleutnant* or gunner fallen asleep, his finger resting on a firing button? We shall never know, but I still wonder. Rees was completely covered in cloud, and why we dropped bombs on a field near the Rhine is probably intriguing a few aged residents even to this day.

Once the brief bombing interlude was over, 38 Group resumed SOE operations in earnest, particularly over Denmark. But by early March they were gearing up for the next great adventure: Operation *Varsity*, the crossing of the Rhine.

This Stirling of Matching's ORTU participated in operation Varsity carrying the operation assembly number '207'. (McCleod)

For about a month before this started, watchers in eastern England were treated to an impressive spectacle as lines of Stirlings towing Horsas participated in exercises which had intriguing names. Gradually the numbers involved increased, and so did the duration of the flights. By mid-March all was set for the final glider assault.

At each of three Stirling bases some sixty Horsas awaited their tugs with the task being to tow them to four LZs and to this pattern:

LZ 'A': 299 Sqn + 15 Horsas, 620 Sqn + 6 Horsas
LZ 'B': 196 Sqn + 2 Horsas, 299 Sqn + 15 Horsas, 620 Sqn + 2 Horsas
LZ 'P': 190 Sqn + 6 Horsas, 196 Sqn + 28 Horsas, 295 Sqn + 5 Horsas, 570 Sqn + 30 Horsas: 620 Sqn + 18 Horsas
LZ 'R': 190 Sqn + 2 Horsas, 196 Sqn + 14 Horsas

The effectiveness of British participation in the operation may be judged by the fact that 319 of the prepared 320 gliders set off, of which 237 were successfully released. Aborts totalled thirty-one, there were fourteen premature releases, seven broken tow ropes, flak claimed nineteen, nine were otherwise brought down and two landed away from LZs. Enemy fighters never approached the armada.

A summary of loads carried in the gliders showed that 190 Squadron was responsible for airlifting 318 troops, 196 Squadron was responsible for 89, 295 Squadron for 222, 299 Squadron for 103, 570 Squadron for 275 and 620 Squadron for 138 in addition to which many vehicles were carried in the gliders. Quite a high proportion of aircrew involved had served with 38 Group since early 1944 and were to achieve the longest tours of any. *Varsity* was a model of efficiency, as I A Downie found:

The crossing of the Rhine seemed to me the culmination of four and half years of preparation. Rumour on the airfield was that complete plans of the Rhine crossing operation were in German hands, and that we should prepare for massive resistance. Instead, the operation was magnificent. We had a front row view and an armchair comfort feeling of being on the winning side at last.

On the morning of **24 March,** 196 Squadron seemed tuned to give its maximum performance. Every Stirling that could flew that day. Gliders were parked on either side of the main runway, angled to preserve precious runway length, and there was little wind as we boarded 'E-Easy'. The sun started to light the scene, the air was clear, cloud slight and high, as we sat awaiting the signal to start engines. All was in such strange contrast to the danger, destruction, disaster and death that we were to effect that day.

I pressed the start buttons and my Hercules engines coughed and grumbled into life. The plane in front was only halfway down the runway when my throttles were fully open, and my bomb aimer, Lou Chevron, had clamped them tight. It seemed an age before I could feel the glider becoming airborne, but soon 'wheels up' was given. We circled, cutting the corner until we were in

8Z-E 'Thunderbird', Flt Lt Session's aircraft of 295 Squadron. ('Cherry' Cherrington)

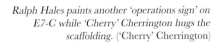

Ralph Hales paints another 'operations sign' on E7-C while 'Cherry' Cherrington hugs the scaffolding. ('Cherry' Cherrington)

Flt Lt W Pearson and crew with their 8Z-V of 295 Squadron. ('Cherry' Cherrington)

'Cherry' Cherrington adds nose art to LJ612 E7-L: 'L's A COMIN''

Varying motifs on LJ612 relate to glider, dagger (SOE sortie), anchor (ASR) and bomb.

formation, following the leaders to the south coast. It was only as we flew on that the realisation came to us of the immensity of the operation.

Our squadron was soon joined from port and starboard by others knitting into a fast expanding stream. Altitude was low, somewhere near 1,800ft, and the stream soon stretched to the horizon. Halfway across France dots appeared on the port side - aircraft returning from the Rhine. It was an amazing sight, overshadowing all the Westerns I had seen.

We crossed the Rhine, and map reading became more intensive as the bomb aimer and navigator kept us exactly on course. I had already worked out my tactics for getting out of what might be a tricky situation. We released the glider at 500ft which seemed extremely dangerous in view of ack-ack fire from small arms on the ground. Then I went into a climbing turn for home, viewing the continuous stream of more aircraft arriving. We were halfway back across France before we passed its ending. Over the Channel we dropped our towrope, the Scottish member of the crew considering that to be a great waste and reckoning a farmer or fisherman would have benefited front it.

John Graf also has memories of **24 March 1945** which he recalls was:

A beautiful day when the air was fresh and clear, the sky was a bright blue and there was very little cloud. The stream of tugs and their matchboxes (gliders) stretched two-by-two like animals heading for the 'Ark' as far ahead as the eye could see – and the tail gunner reported a similar view astern. The Press later reported a stream 200 miles long.

We were flying Stirling, 7T L powered by Hercules XVI engines in which fuel/air mixture regulation was achieved automatically by reference to throttle setting. At +2lb boost per square inch economical cruising was obtained. The setting +6lb boost per square inch (rated boost) provided climbing conditions or, for a limited period of combat flying conditions. Intermediate settings, ie. between +2 and +6, were prohibited for they would have brought rich mixture jets into operation adversely affecting the engines and playing havoc with fuel consumption and reduced flight endurance.

Stirling 7T L had seen more youthful days and towed with rather less zest than many

LJ890 8E-L tows a Horsa out of Rivenhall.
('Cherry' Cherrington)

*Flt Lt Hudson's crew with LK150 V8-H of 570
Squadron.* ('Cherry' Cherrington)

*LK199 V8-L with pilot Flt Lt Brierley and crew
alongside.* ('Cherry' Cherrington)

*LJ995 8Z-H 'The Bushwacker' of 295 Squadron
crashed when taking off from Rivenhall on 4
February 1945 and carrying 24 x 500lb HEs.*
('Cherry' Cherrington)

other aircraft of its type. At maximum permitted cruising boost (+2lb) 7T L was able to maintain station in the stream, but it could not maintain briefed altitude – except by steadily dropping astern. In the event I settled for maintaining station by a succession of very large 'hops' – +2lb cruising boost and putting the aircraft in a gentle dive to keep the airspeed up to that of other aircraft.

When we had lost about 1,000ft, throttles were advanced to +6lb climbing boost, we climbed back to a couple of hundred feet above our station in the stream, and we then started the process over again. The glider pilot and his companions must have wearied of our antics, yet in this unorthodox fashion we maintained our position and time keeping until our final run in to the release for the landing zone on the far side of the Rhine. Over the intercom wired through the tow rope we wished our glider crew well, and they released, on time. By then the ground below was strewn with gliders and at low altitude the air seemed full of gliders losing height and jockeying on to their individual approaches to what they had selected as their landing spaces. Above, the air was full of tugs now lightened of their loads banking and turning away trailing empty tow ropes.

I was not aware of AA fire, but as we settled on to our return course I noted against the sunlight, and still some distance away, a formation of three single-engined fighters swiftly approaching us head-on. This view concentrated the attention wonderfully until at closer range they could be seen to be friendly Mustangs.

We landed back at base 5 hours 35 minutes after take-off. Marshalled nose to tail around the perimeter track, all the aircraft were subjected to close external scrutiny by engineering officers, flight sergeants and ground crews. When cleared as undamaged the aircraft were positioned for a re-supply operation which was not needed.

To the best of my recollection 196 Squadron lost only one aircraft on the Rhine crossing hit by flak, and which was safely crash-landed close to the Rhine by the Australian Flight Lieutenant pilot. One member of the crew – the wireless operator I think – was badly wounded, but happily he survived and some months later and back in the UK was moving around again rather well. The rest of the crew were uninjured.

For operation *Varsity*, Stirling squadrons are known to have fielded the following aircraft:

190 Squadron, Great Dunmow: EE962-D, EF242-Q, EF264-Z, EF273-C, EF316-L, LJ271-P, LJ276-Y, LJ281-R, LJ653-C, LJ818-X, LJ826-J, LJ832-U, LJ895-K, LJ898-M, LJ930-A (Wg Cdr R H Bunker), LJ997-T, LK196-B, LK227-A, LK275-V, LK336-Q, LK431-F, LK433-E, LK566-G, LK889-N, LK336-Q, LK275-V, TS265-O

196 Squadron, Shepherd's Grove: EF276, EF309, EF318, EF392, LJ583, LJ643, LJ835, LJ838, LJ876, LJ888, LJ923, LJ926, LJ931, LJ979, LJ998, LK128, LK146, LK147, LK152, LK193, LK197, LK201, LK205, LK256, LK302, LK320, LK345, LK362, LK389

295 Squadron, Rivenhall: EF446, LJ575 (570 Sqn), LJ576, LJ652, LJ890, LJ922, LJ929, LJ950, LJ951, LJ976, LK120, LK122, LK129, LK132, LK136, LK144, LK287, LK288, LK290, LK346, LK351, LK355, LK513, LK543, LK553, LK558, PK226, '246' and '495'

299 Squadron, Shepherd's Grove: EF237-X9:N, EF272-5G:N, EF323-5G:F, EH950-5G:D, LJ629-X9:B, LJ821-5G:G, LJ844-5G:E, LJ874-5G:I, LJ893-X9:J, LJ942-X9:I, LJ955-X9:K, LJ956-X9:D, LJ971-X9:0, LK118-X9:G, LK124-5G:B, LK130-5G:H, LK135-X9:A, LK148-X9:E, LK239-X9:C, LK254-5G:A, LK282-5G:K, LK284-X9:H, LK331-X9:R, LK332-5G:R, LK428-5G:J, LK509-5G:C, PK225-5G:Q, PK235-5G:S, PW403-X9:Q

570 Squadron, Rivenhall: LJ596-V8:K, LJ612-E7:L, LJ615-V8:P, LJ616-V8-D, LJ620-E7:0, LJ622-V8:M, LJ640-V8:B, LJ645-E7:M, LJ650-E7:W, LJ992-V8:N, LK150-V8:H, LK154-E7:P, LK156-V8:I, LK190-V8:J, LK199-V8-L, LK202-E7:X, LK280-V8:F, LK286-E7:T, LK289-V8:G, LK291-V8:A, LK292-E7:V, LK549-E7:J, LK555-E7:S, LK559-V8:Q, LK636-E7:N

620 Squadron, Great Dunmow: EF277, EF303, LJ554, LJ588, LJ627, LJ847, LJ865, LJ866, LJ887, LJ899, LJ921, LJ932, LJ935, LJ948, LJ952, LJ973, LJ977, LJ980, LJ983, LJ977, LK117, LK123, LK134, LK250, LK294, LK296, LK304, LK410, LK432 and one not known

Operational Refresher Training Unit, Matching: fifteen Stirlings (identities uncertain) operated from here. Some may have been on detachment from 1665 Conversion Unit, and each one towed a Horsa.

As soon as *Varsity* was over, the round of SOE operations was resumed with flights to Scandinavia. These extended through **April.** An interesting and little known action in which 38 Group took part was operation *Amherst*, a paratroop invasion of north-east Holland in which 690 troops of 2nd SAS Brigade were dropped. Their purpose was to capture bridges to aid the armoured spearhead of 2nd Canadian Division. Within the airlift force were eight Stirlings of 570 Squadron, each taking fifteen paratroops and four containers, and which were to be dropped south of Groningen from heights of between 800ft and 1,500ft depending upon cloud conditions, or if necessary dropped after location of the DZ using *Gee* fixes. All eight proceeded singly, flying at 2,000ft to 3,000ft and being routed over recaptured territory. Eventually, the troops jumped from 1,000ft into dense stratus. This was the first occasion that paratroops were dropped blind on exercise, or operations, by 38 Group.

Almost to the close of hostilities, the work of contacting the Resistance continued. The workload for 38 Group increased, for the Stirlings ferried mail, supplies and petrol to forces on the Continent. On 5 May, 299 Squadron took troops in nineteen Stirlings to Copenhagen, then came the carriage of others to Oslo and Stavanger.

Bomb craters and rough airfields like Rheine claimed Stirlings like QS-E, ferrying supplies and sometimes fuel in support of advancing Allied forces.

LK286 E7-T crashed at Rivenhall on 2 April 1945. The crash was caused by a burst tyre. ('Cherry' Cherrington)

A Mk IV of 620 Squadron, Great Dunmow, prepares to convey twelve troops of 1st Airborne Division, two motorbikes and six containers to Gardemoen, Norway, on 11 May 1945. (Noel Chaffey)

Stirlings assembled at Rivenhall – a typical temporary wartime airfield – preparing for the airlift to Norway. ('Cherry' Cherrington)

Flying to Norway was often hazardous due to extremes and sudden changes in weather conditions. Between 2 November 1944 and 14 February 1945 alone, seventeen Stirlings failed to return from SOE sorties despatched to Norway, of which at least seven were shot down by German fighters. LK171 of 295 Squadron flown by Gp Capt Surplice was despatched to make a drop to Resistance forces at DZ252 Lake Ekksund and so severe was the weather that after aborting the mission carburettors of all four engines froze over. As the aircraft lost height, six of the crew baled out. Surplice, unable to do so, was killed when the aircraft crashed at Kalvhold Telemark.

To prevent German forces continuing the fight in Norway, operation *Domesday* was mounted in **May 1945.** Its plan involved the use of twenty-five Stirlings to airlift 1st Airborne Division to Gardermoen. Movement began on **10 May 1945** using Stirlings of 190 Squadron which, as they crossed the North Sea, entered bad weather associated with a front. As a result only fifteen aircraft landed in Norway. The other nine turned about for Britain – except for two which crashed. Aboard one of those, LK566 flown by Sqn Ldr Robertson, was Air Vice-Marshal Scarlett-Streatfield, AOC 38 Group, who was killed along with all the others when the Stirling crashed at sea. A third Stirling also crashed during the deployment whose need was reduced when German forces in Norway surrendered. On **29 May,** 299 Squadron carried much needed nursing staff and blankets from East Fortune to Norway; and soon was engaged in daily mail runs to Italy and the Middle East.

Repatriation of prisoners of war was also under way. John Graf recalls:

The Stirling Mk IV carried out the transport role with some success, taking up to twenty-four fully armed troops, though admittedly in little comfort. On one occasion we brought back from Prague to Crosby thirty-nine children and six adults, all Jewish ex-inmates of concentration camps. About this time some primitive seating was installed in the rear fuselage of the Mk IV – a row of tubular frames with canvas seats and backs along each side of the fuselage facing inboard.

Restricted entrance to the box-like rear fuselage made loading difficult, and only limited cargo lifts were possible. A notable exception to this had been the ferrying of jerry cans carrying 100-octane fuel to forward airfields. Since the load was concentrated in the rear fuselage the cg shifted making take-off and landing more difficult. Destination airfields were liberally cratered, which meant that this detail was not entirely popular with Stirling crews.

A proposed move of 38 Group to the Far East never came about. Instead, its Stirlings performed a multitude of transport tasks within Europe and around its perimeter. Replacement troops were flown to captured territories to relieve those who had seen battle. Mail and newspaper runs were made to Cairo, and stores were transported to such places as Castel Benito, Libya, as well as to Italy and India. Often, such flights set off from Lyneham, and were frequently routed through St Mawgan.

The closing months of the war saw the Halifax taking a greater part in such operations, two Stirling squadrons re-equipping with them soon after hostilities in Europe ceased.

Post-war Stirlings usually wore white identity letters, like LK304 D4-W seen here.

Bold under-wing white serial numbers were featured post-war on Mk IVs, like 299 Squadron's PW443 5G-Q pictured refuelling at Shaibah in September 1945.

LK554 X9-M at El Adem in October 1945 has a completely unpainted transparent nose.

January 1946 brought the end for the Stirling in 38 Group when the squadrons disbanded. Demobilisation had played havoc with squadron air and groundcrew strength, and in January 1946 many Stirling transports retired to 23 MU Aldergrove or the MU at Polebrook there to await demise. Those remaining were struck off charge soon after the widespread aircraft census of 21 June 1947.

General transport duties post-war took the Mk IVs throughout Europe. LK146 ZO-F is seen here at Templehof.
(J P Holden)

PK237 – the 1,000th Belfast-built Stirling. Propeller spinners and engine cooling fans mean that it is suited to tropical service. (Shorts)

Chapter 21
Passenger and Freight

O N the day prior to the Arnhem operation two strange-looking Stirlings wearing the overseas colour scheme of grey, green and blue joined the RAF at 13 MU Aldergrove. These were the first two production Mk Vs, PJ878 and PJ879. Devoid of turrets and with streamlined noses, they were not only the ultimate outcome of plans for the 'C' Stirling, but also embodied Short's hopes for a peacetime civilian Stirling transport.

Designed to Specification C.18/43 for a long-range, passenger-cum-freight transport to serve Empire routes, its crew numbered five, and as many as forty passengers could, theoretically, be carried. Alternatively, twenty paratroops, twelve stretchers or fourteen sitting cases seated aft of the main spar could be accommodated (Initially, Shorts had envisaged a completely new aircraft based upon the Super Stirling). Two such prototypes were contracted for in September 1943 as RG336 and RG341 news of which produced much excitement in Shorts factories. At Sebro Bourn where repaired Stirlings were test flown, rumours of the 'Silver Super Stirling' and even a six-engined sister-ship to the Shetland flying-boat greatly boosted morale. Eventually the Short C.18/43 emerged as a far less ambitious machine – just a modified Stirling the prototype of which, LJ530, was a converted Mk III airframe.

John Graf recalls that:

> The Stirling Mk V had a cargo door 9ft 6in x 5ft 1in on the starboard rear side hinged at the bottom so that it opened to form a ramp. Bulkier loads could now be taken into the rear fuselage while loading through the elongated nose hinged at the top was afforded by using a fitted beam block and tackle. Thus, balanced loading could be achieved, and cargo stabilised to within acceptable limits although the arithmetical calculations could be quite critical.
>
> It was a reasonable aircraft to fly, the additional weight of the nose and fuselage loading

Production Mk Vs were finished in Dark Slate Grey and Extra Dark Sea Grey and had Azure Blue under surfaces.

LJ530, the prototype Stirling V passenger/freight aircraft, had side loading doors and a vertically opening nose into which the aircraft's tackle could lift loads. (Shorts)

doors being offset by turret elimination. Bomb aimers, now redundant, were replaced by second pilots – often without much Stirling experience, and to the consternation of all.

The aircraft retained its hereditary characteristics, with the pronounced desire to swing to the right on take-off remaining, likewise the prospect of a tricky landing. It remained light on the controls and, when shorn of camouflage paint, cruised along unladen, economically, at about 185mph to 190mph IAS.

All 160 Mk Vs were powered by Hercules Mk XVIs, and the lengthened nose increased further the disproportionate overall length, in comparison with the wing span, to 90ft 6 3/4in. Empty weight was 43,500lb, and the all-up weight remained 70,000lb. In round figures the performance of the Mk V included a maximum speed of 280mph at 6,000ft, a normal load range of up to 3,000 miles and a service ceiling of 18,000ft.

High hopes were pinned upon PJ958 the so-called 'Silver Stirling'. Expected record runs promoting it for civilian purposes never took place.

Shorts prepared the S.37, commonly called the 'Silver Stirling', as its civilian counterpart. Fully furnished and sound proofed, it was fitted out for thirty passengers, and PJ958 was converted into the prototype. Short's hopes for a BOAC order were dashed when the Halifax quickly established itself as a transport with an advantageous belly pannier. Nevertheless, a dozen Stirling Mk Vs converted for civilian use by Airtech, Thame, in 1947 were sold to Trans Air of Belgium and became 00-XAK to 00-XAV. The charter company used them on routes to the Far East, with Singapore, Hong Kong and Shanghai featuring on itineraries.

Ten Stirling Mk Vs were in RAF hands before 1944 ended, at which time an effective transport force linking the UK with India and SE Asia was being devised. 46 Squadron, commanded by Wg Cdr B A Coventry, equipped with Mk Vs in January and February 1945. Training flights to Maison Blanche in North Africa started on 17 February and the first route flights were undertaken using PJ912 and PJ913 on the 27th. Also at Stoney

Mk V OO-XAK (ex-PK136) of Belgian operator
Trans-Air. Six of them supposedly joined the
Egyptian Air Force then acquired guns poked from
side windows.

OO-XAS at Blackbushe. (R Staton)

Another Belgian Mk V OO-XAV photographed at
Blackbushe. (Author)

Cross was 242 Squadron under Wg Cdr H Burton. They began flying Stirling Mk Vs in
February 1945. Nearly all the crews for the Mk Vs were drawn from Bomber Command.

During March 1945 the first flights to Mauripur were made, and on 3 March, No 46
Squadron flew its first route service destination Castel Benito. From 1 April the squadron
began despatching services to India on alternate days and terminating at Arkonam (via
Poona) or Dum Dum (via Palam).

Abruptly, and with their training largely completed, 242 Squadron was ordered to
re-equip with Avro Yorks, fifteen of which would replace twenty-five Stirlings. The York
with a civilian future also needed service evaluation for the Far East run. It provided far
more comfort than the Stirling, but York production rates did not allow re-equipment of
all squadrons so 46 Squadron continued using Stirling Vs.

By the end of April 1945 three Stirlings had made the return trip to India usually
carrying seventeen passengers. On 27 April new route schedules came in for the Dum
Dum run, laying down arrival and departure times in airline style. A freight service had

A considerable number of Mk Vs served in aluminium finish with PK143 KA-W of 242 Squadron among
them. Later it carried under wing serial numbers.

already been introduced. The flights were certainly not without moments of alarm. PJ901, flown by Fg Off Kczvajer, made the first run to Arkonam and on taking off from Mauripur on 9 April the old bogey of take-off swing seized the aircraft which crashed and resulted in a seriously damaged rear fuselage.

During May 1945 twenty-one Stirlings left Stoney Cross on scheduled flights. One encountered a lightning strike; another had its plastic nose smashed in flight by a vulture. Flt Lt Frowde was caught in a tropical hailstorm which smashed the astro hatch and cockpit Perspex, and badly dented tail leading edges. Stirlings, twelve of which by the end of the month had completed the return trip, took about eighty hours to make the journey without plug changes, though oil coolers needed careful control.

On 19 May 1945, Wg Cdr Coventry flew PJ944 to Belfast for experimental stripping of paint. The result proving acceptable, others followed and as a result the majority of Mk Vs in squadron hands flew in bare metal finish. It is believed that a few were painted white overall, possibly at Pocklington, the Mk V modification centre, in order to reduce cabin temperature.

As soon as the war in Europe ended 4 Group, Bomber Command, was disbanded, some of its squadrons being switched at once to Transport Command. Among them were 51 and 158 Squadrons, both earmarked for Stirling Mk Vs.

On 7 June 1945, plans were circulated from Air Ministry outlining a vast increase in the size of Transport Command whose role in the Far East war was of vital importance. In Europe the Command would also have a heavy workload as it helped to bring same semblance of normality to the chaotic state of the Continent. Additionally, with the European war over, many Commonwealth troops needed to be taken home and British prisoners of war repatriated. A quick decision was made to convert Coastal Command Liberators, and some Liberator bombers from overseas, into home-based transports to rapidly expand the transport force. Tempsford, from where SOE drops had taken place, housed the Transport Aircraft Modification Unit (TAMU), whose task was to modify Liberators at the rate of fifteen a month.

By June that task was under way, while by 11 June Stirling Vs were operating a twelve-day service to India with some flights also returning from Ratmalana. A lot of freight was lifted, but delays were occurring mainly because of engine trouble. Using Stoney Cross as their usual UK starting point, the Stirling Vs established a regular passenger and freight run to Castel Benito and thence to Lydda – Shaibah – Mauripur – Dum Dum, and sometimes flew on to St Thomas's Mount when outbound and before starting back from Dum Dum. Freight loads were averaging about 5,290lb.

PK124s nose identity letters 'JQ' identify it as a 51 Squadron example. (Imperial War Museum)

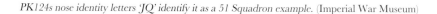

Eight Stirling Vs were delivered to 51 Squadron at the start of June and flying training began while route flying by 46 Squadron entered a settled phase unfortunately punctuated with incidents. Fg Off W Walton took off on Freight Flight SYF41 in PJ981 on 1 June bound for St Thomas's Mount via El Aqir, Castel Benito, Lydda and Shaibah. He proceeded first to El Aqir, and after two days left for Castel Benito, where an engine change took five days. After leaving Shaibah, and as he levelled out at 10,000ft, an unusual noise was heard from the port side. It seemed to be caused by a piece of metal, and a port engine was feathered.

He returned to Shaibah, and after setting out again a starboard engine gave trouble. With the aircraft unable to maintain height, freight had to be jettisoned. Then the starboard inner engine began to overheat and although the aircraft lost height to 200ft they scraped into Shaibah once more. On landing, and after running 200 yards, the port undercarriage leg collapsed; nevertheless the crew escaped unscathed. On the same day 158 Squadron began flying training on Stirling Mk Vs.

By the end of June, two crews of 51 Squadron had converted to Mk Vs, and nineteen aircraft were on strength. Scheduled flights were currently being made to Dum Dum, St. Thomas's Mount and Ratmalana, along with shuttle runs between Cairo and Mauripur – all by 46 Squadron. Most flights now began at Lyneham, and there was still much engine trouble on the routes.

Suddenly, all the Yorks were withdrawn from 242 Squadron which reverted to using Stirling Vs. Training flights were resumed, while 46 Squadron now flew to the Middle East and North Africa as well as operating the India trunk route. On 16 July, 51 Squadron despatched their first overseas training flight, to Castel Benito, and by the end of the month they were route flying to India.

Although 242 Squadron had been ordered to convert to Yorks they had continued limited Stirling flying so, when the Yorks were withdrawn, were able to function operationally. By August they, too, were generating scheduled flights to India, and began a service to the Azores on 19 August 1945. The squadron's training programme included twelve days of ground school and twenty hours of conversion flying, after which came a 'screened' flight to India.

Quite unexpectedly, and to the squadron's dismay, they began to receive Stirling Mk IVs, quite unsuited to route flying, and with poor cargo capacity. Attempts to load these aircraft resulted in some alarming moments if the load was not well distributed, but they were able to carry passengers, albeit in discomfort. Understandably, 242 Squadron wanted Yorks back – and so did their customers!

That rapid expansion of Transport Command was achieved by not only switching ex-4 Group Halifax squadrons onto its books, but also by increasing aircraft UE to thirty and posting in personnel to handle it. That change became effective for 51 and 158 Squadrons on 1 July 1945. Nos 46 and 242 would have to wait until September.

Not only did squadrons change roles and bases, stations changed to other Group control. At noon on 1 August 1945, 47 Group took over Stradishall from 3 Group as a home for 51 and 158 Squadrons and Stirlings thereby returned to one of their long-time homes.

51 Squadron commenced route flying to the Middle East on 1 October as PK115 and PJ953 left for Mauripur. On the same day the squadron started to lift a large number of troops from Brussels to India. October brought to Transport Command a quite mammoth task, operation *Sketch*, the movement of 10,000 troops of 52 Division to the Middle East. Undertaken between the 15th and 24th, they were conveyed from Britain over the next seven days, then 10,000 Indians were flown from Shallufa to Arkonam which allowed the return to the UK of a similar number of troops. To enable this mammoth airlift to be achieved six squadrons of Liberators, two of Dakotas and 51 and 158 Stirling Squadrons were employed, along with 295 Squadron of 38 Group.

The Stradishall squadrons operated the regular LTS service from their home base to Melsbroek – Castel Benito – Shallufa – Lydda – Shaibah – Mauripur – Arkonam – Mauripur and home in reverse route. 295 Squadron flew only from its base to Brussels – Castel Benito – Shallufa and back. Stirling Vs each carried up to twenty-four troops and 500lb of freight, the Mk IVs only twenty troops, and slip crews took over flying at Castel Benito.

Another troop deployment, operation *Annexe*, took place in November. During that period a major accident befell PJ950. Captained by Flt Lt C R Wilson and carrying twenty-two passengers, the aircraft had taken off from Castel Benito shortly after midnight on 11 November. It was believed to have collided – for reasons unknown – with the lead-out funnel lighting on this cloudy, dark night. Apparently, it attained 200ft before crashing in line with the runway. All aboard were killed except for three passengers, two of whom later died in hospital.

A bad accident also occurred at Lyneham on 23 November. Flt Lt Gray arrived overhead late in the afternoon and lined up for a GCA landing. He apparently came in on a wrong heading and his aircraft careered into the control block and civilian canteen. Miraculously, none of the crew was injured in the resulting fire, but two others were killed and three seriously injured.

Some crews from 242 Squadron were now switched to 46 which, at the end of November 1945, held thirty Stirlings. Most flights were now terminating in the Middle East. On 1 November 1945, 51 and 158 Squadrons were placed under 48 Group control as strategic mobility squadrons but for a short time only.

Serial numbers on camouflaged Mk Vs were Dull Red, as on PJ996 DK-H (nose identity O-H) photographed at Delhi in 1945.

Trooping using Stirling Vs of 51 and 158 Squadrons ceased on 3 December 1945, as a result of Transport Command Operations Instruction 86/1945 ordering all Stirlings to be withdrawn from trooping on that date. By January 1946 a number of crews of 158 (reduced to a number-only basis on 1 January 1946) had been posted to 51 Squadron which was revitalised on 16 January 1946, when it received its first Avro York. By the end of February the squadron held twelve examples, and in April its Stirling Vs were allotted away, the last languishing long at Istres and needing major attention.

Mk V PK144 ZO-F of 196 Squadron. (M D Stimson)

196 Squadron had a brief flirtation with Mk Vs early in 1946, but it was 46 which was the last squadron to fly them. Such activity ceased in March 1945, by which time Yorks had taken over services to India.

Two other users of the Mk V deserving mention are 1588 and 1589 Heavy Freight Flights. Their tasks were vitally important on the Indian trunk-route, for they were

Nose letters ORT-C identify this Mk V PK151 as belonging to 1588 Heavy Freight Flight.

Among the many that ended life at 273 MU Polebrook was KY-W.

Only disappointment has rewarded those trying to retrieve a Stirling. One of the most intact was BF523 which crashed in the IJsselmeer on 13/14 May 1943. Wreckage recovery by the Royal Netherlands Air Force revealed power plants. Among that team pictured here is Gerrit Zwanenburg (standing) who, in the 1960s, pioneered 'aviation archaeology'.
(G J Zwanenburg)

It is unlikely that an intact Stirling will ever be seen again. This tail chassis with healthy tyres was discovered among the remains on BF523.
(G J Zwanenburg)

employed to carry components to stations along the line anywhere along the line where transport aircraft needed them. 1588 Flight operated between the Middle East and India, and 1589 between Britain and the Middle East.

One particularly unpleasant accident befell Fg Off Owen in PJ947 as he took off from Lydda on 27 October 1945. The inevitable swing overtook the Stirling, which rammed itself into Anson SU-ACX of the Egyptian airline *Misr*, causing fatal casualties. These two flights were small, each holding five Stirlings, but 1588 Flight has a special place in the Stirling story, for it was the last front line and operational RAF unit to fly them.

On 17 July 1946, a signal was sent to Santa Cruz ordering that no more maintenance was to be undertaken on the Stirlings of 1588 Flight, which were to be immediately struck off charge. Theirs were not the last Stirlings in RAF hands. That distinction probably fell to a Mk V in storage at Polebrook.

One of the great characters from Stirling days, Group Captain Hamish Mahaddie DSO DFC AFC, first President of the Stirling Association.

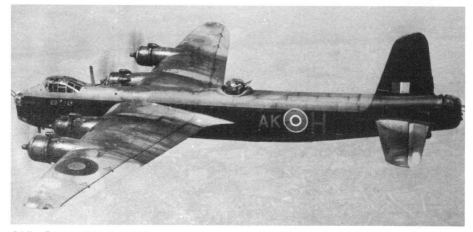

Stirling R9144 AK-H of 1657 Conversion Unit manned by Sqn Ldr Elliott and crew flying over London on 17 July 1943, possibly during a daylight 'Bullseye' to train defence forces.
(Sqn Ldr R B Spear DFC, RNZAF via Jock Whitehouse)

Three Stirlings (AK-V, AK-T and AK-N) of No 1657 Conversion Unit. Each is fitted with an H2S radome because the unit was already training crews for Lancaster as well as Stirling squadrons.
(Sqn Ldr R B Spear DFC, RNZAF via Jock Whitehouse)

Stirling Mk IIIs BF527 AK-B andLK508 AK-S of No 1657 Conversion Unit (variously known as No 1657 Heavy Conversion Unit or 1657 CU(H)). Both feature H2S radomes.
(Sqn Ldr R B Spear DFC, RNZAF via Jock Whitehouse)

Aerial view of No 1657 Conversion Unit Stradishall on 21 March 1944 showing thirteen Stirlings. Smoke had been released to direct attention to a change of active runway. Relatively few Stirling squadrons and units were based at Permanent RAF stations. (Plt Off Earl Bedford RCAF via Jock Whitehouse)

Stirling III R9145 BU-K served with No 214 Squadron at both Stradishall and Chedburgh in 1942-1943. After twenty-eight operations it was shot down on 2 March 1943 during a raid on Kiel. (Photograph by Bob Hook, only survivor, via Jock Whitehouse)

Appendix 1

Performance Graphs

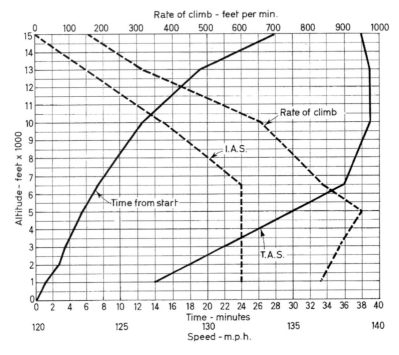

1.   A&AEE performance finding for Mk I, N3635 (Hercules II) with take-off weight of 57,400lb.

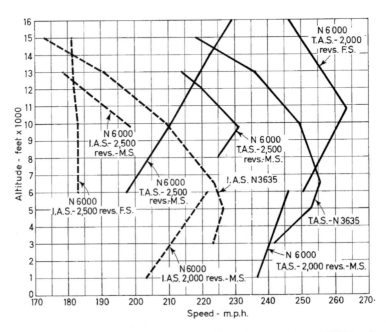

2.   Maximum speeds recorded by A&AEE using Mk I, N6000, fitted with dorsal FN 7 and ventral turrets with take-off weight of 70,000lb.

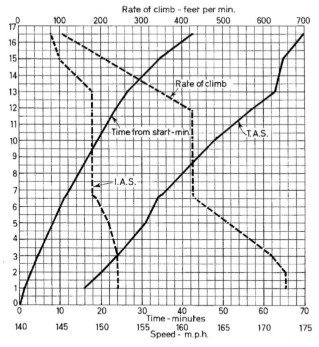

3. Performance characteristics of Mk I (Hercules XI) without dorsal turret with take-off weight of 70,000lb.

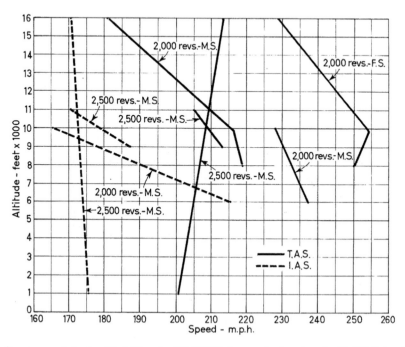

4. Speeds recorded using Mk I (Hercules XI) N3662, first production aircraft with FN 7 dorsal turret and take-off weight 70,000lb.

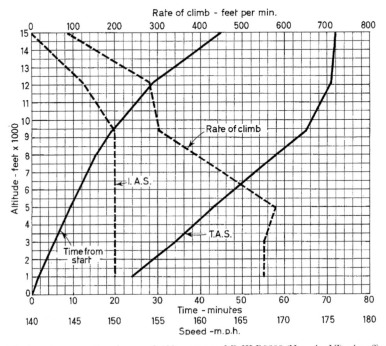

5. Climb performance at engine revs 2,400, prototype Mk III R9309 (Hercules VI) take-off weight 70,000lb.

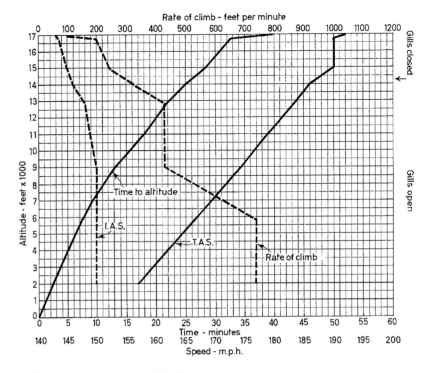

6. Climb performance of second Mk III.

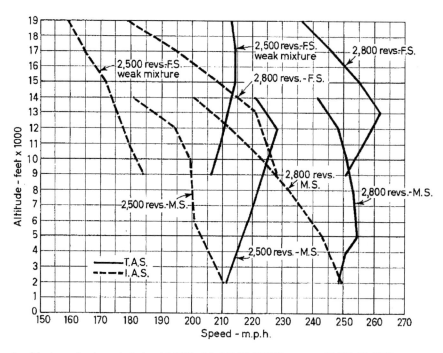

7.   Maximum level speeds during A&AEE trials, Mk III BK649, mean at 60,000–70,000lb.

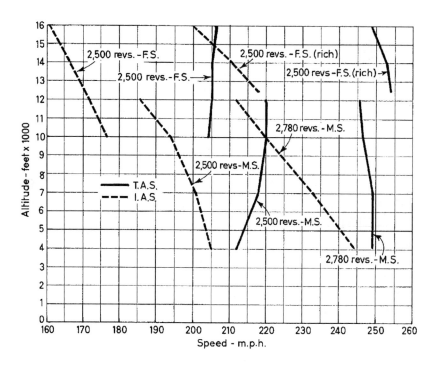

8.   A&AEE performance recorded using second production Mk III, BK761 (Hercules VI). Fitted
     with FN 5A, FN 50A dorsal and FN 20A tail turrets, take-off weight 70,000lb.

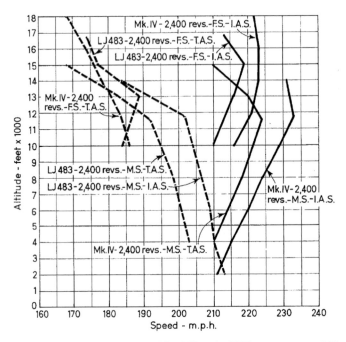

9. A&AEE level speeds recorded using Mk IV LJ483 (Hercules XVI), turrets removed/faired over. Take-off weight 70,000lb.

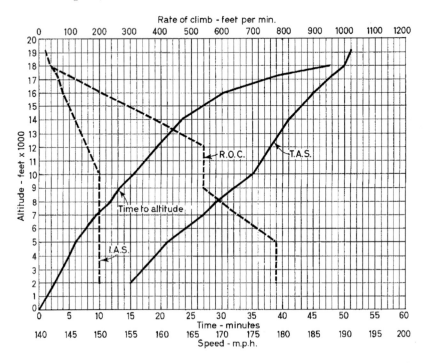

10. A&AEE trials using production Mk IV with turrets removed and faired over, engine cowling gills open, at 2,400 revs and 70,000lb take-off weight.

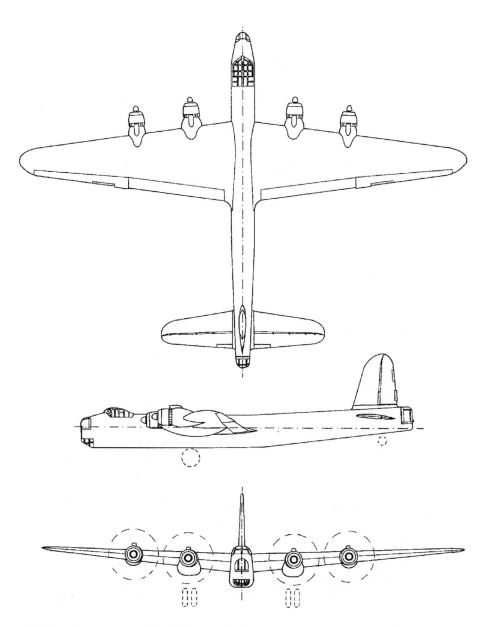

11. General arrangement, Short S.36 to Specification B.8/41. Mainplane related to the Shetland
    flying-boat.
No performance figures were ever recorded as this 'the Super Stirling' was cancelled.

Appendix 2
Production Graphs

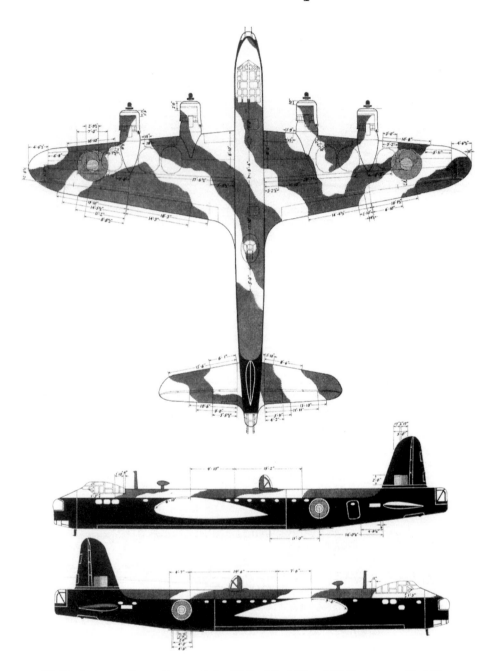

12. Standard camouflage pattern applied to Stirling Mks I, III and IV. Shaded areas Dark Green, clear areas Dark Earth; solid areas Night (black), the latter being ultra-matt in finish at the start of 1941. Roundels were standard – no evidence of white ever being painted over black. Serial numbers Dull Red.

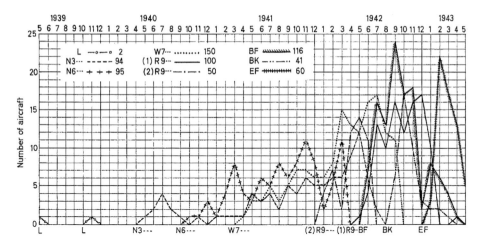

13. Monthly production deliveries, Mk I.

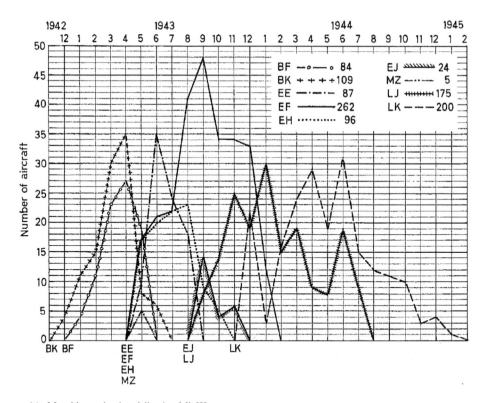

14. Monthly production deliveries, Mk III.

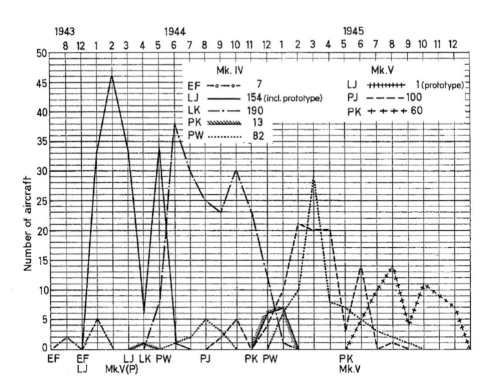

15. Monthly production deliveries, Mks IV and V. Not included are Mk III conversions to Mk IV.

Appendix 3
Loss and Accident Graphs

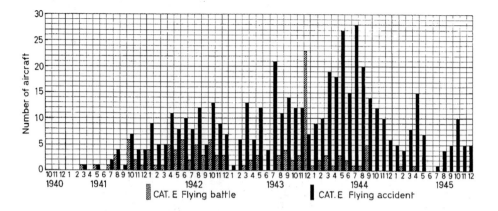

16. Monthly flying accidents involving Stirlings. Interesting are the summer peaks and the steady increase and fall related to the increased number of aircraft in use.

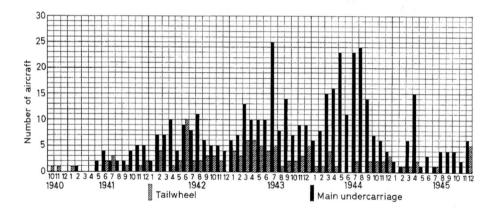

17. Accidents to Stirling bombers attributed to main undercarriage and tailwheel assembly problems during take-offs and landings.

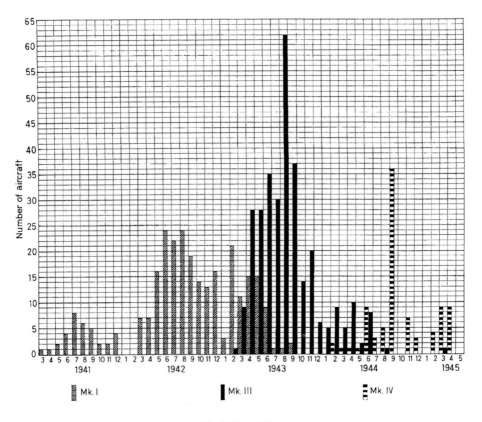

18. Monthly losses during operations, Mks I, III and IV.

Appendix 4
Primary Weapons

The Stirling was designed to carry 250lb and 500lb General Purpose (GP) and 2,000lb Armour Piercing (AP) bombs, weight being the gross of bomb and content. General-purpose bombs of 1920s design failed to equal the performance of such bombers, and APs were unsuitable for use by low-ceiling aircraft. Most effective was the 1934-designed 4lb incendiary, container carried, but not envisaged for the B.12/36.

Bombs have four main features – case, charge, fuse and tail. Much of the explosive force of the charge hurls shrapnel for destructive purposes. Mixing sharp, heavy metal chunks with blast effect caused by the explosion and ensuing implosion as moving air quickly returns to fill the vacuum created by the explosion resulting in two rapid damage phases. Thicker casing is featured by penetration weapons whereas thinner casing, blown apart easily, produces more blast damage and less shrapnel effect. Such weapons are susceptible to breaking up on impact and malfunction.

The fuse striking the detonator on impact sets off the explosive which, in 1941, was usually Amatol. A retarder could be fitted between the detonator cap and its filling to delay action. To improve an explosion certainty many wartime bombs could carry both nose and tail fuses effecting more reliability. Fuses could take account of needs for buried, surface or above ground bursting.

To stabilise a falling bomb, a tail is usually fastened to the charge case, tails in wartime often being packed separately for transit. Assembly demanded that they were securely attached to the bomb's case. High altitude release often meant stability loss resulting in reduced accuracy.

It was largely with 500lb GPs supplemented from **March 1941** by the 1,000lb version, that the Stirling began operations. During 1941 the GP family included the 1,900lb (sometimes called 2,000lb) varieties relying upon case weight for maximum penetration. Curvaceous and quite elegant-looking – if such a term could be applied to a bomb – their ballistics were not good. Indeed, there were many instances when their fuses were torn away in flight and elaborate tails easily damaged. Many did not explode, and they comprised too much metal encasing too little explosive, a one-third charge/weight ratio. By late 1941 nearly 100 thin-cased '2,000lb' high capacity (HC) blast bombs had reached Oakington for 1942 use, but the 1,900lb bomb was reckoned even less effective than the 1,000lb type! Stirlings often carried 5 x 1,000lb bombs supplemented by 500-pounders, a typical operation against Cologne on **27/28 March 1941** being carried out using loads of 5 x 1,000lb and 6 x 500lb GPs.

The Air Staff were aware by 1941 that inability of crews to hit precise targets at night, was further confounded by poor weapon qualities. Autumn 1941 saw the Medium Capacity (MC) type enter production. Explosive filling now equated half the bomb's weight which, in the High Capacity (HC and sometimes called High Charge) range of blast weapons, represented about 75 percent. MC type, reminiscent in appearance of common German bombs, had improved ballistic qualities producing improved accuracy. Useful for long-delay, they were able to penetrate most buildings without breaking apart too soon, and suitable for shallow earth penetration. The 500lb and 1,000lb MC HE bombs were introduced operationally by 1943, forged case examples proving best and, having a 50 percent charge/weight ratio, were used against strong buildings and when long-delay fusing was required. Cast variants had only 42 percent filling by weight. The first, and possibly trials use, of MC bombs by Stirlings occurred in summer 1942.

Highly specialised, relatively few in number and first dropped by Stirlings on Brest during the raid of **22/23 April 1942**, was the 2,000lb Armour Piercing (AP) bomb. The Stirling usually conveyed five and for first use two aircraft dropped eleven between them along with 2 x 500lb bombs. On **28/29 April**, three Stirlings raiding Brest dropped 12 x 2,000lb APs. To penetrate warship armour plating, the bomb case was very thick and its 10 percent charge/weight ratio rendered of little value. Release from the greatest possible height was essential, but scoring a hit on a warship became even more difficult. The Semi-Armour Piercing (SAP) bomb, the first examples of which were 500lb type, were aimed at warships in Brest on **24/25 February 1941**. They were carried by Stirlings on **12 February 1942** during the 'Channel Dash' by capital ships.

Most effective was the Stirling's incendiary load capacity, the common type chosen in summer 1936 having been introduced to service the following year. Slender, hexagonal in cross-section and $21\frac{1}{2}$in long, the black-painted, red-nosed, hexagonal, magnesium zinc alloy fire bomb weighing 4lb was one of Bomber Command's most potent offensive stores. The thermite filling was ignited by an internal striker activated by another example alongside as it fell from the container in which the bombs were tightly packed. Its hexagonal section which aided tessellation during packing caused it to easily lodge on buildings whereas the equivalent German 2kg incendiary, round in section, easily rolled off. A tin plate tail gave limited stability during fall, the flat-nose facilitating exit from the Small Bomb Container (SBC). A small explosive charge added to some 4lb Incendiary Bomb Mk 1 examples was intended to discourage fire fighters. The Mk II with shorter tail fitted more easily into the SBC, and the 1941 Mk III, slightly smaller, contained the same amount of thermite filling. To conserve materials, a Mk IV with reduced filling proved to be no less effective. The 'X' (ie. explosive) variety had a delayed action explosive component incorporated near the nose.

Incendiary bombs were first dropped from Stirlings on **16/17 June 1941**, their use being limited until March 1942. Initially, they formed part of a mixed load, as on **7/8 July 1941** when 15 x 1,000lb GPs, 21 x 500lb GPs and only 720 x 4lb incendiaries were aimed at Frankfurt. Incendiaries were electrically released in showers from containers, the first extensive use by Stirlings taking place on **8/9 March 1942** when the load dropped included 13,050 x 4lb and forty-eight of the less common 250lb incendiaries. The first peak drops occurred during the 'Thousand Plan' raids of May and June 1942 and during the latter month Stirlings dropped 2,000lb HC weapons for the first time.

Very different was the 50lb Incendiary, a modified 5-gallon petrol can containing a rubber-phosphor filling intended for spontaneous combustion on impact. Some 10,000 were made in mid-1941, their first use by Stirlings coming on **7/8 September 1941**, when they were dropped upon Berlin and Kiel. On **10/11 September** another 132 fell in the Turin area. Use by Stirlings was brief, for they were no more precision weapons than the 40lb HE anti-personnel bombs aimed at AA and searchlight sites. Initial use of those by Stirlings took place on **20/21 October 1941**, during a Bremen raid.

Much more effective was the 1940-designed 30lb Phosphor light-case bomb containing 1 1/2lb of liquid phosphorus (later white phosphorus) and 6lb of a rubber-benzol mix controlled to ensure slow burning. On impact the fuse igniter burst, blew off the tail and front base plate and the bomb's fiery contents were ejected over forty yards. In June 1941, a batch of 400,000 was ordered and they proved so effective that production was stepped up to 5,000 a week. German cities, industry and the country's docks, all were incinerated by 4 and 30-pound fire bombs, which Stirlings are believed to have dropped for the first time during a Hamburg raid on **3/4 May 1942**.

Ruthlessly effective incendiary weapons destroyed 30 percent of Lübeck's old town in April 1942, much of the 60 percent incendiary load consisting of 30lb weapons. Against the Heinkel works at Rostock powerfully penetrative 30-pounders proved very effective while about 60 percent of Rostock town was badly damaged by fire.

Developed 30lb bombs were soon in vogue, the Mk II having a drawn steel case, the Mk III a welded body and the Mk IV a thinner case enclosing acetate-cellulose filling. Even so, the 30lb bomb was never quite so effective as its small relation, as it emitted great quantities of black smoke which interfered with high explosive bomb aiming.

A third type of incendiary somewhat akin to the German oil bomb was the adaptation of the 250lb light-case (LC) gas container. Devised in 1940 to cause forest fires, it was modified in 1941 to contain rubber-benzol and dropped by Bomber Command in a number of 1942 and 1943 raids, including the July 1943 attacks upon Hamburg. Stirlings first dropped them in April 1942.

During 1942's Main Force operations, incendiaries usually formed about 40 percent of the overall load; by 1943 they sometimes represented over 60 percent, and formed 50 percent of the bombs released upon Hamburg in July–August 1943.

In March 1943, when the Essen raid signalled the start of the punishing onslaught attacks upon German industry and cities, Stirling squadrons started demonstrating their real potential. It has always been fashionable to look upon these 'flying battleships' as outclassed because they could not accommodate the 4,000lb 'cookie'. Although that is true, Stirlings performed as well as the Halifaxes except where altitude was concerned, but by way of compensation they often delivered heavier loads to the Ruhr. Even against distant Nuremberg on **8/9 March 1943**, the Stirlings' offensive loads included 29 x 2,000lb HCs, 3 x 1,900lb, 29 x 1,000lb and 17 x 500lb HEs, along with 896 x 30lb, 20,970 x 4lb and 1,440 x 4lb 'X' incendiaries, all of which were recorded as being delivered to the target area. Compared with later 1943 raids this appears small. During the Kassel raid of **3/4 October 1943**, Stirlings are known to have dropped 80,689 incendiary bombs out of the gruesome total of 377,263 used. Of the 176 Stirlings available for operations 96/113 are recorded as having bombed Kassel, and the precise load dropped may have been even greater.

The awesome effectiveness of the 1943 and subsequent raids on German towns and industry owed much to the Pathfinder Force, which came into existence on 15 August 1942 and which became 8 (PFF) Group with effect from 8 January 1943. On the **30th/31st** of that month Stirlings of 7 Squadron PFF, fitted with *H2S* land-scanning radar for target location, operated for the first time and headed an attack made on Hamburg. *H2S* presented the navigator with a radar map upon which the aircraft's position was central.

Stirlings equipped with *H2S* next participated in the **2/3 February** raid on Cologne. A night fighter tackled one of the 7 Squadron Stirlings and damaged it after which came a forced landing in the Netherlands. German investigators found the *H2S* set fairly intact, the enemy quickly developing *NAXOS* equipment enabling a night fighter to home on radar pulses from *H2S*. Soon, *H2S* was used only for brief periods as a navigation and sometimes a bombing aid.

PFF located and marked targets with ever increasing skill, good weather, accurate timing, careful routing, 'spoof' operations to mislead the enemy all playing an ever increasing part in Bomber Command's 1943 operations. Complexity of PFF operations involved 7 Squadron in 'route marker', 'backer up', showering flares and brightly coloured TIs on to already marked targets to keep them evident and as 'supporter' dropping mixed incendiary and HE loads on marked targets. The latter was to discourage enemy interference with ground burning TIs.

Prominent among special target-marking weapons was the Target Indicator utilising a 250lb incendiary bomb case for a flammable liquid to produce a brightly coloured ground fire. Stirlings first used 250lb TIs, eight of them along with a dozen marker flares, during the Hamburg raid of **30/31 January 1943**.

Marker flares were adapted 4.5in reconnaissance flares parachute suspended for use as Sky Markers. Within the flare canister candles were tightly packed to function in clusters, or used singly, to produce coloured smoke, stars etc. A variation was the drip type from which burning particles fell during a slow burn. That made them particularly useful for route marking.

Many of the weapons were developed after the Stirling entered service, so it is perhaps worth recalling the aircraft's original load capacity and associated loading plans.

Specification B.12/36 called for a basic load of 28 x 500lb or 250lb GP HE bombs. The Stirling could carry twenty-four of either, utilising eighteen bomb carriers three-abreast in the fuselage cells and three in each of the two inner mainplane cells. Viewed from above the bomb stations from fore to aft were numbered from right to left 1-2-3, 4-5-6, et seq. to 19, 20, 21 in the fuselage with 22, 23, 24 being in the starboard mainplane and 25, 26, 27 in the port mainplane. Twelve loading cases specified were:

Case 1: 2,000lb load: 8 x 250lb on stations 1, 2, 3, 4, 5, 6, 7, 8, 9
Case 2: 2,000lb load: 4 x 500lb on stations 1, 3, 7, 9
Case 3: 4,000lb load: 16 x 250lb or maximum of ten containers, on stations 1, 2, 3, 4, 7, 8, 9, 16, 18, 22, 23, 24, 25, 26, 27
Case 4: 4,000lb load: 8 x 500lb on stations 1, 2, 3, 7, 8, 9, 16, 18
Case 5: 8,000lb load: 16 x 500lb on stations 1, 2, 3, 4, 6, 7, 8, 9, 16, 18, 22, 23, 24, 25, 26, 27
Case 6: 8,000lb load: 4 x 2,000lb on stations 4, 6, 10, 12
Case 7: 14,000lb load: 7 x 2,000lb AP on stations 4, 5, 6, 10, 11, 12, 17
Case 8: 10,000lb load: 20 x 500lb on stations 1 to 9, 13 to 16, 18, 23 to 27
Case 9: 9,000lb load: 10 x 250lb and 14 x 500lb
Case 10: 12,000lb load: 24 x 500lb or 6 x 1,000lb + 24 x 250lb, on stations 1 to 9, 13 to 16, 18 to 27
Case 11: 3 x SCIs: on stations 4, 5, 6
Case 12: 8,000lb load: 6 x 500lb or 6 x 250lb or 5 x 1,000lb on stations 4, 5, 10, 12, 22 to 27

Release order varied, with the seven 2,000lb AP load falling in one stick, 24 x 500lb in six sticks of four or two of twelve bombs. The 24 x 250lb load could be dropped as four sticks of six and two of twelve. In the case of mixed loads including 1,000lb, 500lb and 250lb GPs/SAPs the drop grouping was 5 x 1,000lb or 6 x 500lb, or two sticks of three small bombs and two large. In the case of the '250s' one stick was dropped comprising 3, 2, 3, 3 bombs.

Containers were generally carried in the fuselage cells because if incendiaries were released from the wing cells they, also flares, passed too near the tailplane for safety. In October 1941 a trial drop of twenty-four containers of incendiaries showed that it was not possible because it overloaded the aircraft's accumulators.

Numerous changes in possible loads for the Stirling were made once it had settled in to service. In January 1942, for instance, a modified 2,000lb carrier made it able to carry 7 x 1,000lb GPs or 7 x 1,900lb GPs. Further modifications allowed 9 x 1,000 GPs to be carried on stations 4, 5, 6, 10, 11, 12, 16, 17, 18 and six in the wing cells, a useful potential load which did not cross the cg limits.

Summary of bombs and flares carried by Stirlings of Bomber Command

Type	Length less tail	Max girth	Terminal velocity (fps)	Remarks
High explosive				
2,000lb HC	13ft 5.5in*	1ft 6.5in	?	Hessian parachute can replace tail
1,900lb GP	8ft 2in*	1ft 6.7in	2,100	450lb Amatol filling, 1,288lb body weight
1,000lb GP	7ft 23.5in	1ft 4.15in	1,840	333lb Amatol filling
500lb GP	5ft 10.5in	1ft 1in	?	Long or short tail
250lb GP	4ft 8in*	10.75in	?	Long or short tail
40lb GP	2ft 3.25in	5.01in	1,070	6.3lb Amatol filling, carried in 250lb SBC or on light series carrier. Body weight 27lb 5oz
1,000lb MC Mk I/II	6ft*	1ft 5in	1,600	475lb Amatol, 477lb Amatex or 502lb RDX/TNT
500lb MC Mk III	5ft 11in	1ft 4.15in	1,600	401lb RDX/TNT 60-40 or 366lb DI or 430lb Torpex
2,000lb AP	9ft 4.7in	1ft 1.5in	2,810	Body weight 1,650lb, Shellite filling
500lb SAP	5ft 2in	11.5in	?	Long or short tail
250lb SAP	4ft 1in	9.2in	1,440	40.5lb TNT filling, body weight 177.5lb
500lb US	3ft 11.2in	14.1in	1,310	Designated AN-M43 and AN-64 236lb Amatol filling, 24.4lb TNT and usual weight 494lb. 14in long tail
Flares/Target Indicators				
250lbTI	34.25in	12in	-	Actual complete wt 205 to 230lb
4.5in Flare Mk I	33in	4.5in	500 on parachute	Red, green, yellow stars, emits 7 at regular intervals
4.5in Flare, Sky Marker Mk I	33in	4.5in	600 on 11ft dia Mk VI parachute	Drip duration 120 seconds
Incendiaries				
250lb	5ft*	12in	?	Liquid fuel and phosphorus
50lb	1ft 4.5in	9 x 9in	?	Cloth drogue to control fall
30lb	2ft 8.75in	4.75in	?	Weapon 1ft 6in long; tail screwed on
4lb	1ft 9.5in	1.75in (hexagonal)	?	Tinplate hexagonal tail unit
4lb 'X'	1ft 9.5in	1.75in (hexagonal)	?	Explosive component

Notes

1,900lb GP Mk I body similar to 1,000lb GP but differs in weight and dimensions

* = includes tail and nose, represents length overall

Appendix 5
Summary of Stirling Squadrons and Bases

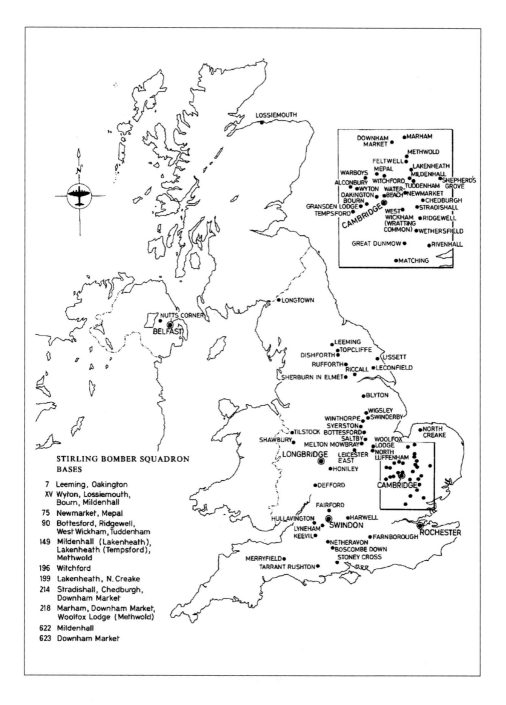

STIRLING BOMBER SQUADRON BASES

7	Leeming, Oakington
XV	Wyton, Lossiemouth, Bourn, Mildenhall
75	Newmarket, Mepal
90	Bottesford, Ridgewell, West Wickham, Tuddenham
149	Mildenhall (Lakenheath), Lakenheath (Tempsford), Methwold
196	Witchford
199	Lakenheath, N. Creake
214	Stradishall, Chedburgh, Downham Market
218	Marham, Downham Market, Woolfox Lodge (Methwold)
622	Mildenhall
623	Downham Market

Stirling Bomber Squadrons

7 Squadron (Identity letters MG)
Reformed Leeming 2.8.40; Oakington 29.10.40 – 8.43 (detached Newmarket 27.3.41–27.4.41: satellite Bourn 6.41 – 7.42). **Mk I** 3.8.40 – 29.8.43: first operation 10.2.41; last operation 10.8.43. **Mk III** 24.3.43 – 29.8.43: first operation 4.4.43, last operation 10.8.43. To Pathfinder Force 8.42: first sorties 24.8.42

7 Conversion Flight (MG)
Formed Oakington 16.1.42: first operation 30.5.42, last operation 31.7.42. To Stradishall 4.10.42. Absorbed by 1657 CU

XV Squadron (LS, 'C' Flt DJ)
Wyton 14.3.41 – 13.8.42 (satellites Alconbury; Warboys). Detached Lossiemouth 28.1.42 – 7.2.42, Bourn 13.8.42 – 14.4.43, Mildenhall 14.4.43 – 12.43. **Mk I** used 14.3.41 –28.12.43: first operation 30.4.41, last operation 19.5.43. **Mk III** used 31.12.42 – 27.12.43: first operation 14.2.43, last operation 22.12.43

XV Conversion Flight (LS)
Alconbury 26.1.42 – 4.10.42

46 Squadron (XK)
Stoney Cross 7.1.45 – 4.46. **Mk I** (LK555 only) 28.11.45 – 9.1.46. **Mk V** used 1.45 –12.4.46

51 Squadron (TB)
Leconfield 6.45 – 20.8.45, Stradishall 20.8.45 – 3.46. **Mk IV** used 27.11.45 – 16.1.46. **Mk V** used 1.6.45 – 25.7.46

75 Squadron (AA, 'C' Flight JN)
Mildenhall 10.42 – 1.11.42 (detached Oakington 15.10.42 – 12.42 for conversion), Newmarket 1.11.42 – 29.6.43, Mepal 29.6.43 – 4.44. **Mk I**: first operation 20.11.42, last operation 12.8.43. **Mk III** used 13.2.43 – 28.4.44: first operation 1.3.43, last operation 23.4.44

90 Squadron (WP, 'C' Flight XY)
Reformed Bottesford 1.12.42, to Ridgewell 29.12.42, West Wickham 31.5.43 (renamed Wratting Common 21.8.43), Tuddenham 13.10.43 – 6.44. **Mk I** used 1.12.42 – 30.11.43: first operation 8.1.43, last operation 24/25.6.43. **Mk III** used 10.2.43 – 24.6.44: first operation 13.2.43, last operation 7.6.44

101 Conversion Flight (SR)
Attached Oakington 4.42 – 10.42. **Mk I** used

115 Conversion Flight (KO)
Oakington 8.12.42 – 31.12.42. **Mk I** used

138 Squadron (NF)
Tempsford 6.44 – 3.45. **Mk IV** used 11.6.44 – 10.3.45: first operation 28.8.44. last 4.3.45

148 Squadron (-)
Brindisi 11.44 to 12.44

149 Squadron (OJ, 'C' Flight TK)
Mildenhall 11.41 – 4.42 (detachments and operations to/from Lakenheath during period), Lakenheath 4.42 – 15.5.44 (detached Tempsford 1.44 – 2.44), Methwold 15.4.44 – 9.44. **Mk I** used 2.11.41 – 1.10.43: first operation 26.11.41, last operation 29.7.43. **Mk III** used 16.2.43 – 13.9.44: first operation 28.2.43, last operation 8.9.44

149 Conversion Flight (OJ)
Lakenheath 21.1.42 – 2.10.42. Participated in a few operations

158 Squadron (DK)
Lissett 6.45, Stradishall 17.8.45, disbanded there 1.1.46. **Mk IV** used 27.11.45 – 1.46. **Mk V** used 29.5.45 – 1.46

161 Squadron (MA)
Tempsford. **Mk IV** used 5.9.44 –12.7.45: first operation 8.9.44, last operation 2.5.45

171 Squadron (6Y)
Reformed North Creake 8.9.44 by raising 'C' Flight, 199 Squadron, to squadron status. **Mk III** used 8.9.44 – 31.3.45 (although re-equipment with Halifax III began 10.44): first operation 15.9.44, last operation 8.10.44

190 Squadron (G5, L9)
Reformed Leicester East 5.1.44, Fairford 25.3.44, Great Dunmow 14.10.44 – 13.5.45. **Mk IV** used 5.1.44 – 3.5.45: first operation 31.3.44, last operation 25.4.45

196 Squadron (ZO on bombers, ZO and 7T on transports)
Witchford 8.43, Leicester East 18.11.43, Tarrant Rushton 7.1.44, Keevil 15.3.44, Wethersfield 9.10.44, Shepherd's Grove 29.1.45 – 3.46. **Mk III** used 22.7.43 – 1.44: first operation 26.8.43, last operation 10.11.43. **Mk IV** used 27.1.44 – 3.46: first operation 3.3.44. **Mk V** used 30.1.46 – 7.3.46

199 Squadron (EX)
Lakenheath 20.6.43 (using Wellingtons). **Mk III** used 5.7.43 – 8.3.45: first operation 30.7.43, last Main Force operation 1.12.43. Mining and SOE operations followed until 21.2.44, then began preparing for RCM duty. Moved to North Creake and 100 Group 1. 5.44: first *Mandrel* operation 5/6.6.44, last Stirling operation 14.3.45

214 Squadron (BU, 'C' Flight PX)
Stradishall 4.42. Chedburgh 1.10.42. Downham Market 1.12.43 – 17.1.44. **Mk I** used 5.4.42 –10.2.44: first operation 18.5.42, last operation 19.11.43. **Mk III** used 10.2.43 – 16.7.44 (most given up 1.44): first operation 10.2.43, last operation 31.12.43

214 Conversion Flight (BU)
Formed Waterbeach 10.4.42, Stradishall 4.5.42, Waterbeach 7.8.42 and absorbed by 1651 C.U. **Mk I** used

218 Squadron (HA)
Marham 12.41, Downham Market 10.7.42, Methwold 4.8.44. **Mk I** used 16.12.41 – 18.8.43: first operation 12.2.42, last operation 25.7.43. **Mk III** used 6.2.43 –17.8.44: first operation 13.2.43, last operation 2.8.44

218 Conversion Flight (HA)
Formed Marham 28.2.42, Lakenheath 3.3.42, Marham 3.42, Stradishall 2.10.42 and absorbed by 1657 CU. **Mk I** used

242 Squadron (KY)
Stoney Cross 2.45, Merryfield 9.12.45. **Mk IV** used 15.2.45 – 1.5.46. **Mk V** used 15.2.45 – 1.5.46. Following training flights 27.2.45 – 4.45 ordered to equip with Yorks used alongside Stirlings. Yorks withdrawn 7.45. Stirlings continued to operate until 10.11.45

295 Squadron (8Z 'A' Flight, 8E 'B' Flight)
Harwell 6.44, Rivenhall 17.10.44, Tarrant Rushton 12.45, disbanded 15.1.46. **Mk IV** used 14.6.44 – 1.46: first operation 27.7.7.44, last front line flying 1.46

299 Squadron (5G, X9)
Formed Stoney Cross 4.11.43, Keevil 28.2.44, Wethersfield 9.10.44, Shepherd's Grove 25.1.45, disbanded 30.3.46. **Mk IV** used 7.1.44 – 19.3.46: first operation 5.4.44, last front line flying, mail carrying 3.46. **Mk V** 15.1.45 – 12.3.46: two aircraft only

513 Squadron (JC)
Formed Witchford 15.9.43, disbanded 24.12.43. **Mk III** used 21.10.43 – 24.12.43: no operational flying

525 Squadron (-)
Lyneham, one **Mk IV** (LJ512) 29.5.44 – 27.7.44

570 Squadron (V8, E7)
Harwell 6.44, Rivenhall 7.10.44, disbanded 8.1.46. **Mk IV** used 30.6.44 – 1.46: first operation 27.7.44, last front line flying 8.1.46

620 Squadron (QS on bombers. QS and D4 on transports)
Formed Chedburgh 17.6.43. **Mk I** used 19.6.43 – 29.7.43, no operational flying. **Mk III** used 19.6.43 – 2.44: first operation 19.6.43, last operation 19.11.43. To Leicester East 23.11.43, Fairford 18.3.44, Great Dunmow 17.10.44. **Mk IV** used 4.2.44 – 9.7.45: first operation 11.2.44, last front line flying 10.6.45

622 Squadron (GI)
Mildenhall 10.8.43, formed from 'C' Flight. XV Squadron. **Mk III** used 10.8.43 – 9.1.44: first operation 10.8.43, last operation 20.12.43

623 Squadron (IC)
Downham Market 10.8.43, formed from 'C' Flight, 218 Squadron. **Mk III** used 10.8.43 –10.2.44: first operation 10.8.43, last operation 4.12.43

624 Squadron (-)
Blida, North Africa 6.44, disbanded 24.9.44. **Mk IV** used 7.6.44 – 24.9.44: first operation 29.7.44, last operation 4.9.44

NB: Dates are mostly those listed as 'effective'. Movement took place over a number of days.

Appendix 6

Summary of Stirling Training and Miscellaneous Units

1651 Conversion Unit (individual letters only to early 1943, then unit letters BS, GG, QQ, YZ)
Formed Waterbeach 2.1.42 from 26 Conversion Flight. Upgraded to three-flight strength 1.12.42. To Wratting Common (73 Base) 11.11.43, Woolfox Lodge 10.11.44. Converted immediately to Lancasters. **Mk I** used 1.42 – 6.11.44, **Mk III** 8.7.43 – 5.1.45: first operation 30.5.42, last operated during night diversion sweeps circa 8.44

1652 Conversion Unit
Marston Moor 12.43 – 2.45. Held one **Mk III** LJ464 possibly used as a ground trainer

1653 Conversion Unit (A3, H4)
Reformed Chedburgh 21.11.43. To North Luffenham 12.44. Stirling then phased out. Used **Mk I** 21.11.43 – 6.11.44, **Mk III** 10.12.43 – 7.12.44

1654 Conversion Unit (JF, UG)
Wigsley. Used only one **Mk I** (BK615) 10.5.44 – 24.5.44. **Mk III** 29.11.43 – 18.3.45

1657 Conversion Unit (AK, XT)
Formed 10.42 incorporating Conversion Flights at Oakington. Immediately to Stradishall. Became 1657 (Heavy) Conversion Unit 4.44. Stirling phased out 12.44. Shepherd's Grove used as satellite in 1944. Used **Mk I** 2.10.42 – 17.10.44, **Mk III** 18.5.43 – 24.2.45

1659 Conversion Unit
Topcliffe. Used only two **Mk IV**, N6049 6.43 –12.43 and R9289 in 8.43. Ground trainers

1660 Conversion Unit (TV, YW)
Swinderby. Used **Mk III** 27.11.43 – 3.3.45, phased out over period 12.44 – 2.45

1661 Conversion Unit (GP)
Winthorpe. Used **Mk III** 9.11.43 – 28.2.45, phased out as main equipment circa 12.44

1662 Conversion Unit
Blyton. Used only two **Mk III**s EF391 in 8.43 and LJ463 2.45 – 3.45. Probable ground trainers

1663 Conversion Unit
Rufforth. Used only one **Mk I** (W7623) 6.11.43

1665 Conversion Unit (NY, OG)
Formed Waterbeach 1.5.43. To Woolfox Lodge 5.6.43, Tilstock for the training of crews for airborne forces 23.1.44. Later amalgamated with 1332 HTCU. Stirling phased out circa 3.46. Used **Mk I** (NY) 20.5.43 – 26.4.45, **Mk III** (OG) 17.5.43 – 25.2.46, **Mk IV** 20.1.44 – 31.3.46

1332 Heavy Transport Conversion Unit
Formed Longtown 5.9.44, Nutt's Corner 7 10.44, Riccall 25.4.45. Trained crews for 46, 242, 246, 511 Squadrons. Used **Mk IV**

Operational and Refresher Training Unit (individual letter only)
Matching. Gave flying practice in operational roles for aircrew. Stirling **Mk IV** received 3.45, towed fourteen Horsas during operation Varsity. Re-equipped mainly with Halifax 4.45, retained a flight of Stirlings. To Wethersfield 15.10.45. Became **1385 HTSCU** 1.4.46 at which time it gave up Stirlings

Central Navigational School, Shawbury
Used only LK508 5.44 – 5.45 and LK589 5.44 – 6.44. Both made trans-Atlantic flights

1427 Flight
Afforded flying experience on Stirlings to ATA and maintenance unit crews. Formed Thruxton 12.41, to Hullavington 18.5.42 (held two Stirlings), Marham early 8.42, Stradishall 2.10.43, and absorbed by 1657 CU

1588 Heavy Freight Flight (previously 'K' Flight)
Formed Melton Mowbray 16.9.45. Transferred to 229 Group. Drigh Road 10.45, Santa Cruz 13.10.45. Used **Mk V** 22.9.45 – 20.5.46 on UK-India run. Disbanded 20.5.46

1589 Heavy Freight Flight (previously 'J' Flight)
Formed Melton Mowbray 28.9.45, to transport spares and groundcrews to maintain any type of aircraft on trunk routes. To Cairo West 10.10.45. Operated four Stirlings supplemented by five Dakotas from 12.45. Disbanded 30.4.46. Used **Mk V** 9.45 – 4.46

Air Transport Trials and Development Unit, Netheravon
Used **Mk V** LJ958 only, 6 – 10.45

Bomber Development Unit (Individual letter only)

Reformed Gransden Lodge 21.7.42. Tested bomber aircraft and their equipment. Tested Stirling **Mk I** from 10.42 (testing Mk VIII autopilot, *H2S* Mk IIG, rotating astrodome. Mk IX integrating sextant, etc). Used BK594 23.9.42 – 13.2.44; EF403 23.5.43 – 4.7.43. To Feltwell 6.4.43; Newmarket 13.9.43. Trials of *Monica*, flame damping exhausts, *Boozer*, *Fishpond*. R9239 used for photoelectric sun compass tests. BK594 for downward search for under defence in night bombers. On 1.10.43 commenced *H2S*, *Fishpond* and *Oboe* **Mk II** and later *Gee–H* training. Used R9277 5.8.43 – 14.11.43; R9280 24.4.43 – 4.2.44; EE968 22.8.43 – 14.12.43; EF405 26.5.43 – 4.7.43; EF466 5.8.43 – 18.9.43

Pathfinder Force Navigational Training Unit (previously Gransden Navigational Training Unit) (individual letters only)

Formed 10.4.43, to Upwood and Warboys 6.43, to Warboys 5.3.44. Used R9252 13.4.43 – 22.12.43; R9269 6.6.43 – 26.7.43; R9277 9.5.43 – 26.7.43; EF404 28.5.43 – 7.43

Royal Aircraft Establishment, Farnborough

Used for research and trials: L7605 28.10.41 – 28.10.42; N3635 28.5.41 – 16.8.41 (RATO trials, written off 1.1.42); N3639 2.8.42 – struck off charge 30.11.44; N3728 2.4.42 – 7.4.42; BK615 7.1.43 – 21.6.43 (*H2S* tests); EF434 7.7.43 – 24.4.44

Signals Flying Unit, Honiley

Used LK460 13.11.44 – 17.1.45; PJ956 28.2.46 – 18.8.47

Telecommunications Flying Unit, Defford

Fitted out Stirlings for radio warfare, eg. 7 Squadron, 199 Squadron

Aeroplane and Armament Experimental Establishment, Boscombe Down

Used for service trials: L7605 22.2.40 – 19.8.40, 4.1.41 – 28.4.41, 10.10.41 – 23.10.41; N3635 21.5.40 – 28.5.41; N3637 6.40 – 20.12.40; N3639 4.1.42 – 7.42; N3643 1.8.40 – 3.1.41; N3657 (**Mk II**) 17.7.41 – 11.9.41, 27.7.42 – 31.5.43; N3662 23.5.41 – undercarriage collapsed on landing, struck off charge 23.3.42; N3678 27.1.42 – 8.7.42; N3702 8.3.42 – 11.3.43; N6000 25.10.40 – 11.40, 11.3.41 – 25.6.41; N6001 23.11.40 – missing on test flight 30.6.41; N6008 15.2.41 – 10.10.41; R9309 14.7.42 – written off 6.9.42; BF382 2.10.42 – 7.11.43; BK649 8.12.42 – 27.3.44; BK651 21.9.43 – 14.3.44; EF466 18.9.43 – 10.10.43; EF503 (**Mk IV**) 2.9.43 – 21.2.44; LJ571 31.8.44 – 15.12.44

Airborne Forces Experimental Establishment

Ringway, Sherburn-in-Elmet and Beaulieu. **Mks I**, **III** and **IV** used mainly for equipment, performance and glider towing trials. Examples: N3702 8.3.42 – 11.3.43; several **Mk IV**s 18.10.43 – 28.2.44

Appendix 7
Summary of Stirling Bombing Sorties

Daylight bombing sorties

Despatched	290
Attacking	208
HE loads dropped (tons)	876.6
Incendiaries (tons)	1.9
Missing	13
Cat EFB	1

Comparative loads of bombs carried – lb per aircraft – attacking by day

Stirling	9,482
Halifax	8,764
Lancaster	11,610
Wellington	3,338

Night bombing sorties

Despatched	10,784
Attacking	9,201
HE (tons)	12,162.2
Incendiary (tons)	14,809.3
Missing	474
Cat E 'A'	28
Cat E 'N'	90

Overall loss rate 4.7 percent. Other types: Halifax 3.3 percent, Lancaster 2.9 percent, Mosquito 0.5 percent

Comparative loads of bombs carried – lb per aircraft – during night operations

Stirling	6,557
Halifax	7,849
Lancaster	9,525
Wellington	2,954

PFF Night sorties by Stirlings, from the formation of 8 Group, 25 January 1943

Despatched	513
Attacking	434
HE (tons)	520.4
Incendiaries (tons)	353.1
Missing	24
Cat E 'N'	4

Overall loss rate 4.7 percent. Other types: Halifax 4.5 percent, Lancaster 3.2 percent, Mosquito 1.1 percent

Appendix 8
Number and Types of Bombs Listed as Dropped by Stirlings

Bomber Command ORS Yearly Totals as listed in Air Ministry War Room, 1945 Summary

(Figures relate to loads known to have been dropped on enemy territory taking no account of others possibly dropped by aircraft which failed to return or jettisoned)

			General Purpose		
	1,900lb	1,000lb	500lb	250lb	40lb
1941	-	1,930	3,989	112	24
1942	490	2,253	2,960	283	-
1943	27	4,398	1,143	32	328
1944	-	-	1,584	-	-
Totals	517	8,581	9,676	427	352

	MC 1,000lb	HC 500lb	AP 2,000lb	SAP 2,000lb	500lb	250lb
1941	-	-	-	461	296	11
1942	-	-	991	41	306	-
1943	831	2,039	1,368	-	-	-
1944	145	12,239	-	-	-	-
Totals	976	14,278	2,359	502	602	11

	RDX 1,900lb	USA Bombs 1,000lb	500lb
1942	7	211	-
1943	-	-	-
1944	-	-	401
Totals	7	211	401

		Incendiaries and Target Indicators			
	250lb TI	250lb	50lb	30lb	4lb	4lb 'X'
1941	-	-	354	-	42,080	-
1942	-	4,554	-	89,285	1,602,008	-
1943	883	8	-	276,418	3,341,538	226,119
1944	-	-	-	-	-	-
Totals	883	4,562	354	365,703	4,985,626	226,119

Total bombs recorded as dropped on enemy territory during operations from the UK by other Bomber Command aircraft types – representative selection

Bomb type	Halifax	Lancaster	Wellington
8,000 HC	1	1,087	-
4,000 HC	467	64,391	1,927
2,000 HC	12,875	13,044	3
1,900 GP	-	665	30
1,000 GP	28,592	30,072	6,352
500 GP	198,343	222,750	67,745
250 GP	19,986	15,795	48,544
USA 500	84,310	140,269	-
30lb Incendiary	631,255	1,863,952*	144,297
4lb Incendiary	10,919,441	38,653,351	5,710,135
4lb 'X' Incendiary	813,715	2,536,368	82,617

*Additionally, Halifaxes and Lancasters delivered various types of incendiary Cluster: the No 14 released 106 x 4lb; No 15, 158 x 4lb; No 16, 236 x 4lb and No 17, 110 x 4lb – with 4 X bombs as alternatives. Clusters, in the case of the Lancaster, added another 8,016,434 x 4lb incendiaries.

Appendix 9
Downward Defence Positions
in Stirling Bombers

In 1943 the Bomber Development Unit, Feltwell, experimented with a ventral gun position for heavy bombers. On 13 June 1943 a .50in Browning gun was installed in lieu of the aft escape hatch in a Stirling, and a protective plastic shield was fitted ahead of the position. On 6 July the installation was discussed at HQ Bomber Command before viewing took place at Feltwell on 20 July. It was suitable also for Halifaxes and Lancasters not fitted with *H2S*. In case the flash from the .50in gun was considered excessive, an alternative 2 x .303in installation was to be tried.

On 6 June 1943, at a meeting of the Airframes Modification Committee, MAP, arrangements had tentatively been made for Short, Austin Motors and Sebro to supply working parties to incorporate Modification 1073, the under-defence gun position, in about 260 Stirlings in Bomber Command. The equipment comprised a .50in. Browning Mk II gun, a free gun reflector sight Mk IIIA with a two-way socket Type F and flash eliminator Mk II. Aircraft of the two squadrons earmarked for 38 Group, Nos 196 and 620, were not so fitted.

Stirling EF466, surplus to CRD needs at Rochester, was chosen on 4 August to transfer to Feltwell for full under-gun trials. Following acceptance, 300 gun mounts (200 for Stirlings, 100 for other bombers) were ordered to be available by the end of October 1943. Night firing had shown the F Type flash eliminator acceptable.

Parts were rapidly manufactured during November, eighty sets going to Mildenhall, and forty each to Stradishall, Downham Market and Waterbeach.

In November 1943 the question of who should man the under gun was raised. The aircraft's Air Bomber was number one choice, but he would need to leave the position about twenty minutes before bomb release time – and at the most likely time for fighter attack.

Implementation of the scheme was slow due to plans to replace the Stirling bomber. By January 1944 only one 3 Group Stirling of 75 Squadron had been fully modified – and that had crashed. During the month, however, Shorts partly modified nearly all of Lakenheath's Stirlings and Mildenhall's and modified aircraft became operational during the month. An investigative check on an installation in a 199 Squadron aircraft took place on 19 January 1944, then in February seven aircraft were completely equipped at Stradishall and another eleven made ready for the gun position to be fitted.

However, the picture was brighter than it might seem for, by 12 December 1943, some of the necessary modifications had been incorporated in twenty-six Lakenheath aircraft, eleven at Tuddenham, fourteen at Mildenhall, two of 1657 CU and four at Chedburgh. Work had been limited by availability of parts making it impossible to modify all the 3 Group aircraft. On-site work was undertaken by parties each of four men from Austin, the first arriving at Swinderby on 25 March 1944 and the second at Wigsley on 30 March. By 5 April 1944 all except four of Stradishall's Mk IIIs had been modified.

The 268 known to have been modified, possibly in the order listed here, were:

By Short & Harland

1657 CU: BF517, BF532, BF468, BF527, BF404, BF350, BF435, BF324, BF344, BF323, BF452, BF342, N6089, N6039, N6079, N6104, N6065

149 Squadron: EE989, EE963, BF509, EF202, EE943, EE957, EE910, EE953

Mildenhall: EF460, EF459, EF122, EF127, EF161

75 Squadron: BF473, EF137, EF152, EF148, EF163

214 Squadron: EE950, EE967, EE960, EE961, EF115, EF125, EF120, EE956

1651 CU Wratting Common: BF302 R9302, BK443, BF439, BF385, BF402, BF354, N6048, N6049, BF394, BF377, BF325, BF397, N6128, N6044

218 Squadron: EE884, EF180, EF141, EE888, EF185, EF124, EF184, EE944, MZ263, BF568, EE899, EF199, EF155, EF157, EE876, EF194, EF204

90 Squadron: BF524, EF159, BF526, EF147, EF162, EF196, EF188, EF102, EE896, BF574, EF191, EF193

By Shorts

1657 CU: EF334, R9237, R9269, R9251, R9195, EF353, EF332, R9353, R9297, R9298, R9144, N3675, N3682, N3758, N3765, N3708

149 Squadron: EF502, EF411, EF412

199 Squadron: EF154, EF138, EF450, EF508, EF153, EF455

75 Squadron: BE512, BF514, BF513, BF507, BF462, LJ441, LJ442, EF454, EF466, LJ457, LJ462, LJ473, LJ453

90 Squadron: EF511, EF431, EF443, EF441, EF509, LJ460, LJ470

214 Squadron: EF406, EF405, EF368, EF444, R9289, EF447, EF403, EF463, EF388, EF385, EF498, EF433

1651 CU: R9157, N3766, R9196, R9244, N3671, EF396, EF358, R9243, EF395, R9148, R9147, R9152, R9287, R9186, BF386, R9236, R9191, R9193, EF389, N3721

1665 CU: R9143, R9285, EF350, EF351, EF384

218 Squadron: LJ446, EF410, LJ452, EF449, LJ449, LJ447, EF442, BF504

623 Squadron: BF489, LJ443, EF413, EF493

By Austin Motors

1657 CU: W7574, W7570, BF772, BK601, BK613, W7460, W7439, W7581, W7463, W7561, W7633, W7622, W7465, W7575, W7510

149 Squadron: EH943, FJ109, FJ107, EH993, EH922, EH904

199 Squadron: BF481, EH926, EJ111, EH995, EJ115, BK762, LK385, LK397

75 Squadron: EH880, EH948, BK771, BK695, EH949, EH939, EH955, EH901, EJl08, LK378, LK389, LK396, LK384

214 Squadron: EH953, EH959, EH978, EH933, EH977, EH951

1651 CU: BK605, W7615, W7577, W7625, W7522, W7468, W7532, BK600, BK622, BK623, EH879

1665 CU: W7623, W7447, BK652

218 Squadron: LJ125, EH923, EH942, BK761, EJ112

623 Squadron: EJ123, EJ124, EH979, EH957, LK387, EJ121, BK727, BK803

90 Squadron: EJ122, BK379, EH996, EH958, BK784, EH947, EH906, EH908, LK383, BK811, BK781, LK392

Appendix 10
Stirling Airframe Serial Numbers, Associated Mark Numbers and Engine Marks

Contract 67299/37: Short, Rochester

L7600 prototype; L7605, second prototype, became 3443M

Contract 763825/38: Short, Rochester

N3635–3644 inclusive: ten Stirling Trainer, Hercules II (N3644 re–engined with Hercules III); N3636 became 3056M; N3637 – 3361M; N3639 – 3031M; N3639 – 3389M; N3641 – 3010M; N3642 – 3012M; N3645 destroyed by bombing; N3646 Hercules III; N3647 to N3651 destroyed by bombing; N3652 Hercules I (?) became 3444M; N3653–3656 Hercules III; N3657 Mk II prototype (Cyclone); N3658–3663 (N3662 first with dorsal turret, fitted to all subsequent in the batch, Hercules XI; previous ones Hercules III), N3664–3684; N3700–3710; N3711 Mk II (Cyclone); N3712–3729; N3750–3769 (following bombing of Rochester 15 August 1940 some completed elsewhere: at South Marston N3673, 3676, 3678, 3679, 3682, 3700, 3704, 3705, 3706, 3708, 3709, 3710, 3712, 3721, 3762 and possibly others). Completed at Hucclecote: N3680, N3681 and possibly others

Contract 774677/38: Short & Harland, Belfast

N6000 Hercules XI, became 3768M; N6001–6003 Hercules X; N6004 Hercules III; N6005 Hercules X; N6006 Hercules X, became 4165M; N6007–6019; N6020–6024 Hercules XI; N6025–6028 destroyed by bombing; N6029–6030 Hercules XI; N6031 destroyed by bombing; N6032–6049 Hercules XI (dorsal turret probably on N6032 et seq); N6065–6084 Hercules XI, completed at Aldergrove; N6085–6104; N6120–6129 Hercules XI

Contract 763825/38: Short, Rochester

(Ranging R9141–9290)

Contract 774677/38: Short & Harland, Belfast

(Ranging R9295–9358): Mk I Hercules XI: R9141–9170; R9184–9203; R9241–9290; R9295–9334; R9349–9358. (R9188 first with Cyclone GR-2600, later converted to Mk III)

Contract 98239/39: Austin Motors, Birmingham

Mk I, Hercules XI: W7426–7475 (W7432 and W7455 converted to Mk III) W7500–7539; W7560–7589; W7610–7639

Contract 774677/38: Short & Harland, Belfast

Mk I, Hercules XI to BF454, then et seq Mk III, Hercules VI BF309–358 (BF355 converted to Mk III); BF372–416; BF434–454; BF455–483 (BF464 and BF468 converted to Mk IV); BF500–534 (BF532 converted to Mk IV; BF561–580 (BF575 converted to Mk IV Hercules XVI, BF580 converted to Mk IV Hercules VI)

Contract B.982939/C36: Austin Motors, Birmingham

Mk I, Hercules XI: BK592–628; BK644–647; then BK648–650 and remainder of batch Mk III, Hercules VI (except BK651 Hercules XVI); BK652–667; BK686–727; BK759–784; BK798–818

Contract 763825/38: Short, Rochester

DJ972–977 Hercules XI (replacing N3645 and N3647–3651 destroyed by bombing)

Contract 774677/38: Short & Harland, Belfast

Mk III: EE871–918 Hercules VI (EE889 and EE900 converted to Mk IV), EE937–975 Hercules VI (EE961 and EE966 converted to Mk IV), EF114–163 Hercules VI (EF141 converted to Mk IV), EF177–217 Hercules VI (EF213 and EF214 converted to Mk IV), EF231–277 Hercules VI (converted to Mk IV: EF234, EF237, EF241–244, EF248, EF256, EF260, EF263, EF265, EF267–269, EF270, EF272, EF277). Hercules XVI in EF250 et seq, except EF253 and EF259 fitted with Hercules VI. EF289–323 Hercules VI (converted to Mk IV: EF293, EF295, EF298, EF303, EF305–306, EF309, EF311, EF314, EF316–323)

Contract 763825/38: Short, Rochester and South Marston

Mk I: EF327–369 Hercules XI; EF384–400 Hercules XI; Mk III: EF401–412 Hercules VI (EF404 converted to Mk IV); EF413 Mk I Hercules XI; Mk III: EF425–470 Hercules VI; EF488–518 Hercules VI (converted to Mk IV: EF429, EF435, EF441, EF470, EF506)

Contract B.982828/39: Austin Motors, Birmingham

Mk III: all completed fitted with Hercules VI: EH875–909 (EH897 converted to Mk IV), EH921–961 (EH950 converted to Mk IV), EH977–996; EJ104–127 (EJ116 converted to Mk IV)

Contract 2008/C4(c): Short, South Marston

Mk III: LJ440–483 Hercules VI (but Hercules XVI: LJ469, LJ474, LJ475; LJ477 et seq); (LJ461 and LJ475 converted to Mk IV), LJ501–544 Hercules XVI (LJ512 converted to Mk IV prototype, LJ530 converted to Mk V prototype); LJ557–596 Hercules XVI (conversions to Mk IV: LJ536, LJ566, LJ569, LJ572, LJ575 which became TS266, LJ576, LJ583, LJ588, LJ590, LJ591, LJ594, LJ596), LJ611–653 Hercules XVI; LJ667–670 Hercules XVI

Contract 2009/C4(c): Short & Harland, Belfast

Mk IV, Hercules XVI: LJ810–851; LJ864–899; LJ913–956; IJ969–999; LK114–156; LK169–211; LK226–257; LK270–313; LK326–370. Built as Mk IV (Special Duty): LK125, LK131, LK145, LK192, LJK194, LK198, LK200, LK204, LK206–210, LK232, LK238, LK278–279, LK285, LK309, LK327, LK329, LK359. Built as Mk IV (Special Duty, Tropical): LK151, LK172–189, LK211, LK226–231, LK233–237, LK240, LK342, LK343

Contract B982939/C36(a): Austin Motors, Birmingham

Mk III, Hercules XVI unless stated: LK375–397 Hercules VI; LK398–402; LK403–411 Hercules VI; LK425–435 Hercules VI; LK436–438, LK439–440 Mk IV; LK441–458 Mk IV; LK459 Hercules VI; LK460–466; LK479–485; LK486 Mk IV; LK487–497; LK498 Mk IV; LK499 Mk IV; LK500 became Mk IV TS262; LK501–503; LK504 Mk IV; LK506–509; LK510 Mk IV; LK511, LK512 Mk IV became TS264; LK513 Mk IV; LK514–521; LK535–541; LK542 Mk IV; LK543 Mk IV; LK544; LK545–549 Mk IV; LK550; LK551 Mk IV; LK552; LK553–560 Mk IV; LK561; LK562 became Mk IV TS265; LK563–565; LK566–567 Mk IV; LK568–572; LK573 Mk IV; LK574–576; LK589 Mk IV; LK590–605; LK607–624 Mk IV

Contract 774677/38: Short & Harland, Belfast

MZ260–264 Mk III replacing five destroyed by bombing at Rochester

Contract 2009/C4(c): Short & Harland, Belfast

Mk V unless stated: PJ878–923; PJ935–959; PJ971–999; PK115–118; PK171–186; PK187–205 and PK217–224 cancelled Mk V. PK225–236 Mk IV; PK237 Mk IV (Special Duties)

Contract 2008/C4(c): Short, South Marston

Mk IV PW255-266; PW267–380 cancelled

Contract 2009/C4(c): Short & Harland, Belfast

Mk IV, Hercules XVI: PW384: PW385 (Special Duties): PW386–425; PW438–465. Cancelled aircraft: Mk IV: PW466–479; PW493–525; PW539–580; PW593–599; Mk V: PW600–637 TS261–266: not built as such, but earlier aircraft rebuilt and renumbered

Production – by Marks

Version	Source	No	Total built
B.12/36	Prototypes	2	2
Mk I	Short	264	
	Short & Harland	265	
	Austin	191	720
Mk II	–	–	3
Mk III	Short	264	
	Short & Harland	343	
	Austin	429	1,036
Mk IV	Short	11	
	Short & Harland	450	461
Mk V	Short	1	
	Short & Harland	160	161
Total			2,383

Note: 134 Mk IIIs were converted to Mk IV

Appendix 11
Individual Aircraft Histories

Listings are based upon the Form 78 Aircraft Movement Cards held by the Ministry of Defence, copies of which may be viewed at the Royal Air Force Museum, Hendon. Many of the cards detail allocation and movement dates, along with units and squadrons involved. For accounting purposes, these cards do not have Historical Document status of Form 540/541s. Most give an accurate account of an aircraft's career, but precise movement dates and sometimes fate and the date of such an event may differ from others that are listed in other documents.

Where such differences are certain, and only when they are certain, I have not used the Form 78 data. It will be found supplemented by aircraft individual letters and squadron identity letters – those never were code letters in the true sense – and details of the sites where aircraft crashed or were brought down – if known with a good degree of certainty. Wreckage fell widely in some cases.

Abbreviations used within the listing

A&AEE	Aeroplane & Armament Experimental Establishment
AA	Anti-aircraft
AAS	Air Armament School
AC	Aircraft repairable on site by contractor
AFEE	Airborne Forces Experimental Establishment
BBOC	Brought back on charge
CF	Conversion Flight
CFS	Central Flying School
CRD	Controller Research & Development
cv	Converted
H/CU	Heavy/Conversion Unit
E	Categorised E – write-off
E/7 Sqn, etc	Aircraft letter 'E' of 7 Squadron
E7–K/570 Sqn, etc	Where squadrons used two sets of squadron identity letters these appear – where known for certain. Bomber squadrons had a second letter used by the third or 'C' Flight Transport squadrons had two squadron identity letter allocations because they held so many aircraft
EFA	Write-off as a result of flying accident during non-operational flying
EFAO	Write-off as a result of flying accident during operational flying
EFB	Write off as a result of battle damage
FA	Flying accident
FH	Total flying time (hours/minutes)
FTR	Failed to return
GA	Ground accident
HFF	Heavy Freight Flight
MR	Major Repair
MU	Maintenance Unit
OADU	Overseas Aircraft Despatch Unit (No 2 at St Mawgan in 1944)
OAPU	Overseas Aircraft Preparation Unit (No 4 at Melton Mowbray in 1944)
PSO	Presumed struck off
RAE	Royal Aircraft Establishment
RIW	Repaired in Works
ROS	Repaired on Site
RTP	Reduced to Produce
SB	Short/Belfast
SD	Special Duties
SH	Short Bros
SLG	Satellite Landing Ground
SO	Sebro
SOC	Struck off charge
STT	School of Technical Training
u/c	Undercarriage

Individual Aircraft Histories

L7600 and L7605 Prototypes

L7600 Crashed 14.5.39

L7605 AAEE 22.4.40, Ringway 19.8.40, SH 2.9.40, AAEE 4.1.41, SH 28.4.41, AAEE 10.10.41, 7 Sqn 23.10.41, service trials of modified u/c, RAE 28.10.41, AC 28.10.42, tailwheel collapse, soon became 3443M

N3635 – N3769, 100 aircraft ordered from Shorts, Rochester 11 April 1938

N3635 AAEE 21.5.40, RAE 28.5.41, damaged 16.8.41, premature firing of assisted take-off rockets during trials, Cat E 1.1.42

N3636 10 MU 3.9.40, A/7 Sqn 24.9.40, tyre burst, and damaged again under repair 7.8.41, SO 11.9.41, E 26.10.41, became a synthetic trainer for 7 Sqn as 3056M

N3637 CFS (handling notes) 29.5.40, AAEE 30.5.40 (intensive flying) K,G/7 Sqn 20.12.40, AC 18.1.41, SH 27.8.41, AFEE 18.4.42, 2 STT 15.9.42 (3316M), SOC 16.2.45

N3638 22 MU 8.6.40, SB 13.7.40, C,L/7 Sqn 10.9.40, XV Sqn 13.6.41, 149 Sqn 24.11.41, 106 CF 3.1.42, 4 STT (3013M)

N3639 AAEE 7.40, 10 MU 17.11.40, DGRD SH 28.11.40, AAEE 4.1.42, RAE 2.8.42, became 3389M, SOC 30.11.44

N3640 10 MU 8.7.40, 7 Sqn 2.8.40, EFA 29.9.40 Hodge Branding, Westmorland, engine failed

N3641 48 MU 20.7.40, D/7 Sqn 12.8.40, tailwheel tyre burst 14.7.41, ROS, 1651 CU 6.10.41, tailwheel collapse 18.2.42, ROS and re-cat B 18.4.42. Became 3010M

N3642 19 MU 25.7.40, E/7 Sqn 29.8.40, XV Sqn 16.4.41, 1651 CU 6.10.41, 4 STT (3012M) 20.4.42, 78 MU 19.8.44 and SOC

N3643 22 MU 31.7.40, AAEE 1.8.40, G/7 Sqn 3.1.41, hit HT cables Halewood Common, Suffolk, returning from Rotterdam 24.3.41, EFAO

N3644 10 MU 9.8.40, H/7 Sqn 25.9.40, XV Sqn 10.4.41 (first one to squadron), u/c collapsed taxiing 21.5.41, SOC 17.6.41

N3645 destroyed by bombing, Rochester

N3646 damaged by bombing, late delivery, R,S/XV Sqn 26.9.41–15.1.42, ROS, XV Sqn 31.3.42, 214 Sqn 13.4.42, EFA swung on take off, 25.4.42

N3647 – N3651 destroyed by bombing, Rochester

N3652 19 MU 17.1.41, M/7 Sqn 6.2.41, damaged by machine gun fire 27.2.41, AC 25.6.41, u/c collapsed (first with Turner oleo legs), M/1651 CU 18.2.42, u/c collapsed landing Waterbeach 25.3.42, ROS, D/1651 CU 1.6.42, became 3444M 20.11.42

N3653 7 Sqn 24.2.41, FTR 3/4.3.41 (Brest, lost at sea)

N3654 SH DGRD 5.11.40, 19 MU 13.2.41, AAEE DGRD 21.3.41, B/XV Sqn 16.4.41, FTR 10/11.5.41 from Berlin, crashed at Opmeer, Netherlands

N3655 10 MU 2.41, 7 Sqn 30.3.41, u/c collapsed on landing 21.10.41, repaired, 7 Sqn 3.4.42, T/1651 CU 12.5.42, FTR 28/29.7.42 from Hamburg

N3656 Wyton 27.4.41, H/XV Sqn 2.5.41, damaged on day raid 21.7.41, shot up 12/13.8.41 and EFB in crash landing at Honington

N3657 Mk II DGRD SH 13.2.41, AAEE 17.7.41, SH 11.9.41, CRD AAEE 27.7.42, 10 MU 31.5.43, ECFS 24.12.43, 10 MU 21.3.44, SOC 16.9.46. [Believed cv to Mk I in 1943]

N3658 19 MU 2.41, E/XV Sqn, FTR 7/8.8.41 from Essen, shot down by AA fire at Overasselt, Netherlands

N3659 Wyton 28.5.41, N/XV Sqn 6.6.41, FTR 12.8.41 from Berlin, crashed Berxen, Germany

N3660 Wyton 11.6.41, W/XV Sqn 19.6.41, landing accident 27.6.41 ROS, XV Sqn 25.8.41, overshot Warboys landing 28.9.41, SO 6.10.41, Cat E 15.2.42

N3661 Wyton 3.7.41, Q/XV Sqn, u/c collapsed landing 11.7.41, SH 14.7.41, Cat E 29.9.41

N3662 DGRD AAEE, first with FN 7 turret, FN 50 later. Crashed on landing AAEE, u/c trouble after flight to assess operating at 70,000lb

N3663 Wyton 1.6.41, 7 Sqn 5.6.41, first to a squadron with FN 7, FTR 2/3.8.41 from Berlin, crashed at Werder, Germany

N3664 Wyton 18.6.41, 7 Sqn 24.6.41, XV Sqn 30.6.41, fate uncertain (FH 9.05)

N3665 B,S/XV Sqn 4.7.41, FTR 18.12.41, last seen off Brest engine burning, being attacked by Bf109s

N3666 Z/7 Sqn 30.7.41, EFB shot up during ops 28/29.8.41, crash landed Newmarket

N3667 T/XV Sqn 8.8.41, EFB 12.10.41, overshot, hit obstruction, from Nuremberg raid

N3668 B/7 Sqn 3.9.41, XV Sqn 4.1.42, u/c collapsed Alconbury 8.1.42, Cat E 15.2.42

N3669 H/7 Sqn 25.8.41, 26 CF 31.12.41, tailwheel damage 29.1.42, ROS, C/XV Sqn 27.2.42, damaged landing from ops 13.4.42, H/XV Sqn 16.5.42, fate uncertain but later used at 1 AAS

N3670 V/XV Sqn 7.9.41, Cat B, RIW 24.2.42, 7 Sqn 9.9.42, 101 CF 14.9.42, 1657 CU 6.10.42, 1665 CU 10.1.44, 6 MU 6.4.44, SOC 14.1.45

N3671 H/XV Sqn 25.9.41, Cat B u/c collapsed landing, SO 31.12.41, 44 MU 14.6.42, BS-F/ 1651 CU 18.5.43, FA 22.4.44 crashed Woodbridge u/c trouble and Cat E 9.5.44

N3672 M,U/7 Sqn 30.9.41, heavy landing 14.1.42, SO 18.2.42, Cat E 19.3.42

N3673 D/XV Sqn 30.9.41, FM 9.3.42 shot down by Nr 2 Bat, Res Flak 155 at 0305 hrs, near Apeldoorn, Netherlands

N3674 XV Sqn 15.10.41, X/214 CF 8.7.42, 1651 CU 7.10.42, FA 13.10.42 & RIW SO 11.10.42, became 4671M for PTS Ringway 12.3.44

N3675 S/XV Sqn 2.10.41, 15 CF 22.1.42, FA 1.3.42 and RIW SO 10.4.42, 19 MU 31.7.42, 1427 Flt 8.9.42, 1657 CU 2.10.42, EFA 4.1.44 crashed SW of Hundon, Suffolk, stalled and caught fire in crash

N3676 U/XV Sqn 26.10.41, S/1651 CU 8.4.42, crashed on take-off Waterbeach 30.7.42

N3677 DGRD SH 21.5.41, J/7 Sqn 12.10.41, FTR 7/8.11.41 crashed near Duisburg

N3678 CRD SH at Wyton 2.11.41. AAEE 27.1.42, 214 CF 8.7.42, EFA 2.10.42 swung on take-off at Waterbeach, Cat E at SO 19.10.42

N3679 D/7 Sqn 24.2.42, 13.4.42 crash landed one u/c leg up, Newmarket, returning from Essen

N3680 149 Sqn 27.10.41, tailwheel damage 1.11.41, SH Wyton 7.11.41, Y/7 Sqn 24.11.41, FTR 18.12.41 from Brest raid

N3681 CM SH 9.11.41, 1651 CU 8.10.42, EFA crashed landing Waterbeach 19.10.42

N3682 F,U/149 Sqn 23.11.41, 149 CF 23.4.42, 1657 CU 3.10.42, hit BF355 landing 5.8.43 Cat AC, 1657 CU 8.2.44, u/c collapsed landing 24.1.44, 1657 CU 8.2.44, MI 18.3.44 then Cat E13.4.44

N3683 XV Sqn 18.11.41, badly damaged 22/23.1.42 when hit by taxiing Wellington W5718 Alconbury, ROS, C/XV Sqn 28.7.42, 7 CF 22.8.42, damaged 21.9.42 low flying, ROS, B/75 Sqn 15.1.43, 1657 CU 19.5.43, u/c collapsed on take-off 3.10.43, SO 23.10.43, became 4668M for 8 Parachute Bn, Bulford, 12.3.44

N3684 149 Sqn 15.3.42, FA 26.3.42, SO RIW 4.5.42, XV CF 31.8.42, EFA Feltwell 13.9.42

N3700 A/7 Sqn 26.11.41, O/218 Sqn 16.1.420, XT:V/1657 CU 2.10.42, SO 27.8.43 after belly landing Newmarket 12.8.43, became 4669M for 8 Parachute Bn, Bulford 12.3.44

N3701 7 Sqn 22.11.41, EFA 1.12.41 hit obstruction landing Oakington in poor visibility

N3702 SH CRD 16.12.41, AFEE Ringway, prototype markings, 8.3.42, 10 MU 11.3.43, A3-J/1653 CU 19.12.43, EFA 6.5.44 after stall during landing

N3703 G/XV Sqn 1.4.42, EFB 10/11.4.42 badly shot up by intruder near Cambridge, back from Essen, crashed near Godmanchester

N3704 A/XV Sqn 1.12.41. V/75 Sqn 16.10.42, 115 Sqn 10.12.42, E/1651 CU 15.1.43, u/c collapse Waterbeach 19.3.43, ROS, 1651 CU 8.5.43, FA 29.10.43 u/c up landing Waterbeach, Cat E 6.12.43

N3705 10 MU 13.12.41, R, F/7 Sqn 31.1.42, FTR forced landed 0658 hrs 16.8.42 near Castle Loevenstein Netherlands. Test flown by *Luftwaffe* from Rechlin

N3706 218 Sqn 27.12.41, Y/7 Sqn 16.1.42, damaged by falling incendiary bomb 5/6.4.42, S/7 Sqn 16.5.42, FTR 29/30.6.42 from Bremen, ditched 50 miles off Cromer

N3707 Nl/XV Sqn 25.4.42, belly landed 28.8.42 electrical fault, RIW SO 23.9.42, 1651 CU 5.4.43, EFA crashed into EE966 on take off Downham Market 21.9.43, to SO 21.9.43, became Cat E 6.12.43

N3708 218 Sqn 26.12.41, E/7 Sqn 26.1.42, 1657 CU 12.8.42, 1653 CU 17.1.44, Cat E MR 1.5.44

N3709 218 Sqn 2.1.42, S,K/7 Sqn 16.1.42, FTR 26.3.42, crashed Gendringham, Netherlands, from Essen

N3710 218 Sqn 3.1.42, M/7 Sqn 5.1.42, FTR 16.5.42, crashed Wailers, France

N3711 Mk II CRD, AAEE 17.5.42, SH CRD 17.8.42, 10 MU 14.7.42, converted to Mk I, SOC 30.11.44

N3712 Y/218 Sqn 26.1.42, EFB 3.3.42, blew up on landing from Billancourt, hung up bombs

N3713 218 Sqn 6.2.42, 1 FA 13.2.42, SO RIW 14.3.42, SOC 21.4.43 RTP

N3714 218 Sqn 31.1.42, u/c up landing Marham 16.2.42, Q/218 Sqn 19.8.42, FTR 2.9.42 from Saarbrucken

N3715 218 Sqn 31.1.42, u/c collapsed landing Marham 27.2.42, RTP 16.3.42

N3716 O,A/7 Sqn 18.4.42, ETR 20.5.42 from Mannheim crashed Oostakker, Belgium

N3717 S/218 Sqn 6.2.42, Cat E after hitting Spitfire AB566 and Albacore X9112 at Manston due to lighting glare, 29.8.42

N3718 218 Sqn 11.2.42, u/c collapsed landing Marham 17.2.42, C/218 Sqn 27.6.42, FTR 2/3.7.42 from Bremen

N3719 S/149 Sqn 1.4.42, swung landing 23.4.42, SOC 27.4.42

N3720 7 Sqn 21.2.42, B/218 Sqn 2.42, SO Cat B 9.10.42, 1651 CU 22.3.43, overshot Waterbeach 4.6.43 starboard u/c torn off, Cat AC 4.6.43, BS:Q/1651 CU 21.7.43, 6 MU 24.4.44, SOC 14.1.45

N3721 C,S,P,J,/218 Sqn 23.2.42, 1651 CU 1.11.43, landed u/c up 4.11.43, not repaired, SOC 1.5.44

N3722 E/218 Sqn 8.3.42, Cat B 9.6.42, 218 Sqn 15.8.42, E/218 CF 7.9.42, 1657 CU 2.10.42, u/c collapsed landing Lakenheath 7.7.43, SOC

N3723 E/149 Sqn 8.3.42, H/149 Sqn EFB 7.12.42 flak damage, crashed near Ascot from Mannheim

N3724 SH CRD 21.7.42, TFU Defford 27.8.42, BMR 27.2.44, Cat E 11.5.44

N3725 D/218 Sqn 15.3.42, ROS 17.7.42, D/218 Sqn 1.9.42, crashed 1 mile E Stoke Ferry 0005 hrs 15.9.42 from Wilhelmshaven

N3726 G/149 Sqn 18.3.42, u/c collapsed landing, fighter damage near Aachen, 6/7.4.42 Cat E 2.5.42

N3727 149 Sqn 28.3.42, G/7 Sqn 29.3.42, FTR 27.4.42 from mining Heligoland

N3728 RAE 2.4.42, T/XV Sqn 7.4.42, FTR 2/3.6.42 from Essen, shot down by II/NJG2 0225 hrs at Herkenbosch, Netherlands

N3729 214 Sqn 19.4.42, Cat E 7.8.42 on undershooting Stradishall

N3750 D/7 Sqn 15.4.42, FTR 1/2.6.42 from Essen, in N Sea

N3751 P/214 Sqn 13.4.42, EFB 27/28.6.42 crash landed from Bremen, fighter damage

N3752 O/149 Sqn 1.5.42, FTR 17/18.5.42, mining in Baltic, crashed Risegaards, Denmark

N3753 218 Sqn 14.5.42 undershot Marham into trees 0030 hrs 2.6.42, from Essen

N3754 O/7 Sqn 14.5.42, FTR 25/26.6.42 from Bremen, shot down at Lugthoch, Germany

N3755 U/218 Sqn 18.5.42 S/149 Sqn 14.6.42, 149 CF 20.8.42, S/149 Sqn 26.8.42, EFB 5.10.42 crashed fuel short Arnold's Oak Farm, East Ling, Kent

N3756 214 Sqn 19.5.42, C/XV Sqn 23.5.42, EFB 11/12.8.42 crashed near Sudbury 0337 hrs from Mainz

N3757 7 Sqn 28.5.42, GIXV Sqn 5.42, FTR 29/30.6.42 from Bremen, shot down by AA, Hartward, Germany

N3758 V/XV Sqn 26.5.42, FA 14.9.42, SO, RIW 14.9.42, XT:K/1657 CU 4.6.43, FA 29.12.43, 1657 CU 30.1.44, EMI 12.6.44

N3759 Q/XV Sqn 30.5.42, FTR 19.9.42 from mining Baltic

N3760 D/7 Sqn 30.5.42, RIW SO 24.6.42 after accidental ground firing, 1657 CU 8.2.43, BFA 21.10.43 landed u/c up, SO RTP, became 4670M for 12 Parachute Bn 12.3.44

N3761 E/214 Sqn, FTR 6/7.6.42?

N3762 C/214 Sqn 8.6.42, FTR 19/20.6.42 from Osnabrück

N3763 44 MU 11.6.42, Q/218 Sqn 24.6.42, FTR 1/2.10.42 from Lübeck

N3764 7 Sqn 19.6.42, XV Sqn, 214 Sqn 5.7.42, J/7 Sqn, FTR 9.11.42 from Hamburg, shot down near target

N3765 7 Sqn 19.6.42, port wheel fell off in flight, crash landed Oakington 20.7.42, SO, 1657 CU 17.4.43, tailwheel up landing 17.5.43, AC FA 9.3.44 starboard u/c collapsed landing, 1657 CU 17.4.44, MU 12.5.44 and RTP Cat E 11.6.44

N3766 149 Sqn 3.6.42, 214 Sqn 5.6.42, Cat B SO RIW 14.7.42, 15 MU 9.1.43, 1651 CU 9.2.43, EFA 12.4.44, swung landing Wratting Common, into trees

N3767 214 Sqn 7.42, u/c up landing Stradishall 12.7.42, RIW SO 24.8.42, 1657 CU 9.3.43, EFA 12.11.43, u/c collapsed Stradishall

N3768 214 Sqn 9.6.42, crashed Stradishall taking off for St Nazaire 17.6.42

N3769 214 Sqn 1.5.42, 214 CF 1.7.42, 15 CF27.8.42, 1651 CU 7.10.42, brake trouble, burnt out after touchdown at Waterbeach 15.1.43

N6000 – N6129: 100 aircraft ordered from Short & Harland, Belfast

Note: N6000 Hercules III, N6001 to N6019 Hercules X, rest Hercules XI. N6004 converted to Stirling Mk III from Mk I (Hercules X)

N6000 AAEE 25.10.40, DGRD SH, AAEE 11.3.41 1427 Flt 1657 CU 6.4.42, became 3768M 5.43, SOC 5.4.44

N6001 AAEE 23.11.40, damaged during ferry flight by 1 FPP 26.11.40, 7 Sqn, FTR 30.6 .41 crashed Wesermunde

N6002 22 MU 17.12.40, 10 MU 22.12.40, DGRD SH 9.5.41, intensive flying, heating trials, EFA Castle Coombe 16.4.41

N6003 19 MU 17.12.40, V/7 Sqn 22.1.41, wheels up landing Oakington 9.2.41, repaired, intensive flying, RAE 26.12.41, 7 Sqn 31.12.41, 26 CF 31.12.41, K/1651 CU 24.3.42, swung on take off Waterbeach 9.42, Cat E 22.9.42

N6004 10 MU 30.12.40, 7 Sqn 24.3.41, F/XV Sqn 25.4.41, u/c collapsed on overshoot Wyton 12.6.41, ROS, SO 31.12.41, 10 MU 13.5.42, 1427 Flt 17.9.42, 1657 CU 2.10.42, FA 16.12.42, SO 23.12.42, modified to Mk III, 10 MU 29.5.43, RAF Northolt 27.7.43, 10 MU 9.8.43, SOC 13.9.46 obsolete

N6005 10 MU 10.1.41, 27 MU 18.1.41, Wyton 23.2.41, G/7 Sqn 3.3.41, F/26 CF 1651 CU 3.10.41, heavy landing 1.4.42, D2/1651 CU, u/c collapsed landing Waterbeach 16.8.42, ROS, stalled 1 mile N Shippea Hill 31.8.43 or 1.9.43, burnt out

N6006 22 MU 4.2.41, Wyton 22.2.41, G/7 Sqn 12.3.41, 26 CF, hit tree during unauthorised low flying near Kempston 15.12.41, SR:Y/101 CF 13.5.42, became 4165M at 4 STT 25.8.42

N6007 10 MU 10.2.41, XV Sqn 16.4.41, 7 Sqn 27.4.41, FTR 28.6.41 shot down at sea

N6008 A&AEE 15.2.41, 19 MU 10.10.41, 1427 Flt 23.3.42, 10 MU 19.5.42, 1427 Flt 23.12.42, FA 10.2.43, fuel starvation, crashed at Kedington, Suffolk

N6009 22 MU 10.2.41, Wyton 23.2.41, 7 Sqn 14.3.41, crashed at Stanbourne Q Site 16.4.41 or 1.4.41?

N6010 Wyton 14.3.41, 7 Sqn 30.3.41, FTR 10.5.41 from Berlin, crashed at Cloppenburg

N6011 Wyton 8.3.41, 7 Sqn 26.3.41, FTR 9/10.4.41 from Berlin, shot down by NF, Lingen

N6012 7 Sqn 29.3.41, hit trees on low approach returning from Hamburg 2/3.5.41, burnt

N6013 10 MU 15.3.41, A/7 Sqn 24.3.41, shot down by fighters off Borkum 1.5.41

N6014 Wyton 24.3.41, 7 Sqn 31.3.41, forced landed Wenhaston, Suffolk, suspected fuel short, badly damaged. To Shorts 14.5.41, SO 31.12.41, re-cat E 15.2.42

N6015 Wyton 24.3.41, A/XV Sqn 14.4.41, FTR 29/30.6.41, ditched

N6016 22 MU 29.3.41, Wyton 7.5.41, G/XV Sqn 17.5.41, FTR 29/30.6.41, shot down Ellerbeck, Germany

N6017 22 MU 30.3.41, 7 Sqn 30.6.41, FTR 10.7.41 shot down in sea 5 miles off Hardelot

N6018 Wyton 5.4.41, C/XV Sqn 16.4.41, FTR 19.7.41 shot down by AA near Dunkirk

N6019 Wyton 6.4.41, 7 Sqn 25.4.41, EFA, engine cut on take off Oakington 9.5.41, crashed 1 mile NE of base. (FH 32)

N6020 Wyton 29.4.41, B/7 Sqn 5.5.41, FTR 26.8.41, crashed near Trier. (FH 88.10)

N6021 Wyton 29.4.41, D/XV Sqn 7.5.41, 15/16.9.41, shot down at Henshingen, Germany

N6022 Wyton 3.5.41, D/7 Sqn, EFB 14/15.7.41 fuel short, crashed Newton Flotman

N6023 10 MU 9.5.41, DGRD SH Wyton 2.6.41, 7 Sqn 29.10.41, T/26 CF 22.12.41, T/1651 CU, EFA 16.2.42 as result of heavy night belly landing at Newmarket Heath

N6024 Wyton 18.5.41, XV Sqn 22.5.41, SH repair 11.6.41, SO 31.12.41, XV Sqn 3.4.42, 1651 CU 3.4.42, heavy landing 6.8.42 ROS, 1651 CU 27.8.42, EFA 10.3.43 swung on landing at Waterbeach

N6025 – N6028 inclusive and **N6031** destroyed by air attack on Belfast 14.8.40

N6029 Wyton 10.6.41, G, K/XV Sqn 15.6.41, FTR 25/26.7.41 ditched. (FH 60.30)

N6030 Wyton 16.6.41, P/XV Sqn 25.6.41, FTR 18.7.41, ditched, last heard by Wyton QDM 290 0506 hrs. (FH 33.55)

N6032 Wyton 2.6.41, T/7 Sqn 3.6.41, belly landing electrics failed 27.6.41, ROS, 7 CF 11.41, u/c collapsed landing 21.4.42, ROS SO, 7 CF 14.7.42, 101 CF 25.7.42, 1651 CU 26.8.42, SO 25.1.43 ROS, 1651 CU 6.2.43, belly landed Newmarket 10.3.43, 23 MU 27.8.43, 8 MU 16.9.44, SOC 2.12.44

N6033 Wyton 19.6.41, 7 Sqn 28.6.41, EFB 15.7.41, crashed in Northampton. (FH 14.10)

N6034 Wyton, XV Sqn 27.6.41, FTR 8.7.41, shot down by AA near Bethune

N6035 Wyton 1.7.41, 7 Sqn 4.7.41, FTR 25/26.7.41, crashed at Georee, Netherlands

N6036 Q/7 Sqn 30.6.41, 214 CF 30.5.42, 1657 CU 8.10.42, u/c collapsed landing 28.2.43 ROS, 8.10.42, 1665 CU 19.6.43, 6 MU 6.4.44, SOC 14.1.45

N6037 7 Sqn 10.7.41, u/c collapsed in overshoot Docking 15.7.41, Waterbeach 2.11.41, 26 CF 30.12.41, SO RIW 17.8.43, 6 MU SLG Woburn 3.3.44, SOC 19.7.45

N6038 R/XV Sqn 14.7.41, FTR 23.7.41, ditched 50 miles off Milford Haven

N6039 7 Sqn 22.7.41, u/c collapsed landing 13.8.41, ROS, SR:Z/101 CF 28.5.42, 1657 CU 5.43, E MR 22.6.44

N6040 C/XV Sqn 27.7.41, u/c collapsed landing Wyton 25.10.41, SO 28.10.41, Cat E 2.12.41

N6041 7 Sqn 2.8.41, damaged in overshoot due to throttle malfunction after ops 15.8.41. SOC 20.8.41

N6042 7 Sqn 6.8.41, fouled runway obstructions when landing at Graveley to avoid intruder activity 15.8.41, SO 31.12.41, RTP

N6043 G/XV Sqn 10.8.41, u/c would not retract after take off on ops. Bombs jettisoned at sea, then crashed near Ramsey, 14.8.41

N6044 0, E /XV Sqn 16.8.41, 15 CF 27.3.42, u/c collapsed landing15.12.41 again on 24.8.42 and on 22.1.43. 1651 CU from 6.10.42 as 'B', 1651 CU 22.6.43, hit obstruction taxiing 25.4.43, RIWSO 25.6.43, 1651 CU 27.10.43, tyre burst in heavy landing Wratting Common 24.5.44, Cat E 16.6.44

N6045 U/XV Sqn 22.8.41, FTR 7/8.9.41, crashed near Steenderen, Netherland. (FH 31.15)

N6046 7 Sqn 25.8.41, FTR 7/8.9.41, shot down near Recklinghausen. (FH 34.50)

N6047 7 Sqn 28.8.41, P/XV Sqn 11.9.41, spar fracture suspected 3.10.41, FTR 12/13.10.41 shot down near Marienbourg, Belgium, 12/13.10.41. (FH 23.20)

N6048 XV Sqn 31.8.41, 7 Sqn 1.9.41, accident damage 3.10.41, 7 Sqn 28.2.42, 7 CF 25.3.42, overshot Oakington u/c collapsed 7.6.42, RIW SO 19.6.42 19 MU 5.12.42, BS-P/1651 CU 21.1.43, SO 2.44, E 15.3.44. (FH 543.30)

N6049 V,Z/7 Sqn 4.9.41, battle damage 16.10.41, 7 Sqn 31.12.41, loaned 26 CF 31.12.41, 218 Sqn 5.1.42, A/1651 CU 2.3.42, u/c collapsed during engine runs 25.3.42, ROS, 1651 CU 13.6.42, tailwheel collapse on landing 30.6.42, 1651 CU 29.7.42, heavy landing 26.9.42, CC/1651 CU 29.10.42, u/c collapse landing 21.3.43, 1651 CU 29.4.43, 1659 CU 6.43, 1653 CU 28.12.43, E MR 13.4.44

N6065 7 Sqn 1.10.41, G/XV Sqn 2.10.41, taxiing damage 30.10.41, D/XV Sqn 5.2.42, Z/149 Sqn 8.7.42, 1657 CU 4.10.42, RIW S&H 29.4.43, 23 MU 26.11.43, S&H 24.3.45, 23 MU, SOC MR 18.4.45

N6066 149 Sqn 23.11.41, 126 CF 25.11.41, EFA 24.12.41 crashed Kempston during low flying, port aileron fractured upon hitting a tree

N6067 22 MU 12.12.41, 46 MU 8.2.42, E/XV Sqn 9.2.42, EFB 26.2.42, crashed due to flak damage and fuel shortage, Beck Lodge Farm, Mildenhall

N6068 T/149 Sqn 29.1.42, FTR 15/16.4.42. crashed Steene, Belgium. (FH 63.40)

N6069 G/1651 CU 1.3.42, FTR 28/29.7.42. (FH 186.45)

N6070 A/218 Sqn 17.2.42, FTR 5.5.42, crashed Frankfurt

N6071 G/218 Sqn 24.2.42, FTR 17/18.5.42, crashed Lyne, Denmark

N6072 J,P/218 Sqn 24.2.42, FTR 7.8.42, shot down by night fighter near Kessel, Netherlands

N6073 Y/7 Sqn 25.2.42, FTR 19/20.5.42, crashed near Mannheim–Neumuller

N6074 G/7 Sqn 27.2.42, FTR 26.3.42 ditched off Barmouth 0200 hrs, off track. (FH 14)

N6075 A/7 Sqn 8.3.42, damaged 15.4.42 ROS, 7 Sqn 23.5.42, SR-W/101 CF 25.5.42, hit 1,600-foot hill between Leek and Longmoore, Staffs, 13.7.42 and EFA. (FH 94.40)

N6076 218 Sqn 10.3.42. D/XV Sqn 12.3.42, crash landed 15.4.42, RIW SO 8.5.42 Cat E 22.5.42

N6077 V/218 Sqn 8.3.42, SO 31.3.42, V/218 Sqn 6.5.42, overshot Marham after ops 27.7.42, ROS, 218 Sqn 30.9.42, FTR 28.1.43 crashed Dassel, Germany. (FH 201.45)

N6078 P/218 Sqn 21.3.42, FTR 22/23.6.42 ditched off Netherlands. (FH 100.50)

N6079 F/149 Sqn 20.3.420, 149 CF 16.8.42, 1657 CU 3.10.42, 6 MU 24.4.44, E MR 1.5.44. (FH 726.30)

N6080 G/149 Sqn 23.3.42, serious battle damage 17.6.42, RIW SO 2.7.42, 19 MU 29.11.42, /1657 CU 26.1.43, crash landed Stradishall 11.8.43, SOC 25.8.43 (FH 221.40)

N6081 G, H/149 Sqn 25.3.42, FTR 29.8.42, shot down Airlenbach, Germany

N6082 Q/149 Sqn 25.3.42, FTR 7.7.42, in IJsselmeer. (FH 139.30)

N6083 N/149 Sqn 27.3.42, crashed soon after take-off Lakenheath 24.8.42 1 mile SE due to engine fire

N6084 C/149 Sqn 27.3.42, FTR 8/9.6.42 crashed near Gelsenkirchen. (FH 83.35)

N6085 H/7 Sqn 10.9.41, shot down near Bourn 3.10.41 by Ju 88, wreckage to 1 PRD Cowley. (FH 135.40)

N6086 R,F/XV Sqn 'MacRobert's Reply', 8.4.42, 101 CF 13.10.42, J/1651 CU 21.11.42, u/c collapsed Waterbeach 15.1.43, ROS, 1651 CU 22.2.43, crashed at Oakington village 14.3.43. (FH 194.15)

N6087 M/7 Sqn 21.9.41, engine fire returning from ops 18.11.41, crashed at Willingham

N6088 G, Q,X/XV Sqn 25.9.41, 15 CF 22.1.42, caught fire on day cross country flight 21 miles N of Retford 16.6.42. (FH 244)

N6089 L/7 Sqn 1.10.41, 26 CF 31.12.41, L/218 Sqn 5.1.42, tailwheel collapse 27.2.42, ROS SO,Y/218 Sqn 7.4.42, u/c collapsed on landing 20.2.43, RIW SO 2.3.43, XT-G/1657 CU 16.7.43, EFA 11.5.44, swung on take off Stradishall, u/c collapsed

N6090 Y/7 Sqn 30.9.41, AAEE *Trinity* Trials, overshot Boscombe in poor visibility 20.11.41, returned to 7 Sqn, Z/15 CF, EFA swung off Alconbury runway 18.4.42, SO, RTP 1.5.42

N6091 K/7 Sqn 2.10.41, FTR 7/8.11.41, shot down by light flak at Hekelingen, Netherlands

N6092 7 Sqn?, O/XV Sqn 6.10.41, 214 Sqn 5.4.42, over-corrected take-off swing at Stradishall 5.5.42

N6093 149 Sqn 12.10.41, 7 Sqn 14.10.41, P, C/XV Sqn 15.10.41, serious battle damage 2/23.1.42, SO 26.1.42 and SOC. (FH 75.25)

N6094 149 Sqn 22.10.41 then re-allocated and became G/7 Sqn 23.10.41, R/XV Sqn 14.1.42, EFA overshot Wyton 25.3.42

N6095 149 Sqn 24.10.41, K/7 Sqn 8.11.41, EFB 18.12.41, written off due to serious damage during Brest attack

N6096 C/XV Sqn 26.10.41, Waterbeach/1651 CU 1.11.41, damaged on take-off 14.1.42, ROS, 1651 CU 11.4.42, u/c collapsed on landing 11.10.42, EFA 20.4.43 after swinging on take-off at Stradishall. (FH 295.25)

N6097 C/XV Sqn 1.11.41, failed to get airborne from Warboys 15.11.41, ice accretion suggested

N6098 G/XV Sqn 1.11.41, burnt out refuelling at Lossiemouth 29.1.42

N6099 C/149 Sqn 2.11.41, P/1651 CU 28.3.42, EFA after hitting N6127 when taking off from cross runway at Waterbeach. (FH 189.20)

N6100 149 Sqn 3.11.41, A/26 CF 6.11.41, swung on landing to avoid crashed aircraft at Waterbeach 18.12.41 and written off

N6101 149 Sqn 3.11.41, E/26 CF 6.11.41, u/c collapsed on touch down 23.11.41, ROS, 149 Sqn 23.3.42, 1651 CU 3.4.42, EFA 9.12.42 crashed by runway and burnt out. (FH 296)

N6102 G/149 Sqn 18.11.41, battle damage, u/c collapsed on landing 12.2.42, RIW SO, B/1651 CU 19.7.42, FTR 29.7.42. (FH 85.35)

N6103 E/149 Sqn 23.11.41, O/1651 CU 10.5.42, EFA crashed on take-off Waterbeach 2.9.42

N6104 149 Sqn 25.11.41, R/26 CF 11.12.419, overshot Waterbeach 15.12.41, 26 CF 26.5.42, R/218 CF 4.8.42, XT-R/1657 CU 2.10.42, EFA 31.3.44, brought down probably by ice accretion 1 mile N of Cavendish

N6120 V/7 Sqn 26.11.41, EFB 17.1.42, prop shot off by fire from 'friendly' convoy, crashed on railway by Oakington

N6121 W/7 Sqn 30.11.41, battle damaged 18.12.41, ROS, 7 Sqn 25.7.42, SR-W/101 CF 25.7.42, hit Wellington X3668/101 Sqn on operational climb-out 28.7.42 and crashed near Cottenham

N6122 XV Sqn 8.12.41, Q/149 Sqn 9.12.41, Y/149 CF 15.6.42, EFA, u/c collapsed landing Mildenhall 21.6.42

N6123 P/149 Sqn 7.12.41, 149 CF 3.9.42, Q/75 Sqn 15.1.43, FTR, ditched 4.3.43. (FH 159.05)

N6124 R/149 Sqn 11.12.41, FTR 5.5.42, crashed near Agincourt

N6125 149 Sqn 13.12.41, Z/149 CF 18.1.42, Y/214 Sqn 30.5.42, 1651 CU 17.12.42, u/c collapsed taxiing at Graveley 29.7.43, RIW SO 4.8.43, 27 MU 9.4.44, SOC obsolete 29.11.45

N6126 218 Sqn 17.12.41, U/149 Sqn 14.2.42. 10/11.3.42 brought down at Nutterden–Materborn

N6127 218 Sqn 16.12.41, N/149 Sqn 15.2.42, V/1651 CU 28.3.42, EFA 12.8.42 take-off on wrong runway Waterbeach, hit N6099 at intersection, 30.5.42

N6128 218 Sqn 23.12.41, 7 Sqn 24.12.41 (loaned to 26 CF), T/218 Sqn 16.1.42, 218 CF 28.2.42, 15 CF 7.7.42, swung taking off Waterbeach 2.6.43 and port wing torn off, RIW SO 12.6.43, L/1651 CU 8.10.43, E MR 5.7.44

N6129 7 Sqn 5.1.42, 218 Sqn 8.1.42, X/218 CF 28.2.42, FTR 28/29.7.42, ditched off Roemoe, Denmark

R9141 – R9358 150 Mk Is. (Designated series ii from R9295)

R9141 G/214 Sqn 26.6.42, u/c trouble Stradishall, to SB RIW 17.8.42. K,PP/1651 CU 31.3.43, swung taking off from Waterbeach 18.9.43, SOC 6.12.43

R9142 B/149 Sqn 27.6.42, u/c collapsed landing at Lakenheath 17.8.42, SB RIW. 1657 CU 12.3.43, u/c collapsed taking off 24.9.43, Cat B, Re-cat E 3.4.44

R9143 7 Sqn 28.6.42, O/149 Sqn 1.7.42, 1665 CU 6.7.43, 6 MU 8.3.44, SOC 14.1.45

R9144 Q, R/XV Sqn 2.7.42, battle damage and belly landing at Newmarket 8.12.42, SB RIW 20.12.42. XT-W/1657 CU 29.5.43, 1665 CU 30.11.43, 6 MU 26.3.44, SOC 14.1.45

R9145 19 MU 18.7.42, K/214 Sqn 29.7.42, FTR 1/2.3.43 from Berlin

R9146 S/214 Sqn 25.7.42, FTR 15/16.10.42 from Cologne, shot down at 2254 hrs by fighter at Oss, Netherlands

R9147 10 MU 17.7.42, K/7 Sqn 23.7.42, RIW SB 1.8.42 after overshooting Honeybourne. BS-U/1651 CU 23.1.43, SOC 15.8.44

R9148 10 MU 19.7.42, J/214 Sqn 19.7.42, J,V,BS-L/1651 CU 13.8.42, FA 2.9.42, SB RIW 5.10.42. 1651 CU 31.3.43, 1665 CU 30.11.43, 6 MU 22.4.44, SOC 14.1.45

R9149 B/7 Sqn 17.8.42, FTR 9/10.3.43 from Munich, shot down at Elan, France

R9150 A/7 Sqn 29.7.42, FA damage 6.8.42, O/7 Sqn, FTR 29/30.11.42 from Turin, shot down at Pecy, France

R9151 O/XV Sqn 23.7.42, flak damage caused forced landed at Docking 18.8.42, SOC 31.8.42

R9152 C/214 Sqn 25.7.42, X,G,JJ/1651 CU 30.1.43, FA 28.11.43, 1653 CU 22.12.43, Cat E on Major inspection 1.8.44

R9153 U/XV Sqn 31.7.42, FTR 28/29.8.42 from Nuremberg, crashed at Mesmont, France

R9168 T/XV Sqn 26.8.42, FTR 16/17.12.42 en route Turin. Shot down by III/NJG1 at 2009 hrs, at Epe, Netherlands

R9169 Y/7 Sqn 1.9.42, FTR 10.11.42 from Hamburg

R9170 H/149 Sqn 31.8.42. On 10.11.9.42 set out for Düsseldorf, shot down by fighter at Ooltgemsplaar, Netherlands

R9184 U/218 Sqn 1.9.42, FTR 23/24.10.42 Genoa, ditched off Dieppe

R9185 Y/218 Sqn 3.9.42, FTR 6/7.11.42 from mining the Gironde Estuary. Shot down west of St Brieuc, France

R9186 F,T/214 Sqn 6.9.42, weather 6.5.43 then RIW SB, 11.7.44, Cat E during major inspection 1.8.44

R9187 A/218 Sqn 12.9.42, FTR 23/24.9.42 from Vegesack

R9188 initially completed as a Mk II (Cyclone engines). CRD Shorts 16.9.42. Converted to Mk III. RAE 9.1.43. Became 3970M and held at 4 STT from 12.43 to 16.10.46 when SOC

R9189 K/218 Sqn 13.9.42, swung during take-off from Downham Market 28.2.43, u/c collapsed, SOC 20.4.43

R9190 E/218 Sqn 16.9.42, FTR 11/12.10.42 from mining, crashed near Sioe Island, Denmark

R9191 O/214 Sqn 15.9.42, SB 15.2.43, QQ-L/1651 CU 28.6.43, 1665 CU 30.11.43, 6 MU 20.3.44, SOC 14.1.45

R9192 7 Sqn 21.9.42, E/XV Sqn 24.9.42, RIW 29.11.43, AK-B/1657 CU 12.5.43, FA 6.11.43, 12.6.44. (FH 412.15)

R9193 7 Sqn 22.9.42, S/XV Sqn 24.9.42, BS-P/1651 CU 5.10.43, heavy landing at Wratting Common 5.7.44, SOC 19.7.44

R9194 N/214 Sqn 22.9.42, FTR 28/29.11.42 from Turin. Crashed at Sinceny, France

R9195 P/XV Sqn 6.11.42, RIW SB 18.12.42. F/1657 CU 21.5.43, EFA 14.5.44, u/c trouble resulted in belly landing

R9196 G,U/218 Sqn 26.9.42, BS-B/1651 CU 9.8.43, 1665 CU 30.11.43, 6 MU 28.4.44, SOC 14.1.45 **R9197** V/214 Sqn 24.9.42, FTR 3/4.2.43 from Hamburg, shot down night fighter at 2004 hrs at Lienden, Netherlands

R9198 M/214 Sqn 30.9.42. On 8.11.42 swung on take off and wheels were caught in a ditch, SB RIW 9.11.42. 90 Sqn 10.5.43, 1665 CU 20.5.43, 1657 CU 9.6.43. SOC after take-off swing caused collapse 26.6.43

R9199 214 Sqn 1.10.42, F,T/7 Sqn date uncertain, FTR 8/9.4.43 from Duisburg

R9200 Allocated to 214 Sqn 3.10.42, became P/149 Sqn 9.10. 42, AA-S/75 Sqn 1.3.43, FA Cat B at Jurby 21.4.43. 214 Sqn, u/c collapsed during take off swing 16.7.43, SB RIW. 10 MU 2.12.43, 6 MU 2.12.44, SOC 19.7.45

R9201 U/XV Sqn 1.10.42, FTR 6/7.11.42 from mining Gironde. Crashed at St Andre des Eaux, France

R9202 K/149 Sqn 13.10.42, FTR 29/30.11.42 Crashed at Trasco–Finerola, Italy

R9203 D/149 Sqn 11.10.42. During low flying off Holkam in poor visibility on 23.10.42 wing tip hit water. D/218 Sqn 18.2.43, X/214 Sqn 13.4.43, FA 14.5.43, 214 Sqn 2.11.43. Became 4240M for 1651 CU 28.10.43

R9241 7 CF 9.10.42, L/218 Sqn 11.10.42. En route for Milan an engine fire caused aircraft to crash at 1925 hrs near Brantham, east of Colchester

R9242 B/149 Sqn 21.10.42, O/214 Sqn 23.3.43. FTR on 14.5.43, shot down by fighter at Heerlerheide, Netherlands

R9243 Y,C/75 Sqn 2.10.42, BS-K, W-K/1651 CU 27.9.43, EFA Waterbeach 6.8.44, u/c torn off as a result of take-off swing

R9244 W,S/ 218 Sqn 15.10.42, BS-D, BS-L/1651 CU 28.9.43, EFA 10.5.44, starboard u/c collapsed during landing at Wratting Common. SOC 15.8.44. (FH 604.50)

R9245 N/75 Sqn 25.10.42, EFB 17.12.42 hit Devil's Dyke during take off from Newmarket. Engine failure a possible cause. En route for Gironde Estuary. Two mines exploded

R9246 S/75 Sqn 31.10.42, EFA 24.11.42, belly landed near Holm, Cambs

R9247 W/75 Sqn 21.10.42, FTR 17/18.12.42 from Fallersleben, shot down by flak at Vechta, Germany

R9248 H/75 Sqn 7.11.42, FTR 23/24.1.43 from Lorient. Shot down at St. Tregonner

R9249 44 MU 20.11.42, TFU 31.12.42, A,H/7 Sqn 14.3.43, 1657 CU 29.7.43. EFA 22.10.43, crashed and burnt out during landing Chipping Warden

R9250 C,W/75 Sqn 2.11.42, FTR 3/4.4.43 from Hamburg, shot down at Elst, Netherlands, at 2000 hrs

R9251 32 MU 7.4.43, 7 Sqn 7.5.43, 1657 CU 13.3.43, MI SB 9.5.43, 1657 CU 17.5.44, MI SB 5.7.44, 1657 CU 31.8.44, 1651 CU 17.10.44, 6 MU 6.11.44, SOC 19.7.45

R9252 10 MU 15.11.42, TFU 23.11.42, L/7 Sqn 13.12.42, NTU Gransden 13.4.43, 1651 CU 22.12.43, SOC 15.8.44. (FH 311.25)

R9253 C/149 Sqn 17.11.42, FTR 9.12.42 from mining off Warnemunde. Crashed at Westermarsch, Germany

R9254 A&AEE 20.11.42, 10 MU 6.6.43, 32 MU 10.10.43, 214 Sqn 22.10.43, 1653 CU 10.12.43, EFA 13.8.44, tyre burst during take-off from Chedburgh

R9255 19 MU 17.11.42, TFU 2.12.42, G/7 Sqn 21.12.42, EFB 28.3.43 due to flak damage sustained during Berlin raid, u/c collapsed landing at Oakington

R9256 G,C/90 Sqn 28.11.42, FA, port tyre burst during heavy landing 1.2.43, RIW SB 1.2.43. 1651 CU 22.6.43, 1665 CU 30.11.43, 6 MU 30.3.44, SOC 14.1.45

R9257 44 MU 28.11.42, TFU 30.12.42, C,E, XU-R/7 Sqn 14.1.43, 1657 CU 17.7.43, 214 Sqn 25.7.43, EFB 12.8.43 swung during take off at Chedburgh for Turin, u/c collapsed

R9258 19 MU 29.11.42, 32 MU 10.12.42, K/7 Sqn 2.1.43, W/214 Sqn 1.8.43, FTR 21/22.9.43, crashed at Bremerode, Germany

R9259 J/7 Sqn 17.11.42, FTR 6/7.12.42 from Mannheim, shot down at Saveniere, Belgium

R9260 44 MU 8.12.42, TFU 9.12.42, O/7 Sqn 21.12.42, EFB 2/3.8.43 engine trouble after take off for Hamburg, landed back, u/c collapsed due to swing

R9261 10 MU 29.11.42, 32 MU 29.12.42, M/7 Sqn 31.12.42. FTR 20/21.4.43 from Stettin, shot down at Kongsmark, Denmark

R9262 A/7 Sqn 22.11.42, FTR 21/22.12.42 from Munich, shot down at Searincourt, France

R9263 44 MU 5.12.42, TFU 23.12.42, D/7 Sqn 29.12.42, FTR 1.5.43 from Bocholt, shot down at Akkerwoude 0252 hrs

R9264/G 10 MU 29.11.42, 32 MU 11.12.42, L/7 Sqn, FTR 2/3.2.43. Shot down at 2205 hrs by night fighter possibly of I/NJG 1 at Hendrik–Ido–Ambacht. Germans retrieved for first time an *H2S* set

R9265 N/149 Sqn 1.12.42, EFA 19.12.42. Wing structural failure during high load test, crashed near Gransden, Cambs

R9266 44 MU 8.12.42, TFU 9.12.42, 10 MU 29.1.43, TFU 18.2.43, J/7 Sqn 18.2.43, FTR 21/22.6.43 from Krefeld. Shot down near target

R9267 10 MU 30.11.42, 32 MU 17.12.42, S/7 Sqn 24.12.42, EFA 14.6.43. Throttle trouble preceded wheels-up landing in a field near Hatley St George, Cambs

R9268 R.,F/XV Sqn 6.12.42, 1665 CU 5.6.43, 6 MU 23.4.44, SOC 14.1.45

R9269 10 MU 4.12.42, 19 MU 11.4.43, 32 MU 24.4.43, NTU 6.6.43, 214 Sqn 26.7.43, 1653 CU 1.8.43, 1657 CU, 1653 CU 3.3.44, EFA 30.6.44. Bounced on landing, starboard u/c collapsed during second landing attempt

R9270 G/TFU 9.12.42, 32 MU 15.12.42, S,Q/7 Sqn 22.12.42, FTR 8/9.3.43 from Nuremberg, crashed at Iles Souhesmes, France

R9271 K/149 Sqn 20.12.42, Q/90 Sqn 23.2.43, FTR 5/6.3.43 from Essen, crashed at St Peter, Germany

R9272 TFU 23.12.42, W/7 Sqn 29.12.42, FTR 21/22.6.43 from Krefeld, crashed at Gilze, Netherlands

R9273 TFU 15.12.42, C/7 Sqn 21.12.42, RIW SB 3.2.43. XT-W1657 CU 5.8.43, EFA 9.5.4. Port wing drop on approach, control lost, crashed at Stradishall

R9274 B/XV Sqn 29.12.42, FTR 3/4.2.43 from Hamburg. Shot down by fighter at Renkum, Netherlands, at 2054 hrs

R9275 TFU 24.12.42, Y/7 Sqn 31.12.42, FTR 10/11.4.43 from Frankfurt, crashed at Koerich, Luxembourg

R9276 F/149 Sqn 29.12.42, G/90 Sqn, FTR 19/20.2.43 from Wilhelmshaven. Probably shot down at sea

R9277 32 MU 20.12.42, P,T, XU-T/7 Sqn 24.12.42, NTU 9.5.43, 214 Sqn 26.7.43, BDU 5.8.43, 1657 CU 14.11.43. FA 11.2.44 arising from control problems and hit ditch. RIW SB 11.2.44 intended, declared Cat E instead on 11.5.44

R9278 TFU 24.12.42, J,E/7 Sqn 31.12.42, FTR 14/15.4.43 from Stuttgart, crashed at St Souplet, France

R9279 J/XV Sqn 8.1.43, FTR 26/27.2.43 from Cologne, fate uncertain

R9280 32 MU 3.1.43, E/7 Sqn 18.2.43, FA 22.3.43, overshot landing, RIW SB 26.3.43. BDU 24.7.43, A3-Z/1653 CU 4.2.44, FA 22.3.44. Engine problem induced swing on take off, port wing and u/c torn off, Chedburgh. Re-cat E 12.6.44

R9281 32 MU 30.12.42, V/7 Sqn 2.4.43, FTR 24/25.6.43 from Elberfeld, shot down off Netherlands

R9282 Q/214 Sqn 2.1.43, FTR 3/4.4.43 from Hamburg. Shot down at Benschop 2330 hrs by fighter

R9283 32 MU 31.12.42, Q/7 Sqn 19.3.43, R,J/214 Sqn 25.8.43, XT-H/1657 CU 31.12.43, Cat E/SOC 26.6.44

R9284 10 MU 18.1.43, 19 MU 11.4.43, 32 MU 28.6.43, 7 Sqn 5.7.43, W/214 Sqn 20.8.43, 1651 CU 22.12.43, SOC 15.8.44

R9285 J/214 Sqn 26.1.43, FA Chedburgh 12.3.43, swing led to detached starboard wheel, RIW SB 12.3.43. 214 Sqn 19.6.43, OG-U/1665 CU 12.7.43, 6 MU 19.3.44, SOC 14.1.45

R9286 32 MU 2.1.43, C/7 Sqn 21.3.43, FTR 11/12.6.43 from Munster. Shot down by flak 25 km SW Den Helder 0304 hrs

R9287 A/149 Sqn 21.1.43, N/218 Sqn 4.3.43, 00, NN, BS-Y/1651 CU 26.3.43, 1653 CU 26.1.44, 8 MU 8.8.44, SOC 15.8.44

R9288 32 MU 27.1.43, Z,P/7 Sqn 27.3.43, Q/214 Sqn 1.8.43, EFB 8.9.43. Swing on take off at Chedburgh took aircraft through bomb dump, Boulogne bound

R9289 19 MU 21.1.43, 32 MU 1.4.43, F/7 Sqn 19.4.43, F,O/214 Sqn 23.8.43, EFB 10.12.43. Swung on take off from Tempsford, u/c collapsed

R9290 Y,X/75 Sqn 29.1.43, FTR 28/29.4.43 from mining Kiel Bay. Crashed at Osterso Veaternas Laaland, Denmark

R9295 (East India III) G/7 Sqn 5.1.42, 218 Sqn, G/149 Sqn 14.2.42, EFB 11.3.42. Burnt out, crashed at Holywell Row returning from Essen when damaged

R9296 7 Sqn 22.1.42, 218 Sqn, D,Q/149 Sqn 13.2.42, /149 CF 26.3.42, 1657 CU 4.10.42, EFA 22.7.43, swung when taking off from Stradishall

R9297 P/7 Sqn 28.1.42, XT-B, XT-E/ 1657 CU, FA Stradishall 10.1.44, overshot, port u/c collapsed, RIW SB 10.1.44. 10 MU 10.6.44, 6 MU 9.12.44, SOC 19.7.45

R9298 218 CF 28.1.42, 7 Sqn 7.2.42, Q/1651 CU 27.2.42, RIW SB 22.4.42. A&AEE 27.8.42, 1657 CU 5.11.43, EFB 29.5.44, shot down on approach to Shepherd's Grove by an Me 410 intruder. Hit LK506

R9299 149 Sqn 11.2.42, Y/149 CF 19.2.42, EFA 16.7.42. Oil entering starboard outer exhaust caused fire. Aircraft spun in and exploded on impact near Swaffham Bulbeck, Cambs

R9300 L/7 Sqn 7.2.42, 7 CF 16.5.42, GA at Little Rissington 4.6.42, heat ignited nose ammunition.1657 CU, 13.10.42, tailwheel collapse Stradishall, 22.12.42 u/c collapsed during take off swing, RIW SB 8.1.43.1657 CU, EFA, u/c collapsed during take off swing

R9301 Q/7 Sqn 5.2.42, 7 CF, 1657 CU 31.10.42, FA 9.2.43, u/c collapse on take off. EFA 21.5.43, take off swing, u/c collapsed

R9302 F/XV Sqn 5.2.42, Z/15 CF 5.5.42, Z/1651 CU 7.10.42? GA 24.6.43, u/c collapse during taxying, 1665 CU 30.11.43, 6 MU 10.4.44, SOC 14.1.45

R9303 P/XV Sqn 11.2.42, 214 Sqn 5.4.42, Z/214 CF 4.10.42, RIW SB 20.4.43 following wheels-up landing. 1665 CU 29.8.43, 6 MU 5.4.44, SOC 14.1.45

R9304 U/XV Sqn 15.2.42, U, 0 /1651 CU 5.4.42, EFA 28.2.43, swung on landing at Waterbeach, u/c collapsed

R9305 R,V/7 Sqn 16.2.42, FTR 28.3.42 from Lübeck, crashed Ahrensburg, Germany

R9306 V/7 Sqn 29.3.42, RIW SB 29.6.42. 19 MU 30.11.42, J/90 Sqn 21.1.43, EFB 16.2.43, fuel starvation caused crash near Blandford, Dorset, when returning from Lorient

R9307 149 Sqn 29.3.42, EFB 22.4.42, swung on to soft ground, taking off from Lakenheath for Le Havre

R9308 P/XV Sqn 1.4.42, EFB 20.7.42, overshot Waterbeach landing in poor visibility after Ju 88 engagement during Vegesack raid

R9309 converted to Mk III for S&H CRD trials wef 27.6.42. A&AEE 14.7.42, EFA 6.9.42, engine cylinder fracture during high load trials led to engine fire. Crashed in wood on edge of Porton Range

R9310 XV Sqn 2.4.42, P/149 Sqn 12.4.42, FTR 17/18.5.42 from mining in Baltic, crashed near Asnaes, Denmark

R9311 XV Sqn 3.4.42, L/218 Sqn 6.4.42, EFB 31.5.42, port u/c would not retract, hit hill just beyond runway. Belly landed en return from Cologne

R9312 H,C/XV Sqn 4.4.42, FA 22.5.42, overshot and smashed into W7536 which had crashed on runway, ROS. FTR 16/17.10.42 from mining off Bayonne, crashed at Pont du Cens, Nantes, France

R9313 XV Sqn 5.4.42, Q/218 Sqn 7.4.42, EFB 5.5.42, shot down by British fighter on return from Laon, crashed on Gatehouse Farm 5 miles N of Petworth, Surrey

R9314 XV Sqn 21.4.42, T/149 Sqn 12.5.42, FTR 5/6.6.42 from Essen, collided with another aircraft reported as either a Bf 110 or a Wellington, ditched off Belgium. Crew rescued

R9315 O/XV Sqn 14/4/42, O/1657 CU 17.11.42, EFA 9.9.43, u/c collapsed during swing on landing at Stradishall

R9316 23 MU 17.4.42, 214 Sqn 21.4.42, RIW SB 20.6.42. 10 MU 6.11.42, K/75 Sqn 23.1.43, FTR 13/14.2.43 from Lorient, crashed at Plouay, France

R9317 U/214 Sqn 19.4.42, EFB 4.6.42, overshot Stradishall, port inner engine gave trouble, aborted en route Bremen

R9318 B/XV Sqn 24.4.42, J/XV Sqn, FTR 14/15.9.42 from Wilhelmshaven. Shot down near Amsterdam

R9319 XV Sqn 26.4.42, S/214 Sqn 28.4.42, EFB 20.6.42, engine failed, bombs jettisoned, landed too fast and, in avoiding R9350, u/c collapsed. RIW SB 21.6.42 but SOC 29.8.42

R9320 S/149 Sqn 29.4.42, FTR 17/18.5.42 from Baltic mining, crashed in Ferne Belt

R9321 R/149 Sqn 1.5.42, 1 FTR 5/6.6.42 from Essen, shot down at Duisburg–Wanheierort, Germany

R9322 C/214 Sqn 3.5.42, GA 3.6.42, Stradishall. Part of bomb load fell off, electrical defect during test. Burnt out

R9323 C,R/214 Sqn 3.5.42, 1665 CU 5.8.43. Declared Cat E during MI 16.5.44 and SOC

R9324 M,X/7 Sqn 5.5.42, FTR 16.6.42 from Essen, crashed at St Remy du Nord

R9325 F/214 Sqn 15.5.42, EFB 31.5.42, engine failure returning from Cologne. Swung off runway

R9326 G/214 Sqn 15.5.42, FTR 11.6.42 from mining *Nectarine II*. Crashed on Memmert Island, Germany

R9327 CRD RAE 19.5.42, SB RIW Cat B 8.6.42. 44MU 22.11.42, U,W/149 Sqn 26.1.43, FTR 4/5.4.43 from Kiel. Crashed at Obbekaer, Germany

R9328 149 Sqn 19.5.42, 214 Sqn 22.5.42, A/7 Sqn 23.5.42, FTR 26/27.7.42 from Hamburg. Crashed in river Elbe at Brunsbuttelkoog, Germany

R9329 214 Sqn 21.5.42, V/149 Sqn 29.5.42, EFB 27.8.42 at Gibhall Horestry, Cornwood, S Devon. Returning from mining hit high ground 0325 hrs. Flak damaged

R9330 O/149 Sqn 24.5.42, EFB 30.6.42, crashed on take off

R9331 Y/7 Sqn 28.5.42, EFA 14.7.42, bounced on landing and overshot Waterbeach

R9332 G/218 Sqn 30.5.42, 218 CF, EFA 31.7.42 at Marham. Caught fire after third landing attempt and u/c collapsed

R9333 F,Y/218 Sqn 31.5.42, RIW SB 28.6.42. 19 MU 29.11.42, Y/218 Sqn 23.1.43, FTR 5/6.3.43 from Essen, crashed near target

R9334 P, G/149 Sqn 29.5.42, EFA 3.1.43. Crashed and burnt out during night bombing practice near Lakenheath. Altimeter problem

R9349 218 Sqn 2.6.42, RIW SB 8.6.42. 23 MU 31.12.42, U/90 Sqn 29.1.43, FTR 28.2/1.3.43 from St Nazaire. Crashed at Clos sous les Bois

R9350 149 Sqn 3.6.42, U,T/214 Sqn 4.6.42, FTR16/17.9.42 from Essen, crashed at Bowal, Belgium

R9351 R/XV Sqn 3.6.42, FTR 17/18.9.42? from mining. Reported crashed in Great Belt. On 1.9.42 reported to have collided with a Whitley between Gransden and Bourn at 2310 hrs(?)

R9352 T/XV Sqn 4.6.42, FTR 19/20.6.42 from Essen. Crashed at Siemolten, Germany

R9353 B/XV Sqn 5.6.42, 1657 CU, FA 20.9.42 when landing at Stradishall in heavy rain. Ran off runway to avoid obstruction and u/c collapsed, RIW SB 30.9.42. 1657 CU 29.1.43, EFA 20.4.44 Stradishall, bounced during landing, opened up, wing dropped, dived into ground

R9354 N/218 Sqn 6.6.42, EFB 28.7.42, heavy landing at Downham Market back from Hamburg and u/c collapsed

R9355 46 MU 11.6.42, O/214 Sqn 23.6.42, EFB 9.9.42, flak damage, crash landed Manston (FH 150.15)

R9356 46 MU 13.6.42, U/214 Sqn 24.6.42, FTR 19/20.9.42 from Munich, crashed Hader, Germany (FH 137.25)

R9357 0 MU 14.6.42, E/218 Sqn 24.6.42, FTR 11.9.42 from Düsseldorf. Much of fuselage blown away during attack, starboard inner failed, aircraft ditched when two other engines cut 30 miles off Dutch coast

R9358 149 Sqn 19.6.42, A/214 Sqn 24.6.42, EFB 9.3.43 crashed 1 mile NW of Chedburgh, port u/c failed to retract, hit house and tree

W7426 – W7639 150 Mk I (Hercules XI) built by Austin Motors, Longbridge, Birmingham

W7426 Wyton 6.5.41, V/XV Sqn 9.8.41, Waterbeach V/1651 CU 6.10.41, u/c problem when landing at Newmarket 10.3.42, RIW SO 10.4.42 but SOC 3.5.42

W7427 Wyton 10.7.41, B/XV Sqn 16.7.41, B/26 CF 9.10.41, flying accident 20.4.42, RIW SO 2.5.42, 7 CF 25.9.42, 1657 CU 30.11.42, EFA, forced landed approaching Stradishall 13.9.43

W7428 F,Z/XV Sqn 20.6.41, FTR 18.12.41, lost at sea

W7429 19 MU 20.4.41, J, X/XV Sqn 31.5.41, flak damage caused u/c collapse when landing at Warboys 29.10.41

W7430 Wyton 10.5.41, 7 Sqn 18.5.41, FTR 2/3.6.41, shot down en route Berlin

W7431 Wyton 18.5.41, A/XV Sqn 10.7.41, EFB 21.10.41, u/c up landing on Catsholne Farm, Methwold due to fuel shortage

W7432 Wyton 1.6.41, L/XV Sqn 4.7.41, H/1651 CU 16.1.42, heavy landing 13.3.42, 651 CU 27.6.42, 10 MU 16.5.43, SOC 13.9.46

W7433 Wyton 14.6.41, U/7 Sqn 13.6.41, FTR 29.9.41, hit over Stettin, ditched, one body recovered off Lowestoft

W7434 XV Sqn 4.7.41, E/7 Sqn 11.7.41, u/c collapsed during heavy landing at Oakington 15.8.41, SO but RTP 23.8.41

W7435 Wyton 16.7.41, 7 Sqn 19.7.41, W/XV Sqn 10.8.41, u/c collapsed during take-off for Magdeburg from Alconbury 14.8.41, SH and SO for repair but SOC 15.3.42

W7436 Wyton 22.7.41, D/7 Sqn 23.7.41, FTR 18.12.41, crashed at Plouguernau, France

W7437 L/XV Sqn 30.7.41, FTR 14.8.41, crashed in Belgium?

W7438 7 Sqn 6.8.41, FTR 28/29.8.41, crashed at Kaart, Germany

W7439 N,U/XV Sqn 22.8.41, hit obstruction when landing at Warboys 12.10.41, XV Sqn 4.12.41, 26 CF 15.12.41, 106 CF 3.1.42, 1651 CU, u/c collapsed during landing at Waterbeach 18.4.42, SOC 4.5.42

W7440 W/7 Sqn 30.8.41, SR-X/101 CF 16.5.42, XT-C/1657 CU 26.3.43, u/c collapsed when landing at Stradishall, RIW SO 16.7.43, 27 MU 20.4.44 and SOC as obsolete 29.11.45

W7441 J,Y/7 Sqn 8.9.41, FTR 29.9.41 ditched (off Hook of Holland?). (FH 38.25)

W7442 M/7 Sqn 15.9.41, u/c trouble 30.1.42, ROS SO, 7 Sqn 30.5.42, E,B/1651 CU, FTR 26.6.42, crashed in Waddensee

W7443 7 Sqn 25.9.41, W,J/XV Sqn 9.41, E,J/1651 CU 21.1.42, 44 MU 14.5.43, 23 MU 6.8.43, SH 24.3.45, SOC 24.4.45

W7444 G, L/7 Sqn 25.9.41, EFB in heavy landing on return from ops, u/c collapsed, 31.10.41

W7445 V/7 Sqn 29.9.41, flak damaged so landed Detling 13/14.10.41, SO Ros, crashed on take-off for Kiel 15.11.41 due to icing problem

W7446 S/7 Sqn 1.10.41, u/c collapsed due to braking problem 18.11.41

W7447 CRD Wyton 3.10.41, XV Sqn 16.10.41, TFU Hurn 8.12.41, L/1651 CU 17.2.42, FA 25.3.42, RIW, 1651 CU 27.8.42, SR-Y/101 CF 1.9.42, G,W/1657 CU, 6.10.42, S,B/1665 CU 6.7.43, Cat E MR 29.4.44

W7448 149 Sqn 12.10.41, Z/7 Sqn 14.10.41, W/26 CF loan 31.12.41, E,N/XV Sqn 4.1.42, Y/15 CF 27.2.42, FTR 6/7.4.42, ditched

W7449 149 Sqn 15.10.41, J/7 Sqn 19.10.41, 214 Sqn 10.6.42, 214 CF, Y/218 CF 5.8.42, RIW SO 27.8.42, A,I,P, XT-R/1657 CU 25.2.43, E MI 14.6.44

W7450 149 Sqn 20.10.41, A/XV Sqn 23.10.41, damaged landing after ops 25.11.41, SP RIW 26.12.41 but made Cat E 23.2.42

W7451 149 Sqn 26.10.41, D/7 Sqn 8.11.41, 7 CF 18.3.42, seriously damaged in overshoot 15.5.42, SO RIW 4.6.42, S/218 CF 14.8.42, S/1657 CU 2.10.42, engine trouble led to wheels-down forced landing in a field 3 miles S of King's Lynn (Saddle Bow) 14.2.43, RIW SO 19.3.43 but instead made Cat E 23.3.43

W7452 A/149 Sqn 31.10.41, overshot Heathfield (Ayr), u/c collapsed and aircraft SOC 9.3.42

W7453 O/149 Sqn 3.11.41, G/26 CF, landed with tailwheels retracted 9.11.41, landed wheels up 17.12.41, made Cat E 31.12.41

W7454 S/7 Sqn 8.11.41, G/218 Sqn 16.1.42, W/218 CF 28.2.42, 1657 CU 2.10.42, u/c collapsed on landing 15.1.43, RIW SO 29.1.43, 10 MU 6.6.43, ECFS 16.11.43, 10 MU 3.12.43, SOC 16.9.46 (sometime converted to B Mk III)

W7455 B/149 Sqn 9.11.41, X/149 CF 10.2.42, u/c collapsed landing and starboard wing sheered off 20.6.42, SO RIW, 44 MU 20.12.42, 75 Sqn 29.1.43, 214 Sqn 1.2.43, 1657 CU 5.2.43, tail-chassis collapsed 6.5.43, ROS, EFA 1 1/2 mile SE Wratting Common 7.9.43

W7456 149 Sqn 15.11.41, 149 CF, starboard wing caught fire, belly landed Boxworth, Cambs, 22.11.41, SOC

W7457 149 Sqn 18.11.41, tailwheels collapsed landing 8.12.41, starboard u/c collapsed during landing at Lakenheath 11.2.42, Cat E 2.4.42

W7458 149 Sqn 23.11.41, u/c collapsed during landing at Mildenhall 28.1.42 and declared Cat E by Sebro

W7459 149 Sqn 25.11.41, 26 CF 11.12.41, 218 Sqn 18.12.41, 26 CF 2.1.42, u/c collapsed during landing 3.5.42, RIW SO 8.6.42, 214 Sqn 11.9.42, 214 CF 25.9.42, O/1651 CU 7.10.42, tailwheel collapsed taxying 3.1.43, BS:A/1651 CU 20.1.43, SO 3.8.43, 6 MU 21.2.44, SOC 19.7.45

W7460 XV Sqn 5.12.41, 149 Sqn 9.12.41, XV Sqn 23.12.41, O/149 Sqn 1.42, X/149 CF 25.6.42, u/c collapsed during landing 30.8.42, 1657 CU 4.11.42, 149 CF 26.3.43, 1657 CU 26.3.43, port u/c collapsed landing 14.4.43, u/c collapsed taxying 28.2.44, SOC 14.3.44. Passed to 108 Para Bn, Bulford Camp as 4777M

W7461 N/149 Sqn 5.12.42, EFB 15/16.1.42, prop fell away, fuel short, crashed at Todwick Barr, Yorks

W7462 T/149 Sqn 12.12.41, BFB, overshot Lossiemouth 29.1.42, declared Cat E 5.3.42

W7463 149 Sqn 9.12.41, B/XV Sqn 31.12.41, 15 CF 2.6.42, u/c collapsed during landing 3.7.42, RIW SO 8.7.42, 1651 CU 21.7.42, XT:D, X,.M,V,/1657 CU 8.2.43, EFA, belly landed at Woodbridge 5.7.44 written off 19.7.44

W7464 19 MU 16.12.41, H/XV Sqn 1.42, Z/218 Sqn 4.4.42, FTR 28/29.7.42 from Hamburg, ditched

W7465 44 MU 23.12.41, 10 MU, W/1651 CU 7.5.42, RIW SO 17.6.42, 19 MU 31.10.42, V/149 Sqn 2.1.43, W/214 Sqn 28.2.43, 620 Sqn, 1657 CU 24.9.43, tailwheel collapsed during landing at Stradishall 3.3.44, made Cat E on 11.4.44

W7466 218 Sqn 2.1.42, B/7 Sqn 5.1.42, FTR 28.3.42 from Lübeck, crashed at Guntz, Germany

W7467 7 Sqn, EFA, mid-air collision with Hurricane V6885 (56 OTU), crashed 1 mile SW Erith 16.1.42

W7468 218 Sqn 6.1.42, W/7 Sqn 10.1.42, RIW SO 29.6.42, 44 MU 21.12.44, T/1651 CU, EFA u/c collapsed during landing at Wratting Common 13.1.44. Became 4532M

W7469 M/218 Sqn 25.1.42, RIW SO 24.6.42, 19 MU, 149 Sqn 21.1.43, T,O/75 Sqn 28.1.43, FTR 16/17.4.43 from Ludwigshaven, crashed at Katzenbach, Germany

W7470 U/7 Sqn 17.1.42, V/7 CF 26.9.42, H/1657 CU, EFA all engines cut, crashed 27.10.42 at Catley Hill, Motty, Co Durham

W7471 J/7 Sqn 30.1.42, FTR 6/7.6.42 from Emden, crashed near Holwerd N of Leeuwarden 0108 hrs

W7472 C/7 Sqn 16.2.42, landed tailwheels up 8.3.42, FTR 20.21.6.42 from Emden, shot down at sea by II/NJG 2

W7473 F/218 Sqn 11.2.42, EFA 23.4.42, crashed Clenchwarton, near Lynn, engine trouble, after take-off for Rostock

W7474 D/218 Sqn 14.2.42, overshot 9.3.42, K/218 Sqn 6.5.42, FTR 3/4.6.42 from Bremen, shot down in IJsselmeer at 0216 hrs by II/NJG2

W7475 H/218 Sqn 12.2.42, FTR 10.11.42 from Hamburg, crashed at Lashorst, Germany

W7500 B/7 Sqn 14.2.42, FTR 2.6.42 from Essen, ditched

W7501 Z/7 Sqn 17.2.42,1 FTR 28.3.42 from Lübeck, ditched

W7502 N/218 Sqn 3.3.42, FTR 30.31,5,42 from Cologne, crashed at Huppenbroich, Germany

W7503 R/218 Sqn 10.3.42, B/218 Sqn 27.5.42, 25/26.6.42 from Bremen, s/d at 0039 hrs in IJsselmeer

W7504 7 Sqn 9.3.42, A/XV Sqn 13.3.42, EFB, overshot on landing at Wyton 0440 hrs due to battle damage

W7505 7 Sqn 9.3.42, V/XV Sqn 13.3.42, RIW SO 16.5.42, E/1651 CU 31.10.42, tailwheels collapsed on t/o 16.1.43, 1651 CU 21.1.43, hit by R9157 taxying 4.3.43, u/c collapsed whilst taking off 17.5.43, RIW SO, 10 MU 2.12.43, 6 MU 9.2.45, SOC 19.7.45

W7506 K/218 Sqn 27.2.42, FTR 26.4.42 from Pilsen, crashed at Hugelsheim, Germany

W7507 P/218 Sqn 14.3.43, EFB 28.3.42 major flak damage during Lübeck raid

W7508 D/149 Sqn 23.3.42, FTR 5/6.6.42 from Essen, crashed at L'ecluse, Belgium

W7509 149 Sqn 13.3.42, U/149 Sqn 2.4.42, Q/1651 CU 24.5.42, FTR 28/29.7.42 from Hamburg, crashed at Heelsum, Netherlands

W7510 B/149 Sqn 13.3.42, 90 Sqn 18.2.43, G/1657 CU 10.3.43, u/c collapsed during landing at Newmarket 11.12.43, RIW SO 21.12.43, 23 MU 12.6.44, SOC 11.1.46

W7511 T/XV Sqn 25.3.42, EFA 8.4.42,1 swung taking off from Wyton, port u/c collapsed. Caught fire

W7512 A/149 Sqn 17.3.42, FTR 26/27.4.42 from Rostock, crashed at Schonhagen, Netherlands

W7513 R/XV Sqn 27.3.42, RIW SP 2.6.42, 10 MU 7.11.42, W/149 Sqn 21.1.43, G/75 Sqn 4.3.43, FTR 28/29.4.43 from mining Kiel Bay, ditched

W7514 B/XV Sqn 28.3.42, FTR 25/26.4.42 from Rostock, crashed at Kravlund, Denmark

W7515 Q/XV Sqn 27.3.42, FTR 29.5.42

W7516 S/XV Sqn 29.3.42, RIW SO 16.9.42, 1651 CU 11.6.43, swung on take off Tempsford 26.6.43, SO 5.8.43, 1651 CU 19 MU 23.4.44, 38 MU 11.5.44, 19 MU 12.3.45, SOC 24.10.45

W7517 Z,U/7 Sqn 29.3.42, heavy landing from ops 21.6.42, 1657 CU 5.10.42, starboard inner failed on take-off, u/c collapsed 29,12,42. SOC 22.1.43

W7518 C,U,G,W/XV Sqn 2.4.42, overshot Wattisham 14.9.42, FTR 1/2.3.43 from Berlin, crashed at St Maartensdijk, Netherlands at 0104 hrs (FH 309.05)

W7519 O/XV Sqn 3.4.42, FTR 13.4.42 from mining off Wangeroog, ditched

W7520 S/7 Sqn 10.4.42, FTR 19/20.5.42 from Mannheim, and crashed at Brusthem, Belgium

W7521 U/218 Sqn 12.4.42, air blockage in fuel lines back from ops caused aircraft to crash at 0455 hrs near Norwich

W7522 G,K/7 Sqn 3.4.42, shot up by Ju 88 and forced landed Friston 2.12.42, repairs by SO, J/1651 CU 13.1.43, 653 CU 28.12.43, fate uncertain. Passed to 1st Airborne Division as 4837M, from Melton Mowbray

W7523 C/XV Sqn 12.4.42,1 EFA 19.5.42, engine trouble and approached Graveley too low, hit trees, burnt out on road 1 1/12 mile from station

W7524 D/XV Sqn 12.2.42, FTR 16/17.7.42 from Lübeck, ditched off Esbjerg

W7525 E/XV Sqn 19.4 142, EFA 22.8.42, stalled approaching Bourn, engine problem

W7526 149 Sqn 17.4.42, W/214 Sqn 19.4.42, landed from ops tailwheels up 20.7.42, V/149 Sqn 28.8.42, 149 CF 20.9.42, 149 Sqn 29.9.42, FTR 15/16.10.42 from Cologne, shot down at Ingen/Lienden 2333 hrs

W7527 D,B,K /214 Sqn 4.42, landing too fast hit obstruction 21.6.42, landed tailwheels up at Chedburgh 8.12.42, 1665 CU 18.6.43, 6 MU 15.4.44, SOC 14.1.45

W7528 G/XV Sqn 21.4.42, FTR 8/9.5.42 from Warnemunde, crashed at Broderaby, Germany

W7529 R,W/7 Sqn 24.4.42, tailwheel chassis broke during landing 13.4.43, NY-J/1665 CU 2.9.43, 6 MU 10.4.44, SOC 14.1.45

W7530 149 Sqn 30.4.428, Q/218 Sqn 8.5.42, FTR 20/21.6.42 from Emden, crashed NW of Wognum, Netherlands

W7531 E,F/XV Sqn 2.5.42, replacement 'MacRobert's Reply', FTR 17.5.42 from mining Copenhagen Roads

W7532 N/214 Sqn 27.4.42,1 undershot 3.5.42, RIW SO 30.6.42, 19 MU 29.11.42, BB,BS-S/1651 CU 23.1.43, tyre burst on landing at Waterbeach and u/c collapsed 29.4.43,1653 CU 25.12.43, belly landed Newmarket 8.3.44, input for RIW SO 4.4.44 but SOC 11.5.44

W7533 G/75 Sqn 1.5.42, FTR 28/29.7.42 from Hamburg, crashed Klein Horstein, Germany

W7534 E/214 Sqn 10.5.42, FTR 30/31.5.42 from Cologne, crashed near Aachen

W7535 C/218 Sqn 13.5.42, FTR 29.5.42 from Gennevilliers, crashed at Colombes, France

W7536 G/XV Sqn 1.5.42, EFA 22.5.42 overshot into ditch, Wyton and struck by R9312

W7537 H/214 Sqn 16.5.42, FTR 3/4.6.42 from Bremen, crashed at Sustedt, Germany

W7538 T/214 Sqn 17.5.42, seriously damaged by night-fighter action during Bremen raid 26.6.42, RIW SO 26.6.42, but input cancelled, SOC 29.8.42

W7559 214 Sqn 20.5.42, K/7 Sqn 22.5.42, FTR 28/29.6.42 from St Nazaire, ditched in Biscay

W7560 46 MU 28.5.42, C/214 Sqn 24.6.42, 26/27.7.42 from Hamburg, crashed at Westerdeichstrich Busum, Germany

W7561 214 Sqn 21.5.42, F/XV Sqn 21.5.42, RIW SO 9.7.42, KK/1651 CU 13.1.43, belly landed Newmarket 18.7.43, SO RIW 3.8.43, C/1653 CU 22.12.43, 8 MU 8.8.44, SOC 15.8.44

W7562 46 MU 31.5.42, R/218 Sqn 27.6.42, FTR 24/25.8.42 from Frankfurt, crashed at Thyne, Belgium

W7563 M/7 Sqn 24.5.42, EFA 3.7.42 tyre burst landing Oakington, swung, burnt out, 2335 hrs

W7564 46 MU 2.6.42, T/7 Sqn 25.6.42, EFB 11.9.42, flak damaged, crash landed Weeley, Essex, burnt out

W7565 46 MU 4.6.42, B/7 Sqn 28.6.42, FTR 28/29.7.42 from Hamburg, shot down at Aschmoehr, Germany

W7566 10 MU 2.6.42, C/149 Sqn 22.6.42, FTR 16/17.11.42 from mining off Brittany, ditched off Vielle St Girone

W7567 10 MU 2.6.42, 149 Sqn 20.6.42, S/214 Sqn 23.6.42, FTR 23/24.7.42 from Duisburg, shot down by flak at Wekendam

W7568 44 MU 7.6.42, D/218 Sqn 23.7.42, EFA soon after take off for Mainz 11.8.42 outer starboard caught fire over Brandon, crashed 2300 hrs Wilton Hill Wood, Hockwold

W7569 44 MU 8.6.42, D./7 Sqn 29.7.42, FTR 17.9.42, from Essen, crashed in IJsselmeer

W7570 10 MU 12.6.42, T,J/1427 Flt 4.8.42, 218 CF, W/1657 CU 6.4.43, u/c collapse Stradishall 8.7.43, T/1653 CU 12.1.44, EFA belly landed 22.2.44

W7571 10 MU 13.6.42, V/1427 Flt 13.8.42, 218 CF, u/c up landing Marham 4.10.42, 1427 Flt 20.2.43, H/1657 CU 6.4.43, EFA starboard engine failure on take off, crash landed 20.1.44

W7572 10 MU 14.6.42, R/149 Sqn 23.6.42, FM 24/25.8.42 from Frankfurt, crashed Thieulain, Belgium

W7573 19 MU 17.6.42, U/218 Sqn 29.6.42, 21.8.42 from mining Fehmarn Channel, crashed near Geel, Germany

W7574 19 MU 19.6.42, 149 Sqn 28.6.42, N/7 Sqn 1.7.42, EFA 22.7.42, port tyre burst landing from Duisburg 0430 hrs, RIW SO 14.9.42, X,E/1657 CU 15.2.43, R/1653 CU 7.1.44, 8 MU 9.7.44, Cat E 1.8.44

W7575 19 MU 20.6.42, 218 Sqn 16.7.42, F/214 Sqn 19.7.42, O, J/90 Sqn 16.11.42, G/1657 CU 5.43, 1653 CU 3.3.44, SOC 9.8.44, became 4834M and used by 6th Airborne Division

W7576 19 MU 21.6.42, G/XV Sqn 7.7.42, FTR 25/26.7.42 from Duisburg, shot down at Horst, Netherlands, by III/NJG 1

W7577 46 MU 27.6.42, XV Sqn 5.7.42, J/214 Sqn 5.7.42, u/c collapsed on landing 6.5.43, RIW SO 12.5.43, 1651 CU 17.9.43, swung landing Newmarket, u/c collapsed, burnt out 25.4.44

W7578 46 MU 26.6.42, A/XV Sqn 11.8.42, FTR 20.9.42 from Munich, crashed at Noyers-le-Val, France

W7579 46 MU 29.6.42, Y/7 Sqn 16.7.42, FTR 14.8.42 from Kiel, ditched off Denmark

W7580 D/149 Sqn, 2.7.42, FTR 23/24.7.42 from Duisburg, destroyed by I/NJG 1 at Geffen, Netherlands, exploded in the air

W7581 O/7 Sqn 2.7.42, RIW SO 13.10.42, 1657 CU 15.6.43, u/c collapsed landing Stradishall 16.8.43, 1665 CU 13.11.43, 6 MU 26.3.44, SOC 14.1.45

W7582 F, S/7 Sqn 2.7.42, EFA 10.11.42, starboard wing caught fire, dived in at 1657 hrs east of Kingsway, Suffolk

W7583 BS-B/1651 CU 6.7.42, EFA, swung landing Waterbeach 26.7.43 and crashed into R9144

W7584 D/214 Sqn 11.7.42, EFB 21.11.42 Exactor problems, fuel short, crashed 2 miles West of Stradishall, crew baled out at 0342 hrs

W7585 T,U/XV Sqn 10.7.42, EFA 29.12.42, engine fire, lost control on approach and landed short of Bassingbourn 1220 hrs

W7586 44 MU 14.7.42, 214 Sqn 3.6.43, C/1657 CU 9.6.43, EFA 22.7.43 overshot Stradishall

W7587 CRD A&AEE 15.7.42, 44 MU 15.1.43, 1651 CU 29.3.43, overshot landing 26,6,43 and RIW SO, 10 MU 24.11.43, 6 MU 9.12 44, SOC 19.7.45

W7588 19 MU 18.7.42, J/XV Sqn 29.7.42, damaged during first sortie and crashed, burnt out, at Coltishall on return

W7589 P/149 Sqn 21.7.42, damaged by night fighter off Dutch coast on 18.8.42 and crash landed 1/2 mile from Southery, SOC 9.1.43

W7610 B,A/214 Sqn 21.7.42, OG-M/1665 CU 18.6.43, 6 MU 6.4.44, SOC 14.1.45

W7611 F/XV Sqn 24.7.42, FTR 2/3.9.42 from Karlsruhe, crashed 40km West of the Hague at 0308 hrs

W7612 T/218 Sqn 25.7.42, EFB 9.11.42 undershot Tangmere returning from Toulon, hit trees

W7613 N/218 Sqn 26.7.42, u/c collapsed landing 14.9.42, FTR 1/2.10.42 from Lübeck, crashed Skallingen, Denmark

W7614 J/218 Sqn 28.7.42, FM 18.12.42 from Fallersleben, crashed Kaltenwalde-Langenhagen

W7615 M/218 Sqn 29.7.42, FTR 21.8.42 from mining Kiel Roads, ditched in Baltic

W7616 214 Sqn 30.7.42, G/7 Sqn 31.7.42, FTR 25.8.42 from Frankfurt, crashed Berzee, Belgium

W7617 A,K/7 Sqn 9.8.42, FTR 1.3.43 from Stuttgart, crashed Minauaourt, France

W7618 218 Sqn 12.8.42, 218 CF 19.8.42, V/218 Sqn 19.8.42, FTR 18/19.8.42 from Flensburg, in the sea off Esbjerg

W7619 A/149 Sqn 15.8.42, swung on landing from ops, u/c collapsed 22,12,42, RIW SO 29.12.42 1651 CU 9.6.43, EFA 13.12.43 u/c collapsed during take-off

W7620 D,L/7 Sqn 15.8.42, FTR 6/7.11.42 from mining Frisians, ditched

W7621 G/214 Sqn 18.8.42, FTR 5.4.43 from Kiel, in the sea

W7622 7 Sqn 22.8.42, P/218 Sqn 22.8.42, RIW SO 5.10.42, XT-M,S/1657 CU 25.1.43, E on Major Inspection 25.6.44

W7623 CRD Shorts 23.8.42, 90 Sqn 20.5.43, 1665 CU 26.5.43, 1657 CU 9.6.43, 1663 CU 16.6.43, OG-H/1665 CU 30.11.43, 6 MU 28.4.44, SOC 14.1.45

W7624 7 Sqn 23.8.42, E/XV Sqn 23.8.42, FTR 28.8.42 from Kassel, crashed Ambt Delden, Netherlands

W7625 R/218 Sqn 26.8.42, 1651 CU 30.10.42, u/c collapsed landing Waterbeach 12.5.43, RIW SO 25.5.43, Y, QQ-C/1651 CU 1.9.43, 1653 CU 28.12.43, tyre burst after take-off, crashed Woodbridge 26.5.44 and SOC 11.6.44

W7626 J/214 Sqn 26.8.42, crashed soon after take-off Chedburgh 6.10.42 possibly due to lightning strike

W7627 214 Sqn 29.8.42, A,E/90 Sqn 16.11.42, EFA 18.3.43, swung on take-off into BK693

W7628 B/149 Sqn 29.8.42, EFB 24.10.42, crashed into houses at Rye St Cliff, Gravesend, returning from Genoa

W7629 Z/7 Sqn 1.9.42, FTR 6/7.9.42 from Duisburg, crashed near target area

W7630 M/7 Sqn 1.9.42, FTR 10/11.9.42 from Düsseldorf shot down at Sytramprooh, Netherlands, by fighter

W7631 G/214 Sqn 7.9.42, EFB 24.10.42 crashed Chedburgh, fuel shortage after 9 1/2 hour flight, 0406 hrs

W7632 N/7 Sqn 6.9.42, FTR 21/22.12.42 Munich, crashed at Jussecourt, France

W7633 P/XV Sqn 9.9.42, crash landed u/c up at Bradwell 4.10.42 fuel short on return from Genoa, RIW SO 22.11.42, O/1657 CU 14.4.43, EFA 18.3.44 crashed during night circuits, burnt out, Little Thurlow, Suffolk

W7634 G/XV Sqn 9.9.42, FTR 1/2.10.42 from Lübeck in sea off Peenemunde

W7635 V/XV Sqn 12.9.42, FTR 8/9.12.42, mining Baltic, in the sea off Esbjerg

W7636 L/218 Sqn 13.9.42, crashed on take off for Krefeld 2.10.42, at Downham Market

W7637 W/214 Sqn 16.9.42, FTR 15/16.1.43 from Lorient, crashed off Plymouth

W7638 R/149 Sqn 19.9.42, FTR 14/15.2.43 Cologne, shot down by fighter, crashed near Boxmeer, Netherlands, at 2130 hrs

W7639 Q/149 Sqn 19.9.42, EFB 9.12.42 from mining, crashed Hockwold making early return

BF309 – BF580 200 Mk I (to BF454), then Mk III with a few conversions to Mk IV

BF309 W218 Sqn 25.6.42, FTR 28/29.7.42 from Hamburg, in the sea off Busum

BF310 H/149 Sqn 20.6.42, FTR 29/30.6.42 from Berlin, crashed at Makkum, shot down by *Lt* Bethel of III/NJG2

BF311 G/149 Sqn 22.6.42, 75 Sqn 20.10.42, 115 Sqn 10.12.42, 1651 CU 12.1.43, became 3983M 5.7.43

BF312 A/149 Sqn 23.6.42, FTR 16/17.7.42 from Lübeck , shot down by AA fire Steinfeld

BF313 T/214 Sqn 27.6.42, FTR 3/4.7.42 from Bremen, shot down by fighter, in Waddensee off Pieterburen, Netherlands

BF314 N/214 Sqn 28.6.42, Y/214 CF 28.7.42, Y/1651 CU 7.10.42, heavy landing, stalled, Waterbeach 28.10.42, SOC 5.11.42

BF315 F/218 Sqn 28.6.42, FTR 28.8.42 from Kassel, shot down 0104 hrs at Elst, Netherlands

BF316 W7 Sqn 1.7.42, EFB 29.8.42, crashed near Stonehenge returning from Nuremberg, fuel shortage

BF317 D, X/7 Sqn 2.7.42, FTR 27/28.3.43 from Berlin, crashed near Bremen

BF318 H/214 Sqn 6.7.42, Cat B Sebro 21.12.42, OG-F/1665 CU, swung on landing Woolfox Lodge EFA 5.9.43

BF319 C/218 Sqn 5.7.42, FTR 21.8.42 from mining Kiel Roads, crashed Langwedel

BF320 H/149 Sqn 6.7.42, FTR 29/30.7.42 from Saarbrucken, crashed Saarbrucken-Rodenhof

BF321 S/7 Sqn 8.7.42, J/1657 CU 6.10.42, swung on landing Ridgewell 10.8.43, SOC 23.8.43

BF322 F/218 Sqn 4.9.42, lightning strike in thick clouds after take-off for Aachen 5.10.42, crashed Icklingham, Suffolk, burnt out

BF323 149 Sqn 11.7.42, X/1651 CU 13.7.42, swung on landing Waterbeach and hit another aircraft 17.8.42, repaired, XT-E/1657 CU 12.3.43, Cat E on MI 19.6.44, SOC 5.7.44, became 4531M

BF324 44 MU 14.7.42,R/214 Sqn 6.8.42, H/90 Sqn 16.11.42, landed after starboard engine fire 2.1.43 Cat AC, 90 Sqn, swung taking off Ridgewell 23.3.43 u/c collapsed, Sebro RIW, O/1657 CU 25.9.43, u/c collapsed on take-off 20.12.43, Sebro Cat B 28.12.43, re-cat El 31.1.44

BF325 44 MU 19.7.42, A/149 Sqn 20.7.42, attacked by Bf 110 during Mainz raid of 12/13.8.42 and forced down at Broadstairs short of fuel and engine problems, Cat B RIW Sebro 13.8.42, 1651 CU 28.1.43, Cat E on MI 1.8.44, SOC 1.8.44

BF326 L,X/214 Sqn 21.7.42, swung on landing Exeter returning from ops 18.2.43, take-off problems 14.4.43 when bound for Stuttgart, bombs jettisoned, u/c damaged during take-off, collapsed during landing at Chedburgh

BF327 D/XV Sqn 26.7.42, FTR 28/29.8.42 from Kassel, shot down by fighter near Beusichem

BF328 D/149 Sqn 30.7.42,1 FTR 30.9/1.10.42 from mining off Frisians, crashed at sea

BF329 O,A/XV Sqn 28.7.42, FTR 12/13.8.42 from Mainz, shot down by fighter, at Romedenne, Belgium

BF330 H/214 Sqn 29.7.42 FTR 17/18.8.42 from Osnabrück, shot down at 0146 hrs by II/NJG 2 in sea 30km NW of Terschelling

BF331 1651 CU 31.7.42, crashed Waterbeach, swung on take-off, u/c collapsed, 27.8.42, SOC 22.9.42

BF332 Q/1651 CU 31.7.42, tail chassis collapsed landing 20.7.43, landing on three engines Downham 26.11.43 spiralled in from 70 feet and burnt out, Cat EFA, SOC 1.12.43

BF333 R/1651 CU 4.8.42, crashed 22.11.42 1 mile NNE Portobello Farm, Shipston-on-Stour, Warks, after engine failure

BF334 T/149 Sqn 4.8.42,1 R/149 CF 26.8.42, 20.9.42 returning from Munich, ditched off Ramsgate

BF335 E/7 Sqn 6.8.42, crashed Abingdon 25.8.42 due to battle damage, Frankfurt raid, SOC 25.8.42

BF336 Z/7 Sqn 5.8.42, FTR 24/25.8.42 from Frankfurt, crashed Charleville

BF337 B/214 Sqn 13.8.42, FTR 4/5.9.42 from Bremen, shot down at Staphorst Netherlands, by fighter

BF338 Q/218 Sqn 9.8.42, FTR 21.8.42 from mining, crashed at Hoffnungstal, Mariental, Germany

BF339 F,C,L/7 Sqn 12.8.42, 90 Sqn 28.5.43, 1665 CU 29.5.43, 1657 CU 9.6.43, 1665 CU 16.6.43, swung on take-off Woolfox Lodge, but EFA 15.7.43,SOC 10.7.43

BF340 A/7 Sqn 15.8.42, XT-A/1657 CU 3.10.42, 1665 CU 24.6.43, tail chassis damaged taxiing 28.7.43, 6 MU 21.3.44, SOC 14.1.45

BF341 J/214 Sqn 16.8.42, damaged 18.2.43, Cat B Sebro 27.10.43, 27 MU 5.4.44, 6 MU17.1.45, SOC 19.7.45

BF342 E/7 Sqn 1.9.42, 1657 CU 3.10.42, Cat AC FA 14.10.42, 1657 CU 30.10.43, EFA 9.5.44, swung landing Stradishall, both u/c legs collapsed, SOC 1.6.44

BF343 M/218 Sqn 10.10.42, FTR 11/12.3.43 from Stuttgart, crashed near Dieppe

BF344 A/214 Sqn 19.8.42, 1657 CU 19.5.43, AC tailwheel collapse 16.4.43, 1657 CU, AC MI 22.10.43, 1657 CU, became 4374M for 1661 CU

BF345 H/7 Sqn 9.42, wing damage landing 11.9.42, 1657 CU 16.11.42, became 3757M 1.43

BF346 218 Sqn 2.9.42, u/c collapsed landing 18.2.43, G/90 Sqn by 1.4.43, FTR 29.4.43 from mining *Quince*/Langelands Belt, ditched

BF347 J/XV Sqn 27.8.42, EFB burnt out 11.9.42 in crash at West Malling returning from Düsseldorf

BF348 P/149 Sqn 28.8.42, EFB 10.10.42, burnt out, hit trees at Great Cressingham NE of Bodney, Norfolk, during mining sortie

BF349 R/149 Sqn 28.8.42, 218 Sqn 4.3.43, R/1651 CU 18.3.43, 1665 CU 22.7.43, u/c collapsed landing Woolfox 2.10.43, RIW Sebro 2.11.43, 27 MU 19.4.44, SOC 6.7.45

BF350 O/XV Sqn 1.9.42, u/c collapsed landing Newmarket 14.3.43, Sebro RIW 31.3.43, G/1657 CU 29.7.43, RIW Sebro 14.4.44, Cat E 11.5.44

BF351 C/218 Sqn 2.9.42, FTR 11.9.42 from Düsseldorf, shot down 2340 hrs by fighter St Philipsland, Netherlands

BF352 U/XV Sqn 2.9.42, EFB 9.9.42, returning from mining, four crew baled out, u/c collapsed landing Waterbeach after early return, engine trouble

BF353 F/XV Sqn 2.9.42, FTR 16/17.9.42 from Essen, crashed in IJsselmeer

BF354 O/7 Sqn 2.10.42, 1657 CU 16.11.42, heavy landing Newmarket 13.3.43, BS-N/1651 CU 5.8.43, K/1653 CU 22.12.43, 8 MU 8.8.44, SOC 15.8.44

BF355 F/XV Sqn 4.9.42, AC Sebro 17.12.42, XV Sqn 25.2.43, B/1657 CU 12.5.43, Cat B Sebro 5.8.43, converted to Mk III, 10 MU 4.12.43, SOC and scrapped 13.9.46

BF356 D/XV Sqn 4.9.42, EFB 17.12.42, overshot Bourn, engine trouble, returning from mining Frisians

BF357 T/149 Sqn 6.9.42, tyre burst and u/c collapsed on take-off 3.10.42, Q/214 Sqn 23.2.43, EFA 9.3.43, u/c collapsed on take off Chedburgh

BF358 C/7 Sqn 8.9.42, FTR 22.12.42 from Munich, crashed at Void-Vacon, France

BF372 H/149 Sqn 11.9.42, FTR 29.11.42 from Turin, flown by Flt Sgt Middleton VC, ditched off Dymchurch, Kent

BF373 P/214 Sqn 12.9.42, 214 CF 30.9.42, G/1651 CU 1.10.42, tailwheel collapsed landing 4.3.43, G,H/1653 CU 10.12.43, tailwheel collapse taxying at Chedburgh 27.1.44, heavy landing 13.3.44, swung on take-off and hit EF410 and became AC FA 21.4.44, 1653 CU 20.4.44, 8 MU 8.8.44, SOC 15.8.44

BF374 214 Sqn 15.9.42, 214 CF 1.10.42, Y,K/1651 CU 1.10.42, EFA 28.11.42 crashed on Smithy Fen Farm 2 mile N of Cottenham, Cambs

BF375 O/218 Sqn 8.10.42, landed Downham 2.2.43 with tailwheel retracted, Z/214 Sqn 26.4.43, tailwheel tyre burst landing cat AC 25.7.43, BS-G/1651 CU 18.8.43, Cat B FA Sebro 25.9.43, ran into ditch taxying at Mepal, RIW Sebro, 10 MU 25.4.44, 6 MU 4.12.44, SOC 19.7.45

BF376 N/XV Sqn 15.1.43, 90 Sqn 11.3.43, 1657 CU 12.5.43, u/c collapsed landing Lakenheath Cat B 29.5.43 but SOC 10.6.43

BF377 W/214 Sqn 22.9.42, RIW Short & Harland 2.10.42, CRD 17.12.42 after repair, J/75 Sqn 14.4.43, 1651 CU 25.6.43, u/c collapsed landing Waterbeach 7.7.43, 8 MU 11.7.44, Cat B MI 1.8.44 but SOC instead

BF378 E/7 Sqn 17.9.42, T/XV Sqn 30.12.42, FTR 18/19.2.43 from Wilhelmshaven and ditched off Frisians

BF379 D/7 Sqn 22.9.42, FTR 11/12.12.42 from Turin, crashed Fossano, Italy

BF380 B/XV Sqn 23.9.42, EFB 18.12.42, undershot Bourn in bad weather returning from mining, Bayonne

BF381 J,P2/214 Sqn 24.9.42, declared Cat AC on DI 5.4.43, FTR 12/13.5.43 from Duisburg, crashed near target area

BF382 Q/214 Sqn 24.9.42, CRD A&AEE 2.10.42, became 4294M held at 4 STT

BF383 H/90 Sqn 22.11.42, landed tail chassis retracted 22.1.43 Cat AC, T/90 Sqn 13.2.43, FTR 26/27.4.43 from Duisburg, wreckage retrieved from IJsselmeer

BF384 R/XV Sqn 26.9.42, u/c collapsed in strong wind on take-off from Bourn for Turin 18.11.42

BF385 A/218 Sqn 26.9.42, BS-H/1651 CU 13.6.43, ROS Sebro, 1651 CU 12.8.43, Cat BFA RIW Sebro 26.3.44, re-Cat E 2.6.44

BF386 Q/XV Sqn 27.9.42, EFA 29.10.42 Control problem due to possible storm damage, dived in after steep turn and burnt out 5 miles SW of Downham

BF387 U/7 Sqn FTR 9/10.11.42 from Hamburg, crashed at sea

BF388 F/1651 CU 7.10.42, EFA 2.5.43, u/c collapsed landing Waterbeach, throttle and engine problems

BF389 XV Sqn 1,10.42, S/149 Sqn 6.10.42, EFA 28.10.42 swung on take-off during night circuit training at Lakenheath

BF390 A/7 Sqn 1.10.42, EFB 21.10.42, damaged when mining off Frisians, re-entered UK air space well south of ordered entry point, engaged and shot down by Bofors guns at Great Yarmouth, crashed off Wellington Pier

BF391 T/149 Sqn 5.10.42, FTR 8/9.12.42 mining Fehmarn Channel, crashed Dobersdorf, Germany

BF392 XV Sqn 5.10.42, D/149 Sqn 8.10.42, FTR 17.10.42 from mining Gironde Estuary, crashed Ile d'Yeu, France

BF393 V/1651 CU 11.10.42, damaged in heavy landing 26.1.43, hit by 97 Sqn Lancaster landing at Waterbeach 5.5.43, SOC 16.5.43

BF394 T,BS-T/1651 CU 11.10.42, accident damage Cat B 31.5.44, SOC 16.6.44

BF395 Z/218 Sqn 24.10.42, NW1651 CU 26.3.43, EFA 20.8.43, overshot Downham Market, SOC 5.9.43

BF396 1657 CLJ 21.10.42, X/75 Sqn 23.10.42, FTR 18.12.42 from Fallersleben crashed Ankum, Germany

BF397 Z/75 Sqn 23.10.42, BFA, RIW Sebro 23.1.43 after overshooting Newmarket, 1651 CU 6.7.43, heavy landing Oakington 8.9.43 u/c damaged, A3- K/1653 CU 3.1.44, tail chassis damaged landing 10.3.44, EFA 10.4.44, bounced landing, u/c collapsed, Chedburgh

BF398 P,F/75 Sqn 24.10.42, EFA 17.5.43, two engines failed on take-off, crashed Linley Hall Farm near Talke, Staffs

BF399 O/75 Sqn 7.11.42,EFA 28.11.42, stalled on Oakington circuit avoiding another Stirling, crashed on Trinity Farm, Cambridge

BF400 O,G/75 Sqn 30.10.42, FTR 17/18.12.42 from Fallersleben, crashed at Ankum, Germany

BF401 M,N/218 Sqn 8.11.42, EFB 3.12.42, crashed Downham Market returning from Frankfurt, due to fighter damage

BF402 M,BS-V/1651 CU 9.11.42, 1653 CU 28.12.43, Cat AC 2.2.44 u/c damage, 8 MU 9.7.44, SOC 1.12.44

BF403 R/218 Sqn 7.11.42, FTR 17/18.12.42, shot down by German naval flak, 19.10 hrs, off Texel

BF404 218 Sqn 21.11.42, Cat AC 23.11.42, V, A/90 Sqn ?, Cat A Sebro 30.5.43 after wheels-up landing Stradishall, 214 Sqn ?, Cat B 18.8.43, 1657 CU 26.10.43, Cat BFA 29.5.44 re-cat E and SOC 16.6.44

BF405 S,U/218 Sqn 21.11.42, FTR 27/28.5.43 from mining off Frisians, ditched 70km NW Leeuwarden

BF406 Q,E/218 Sqn 18.11.42, FTR 3/4.2.42 from Hamburg, shot down by fighter 2041 hrs over Deelen

BF407 Q,S/90 Sqn 8.2.43, 1657 CU 16.8.43, BFA 23.9.43 bounced on landing, Cat B Sebro RIW 5.10.43 re-cat E 10.11.43 and SOC

BF408 T/218 Sqn 22.11.42, FTR 3/4.2.43 from Hamburg crashed off Dover

BF409 R/90 Sqn 18.11.42,EFA 5.4.43 Ridgewell, throttle problem, came in too high, swung and u/c collapsed. SOC 28.4.43

BF410 E/90 Sqn 26.11.42, FTR 25/26.2.43 Nuremberg, crashed Rastatt, Germany

BF411 A/XV Sqn 29.11.42, FTR 18/19.2.43 from Wilhelmshaven, ditched off Terschelling

BF412 XV Sqn 28.11.42, F,Y/75 Sqn 13.3.43, 1665 CU 18.6.43, Cat AC u/c collapsed landing Woolfox 24.10.43, 6 MU 20.3.44, SOC 14.1.45

BF413 H,T/218 Sqn 16.11.42, FA tyre burst landing 15/16.1.43, 1651 CU 6.7.43, RIW Sebro 27.7.43 after swing on take-off Downham and u/c collapse, 27 MU 9.4.44, SOC 3.11.45

BF414 F,R/90 Sqn 28.11.42, FA 19.5.43, tyre burst landing Ricall and u/c collapsed, Cat E 28.6.43

BF415 S/90 Sqn 28.11.42, FTR 3/4.2.43 from Hamburg, shot down by fighter 2300 hrs Montfoort/Willeskon, Netherlands

BF416 115 Sqn 28.11.42, T/149 Sqn 22.12.42, 218 Sqn 18.2.43, GG/1651 CU 22.3.43, EFA 4.8.43 in heavy landing Waterbeach

BF434 X/75 Sqn 13.4.43, OG-W/1665 CU 28.7.43, tyre burst in flight but landed successfully, 6 MU 10.4.44, SOC 14.1.45

BF435 115 Sqn 29.11.42, P/XV Sqn 2.12.42, X/90 Sqn 11.3.43, 1657 CU 6.6.43, Cat EMR 21.7.44 and SOC

BF436 115 Sqn 29.11.42, E/XV Sqn 2.12.42, O,L/1651 CU 11.3.43, 1665 CU 17.8.43, SOC 26.4.45, became 4037M

BF437 L/75 Sqn 24.1.43, FTR 8/9.3.43 from Nuremberg, crashed Huttenheim, Germany

BF438 D/90 Sqn 26.1.43, FTR 14/15.2.43 from Cologne

BF439 D/XV Sqn 29.12.42, 1653 CU 28.12.43, 8 MU 7.7.44, EMR 1.8.44

BF440 U,J,T/ Sqn 6.2.43, u/c collapsed in heavy landing 31.7.43, SOC 16.8.43

BF441 N/214 Sqn 4.1.43, when collecting a crew swung on take-off at Exeter to avoid another aircraft and u/c collapsed 18.2.43 and SOC

BF442 K/90 Sqn 2.3.43, FTR 20/21.4.43 from Rostock, crashed in Baltic

BF443 V/75 Sqn 2.2.43, 1651 CU 17.8.43, 8 MU 11.7.44, EMR 1.8.44

BF444 G/149 Sqn 13.1.43, N/214 Sqn 3.3.43, 1665 CU 18.5.43, 1657 CU 9.6.43, 1665 CU 16.6.43, FA AC 31.1.44, overshot Tilstock, 1665 CU 19.3.44, 6 MU 21.3.44, SOC 14.1.45

BF445 H/214 Sqn 4.1.43, EFB 26.2.43, overshot Stansted's blocked runway, battle damaged, SOC 17.3.43 BF446 H,C/218 Sqn 15.1.43, 14/15.4.43 fuel tank exploded, 1665 CU 30.7.43, swung landing Woolfox u/c collapsed 4.8.43 and SOC

BF447 F/218 Sqn 7.2.43, FTR 28/29.4.43 from mining, crashed Vroending, Denmark

BF448 T/XV Sqn 29.12.42, FTR 15.2.43 from Cologne, crashed Helchteren, Belgium

BF449 J/90 Sqn 2.3.43, EFB 9/10.3.43 after mining Kattegat, engine surge during landing Ridgewell, u/c collapsed

BF450 X/218 Sqn 15.1.43, FTR 25/26.2.43 from Nuremberg, crashed Mannhein Rheinau, Germany

BF451 J,Z/75 Sqn 13.2.43, FTR 16/17.4.43 from Ludwigshafen, crashed at Chingny-les-Roses, France

BF452 V,M,T/218 Sqn 25.2.43, 13/14.5.43 hit by incendiaries over Bochum, 25/26.7.43 tail chassis collapsed in landing Downham, 1657 CU 25.9.43, EMI 21.7.44, SOC 8.8.44

BF453 L/214 Sqn 13.3.43, FTR 27/28.3.43 from Berlin, crashed Finkenwerder, Germany

BF454 W/90 Sqn 4.3.43, EFA 13.4.43 u/c collapsed, SOC 29.4.43

BF455 and subsequent aircraft in this batch were Mk III (Hercules VI)

BF455 Y/75 Sqn 13.2.43, FTR 10.4.43, battle damaged, ditched 3 miles off Shoreham, from Frankfurt

BF456 23 MU 29.1.43, J/75 Sqn 14.3.43, FTR 10.4.43 from Frankfurt, crashed at Stegg, Germany

BF457 B/XV Sqn 24.1.43, FTR 19.2.43 from Wilhelmshaven, in sea off Frisians

BF458 23 MU 31.1.43, A,JN-P/75 Sqn 2.5.43, FTR 30/31.7.43 from Remscheid, crashed Krefeld-Urdingen, Germany

BF459 23 MU 31.1.43, JN-E,JN-G/75 Sqn 2.5.43, FTR 23.9.43 from Mannheim, crashed Lampertheim, Germany

BF460 23 MU 4.2.43, 90 Sqn 10.4.43, C,F/XV Sqn 11.5.43, FTR 10/11.8.43, shot down by fighter at Doiche, Belgium

BF461 23 MU 13.2.43, B/75 Sqn 2.5.43, FTR 4.11.43 from mining Baltic, crashed Kellerup, Denmark

BF462 P/90 Sqn 27.2.43, FTR 14/15.4.43 from Stuttgart, shot down by fighter at Soude-Notre Dame, France

BF463 Q/90 Sqn 29.3.43, FTR 20/21.4.43 from Rostock, crashed in Baltic

BF464 E,C/90 Sqn 23.2.43, 30/31.8.43 swung taking-off Wratting Common and u/c damaged, Cat B RIW Sebro 21.9.43, cv to Mk IV, 6 MU SLG Woburn 20.3.44, 6 MU 22.3.44, 570 Sqn 2.8.44, 19 MU 4.1.45, SOC 16.12.46

BF465 XV Sqn 28.2.43, JN-K/75 Sqn 2.3.43, FTR 23/24.8.43 from Berlin, crashed at Lanke, Germany

BF466 90 Sqn 23.2.43, B/214 Sqn 26.2.43, 620 Sqn 19.7.43, EFA 13.7.43 overshot Chedburgh on air test, SOC 20.8.43

BF467 W/75 Sqn 15.3.43, FTR 28/29.4.43 from mining Kiel Bay, crashed in Baltic

BF468 K/218 Sqn 28.2.43, RIW Sebro 20.3.43, 1657 CU 27.7.43, AC MI 8.1.44, 1657 CU, EFA 27.10.44 in belly landing at Stradishall when two engines failed on take-off, SOC 15.11.44 but re-cat as B 2.12.44 and cv to Mk IV, 23 MU 4.5.45, SOC 5.6.47

BF469 XV Sqn 28.2.43, W214 Sqn 5.3.43, FTR 11/12.3.43 from Stuttgart, crashed Fagnieres, France

BF470 G/XV Sqn 27.2.43, FTR 3/4.10.43 from Kassel, crashed Haste, Germany

BF471 214 Sqn 31.3.43, EFB 27/28.9.43 from Hannover, forced landed near Manston on return after three engines cut

BF472 V,D/218 Sqn 25.3.43, FTR 27/28.9.43 from Hannover, crashed Bothfeld, Germany

BF473 218 Sqn 28.2.43, D,V,A/90 Sqn 7.3.43, Cat B 13.5.43, F,EPS Sqn 26.9.43, 199 Sqn 14.3.44, 1651 CU 28.4.44, EFA 6.6.44 tyre burst on take-off Wratting, and subsequently hit by Wellington JA619 of 69 Squadron and burnt out, SOC 23.6.44

BF474 H/XV Sqn 15.3.43, FTR 16/17.4.43 from Mannheim, crashed St Erme, France

BF475 T/XV Sqn 4.3.43, FTR 10/11.4.43 from Frankfurt, crashed St Genevieve, France

BF476 P/XV Sqn 4.3.43, FTR 20/21.4.43 from Rostock, crashed Kragelund, Denmark

BF477 H,D,B/149 Sqn 13.3.43, 5/6.7.43 hit by incendiaries during ops, FTR 5/6.9.43 from Mannheim, crashed Sorbon, France

BF478 G/214 Sqn, FTR 23/24.5.43 from Dortmund, crashed in Waddensee

BF479 E/149 Sqn 13.3.43, FTR 13/14.5.43 from Bochum, shot down by fighter at Casterlee, Belgium

BF480 K/218 Sqn 15.3.43, EFB 14.5.43, swung landing back from Bochum, hit control tower at Downham Market

BF481 M/214 Sqn 14.3.43, W,O/199 Sqn 6.7.43, 1654 CU 7.2.44, EFA 18.9.44 engine troubles, bounced on landing Wigsley, u/c collapsed

BF482 R/XV Sqn 15.3.43, FTR 23/24.5.43 from Dortmund shot down by AA fire near target

BF483 C/149 Sqn 14.3.43, FTR 28/29.6.43 from Cologne, SOC 4.7.43

BF500 M/149 Sqn 7.4.43, FTR 14/15.4.43 from Stuttgart, crashed near Tonnes, France

BF501 N/7 Sqn 31.3.43, N/218 Sqn 28.4.43, FTR 24/25.6.43 from Elberfeld, crashed Kaggevinne, Belgium

BF502 P/218 Sqn 23.3.43, FTR 8/9.4.43 from Duisburg

BF503 U/149 Sqn 23.3.43, 90 Sqn 5.4.43, U,H/620 Sqn 21.6.43, 1665 CU 11.2.44, FA AC 16.6.44 u/c collapsed landing Tilstock, 1665 CU 26.10.44, 23 MU 11.1.45, SOC 4.3.46

BF504 F/90 Sqn 4.4.43, EFB 3/4.7.43 overshot Wratting Common returning from Cologne

BF505 Z/218 Sqn 23.3.43, FTR 4/5.5.43 from Dortmund, shot down by fighter 0107 hrs Dekkum, Netherlands

BF506 P/75 Sqn 6.4.43, FTR 21.4.43 from Rostock, crashed Boegballe, Denmark

BF507 S/149 Sqn 31.3.43, FTR 29/30.5.43 from Wuppertal, crashed Dormagen, Germany

BF508 S/90 Sqn 31.3.43,1 FTR 20/21.4.43 from Rostock, in sea between Faeno and mainland of Fyn, Denmark

BF509 N/149 Sqn 31.3.43,1 ROS 25.5.43, B/149 Sqn 28.6.43, ROS 17.8.43 after being run into by EF442 at Boscombe Down, R/149 Sqn 14.9.43, 1653 CU 16.2.44, FA overshot Chedburgh u/c damaged 25.7.44, 6 MU SLG Woburn 24.11.44, SOC 24.4.45

BF510 P/149 Sqn 31.3.43, FTR 22.5.43 from mining, crashed in Biscay

BF511 V/214 Sqn, A/620 Sqn 19.6.43, FTR 26.7.43 from Aachen, crashed Hoenderloo, Netherlands

BF512 E/149 Sqn 31.3.43, EFA 9.8.43 undershot Lakenheath, opened up, crashed 1 mile NE aerodrome

BF513 E/75 Sqn 5.4.43, FTR 14.4.43 from Stuttgart, crashed Oignies, Belgium

BF514 X/218 Sqn 7.4.43, FTR 16.4.43 from Mannheim, crashed Raucourt, France

BF515 N/218 Sqn 7.4.43, FTR 29.,4.43 from mining, crashed Taagerup, Denmark

BF516 75 Sqn 11.4.43, U, E/214 Sqn 4.43, FA AC 5.6.43 in heavy landing Chedburgh, 214 Sqn, FTR 11.8.43 from Nuremberg, crashed in Channel off Bexhill, fuel short

BF517 JN-O/75 Sqn 6.4.43, crashed base with battle damage 26.4.43, RIW Sebro, 1657 CU 1.11.43, 6 MU 11.12.44, SOC 19.7.45

BF518 A,E/75 Sqn 11.4.43, landed downwind at West Malling 31.8.43 and u/c damaged, written off

BF519 E/218 Sqn 14.4.43, FTR 30/31.7.43 from Remscheid, shot down at Numansdorp, Netherlands

BF520 TK-Y/149 Sqn 12.4.43, swung taking off 17.5.43 RIW Sebro 18.5.43, K/196 Sqn 8.10.43, 1665 CU 29.3.44, overshot Tilstock RIW Sebro 13.5.44, 23 MU 25.9.44, SOC 5.6.47

BF521 90 Sqn 19.4.43, P/XV Sqn 11.5.43, H/622 Sqn 10.8.43 , FTR 23/24.8.43 from Berlin and crashed near that city

BF522 F,N/218 Sqn 5.5.43, FTR 23/24.8.43 from Berlin, ditched in North Sea

BF523 G/90 Sqn 28.4.43, FTR 13.5.43 from Duisburg, shot down at 0328 hrs by III/NJG 19km SW of Hardewij

BF524 S,N,A,Z,U/90 Sqn 19.4.43, FTR 9.5.44 from SD operation, crashed St Aignant le Jaillard

BF525 A/214 Sqn 19.4.43, Q/620 Sqn 4.7.43, 1653 CU 10.12.43, FTR 14.1.44 from a navigation training exercise, lost without trace

BF526 M/7 Sqn 23.4.43, R,G,P,S/90 Sqn 28.5.43, 1651 CU, starboard u/c led collapsed causing ground loop, Cat B Methwold 29.5.44, 1651 CU 2.6.44, 6 MU 6.11.44, SOC 24.4.45

BF527 K/90 Sqn 16.4.43, 9.6.43 caught fire on ground, Cat B Sebro 9.6.43, 1657 CU 11.3.43, B FA Shepherd's Grove when swung on take-off, port tyre burst, u/c collapsed, Cat E 14.9.44

BF528 L,L2/214 Sqn 21.4.43, FTR 23/24.5.43 from Dortmund, crashed Mönchengladbach

BF529 Q/90 Sqn 23.4.43, RIW B Sebro 13.5.43, 196 Sqn 13.10.43, 513 Sqn 5.11.43, 1660 CU 27.11.43, B FA 22.5.44, failed to get airborne and belly flopped, 1660 CU 15.7.44, FA AC 24.9.44, 1660 CU 29.9.44, 6 MU 24.2.45, SOC 11.4,45

BF530 B/149 Sqn 5.5.43, FTR 3/4.7.43 from Cologne, shot down by fighter at Geetbetz, Belgium

BF531 W/149 Sqn 21.4.43, EFA 14.6.43 landing swing at Lakenheath, u/c collapsed

BF532 Y/7 Sqn 21.4.43, W,A,X/90 Sqn 28.5.43, 1657 CU 1.11.43, AC MI 20.5.44, 1657 CU 26.5.44, FA 22.9.44, overshot Shepherd's Grove, RIW Sebro and cv to Mk IV 22.9.44, 23 MU 20.6.45, 21 HGCU 2.8.45, SOC 5.6.47

BF533 K/XV Sqn 23.4.43, 1657 CU 11.5.43, 1654 CU 29.11.43, FA B 18.7.44 Wigsley, landed without full flap, u/c collapsed, Sebro RIW, 10 MU 21.12.44, SOC 29.4.45

BF534 L/XV Sqn 23.4.43, FTR 26.5.43 from Düsseldorf, crashed Julich along with EF361, both brought down when a fighter destroyed a 77 Sqn Halifax which exploded

BF561 O/75 Sqn 25.4.43, FTR 29/30.5.43 from Wuppertal, crashed Gladbeck-Rentford, Germany

BF562 Q/214 Sqn 25.5.43, H/622 Sqn 18.8.43, 1661 CU 4.12.43, 6 MU 17.12.43, SOC 19.7.45

BF563 J/214 Sqn 25.4.43, EFA Chedburgh 18.6.43, u/c collapsed landing

BF564 W/75 Sqn 8.5.43, FTR 23/24.8.43 from Berlin, crashed Martensmuhle, Germany

BF565 H/218 Sqn 1.5.43, FTR 30.5.43 from Wuppertal, crashed near Kattenis, Belgium

BF566 T,G/90 Sqn 4.5.43, FA AC 30.5.43, G/90 Sqn 9.7.43, FTR 22/23.9.43 from Hannover, shot down by fighter at Gestorf, Germany

BF567 P/218 Sqn 4.5.43, FTR 24.7.43 from Hamburg, shot down by fighter at Einfield, Germany

BF568 B/218 Sqn 5.5.43, B/623 Sqn 13.8.43, B/214 Sqn 15.12.43, BS-Z,BS-Y/1651 CU 27.1.44, 29.5.44 overshot Wratting Common, 6 MU 8.11.44, SOC 24.4.45

BF569 O,Y,V/XV Sqn 25.5.43, FTR 15/16.9.43 from Montlucon, crashed Vaux, France

BF570 T,H/149 Sqn 25.5.43, 1654 CU 17.8.43, FA AC ROS 27.10.43, 1651 CU 23.11.43, FA AC Bourn 27.10.44, tipped on nose after swing on take-off, 6 MU 22.2.45, SOC 24.4.45

BF571 U/XV Sqn 13.5.43, FTR 11/12.6.43 from Düsseldorf, shot down off Ameland

BF572 K/218 Sqn 7.5.43, FTR 22/23.6.43 from Mulheim, shot down by fighter off Dutch coast

BF573 75 Sqn 6.5.43, W/149 Sqn 20.5.43, W,B,U/620 Sqn 21.6.43, FA AC 12.7.43 heavy landing, 620 Sqn, FA AC ROS 9.10.43, 620 Sqn 20.11.43, 1653 CU 10.12.43, 1657 CU 17.1.44, AC MI ROS 28.5.44, 1657 CU 13.6.43, 23 MU 10.2.45, SOC 28.3.46

BF574 B/214 Sqn 20.5.43, F/90 Sqn 19.8.43, FA AC 19.9.43, tailwheel collapse landing at Llandow, ROS, 90 Sqn 14.10.43, 1660 CU 8.2.44, 23 MU 19.2.45, 101 SLG 19.2.45, SOC 28.2.46

BF575 (Hercules XVI) H/75 Sqn 17.5.43, Sebro Cat B 13.9.43, overshot Market Harborough and u/c collapsed during 130mph landing, cv to Mk IV, 10 MU 18.3.44, 6 MU 16.6.44, 295 Sqn 10.8.44, 23 MU 28.4.45, SOC 5.6.47

BF576 Z,Y/149 Sqn 13.5.43, F/620 Sqn 21.6.43, FTR 28.8.43 from Nuremberg, crashed Irach, Germany

BF577 JN-M/75 Sqn 26.5.43, FTR 3.8.43 from Hamburg crashed Kaiser-Wilhelmskoog after mid-air collision with night fighter

BF578 A/218 Sqn 20.5.43, FTR 30.7.43 from Hamburg, shot down at Ahrensolde

BF579 B/XV Sqn 29.5.43, FTR 4.7.43 from mining and shot down at sea by fighter

BF580 T/149 Sqn 24.5.43, C/620 Sqn 21.6.43, Cat B 4.7.43, and SOC 22.7.43, but re-cat B 29.7.43 and converted to Mk IV (Hercules VI), 6 MU 10.1.44, 620 Sqn 11.6.44, 19 MU 27.11.44, SOC 16.12.44

BK592 – BK818, 150 aircraft, Mk I to BK647, Mk III thereafter

BK592 214 Sqn 21.9.42, M,P/7 Sqn 1.10.42, FTR 12/13.3.43 from Essen

BK593 I,/214 Sqn 21.9.42, EFB, crashed moments after take-off for Turin from Chedburgh, 28/29.11.42, possible fuel starvation

BK594 BDU 23.9.42, Sebro Cat B 13.2.44 after colliding with EF396 on runway at Chedburgh, 23 MU 21.6.44, 6 MU 5.12.44, SOC 19.7.45

BK595 A/XV Sqn 25.9.42, FTR 18/19.11.42 from Turin, crashed at Playa de Oro, Spain

BK596 B/218 Sqn 30.9.42, FTR 20.4.43 from Rostock, crashed Stalsund, Germany

BK597 XV Sqn 30.9.42, F/149 Sqn 6.10.42, Cat AC 5.12.42, 218 Sqn 2.7.43, 1651 CU 8.7.43, 1665 CU 4.8.43, RIW Sebro 17.11.43 after u/c collapsed landing Woolfox 16.11.43, 10 MU 11.5.44, 6 MU 31.12.44, SOC 19.7.45

BK598 G/149 Sqn 1.10.42, N,S/90 Sqn 16.11.42 1657 CU 6.6.43, 1665 CU 5.8.43, tail chassis collapsed 20.12.43, 6 MU 5.4.44, SOC 14.1.45

BK599 R/214 Sqn 2.10.42, FTR 13.10.42 from Kiel, shot down at Felde, Germany

BK600 K/214 Sqn 2.10.42, YZ-R/1651 CU 6.7.43, EFA 26.7.44, swung on take-off Wratting Common, u/c ripped off, fuselage buckled

BK601 214 Sqn 6.10.42, N/149 Sqn 8.10.42, 1657 CU 10.5.43, EFA 28.1.44, swung on take-off Rougham, u/c collapsed, SOC 8.2.44

BK602 B/7 Sqn 9.10.42, R/75 Sqn 21.12.42, FTR 25/26.5.43 from Düsseldorf, crashed in sea

BK603 XT-K/1657 CU 6.10.42, 1665 CU 30.7.43, became 4372M 1.12.43, SOC 16.2.45

BK604 7 CF 8.10.42, S/75 Sqn 15.1.43, FTR 3/4.2.43 from Hamburg, shot dawn by fighter 2013 hrs Markelo, Netherlands

BK605 S.BS-L/1651 CU 11.10.42, 1665 CU 30.11.43, 10 MU 30.3.44, 6 MU 11.4.44, SOC 24.11.44

BK606 N/218 Sqn 13.10.42, EFB 8.11.42, engine failure on circuit Bourn returning from Genoa, crashed on Chiver's Farm, near Cambridge

BK607 X/218 Sqn 14.10.42, EFB 29.11.42 after early return from Turin with engine problem and overshot Downham Market, u/c collapsed

BK608 T/75 Sqn 21.10.42, EFB 28.11.42, engines cut on approach to Stradishall, fuel starvation, became 3565M

BK609 R/75 Sqn 18.10.42, EFB 29/30.11.42, overshot Bradwell Bay when landing back from Turin

BK610 S,V/7 Sqn 21.11.42, FTR 8/9.3.43 from Nuremberg, crashed on sand bank east of Dungeness

BK611 U/XV Sqn 24.12.42, FTR 25/26.5.43 from Düsseldorf, shot down near Grubbenvorst, Netherlands

BK612 E/149 Sqn 14.12.42, H,Z/214 Sqn 28.2.43, FTR 11/12.4.43 from mining Gironde Estuary

BK613 214 Sqn 21.1.43, 1657 CU 30.1.43, on 1.3.43 hit an airman during take-off, airman carried around on tailplane, 1653 CU 3.3.44, EFA 17.3.44, landing Stradishall, swung, u/c torn off

BK614 JN-H/75 Sqn 16.3.43, FTR 6/7.8.43 from mining Gironde

BK615 75 Sqn 28.11.42 , CRD RAE 7.1.43 for fitment of H2S, 10 NU 21.6.43, 1654 CU 10.5.44, 4 OAPU 24.5.44, 12 FU Melton Mowbray, GA Cat E 25.3.45, hit Beaufighter NE823 whilst taxiing, SOC 10.4.45

BK616 CRD TFU Defford 22.10.42, 10 MU 10.7.43, 1657 CU 22.8.44, 1651 CU 17.10.44, 6 MU 6.11.44, SOC 19.7.45

BK617 D/75 Sqn 24.10.42, FTR 5/6.2.43 caught fire 1943 hrs off Cromer en route to mine off Frisians

BK618 Q/75 Sqn 24.10.42, FTR 2/3.12.42 from Frankfurt, shot down at Idar-Oberstein, Germany

BK619 X,O/75 Sqn 3.11.42, 1651 CU 14.10.43, RIW Sebro 23.10.43 after being hit on 23.10.43 by BK623 taxiing, 27 MU 19.,4.44, 6 MU 4.1.45, SOC 19.7.45

BK620 A/75 Sqn 31.10.42, FTR 18.12.42 from Fallerseleben, shot down in Westemberplazsee, Aalsmeer, Netherlands

BK621 Q,N/7 Sqn 3.11.42, R/214 Sqn 29.5.43, V/1651 CU 8.1.43, EFA 24.7.43, swung on take-off, port u/c collapsed, Woolfox Lodge

BK622 H, BS-S/1651 CU 8.11.42, mistook perimeter track for runway at Waterbeach 23.10.43 and ran into a gun post, EFA 13.2.44 swung on take-off and hit obstruction

BK623 F,BS-V/1651 CU 6.11.42, 20.6.43 tail chassis damaged on rough ground, 23.10.43 hit BK619 when taxiing, 4.12.43 u/c collapsed when landing at Witchford, EFA 16.6.44, engine trouble and belly landed Stradishall

BK624 1651 CU 7.11.42, A,R,Y/75 Sqn 15.1.43, 19.4.43 u/c twisted during crosswind landing Newmarket, 1651 CU 25.6.43, 1665 CU 10.1.44, 6 MU 22.4.44, SOC 14.1.45

BK625 D/90 Sqn 17.11.42, Cat B FA 19.12.42 ran off runway Ridgewell, RIW Sebro 29.12.42, Re-Cat E 25.1.43

BK626 C,W/90 Sqn 15.11.42, EFB crashed Shipdham after engine trouble during ASR sortie 25.5.43, RIW Sebro 9.6.43 but soon Re-Cat E

BK627 P/90 Sqn 17.11.42, FTR 19/20.2.43 from Wilhelmshaven, crashed at sea

BK628 Q,G/90 Sqn 17.11.42, u/c collapsed 18.11.42 at dispersal killing one man, Cat AC 18.12.42, 90 Sqn 14.4.43, FTR 24/25.6.43 from Wuppertal

BK644 T/90 Sqn 1.12.42,FTR 6.2.43 from mining Frisians, ditched off Cromer

BK645 CRD AFEE 24.1.43, 10 MU 12.11.43, SOC 30.11.44

BK646 N/75 Sqn 10.2.43, FTR 15.6.43 mining Gironde, shot down at Moulines, France

BK647 75 Sqn 9.2.43, EFB 5.3.43 power lost on take-off Newmarket, crashed one mile W of aerodrome

BK648 and subsequent **BK** aircraft were Mk III (Hercules VI unless otherwise stated)

BK648 19 MU 1.12.42, J/XV Sqn 31.12.42, FTR3/4.7.43 from Cologne, crashed at Menden, Germany

BK649 A&AEE 8.12.42, 1660 CU 27.3.44, FA AC RIW Sebro 24.5.44, 10 MU 23.9.44, SOC 27.8.46

BK650 44 MU 9.12.42, L,T/218 Sqn 6.2.43, 15.4.43 hit pylon when low flying over Luxembourg, FTR 30.8.43 from Mönchengladbach, shot down at Dorpplein Budel, Netherlands

BK651 (Hercules XVI) CRD Shorts 29.12.42, CRD A&AEE 21.9.43, 1654 CU 14.3.44, RIW Sebro after heavy landing Wigsley 26.4.44, u/c collapsed, starboard wing came off, 23 MU 18.9.44, SOC 5.6.47

BK652 Q,V/XV Sqn 3.1.43, 622 Sqn 10.8.43, 1665 CU 16.10.43, 6 MU 10.12.44, SOC 24.4.45

BK653 10 MU 11.1.43, A/214 Sqn 9.3.43, FTR 17.4.43 from Mannheim, shot down at Bonneuil, France

BK654 W/XV Sqn 20.1.43, 1651 CU 4.12.43, EFA 28.6.44, two engined failures, crashed at Gosburton, Lincs., SOC 2.7.44

BK655 44 MU 30.1.43, B/90 Sqn 18.3.43, RIW Sebro 24.5.43, X/90 Sqn 8.43, FTR 8/9.10.43 from Bremen, crashed at Rhade, Germany

BK656 A/XV Sqn 26.1.43, FTR 23.6.43 from Mulheim, shot down at 0207 hrs by III/NJG 1km N of Deelen

BK657 C/XV Sqn 25.1.43, FTR 27.4.43 from Duisburg, shot down by fighter 0208 hrs near Portengen, Netherlands

BK658 K/XV Sqn 21.1.43, FTR 5.5.43 from Dortmund, shot down by fighter at Midwolds, Netherlands

BK659 44 MU 29.1.43, N/214 25/26.5.43 FTR from Düsseldorf

BK660 damaged beyond repair during delivery 10.1.43

BK661 44 MU 30.1.43, O/90 Sqn 29.3.43, FTR13.5.43 from Duisburg

BK662 K/214 Sqn 28.2.43, FTR 5/6.3.43 from Essen shot down by fighter off Texel

BK663 214 Sqn 9.3.43, RIW Sebro 30.3.43 after mid-air collision with EF362, declared Cat E but re-cat B, 196 Sqn 17.8.43, EFB 28.9.43 crashed approaching Witchford in poor weather, 1 mile SE Ely, 0230 hrs

BK664 M/75 Sqn, EFB 16/17.4.43, battle damage caused crash at 0420 hrs into hangar at Newmarket on return from ops, throttles would not close

BK665 149 Sqn 24.2.43, D/90 Sqn 3.3.43, FTR 23.6.43 from Mulheim, crashed Kehrum, Germany

BK666 218 Sqn 10.2.43, EFB 1/2.3.43 flak damaged, crashed approaching Foulsham

BK667 H/XV Sqn 21.1.43, EFB 22.3.43, engine trouble when bound for St Nazaire, aborted, crashed at Clyffe Pypard

BK686 10 MU 29.1.43, C/214 Sqn 9.3.43, FTR 25/26.7.43 from Essen, crashed near Essen

BK687 R/218 Sqn 7.2.43, FTR 8/9.10.43 Bremen, crashed at Ebaradorf, Germany

BK688 A/218 Sqn 10.3.43, FTR 30.5.43 Wuppertal, crashed Schaffen airfield, Belgium

BK689 E/214 Sqn 16.3.43,1 218 Sqn 16.10.43, 1657 CU 29.1.44, EFA 28.5.44, hit EF454 during take-off from Shepherd's Grove and burnt out

BK690 V/214 Sqn 10.2.43, P/620 Sqn 19.6.43, FTR 6/7.8.43 mining Gironde, shot down at Nantes by flak

BK691 F/XV Sqn 10.2.43, FTR 17.4.43 from Mannheim, crashed Hetzerath, Germany

BK692 W/149 Sqn 27.2.43, FTR from Berlin 2.3.43, shot down at Gueuteville, France

BK693 A/90 Sqn 10.2.43, EFB 28.7.43, returning from Hamburg, swung off runway at Stradishall and into another Stirling

BK694 O,C/XV Sqn 28.2.43, FTR 29.6.43 from Cologne, shot down by fighter at Lommel, Belgium

BK695 X,/XV Sqn 28.2.43, RIW Sebro 30.4.43, 75 Sqn 26.9.43, 199 Sqn 17.3.44, 1653 CU 25.4.44, EFA 10.8.44, port tyre burst on take-off Chedburgh, u/c collapsed

BK696 V/149 Sqn 27.2.43, EFB 2.5.43, battle damage, fuel short, storm damage, crew abandoned and aircraft crashed on Windmill Hill, Havant, Hants

BK697 P/XV Sqn 28.2.43, FTR 9.3.43 Nuremberg, crashed Campneuville, France

BK698 XV Sqn 28.2.43, O/149 Sqn 10.3.43, FTR 21.4.43 from Rostock, crashed at sea

BK699 E,W/XV Sqn 1.3.43, FTR 25/26.6.43 Gelsenkirchen, crashed south Ameland, Netherlands

BK700 L/218 Sqn 28/2/43, FTR 22/23.9.43 Hannover, crashed at Neustadt, Germany

BK701 G/149 Sqn 16.2.43, FTR 16/17.5.43 mining off Frisians?

BK702 O/218 Sqn 8.3.43, FTR 30.3.43 from Berlin, crashed at Bremen

BK703 XV Sqn 2.3.43, K/149 Sqn 10.3.43, FTR 28/29.6.43 from Cologne, shot down Netersel/Bladel, Netherlands

BK704 Z/XV Sqn 2.3.43, FTR 14.5.43 from Bochum?

BK705 K/218 Sqn 9.3.43, FTR 12/13.5.43 from Duisburg, crashed at sea

BK706 Y/218 Sqn 8.3.43, FTR 23/24.5.43 from Dortmund, crashed near target

BK707 P/214 Sqn 10.3.43, RIW Sebro 26.5.43 after overshoots at Chedburgh, O,G/XV Sqn 10. 9.43, FTR 18.11.43 from Mannheim, crashed at Souain, Germany

BK708 P/149 Sqn 14.3.43, FTR 29/30.3.43 from Berlin, crashed at Lindenburg, Germany

BK709 P/7 Sqn 29.3.43, FTR 14/15.4.43 Stuttgart, shot down at Biblis, Germany

BK710 A/149 Sqn 31.3.43, FTR 25/26.5.43 from Düsseldorf, shot down at sea by fighter

BK711 O/149 Sqn 12.4.43, FTR 5/6.9.43 from Mannheim, crashed at Hockenheim, Germany

BK712 D/218 Sqn 13.4.43, FTR 21/22.6.43 from Krefeld, shot down at Langdorp, Belgium

BK713 X, N/149 Sqn 15.3.43, E/620 Sqn 21.6.43, FTR 12/13.8.43 from Turin, crashed Mittainvilliers, France

BK714 L/149 Sqn 15.3.43, FTR 21.4.43 from Rostock, shot down at Broendum, Denmark

BK715 D/149 Sqn 15.3.43, EFA 31.3.43, engine fire taking off from Lakenheath, subdued but later caused aircraft to be burnt out

BK716 J/218 Sqn 17.3.43, FTR 30.3.43 from Berlin, crashed at sea off Vlieland, Netherlands

BK717 U/214 Sqn 15.3.43, FTR 3/4.7.43 from Cologne crashed near Zaamslag, Netherlands

BK718 M/90 Sqn 15 4 43, FTR 3/4.7.43 from Cologne shot down at Mehlem, Germany

BK719 B/XV Sqn 22.4.43,1661 CU 13.12.43, 6 MU 19.1.44, SOC 24.4.45

BK720 Y/214 Sqn 28.4.43,620 Sqn 19.6.43, EFB 25.6.43, battle damage, tyre burst during landing at Chedburgh

BK721 Z/75 Sqn 2.5.43, EFB 13.5.43, engine failure taking-off from Newmarket 0038 hrs, swerved into Devil's Dyke

BK722 G/218 Sqn 7.5.43, FTR 22.6.43 from Krefeld, shot down by fighter at Maarhaze, Netherlands

BK723 E/7 Sqn 15.4.43, D/90 Sqn 1.7.43, FTR 3/4.10.43 from Kassel, ditched in North Sea 2020 hrs

BK724 I/7 Sqn 24.3.43, 214 Sqn 29.5.43, 620 Sqn 19.6.43, EFA 2.7.43 during fighter affiliation after collision with EF394, crashed at Stansfield, Suffolk

BK725 M/90 Sqn 31.3.43, FTR 16/17.4.43 from Mannheim, shot down near Commenchon, France

BK726 Z/149 Sqn 24.3.43, FTR 13.5.43 from Bochum, shot down at Immerath, Germany

BK727 218 Sqn 9.6.43, 623 Sqn 13.8.43, 218 Sqn 11.12.43, 1651 CU 25.1.44, 6 MU 6.11.44, SOC 24.4.45

BK759 X/149 Sqn 24.3.430, FTR 15.4.45 from Stuttgart, crashed Studernheirn, Germany

BK760 X/7 Sqn 27.5.43, FTR 10/11.4.43 from Frankfurt, shot down by fighter at Tongerloo, Belgium

BK761 7 Sqn 24.3.43, O/218 Sqn 28.4.43, 30/31.7.43 struck by incendiary bomb whilst being flown by Flt Sgt Aaron, 1661 CU 2.2.44, 6 MU 17.12.44, SOC 19.7.45

BK762 214 Sqn 31.3.43, C,X/199 Sqn 7.7.43, RIW Sebro 30.11.43, 19 MU 8.5.44, 6 MU 2.11.44, SOC 19.7.45

BK763 F/214 Sqn 31.3.43, 3.9.43 overshot North Weald into ditch, RIW Sebro 23.11.43, 27 MU 20.4.44, 1653 CU 24.6.44, EFA 5.10.44 u/c collapsed in emergency landing Woodbridge

BK764 R/XV Sqn 9.5.43, FTR 30/31.8.43 from Mönchengladbach 30/31.8.43, crashed Wassenberg, Germany

BK765 P/149 Sqn 17.5.43, FTR 23/24.8.43 from Berlin, crashed at target

BK766 T/XV Sqn 27.5.43, G/622 Sqn 10.8.43, 1661 CU 8.12.43, 23 MU SLG 14.1.45, SOC 25.4.46

BK767 L/214 Sqn 31.5.43, FTR 25/26.6.43 from Gelsenkirchen, crashed Aalten, Netherlands

BK768 L/75 Sqn 21.5.43, FTR 25/26.6.43 Gelsenkirchen, reported crashed in IJsselmeer

BK769 G/7 Sqn 3.4.43, FTR 14/15.4.43 from Stuttgart, crashed Lembach, Germany

BK770 75 Sqn 4.4.43, EFB 9.4.43, control lost and dived in almost vertically near Bressingham, returning from Duisburg

BK771 L/214 Sqn 5.4.43, 196 Sqn 19.8.43, 28.9.43, hit by incendiary over Hannover, 196 Sqn 16.10.43, EFB 3.2.44, swung taking off Tarrant Rushton for SOE drop, hit Halifax DK199 and burnt out

BK772 T/149 Sqn 27.3.43, A/199 Sqn 6,7.43, 1657 CU 28.10.43, EFA 27.8.44 engine trouble and crashed in a field of Tothill Farm, Haughley, about 1 mile NW Stowmarket

BK773 T/7 Sqn 6.4.43, FTR 4/5.5.43 from Dortmund, shot down by fighter at 0008 hrs 8km S of Enkhuizen, Netherlands

BK774 T,K/XV Sqn 17.4.43, FTR 7.9.43 from mining Kattegat, crashed at sea

BK775 H/90 Sqn 31.3.43, FTR 30/31.7.43 from Remscheid, crashed Koonigshofen, Germany

BK776 B/75 Sqn 8.4.43, FTR 29/30.5.43 from Wuppertal, shot down by fighter 0054 hrs near Roermond

BK777 U/75 Sqn 8.4.43, 1653 CU 3.5.43, 6 MU SLG Woburn 24.11.44, SOC 24.4.45

BK778 U/75 Sqn 4.4.43, FTR 4/5.11.43 from mining Baltic, crashed Berstedgaard, Denmark

BK779 7 Sqn 4.4.43, L/90 Sqn 15.4.43, FTR 24.8.43 from Berlin, ditched

BK780 90 Sqn 13.4.43, EFA 25.4.43 u/c collapsed after landing at Ridgewell

BK781 E/90 Sqn 9.4.43, 149 Sqn 13.7.44, 1651 CU 17.8.44, 6 MU 25.11.44, SOC 24.4.45

BK782 X/XV Sqn 13.4.43, FTR 4/5.5.43 from Dortmund, shot down 0104 hrs at Midwoldar Netherlands

BK783 10 MU 2.5.43, 75 Sqn 1.5.43, FTR 23/24.5.43 from Dortmund, shot down by fighter 0214 hrs at Beesd, Netherlands

BK784 P/90 Sqn 14.4.43, EFB 23.5.44, swung on take-off Tuddenham, for mining off Frisians, clipped a tree and crashed at Chippenham Lodge

BK798 Q/149 Sqn 14.4.43, 31.8.43 hit by falling British incendiary bomb (500lb bomb fell off aircraft during gas exercise on 3.10.43), FTR 20/21.12.43 from mining off Frisians, shot down at sea

BK799 O/149 Sqn 21.4.43, 620 Sqn 19.6.43, FTR 21/22.6.43 from Krefeld, crashed in IJsselmeer

BK800 Z/214 Sqn 22.4.43, 620 Sqn 19.6.43, FTR 25/26.4.43 from Wuppertal, crashed at Haslinghausen

BK801 214 Sqn 18.4.43, 620 Sqn 19.6.43, FTR 23/24.8.43 from Berlin, shot down at Lohm, Germany

BK802 214 Sqn 3.6.43, Z/620 Sqn 9.43, EFA 20.10.43, ice accretion, crashed at White Waltham

BK803 D/218 Sqn 4.6.43, 623 Sqn 13.6.43, 30.9.43 hit in flight by incendiary bomb, 1654 CU 29.11.43, EFA 30.6.44, engine fire crashed Tolling, Mansfield

BK804 J/90 Sqn 9.6.43, FTR 23.6.43 from Mulheim, crashed at Duisburg-Beek, Germany

BK805 U/XV Sqn 12.6.43,FTR 25/26.7.43 from Essen, shot down by fighter at Osterwick, Germany

BK806 V/149 Sqn 17.6.43, S/199 Sqn 2.8.43, FTR 27/28.8.43 from Nuremberg, crashed at Ansbach, Germany

BK807 75 Sqn 21.4.43, FTR 29.4.43 from mining Kiel Bay, crashed at sea

BK808 Q/214 Sqn 19.4.43, FA 19.5.43, tyre burst and u/c collapsed landing Chedburgh

BK809 T/75 Sqn 2.5.43, EFB 8/9.9.43 Mepal, swung off for Boulogne, hit petrol bowser

BK810 G/75 Sqn 2.5.43, FTR 23.6.43 from Mulheim, shot down by fighter at Osstrum, Netherlands

BK811 V/90 Sqn 28.4.43, 1653 CU 6.2.44, 6 MU 21.11.44, SOC 24.4.45

BK812 149 Sqn 29.4.43, EFA 11.5.43 swung taking off Mildenhall, u/c collapsed

BK813 O/90 Sqn 5.5.43, overshot Ridgewell 10.5.43, FTR from Wuppertal 25.6.43, shot down by fighter at Haesrode, Belgium

BK814 T/90 Sqn 28.4.43, FTR 4/5.5.43 from Dortmund, crashed at Derne, Germany

BK815 V/XV Sqn 30.4.43, FTR 21/22.6.43 from Krefeld, crashed at Melsele, Belgium

BK816 Y,E/XV Sqn 29.4.43, B/622 Sqn 10.8.43, R/199 Sqn 9.1.44, B/90 Sqn 5.5.44, S/149 Sqn 12.6.44, FB AC 7.8.44, 149 Sqn 14.10.44, 1651 CU 17.10.44, 6 MU 13.12.44, SOC 19.7.45

BK817 75 Sqn 2.5.43, FTR 11/12.6.43 from Düsseldorf, shot down by fighter at Froidthier, Belgium

BK818 R,O/XV Sqn 7.5.43, 1661 CU 4.12.43, 6 MU 28.32.45, SOC 18.5.45

DJ972 – DJ977 Six aircraft as replacements for Mk Is destroyed by bombing of factories

DJ972 (replacing N3645, Hercules III) 149 Sqn 13.4.42, EFB 7.5.42, crashed after fighter engagement, at Lakenheath after attacking Stuttgart

DJ973 (replacing N3647, Hercules XI) A/214 Sqn 3.5.42,EFB 24/25.6.42, engine failure on St Nazaire raid 30 miles off France, crashed after early return at Hundon, near Stradishall

DJ974 (replacing N3648) T/218 Sqn 1.5.42, FTR 27/28.6.42 from Bremen, crashed in sea due to flak damage

DJ975 (replacing N3649) 214 Sqn 4.6.42, W/1651 CU 7.10.42, EFA 31.10.43, overshot landing at Witchford

DJ976 (replacing N3650) A/218 Sqn 26.9.43, RIW Sebro 16.11.42, 1657 CU 9.3.43, Cat EFA 11.6.43, u/c collapsed landing Stradishall, SOC 26.6.43

DJ977 (replacing N3651) F/218 Sqn 22.4.42, FTR 19/20.5.42 from Mannheim

EE871 – EF518 built as Mk III with conversions Mk IV on the line as well as in service

EE871 P/214 Sqn 27.5.43, Cat AC 21/22.6.43, Z/214 Sqn 17.7.43, Q/90 Sqn 18.8.43, FTR 1.9.43 from Berlin, crashed Reesdorf, Germany

EE872 N/149 Sqn 26.5.43, FTR 5/6.9.43 from Mannheim, shot down by fighter near target

EE873 D,Z/90 Sqn 11.6.43, FTR 13/14.7.43 from Aachen, shot down by fighter at Rothem, Belgium

EE874 G/214 Sqn 5.6.43, S/196 Sqn 17.8.43, OG-F /1665 CU 5.3.44, 19 MU 11.12.44, SOC 27.9.45

EE875 S/149 Sqn 24.5.43,1 A/620 Sqn 21.6.43, FTR 23.6.43 from Mulheim, shot down off Netherlands

EE876 N/214 Sqn 27.5.43, J,T/623 Sqn 18.8.43, 1654 CU 29.11.43, FA 8.2.44, taxying hit nose of EF144, 1654 CU 20.5.44, 23 MU 2.1.45, SOC 25.4.46

EE877 XV Sqn 29.5.43, H,E/149 Sqn 14.6.43, FTR 27/28.8.43 from Nuremberg crashed near Langel, Germany

EE878 F,P/XV Sqn 31.5.43, FTR 31.8.43 from Berlin, crashed at Aabruck, Germany

EE879 G/149 Sqn 29.5.43, FTR 31.8.43 from Berlin, crashed at Sputendorf, Germany

EE880 O/149 Sqn 31.5.43, FTR 27/28.6.43 from Cologne, shot down by fighter at Houwaart, Belgium

EE881 JN-G/75 Sqn 16.6.43, Cat B Sebro 6.9.43, 27 MU 1.5.44, XT-T/1657 CU 7.6.44, 23 MU SLG 10.1.45, SOC 23.4.46

EE882 J/214 Sqn 2.6.43, FTR 3/4.7.43 mining *Nectarine 1*, shot down at sea by fighter

EE883 T/214 Sqn 31.5.430, FTR 24/25.6.43 from Wuppertal, crashed at sea

EE884 X/218 Sqn 31.5.43, FTR 18/19.11.43 from Mannheim, crashed at Hofheim, Germany

EE885 G/218 Sqn 2.6.43, FTR 11.8.43 from Nuremberg, crashed at Offenhausen, Germany

EE886 L/75 Sqn 16.6.43, EFB 14.7.43, back from Aachen landed with flat tyre and ground looped at Oakington

EE887 T/90 Sqn 5.6.43, FTR 21/22.6.43 from Krefeld, shot down by fighter at 0244 hrs at Hoogwoud, Netherlands

EE888 H,K/218 Sqn 24.6.43, FTR 16/17.12.43 from mining off La Pallice, missing at sea

EE889 cv to Mk IV. V/90 Sqn 8.6.43, RIW Sebro 13.10.43, Woburn SLG 12.3.44, 6 MU 17.3.44, 190 Sqn 13.6.44, 1665 CU 16.8.44, CRD Defford 17.12.44, S&H: MI 7.3.45, 23 MU 5.3.46, SOC 5.6.47

EE890 L/75 Sqn 29.6.43, FTR 24/25.7.43 from Hamburg, shot down by fighter at Neumunster, Germany

EE891 Q/75 Sqn 20.6.43, FTR 15/16.8.43 from mining Gironde, crashed at sea

EE892 F/75 Sqn 9.6.42, FTR 26.7.43 from Essen, crashed off Suffolk

EE893 N,M/75 Sqn 9.6.43, FTR 5/6.9.43 from Mannheim, crashed at Schwanheim, Germany

EE894 R/149 Sqn 16.6.43, FTR 24.8.43 from Berlin, crashed near Hannover

EE895 S/218 Sqn 30.6.43, FTR 30.7.43,shot down at Billsted, Germany

EE896 J,O/90 Sqn 13.6.43, 3/4.10.43 hit by falling British incendiaries, 1651 CU 24.6.44, 6 MU 25.11.44, SOC 24.4.45

EE897 G/75 Sqn 29.6.43,1 FTR 4.11.43 mining Kattegat 5.11.43, crashed at sea

EE898 D,N/75 Sqn 15.6.43,Cat B FB 17.11.43, FA 16.12.43 Mepal, swung on take off and u/c collapsed. RIW Sebro, 1651 CU 26.5.44, 6 MU 11.11.44, SOC 24.4.45

EE899 O/214 Sqn 16.6.43,1 C/623 Sqn 18.8.43, FB AC 3/4.10.43 and on 18.11.43 (hit by incendiary during operations), 623 Sqn 8.12.43, JF-B/1654 CU 10.2.44, EFA 2.7.44 after bouncing on landing Winthorpe

EE900 Y/90 Sqn 23.6.43, Sebro 17.8.43, u/c collapsed landing at Biggin Hill, 10 MU 17.3.44, 6 MU 29.4.44, W/190 Sqn 21.5.44, 23 MU 17.5.45, SOC 5.6.47

EE901 L/214 Sqn 19.6.43, U/90 Sqn 18.8.43, FTR 24/25.7.43 from Kassel, crashed near Krefeld

EE902 P/214 Sqn 19.6.43, FTR 24.7.43 from Hamburg, shot down by fighter at Barchel, Germany

EE903 Q/218 Sqn 7.7.43, FTR 30/31.8.43 from Mönchengladbach, crashed in target area

EE904 S/90 Sqn 23.6.43,0, FTR 25/26.7.43 from Essen, shot down by fighter at sea

EE905 S/620 Sqn 3.7.43,9, FTR 30/31.7.43 from Remscheid, shot down by fighter at Willersie, Belgium

EE906 214 Sqn 20.6.43, C/620 Sqn 3.7.43, FTR 26/27.7.43 from Essen, shot down at Lieshout, Netherlands

EE907 C/XV Sqn 23.6.43, 1661 CU 8.12.43, FA AC 7.6.44, had swung on landing and hit LK462, 1661 CU 25.8.44, EFA 28.10.44, crashed near Swinderby

EE908 V/XV Sqn 23.6.43, FTR 17/18.8.43 from Peenemunde, in sea off Griefswalde, Germany

EE909 218 Sqn 29.6.43, H/623 Sqn 13.8.43, FTR 27/28.8.43 from Nuremberg, crashed Birkenfield, Germany

EE910 XV Sqn 28.6.43,Q,K/199 Sqn 19.7.43, 10/11.8.43 hit by falling incendiaries, EFA 22.4.44 u/c collapsed landing, St Athan

EE911 G/199 Sqn 8.7.43, FTR mining La Pallice, crashed at sea

EE912 U/XV Sqn 29.6.43, FTR 31.8.43 from Berlin, crashed Roskow, Germany

EE913 XV Sqn 5.7.43, F/199 Sqn 19.7.43, FTR 27/28.8.43 from Nuremberg, crashed at Futtersee

EE914 32 MU 26.6.43, C/214 Sqn 23.7.43, overshot Chedburgh crashed in field 31.8.43, Sebro RIW, 10 MU 12.5.44, 1654 CU 9.6.44, EFA 14.8.44, engine trouble, crashed in sea between Mablethorpe and Skegness

EE915 X/75 Sqn 30.6.43, FTR 30/31.7.43 from Remscheid, details unknown

EE916 218 Sqn 29.6.43, F/90 Sqn, EFB 29/7/43 swung taking off from Wratting for Hamburg

EE917 L/199 Sqn 6.7.43, FTR 30/31.8.43 from Mönchengladbach, crashed at Neder, Netherlands

EE918 D/75 Sqn 4.7.43, FTR 31.8/1.9.43 from Berlin, crashed at Darenthal, Germany

EE937 A/218 Sqn 29.6.43, FTR 27/28.9.43 from Hannover, crashed Eldagsen, Germany

EE938 X/75 Sqn 16.7.43, FTR 23/24.8.43 from Berlin, crashed at Mahlsdorf, Germany

EE939 90 Sqn 30.6.43, 15.7.43 belly landed Stradishall, RIW Sebro 30.7.43, 10 MU 25.11.43, 1651 CU 17.8.44, 1657 CU 17.10.44, 6 MU 8.12.44, SOC 19.7.45

EE940 199 Sqn 11.7.43, Y/XV Sqn 19.7.43, FTR 27.9.43 from Hannover, crashed at Ronnenberg

EE941 218 Sqn 6.7.43, U/199 Sqn 10.7.43, 4/5.3.44 u/c collapsed on take off, RIW Sebro. 14.3.44, 10 MU 26.7.44, 1332 CU 28.8.44, SOC 7.5.45

EE942 23 MU 29.7.43, R/620 Sqn 5.8.43, FTR 27/28.8.43 from Nuremberg, crashed Halberdsorf, Germany

EE943 218 Sqn 6.7.43, X,V/199 Sqn 5.7.43, 1657 CU 10.5.43, 24.8.44 overshot Halfpenny Green, RIW Sebro 8.9.44, final demise uncertain

EE944 23 MU 23.7.43, O,H/218 Sqn 3.8.43, 27.8.43 swung taking off at Downham, c/u collapsed, EFB 4/5.3.44 insufficient power on overshoot and side slipped in at Tempsford returning from SOE sortie

EE945 Oakington 30.6.43, S/620 Sqn 26.7.43, 1665 CU 30.8.43, 10 MU 24.9.44, converted to 4923M 13.11.44

EE946 P/199 Sqn 5.7.43, FTR 31.8.43 from Berlin, shot down at Weert, Germany

EE947 D/199 Sqn 5.7.43,1 EFB 24/25.9.43 making early return from mining sortie undershot Lakenheath crashed 1 mile NE, two mines exploded

EE948 G/199 Sqn 7.7.43, R1W Sebro 2.12.43, 23 MU 7.6.44, 1332 CU 14.9.44, FA 12.4.45 overshot Nutt's Corner

EE949 218 Sqn 1.8.43, G/623 Sqn 10.8.43, FTR 31.8/1.9.43 from Berlin, crashed at Werbig, Germany

EE950 32 MU 12.8.43, C/214 Sqn 7.9.43, 1660 CU 23.12.43, 12.2.44 u/c collapsed when landing, 23 MU 30.6.44, 1654 CU 21.9.44, SLG Maghaberry 3.2.45, SOC 25.4.46

EE951 B/90 Sqn 8.7.43, EFA 3.9.43 Wratting Common, u/c collapsed, swung on take-off

EE952 F/90 Sqn 8.7.43, EFB 28.9.43 crashed on finals near Horseheath, Cambs 0017 hrs returning from Hannover

EE953 E/199 Sqn 11.7.43, V/149 Sqn 5.5.44, EFB 7.6.44 clipped trees approaching Methwold, u/c collapsed on bounce, overshot, re-cat B 29.11.44 at 19 MU but SOC 12.7.45

EE954 199 Sqn 11.7.43, J/XV Sqn 19.7.43, FTR 4.10.43 from Frankfurt, details unknown

EE955 D/75 Sqn 18.8.43,1 FTR 27/28.8.43 from Nuremberg, crashed at Schwarzenau, Germany

EE956 32 MU 24.7.43, J/214 Sqn 12.8.43, battle damage 27.9.43, 1661 CU, EFA 17.5.44, heavy icing, broke up, crashed in quarry near Rothwell, Northants

EE957 196 Sqn 11.8.43, Q/199 Sqn 27.8.43, FTR 31.3.44 from SOE sortie to Fontaine Française, crashed at Sur Tille

EE958 23 MU 24.7.43, V/75 Sqn 11.8.43, 513 Sqn 22.10.43, A/75 Sqn 25.11.43, 1653 CU 3.5.44, EFA 15.5.44, loss of power, forced landed on trees in Banstead Manor, Cheveley, near Newmarket

EE959 32 MU 27.7.43, E/214 Sqn 12.8.43, FTR 31.8.43 from Berlin, crashed near Capeith, Germany

EE960 32 MU 29.7.43, A,Q/214 Sqn 12.8.43, FA 29.11.43 drifted landing and u/c collapsed, 1653 CU 3.44, 6 MU 10.11.44, SOC 24.4.45

EE961 32 MU 3.8.43, L/214 Sqn 23.8.43, 1653 CU 9.3.44, RIW Sebro 27.7.44 after landing across flarepath at Bungay and striking a B-24, 10 MU 11.11.44, SOC 14.8.46

EE962 Mk III converted to Mk IV, 23 MU 30.7.43, D/190 Sqn 11.5.44, 23 MU 17.5.45, SOC 5.6.47

EE963 32 MU 25.8.43, N/149 Sqn 27.8.43, 1653 CU 29.8.43, 4/5.10.43 hit by falling incendiary over target, 6 MU 8.11.43, SOC 24.4.45

EE964 23 MU 2.8.43, F/196 Sqn 11.8.43, FTR 5/6.9.43 from Mannheim, crashed at Bachenau, Germany

EE965 32 MU 24.8.43, 214 Sqn 23.9.43, 1660 CU 10.12.43, P/1661 CU 30.12.43, 23 MU 14.1.45, SOC 15.3.46

EE966 (*H2S* fitted), converted to Mk IV, 218 Sqn 1.8.43, E/623 Sqn 10.8.43, FA and RIW Sebro 21.9.43, Shorts Swindon 18.5.44, 6 MU 10.6.44, 299 Sqn 15.8.44, EFA 11.5.45 Gardemoen, over-corrected take-off swing in cross wind, SOC 31.5.45

EE967 32 MU 6.8.43, I,T/214 Sqn 5.9.43, 1660 CU 10.12.43, 1661 CU 7.6.44, EFA 3.8.44 Winthorpe, swung on take off to avoid another aircraft, u/c collapsed

EE968 32 MU 5.8.43, BDU 22.8.43, 19 MU 14.12.43, gale damage 18.1.45, SOC 27.9.45 (obsolete)

EE969 E/149 Sqn 27.8.43, FTR 27/28.1.44 mining Kattegat, loss details unknown

EE970 32 MU 11.8.43, B/214 Sqn 23.8.43, FTR 31.8/1.9.43 from Berlin, crashed Charlottenfelde, Germany

EE971 A/620 Sqn 30.8.43, FA AC 30.11.43, 1665 CU 4.2.44,6 MU 12.2.45, 1665 CU, SOC 25.5.45 (obsolete)

EE972 T/196 Sqn 15.8.43, OG-C/1665 CU 1.4.44, EFA 25.9.44 struck high ground, in cloud, Cheviots near Broaden

EE973 U/196 Sqn 13.8.43, EFB 6.9.43 crashed Witchford with flak damage after raid on Mannheim

EE974 O/XV Sqn 13.8.43, P, W/90 Sqn 23.12.43, EFB 29.4.44, engine fire on return from SOE sortie, crashed 2 miles NE Stradishall 0535 hrs

EE975 G/196 Sqn 11.8.43, FA Witchford 5.11.43 u/c collapsed, ROS, 27 MU 19.4.44, GP-E/1660 CU, EFA 15.8.44, engine trouble, five abandoned, crashed near Skipton, Yorks, two killed, SOC 24.8.44

EF114 H/196 Sqn 12.8.43,1 FTR 16/17.9.43 from Modane, crashed at Heurtevent, France

EF115 32 MU 16.8.43, K,V/214 Sqn 18.9.43, 3/4.10.43 hit by falling incendiaries, 1660 CU 10.12.43, 1661 CU 30.12.43, 1654 CU 26.7.44, EFA 20.9.44 Wigsley, swung and landed off runway hitting a tree trunk

EF116 J/196 Sqn 14.8.43, 15/16.9.43 hit by falling incendiaries, 513 Sqn 5.11.43, 196 Sqn 30.11.43, OG-G/1665 CU 3.3.44, 6 MU 27.2.45, SOC 8.3.45

EF117 X/620 Sqn 15.8.43, battle damaged 23.9.43, 620 Sqn 30.10.43, 1665 CU 11.2.44, EFA 5.5.44, engine fire then belly landed in field at Tilstock

EF118 O/199 Sqn 17.8.43, FTR 27/28.9.43 from Hannover, crashed at Ramlingen, Germany

EF119 Q/622 Sqn 20.8.43, FTR 31.8.43 from Berlin, shot down by fighter at Waltershuisen Kreis Osterode, Germany

EF120 32 MU 18.8.43, Y/214 Sqn 20.9.43, W/1660 CU 10.12.43, EFA 23.3.44, engine trouble, overshot airfield and crashed wheels up near Norton Disney, Lincs

EF121 F/620 Sqn 22.8.43, 214 Sqn 22.8.43 ?,620 Sqn 30.11.43, OG-B/1665 CU 30.3.44, EFA 28.5.44, swung on landing at Tilstock, u/c collapsed

EF122 N/622 Sqn 20.8.43, GP-Q/1661 CU 4.12.43, swung taxying on grass 18.2.44, 1661 CU 12.6.44, FA 10.11.44, overshot and hit vehicle, Carnaby, ROS Sebro 10.11.44 but repaired not completed

EF123 A/622 Sqn 30.8.43, EFB 19.11.43, crashed, returning from Mannheim Leverkusen, at Isleham and in low visibility

EF124 K,R/218 Sqn 3.9.43, K/149 Sqn 17.8.43, 1653 CU 12.9.43, 6 MU 6.11.44, SOC 19.7.45

EF125 32 MU 24.8.43, X/214 Sqn 21.9.43, 1660 CU 10.12.43, 1661 CU 30.12.43, 1657 CU 26.7.44, 1654 CU 23.9.44, 6 MU 5.12.44, SLG Maghaberry 22.1.45, SOC 25.4.46

EF126 Q,F/622 Sqn 25.8.43, EFB 21.9.43, swung taking off from Mildenhall for mining, u/c collapsed

EF127 N/622 Sqn 26.8.43, 1661 CU 8.12.43, EFA 26.2.44, crashed at Edinwinstoe, Mansfield, possibly due to fuel starvation

EF128 D/622, Sqn 30.8.43, FTR 18/19.11.43 from Mannheim, crashed at La Challande, France

EF129 Q/90 Sqn 27.8.43, FTR 5/6.9.43 from Mannheim, crashed at Limbergerhof, Germany

EF130 JN-M/75 Sqn 27.8.43, FTR 4/5.10.43 Frankfurt, crashed at Russelheim, Germany

EF131 XV Sqn 30.8.43, EFA 19.9.43 overshot Mildenhall, too high approach

EF132 Q/622 Sqn 14.9.43, 27/28.9.43 hit by falling incendiaries and overshot when landing, 622 Sqn 20.10.43, 1654 CU 2.12.43, SLG Maghaberry 3.2.45, SOC 25.4.46

EF133 U/XV Sqn 24.9.43, A/218 Sqn 23.12.43,R/149 Sqn 17.8.44, 1651 CU 13.9.44, 6 MU 6.11.44, SOC 24.4.45

EF134 G/620 Sqn 30.8.43, 1665 CU 11.2.44, 6 MU 12.2.45, SOC obsolete 22.3.45

EF135 T,W/75 Sqn 2.9.43, FA 28.9.43 stalled landing and u/c collapsed, ROS Sebro, 75 Sqn 26.9.43, EFB 28.9.43 battle damaged, stall landed at Mepal, u/c collapsed

EF136 620 Sqn 30.8.43, EFB 8.9.43, swung on take off for Pas de Calais, u/c collapsed

EF137 Y,E/75 Sqn 2.9.43, FTR 23/24.4.44 from mining, crashed Vemmenaes, Denmark

EF138 S/199 Sqn 2.9.43, collided in flight with EH958 22.1.44, Y/199 Sqn 29.1.44, EFB 10.4.44 pilot fatigue after 9 hour flight, damaged in overshoot

EF139 623 Sqn 2.9.43, B/218 Sqn, FTR from Hannover 23.9.43, crashed at Lauenau, Germany

EF140 A/149 Sqn 8.9.43, struck on dispersal at Chedburgh by BF373 on 21.4.44, FTR 25.6.44 from Rousseauville, crashed off Boulogne

EF141 (cv to Mk IV) H,N/218 Sqn 3.9.43, battle damaged 23.11.43, 218 Sqn 8.1.44, 1654 CU 11.2.44, RIW Sebro after heavy landing at Wigsley on 14.11.44, SOC 14.12.44, but BBOC and modified to Mk IV at Bourn, 23 MU 30.5.45, SOC 5.6.47

EF142 C/75 Sqn 24.9.43, EFB 24.10.43, overshot Mepal returning from mining, crashed 1 1/2 miles SW airfield

EF143 23 MU 1.8.43, C/620 Sqn 3.8.43, 1653 CU 9.3.44, 6 MU Woburn 25.11.44, SOC 24.4.45

EF144 S/620 Sqn 14.9.43, 622 Sqn 15.9.43, 1654 CU 1.12.43, RIW Sebro 8.2.44, 23 MU 30.6.44, 1657 CU 20.7.44, FA u/c collapsed during landing, 1657 CU 5.10.44, FA port u/c collapsed landing Witchford and after manual extension, 1657 CU 28.2.45, SOC obsolete 6.5.45

EF145 D/622 Sqn 21.9.43, 1653 CU 1.1.44, 6 MU 25.11.44, SOC 24.4.45

EF146 196 Sqn 9.9.43, 513 Sqn 5.11.43, B/1660 CU 27.11.43, FA 8.3.44 u/c collapse landing, RIW Sebro, 10 MU 23.7.44, 1332 CU 28.8.44, SOC 18.5.45

EF147 J/90 Sqn 29.9.43, FTR 6.3.44 from SOE op, crashed Bellancourt, France

EF148 R/75 Sqn 15.9.43, FTR 22.11.43 from Berlin, crashed at Rulle, Germany

EF149 X/620 Sqn 14.9.43, EFA 15.10.43 swung taking off, Chedburgh

EF150 E/622 Sqn 17.9.430, FTR 22/23.11.43 from Berlin, crashed Derstenhausen, Germany

EF151 P/622 Sqn 16.9.43, 1661 CU 8.12.43, crashed at Brough, Notts, u/c not fully extended

EF152 T,J,V/ 75 Sqn 15.9.43, H4-Z/1653 CU 30.4.43, 6 MU 6.12.44, SOC 19.7.45

EF153 622 Sqn 16.9.43,1 D/199 Sqn 26.9.43, EFB 10.2.44 crashed soon after take-off on SOE op, at Shakers Road, Lakenheath

EF154 622 Sqn 29.9.43, V/199 Sqn 8.10.43, FTR 1.12.43 from mining Kattegat, shot down by AA, off Frederickshafen

EF155 O/623 Sqn 22.9.43, FTR 18/19.11.43 from Mannheim, crashed at Edenkoben, Germany

EF156 E/623 Sqn 22.9.43, FTR 7/8.11.43 from mining Gironde, crashed at sea

EF157 R/623 Sqn 22.9.43, 1654 CU 2.12.43, FA 25.2.44, bounced on landing at Wigsley, RIW Sebro 25.2.44, 23 MU 12.7.44, 1651 CU 2.8.44, 6 MU 10.11.44, SOC 24.4.45

EF158 623 Sqn 23.9.43, FTR 4.10.43 from Kassel, crashed in target area

EF159 620 Sqn 23.9.43, B/90 Sqn 24.9.43, FTR 23/24.4.44 from Laon, shot down by fighter at Vivieres, France

EF160 P/196 Sqn 23.9.43, 1665 CU, SOC 20.3.45

EF161 622 Sqn 22.9.43, Y/XV Sqn 27.9.43, Z/199 Sqn 23.12.43, R/149 Sqn 5.5.44, 1657 CU 29.8.44, 101 SLG of 23 MU 5.2.45, SOC 4.3.46

EF162 K/90 Sqn 24.9.43, FTR 13.4.44 from SOE op, crashed at Fourdrain, France

EF163 JN-L/75 Sqn 26.9.43, EFB 17.12.43, crashed near Sutton, Cambs, returning from mining

EF177 622 Sqn 5.10.43, S/XV Sqn 8.10.43, 1661 CU 8.12.43, EFA 30.10.44, engine problems, spinner flew off hitting aircraft, which crashed east of Alveston, Glos

EF178 H/196 Sqn 23.9.43, NY-R/1665 CU 3.2.44, 19 MU 11.12.44, SOC obsolete 27.9.45

EF179 V/90 Sqn 29.9.43, FTR 7/8.10.43, engaged at sea by fighter, crashed 10 miles east of Cromer returning from mining *Nectarine 1*

EF180 D/218 Sqn 29.9.43, FTR 22/23.11.43 from Berlin, crashed in target area

EF181 JN-S/75 Sqn 24.9.43, J/218 Sqn 25.3.44, EFB 13.6.44 Woolfox, tyre burst on take-off, starboard u/c collapsed

EF182 V,M/90 Sqn 8.10.43, battle damaged 11.4.44 and SOC 27.4.44 then BBOC, 1651 CU 31.8.44, 6 MU 10.1.44, SOC 24.4.45

EF183 D/XV Sqn 29.9.43, Z,T/90 Sqn 9.1.44, 1657 CU 4.6.44, 6 MU 9.12.44, SOC 24.4.45

EF184 L,I,P/218 Sqn 5.10.43, EFB 1/2.5.44, crash landed Woodbridge after attack by two Ju 88s

EF185 L/218 Sqn 27.9.43, L/149 Sqn 17.8.44, 1653 CU 23.8.44, FA ROS 5.9.44, starboard tyre burst on landing, lt53 CU 21.9.44, 6 MU 6.11.44, SOC 24.4.45

EF186 622 Sqn 5.10.43, W/XV Sqn 18.10.43, GP-V /1661 CU 8.12.43, EFA 4.12.44 crashed near Grantham after emergence from cumulo-nimbus cloud on dark night

EF187 C/149 Sqn 5.10.43, FTR 5/6.2.44 from SOE sortie, crashed Cussy les Forges, France

EF188 R/90 Sqn 29.9.43,1 M/149 Sqn 12.6.44, FTR 23/24.6.44 from mining Brest, crashed at Plougonvelin, France

EF189 W/620 Sqn 5.10.43, 1653 CU 18.12.43, 1653 CU 12.1.11 FA 7.11.44 ROS, bounced landing and u/c collapsed, 1657 CU 24.12.44, 23 MU 4.2.45, 101 SLG 18.3.45, SOC 28.3.46

EF190 X/196 Sqn 21.10.43, 1665 CU 1.4.4, 23 MU SLG 11.1.45, SOC 28.4.46

EF191 H/90 Sqn 14.10.43, 1/2.12.43 from mining Kattegat, crashed at Houen Henmt, Denmark

EF192 J/199 Sqn 30.9.43, S,F/149 Sqn 5.5.44, 1653 CU 17.8.44, EFA 12.8.44, swung taking off from Chedburgh, u/c collapsed

EF193 Q,R./90 Sqn 14.10.43, T,D/149 Sqn 31.5.44, 1653 CU 17.8.44, tail chassis damaged 3.9.44, 1653 CU 28.10.44, 6 MU 8.11.44, SOC 24.4.45

EF194 W/623 Sqn 14.10.43, 1654 CU 2.12.43, GP-U of 1661 CU 24.7.44, 23 MU SLG 5.1.45, SOC 25.4.46

EF195 XV Sqn 5.10.43, EFA 15.10.43 Mildenhall, u/c collapsed on take off when aircraft swung on to rough ground

EF196 L/90 Sqn 18.10.43, 1651 CU 24.6.44, 6 MU 8.11.44, SOC 24.4.45

EF197 Z/620 Sqn 14.10.43, 1665 CU 30.3.44, SOC 22.3.45

EF198 F,H/90 Sqn 21.10.43, EFB 26.2.44, crashed at Denham Castle 4 miles N of Chedburgh, uncertain of position when returning from mining, hit trees, burnt out

EF199 I/623 Sqn 9.10.43, I/214 Sqn 15.12.43, 1651 CU 27.1.44, 6 MU 6.11.44, SOC 24.4.45

EF200 75 Sqn 21.10.43, 513 Sqn 7.11.43, 1660 CU 27.11.43, EFA 30.8.44, crashed near Hardwick, Notts, on overshoot after three-engined landing attempt

EF201 75 Sqn 21.10.43, 513 Sqn 4.11.43, 1660 CU 27.11.43, EFA 22.11.44 engine trouble, crashed near Northleach, Glos

EF202 L/149 Sqn 14.10.43, FTR 25/26.11.43 from mining Gironde, crashed at St. Etienne-de-Montluc, France

EF203 Q/620 Sqn 21.10.43, Cat B 9.2.44, 1654 CU 26.6.44, 23 MU SLG 22.1.45, SOC 22.3.46

EF204 E/623 Sqn 22.10.43, 1654 CU 2.12.43, EFA 14.1.45, Barnby-in-the Willows, flew into ground in poor visibility, 2325 hrs

EF205 75 Sqn 21.10.43,1 513 Sqn 3.11.43, 1660 CU 27.11.43, 23 MU SLG 5.1.45, SOC 22.3.46

EF206 75 Sqn 22.10.43, 513 Sqn 4.11.43, TV-F/1660 CU 27.11.43, 6 MU 24.2.44, SOC 24.4.45

EF207 B/75 Sqn 23.10.43, F/218 Sqn 4.5.44, F/149 Sqn 17.8.44, 1653 CU 29.8.44, 6 MU 25.11.44, SOC 24.4.45

EF208 622 Sqn 22.10.43, 1661 CU 8.12.44 EFA 10.12.44 Wiggenhall St Peter, Norfolk, engine problems and force-landed in field

EF209 23 MU 31.10.43, 90 Sqn 29.11.43, TV-H/1660 CU 31.12.43, EFA 17.6.44, landing problem, height lost and crashed, burnt out in field at Stapleford, near Swinderby

EF210 196 Sqn 22.10.43, NY-P/1665 CU 3.2.44, EFA 12.8.44, crashed on overshoot onto railway bridge at Alne, Yorks, burnt out

EF211 75 Sqn 2.10.43, 513 Sqn 3.11.43, 1660 CU 27.11.43, FA RIW Sebro 3.6.44 after hitting tree when low flying, 10 MU 19.10.44, SOC 2.9.46

EF212 23 MU 31.10.43, 90 Sqn 21.12.43, TV-U/1660 CU 23.12.43, EFA 30.10.44 landing in poor visibility, u/c collapsed, SOC 9.11.44

EF213 (Mk III with *H2S*, cv to Mk IV) 10 MU 31.10.43, AWA 2.2.44, 1660 CU 6.3.44, RIW Sebro 2.6.44, 1660 CU ?, 6 MU 26.2.45, SOC 19.7.45

EF214 (cv to Mk IV) PB 23 MU 31.10.43, L/190 Sqn 29.1.44, SOC 9.12.46

EF215 23 MU 30.10.43, W214 Sqn 15.12.43, M/-75 Sqn 1.2.44, FTR 5.3.44 from SOE sortie, crashed Rochefort-Montague, France

EF216 (Mk III with *H2S*) 10 MU 31.10.43, AWA Swindon 24.1.44, 1660 CU 6.3.44, 6 MU 25.2.45, SOC 4.4.45

EF217 622 Sqn 24.10.43, G/75 Sqn 9.11.43, 1653 CU 31.3.44, FA 23.7.44, tyre burst during three-engined landing, 1653 CU 22.8.44, 6 MU 26.11.44, SOC 24.4.45

EF231 (Mk III with *H2S*) PB 10 MU 5.11.43, AWA Swindon 23.1.44, 1660 CU 8.3.44, 23 MU SLG 18.3.45, SOC 27.12.45

EF232 10 MU 4.1.43, XV Sqn 26.11.43, 1660 CU 13.12.43, EFA 31.1.44, control lost after take-off and crashed at Carleton-le-Moorland, Lincs

EF233 10 MU 4.11.43, 620 Sqn 15.12.43, 214 Sqn 20.12.43, L/75 Sqn 30.1.44, D/218 Sqn 29.4.44, D/149 Sqn 17.8.44, 1657 CU 18.9.44, 6 MU 8.12.44, SOC 24.4.45

EF234 (cv to Mk IV) 23 MU 31.10.43, P/196 Sqn 19.4.44, FTR 9.11.44 from SOE sortie to Netherlands, crashed in sea

EF235 10 MU 4.11.43, 1660 CU 13.12.43, 1332 CU 9.12.44, SOC 7.5.45

EF236 0 MU 8.11.43, J/75 Sqn 4.12.43, EFB 15.3.44, during mining sortie, aileron control broke in flight, overshot Castle Combe, Wilts, mines exploded

EF237 (cv to Mk IV) 23 MU 8.11.43,W/620 Sqn 7.2.44, RIW Sebro 13.12.44, cv Mk IV, 23 MU 24.2.45, X9-N/299 Sqn ?, FA 5.4.45, undershot Shepherd's Grove and starboard u/c entered ditch, to Sebro 2.5.45, 23 MU 14.1.46, SOC 5.6.47

EF238 10 MU 8.11.43, H/149 Sqn 1.3.44, EFB 29.4.44, battle damaged, crash landed Methwold

EF239 23 MU 11.11.43, 218 Sqn 29.11.43, 1660 CU 13.12.43, 6 MU 27.2.45, SOC 24.4.45

EF240 10 MU 8.11.43, 1654 CU 5.10.43, 23 MU 8.2.45, SOC 22.3.46

EF241 (cv to Mk IV) 23 MU 11.11.43, 623 Sqn 2.12.43, 1660 CU 13.12.43, FA 16.10.44 landed one leg down at Woodbridge and RIW Sebro 16.10.44, cv Mk IV, 23 MU 5.4.45, SOC 5.6.47

EF242 (cv to Mk IV) 23 MU 13.11.43, Q/.190 Sqn 11.5.44, 23 MU 17.5.45, SOC 5.6.47

EF243 (cv to Mk IV) 23 MU 31.10.43, 299 Sqn 30.4.44, 1665 CU 31.8.44, 23 MU 7.2.46, SOC 5.6.43

EF244 (cv to Mk IV) 23 MU 13.11.43, 620 Sqn 27.3.44, EFA 19.5.44, hit by glider tow rope from LJ880 dropped in LZ area during exercise and crashed 1 mile from Kempsford, Glos

EF245 23 MU 17.11.43, 161 Sqn 23.11.43, 214 Sqn 9.12.43, 1653 CU 18.12.43, 6 MU 6.11.44, SOC 30.1.45

EF246 23 MU 17.11.43, 623 Sqn 29.11.43, C/1660 CU 13.12.43, EFA 10.1.44, crashed in Humber during *Bullseye* exercise

EF247 10 MU 11.11.43, 1651 CU 16.1.44, FA 13.2.44, u/c trouble and belly landed Newmarket, 23 MU 19.7.44, SOC 5.6.47

EF248 (cv to Mk IV) 23 MU 17.11.43, V/196 Sqn 7.2.44, FTR 19.9.44 from *Market III*, hit by flak, three engines on fire and crew baled out into German front line, crashed near Arnhem (Schaarsbergen?)

EF249 23 MU 22.11.43, Y,H/218 Sqn 16.12.43, EFB 9.5.44 Woolfox Lodge, engine trouble after mining Gironde, overshot in flapless landing, u/c collapsed

EF250 10 MU 8.11.43, 622 Sqn 27.11.43, TV-S/1660 CU 13.12.43, 23 MU 2.3.45, SOC 25.4.46

EF251 23 MU 21.11.43, JN-M/75 Sqn 21.12.43, P/90 Sqn 21.3.44, 1653 CU 24.6.44, 6 MU (Woburn) 25.11.44, SOC 24.4.45

EF252 23 MU 25.11.43, 623 Sqn 7.1.44, 1657 CU 9.2.44, EFA 26.7.44 Shepherd's Grove, starboard outer failed, swung into watch office on take-off

EF253 10 MU 11.11.43, 1661 CU 23.11.43, 23 MU SLG 12.1.45, SOC 28.2.46

EF254 23 MU 25.11.43, R/75 Sqn 1.1.44, Q/90 Sqn 30.3.44, FTR 10.5.44 from SOE sortie, crashed Villabon, France

EF255 10 MU 30.11.43, 1653 CU 21.6.44, FA 23.7.44 tailwheels partly down, Witchford, H4-K/1653 CU 28.7.44, 6 MU 15.11.44, SOC 24.4.45

EF256 (cv to Mk IV) 23 MU 13.11.43, 620 Sqn 7.2.44, FTR 10.8.44, crashed in Channel

EF257 10 MU 30.11.43, 1654 CU 8.3.44, 23 MU 2.1.45, SOC 27.12.45

EF258 10 MU 25.11.43, 1653 CU 6.3.44, 1657 CU 10.3.44, RIW Sebro 14.4.44 after swing on take-off and u/c collapse, 10 MU 2.8.44, 1332 CU 4.9.44, SOC 22.5.45

EF259 23 MU 23.11.43, G/218 Sqn 28.12.44, FTR 2.5.44 from Chambly, crashed at La Houssaye, France

EF260 (cv to Mk IV) Sebro 30.11.43 for cv, 6 MU 7.1.44, O/190 Sqn 10.2.44, FTR 21.9.44 from Market IV, shot down by AA, caught fire, all baled out, at Arnhem

EF261 Sebro 30.11.43, 299 Sqn 22.1.44, ZO-I/196 Sqn 27.4.44, FA 8.12.44, 7T-F/196 Sqn 30.12.44, 1665 CU 4.1.45, FA 14.11.45 port u/c collapsed landing Linton-on-Ouse, ROS, 1665 CU 23.1.46, 23 MU 11.2.46, SOC 5.6.47

EF262 23 MU 21.11.43, 623 Sqn 5.1.44, 214 Sqn 14.1.44, V/149 Sqn 27.1.44, D/199 Sqn 7.2.44, B,G/149 Sqn 26.4.44, 1653 CU 17.8.44, FA 1.9.44 Chedburgh, tyre burst on take off, belly landed

EF263 (cv to Mk IV) 23 MU 30.12.43, 190 Sqn 8.5.44, ETR 19.9.44 from *Market III*, hit by AA, crashed at St Michielsgestel, Netherlands

EF264 (cv to Mk IV) Sebro 30.11.43, 6 MU 11.1.44, O,Z/190 Sqn 27.4.44, 23 MU 20.4.44, SOC 14.1.46

EF265 (cv to Mk IV) 23 MU 30.11.43, FA 20.4.44, 23 MU 6.11.44, SOC 5.6.47

EF266 10 MU 8.12.43, 1661 CU 31.5.44, EFA 4.11.44 Winthorpe, heavy landing, swung off runway

EF267 (cv to Mk IV) Sebro 5.12.43, X9-C/299 Sqn 22.1.44, FTR 19.9.44 from *Market III*, shot down at Arnhem

EF268 (cv to Mk IV) 23 MU 25.11.43, 620 Sqn 30.4.44, FTR 6.6.44, shot down at Dives-sur-Mer during Op *Mallard*, by small arms fire

EF269 (cv to Mk IV) 23 MU 25.11.43, 299 Sqn 22.1.44, EFA 25.4.44, Rowde, Wilts, dinghy released and wrapped around rudder, crew vacated

EF270 (cv to Mk IV) Sebro 8.12.43, K/190 Sqn 23.1.44, FA 3.8.44, 190 Sqn 6.10.44, 1665 CU 1.2.45, 23 MU 18.2.46, SOC 5.6.47

EF271 23 MU 30.11.43, 623 Sqn 23.12.43, G/214 14.10.43, F/199 Sqn 30.1.44, FTR 16.2.44 from sortie, crashed at Vergt, France

EF272 (cv to Mk IV) Sebro 16.12.43, Y/196 Sqn 31.1.44, GA 31.5.44 jumped chocks at Keevil, 196 Sqn 9.8.44, FB damage 21.9.44 during Market V, C/196 Sqn 18.11.44, 299 Sqn, EFB 13.4.45, port u/c collapsed taking off from Shepherd's Grove for supply drop

EF273 (cv to Mk IV) Sebro 12.12.43, 196 Sqn 29.1.44, FA u/c trouble RIW Sebro 17.4.44, 6 MU 18.8.44, C/190 Sqn 27.9.44, 23 MU 31.5.46, SOC 5.6.47

EF274 (cv to Mk IV) 23 MU 6.12.43, 196 Sqn 2.2.44, FA swung landing u/c collapsed, RIW Sebro 27.3.44, 6 MU 22.7.44, 8Z-M/295 Sqn 23.9.44, EFA 18.4.45, starboard u/c collapsed, taking off from Rivenhall

EF275 (cv to Mk IV) Sebro 12.12.43, 620 Sqn 27.2.44, FA 21.8.44, pitot head covers not removed and take off abandoned, RIW Sebro 1.9.44, 10 MU 3.2.45, E7-Y/570 Sqn 10.5.45, Cat AC Sebro 3.9.45, 23 MU 20.2.46, SOC 5.6.47

EF276 (cv to Mk IV) 23 MU 19.12.43, 7T-L./196 Sqn 20.4.44, 23 MU 20.7.45, SOC 5.6.47

EF277 (cv to Mk IV) Sebro 5.12.43, 6 MU 11.1.44, V/299 Sqn 25.1.44, FA Keevil 7.5.44, tyre burst on take-off u/c collapsed, RIW Sebro 16.5.44, 23 MU 17.9.44, 620 Sqn 3.10.44, 23 MU 9.7.45, SOC 5.6.47

EF289 10 MU 21.12.43, GP-D/1661 CU 9.6.44, 23 MU SLG 15.1.45, SOC 27.12.45

EF290 10 MU 25.12.43, GP-Y/1661 CU 21.5.44, 23 MU 12.1.45, SOC 31.1.46

EF291 F/214 Sqn 15.12.43, 218 Sqn 4.44, C/218 FA 16.7.44, overshot into ditch, 218 Sqn 18.8.44, 1653 CU 28.8.44, 6 MU 23.11.44, SOC 24.4.45

EF292 Sebro 25.12.43, 6 MU 15.2.44, V8-G/570 Sqn 2.7.44, battle damaged 21.9.44, 570 Sqn 4.11.44, 295 Sqn 9.11.44, ZO-C/196 Sqn 11.1.45, 23 MU 15.2.46, SOC 5.6.47

EF293 (cv to Mk IV) Sebro 23.12.43, 620 Sqn 4.2.44, 23 MU 9.7.44, 295 Sqn 2.12.44, 23 MU 4.12.44, 295 Sqn 11.12.44, 299 Sqn 30.1.45, 196 Sqn 1.2.46, 23 MU 19.3.46, SOC 5.6.47

EF294 10 MU 31.12.43, G,B/90 Sqn 20.4.44, FTR 3.6.44 from SOE sortie, shot down at Bayonvilliers, France

EF295 (cv to Mk IV) 23 MU 24.12.43, 620 Sqn 7.2.44, FA 3.4.44 belly landed after hitting gun post on approach, 620 Sqn, FTR 5/6.6.44, Caen drop, crashed at Chateau de Grangues, France

EF296 (cv to Mk IV) 23 MU 19.12.43, 620 Sqn 8.2.44, EFA 6.9.44 Fairford, tyre burst landing, port wing broken off, RIW Sebro abandoned 14.10.44

EF297 (cv to Mk IV) Sebro 16.12.43, 296 Sqn 29.1.44, EFA 29.2.44, Netheravon, port tyre burst landing, became 4775M

EF298 (cv to Mk IV) 23 MU 23.12.43, 190 Sqn 24.2.44, FA 3.4.44, 190 Sqn 14.7.44, 6 MU 23.7.44, V8-T/570 Sqn 10.8.44, FTR 23.9.44 from *Market VI*, four aircraft shot down over Arnhem possibly included this one, crashed near Wolfheze, Netherlands

EF299 Stradishall 27.12.43, Z/218 Sqn 14.1.44, EFA 13.6.44, Woolfox, overshot landing from Le Havre, hit ridge, u/c collapsed, SOC 21.6.44

EF300 23 MU 30.12.43, 199 Sqn 1.1.44, 1653 CU 6.1.44, FA 23.2.44 damaged hitting tree top on circuit Tuddenham, H4-U/1653 CU 24.3.440, FA 31.8.44, u/c problems at Woodbridge, 1653 CU 22.9.44, 6 MU 25.11.44, SOC 24.4.45

EF301 23 MU 30.12.43, 199 Sqn 1.1.44, 1653 CU 6.1.44, 1657 CU 20.1.44, FA 11.7.44 overshot Shepherd's Grove landing, 1657 CU 31.7.44, 1651 CU 17.10.44, 4 STT St Athan as 4925M, SOC 16.11.45

EF302 23 MU 27.12.43, 90 Sqn 5.1.44, 1651 CU 2.44, 6 MU 8.11.44, SOC 24.4.45

EF303 (cv to Mk IV) 23 MU 10.12.43, Q/620 Sqn 10.2.44, 23 MU 9.7.44, gale damaged 21.9.45, SOC 5.6.47

EF304 23 MU 30.12.43, 199 Sqn 1.1.44, H4-H/1653 CU 6.1.44, 6 MU 26.11.44, SOC 24.4.45

EF305 (cv to Mk IV) 23 MU 20.12.43, 5G-R/299 Sqn 24.2.44, EFA 7.8.44 Keevil, u/c collapsed on overshoot

EF306 (cv to Mk IV) 23 MU 31.12.43, 10 MU 25.3.44, 6 MU 7.6.44, E7-Y/570 Sqn 28.7.44, FB damage on *Market IV*, 570 Sqn 23.10.44, 19 MU 4.1.45, SOC 18.11.46

EF307 E/149 Sqn 30.12.43, FTR 25.2.44 from mining Kiel Bay, crashed in sea

EF308 V,R/149 Sqn 31.12.43, YM 26/26.2.44 from mining Baltic, crashed in sea

EF309 (cv to Mk IV) 23 MU 28.1.44, 7T-P/196 Sqn 25.4.44, FA 19.7.44 belly landed Keevil, RIW Sebro 19.8.44, 10 MU 12.2.45, 196 Sqn 11.3.45, 23 MU 9.2.46, SOC 5.6.47

EF310 1654 CU 6.1.44, 23 MU 2.1.45, SOC 22.5.46

EF311 (cv to Mk IV) 23 MU 31.12.43, 10 MU 15.3.44, 6 MU 3.5.44, I/196 Sqn 19.5.44, FTR 30.8.44 from SOE sortie, engine problem, ditched off Selsey Bill

EF312 19 MU 17.1.44, 1651 CU 31.5.44, 6 MU 6.11.44, SOC 19.7.45

EF313 1654 CU 6.1.44, 16576 CU 19.6.44, 6 MU 13.12.44, SOC 24.4.45

EF314 (cv to Mk IV) 19 MU 11.1.44, 6 MU 4.8.44, 1657 CU 30.8.44, EFA 28.10.44, Stradishall, swung on take-off, SOC 16.11.44

EF315 1654 CU 6.1.44, RIW Sebro 31.3.44 after u/c collapsed during landing at Winthorpe, 23 MU 19.9.44, SOC 5.6.47

EF316 (cv to Mk IV) 23 MU 15.1.46, L/190 Sqn 23.4.44, 23 MU 20.4.45, SOC 5.6.47

EF317 (cv to Mk IV) CRD Shorts 13.12.43, CRD TRE Defford 28.12.43, CRD Short & Harland 19.10.44, RIW 17.3.45, 23 MU 21.3.46, SOC 5.6.47

EF318 (cv to Mk IV) 299 Sqn 5.1.44, ZO-U/196 Sqn 16.6.44, FB accident 20.9.44, 7T-U/196 Sqn 7.10.44, 23 MU 20.7.45, SOC 5.6.47

EF319 (cv to Mk IV) 19 MU 31.12.43, 5G-N/299 Sqn 7.1.44, FTR 19.9.44, hit by flak and crashed in woodland near Schaarsbergen

EF320 (cv to Mk IV) 5G-O,R/299 Sqn 7.1.44, 6 MU 17.11.44, MI Sebro 7.3.45, 23 MU 19.7.45, SOC 5.6.47

EF321 (cv to Mk IV) X9-A/299 Sqn 7.1.44, 23 MU 20.7.45, SOC 5.6.47

EF322 (cv to Mk IV) 5G-B/299 Sqn 8.1.44, 23 MU 3.4.45, SOC 5.6.47

EF323 (cv to Mk IV) 299 Sqn 7.1.44, FA 14/15.2.45 port inner exploded in flight, MI Vickers Shawbury, 23 MU 29.9.45, 1665 CU 19.11.45, 23 MU 4.2.46, SOC 5.6.47

Mk I:

EF327 75 Sqn 29.1.43, M/149 Sqn 20.2.43, EFB 11/12.3.43 on return from Stuttgart, throttle jammed when landing, swung, u/c collapsed, Cat E 30.3.43

EF328 G/90 Sqn 4.2.43, EFB 9.3.43 crash landed with engine trouble, near Sudbury

EF329 C/214 Sqn 14.2.43, 1 ETR 3/4.3.43 FTR from Hamburg, in sea off Texel

EF330 P/149 Sqn, FTR 13.3.43 from Essen, shot down by fighter at Bergh, Netherlands at 2203 hrs

EF331 H/214 Sqn 28.2.43, FTR 14/15.4.43 from Stuttgart, shot down by fighter at Sept Saulx, France

EF332 W/214 Sqn 4.2.43, T/149 Sqn 16.2.43, D/.75 Sqn 24.3.43, 1657 CU 18.5.43, 8 MU 6.8.44, SOC 15.8.44

EF333 X/XV Sqn 16.2.43, 1/2.3.43 from Berlin, in sea off Ameland

EF334 B V,U/90 Sqn 27.1.43, 1657 CU 16.8.43, 1653 CU 3.3.44, EFA 24.6.44 Chedburgh, swung on take-off

EF335 Z/214 Sqn 5.2.43, E,H/149 Sqn 28.2.43, 1665 CU 21.6.43, 6 MU 21.3.44, SOC 14.1.45

EF336 90 Sqn 6.2.43, F/149 Sqn 4.3.43, D/620 Sqn 21.6.43, EFA 298.7.43, Chedburgh, swung on take-off, u/c collapsed

EF337 G/75 Sqn 1.2.43, 1 149 Sqn 2.3.43, 1657 CU 17.5.43, 1665 CU 16.6.43, EFA 29.7.43, hit obstruction when landing, Woolfox, u/c collapsed

EF338 Q,Z/149 Sqn 16.2.43, G/620 Sqn 21.6.43, 1657 CU 5.7.43, EFA 26.7.43, Stradishall, starboard tyre burst landing, u/c collapsed

EF339 Y/XV Sqn EFB 30.7.43, engine trouble, belly landed Coltishall

EF340 218 Sqn 5.2.43, D.149 Sqn 16.2.43, Q/75 Sqn 24.3.43, FTR 5/6.5.43 from mining off Frisians, ditched

EF341 149 Sqn 10.2.43, 1665 CU 17.5.43, 6 MU 198.3.44, SOC 14.1.45

EF342 A/149 Sqn 7.2.43, FA 7.3.43 tyre burst, hit gun post, Coltishall, 1665 CU 17.5.43, RIW Sebro 5.8.43, swung on landing hitting obstruction, 27 MU 5.4.44, GA 11.9.44 port u/c collapsed during engine run up

EF343 B/149 Sqn 13.2.43, FM 4/5.5.43 from Dortmund, shot down by fighter at Ypescolga, Netherlands, at 0018 hrs

EF344 R/149 Sqn 16.2.43, 1657 CU 18.7.43, EFA 27.7.43, tyre burst, u/c collapsed landing Stradishall

EF345 M/XV Sqn 26.2.43, FTR 4/5.5.43 from Dortmund, crashed Anholt, Germany

EF346 218 Sqn 28.2.43,1 G/90 Sqn 7.3.43, 1665 CU 30.11.43, fate uncertain

EF347 T/XV Sqn 28.2.43, 1/2.3.43 from Berlin, shot down by fighter at Mantgum, Netherlands, at 0059 hrs

EF348 N/XV Sqn 2.3.43, FTR 23.6.43 from Mulheim, shot down by fighter at Kessenich, Belgium

EF349 218 Sqn 28.2.43, Y/90 Sqn 7.3.43, 29/30.5.43 from Wuppertal, crashed at Cambrai

EF350 D/214 Sqn 16.3.43, RIW Sebro 7.5.43, CU 14.8.43, EFA 12.2.44, swung landing Hawarden, hit shelter

EF351 L/XV Sqn 27.2.43, 622 Sqn 10.8.43, D/1665 CU 17.8.43, 6 KJ 26.3.44, SOC 14.1.45

EF352 Q/218 Sqn 28.2.43, 1657 CU 18.8.43, EFA 22.10.43, crashed on Rose Moor Farm, Preston-on-Wye

EF353 O,C/218 Sqn 28.2.43, FA 16/17.5.43 Downham Market, starboard engine cut on take-off, crashed into crew room, repaired by Sebro, 1657 CU 3.11.43, 8 MU 6.8.44, SOC 15.8.44

EF354 Q,C/XV Sqn 1.3.43, 1665 CU 6.6.43, EFA 25.7./43, u/c collapsed landing Woolfox

EF355 X,A/XV Sqn 8.3.43, 1665 CU 21.6.43, 30.3.43, 6 MU 11 4 44, SOC 28.11.44

EF356 S,O/218 Sqn 1.3.43, FTR 29.5.43 mining, crashed at Oddm, Denmark

EF357 V/149 Sqn 14.3.43, FTR 12/13.5.43 from Duisburg, shot down by fighter at Rotterdam 0335 hrs

EF358 Q/214 Sqn 14.3.43, RIW Sebro 17.4.43, 1651 CU 8.11.43, Cat E MI 1.8.44

EF359 B/XV Sqn 6.3.43, FTR 8/9.4.43 from Duisburg, crashed at Woltershoff, Germany

EF360 R/149 Sqn 14.3.43, 1651 CU 5.10.43, 4 OAPU 23.5.44, Cat E 14.11.44

EF361 32 MU 24.3.43, B/7 Sqn 6.4.43, FTR 25/26.5.43 from Dortmund, destroyed when 77 Sqn Halifax exploded on being shot down near Julich, along with BF534

EF362 N/214 Sqn 18.3.43, EFB 30.3.43, made early return, collided on circuit with BK663 and crashed near Hadleigh

EF363 19 MU 24.3.43, 32 MU, G/7 Sqn 10.4.43, G,S/214 Sqn 23.8.43, 1653 CU 9.3.44, FA 11.5.44, port tyre burst in air, u/c collapsed landing at Chedburgh

EF364 32 MU 30.3.43, X/7 Sqn 19.4.43, FTR 29/30.7.43 from Hamburg, fate uncertain

EF365 G/218 Sqn 24.3.43, EFA 21.5.43 engine failure followed by belly landing on Bank House Farm, Downham Market

EF366 32 MU 28.3.43, L/7 Sqn 6.4.43, FTR 21/22.6.43 from Krefeld, crashed at Neerpelt, Belgium

EF367 G/218 Sqn 27.4.43, EFB 14.5.43 near Chedburgh, crashed on return from Bochum

EF368 32 MU 30.3.43, A/7 Sqn 13.4.43, V/214 Sqn 29.8.43, 1653 CU 10.2.44, 1657 CU 13.2.44, SOC 4.9.44

EF369 32 MU 31.3.43, Z/7 Sqn 13.4.43, EFB 27/28.7.43 crashed Oakington, power failing on approach, hit obstruction on base

EF384 U/7 Sqn 9.4.43, FA 25.5.43, RIW Sebro, NY-G/1665 CU 21.10.43, 6 MU 15.4.44, SOC 14.1.45

EF385 32 MU 5.4.43, 19 MU 8.4.43, 32 MU 27.7.43, N/214 Sqn 7.8.43, FA 4.10.43 tailwheels-up landing, 214 Sqn 27.11.43, 1651 CU 22.12.43, FA 26.3.44 swung on take-off and hit obstruction, heavy landing Wratting 25.5.44, SOC date unknown

EF386 7 Sqn 13.4.43, Stradishall 16.5.43, W-E/1651 CU 8.7.43, 1665 CU 30.11.43, 6 MU 25.3.44, SOC 14.1.45

EF387 32 MU 1.4.43, D/7 Sqn 19.4.43, 21/22.6.43 from Krefeld, shot down by fighter 10km S of Gilze Rijen at 0114 hrs

EF388 32 KJ 10.4.43, M/7 Sqn 7.5.43, M/214 Sqn 22.8.43, QQ-G/1651 CU 22.12.43, FA 28.3.44, swung landing Wratting, u/c collapsed, hit hut

EF389 Q/149 Sqn 22.4.43, YZ-T/1651 CU 7.8.43, FA 26.3.44 heavy landing Wratting, Cat E on major repair, SOC 1.8.44

EF390 32 MU 8.4.43, T/7 Sqn 21.4.43, A/214 Sqn 1.8.43, FTR 12/13.8.43 from Turin, crashed at La Bussiere, France

EF391 M,N/XV Sqn 18.4.43, 622 Sqn 10.8.43, 1665 CU 17.8.43, 6 MU 4.4.44, SOC 14.1.45

EF392 32 MU 12.4.43, N/7 Sqn 9.5.43, FTR 25.6.43 from Elberfeld, at sea

EF393 32 MU 3.4.43, W/7 Sqn 18.5.43, R/214 Sqn 23.8.43, FTR 22.9.43 from Hannover, crashed near target area

EF394 H/214 Sqn 18.4.43, 620 Sqn 19.6.43, EFA 2/7/43 collided in formation with BK724, crashed at Stansfield near Chedburgh

EF395 L/149 Sqn 21.4.43, RIW Sebro 13.7.43 after hitting vehicle on landing Lakenheath on 22.6.43, 1651 CU 8.11.43, SOC 21.8.44

EF396 G,E/149 Sqn 20.5.43, FA seriously damaged swinging on take-off Lakenheath, 1651 CU 28.9.43, A3-G/1653 CU 22.12.43, EFA 5.2.44, when landing hit BK594

EF397 K/90 Sqn 16.5.43, EFB 29/30.5.43 crashed back from Wuppertal, flying low in circuit, 2 miles N of Stradishall

EF398 A/75 Sqn 5.5.43, FTR 29/30.5.43 from Wuppertal, shot down near Roermond, Netherlands

EF399 Y/XV Sqn 21.5.43, O/75 Sqn 6.6.43, 7M 22/23.6.43 from Mulheim, shot down at Markelo, Netherlands

EF400 75 Sqn 23.5.43, C/149 Sqn 30.6.43, EFB 3/4.7.43 swung on landing Lakenheath, u/c collapsed

EF401 G/7 Sqn 3.5.43, PFF NTU 16.6.43, 214 Sqn, FTR 12/13.8.43 from Turin? or FTR 1.9.43 from Berlin?

EF402 32 MU 5.5.43, Y/7 Sqn 18.8.43, E/214 Sqn 29.8.43, FTR 27/28.9.43 from Hannover, crashed at Galtho, Germany

EF403 32 MU 13.5.43, BDU 23.5.43, H/214 Sqn 4.7.43, 1660 CU 11.12.43, 6 MU 24.2.45, SOC 24.4.45

EF404 32 MU 20.5.43, M/PFF NTU 28.5.43, Z/214 Sqn, Sebro 18.8.43, 6 MU 31.3.44, 29.5.44 tyre burst on take off, belly landing Woodbridge, 1657 CU 25.8.44, FA 29.10.44 engine cut, u/c collapsed when landing at Stradishall, 6 MU 18.2.45, SOC 24.4.45

EF405 32 MU 17.5.43, BDU 26.5.43, R/214 Sqn 4.7.43, 1660 CU 16.12.43, 1661 CU 2.1.44, FA 24.2.44, overshot Docking landing after engine fire, Cat E 29.2.44, but BBOC, 10 MU 28.7.44, 1332 CU 6.9.44, EFA 24.10.44, swung on take-off Nutt's Corner, u/c collapsed, became 4902M 4.11.44

EF406 32 KJ 17.5.43, U/7 Sqn 30.5.43, A/214 Sqn 25.8.43, TV-M/1660 CU 11.12.43, 1654 CU 19.7.44, 6 MU Woburn 8.2.45, SOC 24.4.45

EF407 A/214 Sqn 29.5.43, FTR 29/30.7.43 from Hamburg, shot down off Frisians

EF408 P/75 Sqn 21.5.43, FTR 22/23.6.43 from Mulheim, shot down in IJsselmeer 8km off Oosterland, had twin Todd brothers aboard

EF409 L,V/214 Sqn 24.5.43, FTR 2/3.8.43 from Hamburg, crashed at sea

EF410 Z,I/218 Sqn 21.5.43, 1653 CU 27.1.44, 6 MU 25.11.44, SOC 24.4.45

EF411 XV Sqn 31.5.43, M,K,Y/149 Sqn 21.6.43, 1653 CU 29.8.44, 6 MU 23.11.43, SOC 24.4.45

EF412 XV Sqn 27.5.43, F/149 Sqn 14.6.43, EFA 13.11.43, EFA 13.11.43, port tyre burst on take-off Lakenheath, u/c collapsed, 1235 hrs

EF413 218 Sqn 31.5.43,, FA 4.6.43, swung and hit gun post on take-off Downham, Sebro ROS, 218 Sqn 16.10.43, 1654 CU 29.11.43, 23 MU SLG 3.2.45, SOC 28.3.46

EF425 U,C/218 Sqn, EFA 15.9.43, swung on take-off Downham Market, u/c collapsed

EF426 S/90 Sqn 25.5.43, battle damaged 26.6.43, W/90 Sqn 30.7.43, EFA 9.10.43, overshot Wratting

EF427 A/XV Sqn 31.5.43, FTR 30/31.7.43 from Remscheid, shot down near Mannheim

EF428 N/XV Sqn 31.5.43, FTR 30/31.7.43 from Remscheid, crashed at Kleinenbroich, Germany

EF429 R/214 Sqn 13.5.43, R/620 Sqn 19.6.43, FA 16.9.43, wheels up landing at Newmarket, RIW Sebro 28.9.43 and cv Mk IV, 6 MU 24.3.44, 7T-P/196 Sqn 19.5.44, 23 MU 9.2.46, SOC 5.6.47

EF430 W/218 Sqn 3.6.43, FM 25/26.6.43 from Gelsenkirchen, shot down by fighter at Empe, Netherlands

EF431 X,Q/90 Sqn 8.6.43, B/149 Sqn 2.6.43, 1651 CU 25.8.43, 6 MU 9.11.44, SOC 24.4.45

EF432 10 MU 4.6.43, AFEE CRD 3.7.43, SOC MR 26.1.45

EF433 U/214 Sqn 5.6.43, W,S/620 Sqn 19.6.43, OG- N/1665 CU 11.2.44, 6 MU 18.1.45, SOC 24.4.45

EF434 CRD Dowty, Staverton 12.6.43, CRD RAE 7.7.43, 1657 CU 24.4.44, 1651 CU 17.10.44, 6 MU 10.11.44, SOC 24.4.45

EF435 (cv to Mk IV) JN-J/75 Sqn 12.6.43, Sebro 24.8.43, 10 MU 29.3.44, 6 MU 4.6.44, 10 MU 13.2.45, 20 MU 20.6.45, SOC 5.6.47

EF436 A/75 Sqn 12.6.43, FTR 5/6.7.43 from mining Frisians, shot down at sea

EF437 Z/XV Sqn 18.6.43, EFB 28.7.43, crashed near Mildenhall returning from Hamburg

EF438 D/149 Sqn 14.6.43, FTR 30.31.8.43 from Mönchengladbach, crashed near target

EF439 H/90 Sqn 19.6.43, FTR 27/28.8.43 from Nuremberg, crashed Hesselberg, Germany

EF440 75 Sqn 8.7.43, B/620 Sqn 19.7.43, FA 30.11.43 overshot Leicester East into ditch, 1653 CU 29.5.44, FA 2.6.44, swung on take-off, Sebro 21.6.44, 23 MU 26.10.44, SOC 5.6.47

EF441 G,N/90 Sqn, 1653 CU 13.7.43, 6 MU 15.11.44, SOC 24.4.45

EF442 BDU 25.6.43, O,J/620 Sqn 30.6.43, 1653 CU 10.12.43, 6 MU 29.11.44, SOC 24.4.45

EF443 M/90 Sqn 27.6.43, FTR 28/29.1.44 from mining Kiel Bay, ditched

EF444 (cv to Mk IV) 32 MU 29.6.43, D/214 Sqn 3.8.43, 1660 CU 10.12.43, 1661 CU 4.1.44, EFA 20.7.44, Dawson's Corner, Farsley, Leeds, two engines gave trouble, crash landed in field

EF445 32 MU 25.6.43, K,J/214 Sqn 24.7.43, FM 22/23.11.43 from Berlin, icing and engine problems returning, ditched

EF446 (cv to Mk IV, Hercules replaced by XVIs) O/90 Sqn 27.6.43, FA 16/17.9.43 overshot into ditch at Wratting, RIW Sebro 22.9.43, 10 MU 29.3.44, 6 MU 4.5.44, 570 Sqn 19.7.44, 8Z-O, 8E-O/295 Sqn 3.8.44, 23 MU 20.7.45. SOC 5.6.47

EF447 32 MU 3.7.43, P/214 Sqn 11.8.43, 1660 CU 10.12.43, 1661 CU 29.12.43, FA 12.4.44 landed off runway at Winthorpe, hit wind sock, 1661 CU 18.6.44, 23 MU SLG 12.1.45, SOC 29.2.46

EF448 P/218 Sqn 30.6.43, FM 27/28.8.43 from Nuremberg, crashed at Munster Maifeld, Germany

EF449 J,D/218 Sqn 29.6.43, FA FB 16.12.43 crashed landed in bad weather and overshot base, X/218 Sqn 4.1.44, 1660 CU 31.1.44, EFA 6.5.44, Exeter, engine trouble and flap problem, overshot

EF450 149 Sqn 3.7.43, N/199 Sqn 6.7.43, EFB 18/19.11.43, returning from Mannheim engine and icing problem, swung landing, port outer caught fire, at Lakenheath

EF451 75 Sqn 8.7.43, D/620 Sqn 19.7.43, FTR 28.8.43 from Nuremberg, crashed Greussenheim, Germany

EF452 O/218 Sqn 30.7.43, EFB 12/13.8.43, Bone, Algeria, belly landed (Aaron's aircraft)

EF453 XV Sqn 5.7.43, F/199 Sqn 24.7.43, FA 30.7.43 overshot Lakenheath landing, FTR 4/5.11.43 from mining Kattegat, crashed at sea

EF454 re-built as **TS261** A,C/75 Sqn 16.7.43, 1657 CU 6.4.44, 1657 CU 26.5.44, EFA 28.5.44 at Shepherd's Grove, hit by BK689 which swung off runway burnt, re-Cat E1 15.6.44, rebuilt by Shorts, fate uncertain

EF455 B,W/199 Sqn 5.6.43, 1651 CU 5.5.44, 6 MU 15.11.44, SOC 24.4.45

EF456 75 Sqn 14.7.43, G,R/620 Sqn 26.7.43, FA 3.3.44 at Welford, swung landing and hit Horsa LH174, CU 21.5.44, EFA 10.12.44 Tilstock, port u/c collapsed after landing

EF457 32 MU 7.7.43, A/620 Sqn 11.7.43, FTR 17/18.8.43 from Peenemunde, crashed at Wasterhusen, Germany

EF458 75 Sqn 19.7.43, Y/90 Sqn 1.8.43, FTR 24.9.43 from Mannheim, crashed at Kaifenheim, Germany

EF459 10 MU 27.7.43, S/XV Sqn 3.8.43, 90 Sqn 23.12.43, Z,X/199 Sqn 20.1.44, H4-Y/1653 CU 28.7.44, became 4917M 2.11.44 for 4 S of TT

EF460 199 Sqn 20.7.43, B/XV Sqn 19.7.43, 622 Sqn 10.12.43, 1653 CU 27.12.43, 1651 CU 3.1.44, 6 MU 10.11.44, SOC 24.4.45

EF461 10 MU 29.7.43, XV Sqn 7.8.43, C/623 Sqn 14.8.43, 1661 CU 4.12.43, 6 MU 15.1.45, SOC 15.3.46

EF462 Y,W/75 Sqn 22.7.43, FA 26.4.44, starboard u/c collapsed landing, 218 Sqn 24.6.44, 1653 CU 28.7.44, 6 MU 6.11.44, SOC 24.4.45

EF463 32 MU 28.7.43, Z/214 Sqn 18.8.43, 1660 CU 10.1.44, EFA 13.3.44, u/c torn off in landing at Swinderby after engine trouble

EF464 P/196 Sqn 23.6.43, EFB 3/4.10.43 after raiding Kassel trouble with two engines, undershot Coltishall, crashed near Scottow

EF465 H/75 Sqn 16.7.43,1 513 Sqn 26.10.43, K/75 Sqn 28.11.43, QQ-G/30.3.44, 1657 CU 17.10.44, 6 MU 13.12.44, SOC 19.7.45

EF466 CRD Shorts 29.7.43, BDU 5.8.43, A&AEE 18.9.43, K/75 Sqn 10.10.43, FA 23.11.43, V/75 Sqn 1.12.43, GA 8.1.44 u/c collapsed during daily inspection, RIW 25.1.44, 1653 CU 16.6.44, FA 21.6.44 tyre burst landing, 1653 CU 30.6.44, EFA 30.9.44, Chedburgh, swung on take-off, u/c collapsed

EF467 M/196 Sqn 24.7.43, NY-Q/1665 CU 3.3.44, SOC as obsolete 22.3.45

EF468 10 MU 29.7.43, Q/196 Sqn 6.8.43, EFA 21.2.44, crashed during night X-country at Tarrant Gunville, Dorset

EF469 10 MU 31.7.43, B/196 Sqn 7.8.43, FTR 6.2.44, SOE op, crashed at Berg Foret Gehan, France

EF470 (fitted with *H2S*, later cv to Mk IV) 10 MU 29.7 43, E/620 Sqn 3.8.43, RIW Sebro 11.43, 10 MU 25.3.44, Shorts 10.5.44, 6 MU 9.6.44, 8Z-X/295 Sqn 10.8.44, 620 Sqn 11.1.45, 295 Sqn 8.2.45, 23 MU 19.4.45, SOC 5.6.47

EF488 W/196 Sqn 11.8.43, 1653 CU 9.3.44, 6 MU SLG Woburn 24.11.44, SOC 24.4.45

EF489 10 KJ 29.7.43, 218 Sqn 4.8.43, F/623 Sqn 10.8.43, 1654 CU 2.12.43, 23 MU 2.1.45, SOC 15.3.46

EF490 B/XV Sqn 1.8.43, F,B/622 Sqn 10.8.43, 1653 CU 1.1.44, 1651 CU 16.1.44, EFA 6.7.44 after colliding with EF189 in flight, overshot base, u/c torn off

EF491 O/75 Sqn 16.8.430, EFB 31.8/1.9.43, crash landed back from Berlin with battle damage

EF492 10 MU 1.8.43, Y/196 Sqn 7.8.43, NY-N,Y/1665 CU 1.4.44, SOC 22.3.45

EF493 A/623 Sqn 19.8.43, C/214 Sqn 13.12.43,1 1657 CU 27.1.44, 23 MU 29.12.44, SOC 25.4.45

EF494 10 MU 1.8.43, C/196 Sqn 7.8.43, EFB 8/9.10.43 engine trouble on way to Bremen, ditched 200 yards off shore, off Hemsby Gap, Norfolk

EF495 R/149 Sqn 12.8.43, FTR 27/28.9.43 from Hannover, ditched

EF496 CRD Shorts 10.8.43, 23 MU 18.3.45, SOC 5.6.47

EF497 L/90 Sqn 20.8.43, EFA 20.10.43, crashed, wreckage spread over Woodhouse and Rouse Farms, Benson, crashed during low flying

EF498 32 MU 18.8.43, J/214 Sqn 20.9.43, 1660 CU 10.12.43, EFA 22.4.44, collided on approach to Swinderby with EH926 at night

EF499 K/623 Sqn 22.8.43, EFB 25.9.43, crashed at Downham, early return on mining op, u/c collapsed

EF500 CRD Shorts 26.8.43, 1660 CU 25.9.43, 6 MU 27.2.45. SOC 24.4.45

EF501 K/75 Sqn 16.8.43, FTR 31.8.43 from Berlin, shot down at Potsdam, Germany

EF502 F/149 Sqn 27.8.43, FTR 10/11.4.44 from SOE op, crashed at St Jean le Vieux

EF503 (cv to Mk IV) CRD Shorts 28.8.43, CRD A&AEE 2.9.43 performance assessment, CRD Shorts 21.2.44, 23 MU 26.5.44, 1651 CU 26.7.44, 6 MU 6.11.44, SOC 24.4.45

EF504 P/218 Sqn 1.9.43, FTR 2.5.44 from Chambly, crashed at Abancourt, France

EF505 K/199 Sqn 30.8.43, FA 23.9.43 hit by photoflash over target area, R/199 Sqn 9.10.43, FTR 28.1.44 from mining off Denmark, crashed on Romo Island, Denmark

EF506 (cv to Mk IV) CM Shorts 26.8.43, CRD AFEE Sherburn 18.10.43, CRD Shorts 28.2.44, Sebro 20.12.45, 23 MU 21.2.46, SOC 5.6.47

EF507 P/75 Sqn 27.8.43, FA 1.3.44 overshot slippery runway at Graveley, RIW Sebro 5.3.44, 23 MU 21.7.44, 1332 CU 13.11.44, SOC 15.5.45

EF508 G/199 Sqn 29.8.43, 1653 CU 10.5.43, FA 17.5.44 Chedburgh, engine trouble, swung on landing and u/c collapsed, 1653 CU 22.6.43, 6 MU SLG Woburn 24.11.44, SOC 24.4.45

EF509 Q,X/90 Sqn 1.9.43, FTR 9/10.5.44 from SOE op, shot down at Tinchebray, France

EF510 B/90 Sqn 31.8.43, Sebro 14.10.43, 10 MU 7.6.44, 1654 CU 15.7.44, EFA 12.8.44, engine trouble, wheels-up landing on Willow Farm, Metheringham, Lincs

EF511 C/90 Sqn 31.8.43, EFB 26.11.43, returning from mining made two circuits of Rougham, flew into ground in haze

EF512 A/75 Sqn 11.9.43, battle damage 29.1.44, Sebro, 23 MU 28.6.44, 1661 CU 30.8.44, 23 MU SLG 15.1.45, SOC 28.3.46

EF513 E,W/75 Sqn 2.9.43, 1657 CU 6.4.44, RIW Sebro 20.7.44 after overshooting Shepherd's Grove, 19 MU 28.11.44, SOC 12.7.45

EF514 D/75 Sqn 2.9.43, 199 Sqn 21.3.44, 1651 CU 12.5.44, EGA 18.8.44 hit by LK519 when parked at Wratting Common

EF515 F/75 Sqn 11.9.43, FM 27.9.43 from Hannover, crashed near Hameln, Germany

EF516 O/196 Sqn 8.9.43, OG-Z/1665 CU 3.3.44, 19 MU 11.12.44, SOC 15.9.45

EF517 CRD A&AEE 24.9.43, 23 MU 2.12.45, SOB 5.6.47

EF518 P/XV Sqn 23.9.43, GP-E/1661 CU 8.12.43, FA 1.3.44, u/c collapsed after take-off swing and hitting snow bank at Winthorpe, RIW Sebro but re-cat E, SOC 7.4.44

EH875 – EJ127 120 Mk III, some of which were converted to Mk IV

EH875 S/XV Sqn 8.5.43, FTR 23/24.8.43 from Berlin, crashed in target area

EH876 J/90 Sqn 5.5.43, FTR 25/26.5.43 from Düsseldorf, crashed at sea

EH877 JN-C/75 Sqn 8.5.43, FTR 27.9.43 from Hannover, crashed at Sarstedt, Germany

EH878 I/218 Sqn 12.5.43, I/623 Sqn 13.8.43, FTR 5/6.9.43 from Mannheim, crashed at Schouborn, Germany

EH879 XV Sqn 9.5.43, G/149 Sqn 22.5.43, FA hit by five 30lb incendiaries, Sebro 26.5.43, QQ-B/1651 CU 7.9.43, 1661 CU 9.11.43, 23 MU SLG 15.1.45, SOC 28.2.45

EH880 D,J/75 Sqn 14.5.43, EFB 1/2.12.43 returning from mining off Denmark, undershot Acklington by 2 miles, hit farmhouse at Togston, burnt out

EH881 Z/75 Sqn 14.5.43, FTR 29/30.5.43 from Wuppertal, crashed at Gut Deltourserb, Germany

EH882 O/214 Sqn 14.5.43, FTR 23/24.6.43 Mulheim, crashed near Essen

EH883 A/149 Sqn 20.5.43, FTR 23/24.9.43 Mannheim, crashed at Herxheim, Germany

EH884 H,X/218 Sqn 18.5.43, FTR 16/17.8.43 Turin, crashed at Amerieu, France

EH885 V/149 Sqn 17.5.43, EFA 9.6.43, swung on take-off Lakenheath, u/c collapsed

EH886 S/214 Sqn 21.5.43, S/620 Sqn 19.6.43, FA 5.7.43, engine trouble, hit trees during forced landing at Chedburgh, SOC 30.9.43

EH887 Z/218 Sqn 20.5.43, FTR 25/26.5.43 from Düsseldorf, crashed at Duren, Germany

EH888 Z/XV Sqn 25.5.43, FTR 28/29.6.43 from Cologne, shot down at Heeschwijk, Netherlands

EH889 Z/75 Sqn 29.5.43, FTR 22/23.6.43 from Mulheim, shot down in IJsselmeer, Netherlands

EH890 U/XV Sqn 29.5.43, EFB 25.6.43, ditched off Clacton returning from Wuppertal

EH891 214 Sqn 31.5.43, Q,O/620 Sqn 19.6.43, OG-M/1665 CU 30.3.44, 6 MU 27.2.45, SOC obsolete 8.3.45

EH892 U/218 Sqn 3.6.43, FTR 24/25.6.43 from Elberfeld, crashed Neustadt, Germany

EH893 J/XV Sqn 24.6.43, FTR 27/28.7.43 from Hamburg, shot down near target

EH894 D,J,E/620 Sqn 30.6.43, damaged by incendiaries 14.7.43, NY-T/1665 CU 3.2.44, 23 MU SLG 18.1.45, SOC 4.1.46

EH895 32 MU 30.6.43, Q,M/214 Sqn 31.7.43, FTR 23/24.8.43 from Berlin, crashed at Gr Berlitz, Germany

EH896 32 MU 7.7.43, P/620 Sqn 11.7.43, FTR 30/31.7.43 from Remscheid

EH897 (cv to Mk IV) Z/XV Sqn 9.7.43, Z/622 Sqn 2.8.43, EFA 11.8.43 but re-cat BFA, Sebro, 27.8.43, cv to Mk IV, 10 MU 29.2.44, 6 MU 6.5.44, E7-Z/570 Sqn 28.7.44, FTR 19.9.44 *Market III*, crash landed near Arnhem

EH898 G/218 Sqn 9.6.43, FTR 25/26.6.43 from Gelsenkirchen, shot down at Lichtenvoorde, Netherlands

EH899 D,X/214 Sqn 5.6.43, G,R/196 Sqn 23.8.43, OG-A/1665 CU 29.3.44, 19 MU 11.12.44, gale damaged 18.1.45, SOC 15.9.45

EH900 Y/90 Sqn 9.6.43, FTR 25/26.6.43 from Gelsenkirchen, crashed Legden, Germany

EH901 JN-O,N/75 Sqn 10.6.43, 1657 CU 26.3.44, 6 MU 9.12.44, SOC 19.7.45

EH902 K/75 Sqn 10.6.43, FTR 24/25.6.43 from Wuppertal, shot down by fighter near Bergen-op-Zoom, Netherlands

EH903 L/149 Sqn 12.6.43, FTR 18/19.11.43 from Mannheim, crashed in target area

EH904 K,P/149 Sqn 17.6.43,EFA 16.12.43, u/c collapsed when landing at Pembrey, SOC 14.12.44, cv to 4445M , for 1 AGS, on 27.12.44

EH905 R/75 Sqn 17.6.43, FTR 31.8/1.9.43 from Berlin, crashed at Ludwigsfelde, Germany

EH906 T/90 Sqn 18.6.43, FTR 4/5.3.44 from SOE op, crashed at St Hilaire de Gondilly, France

EH907 O/90 Sqn 23.6.43, FTR 3/4.7.43 from Cologne, crashed at Moorsel, Belgium

EH908 R,U/90 Sqn 23.6.43, EFA 12.11.43, control jammed in shallow dive, crashed Hundon near Stradishall, 2127 hrs

EH909 149 Sqn 24.6.43, Z/199 Sqn 6.7.43, EFB 3.10.43, engine failure so aborted, swung on landing Lakenheath, hit rising ground

EH921 J/214 Sqn 26.6.43, D,L/622 Sqn 18.8.43, 1661 CU 4.12.43, 1654 CU 11.8.44, 6 MU SLG Woburn 14.1.45, SOC 24.4.45

EH922 U,K,O,V/149 Sqn 24.6.43, FA 16.12.43(OJ-O) clipped trees on approach, landed safely, 149 Sqn 5.2.44, 1653 CU 4.5.44, 6 MU 22.11.44, SOC 24.4.45

EH923 W,E/218 Sqn 30.6.43, UG-K/1654 CU 2.2.44, FA 16.4.44 u/c collapsed landing Cranwell,1332 CU 21.9.44, FA 16.11.44 tyre burst landing, 18.1.45 gale damage, EFA 13.4.45 after heavy landing Nutt's Corner

EH924 32 MU 30.6.43, B/620 Sqn 11.7.43, FTR 25/26.7.43 from Aachen, crashed at Asperden, Germany

EH925 C/218 Sqn 3.7.43, C/623 Sqn 13.8.43, FTR 23/24.8.43 from Berlin, (218 Sqn crew) crashed at Zossen, Germany

EH926 218 Sqn 3.7.43, T/199 Sqn 5.7.43, 1654 CU 7.2.44, EFA 22.4.44, SOC 2.5.44, collided with EF498 on approach to Swinderby

EH927 149 Sqn 3.7.43, E/199 Sqn 6.7.43, FTR 23/24.8.43 from Berlin, crashed in target area

EH928 A/75 Sqn 6.7.43, FTR 2/3.8.43 from Hamburg, shot down off Denmark

EH929 75 Sqn 14.7.43, F/XV Sqn 28.7.43, 1661 CU 8.12.43, FA 7.8.44 Swinderby, port u/c collapsed in take-off swing 6 MU 17.12.44, SOC 19.7.45

EH930 75 Sqn 20.7.43, A/XV Sqn 28.7.43, N/199 Sqn 27.12.43, 1651 CU 12.5.44, 6 MU 11.11.44, SOC 24.4.45

EH931 O/620 Sqn 8.8.43, FTR 5/6.9.43 from Mannheim, crashed at Altdorf, Germany

EH932 V/196 Sqn 11.8.43, NY-X/1665 CU SOC 22.3.45, obsolete

EH933 32 MU 16.8.43, E/214 Sqn 15.9.43, 23.12.43, EFA 27.1.44, crashed at speed into an 850ft high hill near Exton, Devon

EH934 149 Sqn 7.7.43, K/199 Sqn, FTR 23/24.8.43 from Berlin, crashed at Ruhlsdorf

EH935 K/75 Sqn 8.7.43, FTR 23/24.9.43 from crashed at Edesheim-Knoerringen, Germany

EH936 W/75 Sqn 7.7.43, FTR 23.9.43 Mannheim, crashed at Dirmstein, Germany

EH937 S/90 Sqn 10.7.43, FTR 23/24.8.43 Berlin, shot down by AA off Urk, IJsselmeer

EH938 F/75 Sqn 4.7.43, FTR 30/31.8.43 Mönchengladbach, crashed at Lommel, Belgium

EH939 J,S/75 Sqn 17.8.43, A,M,W/90 Sqn 21.3.44, H4-X/1653 CU 14.6.44, 6 MU 7.12.44, SOC 19.7.45

EH940 H,U/XV Sqn 19.8.43, damaged by falling incendiary 27/28.9.43, T/218 Sqn 23.12.43, 1661 CU 30.1.44, EFA 22.6.44, crashed on Park Farm, Kettlethorpe after engine fire and control loss

EH941 D/XV Sqn 1.9.43, FTR 23.9.43 Mannheim, crashed at Hassloch, Germany

EH942 M/218 Sqn 3.9.43, FTR 22/23.4.44 Laon, shot down by fighter at Mortefontaine, France

EH943 B/149 Sqn 4.9.43, FTR 22/23.4.44 Laon, crashed at Cuissy-et-Geny, France

EH944 A/90 Sqn 11.7.43, EFB 22/23.9.43, battle damaged by fighter, crash landed Lakenheath

EH945 P/620 Sqn 15.7.43, lighting strike in flight 6.8.43, FTR 27.9.43 from Hannover, crashed at Drahne Winkel, Germany

EH946 75 Sqn 16.7.43, P/620 Sqn 26.7.43, FTR 31.8.43 from Berlin, crashed at Looberghe, France

EH947 75 Sqn 15.7.43, U,S/90 Sqn, EFB 11.4.44, returning from SOE op had engine fire, lost control, crashed at Icklingham, Suffolk

EH948 Q/75 Sqn 17.7.43, FTR 24/25.2.44 from mining Kiel Bay, crashed in sea

EH949 P,R,D/75 Sqn 18.7.43, FA 4.12.43, hit tree when low flying, 1651 CU 29.4.44, FA 29.4.44, port u/c collapsed on take-off Witchford, 1660 CU 6.11.44, SOC 24.4.45

EH950 (cv to Mk IV) Z/196 Sqn 21.7.43, RIW Sebro 18.9.43, cv to Mk IV, Woburn 12.3.44, 6 MU 17.3.44, X9-E,5G-D/299 Sqn 19.5.44, MR 23.7.45 after engine problem on 22.7.45, 151 MU 31.1.46, fate uncertain

EH951 32 MU 21.7.43, 214 Sqn 11.8.43, TV-B/1660 CU 10.1.44, 1654 CU, EFA 20.7.44 after two engine fires, crashed east of Clipstone, near Tollerton

EH952 196 Sqn 2.7.43, FTR 24.8.43 from an ASR sortie off Denmark

EH953 32 MU 4.8.43, G/214 Sqn 22.8.43, 1653 CU, 1657 CU 15.2.44, EFA 11.7.44 Shepherd's Grove, overshot after port u/c collapsed, burnt out

EH954 D/196 Sqn 8.9.43, 1665 CU NY-W/1665 CU 5.12.44, 6 MU 12.12.44, SOC 24.4.45

EH955 K/75 Sqn 24.9.43, FTR 18/19.4.44 from mining Kiel Bay, crashed at Jenning, Denmark

EH956 F/622 Sqn 16.9.43, 1653 CU 27.12.43, 1651 CU 28.12.43, 1657 CU 19.6.44, FA 7.10.44 belly landed Shepherd's Grove and RIW Sebro, 23 MU 28.4.45, SOC 5.6.47

EH957 N/623 Sqn 22.9.43, 1654 CU 2.12.43, 23 MU 20.2.45, 101 SLG 20.2.45, SOC 28.3.46

EH958 O/90 Sqn 30.9.43, 21/22.1.44 collided with EF138 in flight, tail unit damage, landed safely at Tuddenham, 1660 CU 15.6.44, 6 MU 27.2.45, SOC 24.4.45

EH959 32 MU 4.8.43, F/214 Sqn 22.8.43, 1660 CU 23.12.43, 6 MU 3.3.45, SOC 24.4.45

EH960 X/196 Sqn 9.8.43, FTR 17.10.43 crashed in The Wash, control problems

EH961 D/196 Sqn 9.8.43, FTR 31.8/1.9.43 from Berlin, shot down by fighter near Enschede, Netherlands

EH977 32 MU 11.8.43, Q,R/214 Sqn 7.9.43, 1660 CU 23.12.43, EFA 5.11.44, crashed Bassingham Fen, Lincolnshire, 0240 hrs during circuit training, engine problem, seven killed

EH978 32 MU 11.8.43, K/214 Sqn 11.9.43, 1660 CU 23.12.43, EFA 24.7.44, Winthorpe, burnt out after hitting tree and damaging tailplane

EH979 H/623 Sqn 6.10.43, 1654 CU 2.12.43, SOC 11.4.46

EH980 XV Sqn 12.10.43, 1654 CU 2.12.43, 23 MU SLG (101) 13.2.45, SOC 18.3.45

EH981 196 15.10.43, NY-E/1665 CU 3.2.44, 19 MU 11.12.44, SOC 27.9.45

EH982 Y/90 Sqn 22.10.43, 218 Sqn 14.6.44, S/149 Sqn 14.7.44, 1653 CU 17.8.44, FA 4.11.44 damaged in overshoot, RIW Sebro 21.12.44, 1653 CU 15.6.45, 23 MU 2.7.45, SOC 5.6.47

EH983 620 Sqn 24.10.43, 1665 CU 30.3.44, 23 MU SLG 18.1.45, SOC 31.1.46

EH984 C/218 Sqn 14.8.43, FTR 3/4.10.43 from Kassel, crashed near Cologne

EH985 O/XV Sqn 13.8.43, FTR 27/28.8.43 from Nuremberg, crashed at Hesselberg, Germany

EH986 X/218 Sqn 14.8.43, FTR 23/24.8.43 from Berlin, crashed on Tempelhof aerodrome

EH987 P/149 Sqn 14.8.43, EFA 4.10.43, u/c collapsed during landing at Lakenheath

EH988 N/218 Sqn 18.8.43, FA 1.9.43, engine trouble taking off from Hartford Bridge, RIW Sebro, 23 MU 8.6.44, 1661 CU 2.9.43, EFA 14.1.45, crashed on Howe Farm, Annesley Park, Notts, on fire crashed out of control 1015 hrs, five killed

EH989 N,P/90 Sqn 26.8.43, EFB 15/16.3.44, returning from Amiens collided with 11 OTU Wellington LN660, caught fire, crashed on approach, at Astwell Park, Northants

EH990 K/XV Sqn 24.8.43, FTR 8.10.43 from mining, lost at sea?

EH991 P/622 Sqn 21.8.43, FTR 27/28.9.43 from Hannover, fate uncertain

EH992 O/622 Sqn 28.8.43, 1661 CU 4.12.43, 1657 CU 17.6.44, 23 MU SLG 14.1.45, SOC 26.12.45

EH993 D/149 Sqn 1.9.43, FA 4.6.44 belly landed Methwold after ops, RIW Sebro 16.7.44, 19 MU 1.12.44, SOC 8.7.45

EH994 P/623 Sqn 27.8.43, FTR 3/4.10.43 from Kassel, crashed at Harleshausen, Germany

EH995 L/199 Sqn 25.8.43, FA 25.11.43 u/c damaged landing at base, H/199 Sqn 30.11.43, Cat E 29.2.44 but re-cat B 25.8.44, 1657 CU 25.8.44, 6 MU 11.12.44, SOC 19.7.45 as 4538M, allocation date uncertain

EH996 H/90 Sqn 30.8.43, 18/19.11.43 from Mannheim, crashed at Fussgonheim, Germany

EJ104 G/218 Sqn 2.9.43, FTR 23/24.9.43 from Mannheim, crashed at Bauwaldthal, Germany

EJ105 N/218 Sqn 3.9.43, EFB 22/23 9.43 battle damaged, crashed on return at Hall Farm, Barrow, all killed

EJ106 O/149 Sqn 8.9.43, FTR 7/8.10.43 from mining off Frisians, crashed in sea at 2026 hrs 50km NW of Vlieland

EJ107 K/149 Sqn 4.9.43, FA 26.2.44 belly landed Coltishall after engine trouble, Cat E 29.2.44, but RIW Sebro 12.4.44, 23 MU 16.7.44, 1657 CU 2.8.44, FA 25.10.44, landed Woodbridge tailwheels up, 1657 CU 1.12.44, 23 MU SLG 29.12.44, SOC 8.3.46

EJ108 O/75 Sqn 4.9.43, 1657 CU 6.4.44, EFA 19.4.44, damaged on take-off Grafton Underwood, crew baled out near Wickham Market, aircraft crashed at Little Glemham, Suffolk

EJ109 H,C,M/149 Sqn 8.9.43, battle damaged 6.3.44, 149 Sqn 21.3.44, 1657 CU 23.9.44, 23 MU SLG 10.1.45, SOC 25.4.46

EJ110 N/196 Sqn 8.9.43, battle damaged 8.11.43, FTR 4/5.2.44 from SOE op, crashed Hauteville, France

EJ111 P/199 Sqn 11.9.43, EFB 23.11.43 at Lakenheath, incendiary set aircraft ablaze during removal after operation

EJ112 Q/218 Sqn 12.9.43, 1651 CU 28.7.44, FA 27.8.44 swung off runway on take-off, damaged, 1651 CU 15.9.44, 6 MU 10.11.44, SOC 24.4.45

EJ113 Q/622 Sqn 15.9.43, FTR 18.11.43 from Mannheim, crashed at Bussy le Chateau, France

EJ114 R/622 Sqn 15.9.43,1 1664 CU 1.12.43, EFA 18.7.44, engine trouble, caught fire and crash landed at Girton near Wigsley, Notts

EJ115 H/199 Sqn 1.10.43, battle damage 6.1.44, C/199 Sqn 2.2.44, battle damage 6.3.44, 199 Sqn 1.9.3.44, K/90 Sqn 5.5.44, battle damage 8.6.44, 149 Sqn 23.7.44, 1653 CU 17.8.44, FA 14.8.44 Chedburgh, port tyre burst, swung, u/c collapsed, RIW Sebro 25.8.44, 19 MU 1.12.44, SOC 12.7.45

EJ116 (cv to Mk IV) 23 MU 29.10.43, 620 Sqn 13.5.44, FTR 5/6.6.44, crashed at Chateau de Grangues, France

EJ117 10 MU 8.11.43, 6 MU 21.9.44, 1660 CU 25.9.44, SOC 23.4.45

EJ118 10 MU 12.11.43, 1661 CU 1.9.44, 23 MU SLG 15.1.45, SOC 4.1.46

EJ119 10 MU 17.11.43, 1657 CU 19.7.44, 23 MU SLG 18.3.45, SOC 28.3.46

EJ120 23 MU 18.11.43, 19 MU 6.1.44, 1657 CU 3.6.44, RIW Sebro 24.8.44 after belly landing Woodbridge, port tyre burst on take-off, 10 MU 3.2.45, SOC 2.9.46

EJ121 Q/623 Sqn 22.9.43, 1654 CU 1.12.43, 23 MU SLG 8.2.45, SOC 28.2.45

EJ122 E/90 Sqn 6.10.43, Q,X/149 Sqn 14.6.44, 1657 CU 29.8.44, 6 MU 8.12.44, became 5223M 28.4.45 for Airborne Forces

EJ123 A/623 Sqn 22.9.43, A/214 Sqn 15.12.43, 1657 CU 27.1.44, 6 MU 13.12.44, SOC 19.7.45

EJ124 D/623 Sqn 22.9.43, Q/214 Sqn 15.12.43, C/149 Sqn 27.1.44, FTR 15/16.3.44 from Amiens, crashed at Baves, France

EJ125 C,J/218 Sqn 1.10.43, FTR 21/22.2.44 from mining, crashed at sea

EJ126 10 MU 27.11.43, 1660 CU 19.5.44, 6 MU 21.2.45, SOC 2.4.45

EJ127 10 MU 30.11.43, AK-W/1657 CU 9.9.44, 23 MU Aldergrove 5.1.45, SOC 25.4.46

LJ440 – LJ670 all Mk III or Mk IV as indicated

LJ440 (cv to Mk IV) V,K/620 Sqn 10.9.43, 1665 CU 30.3.44, 196 Sqn 8.44, damaged 19.9.44, Z/196 Sqn 30.10.44, OG-H/1665 CU, SOC 22.3.45

LJ441 P/75 Sqn 21.9.43, 1653 CU 13.3.44, 6 MU 1.12.44, SOC 24.4.45

LJ442 F/75 Sqn 27.9.43, FTR 19.11.43 from Leverkusen, shot down by fighter at Horrues, Belgium

LJ443 G/623 Sqn 22.9.43, 1654 CU 2.12.43, 1332 CU 6.12.44, FA 13.1.45, swung on take-off Nutt's Corner, nosed over into soft ground, SOC 18.4.45

LJ444 A/622 Sqn 17.9.43, 1653 CU 1.1.44, EFA 3.11.44, two engines failed on approach, hit trees, burnt out, at Stansfield, near Stradishall

LJ445 620 Sqn 24.9.43, FA 21.1.44, 1653 CU 9.3.44, EFA 24.8.44, heavy landing Chedburgh, tyre burst, ground loop and u/c collapse

LJ446 R/218 Sqn 1.10.43, 1653 CU 9.3.44, FA 26.9.44, u/c collapsed on take-off at Chedburgh, RIW Sebro 8.8.44, 23 MU 8.11.44, 1332 CU 13.12.44, FA 7.4.45 overshot Nutt's Corner, damaged tailplane, 1332 CU 23.4.45, SOC 15.5.45

LJ447 F/218 Sqn 29.9.43, 149 Sqn 17.8.44, 1657 CU 29.8.44, 1651 CU 17.10.44, 6 MU 10.11.44, SOC 24.4.45

LJ448 D,A/218 Sqn 29.9.43, FTR 21.4.44 from Chambly, crashed at Asnieres, France

LJ449 E/218 Sqn 1.10.43, H/149 Sqn 17.8.44, 1651 CU 23.8.44, 6 MU 18.11.44, SOC 6.6.45

LJ450 V/623 Sqn 15.10.43, UG-F/1654 CU 2.12.43, EFB 12.4.44, shot down by intruder at Bassingham Range during practice bombing

LJ451 K/XV Sqn 2.10.43, 622 Sqn 15.12.43, 1653 CU 1.1.44, QQ-C/1651 CU 16.1.44, EFA 28.7.44, engines problems, crashed in steep dive near March on 27.7.44

LJ452 S/218 Sqn 21.10.43, 1651 CU 27.1.44, 6 MU 6.11.44, SOC 20.4.45

LJ453 XV Sqn 21.10.43, K/75 Sqn 9.11.43, FTR 22/23.11.43 from Berlin, crashed at Dolberg, Germany

LJ454 E/623 Sqn 15.10.43, FTR 18/19.11.43 from Mannheim, crashed near target

LJ455 E/622 Sqn 21.10.43, H4-C/1653 CU 1.1.44, EFA 20.1.44 lost height in circuit, side-slipped in and burnt out in grounds of Hargrave Hall, Suffolk

LJ456 D/620 Sqn 15.10.43,1 OG-R/1665 CU 11.2.44, 6 MU 27.2.45, SOC 24.4.45

LJ457 V,H/75 Sqn 19.10.43, 1657 CU 26.3.44, 23 MU SLG 21.1.45, SOC 27.10.45

LJ458 10 MU 4.11.43, SOC 2.9.46

LJ459 E/620 Sqn 19.10.43, 1665 CU 11.2.44, FA 10.9.44 Tilstock, tyre burst after take-off, u/c collapsed landing, EFA 24.2.45 heavy landing Tilstock, u/c collapsed and outer mainplane broke away, burnt out

LJ460 E/90 Sqn 5.11.43, FTR 10/11.4.44 from SOE op, crashed at Lion en Sullias, France

LJ461 (cv to Mk IV) CRD Shorts 10.11.43, 23 MU 21.12.43, 196 Sqn 12.5.44, 1665 CU 21.8.44, swung on take-off at Saltby, u/c collapsed

LJ462 XV Sqn 21.10.43, O/75 Sqn 9.11.43, FTR 14.3.44 from mining off west coast of France

LJ463 620 Sqn 7.11.43, NY-Y,M/1665 CU 30.3.44, L662 CU 27.2.45, SOC 3.45

LJ464 XV Sqn 21.10.43, 1652 CU 2.12.43, 23 MU SLG 23.2.45, SOC 15.3.46

LJ465 10 MU 24.10.43, AFTDU 4.12.43, NY-K/1665 CU 20.6.44, SOC 25.1.45

LJ466 10 MU 4.10.43, 623 Sqn 27.11.43, 1660 CU 11.12.43, 6 MU 26.2.45, SOC 24.4.45

LJ467 10 MU 8.12.43, QQ-L/1651 CU 29.9.44, 1657 CU, 23 MU 21.1.45, SOC 20.4.46

LJ468 10 MU 7.12.43, 1661 CU 14.3.44, 23 MU 20.12.44, SOC 13.1.45

LJ469 10 MU 4.11.43, 1661 CU 2.8.44, GA 27.10.44 hit when parked by LK535, 24 MU 20.12.44, 23 MU 13.1.45, SOC 20.12.45

LJ470 C/90 Sqn 5.11.43, RIW Sebro 12.5.44, 6 MU, 1332 CU 14.9.44, EFA 28.11.44, possible icing troubles, forced landed in Atlantic 60 miles west of Isle of Lewis

LJ471 10 MU 5.11.43, H4-O/4.3.44, 6 MU 22.11.44, SOC 24.4.45

LJ472 10 MU 8.11.43, K/218 Sqn 28.11.43, Q/149 Sqn 17.8.44, 1651 CU 14.9.44, 6 MU 6.11.44, SOC 24.4.45

LJ473 R/75 Sqn 5.11.43, EFB 5.1.44 approached Mepal too fast when returning from mining, swung on landing, crashed on belly, caught fire

LJ474 10 MU 4.11.43, 199 Sqn 2.12.43, TV-Q/1660 CU 13.12.43, EFA 28.9.44, forced belly landing at Swinderby

LJ475 (cv to Mk IV) 23 MU 9.12.43, 620 Sqn 27.3.44, EFA 13.4.44 Blackford Farm, Kempsford, dived in after failure to recover from too steep a descent when releasing a Horsa

LJ476 10 MU 4.11.43, SOC 27.8.46

LJ477 10 MU 8.11.43, 623 Sqn, K/214 Sqn 14.1.44, P,H/90 Sqn 24.1.44, M/149 Sqn 14.6.44, EFB 19.5.44, crashed at Thorney Island returning from SOE op

LJ478 10 MU 8.11.43, 1654 CU 19.5.44, 23 MU SLG 11.2.45, SOC 22.4.46

LJ479 10 MU 13.11.43, 1660 CU 21.9.44, FA 17.12.44 Swinderby, u/c collapsed landing, fate uncertain

LJ480 10 MU 18.11.43, 623 Sqn 13.12.43, H/214 Sqn 15.12.43, S/199 Sqn 30.1.44, FTR 11/12.3.44 from mining, crashed at Naujac sur Mer, France

LJ481 B/218 Sqn 1.12.43, U/149 Sqn 17.8.44, 1653 CU 15.9.44, 6 MU 6.11.44, SOC 24.4.45

LJ482 22 MU 26.11.43, 214 Sqn 14.1.44, 623 Sqn 14.1.44, QQ-H/1651 CU 27.1.44, 1657 CU 19.10.44, 6 MU 12.44, SOC 19.4.45

LJ483 XY-V/90 Sqn 2.12.43, FTR from SOE op, crashed at Roye sur Matz, France

LJ501 23 MU 26.11.43, P/214 Sqn 15.12.43, H/199 Sqn 16.1.44, H/149 Sqn 5.5.44, FTR 31.5/1.6.44 from mining off Knocke, crashed near Zeebrugge

LJ502 (cv to Mk IV) 23 MU 9.12.43, ZO-D/196 Sqn 12.3.44, battle damage 29.12.44, 7T-V/196 Sqn 19.1.45, NY-U/1665 CU 1.2.45, 23 MU 14.2.46, SOC 5.6.47

LJ503 (cv to Mk IV) 23 MU 30.11.43, CRD Shorts 16.2.44, Tempsford 2.4.44, Shorts 21.4.44, Tempsford 22.5.44, NF-P/138 Sqn 20.6.44, loaned to 296 Sqn, battle accident 10.8.44, 138 Sqn, FTR 1.9.44 from SOE op, crashed Byans sur Doubs, France

LJ504 10 MU 30.11.43, Q,J,K/149 Sqn 1.12.43, battle damaged 21.1.44, hit on port wing and tailplane by two 500lb HEs over target, FTR 18/19.4.44 from mining Kiel Bay, crashed at sea

LJ505 10 MU 30.11.43, 1657 CU 23.6.44, EFA 25.11.44, port engine failed and u/c would not retract, lost height, crashed 500 yards from Hundon village church

LJ506 10 MU 7.12.43, F/90 Sqn 30.3.44, 218 Sqn 24.6.44, 1657 CU 28.7.44, FA 28.7.44, overshot Shepherd's Grove (pitot head covers not removed), Sebro 3.8.44, SOC 15.9.44

LJ507 10 MU 20.11.43, 1660 CU 4.12.43, 6 MU 17.2.45, SOC 24.4.45

LJ508 10 MU 20.11.43, T/1660 CU 24.12.43, FA 31.7.44 Valley, night landing with engine problem away from base, swung, both u/c legs torn off, Sebro repairs, ready 29.11.44, 10 MU 3.2.45, SOC 29.4.45

LJ509 10 MU 30.11.43, 623 Sqn 4.12.43, R/214 Sqn 15.12.43, F/90 Sqn 24.1.44, FTR 10/11.3.44 from SOE op, crashed at Brazey en Plaine, France

LJ510 10 MU 2.1.44, A/199 Sqn 21.4.44, FA 23.10.44, overshot, engine trouble, port u/c collapsed, 199 Sqn 13.1.45, 6 MU 8.3.45, SOC 24.4.45

LJ511 10 MU 15.12.43, 90 Sqn 1.4.44, Q/149 Sqn 13.4.44, FA 7.7.44 Methwold, swung, take-off abandoned, RIW Sebro 10.7.44, 23 MU 11.11.44, 1332 CU 13.12.44, SOC 30.5.45

LJ512 (cv to Mk IV) CRD Shorts 8.1.44, CRD Pershore 31.3.44, 304 FTU Melton Mowbray 14.4.44, 525 Sqn 29.5.44, RIW Sebro 27.7.44, 525 Sqn 21.3.45, 23 MU 28.4.45, SOC 31.1.46

LJ513 10 MU 10.1.44, E/199 Sqn 22.4.44, 171 10.11.44, 23 MU SLG 20.1.45, SOC 25.4.46

LJ514 10 MU 15.12.43, B/199 Sqn 5.5.44, 6 MU 24.2.45, SOC 4.5.45

LJ515 10 MU 6.12.43, 1665 CU 6.3.44, 23 MU 30.12.44, SOC 25.4.46

LJ516 10 MU 25.12.43, 27 MU 13.4.44, Defford 6.7.44 for *Mandrel* fit, 199 Sqn 17.4.45 (on last *Mandrel* op by 199 Sqn 14.3.45)

LJ517 10 MU 25.12.43, 623 Sqn 29.12.43, J/214 Sqn 14.1.44, U/218 Sqn 6.2.44, 1657 CU 28.7.44, RIW Sebro 4.8.44, 1657 CU 8.9.44, 6 MU 12.12.44 SOC 19.7.45

LJ518 10 MU 22.12.43, K/199 Sqn 29.4.44, EFB 26.9.44, hit trees on approach, rose to vertical, fell at Saxthorpe at 2145 hrs

LJ519 10 MU 23.12.43, 1654 CU 26.3.44, 23 MU SLG 8.2.45, SOC 4.2.46

LJ520 10 MU 25.12.43, Z/199 Sqn 2.5.44, 6 MU 24.2.45, SOC 4.2.46

LJ521 10 MU 24.12.43, 623 Sqn 29.12.43, 214 Sqn 14.1.44, W/218 Sqn 16.7.44, 1657 CU 28.7.44, 23 MU 21.12.44, SOC 24.4.45

LJ522 19 MU 13.1.44, N/218 Sqn 3.4.44, T,N/149 Sqn 27.7.44, 1657 CU 25.8.44, SOC 19.7.45

LJ523 1661 CU 31.12.43, EFA 18.9.44 overshot Harlaxton in bad weather

LJ524 1654 CU 6.1.44, EFA 11.5.44, Wigsley, three-engined overshoot, stalled

LJ525 6 MU 6.1.44, R/199 Sqn 30.4.44, SOC 31.1.45

LJ526 P,S,R/149 Sqn 5.1.44, FTR 23/24.4.44 from mining Fehmarn Belt, crashed at Oster Skerninge, Denmark

LJ527 1661 CU 31.12.43, 23 MU 30.12.44, SOC 25.4.46

LJ528 1654 CU 9.1.44, FA 3.2.44 Wigsley, starboard tyre burst landing, FA 2.7.44 Wigsley, tyre burst landing, swung u/c collapsed, 23 MU SLG 28.2.45, SOC 22.3.46

LJ529 1661 CU 31.12.43, EFA 25.2.44, Port Ellen, thrice tried landing on three engines, crashed behind watch office, SOC 29.2.44

LJ530 Prototype Stirling Mk V CRD Shorts 30.4.44, CRD Defford 25.8.44, Shorts 31.8.44, Belfast 31.5.45, SOC 27.10.46

LJ531 19 MU 13.1.44, N/199 Sqn 29.4.44, FTR 17.6.44 from *Mandrel* op, fate uncertain

LJ532 (cv to Mk IV) GP-E/1661 CU 6.1.44, FA 9.11.44 Winthorpe, fuel starvation, belly landed, RIW Sebro, cv to Mk IV, 23 MU 15.4.45, SOC 5.6.47

LJ533 1661 CU 4.1.44, EFA 21.3.44, engine trouble, force-landed in field near Winthorpe

LJ534 1660 CU 10.1.44, EFA 19.4.44 tyre burst on take-off, u/c collapsed landing, Woodbridge

LJ535 1654 CU 6.1.44, 1661 CU 15.3.44, 1654 CU 22.4.44, 1660 CU 24.7.44, 6 MU 24.2.45, SOC 31.5.45

LJ536 19 MU 7.1.44, P/199 Sqn 26.4.44, FTR 16.9.44?

LJ537 1654 CU 6.1.44, 1660 CU 24.7.44, 23 MU SLG 3.2.45, SOC 25.4.46

LJ538 6 MU 23.1.44, T/199 Sqn 22.5.44, 6 MU 21.2.45, became 5239M 5.5.45 for paratroop training, SOC 5.6.45

LJ539 1654 CU 6.1.44, EFA 19.7.44 Wigsley, vibration led to aborted take-off, part of u/c broke away, belly flopped

LJ540 19 MU 31.1.44, 1661 CU 13.4.44, 23 MU 3.2.45, SOC 28.2.46

LJ541 10 MU 31.1.44, Defford 3.7.44, 199 Sqn 17.7.44, 6Y-N/171 Sqn 17.9.44, 199 Sqn 2.10.44, gale damaged 18.1.45, ROS, 199 Sqn 10.2.45, 6 MU 8.3.45, SOC 24.4.45

LJ542 19 MU 1.44, G/199 Sqn 30.4.44, SOC 31.1.45

LJ543 19 MU 31.1.44, J/199 Sqn 29.4.44, 171 Sqn 6.12.44, 23 MU 22.1.45, SOC 3.46

LJ544 19 MU 31.1.44, D/199 Sqn 29.4.44, 171 Sqn 6.12.44, 23 MU SLG 22.1.45, SOC 28.3.46

LJ557 19 MU 31.1.44, Y/199 Sqn 29.4.44, SOC 31.1.45

LJ558 1654 CU 26.1.44, 1661 CU 27.1.44, EFA 27.5.44, Winthorpe, swung landing, hit buildings on airfield edge and damaged BK766

LJ559 10 MU 3.2.44, 199 Sqn 31.8.44, R,J/171 Sqn 17.9.44, Q/199 Sqn 2.11.44, FA seriously damaged in fast dive to recover from severe icing, RIW 24.1.45, SOC 10.2.45

LJ560 19 MU 31.1.44, H/199 Sqn 30.4.44, EFB 30.8.44, hit obstruction during op take-off, port tyre burst, u/c collapsed, burnt out

LJ561 1654 CU 26.1.44, 1660 CU 27.1.44, 23 MU SLG 5.1.45, SOC 28.2.46

LJ562 10 MU 31.1.44, V/199 Sqn 5.5.44, 171 Sqn 10.11.44, 23 MU SLG 23.1.45, SOC 20.3.46

LJ563 (cv to Mk IV) 23 MU 30.1.44, C,O/190 Sqn 18.5.44, 23 MU 20.2.46, SOC 5.6.47

LJ564 23 MU 31.1.44, 226 MU 21.2.44, 23 MU 27.2.44, ZO-X/196 Sqn 14.5.44, EFB 7.7.44 overshot Keevil returning from SOE op, SOC 26.7.44, be 4845M at HQ Airborne Forces, Signcoat House, Netheravon

LJ565 10 MU 31.1.44, Q/199 Sqn 14.5.44, 171 Sqn 10.11.44, J/199 Sqn 17.11.44, 6 MU 22.2.45, SOC 24.4.45

LJ566 (cv to Mk IV) 23 MU 31.1.44, QS-L/620 Sqn 18.5.44, damaged in action 20.9.44, D4-Y/620 Sqn 4.10.44, GA 31.5.45 at B58 grazed LK123, 151 RU 31.1.46, 36 RU 20.6.46, QS-L/620 Sqn 29.5.46, 29 MU, SOC 16.10.47

LJ567 6 MU 5.2.44, Y/199 Sqn 31.8.44, S/171 Sqn 17.9.44, FA 15.10.44 landed tailwheels-up, C/171 Sqn 5.11.44, X/199 Sqn 10.11.44, GA 21.11.44, damaged by taxying LL351 at Rivenhall, 199 Sqn, FA 5.12.44 hit wall approaching North Creake back from ops, belly landed Woodbridge, Cat E 22.2.45

LJ568 6 MU 3.2.44, 218 Sqn, A/149 Sqn 28.7.44, 199 Sqn 29.8.44, H/171 Sqn 17.9.44, FA 19.10.44, damaged wing of B-17 38420 of 526th BS, USAAF, 171 Sqn 4.11.44, H,L/199 Sqn 10.11.44, 6 MU 6.3.45, SOC 11.4.45

LJ569 (cv to Mk IV) 6 MU 5.2.44, C/199 Sqn 22.5.44, FA 16.9.44 engine trouble taking off on ops 2117 hrs, starboard wing torn off during swing, RIW Sebro 28.9.44, cv to Mk IV, 23 MU 21.4.45, SOC 5.6.47

LJ570 Stradishall 14.2.44, W-K/1651 CU 17.4.44, 1657 CU 17.10.44, 23 MU SLG 12.1.45, SOC 25.4.46

LJ571 CRD Shorts 3.2.44, CRD AWA 23.5.44, Shorts 30.6.44, A&AEE 31.8.44, 6 MU 15.12.44, SOC 24.4.45

LJ572 (cv to Mk IV) 23 MU 5.2.44, X9-T,L/299 Sqn 17.5.44, Sebro 21.6.45, 23 MU 20.2.45, SOC 5.6.47

LJ573 Stradishall 11.2.44, QQ-J/1651 CU 17.4.44, FA 25.8.44 Wratting, landed too far along runway and u/c collapsed, 6 MU 20.11.44, SOC 19.7.45

LJ574 1654 CU 21.2.44, 6 MU SLG Woburn Abbey 8.2.45, SOC 4.4.45

LJ575 (cv to Mk IV, re-numbered TS266) 1654 CU 20.2.44, 1661 CU 6.3.44, EFA 15.5.44 Waddington, port tyre burst on take-off, swung, u/c collapsed, re-cat and RIW Sebro 26.9.44, cv Mk IV, 19 MU 6.12.44, 570 Sqn 15.3.45, GA 9.4.45, 570 Sqn 17.4.45, 23 MU 18.2.46, SOC 5.6.47

LJ576 (cv to Mk IV) 23 MU 21.2.44, FA 23.2.44, 8Z-E,D/295 Sqn 18.8.44, battle damaged 24.9.44, 295 Sqn 2.10.44, 20 MU 25.1.46, SOC 5.6.47

LJ577 E/149 Sqn 21.2.44, 1651 CU 23.8.44, 6 MU 6.11.44, SOC 7.2.45

LJ578 S/199 Sqn 29.2.44, EFB 10.9.44 North Creake, tyre burst on op take-off, u/c collapsed, burnt

LJ579 O/90 Sqn 3.3.44, EFB 23.4.44, u/c collapsed on take-off, re-cat B 25.5.44, 23 MU 18.8.44, ECFS 21.9.44, SOC 9.8.45

LJ580 149 Sqn 29.2.44, X/199 Sqn 11.3.44, SOC 31.1.45

LJ581 1654 CU 4.3.44, 90 Sqn 5.3.44, 1654 CU 11.3.44, 23 MU 15.2.45, SOC 28.2.46

LJ582 149 Sqn 29.2.44, L/199 Sqn 11.3.44, 171 Sqn 10.11.44, 23 MU SLG 31.3.45, SOC 22.2.46

LJ583 (cv to Mk IV) 23 MU 23.3.44, ZO-N, 7T-A/196 Sqn 12.6.44, 299 Sqn, 23 MU 17.6.45, SOC 5.6.47

LJ584 GP-O/1660 CU 18.3.44, 23 MU 30.12.44, SOC 25.4.46

LJ585 1654 CU 9.3.44, EFA 29.7.44, caught fire in the air, engine trouble, crashed Normanton-upon-Trent, Notts, five baled out and four killed

LJ586 GP-Y,X/1661 CU 8.3.44, EFA 28.10.44, icing problems, forced down at Iwerne Minster, Blandford, burnt out

LJ587 1660 CU 31.3.44, FA 24.8.44 Swinderby, landed on three engines, crash landed u/c up, 6 MU 25.2.45, SOC 7.5.45

LJ588 (cv to Mk IV) 23 MU 9.3.44, 620 Sqn 18.5.44, 23 MU 19.4.45, SOC 14.1.46

LJ589 23 MU 22.3.44, 10 MU 9.6.44, FA 20.8.44, 10 7.10.44, 8Z-F/295 Sqn 12.10.44, 570 Sqn 10.12.44, FA 6.3.45, Rivenhall, swung off runway hitting three Horsas RN655, RN621 and PW833, ROS, 570 Sqn 20.3.45, 23 MU 20.4.45, SOC 5.6.47

LJ590 (cv to Mk IV) 23 MU 4.3.44, 6 MU 13.6.44, 8Z-F,C, 8E-G/295 Sqn 13.7.44, 570 Sqn 9.11.44, 19 MU 11.12.44, SOC 26.12.46

LJ591 Mk IV 23 MU 25.3.44, 13 MU 9.6.44, 8Z-J/295 Sqn 2.7.44, battle damage 20.9.44, 295 Sqn 16.10.44, GA 30.9.45 damaged tailplane at B58, SOC 25.10.45

LJ592 GP-X/1661 CU 30.3.44, FA 17.9.44 Winthorpe, landed on three engines, ran off runway, port u/c collapsed, RIW Sebro 18.9.44, fate uncertain, PSO 21.6.47

LJ593 GP-W/1661 CU 30.3.44, 23 MU 3.2.45, SOC 28.2.46

LJ594 Mk IV 23 MU 21.3.44, V8-N/570 Sqn 19.7.44, FTR 18.9.44, crash landed 2–3 miles SE of Oudenbosch, near Breda, Netherlands, two crew baled out, became POWs, rest safe

LJ595 27 MU 13.3.44, Defford for *Mandrel* fit 4.6.44, 199 Sqn 6.7.44, 6 MU 22.2.45, SOC 24.4.45

LJ596 Mk IV 23 MU 25.3.44, V8-K/570 Sqn 28.9.44, 23 MU 20.4.45, SOC 5.6.47

LJ611 27 31.3.44, 6 MU 25.7.44, 199 Sqn 31.8.44, 6Y-E/171 Sqn 17.9.44, A/199 Sqn 26.10.44, 6 MU 8.3.45, SOC 6.6.45

LJ612 Mk IV 27 MU 31.3.44, 23 MU 1.5.44, 570 Sqn 19.7.4, 8Z-V/295 Sqn 3.8.44, E7-L,S/570 Sqn 10.12.44, 23 MU 20.12.45, SOC 5.6.47

LJ613 Mk IV 23 MU 31.3.44, V8-B/570 Sqn 5.7.44, RIW Sebro 2.8.44 after u/c collapse, 570 Sqn 13.8.44, RIW Sebro 18.9.44, 23 MU 16.2.45, SOC 5.6.47

LJ614 27 MU 6.4.44, Defford 2.7.44, 6 MU 13.8.44, S/199 Sqn 30.8.44, 6 MU 8.3.45, SOC 24.4.45

LJ615 (cv to Mk IV) 6 MU 5.6.44, V8-H,P/570 Sqn 19.7.44, 1665 CU 24.5.45, 23 MU 9.2.46, SOC 5.6.47

LJ616 (cv to Mk IV) 23 MU 13.4.44, V8-D, E/570 Sqn 1.8.44, 242 Sqn 2.10.45, 23 MU 9.1.46, SOC 5.6.47

LJ617 27 MU 13.4.44, 6 MU 5.7.44, 199 Sqn 30.8.44, P,K/171 Sqn 17.9.44, 199 Sqn 10.11.44, FTR 5/6.3.45, shot down by American AA fire during *Mandrel* operation, crashed at Thionville

LJ618 Mk IV 6 MU 16.6.44, 295 Sqn 28.8.44, FTR 20.9.44 from *Market IV*, shot down at Nimegen, crashed on south bank of Waal west of town at Puifluik, Netherlands

LJ619 27 MU 20.4.44, 23 MU 11.5.44, H4-J/1653 CU 18.6.44, 6 MU 26.11.44, SOC 24.4.45

LJ620 (Mk III with *H2S*, cv to Mk IV) 6 MU 16.6.44, V8-O/570 Sqn 16.8.44, battle damage 24.9.44, 570 Sqn 20.10.44, GA nose damaged when taxying, E7-O/13.2.45, 20 MU 19.4.45, SOC 5.6.47

LJ621 M/149 Sqn 19.4.44, FTR 5/6.6.44 from D-Day feint, crashed at Marcelet, France

LJ622 (Mk III with *H2S*, cv to Mk IV) 6 MU 10.6.44, V8-W/570 Sqn 9.7.44, battle damaged 24.9.44, 570 Sqn 4.11.44, 295 Sqn 9.11.44, NY-X/1665 CU 24.5.44, EFA 9.10.45, Tockwith, Yorks, possibly crashed at night making a stall turn, crashed and burnt out in a row of houses

LJ623 P/149 Sqn 27.4.44, 17.7.44, hit in wings over target by three falling 500lb HEs, 149 Sqn 19.8.44, 1651 CU 25.8.44, 6 MU 22.11.44, SOC 24.4.45

LJ624 TV-C/1660 CU 5.6.44, EFA 5.10.44, Swinderby, on landing off runway clipped LK389

LJ625 D,T,N/90 Sqn 25.4.44, S,G/218 Sqn 24.6.44, O/149 Sqn 26.7.44, 1657 CU 25.8.44, 6 MU 12.12.44, SOC 19.7.45

LJ626 1660 CU 13.4.44, FA 5.8.44, 1660 CU 31.12.44, SOC 21.2.45, to instructional 5240M 5.5.45,

LJ627 (cv to Mk IV) 6 MU 25.6.44, 620 Sqn 10.9.44, FA 8.11.44, 620 Sqn, EFA 21.4.45, swung landing at Rhine into bomb crater, u/c collapsed

LJ628 1660 CU 18.6.44, 1654 CU 12.5.44, EFA 21.7.44 dived out of cloud, hit Marjory's Hill, Midfield, Yorks

LJ629 (Mk III with *H2S*, cv to Mk IV) 6 MU 18.6.44, 5G- 0. X9-B/299 Sqn 3.9.44, FA 10.11.44 taxied into EE966 at Wethersfield, 299 Sqn 9.12.44, FA 22.4.45, u/c collapsed at B112 Hopsten, Germany, during cross-wind landing

LJ630 1654 CU 19.5.44, EFA 31.8.44, possible engine fire, crashed at Stanton-by-Dale near Hucknall, all killed

LJ631 Mk IV V8-Q/570 Sqn 10.8.44, EFB 25.8.44 from SOE op, damaged by Allied AA fire, crashed at Belleme, France, SOC 4.9.44

LJ632 G/218 Sqn 9.5.44, P/149 Sqn 26.7.44, 1653 CU 12.9.44, 6 MU 6.11.44, SOC 19.7.45

LJ633 Mk IV 6 MU 26.6.44, 8E-F/295 Sqn 10.8.44, E7-R/570 Sqn 10.12.44, 23 MU 4.1.46, SOC 5.6.47

LJ634 Syerston 13.5.44, ECNS Shawbury 24.5.44, SOC 4.1.45, Sebro (Bourn) 5.4.45 for cannibalisation

LJ635 TV-E/23.5.44, 1332 CU 5.12.44, SOC 15.5.45

LJ636 (Mk III with *H2S*, cv to Mk IV) 6 MU 10.7.44, V8-N, E7-N/570 Sqn 22.9.44, 23 MU 9.1.46, SOC 5.6.47

LJ637 1660 CU 23.5.44, EFA 31.8.44 Swinderby, engine problem, bounced on landing, swung, u/c collapsed

LJ638 (Mk III with *H2S*, cv to Mk IV) 6 MU 10.7.44, 8Z-I/295 Sqn 1.8.44, battle damage 25.9.44, 295 Sqn 30.9.44, E7-Y/570 Sqn 21.12.44, GA 10.1.45, hit LJ612 when taxying, ROS, 570 Sqn 24.1.45, FTR 11/12.2.45 from SOE drop *Nico 1*, crashed near Nieuwerkirk, by IJsselmeer, Netherlands

LJ639 1653 CU 26.5.44, 6 MU Woburn 24.11.44, SOC 24.4.45

LJ640 Mk IV 6 MU 10.7.44, 295 Sqn 25.9.44, V8-B/570 Sqn 10.12.44, 23 MU 20.12.45, SOC 5.6.47

LJ641 1653 CU 28.5.44, FA 1.8.41, port tyre burst when landing at Chedburgh, swung and u/c collapsed, 6 MU 3.11.44, SOC 24.4.45

LJ642 1657 CU 3.6.44, 6 MU 13.12.44, SOC 19.7.45

LJ643 (Mk III with *H2S*, cv to Mk IV) 6 MU 10.7.44, ZO-X, 7T-J/196 Sqn 27.9.44, FA 24.10.45, 108 RSU 1.11.45, 23 MU 21.3.46, SOC 5.6.47

LJ644 1654 CU 5.6.44, 23 MU 2.1.45, SOC 28.2.46

LJ645 Mk IV 6 MU 14.6.44, 570 Sqn 23.8.44, flying battle damage 24.9.44, E7-M/570 Sqn 14.10.44, MR 22/23.4.45 from SOE drops in Denmark, shot down by AA at Skaering, Denmark

LJ646 1654 CU 14.6.44, 23 MU SLG 22.1.45, SOC 4.1.46

LJ647 Mk IV 6 MU 14.6.44, V8-U/570 Sqn 16.8.44, FTR 19.9.44 from *Market III*, forced landed at Haren, near Megan, Netherlands, crew returned home by 24th, helped out by Dutch Underground

LJ648 1660 CU 15.6.44, FA 29.6.44, port inner engine on fire after landing, u/c collapsed, 10 MU 3.2.45, SOC 13.9.46

LJ649 23 MU 30.6.44, Defford for *Mandrel* 3.7.44, 6 MU 3.8.44, 199 Sqn 30.8.44, 171 Sqn 17.9.44, P/199 Sqn 2.10.44, SOC 24.2.45

LJ650 Mk IV 6 MU 25.6.44, V8-L/570 Sqn 16.8.44, 190 Sqn 16.11.44, E7-W/570 Sqn 23.11.44, 299 Sqn 9.1.46, 23 MU 7.3.46, SOC 5.6.47

LJ651 23 MU 30.6.44, Defford for *Mandrel* 17.7.44, 6 MU 3.8.44, 199 Sqn 30.8.44, 171 Sqn 17.9.44, C/199 Sqn 2.10.44, GA gale damage 18.1.45, ROS, 199 Sqn 3.2.45, 6 MU 8.3.45, SOC 6.6.45

LJ652 Mk IV 6 MU 26.6.44, 8E-X/295 Sqn 16.8.44, battle damage 19.9.44, 295 Sqn 17.11.44, 51 Sqn 6.12.45, 23 MU 16.1.46, SOC 5.6.47

LJ653 23 MU 13.7.44, SOC 27.12.45

LJ667 Mk IV 6 MU 10.7.44, V8-U, E7-U,L/570 Sqn 22.9.44, FA 13.9.45, ROS, 299 Sqn 11.1.46, 273 MU 29.3.46, SOC 16.10.47

LJ668 (Mk III with *H2S*, cv to Mk IV) 6 MU 10.7.44, 23 MU 6.11.44, 620 Sqn 18.3.45, 5G-J/299 Sqn 31.5.45, EFA 6.10.45 crashed after trying to locate airfield near Rennes, France, very low cloud, twenty-six killed

LJ669 Mk IV 6 MU 16.7.44, SG-M/299 Sqn 22.9.44, 242 Sqn 23.9.45, 23 MU 9.1.46, SOC 5.6.47

LJ670 23 MU 24.7.44, 199 Sqn 29.9.44, 171 Sqn 2.10.44, 6 MU 18.12.44, SOC 19.7.45

LJ810 – LJ999 All Mk IV transports

LJ810 299 Sqn 7.1.44, ZO-B/196 Sqn 20.4.44, FT 21.9.44 from *Market V*, shot down by AA and fighters, crashed at Wychen, Netherlands

LJ811 299 Sqn 18.1.44, FA Keevil 7.8.44, swung on take-off, RIW Sebro 8.8.44, 19 MU 20.12.44, 295 Sqn 16.3.45, 1665 CU 5.4.45, 5G-G/299 Sqn 26.4.45, 23 MU 17.3.44, SOC 5.6.47

LJ812 5G-P, X9-Z/299 Sqn 8.1.44, 1665 CU 1.2.45, 23 MU 5.2.46, SOC 5.6.47

LJ813 13.1.44, 196 Sqn 29.4.44, 5G-E/299 Sqn, FTR 21.6.44 on SOE op, crashed at St Germain-des-Pres

LJ814 5G-R/299 Sqn 18.1.44, EFA 26.3.44, oil leak on starboard outer engine, could not maintain height, crashed at Brize Norton

LJ815 5G-E/299 Sqn 12.1.44, 10 MU 24.2.45, 23 MU 24.5.45, SOC 5.6.47

LJ816 190 Sqn 21.1.44, battle damaged 22.9.44, 190 Sqn 30.9.44, 620 Sqn 5.10.44, 190 Sqn 8.10.44, 19 MU 11.12.44, SOC 20.12.46

LJ817 5G-S/299 Sqn 18.1.44, FA Keevil 2.5.44, swung after landing in gusty weather, port u/c collapsed, RIW Sebro 2.5.44, 23 MU 21.9.44, 620 Sqn 5.10.44, 1665 CU 4.1.45, Sebro 15.11.45, Cat E 14.1.46 at Bourn, SOC 22.1.46

LJ818 X/190 Sqn 28.1.44, SOC and to instructional 5051M on 24.2.45, for use by 3 Para Brigade

LJ819 5G-H,K/299 Sqn 21.1.44, FTR 6.6.44 shot down during Op *Mallard*

LJ820 190 Sqn 21.1.44, 19 MU 27.11.44, SOC 14.11.46

LJ821 5G-G,H/299 Sqn 24.1.44, RIW Sebro 17.4.45, 23 MU 15.9.45, 299 Sqn 8.11.45, 23 MU 29.1.46, 196 Sqn 3.3.46, 23 MU 22.3.46, SOC 5.6.47

LJ822 190 Sqn 21.1.44, EFB 11/12.4.44 crashed on Knighton Farm, Hampreston, Dorset, from a stall turn during SOE sortie, SOC 2.5.44

LJ823 190 Sqn 24.1.44, FTR 21.9.44 from *Market V*, hit by flak over DZ then attacked by fighters; turned south and aircraft caught fire, crew baled out south of River Waal, crashed at Horssen, Netherlands

LJ824 190 Sqn 26.1.44, 23 MU 31.5.44, S&H 8.12.45, SOC 14.1.46

LJ825 H/190 Sqn 26.1.44, 23 MU 20.4.45, SOC 5.6.47

LJ826 190 Sqn 27.1.44, FA 10.5.44 port tyre burst on landing, swung, port u/c collapsed, J/190 Sqn 12.8.44, FA 26.2.45 tail chassis damaged in crosswind landing, 23 MU 17.5.44, SOC 5.6,47

LJ827 190 Sqn 24.1.44, FTR 26.8.44, from SOE drop, crashed at Villebougis, France

LJ828 190 Sqn 28.1.44, GA 14.6.44 taxied into LJ829 on dispersal, 620 Sqn 15.7.44, 1665 CU 16.8.44, battle damaged 21.9.44, NY-A/1665 CU 20.11.44, EFA 22.9.45 Marston Moor, tyre burst on landing, u/c collapsed

LJ829 190 Sqn 26.1.44, FTR 21.9.44 from *Market V*, crashed 5 miles W of Arnhem, nine personnel aboard killed

LJ830 190 Sqn 31.1.44, 620 Sqn 23.6.44, FTR 21.9.44 from *Market V*, total wreck after crash landing 3 miles west of Arnhem, one killed, five survived

LJ831 190 Sqn 26.1.44, EFB 21.9.44, flak damaged and belly landed on Ghent airfield, Belgium

LJ832 U/190 Sqn 27.1.44, 23 MU 20.4.45, SOC 5.6.47

LJ833 190 Sqn 2.2.44, FTR 21.9.44 from *Market V*, hit by flak, attacked by two Bf 109s, caught fire, crash landed in River Waal, near Appeltern, three survivors (one died)

LJ834 196 Sqn 27.1.44, EFA 16.3.44, overshot Tarrant Rushton in poor visibility, u/c collapsed, SOC 31.3.44, became 4776M 4.5.44 for PTS Ringway

LJ835 ZO-W196 Sqn 28.1.44, 299 Sqn 9.44?, 23 MU 23.6.45, SOC 23.1.46

LJ836 ZO-G/196 Sqn 2.2.44, 10 MU 22.2.45, 299 Sqn 10.5.45, 23 MU 12.7.45, SOC 5.6.47

LJ837 ZO-Q/196 Sqn 30.1.44, Sebro 22.2.45, 23 MU 26.6.45, 21 HGCU 2.8.45, 23 MU SLG 28.9.45, 1665 CU 28.11.45, 23 MU 4.2.46, SOC 5.6.47

LJ838 196 Sqn 5.2.44, RIW Sebro after battle damage on 6.6.44, 23 MU 3.3.45, ZO-N/196 Sqn 8.3.45, battle damage 24.3.45, Cat E 14.1.46, SOC 22.1.46

LJ839 ZO-N/196 Sqn 8.2.44, EFA 28.3.44, overshot Marham and hit aged hangar

LJ840 ZO-C, 7T-G/196 Sqn 31.1.44, M 20.9.44, hit over DZ during *Market IV*, crew baled out, crashed at Batenburg, Netherlands

LJ841 196 Sqn 31.1.44, FTR 5/6.6.44 from Op *Tonga IV*, crashed at Cagny, France

LJ842 ZO-S,K/196 Sqn 7.2.44, EFA 4.4.44, glider towing low in bad weather, clipped trees, stalled, burnt out 1 mile SW of Romsey, Hants

LJ843 ZO-R/196 Sqn, 31.1.44, FTR 21.9.44 from *Market V*, crashed at Oranje-Nassau Oord Renkum, eight killed

LJ844 6 MU 24.2.44, 5G-E/299 Sqn 9.5.44, 23 MU 23.6.44, SOC 5.6.47

LJ845 ZO-L/196 Sqn 31.1.44, FA 26.4.44 damaged landing at Keevil, RIW Sebro 14.5.44, 6 MU 13.9.44, 299 Sqn 27.9.44, NY-K/1665 CU 24.5.44, 23 MU 9.2.46, SOC 5.6.47

LJ846 ZO-S,7T-S/196 Sqn 2.2.44, 23 MU 2.7.45, Sebro 12.8.45, 23 MU 22.2.46, SOC 5.6.47

LJ847 D4-X/620 Sqn 7.2.44, 23 MU 20.4.45, SOC 5.6.47

LJ848 ZO-O/196 Sqn 31.1.44, 10 MU 4.1.45, 23 MU 25.5.45, SOC 5.6.47

LJ849 620 Sqn 8.2.44, FTR 6.6.44, crashed in drop zone

LJ850 620 Sqn 11.2.44, FTR 17.6.44 from SOE drop in France

LJ851 ZO-E/196 Sqn 3.2.44, *Market IV*, circumstances of loss uncertain, probable forced landing, crashed S of Eindhoven on route to DZ

LJ864 620 Sqn 7.2.44, FTR 22.7.44 from SOE op, crashed at Brillac, France

LJ865 620 Sqn 10.2.44, 23 MU 9.7.45, SOC 5.6.47

LJ866 QS-E,F/620 Sqn 7.2.44, 23 MU 20.4.45, became 5246M 12.5.45

LJ867 620 Sqn 7.2.44, FTR 11.4.44 from SOE op, crashed in western France

LJ868 6 MU 24.2.44, 5G-R/299 Sqn 28.5.44, FTR 19.9.44, crashed on bank of Dutch Rhine 200 yards from rail bridge between Arnhem and Driel, crew saved

LJ869 620 Sqn 7.2.44, FA 9.6.44 damaged in collision with Horsa LH562, RIW Sebro 9.6.44, 23 MU 27.9.44, 295 Sqn 1.10.44, 190 Sqn, 23 MU 31.5.45, SOC 5.6.47

LJ870 6 NU 23.3.44, ZO-G/196 Sqn 29.4.44, FA 27.5.44 tyre burst on take-off, u/c collapsed, Keevil, 196 Sqn 12.11.44, EFA 19.2.45 fast landing at Shepherd's Grove with engine trouble, swung, u/c collapsed

LJ871 6 MU 24.2.44, 620 Sqn 11.6.44, 299 Sqn 19.10.44, 620 Sqn, GA gale damage at Dunmow 18.2.45, ROS Sebro, 620 Sqn 12.2.45, battle damage 24.3.45, RIW Sebro 20.4.45, 23 MU 27.8.56, SOC 5.6.47

LJ872 QS-V/ 620 Sqn 8.2.44, 23 MU 20.4.45, Sebro 12.11.45, SOC 22.1.46

LJ873 QS-H/620 Sqn 10.2.44, FTR 23.9.44 from *Market VII*, believed to have crashed near Oss, Netherlands, crew all saved, loss details uncertain

LJ874 6 MU 19.2.44, 5G-I/299 Sqn 1.9.44, 196 Sqn 5.4.45, 23 MU 23.6.45, SOC 5.6.47

LJ875 620 Sqn 8.2.44, Sebro 13.3.45, 23 MU 2.8.45, SOC 5.6.47

LJ876 6 MU 24.2.44, 299 Sqn 15.8.44, ZO-K,7T-K/196 Sqn 1.11.44, 242 Sqn 23.9.45, 23 MU 14.1.46, SOC 5.6.47

LJ877 6 MU 15.2.44, 299 Sqn 24.2.44, 6 MU 17.11.44, SOC 14.1.46

LJ878 6 MU 6.3.44, 5G-T/299 Sqn 1.5.44, FTR 6.8.44 from SOE op, crashed at Auray-Plougoumelen, France

LJ879 5G-W/299 Sqn 25.2.44, Sebro MI 23.2.45, 23 MU 3.6.45, 5G-F/299 Sqn 22.10.45, 196 Sqn 10.3.46, 273 MU 28.3.46, SOC 30.1.47

LJ880 620 Sqn 11.2.44, EFA 19.5.44, hit at 400ft by EF244 over tow rope drop zone, crashed, broke up on impact, burnt out, 1 mile WSW of Kempsford, Glos

LJ881 6 MU 11.2.44, 190 Sqn 17.5.44, FTR 21.9.44 from *Market V*, crashed 1 1/2 miles NE of Hemmen, claimed by AA and fighters, two survivors baled out then aircraft broke up

LJ882 6 MU 6.3.44, 190 Sqn 2.5.44, 620 Sqn 11.5.44, 190 Sqn, FTR 22.7.44, crashed at Graffigny-Chemin, France

LJ883 6 MU 15.2.44, V8-K/570 Sqn 9.7.44, FTR 23.9.44 from *Market VII*, shot down at Planken Wambuis, 6 miles NW Arnhem, six killed

LJ884 6 MU 15.2.44, 5G-M/299 Sqn 2.3.44, battle damage 21.9.44, 299 Sqn 21.10.44, 196 Sqn 1.11.44, RIW Sebro 3.12.44, 10 MU 12.2.45, 8Z-L/295 Sqn 10.5.45, 299 Sqn 24.1.46, 570 Sqn 23.2.46, 23 MU 27.2.46, SOC 5.6.47

LJ885 5G-K,C/299 Sqn 25.2.44, FTR 6.6.44, crashed at Hermanville, France

LJ886 6 MU 17.2.44, 620 Sqn 24.4.44, FTR 7/8.5.44 from SOE op, crashed at Poissons, France

LJ887 6 MU 17.2.44, 620 Sqn 21.5.44, 23 MU 9.7.45, SOC 5.6.47

LJ888 6 MU 6.3.44, 7T-X,ZO-X/196 Sqn 14.5.44, battle damage 17.9.44, ZO-T/196 Sqn 29.9.44, 7M 30/31.3.45 from SOE op to Norway, shot down by fighter at Ostre-Moland, Arendal, Norway

LJ889 6 MU 19.2.44, N/190 Sqn 19.5.44, 23 MU 31.5.45, gale damage 24.10.45, 23 MU 26.11.45, SOC 5.6.47

LJ890 (SD) 6 MU 31.3.44, 10 MU 8.5.44, 6 MU 17.6.44, V8-W/570 Sqn 11.8.44, 8E-L,O/295 Sqn 10.12.44, GA 15.4.45, hit LK330 parking, 23 MU 26.1.46, SOC 5.6.47

LJ891 5G-D/299 Sqn 25.2.44, battle damage 24.9.44, RIW Sebro 27.9.44, 299 Sqn 9.10.44, EFA 20.11.44, Wethersfield, engine trouble, starboard tyre burst on landing, u/c collapsed, became 4942M 2.12.44

LJ892 6 MU Woburn 10.3.44, QS-T/620 Sqn 24.4.44, battle damage 21.9.44, 620 Sqn 17.10.44, 19 MU 7.12.44, SOC 22.10.46

LJ893 6 MU 19.1.44, 5G-Y, X9-J/299 Sqn 9.5.44, battle damage 22.9.44, RIW Sebro 27.9.44, 299 Sqn 4.10.44, 1665 CU 25.5.45, 23 MU 2.7.45, SOC 5.6.47

LJ894 6 MU 24.2.44, 7T-W/196 Sqn 17.5.44, FTR 21/22.2.45 from Rees, shot down by AA at De Rips, Netherlands

LJ895 6 MU Woburn 10.3.44, K/190 Sqn 17.5.44, 23 MU 24.5.45, SOC 5.6.47

LJ896 6 MU 19.2.44, 5G-C/299 Sqn 1.5.44, 21/22.2.45 from Rees, shot down by AA at Goch

LJ897 6 MU 24.2.44, 299 Sqn 1.3.44, EFA 4.7.44, landed on blind runway at Tarrant Rushton, overshot, u/c collapsed, SOC 18.7.44

LJ898 6 MU for Woburn 18.3.44, M/190 Sqn 4.5.44, 23 MU 25.5.45, SOC 5.6.47

LJ899 A&AEE trials at Leicester East 28.2.44, 620 Sqn, 190 Sqn 21.5.44, 620 Sqn, 190 Sqn FTR 11.5.45, loss of control in poor visibility, ditched in Rujdafors Lake near Torsky, Sweden, troops aboard

LJ913 6 MU 24.2.44, V8-P/570 Sqn 19.7.44, FTR 18.9.44, crash landed at 52°01N/05°54E, all aboard became POWs

LJ914 6 MU Woburn 17.3.44, 620 Sqn 11.5.44, FTR 1.12.44 from SOE op to Norway, possibly shot down by AA on route, at sea

LJ915 5G-Y/299 Sqn 25.2.44, battle damage 24.9.44, SOC 30.9.44 then BBOC for RIW Sebro 29.3.45, 23 MU 4.10.45, 1665 CU 3.11.45, 23 MU 5.2.46, SOC 5.6.47

LJ916 10 MU 6.3.44, 6 MU 22.4.44, 190 Sqn 24.5.44, FTR 21.9.44 from *Market V*, force landed between Tilburg and Eindhoven, crew became POWs

LJ917 10 MU 31.3.44, 6 MU 23.4.44, 620 Sqn 2.5.44, battle damage 21.9.44, 620 Sqn 18.10.44, 19 MU 7.12.44, SOC 25.11.46

LJ918 6 MU 29.2.44, 620 Sqn 21.5.44, battle damage 21.9.44, 620 Sqn 23.10.44, 19 MU 16.11.44, SOC 14.2.47

LJ919 10 MU 25.2.44, 6 MU 27.4.44, 5G-S/ 299 Sqn 17.5.44, 1665 CU 11.1.45, EFA 22.8.45 Marston Moor, u/c already strained collapsed during take-off swing

LJ920 6 MU Woburn 18.3.44, 620 Sqn 17.5.44, FTR 4/5.8.44, crashed at Notre Dame de Livaye, France

LJ921 10 MU 29.2.44, 6 MU 22.4.44, 620 Sqn 9.5.44, 23 MU 7.6.44, SOC 5.6.47

LJ922 10 MU 28.2.44, Shorts Swindon 20.4.44, 7T-E/196 Sqn 19.5.44, 570 Sqn 3.12.44, Rivenhall 5.12.44, 8Z-F, I/295 Sqn 21.12.44, 23 MU 21.1.45, SOC 5.6.47

LJ923 10 MU 31.3.44, 6 MU 23.4.44, ZO-D/196 Sqn 7.5.44, FA 21.4.45 at B108 landing in crosswind, swung and u/c damage in hollow area of airfield, SOC 3.5.45, BBOC 14.1.46, 23 MU 19.1.46, SOC 5.6.47

LJ924 6 MU 29.2.44, ZO-W/196 Sqn 25.4.44, RIW Sebro 10.6.44 after battle damage, 23 MU 6.11.44, gale damage 21.9.45, Short & Harland 26.9.45, 23 MU 8.1.46, SOC 5.6.47

LJ925 10 MU 29.2.44, Shorts 14.4.44, ZO-J/196 Sqn 19.5.44, FTR 26.2.45 from SOE op to Norway, crashed in Holen Lake, Arendal, Norway

LJ926 6 MU Woburn 9.3.44, 299 Sqn 1.5.44, 196 Sqn 7.7.44, FA 22.9.44, ZO-L,7T-G/196 Sqn 21.10.44, FA 1.3.45, starboard u/c fractured in bouncy landing, ZO-K/196 Sqn 7.3.45, 23 MU 27.2.46, Cat E 29.5.46

LJ927 6 MU 15.4.44, 190 Sqn 27.4.44, battle damage 6.6.44, 620 Sqn 22.7.44, GA 13.3.45 taxied into by LJ935, 620 Sqn 14.4.45, 23 MU 9.7.45, gale damage 21.9.45, ROS, Short & Harland 26.9.45, 23 MU 1.1.46, SOC 5.6.47

LJ928 6 MU 6.3.44, ZO-L/196 Sqn 29.4.44, FTR 21.9.44 from *Market V*, crashed 1/4 mile from Heveadorp, total wreck, seven killed, one POW

LJ929 'S.T.IV', 10 MU 8.3.44, Shorts Swindon 27.4.44, 6 MU 27.5.44, V8-E,X/570 Sqn 2.7.44, GA 25.8.44 hit by LJ985 whilst parked, 570 Sqn 4.10.44, 8E-T/295 Sqn 10.12.44, 23 MU 18.2.46, SOC 5.6.47

LJ930 10 MU 9.3.44, 6 MU 30.4.44, QS-A/620 Sqn 21.5.44, battle damage 24.9.44, 620 Sqn 12.10.44, A/190 Sqn 21.12.44, EFA 20.4.45, took off with flat tailwheel tyre, flying low tail unit caught fire and aircraft fell out of control after turret broke away, crashed at Woodlands Lane, Berks

LJ931 10 MU 9.3.44, Shorts 22.4.44, 10 MU 24.5.44, 6 MU 6.5.44, 8E-O/295 Sqn 13.7.44, FA 5.8.44 landed u/c only partly down after engine trouble, RIW Sebro 16.8.44, 6 MU 13.12.44, ZO-J/196 Sqn 6.3.45, FA 13.4.45, swung on take-off and u/c collapsed, RIW Sebro 14.5.45, 23 MU 10.11.45, 7T-D/196 Sqn 3.12.45, 273 MU 28.3.46, SOC 3.3.47

LJ932 10 MU 8.5.44, NF-W/138 Sqn 20.6.44, EFB 29.9.44 damaged by fighter on SOE op to Denmark and crash-landed Ludford Magna

LJ933 10 MU 11.3.44, Shorts Swindon 19.5.44, 190 Sqn 14.6.44, battle damage 24.9.44, ROS Sebro 27.9.44, V/190 Sqn 30.9.44, 23 MU 31.5.45, SOC 5.6.47

LJ934 10 MU 15.3.44, Shorts Swindon 20.4.44, 190 Sqn, battle damage 24.9.44, Y/190 Sqn 6.10.44, 23 MU 31.5.45, SOC 5.6.47

LJ935 6 MU 13.4.44, 620 Sqn 9.5.44, 23 NU 9.7.45, 1665 CU 28.11.45, GA 30.12.45 u/c collapsed whilst taxying at Linton-on-Ouse, SOC 10.1.46

LJ936 10 MU 17.3.44, Swindon 20.4.44, 5G-N/190 Sqn 21.5.44, 23 MU 25.5.45, SOC 5.6.47

LJ937 6 MU Woburn 23.3.44, ZO-K/196 Sqn 18.4.44, 10 MU 11.1.45, 190 Sqn, FA 23.5.45, 23 MU 12.3.46, SOC 5.6.47

LJ938 (SD/Tropical) 10 MU 10.5.44, 4 OAPU 28.5.44, 2 OADU 29.6.44, to ME 4.7.44, D/624 Sqn, GA 23.12.44 at 144 MU collided with Walrus Z1761 taxying, left ME 20.2.45, arrived St Mawgan 23.4.45 to 10 MU, SOC 25.7.46

LJ939 6 MU Woburn 21.3.44, A/196 Sqn 17.5.44, FTR 19.9.44 from *Market III*, shot down by AA fire and crashed near Schaarsbergen, near Arnhem

LJ940 (SD) 6 MU Woburn 23.3.44, FA 19.3.44, Short & Harland, 6 MU Woburn 4.4.44, X9-B/299 Sqn 14.5.44, FTR 14/15.8.44 from SOE op, crashed at Mereau, France

LJ941 (SD/Tropical) 10 MU 7.5.44, 4 OAPU 31.5.44, St Mawgan 19.6.44, to MAAF 21.6.44, B/624 Sqn, returned via St Mawgan to 10 MU 2.3.45, SOC 25.9.46

LJ942 6 MU 23.3.44, 5G-X, X9-I/299 Sqn 14.5.44, fuselage damaged during maintenance 18.7.44, FTR 2/3.4.45 from SOE op, crashed at Roskilde Fjord, Frederikssund, Denmark

LJ943 6 MU Woburn 23.3.44, 190 Sqn 27.4.44, FTR 21.9.44 from *Market V*, crashed near Zetten, hit by flak and on fire in the air, two baled out from 400ft, rest killed in crash

LJ944 6 MU Woburn 27.3.44, ZO-H/196 Sqn 25.4.44, 10 MU 2.6.44, V8-I/570 Sqn 8.7.44, EFB 19.9.44 on *Market III*, belly landed, Ghent airfield, Belgium

LJ945 6 MU 23.3.44, ZO-F/196 Sqn 18.4.44, serious battle damage 20.9.44 on *Market IV*, 23 MU 3.3.45, SOC 5.6.47

LJ946 10 MU 24.3.44, Shorts 14.4.44, 620 Sqn 17.5.44, FTR 21.9.44 from *Market V*, set on fire by flak and crashed near Bennekom, crew baled out

LJ947 10 MU 31.3.44, 6 MU 25.4.44, 7T-Z,ZO-S/196 Sqn 9.5.44, EFB 20.9.44 on *Market IV*, flak damage to port engines, crash landed at Alost, Belgium

LJ948 10 MU 31.3.44, 6 MU 3.5.44, X9-W/299 Sqn 17.5.44, 570 Sqn 3.12.44, 295 Sqn 21.12.44, 620 Sqn 8.2.45, 23 MU 9.7.47, gale damage 21.9.45, ROS, SOC 5.6.47

LJ949 6 MU for Ovesley 31.3.44, 7T-U,ZO-U/196 Sqn 19.5.44, FTR 23.9.44 from *Market VII*, damaged by flak then forced landed in friendly territory 2–3 miles south of Eindhoven, two injured

LJ950 6 MU 31.3.44, 10 MU 2.6.44, 6 MU 6.6.44, 8Z-U/295 Sqn 9.7.44, FTR 26/27.4.45 from SOE op, hit sea off Denmark 55°54N/08°15E in steep turn at 0015 hrs in moonlight and crashed, near Tipperne

LJ951 10 MU 31.3.44, 6 MU 14.5.44, 10 MU 2.6.44, 6 MU 6.6.44, 8E-C,R,W/295 Sqn 2.7.44, 23 MU 11.2.46, SOC 5.6.47

LJ952 6 MU 26.4.44, QS-Y/620 Sqn 17.5.44, 23 MU 26.4.45, became 5247M 12.5.45, SOC 12.3.46

LJ953 (SD/Tropical) 10 MU 10.5.44, 4 OAPU 31.5.44, MAAF 24.6.44 via St Mawgan, 624 Sqn, returned to 10 MU 9.3.45, SOC 27.6.46,

LJ954 6 MU 26.4.44, 7T-X/196 Sqn 17.5.44, GA 7.6.44 hit by tractor, 196 Sqn 1.7.44, FTR 20.9.44 from *Market IV*, crash landed near Brussels with flak damage

LJ955 6 MU 28.4.44, 5G-Z/299 Sqn 14.5.44, battle damage 21.9.44, X9-K/299 Sqn 24.10.44, 23 MU 20.7.45, SOC 5.6.47

LJ956 6 MU 3.5.44, 5G-Q, X9-D/299 Sqn 17.5.44, 23 MU 24.5.45, Shorts 30.11.45, SOC 14.1.46

LJ969 10 MU 8.5.44, 4 OAPU 25.5.44, St Mawgan 19.6.44, to MAAF/ME 21.6.44, 624 Sqn, SOC 31.8.44

LJ970 6 MU 30.4.44, QS-S/620 Sqn 18.5.44, FIR 28/29.12.44 from SOE op to Norway, crashed at Sande-in-Vestfold, Norway

LJ971 6 MU 8.44, X9-X,U/299 Sqn 19.5.44, 23 MU 29.1.46, SOC 5.6.47

LJ972 10 MU 15.5.44, 4 OAPU 4.6.44, 2 OADU 24.6.44, to MW 9.7.44, S/624 Sqn, returned to 10 MU via St Mawgan 8.4.45, RTP 11.11.46

LJ973 6 MU 3.5.44, 620 Sqn 11.6.44, 23 MU 9.7.45, SOC 5.6.47

LJ974 (SD/Tropical) 10 MU 24.5.44, 4 OAPU 31.5.44, St Mawgan 21.6.44, MAAF 3.6.44, Q/624 Sqn, EFB 7.8.44

LJ975 6 MU 8.5.44, 10 MU 2.6.44, 6 MU 570 Sqn 28.7.44, 8Z-D/295 Sqn 3.8.44, 13.7.44, 23 MU 25.1.46, SOC 5.6.47

LJ976 6 MU 6.5.44, 8Z-O,8E-Q/295 Sqn, 23 MU 25.1.46, SOC 5.6.47

LJ977 10 MU 20.5.44, 6 MU 16.6.44, V8-B/570 Sqn 10.8.44, battle damage 24.9.44, 570 Sqn 18.10.44, 8Z-G/295 Sqn 10.12.44, 620 Sqn 8.2.45, 196 Sqn 14.6.45, 23 MU 25.2.46, SOC 5.6.47

LJ978 6 MU 20.5.44, 4 OAPU 4.6.44, St Mawgan 21.6.44, MAAF 23.6.44, 624 Sqn, SOC 31.8.44

LJ979 6 M 10.5.44, Handling Squadron ECFS 11.6.44, 6 MU 24.7.44, ZO-U,7T-F/196 Sqn 27.9.44, EFB 24.3.45, flak damage, forced landed at Overloon, Netherlands

LJ980 6 MU 10.5.44, 620 Sqn 11.6.44, 570 Sqn 10.8.44, battle damage 21.9.44, 570 Sqn 2.11.44, 8Z-F/295 Sqn 14.6.45, 158 Sqn 27.11.45, 23 MU 16.1.46, SOC 5.6.47

LJ981 (SD/Tropical) 10 MU 24.5.44, 4 OAPU 4.6.44, St Mawgan 21.6.44, MAAF 23.6.44, returned to 10 MU via St Mawgan 10.1.45, ROS Sebro 7.2.45, 10 MU 27.2.45, SOC 14.8.46

LJ982 10 MU 15.5.44, 10 MU 2.6.44, 6 MU 6.6.44, 190 Sqn 11.6.44, FTR 21.9.44 from *Market V*, believed crashed near Zetten, Netherlands, details uncertain

LJ983 10 MU 20.5.44, 6 MU 25.6.44, 620 Sqn 27.9.44, 23 MU 9.7.44, SOC 5.6.47

LJ984 10 MU 20.5.44, 4 OAPU 2.6.44, to MAAF 24.6.44, EFB 18.8.44, crashed 5 miles W of Reghaia, North Africa, after SOE op to Quincaille in Vichy France

LJ985 6 MU 18.5.44, 10 MU 4.6.44, 6 MU 6.6.44, V8-W 30.6.44, GA 25.8.44, hit LJ929 taxying, 570 Sqn, 23 MU 4.1.45, SOC 5.6.47

LJ986 6 MU 15.5.44, 10 MU 4.6.44, 6 MU 6.6.44, 8Z-Y/295 Sqn 2.7.44, battle damage 25.9.44, 295 Sqn 13.11.44, EFB 1.1.45 destroyed on ground by enemy strafing at Ghent

LJ987 (SD/Tropical) 10 MU 24.5.44, 4 OAPU 4.6.44, 2 OADU 26.6.44, MAAF 4.7.44, X/624 Sqn, returned to 10 MU via St Mawgan 14.2.45, scrap 14.10.46

LJ988 6 MU 15.5.44, ZO-T/196 Sqn 28.5.44, FTR 20.9.44 from *Market IV*, crashed 6 miles west of Arnhem on edge of a boating lake, near Heteren, seven killed

LJ989 CRD R Malcolm of White Waltham 16.5.44, AFEE Beaulieu 18.3.45, used for glider snatch/pick-up cable trials, CRD Malcolm 18.1.46, SOC 19.6.46

LJ990 (SD) 10 MU 28.5.44, NF-O/138 Sqn 11.6.44, 38 Gp 10.3.45, 23 MU 20.7.45, SOC 5.6.47

LJ991 10 MU 18.5.44, 6 MU 1.7.44, E7-W/570 Sqn 10.8.44, FTR 23.9.44 from *Market VII*, crashed at 51°57N/05°46E, hit by AA fire, four killed

LJ992 10 MU 24.5.44, 6 MU 3.6.44, E7-K/570 Sqn 3.9.44, battle damage 19.9.44, 570 Sqn 16.10.44, FA 21.11.44 overshot Rivenhall u/c damaged, V8-N/570 Sqn 20.2.45, FA 4.5.45, ROS, 570 Sqn 15.6.45, 23 MU 22.6.45, SOC 5.6.47

LJ993 (SD) 10 MU 31.5.44, NF-M/138 Sqn 16.6.44, FTR 9.11.44 from SOE op to Norway

LJ994 10 MU 24.5.44, Shorts Swindon 30.5.44, 6 MU 9.6.44, E7-L/570 Sqn 19.7.44, 23 MU 4.1.45, SOC 5.6.47

LJ995 10 MU 20.5.44, 6 MU 26.6.44, 8Z-H/295 Sqn 1.8.44, EFB 4.2.45, swung taking off from Rivenhall, lost height, hit tree, exploded at Lamblas Green, Essex

LJ996 (SD) 10 MU 31.5.44, 6 MU 26.6.44, E7-X/570 Sqn 3.9.44, FB 23.9.44 crash landed at Ghent, 570 Sqn 26.10.44, 5G-W,X9-N/299 Sqn 12.4.44, 6 MU 26.6.44, E7-X/570 Sqn 3.9.44, FB 23.9.44 crash landed at Ghent, 570 Sqn 26.10.44, 5G-W, X9-N/299 Sqn 10.12.44, FTR 2/3.3.45 from SOE op to Norway

LJ997 10 MU 24.5.44, 6 MU 26.8.44, T/190 Sqn 22.9.44, EFA 24.3.45, crashed taking off from Dunmow with glider in tow, swung, u/c collapsed SOC 29.3.45

LJ998 10 MU 24.5.44, 6 MU 10.7.44, 7T-G,O/196 Sqn 27.9.44, battle damage 30/31.3.45, ROS, 196 Sqn 27.4.45, 23 MU 19.2.46, SOC 5.6.47

LJ999 (SD) 10 MU 10.6.44, Short & Harland 9.6.44, NF-Q/138 Sqn 20.6.44, FTR 5/6.3.45 from SOE op to Denmark, crashed in Ringkobing Fjord

LK114 10 MU 25.5.44, AFTDU 19.6.44, TCDU Brize Norton 21.3.46, 238 OCU Polebrook 26.4.46, SOC 16.10.47

LK115 6 MU 31.5.44, 8Z-M/295 Sqn 23.8.44, FTR 21.9.44 from *Market V*, force-landed, two engines burning, near Ede, Netherlands, crew became POWs

LK116 6 MU 10.6.44, 620 Sqn 15.8.44, battle damage 21.9.44, 620 Sqn 5.10.44, EFB 20/21.3.45, shot down near Great Dunmow by intruder after return from SOE drop over Norway

LK117 10 MU 28.5.44, 6 MU 2.6.44, V8-F/570 Sqn 9.7.44, battle damage led to RIW Sebro 24.9.44, 23 MU 24.2.45, 190 Sqn 18.3.45, 620 Sqn, 7T-B/196 Sqn 31.5.45, 23 MU 19.3.46, SOC 5.6.47

LK118 10 MU 31.5.44, 6 MU 8.6.44, 5G-U/299 Sqn 29.8.44, FA 15.11.44 Keevil, tailwheel damage, X9-C/299 Sqn 22.11.44, 242 Sqn 23.9.45, FA 9.10.45 hit by LK152 landing at Stoney Cross, Cat E 14.1.46

LK119 (SD) 10 MU 28.6.44, FA 6.7.44 Hullavington, heavy landing caused mainplane damage, 10 MU, NF-R/138 Sqn 17.7.44, MA-Y/161 Sqn, FTR 30/31.3.45 from SOE op Norway, shot down by fighter at Hegland-in-Holt, Norway

LK120 10 MU 27.5.44, 6 MU 3.6.44, 570 Sqn 19.7.44, 8Z-W,8E-W/295 Sqn 3.8.44, FA Woodbridge 27.8.45, tyre burst in flight and belly landed, SOC 22.1.46

LK121 6 MU 20.6.44, V8-H/570 Sqn 28.8.44, FTR 18.9.44, hit by AA fire at Overflakkee, crash landed after releasing Horsa at Opheusden, Netherlands, and all killed

LK122 6 MU 10.6.44, V8-R/570 Sqn 23.8.44, 8E-D,8Z-F/295 Sqn 10.12.44, FA 1.6.45, port tyre burst during landing at B58 Brussels, 151 RU 31.1.46, 3 BRU 11.3.46, SOC 21.6.47

LK123 6 MU 8.6.44, 620 Sqn 15.8.44, FA 2.6.44, 620 Sqn GA 31.5.45, hit LJ566 when taxiying, 151 RU 31.1.46, SOC 21.6.47

LK124 6 MU 31.5.44, X9-B,5G-B/299 Sqn 25.8.44, 23 MU 12.3.46, SOC 5.6.47

LK125 10 MU 10.6.44, NF-S/138 Sqn 20.6.44, 38 Gp 10.3.45, 23 MU 29.3.45, SOC 5.6.47

LK126 10 MU 31.5.44, 6 MU 9.6.44, V8-C/570 Sqn 9.7.44, battle damage 20.9.44, RIW Sebro 27.9.44, 570 Sqn 8.10.44, 196 Sqn 3.12.44, EFB 21/22.2.45 attacked by intruder when landing at Shepherd's Grove, back from Rees

LK127 6 MU 31.5.44, QS-O/620 Sqn 15.8.44, 20.9.44 from *Market IV*, fate uncertain, officially listed as crashing 'near Heteren, Netherlands', possible that wreckage recovered in 1964 by RNethAF in the area came from LK127

LK128 6 MU 7.6.44, 8Z-S/295 Sqn 9.7.44, battle damage 24.9.44 and SOC 30.10.44, BBOC, RIW Sebro 9.11.44, 7T-M/196 Sqn 5.3.45, CA 14.10.45 when taxiying at Coltishall, ROS, 23 MU 16.2.46, SOC 5.6.47

LK129 6 MU 20.6.44, 8Z-B/295 Sqn 14.8.44, GA 13.4.45, taxied into by LJ616, 295 Sqn 23.4.45, 23 MU 25.1.46, SOC 5.6.47

LK130 6 MU 8.6.44, 5G-H/299 Sqn 25.8.44, 196 Sqn 9.44, 23 MU 20.7.45, SOC 5.6.47

LK131 10 MU 12.6.44, NF-T/138 Sqn 20.6.44, EFB 1.9.44, crashed at Gilze-Rijen during SOE op

LK132 6 MU 8.6.44, 8E-A,8Z-N/295 Sqn 23.8.44, FA 18.4.45, overshot at B108 Rheine, Germany, into bomb crater and starboard u/c stuck in soft ground, PSO 21.6.47

LK133 6 MU 8.6.44, V8-J/570 Sqn 19.7.44, FM 28/29.7.44 from SOE op, crashed at Orleans, France

LK134 6 MU 8.6.44, 8Z-F/295 Sqn 23.8.44, 620 Sqn 11.1.45, 196 Sqn 31.5.45, 242 Sqn 29.9.45, 46 Sqn 28.11.45, 23 MU 30.1.46, SOC 5.6.47

LK135 6 MU 16.6.44, 5G-N,X9-A, U/299 Sqn 3.9.44, 23 MU 29.1.46, SOC 5.6.47

LK136 6 MU 10.6.44, V8-Y/570 Sqn 23.8.4, battle damage 20.9.44, 570 Sqn 30.9.44, 8E-V/295 Sqn 10.12.44, 23 MU 4.1.46, SOC 5.6.47

LK137 6 MU 20.6.44, 8E-J/25.8.44, battle damage 19.9.44, ROS Sebro 27.9.44, 295 Sqn 30.9.44, FTR 24.3.45, hit by AA fire during Rhine Crossing, crashed at Kervenheim, Germany

LK138 6 MU 20.6.44, V8-Q/28.8.44, battle damage 21.9.44, 570 Sqn 30.9.44, 23 MU 4.1.45, SOC 5.6.47

LK139 (SD) 10 MU 25.6.44, NF-A/138 Sqn 12.7.44, 38 Gp 10.3.45, 23 MU 9.7.45, SOC 5.6.47

LK140 6 MU 21.6.44, V8-E/570 Sqn 28.8.44, 8E-B, 8Z-O/295 Sqn 10.12.44, 23 MU 19.4.45, SOC 5.6.47

LK141 6 MU 21.6.44, 8E-N,K/295 Sqn 28.8.44, battle damage 19.9.44, 295 Sqn 14.10.44, 23 MU 9.1.46, SOC 5.6.47

LK142 6 MU 25.6.44, 7T-A/196 Sqn 3.9.44, FTR 24/25.9.44, crashed near Spincourt during SOE drop to French

LK143 10 MU 25.6.44, NF-B/138 Sqn 15.7.44, FTR 3.12.44 from SOE run to Denmark, crashed at sea

LK144 6 MU 26.6.44, 8E-Q,M/295 Sqn 10.8.44, battle damage 19.9.44, 295 Sqn 11.10.44, 23 MU 19.4.45, SOC 5.6.47

LK145 10 MU, 26.6.44, NF-C/138 Sqn 8.7.44, 38 Gp 10.3.45, 23 MU 29.3.45, SOC 5.6.47

LK146 6 MU 20.6.44, 7T-B/196 Sqn 3.9.44, battle damage 30/31.3.45, 196 Sqn 28.4.45, 23 MU 11.2.46, SOC 5.6.47

LK147 6 MU 28.6.44, ZO-Z/196 Sqn 23.9.44, battle damage 23.9.44, ZO-Q/196 Sqn 28.10.44, EFA 10.5.45, loss of control in bad visibility, broke cloud too low like LJ899 and LK297 when approaching Gardermoen, Norway, stalled and crashed 2 miles SW of airfield

LK148 6 MU 28.6.44, 299 Sqn 22.9.44, 242 Sqn 29.9.45, 51 Sqn 27.11.45, 23 MU 14.1.46, SOC 5.6.47

LK149 (SD/Tropical) 10 MU 30.6.44, NF-D/138 Sqn 24.7.44, FTR 23/24.2.45 from SOE drop Denmark, crashed at sea

LK150 6 MU 28.6.44, V8-H/22.9.44, FA 31.10.45, 570 Sqn 18.1.46, SOC 5.6.47

LK151 (SD/Tropical) 10 MU 9.7.44, NF-E/138 Sqn 22.7.44, FTR 27.11.44, shot down by fighter during SOE op to Denmark, crashed in Little Belt, near Assens, Denmark

LK152 6 MU 26.6.44, 7T-D/196 Sqn 27.8.44, 242 Sqn 23.9.44, EFA 9.10.45, hit LK118 when landing on runway at Stoney Cross, SOC 11.1.46

LK153 6 MU 28.6.44, X9-X/299 Sqn 15.8.44, FA 29.4.45, overshot at Colerne, 5G-O/299 Sqn 17.5.45, EFA 29.6.45, wing dropped just after take-off, throttled back, aircraft crashed 1/2 mile south of Shepherd's Grove

LK154 6 MU 28.6.44, V8-P/570 Sqn 22.9.44, 23 MU 9.1.45, SOC 5.6.47

LK155 (SD/Tropical) 10 MU 30.6.44, 4 OAPU, 2 OADU 25.7.44, 11 Ferry Unit, to MAAF 30.7.44, 144 MU, returned to Melton Mowbray 27.11.44, Sebro 5.12.44, 10 MU 8.1.45, 23 MU 12.10.45, SOC 5.6.47

LK156 6 MU 30.6.44, V8-I,N/570 Sqn 22.9.44, 299 Sqn 9.1.46, 23 MU 19.3.46, SOC 5.6.47

LK169 (SD/Tropical) 10 MU 7.7.44, 4 OAPU 4.8.44, MAAF 24.8.44, returned to St Mawgan 14.2.45, SOC obsolete 27.6.46

LK170 6 MU 30.6.44, 8E-P/295 Sqn 3.9.44, FTR 19.9.44 from *Market III*, crashed between Brugge and Eede on Dutch/Belgian border, no survivors

LK171 6 MU 9.7.44, 295 Sqn 1.8.44, battle damage 19.9.44, 295 Sqn 5.10.44, ETR 3.11.44 from SOE drop, crashed due to icing, Skarfjell, near Vinkelvaan and Rjukan, Norway

LK172 (SD/Tropical) 10 MU 30.6.44, 4 OAPU 16.7.44, 2 OADU 21.7.44, MW 23.7.44, 624 Sqn, returned St Mawgan 20.1.45, 10 MU 20.1.45, SOC 14.8.46

LK173 (SD/Tropical) 10 MU 30.6.44, 4 OAPU 24.7.44, 2 OADU 26.7.44, MAAF 1.9.44, returned to St Mawgan for 10 MU 20.2.45, SOC 25.7.46

LK174 (SD/Tropical) 10 MU 5.7.44, 4 OAPU 2.8.44, MAAF 21.8.44, returned to St Mawgan for 10 MU 28.3.45, SOC 25.9.46

LK175 (SD/Tropical) 10 MU 6.7.44, 4 OAPU 21.7.44, MAAF 30.7.44, 144 MU, Melton Mowbray 21.11.44, 23 MU 26.11.44, 10 MU 5.1.45, 23 MU 24.1.45, 10 MU, RTP and scrapped 14.10.46

LK176 10 MU 6.7.44, 4 OAPU 29.7.44, MAAF 27.8.44, 148 Sqn, returned to 10 MU via St Mawgan 20.1.45, SOC 20.8.46

LK177 10 MU 7.7.44, 4 OAPU 14.7.44, 2 OADU 21.7.44, MAAF 23.7.44, 624 Sqn, EEB 9.8.44, u/c damaged on take off at Blida, belly landed, SOC 31.8.44

LK178 10 MU 30.6.44, 4 OAPU 14.7.44, 2 OADU 25.7.44, MAAF 27.7.44, EFB 18.8.44, crashed at Beni Mered, Algeria, after ops Vichy France, fuel short, misty conditions

LK179 10 MU 6.7.44, 4 OAPU 19.7.44, MAAF 31.7.44, 624 Sqn, returned to 10 MU via St Mawgan 30.12.44, 23 MU 1.12.45, SOC 5.6.47

LK180 (SD/Tropical) 10 MU 7.7.44, 4 OAPU 21.7.44, 2 OAPU 26.7.44, MAAF 28.7.44, 624 Sqn, returned to 10 MU via St Mawgan 15.3.45, SOC 30.10.46

LK181 (SD/Tropical) 10 MU 5.7.44, 4 OAPU 14.7.44, 2 OADU 23.7.44, MAM 24.7.44, 624 Sqn, 148 Sqn, EFA 18.11.44, swung taking off from Brindisi, u/c collapsed

LK182 (SD/Tropical) 10 MU 9.7.44, 4 OAPU 19.7.44, MAAF 30.7.44, 624 Sqn, EFB 7.8.44 crashed taking off from Blida for southern France

LK183 (SD/Tropical) 10 MU 10.7.44, 4 OAPU 4.8.44, 144 MU, 12 FU 12.12.44, MAAF 25.8.44, 10 MU 21.12.44 SOC 20.8.46

LK184 (SD/Tropical) 10 MU 6.7.44, 4 OAPU 19.7.44, 2 OADU 25.7.44, MAAF 27.7.44, 624 Sqn, returned to 10 MU via St Mawgan 20.1.45, 23 MU 9.11.45, SOC 5.6.47

LK185 (SD/Tropical) 10 MU 27.7.44, 2 OADU 4.8.44, MAAF 21.8.44, 624 Sqn, returned to 10 MU via St Mawgan 20.1.45, scrap 9.10.46

LK186 (SD/Tropical) 10 MU 10.7.44, 4 OADU 24.7.44, 2 OADU 26.7.44, MAAF 17.8.44, returned to 10 MU via St Mawgan 31.12.44, 23 MU 17.10.45, SOC 5.6.47

LK187 (SD/Tropical) 10 MU 10.7.44, 2 OAPU 28.7.44, MAAF 16.8.44, 624 Sqn, EFA 13.9.44, crashed in sea 5 miles off Castiglione

LK188 (SD/Tropical) 10 MU 13.7.44, 2 OAPU 26.7.44, MAAF 17.8.44, returned to 10 MU via St Mawgan 31.3.45, SOC 2.10.46

LK189 (SD/Tropical) 10 MU 21.7.44, 4 OAPU 4.8.44, 2 OADU 28.8.44, MAAF 30.8.44, 148 Sqn, returned to 10 MU via St Mawgan 25.1.45, 23 MU 7.12.45, SOC 20.8.46

LK190 6 MU 23.7.44, V8-J/299 Sqn 15.8.44, 570 Sqn 15.8.44, battle damage 20.9.44, 570 Sqn 4.10.44, GA 18.1.45, taxied into LK543, ROS , 570 Sqn 3.2.45,23 MU 16.1.45, SOC 5.6.47

LK191 6 MU 31.7.44, V8-G/570 Sqn 22.9.44, FTR23.9.44 from *Market VII*, crashed in flames near Andelst south-west of Arnhem

LK192 (SD) 10 MU 29.7.44, NF-F/138 Sqn 13.8.44,38 Gp 10.3.45, 23 MU 20.3.45, SOC 5.6.47

LK193 6 MU 27.7.44, ZO-V/196 Sqn 22.9.44, FTR 2/3.4.45 crashed in sea low-flying off Cromer during SOE sortie

LK194 10 MU 1.8.44, NF-G/138 Sqn 10.8.44, 38 Gp 10.3.45, 23 MU 9.7.45, SOC 5.6.47

LK195 6 MU 27.7.44, A/190 Sqn 25.9.44, FTR 6/7.11.44 from SOE sortie, crashed at Enkhuizen, Netherlands

LK196 6 MU 30.7.44, B/190 Sqn 22.9.44, FA 4.5.45, swung on take-off, u/c collapsed, Cat E 1.6.45

LK197 6 MU 30.7.44, 196 Sqn 25.9.44, FTR 30/31.3.45 from SOE sortie to Norway

LK198 10 MU 31.7.44, NF-H/7.8.44, F7R 9.11.44, crashed at sea

LK199 6 MU 30.7.44, V8-L/570 Sqn 31.8.44, 27 MU 18.2.44, SOC 5.6.47

LK200 10 MU 31.7.44, NF-J/138 Sqn 10.8.44, FTR9.9.44, crashed on Texel

LK201 6 MU 31.7.44, ZO-L/196 Sqn 22.9.44, FA 19.4.44, 7T-I/196 Sqn 31.5.45, FA 18.4.45 tailwheel collapsed when landing at B58, 23 MU 30.1.46, SOC 5.6.47

LK202 6 MU 30.7.44, 8E-P/295 Sqn 22.9.44, E7-X/570 Sqn 10 12.44, EFA 18.4.45, pilot's seat slipped during take-off, u/c collapsed during avoidance action, at B58

LK203 6 MU 2.8.44, 295 Sqn 22.9.44, V8-E/570 Sqn 10.12.44, EFA 9.3.45 crash landed Rivenhall

LK204 10 MU 6.8.44, NF-U/138 Sqn 16.8.44, 38 Gp 10.3.45, 23 MU 29.3.45, SOC 5.6.47

LK205 6 MU 3.8.44, ZO-B,D/196 Sqn 25.9.44, 23 MU 25.2.46, SOC 5.6.47

LK206 10 MU 7.8.44, 138 Sqn 24.8.44, MA-U/161 Sqn 5.9.44, FA u/c collapsed on landing, ROS 27.9.44, 161 Sqn 26.10.44, 38 Gp 10.3.45, 23 MU 9.7.45, SOC 5.6.47

LK207 10 MU 5.8.44, 138 Sqn 24.8.44, MA-W/161 Sqn 5.9.44, EFA 19.10.44 crashed east of Potton eleven minutes after take-off, broke up in air, burnt out

LK208 10 MU 3.8.44, 138 Sqn 17.8.44, MA-X/161 Sqn 5.9.44, EFB, 21.9.44 swung on take-off Tempsford for SOE sortie

LK209 10 MU 7.8.44, 138 Sqn 19.8.44, MA-T/161 Sqn 5.9 44, FA 27.11.44, 161 Sqn 7.1.45, FTR 22/23/3.45 from SOE drop to Netherlands, shot down at Vlieland

LK210 10 MU 20.8.44, 138 Sqn 30.8.44, MA-U/161 Sqn 5.9.44, GA 22.9.44, wing tip damaged taxying at Tangmere, 161 Sqn 3.10.44, 38 Gp 9.3.45, 23 MU 30.7.45, SOC 5.6.47

LK211 10 MU 7.8.44, 4 OAPU 30.8.44, 303 FTU, 2 OADU 20.9.44, MAAF 22.9.44, returned to UK via St Mawgan 18.12.44, 10 MU 20.1.45, SOC 2.10.46

LK226 (SD/Tropical) 10 MU 18.8.44, 4 OAPU 31.8.44, MAAF 17.9.44, returned UK, Melton Mowbray 26.11.44, 10 MU 17.2.45, 299 Sqn, 23 MU 25.1.46, 10 MU, SOC 25.7.46

LK227 10 MU 20.8.44, 4 OAPU 3.9.44, 2 OADU 18.9.44, MAAF 19.9.44, returned UK, St Mawgan, 10 MU 31.12.44, SOC 25.7.46

LK228 (SD/Tropical) 10 MU 23.8.44, 4 OAPU Melton Mowbray 11.9.44, 10 MU 30.10.44, 23 MU 15.7.45, SOC 5.6.47

LK229 10 MU 18.8.44, 4 OAPU 4.9.44, 2 OADU 19.9.44, MAAF 20.9.44, Rabat, St Mawgan 17.1.45, 10 MU 10.2.45, SOC 20.11.46

LK230 (SD/Tropical) 10 MU 23.8.44, 4 OAPU 8.9.44, MAAF 27.9.44, 144 MU, returned UK, FA 4.1.45, ROS, Christchurch, 10 MU 17.3.45, SOC 16.9.46

LK231 (SD/Tropical) 10 MU 18.8.44, 4 OAPU 8.9.44, 2 OADU 18.9.44, MAAF 19.9.44, St Mawgan, 10 MU 24.4.45, 23 MU 5.6.45, SOC 5.6.47

LK232 (SD/Tropical) 10 MU 30.8.44, NF-K/138 Sqn 9.9.44, FA 1.1.45, RIW Sebro 16.3.45, 23 MU 12.7.45, X9-G/299 Sqn 5.11.45, 23 M 18.3.46, SOC 5.6.47

LK233 (SD/Tropical) 10 MU 23.8.44, 4 OAPU 11.9.44, 10 MU 4.7.45, 23 MU 21.8.45, SOC 5.6.47

LK234 (SD/Tropical) 10 MU 23.8.44, 4 OAPU 27.9.44, 10 MU 4.7.45, SOC 27.6.46

LK235 (SD/Tropical) 10 MU 28.8.44, 138 Sqn 11.9.44, 4 OAPU 14.9.44, 2 OADU 23.9.44, MAAF 26.9.44, St Mawgan 25.1.45, 10 MU 24.2.45, SOC 27.6.46

LK236 (SD/Tropical) 10 MU 28.8.44, 138 Sqn 14.9.44, MA-Y/161 Sqn 11.9.44, EFA 14.2.45, unauthorised practice combat with P-51, both crashed and burnt out at Sandy Heath, seven killed

LK237 (SD) 10 MU 31.8.44, 138 Sqn 30.9.44, MA-Z/161 Sqn 28.9.44, 38 Gp 9.3.45, 23 MU 12.7.45, SOC 5.6.47

LK238 (SD) 10 MU 28.8.44, 138 Sqn 29.9.44, MA-Y/161 Sqn 28.9.44, FTR 6.10.44

LK239 6 MU 30.8.44, YP-C,5G-P/299 Sqn 22.9.44, 23 MU 29.1.46, SOC 5.6.47

LK240 (SD/Tropical) 10 MU 30.8.44, 4 OAPU 14.9.44, 2 OADU 24.9.44, MAAF 27.9.44, 10 MU 29.12.44, 570 Sqn, 23 MU 25.1.46, SOC 14.10.46

LK241 299 Sqn, FTR 28.11.44 from SOE sortie to Norway, shot down at sea by fighter

LK242 196 Sqn, SOC 5.6.47

LK243 4 OAPU, SOC 5.6.47

LK244 190 Sqn, SOC 5.6.47

LK245 SOC 5.6.47

LK246 295 Sqn, SOC 5.6.47

LK247 SOC 5.6.47

LK248 4 OAPU, SOC 5.6.47

LK249 4 OAPU, MAAF, 17 FU, SOC 9.10.46

LK250 620 Sqn, 196 Sqn SOC 5.6.47

LK251 4 OAPU, SOC 5.6.47

LK252 4 OAPU, 2 OADU, MAAFO, 12 FU, 196 Sqn, SOC 31.7.46

LK253 4 OAPU, 620 Sqn, SOC 27.6.46

LK254 299 Sqn, SOC 5.6.47

LK255 4 OAPU, SOC 5.6.47

LK256 196 Sqn, SOC 22.1.46

LK257 SOC 5.6.47

LK270 23 MU 15.9.44, E7-W,Q/570 Sqn 28.9.44, GA 15.9.45 hit LK636 taxying Rivenhall, 23 MU 9.1.46, SOC 5.6.47

LK271 23 MU 21.9.44, 190 Sqn 28.9.44, gale damage 18.1.45, 190 Sqn 5.2.45, GA 9.5.45 tailwheel damaged, 190 Sqn 18.5.45, 620 Sqn 24.5.45, 8E-S/295 Sqn 14.6.45, 23 MU 25.1.46, SOC 5.6.47

LK272 (SD/Tropical) 10 MU 18.9.44, NF-P/138 Sqn 2.10.44, FTR 26/27.2.45

LK273 23 MU 21.9.44, E7-K/570 Sqn 28.9.44, FA 3.12.44 Rivenhall, landed on wrong runway, overshot, u/c collapsed, burnt out, SOC 6.3.45

LK274 (SD/Tropical) 10 MU 21.9.44, NF-N/138 Sqn 29.9.44, 38 Gp 10.3.45, 161 Sqn, 23 MU 12.7.45, SOC 5.6.47

LK275 190 Sqn 25.9.44, FA 1.1.45, fuel short, landed downwind at Bungay clipping tree on approach, collided on ground with another aircraft, RIW Sebro 21.2.45, 23 MU 3.7.45, SOC 5.6.47

LK276 23 MU 21.9.44, Y/190 Sqn 28.9.44, EFA 21.11.44 belly landed upwind near Great Dunmow at 2120 hrs

LK277 23 MU 21.9.44, E7-J,V8-O/ 570 Sqn 26.9.44, GA 21.2.45 tyre burst during change, RIW Sebro 19.3.45, 23 MU 21.7.45, SOC 5.6.47

LK278 (SD/Tropical) 10 MU 30.9.44, MA-X/4.10.44, 138 Sqn 6.3.45, 38 Gp 10.3.45, 23 MU 29.3.45, SOC 5.6.47

LK279 10 MU 2.10.44, NF-L/138 Sqn 6.10.44, FTR 10.2.45

LK280 23 MU 21.9.44, V8-G,F/570 Sqn 26.9.44, FA 13.4.45 brakes failed at Rivenhall and starboard u/c collapsed, RIW Sebro 2.5.45, 23 MU 20.10.45, 299 Sqn 2.12.45, SOC 5.12.45, BBOC 1.2.46, SOC 5.6.47

LK281 R/190 Sqn 28.9.44, 23 MU 17.5.45, SOC 5.6.47

LK282 5G-K,X9-K/299 Sqn 28.9.44, 23 MU 7.3.46, SOC 5.6.47

LK283 10 MU 7.10.44, 161 Sqn 28.10.44, NF-J/138 Sqn 29.10.44, FTR 31.12.44 from SOE sortie to Norway, crashed at sea

LK284 299 Sqn 28.9.44, 23 MU 29.1.46, SOC 5.6.47

LK285 10 MU 4.10.44, NF-T/138 Sqn 7.10.44, MA-S/161 Sqn 25.3.45, 23 MU 12.7.45, SOC 5.6.47

LK286 V8-T/570 Sqn 28.9.44, GA 3.12.44 port wing tip hit nose of LJ620, E7-T/570 Sqn 15.12.44, EFA 2.4.45 port tyre burst when landing at Rivenhall, u/c collapsed

LK287 8Z-C/295 Sqn 30.9.44, GA 5.12.44 when collided with LJ975, 295 Sqn 15.12.44, FA 19.7.45 at B58 Brussels, swung on take-off, PSOC 21.6.47

LK288 8Z-Y,C/295 Sqn 30.9.44, FA 20.11.44 tailwheel dragged during drift on take-off, 295 Sqn 1.12.44, GA 9.3.45 taxied into tractor at Rivenhall, 23 MU 9.1.46, SOC 5.6.47

LK289 V8-F,G/570 Sqn 30.9.44, FA 5.10.44, hit by LJ624 when landing, 295 Sqn 9.1.46, X9-L/196 Sqn 3.3.46, 23 MU 25.3.46, SOC 5.6.47

LK290 8Z-Z, 8E-Z/295 Sqn 28.9.44, 570 Sqn, FA 27.10.45 port tyre air burst, belly landed Woodbridge, RIW Sebro 3.12.45, Cat E 6.12.45

LK291 V8-A/570 Sqn 30.9.44, GA 14.2.45 hit trolley when taxying at Rivenhall, ROS, 570 Sqn, FA 19.12.45, port tyre burst on take-off, belly landed Woodbridge

LK292 295 Sqn 30.9.44, E7-V/570 Sqn 21.12.44, 23 MU 25.1.46, SOC 5.6.47

LK293 X/190 Sqn.30.9.44, 23 MU 17.5.45, SOC 5.6.47

LK294 620 Sqn 30.9.44, 296 Sqn 7.6.45, 299 Sqn, FA 11.2.46 crash landed Shepherd's Grove, Cat E 28.3.46

LK295 190 Sqn 7.10.44, gale damaged 18.1.45, ROS, 190 Sqn 22.2.45, V/196 Sqn, damaged 25/26.2.45, ROS 27.9.45, 23 MU 18.10.45, SOC 5.6.47

LK296 620 Sqn 5.10.44, 299 Sqn 14.6.45, 23 MU 29.1.46, SOC 5.6.47

LK297 G/190 Sqn 7.10.44, FTR 10.5.45 from Op *Doomsday*, loss of control in bad weather

LK298 A/190 Sqn 4.10.44, 620 Sqn 21.12.44, 299 Sqn, EFA 15.6.45 starboard u/c collapsed on landing at Shepherd's Grove

LK299 620 Sqn 11.10.44, 23 MU 20.10.44, SOC 5.6.47

LK300 620 Sqn 11.10.44, 8Z-A/295 Sqn 14.6.45, FA 21.10.45 landed one wheel off Istres runway, 108 R&SU 1.11.45, 295 Sqn, 23 MU 29.1.46, SOC 5.6.47

LK301 23 MU 19.10.44. ORTU 8.3.45, X9-F/299 Sqn 19.4.45, 23 MU 18.3.46, SOC 5.6.47

LK302 ZO-B,L/196 Sqn 7.10.44, 23 MU 11.2.46, SOC 5.6.47

LK303 620 Sqn 12.10.44, 23 MU 19.10.44, 620 Sqn 18.3.45, ZO-S/196 Sqn 14.6.45, 23 MU 11.3.46, SOC 5.6.47

LK304 620 Sqn 4.10.44, gale damaged 18.1.45, D4-W/620 Sqn 19.2.45, 299 Sqn 31.8.45, 23 MU 29.1.46, SOC 5.6.47

LK305 23 MU 19.10.44,ZO-S/196 Sqn, FTR 10/11.4.45, shot down off Frisians

LK306 (SD/Tropical) 10 MU 19.10.44, 23 MU 5.6.45, SOC 5.6.47

LK307 (SD/Tropical) 10 MU 28.10.44, 23 MU 14.12.44, 10 MU 10.1.45, SOC 2.10.46

LK308 (SD/Tropical) 10 MU 14.10.44, MA-V/161 Sqn 19.10.44, FA 1.3.45 port u/c. collapsed landing at Tempsford, 161 Sqn 29.3.45, 23 MU 12.7.45, SOC 5.6.47

LK309 (SD/Tropical) 10 MU 17.10.44, 138 Sqn 13.1.45, 23 MU 9.7.45, SOC 5.6.47

LK310 (SD/Tropical) 10 MU 26.10.44, scrap 11.11.46

LK311 (SD/Tropical) 10 MU 22.10.44, scrap 14.10.46

LK312 (SD/Temperate) 10 MU 17.10.44 MA-W/161 Sqn 25.10.44 – FTR 4/5.3.45 crashed in Limfjord, Denmark

LK313 23 MU 26.10.44, SOC 5.6.47

LK326 23 MU 28.10.44, 196 Sqn 15.3.45, EFA 18.9.45 port tyre burst on take-off Mauripur, belly landed, SOC 4.10.45

LK327 (SD/Temperate) 23 MU 5.6.45, SOC 5.6.47

LK328 23 MU 31.10.44, V8-R,C/570 Sqn 15.3.45, 151 RU 31.1.46, 299 Sqn 21.3.46, 23 MU 25.3.46, 273 MU 29.3.46, SOC 10.3.47

LK329 10 MU 11.11.44, NF-E/138 Sqn 1.12.44, 161 Sqn 8.3.45, 38 Gp 9.3.45, 161 Sqn, 32 MU 12.8.45, SOC 5.6.47

LK330 23 MU 31.10.44, 8E-P/295 Sqn 15.3.45 GA 15.4.45- parked, hit by LJ890, 8Z-P/295 Sqn MU 11.2.46, SOC?

LK331 23 MU 26.10.44, X9-R/299 Sqn 15.3.45, FA 3.6.45, swung off runway at Blackbushe and starboard u/c collapsed, RIW Sebro 11.6.45, 23 MU 5.2.46, SOC 5.6.47

LK332 23 MU 31.10.44, 5G-R/299 Sqn, FTR 30/31.3.45 from SOE sortie to Norway, shot down by fighter at Vierli-on-Vegars Moor, Norway

LK333 (SD/Temperate) 10 MU 31.10.44, SOC 27.6.46

LK334 23 MU 5.11.44, ORTU 23.2.45, 23 MU 12.4.45, SOC 5.6.47

LK335 23 MU 31.10.44, Q/190 Sqn 18.3.45, 23 MU 17.5.45, SOC 5.6.47

LK336 23 MU 9.11.44, Q/190 Sqn 18.3.45, 23 MU 25.5.45, gale damage 24.10.45, SOC 5.6.47

LK337 **23 MU 6.11.44, ORTU 23.2.45, 23 MU 14.4.45, SOC 5.6.47**

LK338 23 MU 9.11.44, ORTU 18.3.45, 23 MU 12.4.45, SOC 5.6.47

LK339 23 MU 9.11.44, SOC 5.6.47

LK340 23 MU 6.11.44, ORTU 18.3.45, 570 Sqn 19.4.45, 196 Sqn 26.4.45, GA 12.10.45 hit by taxying PJ978 at Lydda, 273 MU 29.3.46, SOC, 18.2.47

LK341 23 MU 5.11.44, 196 Sqn 20.3.45, 1665 CU 5.4.45, X9-B/299 Sqn 26.4.45, SOC 30.8.45 obsolete

LK342 (SD/Tropical) 10 MU 11.11.44, SOC 9.10.46

LK343 (SD/Tropical) 10 MU 11.11.44, Sebro 27.11.44, 10 MU 20.12.44, 23 MU 5.8.45, SOC 5.6.47

LK344 (SD/Tropical) 10 MU 11.11.44, ORTU 1.3.45, 23 MU 12.9.45, SOC 5.6.47

LK345 23 MU 13.11.44, ZO-R/196 Sqn 15.3.44, EFA 18.4.45 at B120 Hannover, landed on grass and u/c collapsed in swing

LK346 23 MU 5.11.44, 8Z-H/295 Sqn 18.3.45, 23 MU 25.1.46, SOC 5.6.47

LK347 (SD/Tropical) 10 MU 23.11.44, 23 MU 16.6.45, SOC 5.6.47

LK348 (SD/Tropical) 10 MU 23.11.44, SOC 27.6.46

LK349 19 MU 19.11.44, gale damage 18.1.45, SOC 27.3.47

LK350 (SD) 10 MU 23.11.44, 23 MU 12.9.45, SOC 5.6.47

LK351 19 MU 20.11.44, 8E-N/295 Sqn 15.3.45, 158 Sqn 27.11.45, 23 MU 16.1.46, SOC 5.6.47

LK352 (SD) 10 MU 20.11.44, SOC obsolete 25.7.46

LK353 (SD) 10 MU 23.11.44, 23 MU 20.9.45, SOC 5.6.47

LK354 19 MU 20.11.44, SOC 14.11.46

LK355 19 MU 25.11.44, 8E-Y/295 Sqn 12.3.45, 23 MU 16.1.45, SOC 5.6.47

LK356 (SD) 10 MU 1.12.44, 23 MU 25.10.45, SOC 5.6.47

LK357 19 MU 23.11.44, ORTU 11.3.45, 570 Sqn 19.4.45, 7T-E,N/196 Sqn 26.4.45, 273 MU 28.3.46, SOC 3.3.47

LK358 19 MU 1.12.44, ORTU 8.3.45, 23 MU 10.4.45, SOC 5.6.47

LK359 (SD) 10 MU 20.11.444, 23 MU 1.10.45, SOC 5.6.47

LK360 19 MU 7.12.44, SOC 29.10.46

LK361 19 MU 2.12.44, ORTU 8.3.45, GA 5.10.45 hit by PW389 taxying at Matching, ROS Sebro, ORTU 3.12.45, 1385 HTSCU 21.3.46, 273 MU 8.4.46, SOC 10.2.47

LK362 19 MU 8.12.44, 7T-R/196 Sqn 14.3.45, 23 MU 27.2.46, SOC 5.6.47

LK363 19 MU 7.12.44, 190 Sqn 15.3.45, 620 Sqn 22.3.45, 7T-T/196 Sqn 14.6.45, 23 MU 27.3.46. SOC 5.6.47

LK364 19 MU 8.12.44, V8-O/570 Sqn 12.3.45, 299 Sqn 9.1.46, X9-S/196 Sqn 3.3.46, 23 MU 25.3.46, SOC 5.6.47

LK365 10 MU 23.11.44, 23 MU 27.9.45, SOC 5.6.47

LK366 19 MU 9.12.44, ORTU 8.3.45, 1385 HTSCU 21.3.46, 23 MU 5.4.46, scrap 20.12.46

LK367 19 MU 9.12.44, ORTU 8.3.45, 620 Sqn, 23 MU 20.4.45, SOC 5.6.47

LK368 (SD/Tropical) 10 MU 13.12.44, ZO-W96 Sqn 15.3.45, ROS S&H 30.11.45, 23 MU 25.2.46, SOC 5.6.47

LK369 10 MU 21.12.44, 2 OAPU 28.2.45, ORTU 1.3.45, 1385 HTSCU 21.3.46, 273 MU 8.4.46, scrapped 11.1.47

LK370 (SD) 10 MU 6.1.45, 23 MU 25.10.45, SOC 5.6.47

LK375 10 MU 6.12.43, 1651 CU 17.8.43, 1657 CU 17.10.43, 28 MU 24.2.45, 101 SLG 31.3.45, SOC 4.3.46

LK376 10 MU 6.12.43, 1657 CU 13.9.44, 23 MU 7.1.45, SOC 4.1.46

LK377 10 MU 6.12.43, 1660 CU 4.10.43, 1654 CU 2.10.44, 101 SLG 4.2.45, SOC 25.4.46

LK378 JN-G, AA-U,Q/75 Sqn 24.9.43, 1657 CU 1.5.44, 23 MU SLG 7.1.45, SOC 21.1.46

LK379 F/90 Sqn 28.9.43, FTR 18/19.11.43 from Mannheim, crashed at Biedensend-Insel, Germany

LK380 Y/90 Sqn 26.9.43, EFA 9.11.43, collided with Hurricane KW800 of AFDU during fighter affiliation exercise, crashed on Sedge Fen, near Shippea Hill

LK381 Z/199 Sqn 1.10.43, FB accident, belly-landed Mepal after hitting trees and telegraph pole during approach, repaired, 75 Sqn, FB damage 17.12.43, engine trouble, entered a spin and eventually belly-landed at Tempsford, SOC 31.12.43 but BBOC, 1653 CU 29.5.44, 1657 CU 29.5.44, GA 9.7.44, tailwheel collapsed during take-off swing, 1657 CU 29.8.44, 6 MU 8.12.44, SOC 19.7.45

LK382 W,Q/149 Sqn 6.10.43, FTR 9/10.4.44 from SOE drop, crashed at Esmery-Hallon, France

LK383 XY-W/90 Sqn 13.10.43, FB accident 26.3.44, A/90 Sqn 17.4.44, A/149 Sqn 14.6.44, FTR 6/7.8.44, mining off Brest, crashed at sea

LK384 JN-X/75 Sqn 6.10.43, 1653 CU 30.3.44, MI 9.9.44, 1653 CU 3.10.44, 6 MU 26.11.44, SOC 24.4.45

LK385 A/199 Sqn 8.11.43, C/149 Sqn 5.5.44, 5.6.6.44 from feint operation, crashed at Baudres, France

LK386 XV Sqn 8.10.43, P,J,O?/149 Sqn 27.11.43, EFB 24.6.44, overshot Hartford Bridge when returning from mining off Brest, burnt out, SOC 1.7.44

LK387 P/623 Sqn 7.10.43, FTR 4/5.11.43 from mining off Frisians

LK388 N/149 Sqn 9.10.43, FB damage by fire from mid-upper gunner, L/149 Sqn 26.2.44, EFA 17.7.44 Methwold, heavy landing and u/c collapse, overturned and burnt out

LK389 C/75 Sqn 21.10.43, FB damage then to Sebro 27.11.43, cv to Mk IV, 10 MU 12.5.44, 1661 CU 19.5.44, FA 9.7.44, u/c trouble but landed safe at Swinderby, 1661 CU 1.10.44, FA 5.10.44 and declared SOC 17.10.44 but BBOC 5.11.44, 23 MU 2.3.45, ZO-P/196 Sqn 8.3.45, 23 MU 15.2.46, SOC 5.6.47

LK390 513 Sqn 8.11.43, 1660 CU 27.11.43, MI 21.7.44, 1660 CU 30.7.44, 23 MU 4.2.45, SOC 25.4.46

LK391 X/620 Sqn 15.10.43, NY-U/1665 CU 3.2.44, 23 MU SLG 18.1.45, SOC 31.1.46

LK392 A/90 Sqn 17.10.43, BFB 23.11.43, B/90 Sqn, O/149 Sqn 14.6.44, FA 19.7.44 overshot after landing swing, RIW Sebro 19.7.44, 19 MU 22.11.44, SOC 26.7.45

LK393 B/XV Sqn 23.10.43, GP-B/8.12.43,GA 21.8.44 hit trolley-ac during run up, 1661 CU 30.8.44, FA 26.9.44, 1661 CU 31.12.44, 23 MU SLG 15.1.45, SOC 11.1.46

LK394 V,O/149, Sqn 22.10.43, FA 9.4.44, D/149 Sqn 31.5.44, FTR 25.6.44 from Ruisseauville, crashed at Lisbourg, France

LK395 620 Sqn 27.10.43, FTR 4/5.2.44 from SOE sortie, crashed at St Denis de Palin, France

LK396 622 Sqn 24.10.43, JN-U,E/75 Sqn 9.11.43, W218 Sqn 30.4.44, M/149 Sqn 17.8.44, 1657 CU 14.9.44, SOC 15.1.45

LK397 P/199 Sqn 8.11.43, K,C/149 Sqn 26.4.44, FAB 23.6.44 tyre burst on take-off Methwold, belly landed, RIW Sebro 16.7.44, 10 MU 11.11.44, SOC 16.9.46

LK398 19 MU 24.12.43, NY-L/1665 CU 27.5.44, 6 MU 12.2.43, SOC 24.4.45

LK399 UG-G/1654 CU 31.12.43, MI 6.3.44, 1654 CU, FA 5.6.44 u/c trouble and crash-landed Woodbridge, RIW Sebro, 23 MU 15.10.44, SOC 26.7.45

LK400 1660 CU 7.1.44, FA 15.7.44, F/1660 CU 19.8.44, FA 16.11.44, 1660 CU, EFA 29.1.45, both inner engines cut in low flight, belly-landed at 1730 hrs in field near Morton, Swinderby

LK401 6 MU 10.1.44, I/218 Sqn 10.5.44, G/149 Sqn 17.8.44, 1653 CU 12.9.44, 6 MU 6.11.44, SOC 19.7.45

LK402 1654 CU 24.1.44, 1660 CU 25.1.44, FA 1.3.44, hit snow bank when taxying, tail turret damage, 1660 CU 2.5.44, 6 MU 27.2.45, SOC 24.4.45

LK403 622 Sqn 23.10.43, ZO-W/196 Sqn 12.11.43, 1665 CU 1.4.44, EFA 27.3.44, overshot landing, port u/c collapsed, Tilstock

LK404 10 MU 7.11.43, W-P/1661 CU 15.10.43, Sebro 22.1.45, SOC at Bourn as MR 24.1.45

LK405 23 MU 26.10.43, cv to Mk IV, 10 MU 15.3.44, W/190 Sqn 25.3.44, GA 28.1.45, gale damage at Dunmow, 190 Sqn 10.2.45, 23 MU 31.5.45, Short & Harland 27.12.45, SOC 7.2.46

LK406 10 MU 10.11.43, SOC 27.8.46

LK407 10 MU 10.11.43, 1661 CU 8.11.44, 23 MU SLG 15.1.45, SOC 4.3.46

LK408 10 MU 12.11.43, 1654 CU 26.7.44, 23 MU SLG 3.2.45, SOC 8.3.46

LK409 10 MU 12.11.43, 1661 CU 26.7.44, 1654 CU 15.7.44, 23 MU SLG 22.1.45, SOC 25.4.46

LK410 10 MU 12.11.43, 1653 CU 4.8.44, 6 MU 25.11.44, SOC 24.4.45

LK411 10 MU 12.11.43, 1653 CU 14.6.44, FA 16.7.44 tyre burst on take-off Chedburgh, u/c strained in landing, 6 MU 22.11.44, SOC 24.4.45

LK425 10 MU 12.11.43, 1654 CU 17.10.44, 23 MU/101 SLG 13.2.45, SOC 8.3.46

LK426 10 M 13.11.43, 1657 CU 4.8.44, 23 MU SLG 27.1.45, SOC 25.4.46

LK427 10 MU 13.11.43, 1653 CU 4.8.44, 6 MU 25.11.44, SOC 24.4.45

LK428 23 MU 19.11.43, cv to Mk IV, ZO-B/196 Sqn 26.1.44, FA 12.4.44, port u/c collapsed landing, Keevil, 196 Sqn 5.5.44, X9-G,5G-J/299 Sqn, 1665 CU 24.5.45, 23 MU 4.2.46, SOC 5.6.47

LK429 10 MU 14.11.43, 1661 CU 30.8.44, 23 MU/101 SLG 5.2.45, SOC 28.2.46

LK430 10 MU 14.11.43, 1654 CU 20.8.44, 23 MU SLG 22.1.45, SOC 8.3.46

LK431 23 MU 18.11.43, cv to Mk IV, F/190 Sqn 28.1.44, 23 MU SLG 31.5.45, SOC 5.6.47

LK432 23 MU 22.11.43, 620 Sqn 10.2.44, GA gale damage at Dunmow 20.1.45, 620 Sqn 24.2.45, 23 MU 7.6.45, Short & Harland 15.12.45, Cat E 14.1.46

LK433 23 MU 24.11.43, 10 MU 15.3.44, 190 Sqn 25.3.44, battle damage 21.9.44, E/190 Sqn 6.11.44, FA 22.4.45 u/c strain in heavy landing E/190 Sqn 12.5.45, 620 Sqn 17.5.45, 23 MU 9.7.45, SOC 5.6.47

LK434 10 MU 30.11.43, XT-Y/1657 CU 31.5.44, FA 16.7.44 swung on take-off through hedge at Shepherd's Grove, 1657 CU 29.8.44, 23 MU 15.1.45, SOC 28.2.46

LK435 10 MU 24.11.43, SOC 2.5.45

LK436 6 MU 25.1.44, TV-Y/1660 CU 29.3.44, FA 12.9.44, 1660 CU 20.9.44, Sebro MI and SOC 25.1.45

LK437 6 MU 27.1.44, 1657 CU 25.8.44, EFA 15.11.44, engine failure and more power loss during approach to Ridgewell, crashed near church at Tilbury-junxta-Clare

LK438 10 MU 31.1.44, 1661 CU, 6 MU 17.12.44, SOC 19.7.45

LK439 (cv Mk IV) 23 MU 7.2.44, 5G-J/299 Sqn 30.4.44, battle damage 10.8.44, 299 Sqn 2.9.44, 10 MU 20.1.45, 8Z-S/295 Sqn 21.3.45, 23 MU 25.1.46, SOC 5.6.47

LK440 (cv Mk IV) 23 MU 7.2.44, 196 Sqn 25.4.44, damaged returning after and written off but later BBOC, Shorts 27.9.45, 23 MU 7.11.45, SOC 5.6.47

LK441 10 MU 4.12.43, Sebro 19.5.45, SOC 22.5.45

LK442 10 MU 27.11.43, 1654 CU 26.7.44, 23 MU SLG 3.2.45, SOC 21.1.46

LK443 10 MU 13.12.43, Signals Flying Unit Honiley 13.11.44, SOC 18.1.46

LK444 10 MU 30.11.43, 27 MU 13.4.44, 1657 CU 21.6.44, 23 MU 17.1.45, SOC 28.3.46

LK445 D/214 Sqn 15.11.43, C/149 Sqn 30.1.44, 1657 CU 5.5.44, 1651 CU 17.10.44, 6 MU 10.11.44, SOC 24.4.45

LK446 10 MU 13.12.43, AK-D/1657 CU 4.6.44, FTR 23/24.8.44 from a night exercise, crashed at sea?

LK447 10 MU 15.12.43, FA 20.12.43 damaged at 10 MU SLG, 10 MU 20.1.44, 1661 CU 15.10.44, 1651 CU 17.10.44, 23 MU SLG 12.1.45, SOC 20.2.46

LK448 10 MU 13.12.43, 1651 CU 12.4.44, 6 MU 8.11.44, SOC 24.4.45

LK449 10 MU 15.12.43, 1654 CU 15.5.44, GA 21.11.44 port elevator damaged by van, 1654 CU 18.2.45, 6 MU 8.3.45, SOC 24.4.45

LK450 H4-R/1653 MU 24.12.43, FA 11.7.44, ASI failed during take-off run, throttled back, overshot, u/c collapsed in ditch, RIW Sebro 18.7.44 but SOC 1.8.44

LK451 10 MU 21.12.43, FA 27.1.44, 10 MU 19.2.44, SOC 22.5.45

LK452 19 MU 24.12.43, 1651 CU 31.5.44, 6 MU 2.11.44, SOC 24.4.45

LK453 10 MU 24.12.43, 1654 CU 15.5.44, EFA 27.9.44, crashed at night in Wigsley circuit and burnt out

LK454 19 MU 24.12.43, 1657 CU 14.6.44, FA 28.8.44, 1657 CU 11.9.44, RIW Sebro 5.10.44, 1657 CU 14.11.44, FA 4.12.44, 23 MU 17.1.45, 1657 CU 29.1.45, Sebro Bourn 9.2.45, SOC 5.4.45

LK455 19 MU 24.2.44, OG-L/1665 CU 19.5.44, 6 MU 10.1.45, SOC 24.4.45

LK456 W-T/1661 CU 30.12.43, EFA 11.4.44, engine fire in flight then crashed at Winthorpe

LK457 19 MU 10.1.44, 1653 CU 31.5.44, FA 23.8.44, 1653 CU 5.9.44, 6 MU SLG Woburn 25.11.44, SOC 25.4.45

LK458 19 MU 24.12.43, 1653 CU 3.6.44, BFA 5.7.44 starboard tyre burst on take-off, u/c then torn off, at Chedburgh, SOC 2.8.44

LK459 19 MU 24.12.43, 1651 CU 31.5.44, 6 MU 8.11.44, SOC 24.4.45

LK460 GP-O/1661 CU 31.12.43, FA 24.4.44, engine fire in flight and u/c damaged in landing at Winthorpe, RIW Sebro 25.4.44, 10 MU 7.8.44, Signals Flying Unit Honiley 13.11.44, FA 31.12.44, starboard u/c jammed up, belly landed Wittering, declared Cat B 17.1.45, fate uncertain but PSO 21.6.47

LK461 1654 CU 30.12.43, FA 4.5.44 overshot at Wigsley and starboard u/c collapsed, GP-P/1661 CU 5.10.44, FA 31.12.44, collided with lorry at Winthorpe, 1661 CU 2.1.45, 23 MU 5.2.45, SOC 4.3.46

LK462 1661 CU 30.12.43, MI 3.8.44, GP-P/1661 CU 5.10.44, FA 2.12.44 collided with lorry at Winthorpe, 1661 CU 2.1.45, 23 MU 5.2.45, SOC 4.3.46

LK463 19 MU 10.1.44, 1657 CU 5.6.44, 6 MU 7.12.44, SOC 19.7.45

LK464 1660 CU 7.1.44, FA 2.5.44 starboard u/c collapsed after landing, RIW Sebro 23.5.44, 23 MU 29.9.44, Signals Flying Unit Honiley 22.2.45, SOC M 18.1.46

LK465 6 MU 17.1.44, 1657 CU 2.8.44, EFA 12.10.44 crashed, during three engined approach, 1/2 mile north of Chedburgh and burnt out

LK466 19 MU 7.1.44, 1665 CU 19.5.44, FA 24.7.44 port u/c collapsed after swing in landing at Sleap, 1665 CU 9.11.44, 6 MU 21.2.45, SOC 31.5.45

LK479 6 MU 17.1.44, 1657 CU 20.6.44, FA 12.8.44, 1657 CU 12.9.44, 6 MU 12.12.44, SOC 19.7.45

LK480 19 MU 10.1.44, 1653 CU 1.6.44, FA 19.7.44 u/c strained in heavy landing Chedburgh, 1657 CU 11.9.44, 6 MU 12.12.44, SOC 19.7.45

LK481 6 MU 17.1.44, TV-ZX/1660 CU 9.6.44, 23 MU 10.1.45, SOC 28.2.46

LK482 6 MU 17.1.44, 1654 CU 26.6.4, 1332 CU 6.12.44, SOC 22.2.45

LK483 6 MU 24.1.44, 1660 CU 16.6.44, FA 26.7.44 swung on take-off and raised u/c to stop, SOC 16.8.44

LK484 6 MU 25.1.44, 1665 CU 19.6.44, FA 9.8.44, 1665 CU 29.9.44, FA 7.12.44 collided with vehicle at Tilstock, 1665 CU 19.1.45, SOC obsolete 22.3.45

LK485 1654 CU 24.1.44, GP-K/1661 CU 25.1.44, FA 7.4.44, engine trouble and u/c collapsed landing at Ossington, RIW Sebro, 10 MU 31.7.44, 1332 TSCU 28.8.44, gale damage 16/17.11.44, 1332 CU 19.1.45, SOC 22.5.45

LK486 (cv to Mk IV), 6 MU 30.1.44, 1657 CU 23.7.44, FA 8.11.44 tyre burst in flight, belly-landed Woodbridge, RIW Sebro 8.11.44, 23 MU 5.4.45, SOC 5.6.47

LK487 6 MU 25.1.44, TV-R/1660 CU 17.3.44, FA 17.6.44, TV-D,G/1660 CU 3.9.44, 6 MU 25.2.45, SOC 18.5.45

LK488 6 MU 25.1.44, QQ-E/1651 CU 21.6.44, EFA 19.10.44 crashed into Mickle Fell, 16 miles S of Barnard Castle, in poor visibility.

LK489 10 MU 21.1.44, 1654 CU 8.6.44, FA 16.7.44, tyre burst during take-off at Wigsley, swung, u/c collapsed

LK490 6 MU 25.1.44, YV-S/1660 CU 21.3.44, 6 MU 27.2.45, SOC 24.4.45

LK491 6 MU 30.1.44, TV-R/1660 CU 17.3.44, FA 29.7.44, 1661 CU, 1332 CU 5.12.44, 6 MU 26.2.45, SOC 24.4.45

LK492 6 MU 30.1.44, 1651 CU 21.6.44, FA 24.8.44, 1651 CU 8.9.44, 6 MU 10.11.44, SOC 24.4.45

LK493 6 MU 30.1.44, 1651 CU 31.5.44, FA 19.9.44, 1651 CU 30.9.44, 6 MU 10.11.44, SOC 24.4.45

LK494 6 MU 2.2.44, 1654 CU 27.3.44, 1661 CU 29.7.44, EFA 2.8.44 tyre burst on take-off Winthorpe, u/c collapsed, SOC 15.8.44

LK495 6 MU 30.1.44, QQ-U/1651 CU, 6 MU 14.11.44, SOC 24.4.45

LK496 10 MU 31.1.44, 1651 CU 31.5.44, 6 MU 6.11.44, SOC 24.4.45

LK497 10 MU 30.1.44, 1661 CU 17.6.44, 1332 CU 13.12.44, EA 5.1.45 overshot Nutt's Corner, u/c collapsed on icy runway

LK498 (cv to Mk IV), 23 MU 20.2.44, 190 Sqn 23.4.44, FTR 21.9.44, shot down by flak near Grave, Netherlands

LK499 R/149 Sqn 24.2.44, 1653 CU 8.5.44, FA 30.5.44, u/c would not retract, H4-D/1653 CU 15.6.44, EFA 13.9.44, control problem led to rear fuselage structural failure, crashed near Cadover Bridge, Lee Moor, Devon

LK500/TS262 S,F/149 Sqn 29.2.44, EFB 11.5.44 swung taking off from Lakenheath, u/c collapsed, RIW Sebro 24.5.44 and SOC 22.6.44, BBOC 5.10.44 and rebuilt as TS262, awaiting collection 8.2.45, further history uncertain, PSO 21.6.47

LK501 QQ-L/1651 CU 3.3.44, EFA 30.9.44, engine fire soon after take-off, crashed and burnt out near Horseheath

LK502 JF-M/1654 CU 10.3.44, EFA 27.5.44, rudder controls failed and both starboard engines feathered, four baled out, aircraft crashed at Clifton Park, Rudyard, Staffs

LK503 6 MU 2.2.44, 1651 CU, 6 MU 14.11.44, SOC 24.4.45

LK504 6 MU 2.2.44, 1651 CU 31.5.44, FA 23.10.44, 1651 CU 4.11.44, 6 MU 22.11.44, SOC 24.4.45

LK505 (cv to Mk IV) 23 MU 7.2.44, ZO-C/196 Sqn 5.5.44, 27 MU 22.2.45, 23 MU 23.2.45, SOC 5.6.47

LK506 1657 CU 12.2.44, Cat B 29.5.44, Cat E 15.6.44 following ground accident?

LK507 1657 CU 9.2.44, EFA 4.7.44 landing on three engines at Shepherd's Grove swung and u/c collapsed

LK508 XT-T,S/1657 CU 9.2.44, 'U3', 'W3'/ECNS Shawbury 1.5.44, FA AC 21.5.44 engine problem at Long Kesh and landed safely, FA 11.4.45 forced landed Aldergrove with engine trouble, re-cat E2 22.5.45

LK509 (cv to Mk IV) 23 MU 10.2.44, 620 Sqn 2.5.44, 5G-C/299 Sqn 1.3.45, 23 MU 29.1.45, SOC 5.6.47

LK510 (cv to Mk IV) 23 MU 10.2.44, ZO-U,W/196 Sqn 23.4.44, battle damage 5/6.6.44, 10 MU 6.1.45, 190 Sqn 6.5.45, 23 MU 17.5.45, SOC 5.6.47

LK511 1654 CU 16.2.44, 23 MU 20.2.45, 101 SLG 20.2.45, SOC 22.5.46

LK512 (cv to Mk IV) **TS264** 1654 CU 24.2.44, EFA 9.5.44 following engine trouble landed u/c up at Lindholme and classified Cat E1 26.6.44, RIW Sebro and re-cat B 26.9.44, awaiting collection 9.10.44, 23 MU 26.10.44, SOC 5.6.47

LK513 (cv to Mk IV) 23 MU 29.2.44, 190 Sqn 2.5.44, 620 Sqn, FA AC u/c collapsed during take-off for Arnhem, from Fairford, RIW Sebro 4.10.44, 23 MU 24.2.45, 8Z-Q/295 Sqn 15.3.45, 23 MU 16.1.46, SOC 5.6.47

LK514 1654 CU 4.3.44, IV-B/1660 CU 24.7.44, 23 MU 19.2.45, 101 SLG 19.2.45, WOC 25.4.46

LK515 1654 CU 4.3.44, EFA 8.6.44, engine trouble, undershot Crosby

LK516 149 Sqn 29.2.44, J/90 Sqn 11.3.44, 1651 CU 24.6.44, GA 15.10.44 hit LJ449 taxying, 6 MU 6.11.44, SOC 30.1.45

LK517 1654 CU 4.3.44, EFA 31.5.44 control loss in cloud led to structural failure, broke up and crashed at Ticklet Farm, Midridge near Shildon, Co Durham

LK518 1653 CU 4.3.44, EFA 29.5.44 but re-cat B, RIW Sebro 18.6.44, 23 MU 26.10.44, gale damage Aldergrove 7.11.44, 23 MU 30.1.45, SOC 5.6.47

LK519 QQ-O/1651 CU, EFA 18.8.44, u/c and engine control problems landing at Wratting, crashed into EF514

LK520 1651 CU 3.3.44, GA caught fire during refuelling at Wratting, burnt out

LK521 H4-W/1653 CU 4.3.44, EFA 18.7.44, could not maintain height, force landed in field S of Shedburgh, map reference OS M253731

LK535 1661 CU 8.3.44, FA 10.8.44, GP-D/1661 CU 13.9.44, 23 MU SLG 14.1.45, SOC 28.2.46

LK536 1654 CU 9.3.44, FA 21.8.44, 1654 CU 2.9.44, 101 SLG 4.2.45, SOC 25.4.46

LK537 GP-N/1661 CU 9.3.44, FA 20.3.44, u/c collapsed landing Winthorpe, RIW Sebro 21.3.44, 23 MU 23.7.44, 1331 CU 1.10.44, SOC 22.5.45

LK538 GP-J/1661 CU 10.3.44, 101 SLG 22.1.45, SOC 28.2.46

LK539 1660 CU 15.3.44, FA 22.5.44, 1660 CU 31.12.44, 6 MU 3.3.45, SOC 24.4.45

LK540 75 Sqn 13.3.44, QQ-M/1651 CU 16.3.44, 6 MU 10.11.44, SOC 24.4.45

LK541 1661 CU 20.3.44, RIW Sebro 15.6.44, 23 MU 15.10.44, SOC 26.7.45

LK542 (cv to Mk IV) 23 MU 22.3.44, 10 MU 9.6.44, 6 NU 6.6.44, 5G-H/299 Sqn 13.6.44, FB AC 26.8.44 clipped tree on approach and landed away from base, X9-P/299 Sqn 8.2.45, 273 MU 28.3.45, SOC 25.2.47

LK543 (cv to Mk IV) 23 MU 20.3.44, 6 MU 9.6.44, 8Z-V/295 Sqn 30.6.44, GA 18.1.45 hit by LK190 taxying, FA 14/15.2.45 landed with glider, hit light, overshot, ROS Sebro, 295 Sqn 22.2.45, 23 MU 25.1.46, SOC 5.6.47

LK544 (cv to Mk IV) 23 MU 22.3.44, 10 MU 9.6.44, 6 MU 6.6.44, 5G-L/299 Sqn 13.6.44, FB 20.9.44, ROS, 299 Sqn 10.10.44, 1665 CU 4.1.45, EFA 10.5.45, swung on take-off, Saltby, u/c collapsed, SOC 17.5.45

LK545 (cv to Mk IV) 23 MU 22.3.44, 10 MU 9.6.44, 5G-T/299 Sqn 13.6.44, as XG-O, FTR 21.9.44 shot down by flak and crash landed near Veghel, Netherlands

LK546 1661 CU 26.3.44, EFA 19.5.44 overshot Culmhead due to engine trouble, SOC 30.5.44

LK547 1661 CU 24.3.44, FA 3.8.44, GP-H/1661 CU 17.8.44, FA 25.9.44 overshot at Winthorpe, 1661 CU 18.11.44, 101 SLG 12.1.45, SOC 28.2.45

LK548 (cv to Mk IV) 27 MU 31.3.44, 23 MU 13.5.44, 620 Sqn 2.9.44, 20.9.44 hit by flak and at 1600 hrs crashed in flames at Nistelrode after dropping load, four killed

LK549 (cv to Mk IV) 23 MU 29.3.44, V8-Z,E7-J/570 Sqn 23.9.44, 23 MU 25.1.46, SOC 11.4.46

LK550 TV-G/1660 CU 30.3.44, FA 5.10.44, 1660 CU 31.12.44, 6 MU 25.2.45, SOC 6.6.45

LK551 (cv to Mk IV) 23 MU 18.3.44, E7-Z/570 Sqn 28.9.44, 23 MU 20.4.45, SOC 5.6.47

LK552 JF-C/1654 CU 30.3.44, EFA 25.4.44, oil cooler and aileron problem reported, crew baled out, crashed 9 miles E of Birootes, Notts.

LK553 (cv to Mk IV) 23 MU 26.3.44, 8Z-P/295 Sqn 31.7.44, battle damage 20.9.44, 295 Sqn 7.10.44, EFA 10.3.45 control column jammed during take-off from Rivenhall and port u/c collapsed, re-cat 'B', RIW 25.5.45, 23 MU 14.1.46, SOC 5.6.47

LK554 (cv to Mk IV) 23 MU 30.3.44, 620 Sqn 25.9.44, gale damage at Dunmow 18.1.45, 620 Sqn 16.2.45, X9-M/299 Sqn 14.6.45, 273 MU 29.3.46, SOC 30.1.47

LK555 (cv to Mk IV) 27 MU 125.4.44, 23 MU 13.5.44, V8-S,E7-S/570 Sqn 31.7.44, battle damage 18.9.44, 570 Sqn 1.10.44, 242 Sqn 2.10.45, 46 Sqn 28.11.45, 23 MU 9.1.46, SOC 5.6.47

LK556 (cv to Mk IV) 23 MU 30.3.44, ZO-Y/196 Sqn 12.6.44, FTR 20.9.44, force-landed near Nijmegen, one baled out, rest safe

LK557 (cv to Mk IV) 23 MU 30.3.44, ZO-V,H/196 Sqn 12.6.44, FA 12/13.5.45, ROS, 196 Sqn 7.6.45, EFA 14.1.46, 23 MU 21.3.46, SOC 5.6.47

LK558 (cv to Mk IV) 27 MU 5.4.44, 23 MU 27.4.44, 8Z-A,R,P/295 Sqn 1.8.44, battle damage 19.9.44, 295 Sqn 1.10,44, 23 MU 19.4.45, SOC 5.6.47

LK559 (cv to Mk IV) 27 MU 2.4.44, 23 MU 30.4.44, V8-X,E7-W570 Sqn 21.7.44, battle damage 31.7.44, 570 Sqn, battle damage 19.9.44, ROS Sebro 27.9.44, 570 Sqn 30.9.44, 23 MU 16.1.46, 151 RU 31.1.46, 570 Sqn 21.3.46, 273 MU 28.3.46, SOC 30.1.47

LK560 (cv to Mk IV) 27 MU 7.4.44, 23 MU 3.5.44, V8-Z/570 Sqn 19.7.44, EFB 17.9.44 during take-off from Harwell, Horsa glider badly swung, engine trouble also and LK560's u/c collapsed

LK561 GP-A/1661 CU 23.4.44, EFA 25.9.44, prop fell off then port engine gave trouble, crew baled out, crashed near St Osyth, Essex, 0300 hrs

LK562 TS265 Syerston 3.5.44, W-V/1661 CU 27.5.44, GS 7.6.44, run into by EE907, RIW Sebro 7.6.44, repair cancelled and aircraft written off 27.6.44, BBOC as Cat B RIW 26.9.44, modified to Mk IV and rebuilt as **TS265**, 23 MU 31.10.44, 190 Sqn 24.3.45, FTR 14/15.4.45 from SOE sortie to Norway, crashed at sea?

LK563 Syerston 13.5.44, X3/ECNS Shawbury 24.5.44, SOC 2.6.45

LK564 HA-C/1653 CU 27.5.44, EFA 15.7.44, re-cat B, RIW Sebro 10.9.44, 10 MU 7.2.45, SOC 3.5.45

LK565 W-R/1651 CU 15.6.44, EFA 15.7.44, entered spiralling turn, crashed near Wendons Ambo, Essex?

LK566 (cv to Mk IV) 27 MU 13.4.44, 23 MU 13.5.44, G5-G/190 Sqn 28.9.44, 620 Sqn 5.10.44, FM 22/23.2.45 from SOE sortie to Norway, shot down by fighter, at Landdgang-in-Holt, Norway

LK567 (cv to Mk IV) 27 MU 13.4.44, 23 MU 9.5.44, 8Z-L/295 Sqn 13.8.44, battle damage 21.9.44, 295 Sqn 3.10.44, FTR 26/27.4.45 from SOE sortie from Denmark, crashed at St. Alnistock, Plovelund

LK568 149 Sqn 17.4.44, K/90 Sqn 18.4.44, FA 27.4.44 u/c screw jack forced through wing, landed safely Woodbridge, U/90 Sqn 20.5.44, O/218 Sqn 14.6.44, U/149 Sqn 26.7.44, 1653 CU 13.9.44, 6 MU 6.11.44, SOC 24.4.45

LK569 S,K/90 Sqn 19.4.44, battle accident 17.5.44, 1651 CU 24.6.44, 6 MU 6.11.44, SOC 24.4.45

LK570 XY-V,W90 Sqn 10.4.44, 1651 CU 24.6.44, 6 MU8.11.44, SOC 24.4.45

LK571 O/90 Sqn 20.4.44, 1653 CU 24.6.44, 6 MU 15.11.44, SOC 24.4.45

LK572 W-T/1661 CU 26.4.44, FA 23.8.44, 1661 CU 21.10.44, RIW Sebro 18.12.44, 23 MU 15.1.45, SOC 28.2.45

LK573 (cv to Mk IV) GP-F/1661 CU 23.4.44, FA 25.7.44, 1661 CU, FA 26.9.44, 6 MU 23.11.44, SOC 24.4.45, 23 MU 13.6.45, SOC 5.6.47

LK574 1661 CU 26.4.44, FAB 16.5.44, u/c would not lock after manual lowering and port leg collapsed during landing at Woodbridge, RIW Sebro 16.5.44, 23 MU 7.10.44, SOC 5.6.47

LK575 UG-F/1665 CU 27.4.44, FAB 9.5.44, starboard wheel caught in deep hole during take-off from Wigsley and u/c collapsed, RIW Sebro 9.5.44, 10 MU 25.9.44, 8Z-A/295 Sqn, 23 MU 23.4.45, 10 MU, SOC 29.5.45

LK576 Syerston 1.5.44, 1660 CU 13.12.44, 23 MU 4.2.45, SOC 28.2.46

LK589 (cv to Mk IV) Syerston 3.5.44, V3/ECNS 16.5.44, 6 MU 6.6.44, 295 Sqn 9.7.44, 6 MU 28.2.45, 570 Sqn, 23 MU 19.4.45, became 5238M 5.5.45

LK590 Syerston 3.5.44, 1660 CU 21.5.44, 1654 CU 24.7.44, GP-L/1661 CU 11.8.44, 23 MU, 101 SLG 15.1.45, SOC 28.3.46

LK591 Syerston 15.5.44, 1661 CU 27.5.44, 6 MU 6.6.44, 1661 CU, EFA 25.7.44 oxygen failure followed by engine problem, crashed in landing attempt at Gaydon and burnt out

LK592 1654 CU 17.5.44, 101 SLG 3.2.45, SOC 25.4.46

LK593 1654 17.5.44, 6 MU (Woburn SLG) 8.2.45, 101 SLG 23.2.45, SOC 27.12.45

LK594 1654 CU 17.5.44, EFA 7.6.44, crashed Saltby, Leics, possibly due to control problem

LK595 GP-L/1661 CU 23.5.44, FA 7.8.44, starboard tyre burst on take-off Winthorpe swung, starboard wing tailplane and u/c torn off, re-cat B, RIW Sebro 17.8.44, 19 MU 1.12.44, SOC 30.8.45

LK596 1654 CU 24.5.44, 23 MU 13.2.45, SOC 28.2.46

LK597 1657 CU 5.6.44, FA 13.8.44, starboard u/c collapsed when landing Shepherd's Grove, RIW Sebro 1.9.44, 6 MU 20.12.44, SOC 19.7.45

LK598 1660 CU 7.6.44, FA 6.11.44, 1660 CU 31.12.44, 6 MU 3.3.45, SOC 24.4.45

LK599 1661 CU 7.6.44, 6 MU 19.1.45, SOC 24.4.45

LK600 1654 CU 10.6.44, 101 SLG 3.2.45, SOC 28.2.46

LK601 1651 CU 15.6.44, 6 MU 6.11.44, SOC 24.4.45

LK602 PB TV-J/1660 CU 16.6.44, FA 22.11.44, 1660 CU 31.12.44, 23 MU 19.2.45, 101 SLG 19.2.45, SOC 31.1.46

LK603 23 MU 29.6.44, 1660 CU 20.8.44, Cat E on 21.2.45, SOC 5.6.45 becoming 5237M and used by 1st Canadian Parachute Bn

LK604 23 MU 9.7.44, 1657 CU 25.7.44, 23 MU/101 SLG 20.1.45, SOC 25.4.46

LK605 23 NU 28.7.44, FA 27.7.44, 23 MU 4.8.44, 1660 CU 14.8.44, 1651 CU 15.8.44, 101 SLG 5.1.45, SOC 28.3.46

LK606 (cv to Mk IV) 23 MU 31.7.44, 1661 CU 18.8.44, FA 8.9.44, u/c collapse when landing at Woodbridge, declared Cat B 22.10.44, 23 MU 14.4.45, gale damage 21.9.45, SOC 5.6.47

LK607 23 MU 29.9.44, 1332 CU 15.11.44, EFA 12.12.44, swung on landing at Nutt's Corner, starboard u/c collapsed in soft ground, SOC 17.1.45

LK608 XT-X,Z/1657 CU 21.6.44, 23 MU/SLG 14.1.45, SOC 28.2.46

LK609 1654 CU 24.6.44, 6 MU Woburn SLG 22.2.45, SOC 24.4.45

LK610 1657 CU 23.6.44, 6 MU 13.12.44, SOC 19.7.45

LK611 23 MU 2.7.44, 1651 CU 2.8.44, 6 MU 8.11.44, SOC 24.4.45

LK612 23 MU 7.7.44, 1651 CU 8.8.44, 6 MU 8.11.44, SOC 24.4.45

LK613 23 MU 16.7.44, XT-W/1657 CU 18.8.44, GA 30.11.44, starboard u/c damaged in hangar at Stradishall, 1657 CU 18.1.45, Sebro Bourn 5.2.45, SOC 5.4.45

LK614 23 MU 18.7.44, SOC 5.6.47

LK615 23 MU 23.7.44, 11 FU Melton Mowbray, despatched to USSR 28.2.45 and delivered via Shaibah and Teheran arriving mid-March 1945. Replaced LK618

LK616 23 MU 27.7.44, GP-G/1661 CU 18.8.44, EFA 27.8.44, crashed at Hawton AA camp, Notts, after returning from X-country, burnt out

LK617 23 MU 31.7.44, GP-V/1660 CU 18.8.44, EFA 10.10.44, u/c collapsed when landing Woodbridge, earlier retraction problems, SOC 15.10.44

LK618 23 MU 28.9.44, 4 APU 26.12.44, 23 MU, 11 FU Melton Mowbray for despatch to USSR 4.1.45, FA 14.1.45, ASI u/s during take-off, u/c collapsed during remedial action. (See LK615)

LK619 23 MU 16.10.44, 1332 CU 5.1.45, SOC 22.5.45

LK620 1653 CU 26.8.44, 6 MU 22.11.44, SOC 24.4.45

LK621 1332 CU 30.8.44,, F.A 26/27.3.45 landed too far along runway at Nutt's Corner, u/c collapsed, back broken, SOC 19.6.45

LK622 1332 CU 30.8.44, SOC 15.5.45

LK623 1332 CU 3.9.44, gale damage 17.11.44, 1332 CU 17.1.45, SOC 22.5.45

LK624 1332 CU 7.9.44, EFA 9.4.45 Nutt's Corner, port tyre burst during take-off, SOC 19.6.45

MZ260 – MZ264 all Mk III, replacement aircraft for N6025, N6028 and N6031 destroyed by bombing prior to delivery

MZ260 S,C/149 Sqn 31.5.43, EFA 17.11.43, crashed Lakenheath after overshooting on three engines, burnt out, SOC 24.11.43

MZ261 T/214 Sqn 17.5.43, FTR 24.5.43 from Dortmund, crashed at Unna, Germany

MZ262 K/90 Sqn 31.5.43, EFB 22.9.43, after take-off for Hannover starboard inner engine caught fire which spread, dived in at Brockley Green, Suffolk

MZ263 Y,B/218 Sqn 21.5.43, EFB 17.12.43, crash landed St Eval, fuel short and weather bad, returning from mining off La Pallice, crash-landed u/c up

MZ264 DJ-A/XV Sqn 24.5.43, A/622 Sqn 18.8.43, MR 31.8/1.9.43 from Berlin, crashed at Schaepe, Germany

PJ878 – PK186 all completed as Mk V

PJ878 23 MU 16.9.44, Shorts 8.6.45, ZO-I,/196 Sqn 6.2.46, 23 MU 27.3.46, SOC 5.6.47

PJ879 23 MU 16.9.44, Shorts 14.6.45, TB-O/51 Sqn 5.8.45, 23 MU 25.3.46, SOC 5.6.47

PJ880 CRD Short & Harland 28.10.44, SOC 28.8.46

PJ881 23 MU 12.10.44, Shorts 8.6.45, 158 Sqn 1.8.45, 51 Sqn 2.2.46, 273 MU 5.4.46, SOC 26.11.46

PJ882 23 MU 12.10.44, 242 Sqn 18.3.45, Shorts 8.6.45, TB-U/51 Sqn 28.6.45, 46 Sqn 4.1.46, 23 MU 21.3.46, SOC 5.6.47

PJ883 23 MU 3.12.44, Shorts 29.4.45, 23 MU 29.5.45, A,/51 Sqn 2.6.45, FA 31.8.45, u/c strained in heavy landing at Stradishall, ROS, ZO-B/196 Sqn 7.2.46, 273 MU 28.3.46, SOC 16.10.47

PJ884 23 MU 31.10.44, XK-P/46 Sqn 18.3.45, 273 MU 12.4.46, SOC 16.10.47

PJ885 23 MU 31.10.44, Shorts 29.4.45, 23 MU 29,.5.45, TB-A,B/51 Sqn 2.6.45, 7T-V/196 Sqn 30.1.46, 23 MU 25.3.46, SOC 5.6.47

PJ886 23 MU 7.12.44, 242 Sqn 18.3.45, Shorts 8.6.45, 158 Sqn 8.7.45, Pocklington 4.12.45, 46 Sqn 5.2.46, 23 MU 8.3.46, SOC 5.6.47

PJ887 46 Sqn 7.1.45, ZO-H/196 Sqn 18.9.45, 23 MU 26.3.46, SOC 5.6.47

PJ888 46 Sqn 1.45, ROS Sebro 1.5.45, 46 Sqn 11.5.45, St Mawgan 7.10.45, ACSEA for 1588 HFF 11.3.46, SOC 30.5.46

PJ889 23 MU 9.12.44, 242 Sqn 18.3.45, DK-B/158 Sqn 6.9.45, 242 Sqn 27.11.45, 46 Sqn 15.2.46, 23 MU 21.3.46, SOC 5.6.47

PJ890 46 Sqn 12.1.45, GA 8.4.45, heavy fumes encountered during wing inspection after elevator fabric had caught fire, Cat E, GA 29.4.45, port wing caught fire at 17 Staging Post, Castel Benito, Libya, and attributed to electrical trouble

PJ891 46 Sqn 12.1.45, PAB 10.6.45 u/c failed to lock, collapsed on landing at Shaibah, ROS, Pocklington 20.12.45, 23 MU 12.4.46, SOC 16.10.47

PJ892 46 Sqn 16.1.45, Pocklington 20.12.45, 23 MU 4.4.46, SOC 20.11.46

PJ893 46 Sqn 16.1.45, 9.2.45 tail damaged during taxying, Pocklington 27.11.45, 46 Sqn 31.1.46, 23 MU 20.3.46, SOC 5.6.47

PJ894 46 Sqn 22.1.45, AC 27.5.45, RIW Sebro 20.8.45, Pocklington 4.12.45, 46 Sqn 14.2.46, 23 MU 14.3.46, SOC 5.6.47

PJ895 Stoney Cross 22.1.45 for 46 Sqn, 23 MU 21.3.46, SOC 5.6.47

PJ896 46 Sqn 23.1.45, Pocklington 3.12.45, 273 MU 10.4.46, SOC 6.1.47

PJ897 46 Sqn 2.1.45, FA 9.22.45, tailwheels not down, doors ripped off during landing at Stoney Cross, Melton Mowbray 23.9.45, St Mawgan 6.10.45, KY-V/242 Sqn 24.10.45, 51 Sqn, FA 16.11.45, 46 Sqn 17.1.46, 23 MU 7.3.46, SOC 5.6.47

PJ898 46 Sqn 2.1.45, Pocklington 22.12.45, 273 MU 6.5.46, SOC 16.10.47

PJ899 46 Sqn 5.2.45, 273 MU 31.3.46, SOC 16.10.47

PJ900 46 Sqn 9.2.45, FA 4.7.45, Pocklington 27.11.45, 46 Sqn 28.1.46, 23 MU 15.3.46, Shorts 6.6.46, 273 MU 19.6.47, SOC 21.7.47. Sold to Transair became OO-XAH

PJ901 46 Sqn 5.2.45, EFA 9.4.45 at 8 FU, Mauripur, u/c collapse following swing, SOC 13.4.45

PJ902 Initially to Kemble for Command mod programme, 46 Sqn, Pocklington 11.2.46, 273 MU 9.4.46, SOC 16.10.47

PJ903 XK-Y/46 Sqn 15.2.45, 273 MU 28.3.46, SOC 16.10.47

PJ904 242 Sqn 15.2.45, Short & Harland 17.6.45, 242 Sqn 20.8.45, 46 Sqn, FA 30.9.45 hit Dakota KN408/525 Sqn taxying at Lydda, EFA 23.11.45, landed alongside Lyneham runway in poor visibility, hit buildings, burnt out

PJ905 242 Sqn 20.2.45, EGA and SOC 20.4.45, starboard u/c collapsed during taxying at Mauripur

PJ906 242 Sqn 22.2.45, Shorts 17.6.45, 242 Sqn 13.8.45, 299 Sqn 19.9.45, FA 20.12.45, dinghy and port u/c released in flight, port u/c collapsed during taxying at Woodbridge, Cat E 20.2.46

PJ907 242 Sqn 22.2.45, Pocklington 12.12.45, Polebrook 30.4.46, SOC 16.10.47

PJ908 242 Sqn 25.2.45, Shorts 8.6.45, 158 Sqn 1.7.45, FA AC Shaibah 22.3.45, tailwheel collapsed on landing, EFA 5.8.45 swung on take-off Castel Benito, u/c collapsed, burnt out

PJ909 KY-X/242 Sqn 25.2.45, EFA 22.3.45 Mauripur, swung on take-off, u/c collapsed

PJ910 242 Sqn 28.2.45, FA 21.3.45, type burst on landing Le Bourget, returned UK and RIW Sebro 24.4.45, 242 Sqn 11.10.45, 46 Sqn 7.12.45, Pocklington 12.2.46, 273 MU 2.5.46, SOC 16.10.47

PJ911 46 Sqn 9.2q.45, EFA 24.3.45, off track 40 miles SW Perpignan, France, crashed into mountain at 7,800ft

PJ912 242 Sqn 18.2.45, Shorts 8.6.45, 158 Sqn 27.7.45, 7T-L/196 Sqn 28.1.46, 299 Sqn 3.3.46, 23 MU 12.3.46, SOC 5.6.47

PJ913 242 Sqn 18.2.45, EFA 19.3.45, on take-off 14 SP Lydda hit lighting system, u/c collapsed

PJ914 242 Sqn 25.2.45, Pocklington 19.10.45, 158 Sqn 6.12.45, 46 Sqn 31.12.45, 23 MU 20.3.46, SOC 5.6.47

PJ915 242 Sqn 25.2.45, Shorts 8.6.45, 158 Sqn 28.6.45, 51 Sqn 2.2.46, 23 MU 25.3.46, SOC 5.6.47

PJ916 242 Sqn 28.2.45, Shorts 27.8.45, 51 Sqn 25.10.45, 46 Sqn 15.10.45, 23 MU 14.3.46, SOC 5.6.47

PJ917 242 Sqn 28.2.45, FA 29.5.45 throttle jammed open, swung, hit grass cutter, ROS, 242 Sqn 8.6.45, 46 Sqn 3.12.45, 23 MU 20.3.46, SOC 5.6.47

PJ918 242 Sqn 28.2.45, Pocklington 23.12.45, 273 MU 9.4.46, SOC 16.10.47

PJ919 46 Sqn 1.3.45, 273 MU 12.12.45, 273 MU 2.5.46, SOC 16.10.47

PJ920 46 Sqn 1.3.45, FA B 13.4.45 port tyre burst on take-off, belly-landed, RIW Sebro 30.5.45, 242 Sqn 20.10.45, Pocklington 22.12.45, 273 MU 4.4.46, SOC 17.12.46

PJ921 46 Sqn 1.3.45, EFA 25.4.45, At 8 FU Mauripur, landed on taxy-track, starboard wheel sank in soft ground alongside, u/c collapsed

PJ922 242 Sqn 28.2.45, 158 Sqn 31.8.45, Pocklington 29.11.45, 46 Sqn 31.1.46, 23 MU 19.3.46, SOC 5.6.47

PJ923 46 Sqn 6.3.45, FA B 6/7.5.45 landing Lyneham tyre burst, ROS Sebro 23.5.45, 46 Sqn 12.6.45, 23 MU 1.3.46, SOC 5.6.47

PJ935 46 Sqn 6.3.45, 23 MU 1.3.46, SOC 5.6.47

PJ936 XK-X/46 Sqn 8.3.45, Pocklington 11.45, 273 MU 14.5.46, SOC 16.10.47

PJ937 46 Sqn 8.3.45, Pocklington 4.12.45, XK-Y/46 Sqn 5.2.46, 273 MU 4.46, SOC 16.10.47

PJ938 46 Sqn 8.3.45, FA 13.8.45, 46 Sqn, Pocklington 8.1.46, 273 MU 2.4.46, SOC 10.12.46

PJ939 242 Sqn 8.3.45, Shorts 17.6.45, TB-A/51 Sqn 5.8.45, 7T-C/196 Sqn 7.2.46, 23 MU 25.3.46, SOC 5.6.47

PJ940 242 Sqn 15.3.45, TB-B/51 Sqn 8.10.45, Pocklington 2.1.46, 273 MU 15.5.46, SOC 16.10.46

PJ941 242 Sqn 19.3.45, 46 Sqn 12.12.45, 23 MU 25.3.46, SOC 5.6.47

PJ942 242 Sqn 24.3.45, 108 RSU 30.9.45, FA AC 6.9.45, XK-Aw/46 Sqn 4.10.45, Pocklington 15.12.45, 273 MU 8.4.46, SOC 10.10.47

PJ943 242 Sqn 12.3.45, XK-U/46 Sqn , FA AC 2.5.45, gale damage at Dum Dum, 46 Sqn 24.5.45, FA AC 7.10.45, 273 MU 28.3.46, SOC 16.10.47

PJ944 242 Sqn 26.3.45, Pocklington 19.10.45, 46 Sqn 15.12.45, FA AC 11.1.46, 46 Sqn 27.2.46, 23 MU 25.3.46, SOC 5.6.47

PJ945 23 MU 26.3.45, Shorts 30.5.45, TB-W/51 Sqn 27.6.45, Pocklington 15.11.46, 273 MU 4.6.46, SOC 16.10.46

PJ946 23 MU 26.3.45, Shorts 13.6.45, 242 Sqn 1.8.45, 5G-O/299 Sqn 15.1.45, 196 Sqn 3.3.46, 23 MU 27.3.46, SOC 5.6.47

PJ947 23 MU 26.3.45, Shorts 1.6.45, 242 Sqn 21.6.45, 1588 HFF 4.10.45, St Mawgan 6.10.45, FA 18.10.45 hit crated engine at 12 FU Lydda, EFA 26.10.45, at Lydda swung on take-off and crashed into Misr Anson SU-ACX

PJ948 23 MU 30.3.45, Shorts 1.6.45, 158 Sqn 24.6.45, FA 28.7.45, swung on take-off at Castel Benito, ROS, 158 Sqn, 7T-B/196 Sqn 21.3.46, 273 MU 21.3.46, SOC 4.2.47

PJ949 Shorts 22.3.45, AFEE Beaulieu 28.3.45, FA AC 16.1.46, 23 MU 15.3.46, SOC 5.6.47

PJ950 23 MU 31.3.45, Shorts 8.6.45, 158 Sqn 2.7.45, FA AC 16.10.45, hit refuelling bowser when landing at Shaibah, EFA 11.11.45 Castel Benito, failed to climb away, crashed and burnt out

PJ951 23 MU 2.4.45, Shorts 1.6.45, KY-O/242 Sqn 21.6.45, 46 Sqn, FA AC 4.9.45, landing swing in cross-wind Ballykelly, Shorts 23.10.45, 46 Sqn 30.3.46, 273 MU 28.3.46, SOC 16.10.47

PJ952 23 MU 2.4.45, Shorts 1.6.45, Pocklington, 242 Sqn 14.6.45, 273 MU 9.4.46, SOC 16.10.46

PJ953 23 MU 22.4.45, TB-C/51 Sqn 7.6.45, EFA 19.10.45, swung on take-off Castel Benito, u/c collapsed

PJ954 23 MU 8.4.45, Shorts 27.8.45, 158 Sqn 29.5.45, Pocklington 29.11.45, 46 Sqn 9.2.46, 23 MU 20.3.46, SOC 5.6.47

PJ955 23 MU 8.5.45, Shorts 1.6.45, 51 Sqn 24.6.45, ZO-A,U/196 Sqn 1.2.46, 23 MU 26.3.46, SOC 5.6.47

PJ956 Shorts 14.4.45, 23 MU, TB-D/51 Sqn 31.5.45, ZO-C/196 Sqn 14.2.46, SFU 28.2.46, 273 MU 2.7.46, SOC 18.8.47

PJ957 23 MU 8.4.45, 158 Sqn 25.8.45, Pocklington 17.10.45, 158 Sqn 15.12.45, 46 Sqn 31.12.45, 23 MU 15.3.46, SOC 5.6.47

PJ958 23 MU 7.4.45, Shorts 14.4.45, ATTDU Netheravon 10.6.45, 2 TAMU 12.10.45, TCDU Harwell 28.10.45, 2 TAMU 15.11.45, TCDU 10.12.45, EFA 19.12.45, touch down too far along runway, turned off to avoid bomb dump, u/c collapsed, BBOC 17.1.46 and passed to TCDU Brize Norton as 5797M

PJ959 23 MU 14.4.45, Shorts 27.4.45, 23 MU 29.5.45, 158 Sqn 2.6.45, 196 Sqn 20.2.46, 23 MU 22.3.46, SOC 5.6.47

PJ971 23 MU 22.4.45, Shorts 4.5.45, Pocklington 20.12.45, XK-S/46 Sqn 12.2.46, 273 MU 29.3.46, SOC 16.10.47

PJ972 23 MU 24.4.45, Shorts 4.5.45, Pocklington 17.1.46, 273 MU 17.4.46, SOC 16.10.45

PJ973 Shorts 27.4.45, TB-N/51 Sqn 2.6.45, Pocklington 27.11.45, XK-N/46 Sqn 8.1.46, 23 MU 22.3.46, SOC 5.6.47

PJ974 Shorts 29.5.45, TIB-F/51 Sqn 1.6.45, ZO-O/196 Sqn 30.1.46, 23 MU 26.3.46, SOC 5.6.47

PJ975 Shorts 26.4.45, B/1589 HFF 24.9.45, St Mawgan 7.10.45, MEDME 15.11.45 and SOC there 29.8.46

PJ976 Shorts 26.4.45, 158 Sqn 10.6.45, EGA 5.11.45 Mauripur, hit by Liberator KH146 of 53 Sqn

PJ977 Shorts 28.4.45, 158 Sqn 8.6.45, Pocklington 17.1.46, 273 MU 2.4.46, SOC 4.12.46

PJ978 Shorts 28.4.45, DK-Y/158 Sqn 10.6.45, hit LK340 12.6.45 when taxying at Lydda, Pocklington 4.12.45, 273 MU 24.4.46, SOC 16.6.47

PJ979 Shorts 30.4.45, 242 Sqn 6.6.45, 15.8.45 collided with Hurricane LF173 at Dum Dum C/1589 HFF 22.9.45, St Mawgan 6.10.45, MEDME 15.11.45, SOC 25.7.46

PJ980 23 MU 25.4.45, TB-F/51 Sqn 2.6.45, Pocklington 27.12.45, 273 MU 5.4.46, SOC 10.12.46

PJ981 23 MU 20.5.45, TB-H,Bw/51 Sqn 11.6.45, ZO-V/196 Sqn 31.1.46, 23 MU 27.3.46, SOC 5.6.47

PJ982 23 MU 25.4.45, DK-S/158 Sqn 2.6.45, 51 Sqn 2.2.46, 273 MU 21.6.46, SOPC 16.10.47

PJ983 51 Sqn 25.4.45, EGA 21.8.45, fuel overflow on to petrol bowser caused fire which engulfed aircraft, Stradishall

PJ984 158 Sqn 1.6.45, FA AC 17.9.45, 51 Sqn 21.2.46, 273 MU 4.4.46, SOC 4.12.46

PJ985 DK-H/158 Sqn 1.6.45, FA AC 17.9.45, 51 Sqn 21.2.46, 273 MU 4.4.46, SOC 4.12.46

PJ986 158 Sqn 2.6.45, 7T-A/196 Sqn 28.1.46, 23 MU 1.5.46, SOC 5.6.46

PJ987 242 Sqn 6.8.45, EFA 14.9.45, swung on take-off Lydda, u/c collapsed

PJ988 242 Sqn 6.6.45, XK-Bw/46 Sqn 3.12.45. 273 MU 1.4.46, SOC 16.10.47

PJ989 KY-W/242 Sqn 8.6.45, K/1589 HFF 22.9.45, St Mawgan 6.10.45, MEDME 15.11.45, SOC 29.8.46

PJ990 242 Sqn 8.6.45, EFA 26.7.45, dinghy inadvertently released in flight, belly-landed at 42 SP Shaibah

PJ991 KY-Fw/242 Sqn 8.6.45, 46 Sqn 3.12.45, Pocklington 20.12.45, 273 MU 10.4.46, SOC 16.10.47

PJ992 CRD Shorts 25.4.45, TB-J/51 Sqn 8.10.45, 23 MU 25.7.46, SOC 5.6.47

PJ993 242 Sqn 10.6.45, 23 MU 19.3.46, SOC 5.6.47

PJ994 242 Sqn 14.6.45, J/1589 HFF 22.9.45, St Mawgan 6.10.45, MEDME 15.11.45, SOC 29.8.46

PJ995 KY-Y/242 Sqn 14.6.45, FA AC 28.10.45, 46 Sqn, 23 MU 21.3.46, SOC 5.6.47

PJ996 242 Sqn 21.6.45, 1588 HFF 24.9.45, St Mawgan 6.10.45, AC SEA 11.3.46 arrived India 14.3.46, SOC 31.11.46

PJ997 242 Sqn 21.6.45, FA AC 29.9.45, 46 Sqn 3.12.45, Pocklington 31.12.45, 273 MU 6.5.46, SOC 16.10.47

PJ998 158 Sqn 24.6.45, 51 Sqn 2.2.46, 273 MU 4.4.46, SOC 26.11.46

PJ999 51 Sqn 24.6.45, Pocklington 17.10.45, 158 Sqn 6.12.45, 46 Sqn 31.12.45, 23 MU 8.3.46, SOC 5.6.47

PK115 TB-X/51 Sqn 24.6.45, FA 10.9.45, Pocklington 20.12.45, 273 MU 16.4.46, SOC 16.10.47

PK116 158 Sqn 27.6.45, Pocklington 20.12.45, 273 MU 2.4.46, SOC 4.12.46

PK117 TB-V,W/51 Sqn 27.6.45, Pocklington 27.10.45, 46 Sqn 28.1.46, 273 MU 12.4.46, SOC 16.10.47

PK118 158 Sqn 27.6.45, EFA 28.10.45, swung on take-off Lydda, hit pile of stones, u/c collapsed, burnt out

PK119 TB-T/51 Sqn 28.6.45, Pocklington 15.1.46, 273 MU 16.4.46, SOC 16.10.47

PK120 51 Sqn 1.7.45, EFA 31.10.45 Abadan, Iran, u/c torn off when, landing in cross wind, aircraft ran into a gully

PK121 TB-E,R/51 Sqn 1.7.45, Pocklington 20.2.46, St Athan 28.3.46, became 5904M, SOC 15.5.47

PK122 158 Sqn 2.7.45, EFA 25.10.45 extensively damaged during swing on take-off from Lydda

PK123 158 Sqn 5.7.45, 51 Sqn 2.2.46, 23 MU 21.3.46, SOC 5.6.47

PK124 TB-R/51 Sqn 6.7.45, Pocklington 27.11.45, 46 Sqn 28.1.46, 23 MU 22.3.46, SOC 5.6.47

PK125 TB-F/8.7.45, Pocklington 15.1.46, 273 MU 4.4.46, SOC 20.12.46

PK126 TB-L/51 Sqn 8.7.45, 7T-O/196 Sqn 30.1.46, 23 MU 21.3.46, SOC 5.6.47

PK127 158 Sqn 8.7.45, 7T-U/196 Sqn 30.1.46, 23 MU 25.3.46, SOC 5.6.47

PK128 158 Sqn 8.7.45, ZO-A/196 Sqn 28.1.46, 23 MU 26.3.46, SOC 5.6.47

PK129 XK-G/46 Sqn 31/7/45, Pocklington 8.2.46, 273 MU 26.2.46, SOC 16.10.47

PK130 46 Sqn, EFA 31.12.45 Lyneham, serious swing following engine problem on take-off, damaged beyond repair

PK131 SFU Honiley 1.8.45, 273 MU 11.6.46, SOC 16.10.47

PK132 51 Sqn 5.8.45, 23 MU 25.3.46, SOC 5.6.47

PK133 TB-Z/51 Sqn 5.8.45, 273 MU 12.4.46, SOC 16.10.47

PK134 242 Sqn 10.8.45, EFA 2.10.45 Mauripur swing on take-off, u/c collapsed

PK135 KY-U,N/242 Sqn 12.8.45, 46 Sqn 3.12.45, Pocklington 8.2.46, 273 MU 26.4.46, SOC 16.10.47

PK136 CRD A&AEE 20.9.45, Shorts 9.1.46, Pocklington 15.1.46, 273 MU 30.4.46, Sold to Transair Belgium 25.8.47, possibly became OO-XAK?

PK137 242 Sqn 20.8.45, FA 23.8.45 dinghy became wrapped around tailplane but aircraft landed safely at Castel Benito, Pocklington 3.12.45, 46 Sqn 5.2.46, 23 MU 1.3.44, SOC 5.6.47

PK138 242 Sqn 20.8.45, Pocklington 11.2.46, 273 MU 18.4.46, SOC 16.10.47

PK139 242 Sqn 20.8.45, 273 MU 1.4.46, XK-M/46 Sqn 2.12.46, 273 MU, SOC 16.10.47

PK140 242 Sqn 20.8.45, 23 MU 7.3.46, SOC 5.6.47

PK141 242 Sqn 20.8.45, GA 26.10.45 damaged Lyneham by petrol bowser, FA 8.1.46, XK-R/46 12.2.46, Pocklington 22.2.46, SOC 16.10.47

PK142 242 Sqn 14.8.45, Pocklington 19.10.45, Sqn 4.12.45, 23 MU 21.3.46, SOC 5.6.47

PK143 KY-Aw/242 Sqn 31.8.45, 158 Sqn 5.9.45, A/1589 HFF, St Mawgan 6.10.45, MEDME 15.11.45, SOC 25.7.46

PK144 158 Sqn 31.8.45, ZO-F/196 Sqn 6.2.46, 23 MU 27.3.46, SOC 5.6.47

PK145 158 Sqn 6.9.45, 7T-Q/196 Sqn 6.2.46, 23 MU 25.3.46, SOC 5.6.47

PK146 158 Sqn 6.9.45, TB-Cw/51 Sqn 2.2.46, 273 MU 8.4.46, SOC 16.10.47

PK147 DK-Yw/158 Sqn 6.9.45, 1589 HFF 31.12.45, MEDME 11.4.46, SOC 25.7.46

PK148 TB-YW/51 Sqn 5.10.45, 273 MU 8.4.46, sold to Transair Belgium 25.8.47, became OO-XAM but changed to G-AKPC

PK149 DK-Dw/158 Sqn 5.10.45, 1589 Flt 31.12.45, 16 FU 21.3.46, arrived MEDME 11.4.46, SOC 25.7.46

PK150 51 Sqn 11.10.45, 1588 HFF, St Mawgan 12.10.45, ACSEA 11.3.46, SOC in India 31.12.46

PK151 C/1588 HFF 12.11.45, ACSEA 11.3.46, SOC in India 31.12.46

PK152 KY-A/-242 Sqn 13.10.45, 46 Sqn 3.12.45, 273 MU 28.3.46, SOC 16.10.47

PK153 KY-B/242 Sqn 25.11.45, KX-X/46 Sqn 3.12.45, Pocklington 8.2.46, 273 MU 12.4.46, sold to Transair Belgium 25.8.47, became OO-XAS

PK154 242 Sqn 18.10.45, 23 MU 1.5.46, SOC 5.6.47

PK155 51 Sqn 26.10.45, 46 Sqn 17.12.45, 23 MU 15.3.46, SOC 5.6.47

PKI56 242 Sqn 8.10.45, XK-Ow/46 Sqn 27.12.45, 273 MU 1.4.46, SOC 16.10.47

PK157 KY-MR/242 Sqn 25.10.45, Pocklington 20.12.45, 273 MU 8.4.46, sold to Transair Belgium 25.8.47, became OO-XAR?

PK158 Pocklington 24.10.45, XK-Pw/46 Sqn 27.12.45, EFA 7.2.46, undershot Stoney Cross

PK171 Pocklington 19.10.45, 46 Sqn 27.12.45, 23 MU 20.3.46, SOC 5.6.47

PK172 Pocklington 3.11.45, 273 MU 8.4.46, SOC 11.4.47. Sold to Transair, became OO-XPC

PK173 46 Sqn 26.10.45, EFA 13.11.45 St Thomas's Mount, India, swung on taking off and u/c collapsed in boggy ground

PKI74 TB-C/51 Sqn 2.11.45, 273 MU 8.4.46, sold to Transair Belgium 25.8.47, became OO-XAV

PK175 TB-U/51 Sqn 14.11.45, 273 MU 9.4.46, SOC 16.10.47

PK176 51 Sqn 17.11.45, 273 MU 7.4.46, SOC 30.1.47

PK177 51 Sqn 28.11.45, EFA 30.12.45, dinghy released in error, u/c collapsed on landing at Stradishall

PK178 51 Sqn 15.11.45, 1588 HFF 18.12.45, ACSEA 11.2.46 arrived 11.3.46, SOC in India 31.11.46

PK179 TB-N/51 Sqn 1.12.45, 273 MU 8.4.46, SOC 16.10.47

PK180 23 MU 30.11.45, Pocklington 22.12.45, 273 MU 16.4.46, SOC 15.5.47. Sold to Transair, became OO-XAL

PK181 23 MU 8.12.45, Pocklington 22.12.45, 273 MU9.4.46, sold to Transair Belgium 25.8.47, became OO-XAE

PK182 23 MU 1.12.45, Pocklington 22.12.45, 273 MU 10.4.46, sold to Transair Belgium 25.8.47, possibly became OO-XAL

PK183 Pocklington 15.12.45, 273 MU 6.5.46, SOC 16.10.47

PK184 Pocklington 15.12.45, 273 MU 1.4.46, XK-Vw/46 Sqn 5.2.46, 273 MU 1.4.46, SOC 16.10.47

PK185 Pocklington 15.12.45, 46 Sqn 15.2.46, 23 MU 25.3.46, SOC 5.6.47

PK186 Pocklington 15.12.45, 273 MU 9.4.46, SOC 16.10.47

PK225 – PK237 completed as Mk IV

PK225 10 MU 18.12.44, SG-Q/299 Sqn, FTR 30/31.3.45 from SOE sortie to Norway

PK226 19 MU 1.12.44, 8Z-R/295 Sqn 15.3.45, 23 MU 4.2.46, SOC 5.6.47

PK227 10 MU 21.12.44, 190 Sqn, FTR 2/3.4.45 from SOE sortie to Norway

PK228 10 MU 4.1.45, X9-P/295 Sqn 13.3.45, FTR 11/12.4.45 from SOE sortie to Denmark

PK229 10 MU 6.1.45, ORTU 8.3.45, 1665 CU 17.5.45, 1385 CU 31.3.46, 273 MU 5.4.46, SOC 10.12.46

PK230 10 MU 6.1.45, ORTU 25.2.46, 620 Sqn, 23 MU 20.4.45, SOC 5.6.47

PK231 10 MU 9.1.45, 1665 CU 31.1.45, EFA 5.9.45, swung on take-off Marston Moor, both u/c legs collapsed

PK233 10 MU 9.1.45, SOC 20.11.46

PK234 10 MU 23.1.45, V8-E,D/570 Sqn 11.3.45, X9-K/299 Sqn 9.11.45, 196 Sqn 10.3.46, 23 MU 25.3.46, SOC 5.6.47

PK235 19 MU 8.12.44, 5G-S/299 Sqn 17.3.45, 23 MU17.3.46, SOC 5.6.47

PK236 19 MU 8.12.44, SOC 4.2.47

PK237 (SD Mk IV) 10 MU 21.12.44, SOC 9.10.46

PW255 – PW633 224 aircraft of which only 80 within the range PW255 – PW465 were built, as Mk IVs

PW255 6 MU 26.6.44, 8Z-T/295 Sqn 16.8.44, E7-K/570 Sqn 10.12.44, 23 MU 21.1.45, SOC 5.6.47

PW256 23 MU 13.8.44, CRD Shorts 25.9.44, 199 Sqn 25.9.44, 6Y-D/171 Sqn 2.10.44, 6 MU 27.11.44, EX-D/199 Sqn 7.12.44, became 5088M 31.3.45

PW257 6 MU 10.7.44, 190 Sqn 25.9.44, gale damage Dunmow 20.1.45, Z/190 Sqn 31.1.45, 23 MU 25.5.45, SOC 5.6.47

PW258 23 MU 4.8.44, 199 Sqn 12.10.44, 171 Sqn 2.10.44, 6 MU 30.11.44, SOC 19.7.45

PW259 23 MU 14.8.44, 199 Sqn 13.9.44, 6Y-A/171 Sqn 17.9.44, EX-V/199 Sqn 10.11.44, SOC 24.4.45

PW260 23 MU 20.8.44, SOC 22.3.46

PW261 1332 CU 3.9.44, 16/17.11.44 gale damage Nutt's Corner, 1332 CU 29.12.44, SOC 22.2.455

PW262 1332 CU 3.9.44, EFA 2.11.44, overshot unfamiliar airfield, Bishop's Court, in rain, port wing torn off, 226 MU 9.11.44, SOC 1.12.44

PW263 CRD Shorts 13.9.44, CRD Swinderby 3.12.44, 6 MU 27.2.45, SOC 24.4.45

PW264 23 MU 31.7.44, SOC 5.6.47

PW265 Sebro 17.4.45, SOC 21.6.47

PW266 23 MU 3.8.44, SOC 5.6.47

PW384 10 MU 3.1.45, SOC 26.9.46

PW385 (SD) 10 MU 12.1.45, 23 MU 25.10.44, SCC 5.6.47

PW386 10 MU 12.1.45, NY-T/1665 CU 1.2.45, EFA 29.5.45 Saltby, swung on take-off and hit two C-46s

PW387 10 MU 5.2.45, ORTU 8.3.45, 1665 CU 17.5.45, 23 MU SLG 25.2.46, 23 MU 21.3.46, SOC 5.6.47

PW388 10 MU 12.1.45, NY-L/1665 CU 1.2.45, FA 27.8.45 taxying, encountered brake problem, 23 MU 4.2.46, SOC 5.6.47

PW389 10 MU 5.2.45, ORTU 8.3.45, 1665 CU 17.5.45, 1385 CU 21.3.46, 273 MU 8.4.46, SOC 20.12.46

PW390 10 MU 23.1.45, SOC 25.9.46

PW391 10 MU 15.2.45, ORTU 25.2.45, EFA 29.3.45 Thorney Toll, Northants, collided with Master II DM336 of 7 SFTS

PW392 10 MU 24.1.45, ORTU 28.2.45, ZO-G/196 Sqn 1.3.45, 23 MU 27.2.46, SOC 5.6.47

PW393 ORTU 8.3.45, 620 Sqn, 23 MU 20.4.45, SOC 5.6.47

PW394 ORTU 8.3.45, 1665 CU 17.5.45, 1385 CU 21.8.45, 273 MU 8.4.46, SOC 11.1.47

PW395 10 MU 7.2.45, 138 Sqn 18.2.45, MA-X/161 Sqn 6.3.45, 38 Gp 9.3.45, 161 Sqn, 23 MU 12.7.45, storm damage 21.9.45, Cat E 23.1.46

PW396 10 MU 15.2.45, ORTU 2.3.45, 23 MU 14.4.45, SOC 5.6.47

PW397 10 MU 7.2.45, 23 MU 28.11.45, SOC 5.6.47

PW398 10 MU 20.2.45, 13 MU 7.12.45, 23 MU 15.12.45, SOC 5.6.47

PW399 10 MU 22.2.45, SOC 25.7.46

PW400 10 MU 6.2.45, R/ORTU 8.3.45, 23 MU SLG 25.2.46, 23 MU 21.3.46, SOC 5.6.47

PW401 F/190 Sqn 15.3.45, 23 MU 31.5.45, SOC 5.6.47

PW402 10 MU 6.3.45, 23 MU 14.12.45, SOC 5.6.47

PW403 X9-Q/299 Sqn 15.3.45, 273 MU 28.3.46, SOC 25.2.47

PW404 10 MU 1.3.45, SOC 25.9.46

PW405 10 MU 17.2.45, ORTU 2.3.45, 23 MU 1.2.46, SOC 5.6.47

PW406 E7-I,T/570 Sqn 17.3.45, 5G-W/299 Sqn 11.1.46, 23 MU 17.3.46, SOC 5.6.47

PW407 23 MU 1.3.45, ORTU 8.3.45, 23 MU 12.4.45, SOC 5.6.47

PW408 ORTU 17.3.45, FA 13.11.45 ran off runway Wethersfield, tail damaged, ORTU 14.12.45, 1385 CU 21.2.46, 273 MU 5.4.46, SOC 17.12.46

PW409 23 MU 6.3.45, ORTU 8.3.45, 1385 CU 21.3.46, 273 MU 5.4.46, SOC 6.1.47

PW410 620 Sqn 22.3.45, 7T-F/196 Sqn 31.5.45, 23 MU 18.2.46, SOC 5.6.47

PW411 10 MU 11.3.45, SOC 6.11.46

PW412 23 MU 19.3.45, SOC 5.6.47

PW413 23 MU 22.3.45, SOC 5.6.47

PW414 10 MU 15.3.45, SOC 20.11.46

PW415 23 MU 26.3.45, X9-N/299 Sqn 13.5.45, 23 MU 18.3.46, SOC 5.6.47

PW416 23 MU 26.3.45, SOC 5.6.47

PW417 23 MU 30.3.45, SOC 5.6.47

PW418 23 MU 22.3.45, SOC 5.6.47

PW419 23 MU 23.3.45, gale damaged 21.9.45, SOC 11.4.46

PW420 23 MU 31.3.45, ZO-E,N,G/196 Sqn 3.5.45, MU 6.3.46, SOC 5.6.47

PW421 23 MU 26.3.45, SOC 5.6.47

PW422 23 MU 20.3.45, E7-M,U/570 Sqn 3.5.45, EFA 14.11.45 crashed into houses 0745 hrs close to Evere after hitting telegraph pole during newspaper drop

PW423 23 MU 30.3.45, SOC 5.6.47

PW424 23 MU 31.3.45, V8-F/570 Sqn 10.5.45, 23 MU 8.2.46, SOC 5.6.47

PW425 23 MU 26.3.45, 8Z-N/295 Sqn 3.5.45, Sebro 25.1.46, 23 MU 25.1.46, SOC 5.6.47

PW438 23 MU 30.3.45, SOC 5.6.47

PW439 23 MU 9.3.45, 8E-U/295 Sqn 3.5.45, 23 16.1.46, SOC 5.6.47

PW440 23 MU 2.4.45, E7-0,Z/570 Sqn 10.5.45, EFA 28.12.45 Buckeburg B151 port tyre burst after landing, aircraft swung and u/c torn off in ditch

PW441 23 MU 9.3.45, SOC 5.6.47

PW442 23 MU 29.4.45, P/190 Sqn 3.5.45, 23 MU 25.5.45, SOC 5.6.47

PW443 23 MU 9.5.45, 5G-Q/299 Sqn 12.5.45, 23 MU 17.3.46, SOC 5.6.47

PW444 23 MU 3.5.45, 8Z-A/295 Sqn 3.5.45, EFA 30.5.45, swung on take-off at Brussels/Melsbroek, SOC 14.6.46

PW445 23 MU 20.4.45, SOC 5.6.47

PW446 23 MU 22.4.45, V8-W/570 Sqn 10.5.45, 9.1.46, 23 MU 21.3.46, SOC 5.6.47

PW447 23 MU 23.4.45, 190 Sqn 10.5.45, 25.5.45, SOC 5.6.47

PW448 23 MU 28.4.45, X9-P/299 Sqn 10.5.45, 26.1.46, 273 MU 28.3.46, SOC 18.2.47

PW449 23 MU 28.4.45, E7-X/570 Sqn 3.5.45, K/196 Sqn 9.1.46, 23 MU 6.3.46, SOC 5.6.47

PW450 23 MU 29.5.45, SOC 5.6.47

PW451 23 MU 1.6.45, SOC 5.6.47

PW452 23 MU 12.5.45, SOC 5.6.47

PW453 23 MU 26.5.45, SOC 5.6.47

PW454 23 MU 31.5.45, 570 Sqn 4.12.45, ZO-N/196 Sqn 9.1.46, 23 MU 28.3.46, SOC 30.1.47

PW454 6.5.45, 7T-G/196 Sqn 15.12.45, 273 MU 28.3.46, SOC 4.2.47

PW456 23 MU 8.6.45, SOC 5.6.47

PW457 23 MU 10.6.45, SOC 5.6.47

PW458 23 MU 27.6.45, SOC 5.6.47

PW459 23 MU 28.6.45, storm damage 21.9.45, ROS, 23 MU 22.1.46, SOC 5.6.47

PW460 23 MU 5.7.45, SOC 5.6.47

PW461 23 MU 6.7.45, ZO-M/196 Sqn 15.12.45, 23 MU 23.2.46, SOC 5.6.47

PW462 23 MU 6.7.45, SOC 5.6.47

PW463 23 MU 2.8.45, SOC 5.6.47

PW464 23 MU 20.8.45, SOC 5.6.47

PW465 23 MU 8.9.45, 299 Sqn 20.4.45, 295 Sqn 21.11.45, 23 MU 25.1.46, SOC 5.6.47

TS serial aircraft were earlier airframes re-built, TS261 being produced by Shorts possibly at Swindon and remainder by Sebro at Cambridge and Bourn:

TS261 ex-EF454 SOC 21.6.47

TS262 ex-LK500 fate unknown

TS263 origin unknown, fate unknown

TS264 ex-LK512 23 MU, SOC 5.6.47

TS265 ex-LK562 O,H/190 Sqn, FTR 15.4.45, from SOE sortie to Norway

TS266 ex-LJ575 V8-K/570 Sqn, 23 MU, SOC 5.6.47

Index